THE Amazing 10,000 Quiz Challenge

This edition published in 2005

10 9 8 7 6 5 4 3 2 1

A CIP catalogue record for this book is available from the British Library

ISBN 1 84442 466 9

Commissioning editor: Martin Corteel
Project art direction: Luke Griffin
Picture research: Tom Wright
Designer: GetSet Graphic Design Limited
Text: Roy and Sue Preston
Illustrations: CAT Media
Production: Lisa French

Printed in Dubai

THE Amazing 10,000 Quiz Challenge

CARLTON
BOOKS

INTRODUCTION

Can you guess how many quiz questions there are in this book? Here's a clue – the book is called the AMAZING 10,000 QUIZ CHALLENGE! Any nearer?

If you think that there may be a few hundred questions, or if you don't have any ideas, then perhaps this book is not for you! On the other hand, if you like lots of questions – 10,000 of them – and you enjoy a wide variety of quiz types, then this is most definitely the book of your dreams!

There are straightforward quizzes that each contain 20 questions, and all you have to do is answer them! These quizzes are arranged in broad subject areas, such as AT THE MOVIES, TELEVISION and GENERAL KNOWLEDGE. There's a colourful icon above each quiz to help you find your way around the book. In addition, there are some more specialised quizzes. So, for example, in a quiz headed SPORT you could come across a question about anything sporting, whereas some quizzes are about individual sports, such as TENNIS or personalities, such as DAVID BECKHAM.

Throughout the book there are feature quizzes linked to calendar dates and the seasons of the year. We up the question count to 50 for these double page specials.

We like to provide you with different types of quizzes, and you will find plenty of the following . . .

MULTI-CHOICE. You have to decide which of the three given answers is the correct one.

TRUE OR FALSE. Can you call our bluff and decide which statements are true and which are false?

NAME THE YEAR. Identify the year in question from some headliness of the time.

DOUBLE TAKE. A quiz for the two-faced, where two different questions lead to the same answer.

PICTURE QUIZZES. In each quiz we play some tricks with pics! There are famous faces to identify and some crafty connections to track down!

WHO SAID. . . ? Match the quotation to the speaker.

GUESS WHO . . . ? Identify the personalities from the few selected facts.

PLUS many **QUICKFIRE QUIZZES** where you can show your expert knowledge or total ignorance about subjects varying from capital cities to international sports stars.

The quizzes are NOT graded in levels of difficulty. The downright obscure will be found rubbing shoulders with questions that most of us will have no problems in answering. You may have sailed through questions 1 to 19, only to find that you get sunk on the final one. This book is packed with colour and cartoons, highlighting the fact that quizzes are here to entertain you. The main thing about all quizzes is that they are meant to be fun! There is a certain satisfaction in the knowledge that you know more about Bolivian poets than anyone else in the room, but we strongly suggest that the winner-takes-all attitude is not the best one to have . . . and anyone who shows signs of Quiz Rage should have a break from answering questions for a while.

Whether you are a complete quiz novice or an expert, this collection of quizzes will provide you with hours of entertainment.

1 AT THE MOVIES

1. Which Asian country is home to "Bollywood"?
2. Which Emma starred in, and won an Oscar for, the screenplay of, *Sense and Sensibility*?
3. To the nearest hour how long does the movie *Titanic* last?
4. Who directed *Gladiator*?
5. In which 1997 movie did Daniel Day Lewis play a boxer?
6. Who won the Best Actor Oscar for *On The Waterfront*?
7. In which decade of the 20th century was Joan Collins born?
8. Which Nicolas starred in *Face/Off*?
9. Is *Raging Bull* about American Football, boxing or bull fighting?
10. *My Best Friend's Wedding* and *Sleeping With The Enemy* featured which actress?
11. The character Sonny Corleone was in which sequence of movies?
12. *Air Force One* starred which Gary?
13. What is the first name of the *Pulp Fiction* director?
14. Which actor links *Se7en, Sleepers* and *Thelma & Louise*?
15. Which Mike directed *Four Weddings And A Funeral*?
16. Which Tony starred in *Some Like It Hot*?
17. The Secret Life Of which Walter formed a movie title?
18. Which early Spielberg blockbuster featured a shark?
19. Which Ms Ryder had her big break in *Beetlejuice*?
20. Which Oliver won the Best Director Oscar for *Born On The Fourth of July*?

ANSWERS ON PAGE 284

2 POP MUSIC

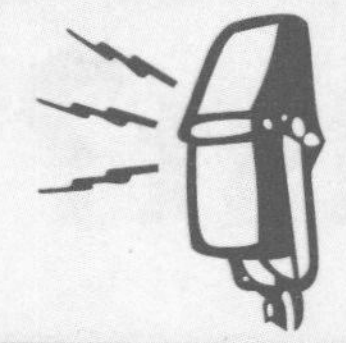
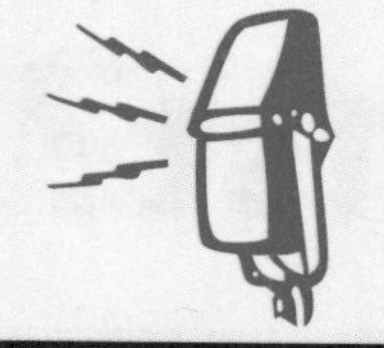
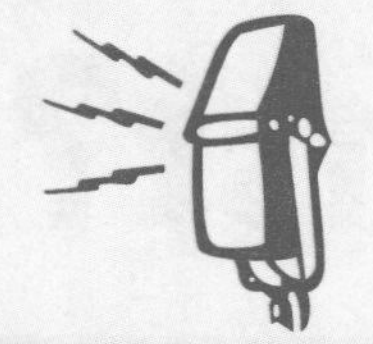

1. How is controversial rapper Marshall Mathers better known?
2. Freddie Mercury led which regal sounding band?
3. *Fallin'* won a Grammy Song Of The Year for which songwriter and singer?
4. What was the Spice Girls' first album called?
5. *Whose Come On Over* album was a top seller in the US and the UK?
6. Whose hits include *Jesus To A Child* and *Outside*?
7. In 2000 U2 received the keys to which capital city?
8. Which former Beatle announced his engagement in 2001?
9. Did Sting front The Firemen, The Nurses or The Police?
10. What goes with *Jagged Little* to complete the title of an Alanis Morissette album?
11. Bjorn Again are a tribute band to which pop superstars?
12. Eric Clapton had a transatlantic hit that stated that "I Shot" which person?
13. What were the Detroit Spinners called in the UK before using this name?
14. What was the only song from the album *Thriller* to reach No 1 as a single in the UK?
15. Who was the only American man to have a million seller single in the UK back in the 1980s?
16. What is the first word of *My Heart Will Go On*?
17. Which female came to fame with the soul album *I Never Loved A Man (the Way I Love You)*?
18. Who killed Marvin Gaye?
19. Which Elton John song was reworked and dedicated to Princess Diana?
20. Who was Paul Simon's long-time singing partner?

ANSWERS ON PAGE 284

3 FAMOUS FIRSTS

1st? 1st? 1st?

1. Who was the first female Prime Minister in Europe?
2. In what decade was the first external heart pacemaker fitted?
3. Who was the first woman to sail around the world?
4. Henry Mill was awarded the first patent for which machine?
5. The first Miss World came from which country?
6. What did Carlton Magee devise in the US for motorists?
7. What was first revealed at Lord's during a cricket match in 1975?
8. Which Marie became the first person to win a Nobel Prize twice?
9. Which two national teams made the first flight over Everest in a hot air balloon?
10. In which country was the first kidney transplant carried out?
11. What was Lester Piggott's first Derby winner back in 1954?
12. Which British bank was the first to issue cash dispenser cards?
13. Who was the first person to make a solo trek to the South Pole on foot?
14. Which support group was founded in Ohio in 1935?
15. What was the first UK and US No 1 for Christina Aguilera?
16. After record-breaking flights to Australia and Cape Town where was Amy Johnson's plane lost?
17. Joseph Mornier patented which building material?
18. Who was the first black American to win the Nobel Peace prize?
19. Who led the team which made the first successful overland crossing of Antarctica?
20. Was the first nuclear reactor built at Chicago or Chernobyl?

ANSWERS ON PAGE 284

4 GENERAL KNOWLEDGE

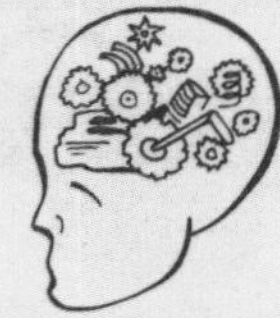
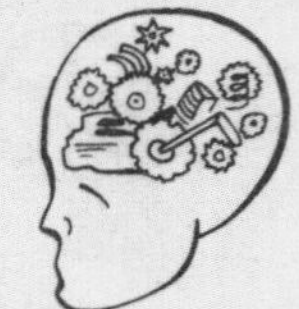
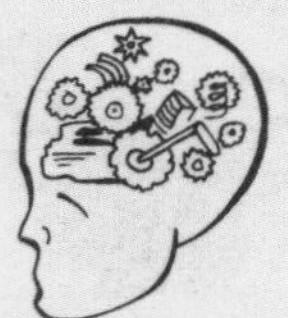

1. How many sides would a dozen dice have in total?
2. What or who was Mitch, the bringer of destruction to Honduras?
3. On which date was the movie *Independence Day* first screened in America?
4. What does the initial J stand for in Bill Clinton's name?
5. Amarillo airport was built in which US state?
6. Who wrote the classic song *I Will Always Love You*?
7. What does the letter D stand for in the initials DTP?
8. In baseball where do the Braves come from?
9. Eric Clapp found fame under which name?
10. What was Walt Disney's first feature length cartoon film?
11. In which decade did American women first vote in elections?
12. Eva Peron was the subject of which film and musical?
13. Capricorn, Libra and Phoenix – which of these is not a sign of the zodiac?
14. Willie Nelson wrote *Always On My Mind* for which pop legend?
15. In which decade of the 20th century was Woody Allen born?
16. The ACS is a charity raising money for what?
17. Crystal Gayle's Eyes were made what colour in the title of a hit song?
18. Which Jack was known as "The Golden Bear"?
19. Who was US President when the Berlin Wall came down?
20. Which country boy recorded *The Red Strokes*?

ANSWERS ON PAGE 284

5 PICTURE QUIZ

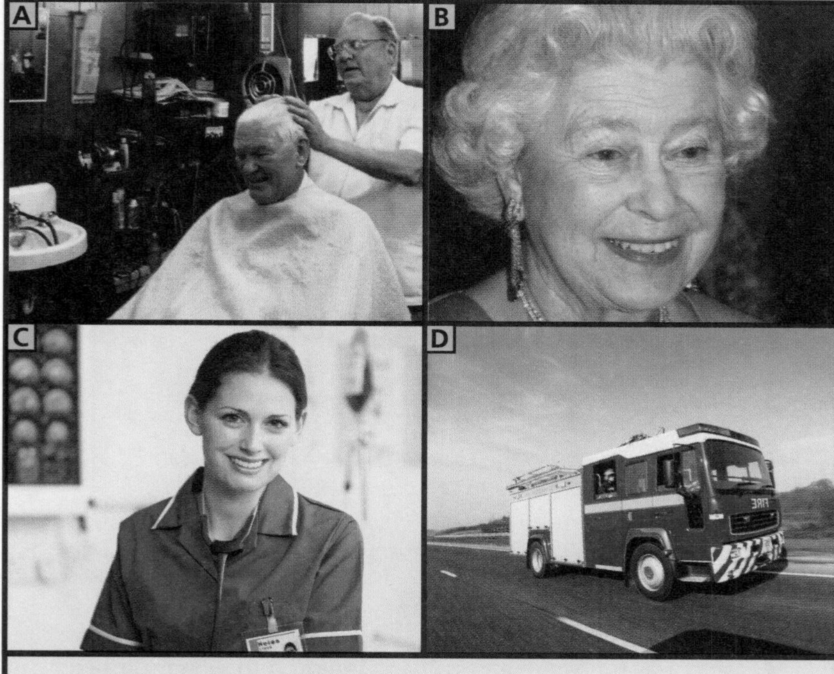

In which song do these people feature?

ANSWERS ON PAGE 284

6 WHO SAID . . . ?

1 "I think most people who have dealt with me think I'm a pretty straight sort of guy – and I am."

2 "I have tried to read Shakespeare, and found it so intolerably dull that it nauseated me."

3 Who when asked what he would spend his Booker Prize money on replied, "Booze, of course, and then curtains."

4 "People are wrong when they say opera isn't what it used to be. It is what it used to be. That's what's wrong with it."

5 "I shall hear in heaven."

6 "I've had 18 straight whiskies. I think that's a record."

7 "Golf is a good walk spoiled."

8 "That's one small step for a man, one giant leap for mankind."

ANSWERS ON PAGE 284

7 CLEVER ANIMALS

1 Which animal's handiwork won first prize in a 1971 Kansas art contest?
☐ Cat ☐ Orang-utan ☐ Parrot

2 Macaques are intelligent, but what are they?
☐ Monkeys ☐ Pigs ☐ Sheep

3 Which of these animals is the most intelligent
☐ Chimpanzee ☐ Elephant ☐ Pig

4 Hyenas communicate and can make which human-like sound?
☐ Laughter ☐ Singing ☐ Whistling

5 Which sea creatures can produce over 32 different sounds
☐ Dolphin ☐ Fish ☐ Shark

6 Which creature was Andre in the film of the same name?
☐ Cat ☐ Dog ☐ Seal

7 Which bird is often described as being wise?
☐ Eagle ☐ Hawk ☐ Owl

8 What was the name of the Lone Ranger's horse?
☐ Hi-ho ☐ Silver ☐ Trigger

9 What was the cat called in *Breakfast At Tiffany's*?
☐ Cat ☐ Felix ☐ Jules

10 Which bear was found at a London railway station?
☐ Paddington ☐ Victoria ☐ Waterloo

11 Who wrote *Animal Farm*?
☐ Blyton ☐ Dickens ☐ Orwell

12 Which fictional animals were both Mutant and Ninja?
☐ Penguins ☐ Turtles ☐ Zebras

13 Who was, "Smarter than the average bear!"?
☐Boo-Boo ☐ Paddington ☐ Yogi

14 Who is the Mystery Cat in *Cats*?
☐ Grizabella ☐ Macavity
☐ Rumpleteazer

15 Which is the most intelligent animal on Earth?
☐ Gorilla
☐ Human
☐ Monkey

ANSWERS ON PAGE 284

8 GEOGRAPHY

 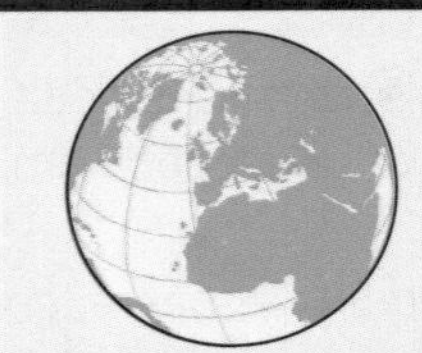 

1 Which long river has White and Blue tributaries?

2 Which religious leader is head of state of the Vatican?

3 Is Perth on the west or east coast of Australia?

4 In which country is Calgary?

5 Does Bombay or Tokyo have the higher population?

6 What sort of Snowman is another name for the Himalayan yeti?

7 What is the world's smallest, flattest and driest continent?

8 Is Argentina in the northern or southern half of South America?

9 Pakistan and Bangladesh both border which country?

10 Which country's name is an anagram of PURE?

11 The West Indies lie in which Sea?

12 Zambia is a neighbour of which country which also begins with Z?

13 Which Egyptian canal links the Red Sea and the Mediterranean?

14 Is Ghana on the African coast or wholly inland?

15 Which ocean is the world's deepest?

16 In Ireland what is a lough?

17 Who is commemorated at Washington's Lincoln Memorial?

18 Which US state has the postal abbreviation AZ?

19 New South Wales is in which country?

20 Which African desert is the world's largest?

ANSWERS ON PAGE 284

9 BRITISH ROYALS

1 In which month of 2005 did Prince Charles announce his engagement to Camilla Parker Bowles?

2 Which prince is the Queen's youngest son?

3 What is Prince Harry's real first name?

4 Which Royal wrote the children's story *The Old Man Of Lochnagar*?

5 Which late princess had a holiday villa on Mustique?

6 What is Prince Charles' Gloucestershire home called?

7 Who was the late Princess Diana referring to when she said her marriage was "a bit crowded"?

8 Which Prince was born on the Greek island of Corfu?

9 Which Scottish school did Princes Charles, Andrew and Edward all attend?

10 Which Princess is the mother of Peter Phillips?

11 How many daughters did the late Queen Mother have?

12 In which cathedral did Prince Charles marry Lady Diana Spencer?

13 Which Royal was once the BBC Sports Personality of the Year?

14 In 2005 Prince Harry controversially wore which fancy dress costume – French maid, Nazi or Pope?

15 Which hair colour is shared by Earl Spencer and his nephew Prince Harry?

16 What is the name of the Spencer ancestral home in Northamptonshire?

17 In which 1980s war did Prince Andrew serve?

18 Which Royal famously appeared in an epsiode of *Friends*?

19 At which English university did Prince Charles study?

20 Which school did Princes William and Harry attend in the late 1990s?

ANSWERS ON PAGE 284

10 PICTURE QUIZ

What links these pictures?

ANSWERS ON PAGE 284

11 NAME THE YEAR

1 The Olympic Games were held in Athens. George W Bush was elected to a second term of office. Yasser Arafat died.

2 Nelson Mandela was released from prison. The Best Picture Oscar went to Kevin Costner's *Dances With Wolves*. Margaret Thatcher was ousted as British Prime Minister

3 Bobbi McCaughey gave birth to septuplets in Iowa, USA. The Spice Girls made their first movie *Spiceworld*. Princess Diana was killed in a car crash in Paris.

4 The Korean War began. Ben Hogan won the US Open. The Best Movie Oscar went to *All About Eve*.

5 Jazz singer Ella Fitzgerald was born. Marie Stopes' controversial book *Married Love* was published. The First World War ended.

6 US inventor Percy Spencer patented a design for a microwave oven. General Patton died from injuries suffered in a car crash. The USA dropped atomic bombs on two Japanese cities.

ANSWERS ON PAGE 284

12 SPORT

1 In basketball where do the Wizards come from?

2 In horse racing which American Triple Crown Stakes race is held on Long Island?

3 In the 1960s what did the letters AFL stand for in sporting terms?

4 Phil Taylor has dominated which sport in recent years?

5 In which city does the Tour de France finish?

6 David Beckham joined which Spanish soccer side from Man Utd?

7 What type of speed event was Eric Heiden famous for?

8 Where does Sumo wrestling originate from?

9 Martina Navratilova has been on the winning side in the Federation Cup for which two countries?

10 Sergei Bubka competed in which athletics event?

11 Who is Jackie Joyner Kersee's famous athlete brother?

12 Which London soccer side is further south – Arsenal or Chelsea?

13 How many players are there in a men's lacrosse team?

14 In which Olympic event did Bob Beamon find fame?

15 The Walker Cup is competed for in which sport?

16 In which US state was boardsailing or windsurfing invented?

17 In boxing which is heavier, flyweight or middleweight?

18 Greg LeMond was a champion in which sport?

19 In which Park was the New York marathon run until 1970?

20 What type of golfers compete for the Curtis Cup?

ANSWERS ON PAGE 284

13 ANIMALS

1 Where does a kangaroo keep its young?

2 Which black and white mammal lives in China's bamboo forests?

3 Where do koalas live?

4 How many legs does an adult insect have?

5 What type of creature is a black widow?

6 Which animal's nickname is the ship of the desert?

7 Which breed of spaniel shares its name with a king?

8 Which sea creature is known as a Portuguese Man O'War?

9 Which deadly snakes can be Egyptian, Indian or Forest?

10 What do carnivorous animals live on?

11 What type of creature is a mandrill?

12 What is a fox's tail called?

13 Which saint is the heaviest breed of dog named after?

14 What is special about a guinea pig's tail?

15 What are pigs' feet called?

16 Which elephants have the smaller ears, African or Indian?

17 What are edible sturgeon eggs called?

18 What name is given to the period of winter sleep by some animals?

19 Approximately how many domestic breeds of dog are there – 200, 350 or 400?

20 What is a young penguin called?

ANSWERS ON PAGE 284

14 HISTORY

1 By which name was silent movie star Joseph Keaton better known?

2 Who was the first black President of South Africa?

3 How was Mao Zedong also known?

4 Which Marx brother had a moustache, cigar and funny walk?

5 According to the Bible who was the mother of Jesus?

6 Which trombonist Glenn became a famous bandleader?

7 Who was Italian dictator between 1926 and 1943?

8 What was the nationality of inventor Marconi?

9 Which of Queen Elizabeth II's Prime Ministers was not even born when she came to the throne?

10 Who was the youngest US President to die in office?

11 As a double agent, Mata Hari was executed by whom?

12 Mrs Meir was the first woman PM in which country?

13 Who was the USA's first Roman Catholic President?

14 Aung San Suu Kyi is an opposition leader in which country?

15 Which Panamanian leader was nicknamed "Pineapple Face"?

16 Which Pass did Hannibal use to cross the Alps?

17 Which lady became President of Ireland in 1997?

18 In which Vietnamese village were 109 civilians massacred by US troops in 1968?

19 Who was the first woman US Secretary of State?

20 Where did Tung Chee-Hwa become chief executive in July 1997?

ANSWERS ON PAGE 284

15 NAME GAME

How are these celebrities better known?

1 MELVIN KAMINSKY

2 ANTHONY BENEDETTO

3 BETTY PERSKE

4 PAUL HEWSON

5 NATASHA GURDIN

6 BRIAN WARNER

7 SAMUEL ROGERS

8 DECLAN McMANUS

9 JULIE ANNE SMITH

10 MARSHALL MATHERS III

ANSWERS ON PAGE 284

16 GUESS WHO . . . ?

1 He was born on 1st July 1961 and won a total of nine Olympic gold medals, from 1984 to 1996.

2 This English novelist died in 1995 after winning acclaim for novels such as *Lucky Jim* and *Jake's Thing*.

3 Daughter of Tony Curtis and Janet Leigh, she married movie director Christopher Guest.

4 She was born in South Africa in 1966 but ran for Great Britain in the 1984 Olympics where she finished seventh in the 3000m.

5 Born in Medina in Italy in 1935 he is the heaviest of the Three Tenors.

6 A former actor, he became Governor of California before reaching the top and entering the White House.

7 Born in St Louis Missouri, he wrote songs, played the guitar and sang *No Particular Place to Go*.

8 Born in the Ukraine in 1963, he dominated pole vaulting throughout his career, but only won one Olympic gold.

9 She starred in blockbuster *Titanic*, married movie director Sam Mendes and co starred with Johnny Depp in *Finding Neverland*.

10 He was born in Georgia in 1930, played piano, sang and was played on film by Jamie Foxx.

ANSWERS ON PAGE 284

17 PIRATES

1 What goes with a skull on a pirate flag?
☐ Crossbones ☐ Parrot ☐ Skeleton

2 The pirate flag is the Jolly what?
☐ Pirate ☐ Roger ☐ Skull

3 The Caribbean in the 16th and 17th centuries was known as the Spanish what?
☐ Doubloon ☐ Graveyard ☐ Main?

4 How was Edward Teach better known as a pirate?
☐ Blackbeard ☐ Calico Jack ☐ Flint

5 In song how many men are on a dead man's chest?
☐ 10 ☐ 15 ☐ 101

6 What was the name of the pirate sword?
☐ Bloodcut ☐ Cutlass ☐ Longsword

7 What was the name of the blind pirate in *Treasure Island*?
☐ Dog ☐ Bones ☐ Pew

8 Boney and Read were what type of rather unusual pirate?
☐ Children ☐ Same person ☐ Women

9 What was the usual pirate pistol called?
☐ Dreadlock ☐ Flintlock ☐ Kickback

10 In fiction who was Peter Pan's greatest foe?
☐ Captain Hook ☐ Captain Blood
☐ Captain Claw

11 When did the dreaded Blackbeard die?
☐ 1618 ☐ 1668 ☐ 1718

12 Where do Gilbert and Sullivan's singing pirates hang out?
☐ Basingstoke ☐ Caribbean
☐ Penzance

13 Scurvy was a disease caused by lack of what?
☐ Vitamin C ☐ Sleep ☐ Fresh water

14 Bartholomew Roberts was a pirate who dressed himself as a what?
☐ Cleric
☐ Gentleman
☐ Woman

15 If a pirate was left on an island, they were said to have been what?
☐ Marooned
☐ Planked
☐ Scuppered

ANSWERS ON PAGE 284

18 MADONNA

1. What is Madonna's real second name?
2. Whose single did she feature on in 2003?
3. Who was Madonna *Desperately Seeking* in her first major film role?
4. Madonna was *Like A* what on her second album?
5. What was Madonna Into on her first UK No 1?
6. Who did Madonna tell not to Preach on her 1986 single?
7. Which actor did Madonna marry in 1985?
8. What type of Ambition describes her world tour in 1990?
9. In which film based on a cartoon character did she co star with Warren Beatty?
10. Which *Collection* album was made up of greatest hits?
11. What name was given to her 1992 album and accompanying book?
12. What type of Girl is Madonna on her 1985 hit?
13. What were Madonna fans wearing on her video *Bedtime Story*?
14. What was Madonna's first hit single to feature the word American in the title?
15. Which True colour was Madonna in 1986?
16. Which magazine shares its name with a 1990 No 1?
17. Robert Hoskins was convicted of which crime against Madonna in January 1996?
18. Did Madonna give birth to a son or a daughter in autumn 1996?
19. *Love Profusion* charted in 2003, but what was the previous single hit to use the word Love in the title?
20. *Like A Prayer* was used to advertise which drink?

ANSWERS ON PAGE 284

19 LUCKY DIP

1. Who released the successful album *Let Go*?
2. Who or what was a Penny Black?
3. Cartoon racer Dick Dastardly exclaims, "Drat and double" what?
4. Which swimming stroke is named after an insect?
5. Which former US President went with George Bush Snr to areas affected by the tsunami of December 2004?
6. What part of your body would a chiropodist look at?
7. Which British royal residence was badly damaged by fire in the early 1990s?
8. Who is the patron saint of Wales?
9. What is a female deer called?
10. In *Cinderella* what turned into a magic coach?
11. What can be an island, a sweater or a potato?
12. What unit is used to measure horses?
13. Which country does opera singer Pavarotti come from?
14. Where did chess originate in the second century?
15. To which country did the Pilgrim Fathers sail in *The Mayflower*?
16. How many tenpin bowling skittles need knocking down for a strike?
17. What is the emblem of Canada?
18. Which Cecil won Oscars for his designs on the classic movies *Gigi* and *My Fair Lady*?
19. What are birds of a feather said to do?
20. In finance, what did Britain abandon in 1931?

ANSWERS ON PAGE 284

20 FANTASY FILMS

1 What was the 2001 *Lord Of The Rings* film called?

2 In which Southern Hemisphere country was *Lord Of The Rings* partly made?

3 Which Disney fantasy featured the song *Be Our Guest*?

4 Who is Harry Potter's female accomplice?

5 Which Robert directed the *Back To The Future* movies?

6 Which Mike was the voice of *Shrek*?

7 Who played Gandalf the Grey in the first *Lord Of The Rings* film?

8 Which ballet music by Tchaikovsky features in Disney's *Fantasia*?

9 Who directed the first *Harry Potter* movie?

10 Who played Frodo Baggins in the first of the *Lord Of The Rings* trilogy?

11 What was the first Harry Potter film called in the USA?

12 In which decade was Disney's magical *Pinocchio* first released?

13 Who wrote the book on which the first *Lord Of The Rings* movie was based?

14 Which brothers wrote the story on which *Snow White And The Seven Dwarfs* was based?

15 Which Charlie's Angel was the voice of Princess Fiona in *Shrek*?

16 In which US state did the classic *Invasion Of The Body Snatchers* take place?

17 Who is the resident giant at Hogwart's school as played by Robbie Coltrane?

18 Who plays Ron in the first *Harry Potter* movie?

19 Which famous Disney character conducts in The Sorcerer's Apprentice in *Fantasia*?

20 What was Richard Harris's character in the first *Harry Potter*?

ANSWERS ON PAGE 284

21 HALF CHANCE

½? ½? ½?

1 In comic book and film which caped hero flew round Metropolis – Batman or Superman?

2 Which fruit goes in the pudding named after opera diva Nellie Melba – cherry or peach?

3 Which was built first – the Eiffel Tower or the Sydney Opera House?

4 What comes after New South in the name of an Australian state – England or Wales?

5 Which of these shapes has more sides a hexagon or a pentagon?

6 What does the e stand for in e-mail – electronic or encoded?

7 What was the name of Christopher Robin's bear – Tigger or Winnie the Pooh?

8 Is coffee produced from beans or leaves?

9 Did turkeys originally come from North America or Turkey?

10 Is Houston in the US state of Arizona or Texas?

11 Which of these zodiac signs represents a human shape – Gemini or Pisces?

12 Which Brothers made the first controlled powered flight – Wright Brothers or Flyte Brothers?

13 In which decade was the first pocket calculator used – 1950s or 1970s?

14 In history were Nina, Pinta and Santa Maria all names of battles or ships?

15 To play a euphonium do you blow into or strum it?

16 If you multiply the length of a rectangle by the width do you get the area or the depth?

17 Does the Roman numeral M represents 50 or a 1000?

18 Are Manx and Marmalade types of cat or computer virus?

19 Following the nursery rhyme recipe, how many blackbirds would be baked in two pies – 36 or 48?

20 What form of transport is the French TGV – a train or a coach?

ANSWERS ON PAGE 284

22 EUROPEAN TOUR

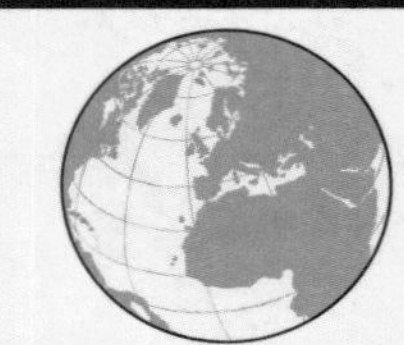

1 Anjou is now part of which French departement?

2 In Austria what is the Fohn?

3 The Campine coalfield is to the east of which country?

4 Which country is to the immediate south of Croatia?

5 Where is the Jotunheimen range of mountains?

6 Which Italian port takes its name from the Greek for elbow?

7 How many countries border the Federal Republic of Germany?

8 Which country is to the north of Slovakia?

9 What is the currency of Slovenia?

10 In which country are the Pripet Marshes?

11 Which is the largest province of Spain?

12 Cadiz has a ferry link with which location which shares its name with a film title?

13 In which department of Basse Normandie is the village where the famous soft cheese is made?

14 In which country are the Bakony Mountains?

15 Where is Switzerland's oldest university?

16 What is Europe's most southerly point?

17 Which country is to the immediate north of the Ukraine?

18 In which Sea are Gotland and Oland?

19 Which city is the burial place of William the Conqueror and Beau Brummel?

20 Which river bisects Andorra?

ANSWERS ON PAGE 284

23 SCIENCE

1 What was the name of the first lamb born to Dolly the first cloned sheep?

2 What would you use Isaac Singer's invention for?

3 In which room would you be most likely to use the inventions of Kenneth Wood – known to his friends as Ken?

4 At what sort of party might you see the invention of Earl W. Tupper?

5 Which frozen confection was originally called Eskimo pie?

6 Which Earl invented a snack of meat between two slices of bread?

7 What was special about the fabric Charles Macintosh invented?

8 Which essential for foreign tourists was invented by American Express?

9 What type of camera did George Eastman invent?

10 What type of aircraft is Sikorsky famous for?

11 What did Crick, Watson and Wilkins determine the structure of?

12 Who formulated a law of electromagnetism and pioneered techniques in measuring electricity?

13 Which French philosopher created analytical geometry?

14 Which English chemist discovered the most elements?

15 Which virus was Robert Gallo one of the first to identify?

16 Which English physicist discovered the neutron?

17 What type of bomb did Edward Teller develop?

18 What sort of tube did William Crookes invent?

19 Who gave his name to the law that states that the pressure of gas is proportional to its volume?

20 Which physicist and chemist gave his name to the law of induction?

ANSWERS ON PAGE 284

24 PICTURE QUIZ

A
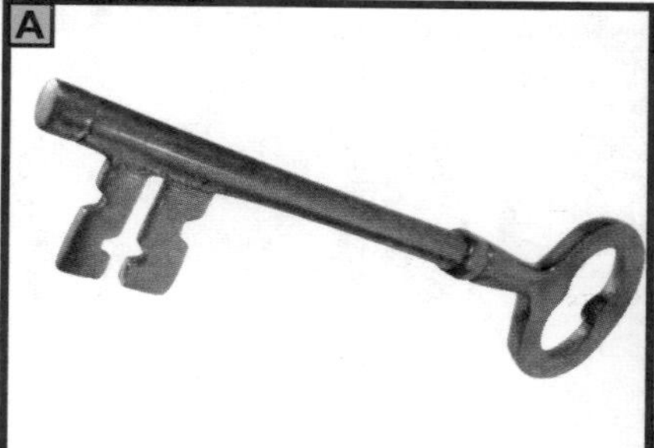

B

C

D

What links these pictures?

ANSWERS ON PAGE

25 NAME THE YEAR

1 *Snow White and the Seven Dwarfs*. Orson Welles' broadcast of *The War of the Worlds* caused panic.

2 *Sputnik I* was the first artificial object to orbit the Earth. The Best Picture Oscar went to *The Bridge On The River Kwai*. Christian Dior died in Italy.

3 Harper Lee's *To Kill A Mockingbird* won the Pulitzer prize. Yuri Gagarin became the first man in space. Rudolf Nureyev defected to the West.

4 The Watergate scandal forced Richard Nixon to resign. Chris Evert and fiancé Jimmy Connors won Wimbledon titles. Heiress Patty Hearst was abducted.

5 Robert Kennedy was assassinated. The Prague Spring was ended by a Soviet invasion. Jackie Kennedy married Aristotle Onassis.

6 The First Gulf War began. Anthony Hopkins won an Oscar for *The Silence of the Lambs*. Mikhail Gorbachev resigned.

ANSWERS ON PAGE 284

26 THE ARTS

1 Which little girl had *Adventures Through the Looking Glass*?

2 How many Musketeers were there in the title of the book by Dumas?

3 Which Robinson was shipwrecked on a desert island?

4 Where is the Wind in the story about Toad and Badger?

5 What was the surname of Ebenezer in *A Christmas Carol*?

6 At which film festival is the prize the Golden Lion awarded?

7 Which popular yellow spring flower did Wordsworth write about?

8 What type of writing is John Betjeman famous for?

9 What is the nationality of Agatha Christie's detective Poirot?

10 What is the religious occupation of medieval detective Cadfael?

11 Which part of the Pacific is the setting for a popular musical?

12 Which class of society is a musical based on *The Philadelphia Story*?

13 *Oh* which Indian city appears in the title of a controversial show?

14 *The Importance Of Being* what is the name of an Oscar Wilde play?

15 Who are with the Guys in the show about gangsters?

16 Which girl is the lecturer educating in the play by Willy Russell?

17 Which *Miss* is a musical set in Vietnam?

18 Which show is often just referred to as *Les Mis*?

19 What do you say to Dolly in the title of the show?

20 Aspects of what are the theme of which Lloyd Webber musical?

ANSWERS ON PAGE 284

NEW YEAR

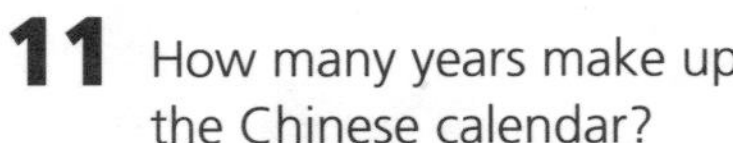

The start of a New Year always brings hope of something good to happen in the months ahead. Here are 50 questions about celebrations and events that took place at the beginning of the calendar year.

1 What is your star sign if you were born on New Year's Day?

2 The first month of the year is dedicated to which god?

3 Which is the only feathered symbol in the Chinese calendar?

4 How many days make up the celebrations of Chinese New Year?

5 Which Oscar winner for the movie *Gandhi* was born on New Year's Eve 1943?

6 In which months can the Hindu New Year fall?

7 King Zog of which country was deposed on the second day of 1946?

8 Work on which Egyptian Dam began during the second week of 1960?

9 If you were born on New Year's Eve what would be your blue birthstone?

10 The Chinese lantern festival falls on which night of the New Year celebrations?

11 How many years make up the Chinese calendar?

12 Where is Hogmanay traditionally celebrated?

13 What name is given to the Sikh New Year?

14 February 2005 saw the start of the Chinese Year of the what?

15 Tear gas was first used on the third day of 1915 in which war?

16 Who seized power in Cuba on New Year's Day 1959?

17 Which HQ of the US Department of Defense was completed in the first month of 1943?

18 If you were born on New Year's Day what is your white birth flower?

19 Which pioneer of an alphabet for the blind was born on the fourth day of 1809?

20 The oldest US President was inaugurated in January 1981. Who was he?

21 Who recorded the single *New Year* in 2000?

22 Who began his famous diary on 1st January 1660?

23 Which country celebrated the Year of the Monkey in 2004?

24 Which rodent is associated with the Chinese year of Shu?

25 Crowned in the first month of 1547, what was the name given to the first Tsar Ivan?

QUIZ

26 Which British newspaper was first published on 1st January 1788?

27 What Scottish ditty is traditionally sung at the stroke of midnight on New Year's Day?

28 He was born in the first month of 1940 and nicknamed the "Golden Bear". Who is he?

29 In which month was New Year's Day in the UK before 1752?

30 Which founder of the FBI was born on New Year's Day 1895?

31 Which future US President married Barbara Pierce on the sixth day of 1945?

32 Which coins ceased to be legal tender in the UK on New Year's Eve 1960?

33 Which Irish band recorded *New Year's Day* in 1983?

34 Which supersonic airliner entered service in the new year of 1976?

35 Which Queen of Disco was born on New Year's Eve 1948?

36 How many days does the first month of the year have?

37 Which author of *Lord Of The Rings* was born on the third day of 1892?

38 The first surviving sextuplets were born in the second week of January 1974 in which country?

39 If you were born on New Year's Eve what is your star sign?

40 Who, born on 1st January 1863, was responsible for reviving the Modern Olympics?

41 What name is given to the Jewish New Year?

42 Which famous US basketball team was founded on the fourth day of 1927?

43 If you were born on New Year's Day what is your birthstone?

44 Which film company was founded by William Fox, born 1st January 1879?

45 Which country celebrated the year Heisei 16 in 2004?

46 Which is the only symbol in the Chinese calendar without legs?

47 Which Island in upper New York Bay became an immigration depot on New Year's Eve 1890?

48 Which star of *The Silence Of The Lambs* was born on New Year's Eve 1937?

49 On the third day of 1959 which area became the largest state of the USA?

50 If you were born on New Year's Eve what would be your yellow birth flower?

ANSWERS ON PAGE 284

28 GENERAL KNOWLEDGE

 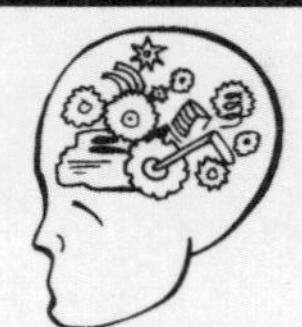 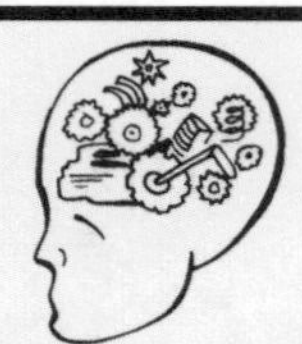

1 In which decade did Bill and Hillary Clinton get married?

2 Which animal name was given to the terrorist Carlos who was tried in 1997?

3 Who did Michael Jackson marry in May 1994?

4 In which decade was prohibition imposed in America?

5 What is the postal abbreviation for Alaska?

6 Which Michael had a huge hit with *How Am I Supposed To Live Without You*?

7 Which Ford first mass produced the car?

8 What completes the lines, "Cruising and playing the radio, With no particular place . . ."?

9 What did Ceylon change its name to in 1970?

10 Which hippie Timothy was Winona Ryder's godfather?

11 In ASCII what does the letter C stand for ?

12 Key West airport was built in which US state?

13 Which Janet had a US No 1 with *Escapade*?

14 Which country won the first Davis Cup?

15 Where was the Tin Lizzy first made?

16 Where did the Boeing 707 make its maiden flight from?

17 Which Californian city was devastated by an earthquake in 1906?

18 Who was *In Disguise* in Elvis Presley's 1963 hit?

19 Django Reinhardt was associated with which musical instrument?

20 Whose first European ad campaign was for Max Factor in 1999?

ANSWERS ON PAGE 284

29 KAROAKE

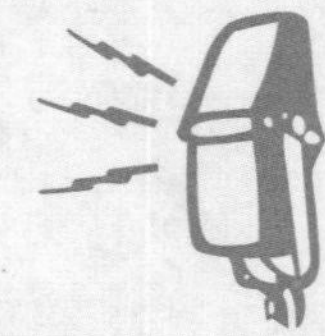 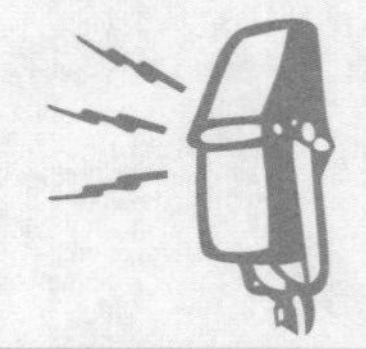 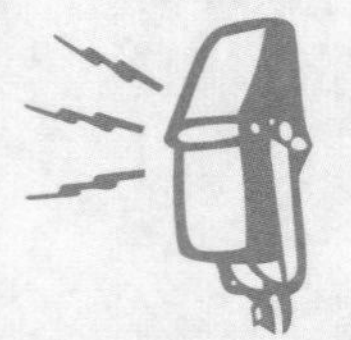

1 Which song starts, "It's a little bit funny, This feeling inside"?

2 Which Shania Twain song includes, "Okay, so you're Brad Pitt"?

3 What is the first word of *She*?

4 Which song begins, "I feel it in my fingers"?

5 Which Cliff Richard hit starts, "Used to think that life was sweet, Used to think we were so complete"?

6 Which Dire Straits song starts, "These mist covered mountains . . ."?

7 Which group declared, "It's fun to stay at the YMCA"?

8 Which chilly Madonna song begins "You only see what your eyes want to see"?

9 Which organ of the body is mentioned in the theme song to *Titanic*?

10 Judy Garland sang about going somewhere over the what?

11 Who Get Going When The Going Gets Tough?

12 Which Queen classic starts, "Is this the real life . . ."?

13 In *Candle In The Wind* 1997 Elton John described the late Princess of Wales as England's what?

14 "It's only words, and words are all I have, to take . . ." what?

15 What number was "Perfect" according to The Beautiful South in 1998?

16 In the Bowie song who was Ground Control trying to make contact with?

17 Who made Little Richard sing "Good Golly"?

18 What's the response to, "See you later, alligator"?

19 Which song starts, "Sometimes it's hard to be a woman"?

20 Which Elton John song has the colour yellow in the title?

ANSWERS ON PAGE 284

30 OLOGIES

What do you study if you pursue the following OLOGIES?

1 AGROSTOLOGY

2 PSEUDOLOGY

3 HOPLOLOGY

4 BRYOLOGY

5 VEXILLOLOGY

6 CRYPTOLOGY

7 PODOLOGY

8 OENOLOGY

9 HYPNOLOGY

10 GRAPHOLOGY

ANSWERS ON PAGE 284

31 DOGS

Is each statement TRUE or FALSE?

T F **1** The Afghan is a member of the greyhound family.

T F **2** The Manchester terrier has a rough coat.

T F **3** The Chesapeake Bay retriever is black and white.

T F **4** Samoyeds hail from western Europe

T F **5** The word "basset" means dwarf in French.

T F **6** The Dandie Dinmont originated in Ireland.

T F **7** A St Bernard typically weighs between 110 and 200 lbs.

T F **8** The Basenji is an ideal domestic pet.

T F **9** The Italian Spinone is smooth-haired.

T F **10** The Beagle is the smallest of the British scent hounds.

ANSWERS ON PAGE 284

32 THE PLANETS

1 How many planets are there in our Solar System?
☐ Seven ☐ Eight ☐ Nine

2 Which planet is closest to the Sun?
☐ Mars ☐ Mercury ☐ Neptune

3 Is Jupiter larger or smaller than Earth?
☐ No ☐ Same size ☐ Yes

4 Which gas in the Earth's atmosphere gives us life?
☐ Helium ☐ Hydrogen ☐ Oxygen

5 An eclipse occurs when the Moon gets between Earth and what?
☐ Mars ☐ Mercury ☐ Sun

6 Which is the seventh planet from the Sun?
☐ Pluto ☐ Saturn ☐ Uranus

7 What is the layer around the Earth called?
☐ Interlink ☐ Atmosphere
☐ Asteroid Belt

8 What is at the centre of our solar system?
☐ Earth ☐ Moon ☐ Sun

9 Who wrote the musical work *The Planets*?
☐ Delius ☐ Holst ☐ Vaughan Williams

10 Ganymede is a moon of which planet?
☐ Jupiter ☐ Pluto ☐ Saturn

11 In 1781 William Herschel discovered which planet?
☐ Neptune ☐ Saturn ☐ Uranus

12 What colour is the Great Spot on Jupiter?
☐ Blue ☐ Green ☐ Red

13 Which planet has two moons called Phobos and Deimos?
☐ Mars ☐ Mercury ☐ Saturn

14 Which planet lies between Venus and Mars?
☐ Earth ☐ Jupiter ☐ Pluto

15 Which of the planets was the last to be discovered from Earth?
☐ Neptune ☐ Pluto ☐ Saturn

ANSWERS ON PAGE 284

33 FOOD AND DRINK

1. What are the tips of asparagus called?
2. Which animal does venison come from?
3. Which garden herb is made into a sauce often eaten with lamb?
4. Schnapps is distilled from what?
5. What is traditionally eaten on Shrove Tuesday?
6. What colour is piccalilli?
7. Which black, gourmet fungus is a native of France's Périgord region?
8. Which country does the dish lasagne originate from?
9. What is done to a herring to make it into a kipper?
10. Which vegetable can be King Edward or Desirée?
11. Which country does Edam cheese originate from?
12. What do you add to milk to make porridge?
13. Arborio is a type of what?
14. What shape is the pasta called fusilli?
15. What colour is vodka?
16. In which country was sherry first made?
17. Which fruit is used to make Calvados?
18. Which nuts are used to make marzipan?
19. Is spotted dick usually eaten hot or cold?
20. Jerome Maubée, a monk was responsible for putting which liqueur on sale?

ANSWERS ON PAGE 285

34 PEOPLE

1. In 2005, who landed Best Supporting Actor Oscar for *Million Dollar Baby*?
2. Who led Iraq into the 1990s Gulf War?
3. Which astronaut said, "Houston we have a problem"?
4. Who was manager of The Beatles?
5. Which Russian introduced policies of glasnost?
6. What was Dan Quayle's Dan short for?
7. Whose dresses raised £2 million for charity in a June 1997 auction?
8. Who designed the Guggenheim Museum?
9. Who was Richard Nixon's Vice President from 1973 to 1974?
10. Who became King of Spain in the 1970s following General Franco's death?
11. Which G B wrote the play *Pygmalion* that was adapted into *My Fair Lady*?
12. Whose ancient tomb was discovered in Egypt in 1922?
13. Who was the ex-peanut farmer who became US President?
14. What was Richard Nixon's middle name?
15. Who was awarded a Nobel Peace Prize for her work with the poor in India?
16. Who led so-called witch hunts against Communists in the USA after WWII?
17. Who was the man who created The Muppets?
18. Where was General Colin Powell born?
19. Who thought that everyone would be famous for 15 minutes?
20. Which pop star married Linda Eastman in the 1960s?

ANSWERS ON PAGE 285

35 PICTURE QUIZ

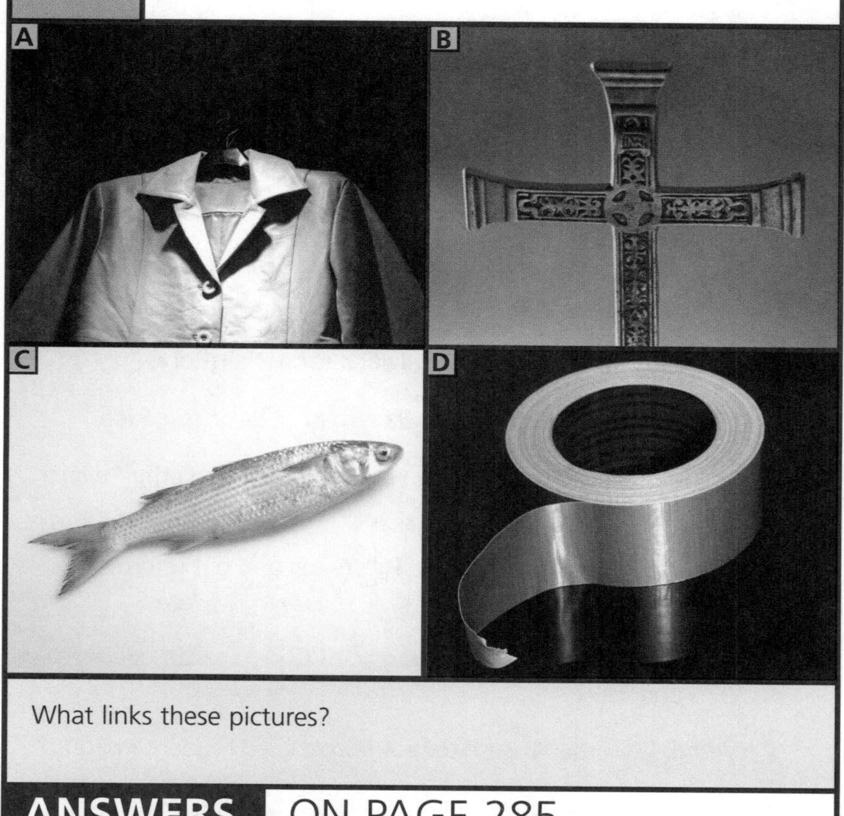

What links these pictures?

ANSWERS ON PAGE 285

36 DOUBLE TAKE

In each case, the two-part quiz question leads to just one answer!

1 Which word describes sailors as well as medicinal minerals?

2 Which word names a brush as well as a shrub?

3 Which word describes both a paragraph and a corridor?

4 Which word for a dissolving substance also means in the black?

5 Which US grunge band shares a name with the Buddhist state of bliss?

6 Which word names a Greek Island and a lettuce?

7 Which word links a chess piece and an ancient soldier?

8 Which planet is also the first name of a 2001 sporting champ?

9 What can be a musical sound or a short letter?

10 Which word meaning talk is the name of a bird?

ANSWERS ON PAGE 285

37 SPIES

1 Who created the most famous spy of them all – James Bond?
☐ Fleming ☐ Francis ☐ Makepeace

2 The word code derives from the Latin codex meaning what?
☐ Book ☐ Code ☐ Symbol

3 What term is used for a network of spies?
☐ Ring ☐ Watch ☐ Web

4 A spy in a position of trust with the enemy is known as a what?
☐ Ferret ☐ Mole ☐ Weasel

5 Which code is based on dots and dashes?
☐ Enigma ☐ Highway ☐ Morse

6 What is the first name of John Le Carré's spy Smiley?
☐ George ☐ John ☐ Simon

7 Which famous figure devised a notable Alphabet code?
☐ Henry VIII ☐ Lenin ☐ Julius Caesar

8 Which heavy did Bond face in *Goldfinger*?
☐ Jaws ☐ Oddjob ☐ Stromberg

9 Which double agent died in Russia in 1988?
☐ Blunt ☐ Burgess ☐ Philby

10 What was a skytale – used by the Spartans in coded messages?
☐ Cylinder ☐ Flare ☐ Strap

11 In which movie did Julia Roberts play a code cracker?
☐ *Enigma* ☐ *Matrix* ☐ *Pretty Woman*

12 Polybius made a letter cipher that took which shape?
☐ Circular ☐ Square ☐ Triangular

13 What nationality was the dancer and secret agent Mata Hari?
☐ Dutch ☐ French ☐ German

14 Which Stella became head of MI5?
☐ Moneypenny ☐ Rimington
☐ Steel

15 In the 16th century the Freemasons used which diagram code?
☐ Cipher disc
☐ Pig Pen
☐ Wheel

ANSWERS ON PAGE 285

38 THE OSCARS

1 Which Oscar winner was a "Beauty", with Annette Bening and Kevin Spacey?

2 In which country was Warren Beatty's political thriller *Reds* set?

3 Which Juliette won Best Supporting Actress for *The English Patient*?

4 Which city was Nicolas Cage *Leaving* in his 1995 winner?

5 Which Ben shared a screenplay Oscar with Matt Damon for *Good Will Hunting*?

6 Which Jennifer did Oscar nominee Brad Pitt marry?

7 In which US city was *The Godfather* set?

8 When Jessica Tandy won an Oscar for *Driving Miss Daisy* was she in her 60s or 80s?

9 Which English Julie, a 1960s winner, was nominated for *Afterglow* in the 1990s?

10 In which film venue were the first Oscars presented?

11 Which blonde cried all the way through her acceptance speech for *Shakespeare In Love*?

12 What type of fighter was the subject of the 2001 winner with Russell Crowe?

13 What was the nationality of the hero of *Braveheart*?

14 Which Hilary won best Supporting Actress for *Boys Don't Cry*?

15 Which was the best earning Oscar winner of the 1990s?

16 Which director won the award for *Million Dollar Baby* in 2005?

17 In which decade was *Cabaret* a winner?

18 What sort of games was *Chariots Of Fire* about?

19 Which John won for *True Grit*?

20 Which Susan played a nun in *Dead Man Walking*?

ANSWERS ON PAGE 285

39 THE HEADLINES

1 What was special about the Kilshaws adopting baby twin girls that made it newsworthy?

2 Bangladesh was created from which former territory?

3 Which political leader had a villa retreat at Berchtesgaden?

4 Who succeeded Harold Wilson as PM and suffered the "winter of discontent"?

5 Bill Clinton appointed his wife Hillary to carry out reforms in which social service?

6 What was the Democratic Republic of Congo called between 1971 and 1997?

7 Who did George W Bush defeat to become President in 2000?

8 What does the M stand for in IMF?

9 What nationality was the England soccer manager who replaced Kevin Keegan?

10 What does A stand for in IRA?

11 Which Israeli leader was assassinated in 1995?

12 Silvio Berlusconi became which country's PM in 1994?

13 Who was the first British writer to receive the Nobel Prize for Literature?

14 Who headed the committee in the US investigating Communist infiltration in public life?

15 What did Joseph Pulitzer give a Prize for?

16 Which country has a news agency called TASS?

17 Who interviewed Princess Diana in her infamous *Panorama* interview when she frankly discussed her marriage?

18 Which Moors were the scene of the so called Moors Murders?

19 In 2001 which country had three kings in as many days when many royals were machine-gunned to death?

20 In which decade did John Logie Baird first demonstrate television?

ANSWERS ON PAGE 285

40 LUCKY DIP

1 Which word connects the FBI and a vacuum cleaner?
2 What are James M Cox and Norman Manley International?
3 Which band made the album *A Rush Of Blood To The Head*?
4 Which part of the mint plant is used to make mint sauce?
5 In which sport is there an eagle, an albatross and a birdie?
6 How many fiddlers did Old King Cole have?
7 In which English county is the town of Ipswich?
8 What do guitars, harps and violins all have?
9 How many pence is the smallest silver-coloured UK coin?
10 Which vegetable is the emblem of Wales?
11 In which End of London are most of the capital's theatres?
12 Which country did the Pharaohs rule?
13 Bob Dylan was born in which decade of last century?
14 According to the proverb, what do many hands do?
15 Which suit of cards sounds like it would be useful in the garden?
16 Which board game is named after a serpent and something to climb up?
17 What type of animal was Babe in the film of the same name?
18 Which Great disaster befell London in 1666?
19 How many colours are there on the Belgian flag?
20 Where would you find a bull's-eye apart from on a bull's face?

ANSWERS ON PAGE 285

41 CLINT EASTWOOD

1 What was the nickname of the westerns he made in Italy?
2 What type of ape features in *Every Which Way But Loose*?
3 *In The Line Of Fire* is about a security agent haunted by his failure to prevent which US President's assassination?
4 Who directed him in *Unforgiven*?
5 *A Fistful Of* what was the title of his first Italian made western?
6 He played opposite Meryl Streep in the *Bridges* of which *County*?
7 With which Kevin did he co star and direct in *A Perfect World*?
8 *Escape From* which prison was the title of a 1979 movie?
9 In which decade was Clint Eastwood born?
10 *Any Which Way You Can* was the sequel to what?
11 Whose *Bluff* was the title of a 1960s movie?
12 In which TV series was he famous in the 1950s and 1960s?
13 What went with *The Good And The Bad* in the 1966 movie?
14 Eastwood won an Oscar for *Unforgiven* in what category?
15 Which Sondra was Eastwood's co star in *Every Which Way But Loose* and his partner off screen?
16 Which Tyne of Cagney and Lacey fame appeared in the Dirty Harry movie *The Enforcer*?
17 What was the surname of *The Outlaw – Josey*?
18 He was elected to which role in Carmel, California in 1986–88?
19 In which western musical starring Lee Marvin did he sing in 1969?
20 *Bird* was about Charlie Parker, famous for what type of music?

ANSWERS ON PAGE 285

42 TRAVEL

1. What is chiefly grown in Alabama's Canebrake country?
2. The Julian and Dinaric Alps extend into which two countries?
3. The Amur river forms much of the boundary between which two countries?
4. What is the Maori name for New Zealand?
5. Speaker's Corner is on the corner of which famous London Park?
6. What is the currency of Malaysia?
7. Which country has the highest density of sheep in the world?
8. Which city has a famous Royal Crescent?
9. Which volcanic peak is west of Cook inlet in Alaska?
10. San Miguel is the main island of which group?
11. What is the capital of the Lazio region of Italy?
12. What is the former name of the capital of Dominica?
13. Which Brazilian state is the centre of Amazonian tin and gold mining?
14. Aqaba is which country's only port?
15. On which island of the Philippines is Manila?
16. What is the world's flattest continent?
17. Which former fort in New York State is the home of the US Military Academy?
18. Which US state capital lies on the river Jordan?
19. In which country is Africa's lowest point?
20. What is the largest primeval forest left in Europe?

ANSWERS ON PAGE 285

43 TELEVISION

1. Who was Martha Huber killed by in *Desperate Housewives*?
2. What is the name of Grace's assistant in *Will and Grace*?
3. Which cop series featured Crockett & Tubbs?
4. In which series did Pamela Anderson shoot to superstardom?
5. In which series did Dr Frasier Crane first appear?
6. 1980's drama *St Elsewhere* was set in what type of institution?
7. In *The Simpsons*, what is the name of Chief Wiggum's son?
8. *South Park* is situated in which US state famous for its ski resorts?
9. In which decade did *All In The Family* premiere?
10. In *Diff'rent Strokes* where did the millionaire hail from?
11. In which city did the cartoon family The Jetsons live?
12. *Riptide* was about veterans from which war?
13. In which family did Morticia have an uncle Fester?
14. What type of aircraft featured in *Airwolf*?
15. In which city was *Car 54 Where Are You?* set?
16. Which Woman did former Miss USA Lynda Carter become?
17. David Cassidy played Keith in which family?
18. How many series of *Sex And The City* were there?
19. Which Tony played Philip Roth in *Vega$*?
20. In *M*A*S*H* how was Benjamin Franklin Pierce better known?

ANSWERS ON PAGE 285

44 NAME GAME

How are these celebrities better known?

1 REGINALD DWIGHT

2 HELEN MIRONOFF

3 GEORGIOS PANAYIOTOU

4 ISSUR DANIEL OVICH

5 ANNIE MAE BULLOCK

6 LUCY JOHNSON

7 JAMES OSTERBERG

8 JULIA WELLS

9 FERDINAND JOSEPH LAMENTHE

10 BERNARD SCHWARTZ

ANSWERS ON PAGE 285

45 GUESS WHO . . .?

1 Born in London in 1956, he broke three world records in 41 days in 1979 and led Britain's Olympic bid for 2012.

2 He played Jack in *Titanic* and was Oscar nominated for his role as Howard Hughes in *The Aviator*.

3 Born in Los Angeles, he found fame as an actor and director, such as in *Dances With Wolves* in 1990.

4 This singer/songwriter guitarist recorded *Song Sung Blue* and starred in *The Jazz Singer* in 1980.

5 Known as Flo Jo, she earned the title of the world's fastest woman and won four gold medals in Seoul in 1988.

6 This novelist who died in 1817 is most famous for creating Mr Darcy in *Pride & Prejudice*.

7 A lawyer by profession, she was the wife of the Governor of Arkansas until she became First lady in the 1990s.

8 He fronted the US group The Doors until his early death in 1971 and is buried in a Paris cemetery.

9 He was born in Jamaica and ran for Olympic gold until he was stripped of the title for taking banned drugs.

10 Born in Syracuse, New York, he married Nicole Kidman and starred with Dustin Hoffman in *Rain Man*.

ANSWERS ON PAGE 285

46 EXTINCT CREATURES

1 What percentage of all creatures that have ever lived are believed to be extinct?
☐ 50.5 ☐ 75.2 ☐ 99.9

2 Dinosaur comes from the Greek meaning Terrible what?
☐ Beast ☐ Lizard ☐ Monster

3 How many million years ago did dinosaurs die out?
☐ 20 ☐ 65 ☐ 100

4 Endangered animal the Giant Panda is native to which country?
☐ China ☐ India ☐ Tibet

5 What was the name of the last passenger pigeon that died in 1914?
☐ Martha ☐ Peter ☐ Postie

6 What did the name dodo mean in Portuguese?
☐ Extinct ☐ Flightless ☐ Stupid

7 On which island was the dodo last sighted?
☐ Borneo ☐ Mauritius ☐ Sumatra

8 The extinct Steller's sea cow was linked to which creature of legend?
☐ Dracula ☐ Mermaid ☐ Wolfman

9 What was the name of the wild European ox last seen in the 17thC?
☐ Aurochs ☐ Deinodon ☐ Samiad

10 The dinosaur Stegosaurus is reckoned to have had the smallest what?
☐ Brain ☐ Ears ☐ Feet

11 In which century were most dinosaur remains excavated?
☐ 10th ☐ 19th ☐ 20th

12 Archaeopteryx is recognized as being the first what?
☐ Bird ☐ Fish ☐ Mammal

13 Marc Bolan used which extinct creature to name his group?
☐ Dodo ☐ Tyrannosaurus Rex
☐ Wolly Mammoth

14 Dinosaurs lived in which geological era?
☐ Cenozoic ☐ Mesozoic
☐ Precambrian

15 What did the gigantic dinosaurs the sauropods feed on?
☐ Insects ☐ Meat ☐ Plants

ANSWERS ON PAGE 285

47 WAR ZONES

1. Which US General along with Schwarzkopf was leader in the Gulf War of the 1990s?
2. The Taliban were a guerrilla group in which country?
3. How long did the Arab Israeli War of 1967 last?
4. Who, during the Vietnam War, was known as Hanoi Jane?
5. Which breakaway Russian republic had Grozny as its capital?
6. Which country's "Spring" was halted by the arrival of Soviet tanks in 1968?
7. Where was the Bay of Pigs whose invasion sparked a world crisis in the 1960s?
8. Which country pulled out of Vietnam in the 1950s?
9. Where did the *Enola Gay* drop a devastating bomb in WWII?
10. In which country is Passchendaele, scene of battle in WWI?
11. Whose forces were defeated at the Battle of Midway in 1942?
12. Who were defeated along with the Germans at El Alamein?
13. During World War 1 what kind of gas was used in the trenches?
14. What Operation was the codename for the D-Day landings?
15. Which major weapon of war was used for the first time in 1916?
16. The Tamil Tigers were fighting for a separate state on which island?
17. Muhammad Ali refused to fight in which war?
18. War broke out in Biafra in the 1960s when it broke away from which country?
19. Where did Nazi leader Rudolf Hess crashland in 1941?
20. The EOKA were a terrorist group operating on which European island?

ANSWERS ON PAGE 285

48 GENERAL KNOWLEDGE

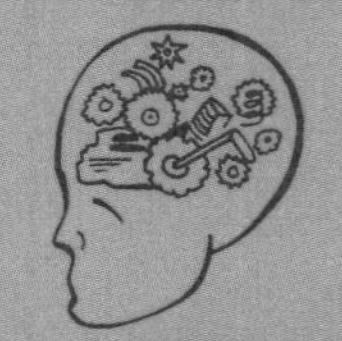
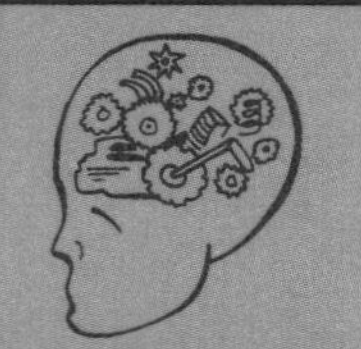

1. What was the name given to the first cloned sheep?
2. What did the letter F stand for in the name of President J F Kennedy?
3. What was the biggest US airbase in South Vietnam?
4. Doris Kapelhoff found fame by adopting which time related name?
5. Where was the presidential retreat where the agreement between Sadat and Begin was signed in 1978?
6. *The Cosby Show* was set in which American city?
7. In an *Evita* song what word follows, "Don't cry for me . . ."?
8. In which city was Gianni Versace shot?
9. Which Tom married Nicole Kidman?
10. What animal was Laika who went into space in 1957?
11. According to the song, what did the Andrew Sisters drink with Rum?
12. Jamie Lee Curtis was born in which decade of the 20th century?
13. *Country House* was a hit for which band?
14. On a computer keyboard what letter is far left on the top row of letters?
15. What type of singer was Mariah Carey's mother?
16. Antonio Carluccio writes about which country's food?
17. Which country does golfer Greg Norman come from?
18. Which was the longest major war of the 20th century?
19. In which country was Ingrid Bergman born?
20. In which country were Fiat cars first produced?

ANSWERS ON PAGE 285

49 LEADING LADIES

1. Which actress links *Gangs Of New York* and *There's Something About Mary*?
2. Who received an Oscar for *Chicago* shortly before giving birth to her second child?
3. Which Ms Roberts received an Oscar for *Erin Brokovich*?
4. What time of day was in the title of Nicole Kidman's first Oscar-winning movie?
5. Which Jennifer starred in *Maid In Manhattan*?
6. Which Ms Berry appeared in *Monster's Ball*?
7. Which Ms Moore starred opposite Anthony Hopkins in *Hannibal*?
8. Sarah Michelle Gellar starred in *Scooby Doo* about a crime fighting what?
9. Andie McDowell moved from *Four Weddings And A Funeral* to advertise what cosmetic?
10. Jennifer Connelly starred opposite Russell Crowe in a what type of *Mind*?
11. Which Ingrid was the mother of Isabella Rossellini?
12. Which Julie was Jamie Bell's teacher in *Billy Elliot*?
13. Which Barrymore starred in *Never Been Kissed* in 1999?
14. Which actress was on the video cover of *Titanic* with Leonardo DiCaprio?
15. Which Ryan starred in *When Harry Met Sally* and *Kate And Leopold*?
16. Who was at the front of the picture on the cover of *The Sound Of Music* DVD?
17. What is the first name of Ms Watson of *Angela's Ashes* fame?
18. Which Bridget of *Kiss Of The Dragon* fame has an actress aunt called Jane?
19. Which Australian leading lady of pop appeared in *Moulin Rouge*?
20. Which Kristin links *The Horse Whisperer* and *Four Weddings And A Funeral*?

ANSWERS ON PAGE 285

50 HALF CHANCE

½? ½? ½?

1. Which vegetable is produced from the plant maize – lentils or sweetcorn?
2. In which part of the UK was Charlotte Church born – Scotland or Wales?
3. Dennis Bergkamp has a phobia about what type of travel – flying or sailing?
4. Mozambique is on which coast of Africa – east or west?
5. Who starred as 007 in *The World is Not Enough* – Pierce Brosnan or Roger Moore?
6. Which superstar did film producer Guy Ritchie marry in 2000 – Madonna or Whitney Houston?
7. Frank Zappa was leader of the group The Mothers Of what – Destiny or Invention?
8. Does a hovercraft move along on a cushion of air or a cushion of water?
9. What is the German word for a motorway – autobahn or autorouten?
10. Are needles or oils applied to the body in acupuncture?
11. In darts, is the difference between the highest single dart treble and the lowest 49 or 57?
12. What colour car does The Pink Panther drive in his cartoon show – pink, red or gold?
13. Which politically incorrect adjective is applied to Thomas The Tank Engine's Controller – fat or ugly?
14. In which month is the London Marathon held – April or June?
15. Is the Acropolis situated in the Greek city of Athens or the city of Patras?
16. Chile is on which coast of South America – east or west?
17. Is the edelweiss a native flower to the Alps or the Andes?
18. Which word goes with Sleep in the title of a classic Bacall and Bogart movie – Big or Deep?
19. What did Jodhpur in India give its name to – a hot curry or riding trousers?
20. In which century was explorer David Livingstone born – the 18th or the19th?

ANSWERS ON PAGE 285

51 POP MUSIC QUIZ

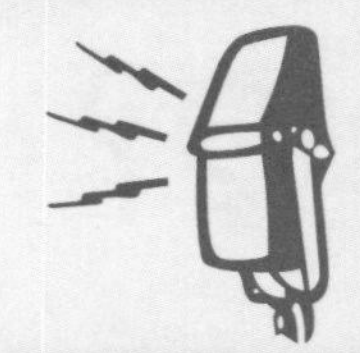
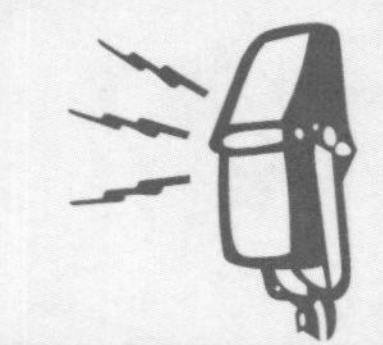
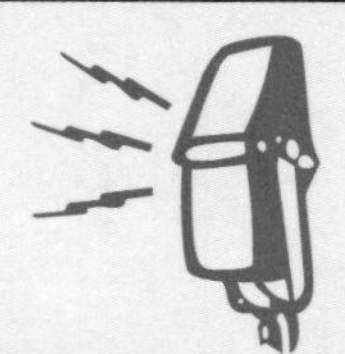

1. Which lady recorded the chart-topping album *Come Away With Me*?
2. Who was *Stripped* at the top of the UK album charts?
3. Who accompanied Boyz II Men on the mega hit *One Sweet Day*?
4. Danny, Joe, Sonnie, Jon and Jordan were better known as which group?
5. Who had a best-selling 1980s album *No Jacket Required*?
6. What was the highly original title of Ashanti's first album?
7. How many people were on the cover of Michael Jackson's *Thriller* album cover?
8. Which group made the album *Nevermind*?
9. Which country singer won a Lifetime Achievement Grammy in 2000?
10. With which late superstar did opera's Montserrat Caballe sing at the Barcelona Olympics?
11. Who recorded the album *Ten Summoner's Tales*?
12. Paul McCartney's *Standing Stone* was premiered in New York and which London venue?
13. Who was the first singer to have No 1 hits in five decades in the UK?
14. Which female vocalist duetted with George Michael on *If I Told You That*?
15. Which former Motown star had a new millennium hit with *Not Over Yet*?
16. Which James Bond theme did Tina Turner sing?
17. How is Lewis Allan Reed better known?
18. Who is Timothy Miles Bindon Rice's most famous musical collaborator?
19. Which Irish band made the album *The Joshua Tree*?
20. Which songstress got to No 1 on both sides of the Atlantic with *Spinning Around*?

ANSWERS ON PAGE 285

52 UK TOUR

1. Is Holy Island off the east or west coast of England?
2. What is a native of Aberdeen called?
3. Is London's Docklands, north, south, east or west of the city?
4. Where do people go to spot Nessie?
5. Which English gorge takes its name from a nearby village famous for its cheese?
6. Which county has the abbreviation Beds?
7. St Annes lies to the south of which British seaside resort?
8. Which Royal residence stands by the river Dee?
9. In which country is the UK's highest mountain?
10. What sort of an institution in London is Bart's?
11. On a London Tube map the Central Line is what colour?
12. In which Scottish city did you find the Gorbals?
13. Where is London's most famous Dog's Home?
14. Which Isle off the south coast of England is a county in its own right?
15. What is Britain's most southerly country?
16. Norwich is the administrative centre of which county?
17. In which city did the National Trust buy the childhood home of Paul McCartney?
18. Which motorway runs almost parallel to the A4?
19. With which profession is London's Harley Street associated?
20. What is Britain's largest international airport?

ANSWERS ON PAGE 285

53 PICTURE QUIZ

A B C D

What links these pictures?

ANSWERS ON PAGE 285

54 BONES

Is each statement TRUE or FALSE?

T F **1** The human skeleton is made up of 206 bones.

T F **2** The sternum is the breast bone.

T F **3** The tibia is in the arm.

T F **4** There are 18 separate bones in the human spine.

T F **5** Around half the human skeleton's bones are in the hands and feet.

T F **6** Cartilage cushions bones in movement.

T F **7** Female bones are usually heavier than male bones.

T F **8** The patella is part of the ankle joint.

T F **9** The scapula is the shoulder blade.

T F **10** The clavicle is the elbow.

ANSWERS ON PAGE 285

55 BEST ACTOR OSCAR

1 Which movie gave Jamie Foxx his first Oscar?
☐ *The Aviator* ☐ *The Incredibles*
☐ *Ray*

2 Which British Rex won in the 1960s?
☐ Ford ☐ Harrison ☐ Laughton

3 Who won back to back awards in 1993 and 1994?
☐ Tom Cruise ☐ Tom Hanks
☐ Al Pacino

4 Russell Crowe won for which combat movie?
☐ *Braveheart* ☐ *Gladiator* ☐ *Matrix*

5 Who won for *Sergeant York* and *High Noon*?
☐ Gary Cooper ☐ James Stewart
☐ Spencer Tracy

6 What type of Day did Denzil Washington star in?
☐ Laundry ☐ Ordinary ☐ Training

7 Which Robert won for *Tender Mercies*?
☐ De Niro ☐ Duvall ☐ Redford

8 What was Bing Crosby's profession in *Going My Way*?
☐ Doctor ☐ Priest ☐ Salesman

9 What type of person did Geoffrey Rush play in *Shine*?
☐ Musician ☐ Soldier ☐ Traveller

10 How many years between Marlon Brando's first and second Oscar?
☐ 10 ☐ 18 ☐ 22

11 Gene Hackman won for a movie set in which country?
☐ Austria ☐ France ☐ Uruguay

12 How many Oscars did Errol Flynn win?
☐ None ☐ One ☐ Three

13 Which Douglas won for *Wall Street*?
☐ Douglas ☐ Kirk ☐ Michael

14 Which Terry did Brando play to win his first award?
☐ Malloy ☐ Thomas ☐ Jones

15 What kind of Man proved a success for Dustin Hoffman?
☐ Hard
☐ Rain
☐ Super

ANSWERS ON PAGE 285

56 LUCKY DIP

1 What does R stand for in the initials HRH?

2 What sort of fruits are limes, lemons and grapefruit?

3 Who did Doctor Jekyll turn into?

4 What are too many cooks said to spoil?

5 Which is not an island – Cyprus, Greece, Sicily?

6 Which animals took Hannibal over the Alps?

7 What do you call a puzzle where interlinking answers are written across and down?

8 In which team game do you try to move backwards all the time?

9 What colour are emeralds?

10 How many aces are there in a pack of cards?

11 Who has to climb a ladder to reach his or her seat at Wimbledon?

12 In the fairy tale, who does The Beast fall in love with?

13 What is the main ingredient in a brick?

14 What hangs down from the roof of cave – a stalagmite or a stalactite?

15 What is the Roman number for ten?

16 How does Saturday's child work for a living according to the rhyme?

17 What language do the people native to Milan speak?

18 How many are there in a baker's dozen?

19 In rhyme, which bell said, "You owe me five farthings"?

20 Which British national daily newspaper of yesterday ceased publication in 1995?

ANSWERS ON PAGE 285

57 WESTERNS

1 Which Val starred in *Tombstone*?

2 During which American war was *Dances With Wolves* set?

3 Which spaghetti western icon was the Good in *The Good, The Bad And The Ugly*?

4 What was big John Wayne's final movie?

5 Which Gary won the Best Actor Oscar for *High Noon*?

6 Which Lee won the Best Actor Oscar for *Cat Ballou*?

7 Which Robert co starred with John Wayne in *El Dorado*?

8 Which 60s folk singer had a minor role in *Pat Garrett And Billy The Kid*?

9 *I Was Born Under A Wandrin' Star* comes from which musical western?

10 In which decade did spaghetti westerns first hit the screens?

11 Westerns were referred to as what type of operas?

12 Which Gene was dubbed the singing cowboy?

13 Which Gene won an Oscar as the Sheriff in *Unforgiven*?

14 In which western did John Wayne famously wear an eye patch?

15 Which western movie was a remake of the *Seven Samurai*?

16 Which Barbara, star of *Forty Guns*, was one of the few female members of the National Cowboy Hall of fame?

17 Which Morgan appeared with Clint Eastwood in *Unforgiven*?

18 Which blue-eyed Paul starred in *Hud*?

19 In which decade was *High Noon* released?

20 "Come back Shane" is the last line of which movie?

ANSWERS ON PAGE 285

58 AT THE MOVIES

1 *Top Gun* and *City Of Angels* featured which actress?

2 The character Vincent Vega appeared in which movie?

3 Which Susan starred in *The Witches Of Eastwick*?

4 In 1998 who separated from her husband Bruce Willis?

5 In which decade was *Godzilla* released after the 1955 movie?

6 Who played Jack in *Titanic*?

7 Which Landings were the subject of *Saving Private Ryan*?

8 Who played the title role in the movie *Citizen Kane*?

9 Which Matt starred in *Wild Things*?

10 Which word links a Hawk and a Wolf to give two film titles?

11 Who played Rosemary in *Rosemary's Baby*?

12 *Was Beverly Hills Cop* first released in the 1960s, 70s or 80s?

13 *Ghostbusters* and *Alien* featured which actress?

14 Who played the police captain in *Casablanca*?

15 Which actress links *The Silence Of The Lambs* and *Taxi Driver*?

16 Which film superhero gets involved with Cat Woman?

17 Who starred in the *Lethal Weapon* series of films?

18 In which decade was *Rain Man* released?

19 Which fruit would complete this movie title, *The* ____ *Of Wrath*?

20 Which Jamie starred in *Halloween*?

ANSWERS ON PAGE 285

59 SPORT

1 Which team won the Super Bowl in 2002 and 2004?

2 Who has won most international soccer caps for England?

3 For how many years was Matt Busby manager of Man Utd?

4 In which sport were Scott Hamilton and Katarina Witt world champions?

5 Which trainer became known as the "Queen of Aintree"?

6 What nationality is tennis player Michael Chang?

7 Which ball scores more points in snooker, the blue or the brown?

8 Which legendary golfer Henry won his first British Open in 1934?

9 For what sport is Ellery Hanley famous?

10 Moving clockwise round a dartboard, what number follows on from 6?

11 Which two sports take place on a piste?

12 At which Grand Prix circuit did Ayrton Senna lose his life?

13 Who was the first swimmer to break a minute for the 100 metres breast stroke?

14 Which sport involved the Miami Dolphins – American football, sailing or swimming?

15 Where was Barry Sheene involved in a 175 mph crash in 1975?

16 Which twisting circuit on the Grand Prix calendar is only 1.95 miles long?

17 Has croquet ever been a sport in the Olympics?

18 Is an own goal allowed for in the rules of hockey?

19 In Rugby Union, who is Australia's record try scorer?

20 In speedway, how many laps of the track does a race consist of?

ANSWERS ON PAGE 285

60 AROUND AMERICA

1 Which state lies to the south of Georgia?

2 Which ocean is off the Californian coast?

3 Which city is the home of jazz?

4 In which city is the Guggenheim Museum?

5 In which state is Harvard University?

6 Which state was called Quinnehtukqut by Native Americans?

7 What is the other main Boston newspaper along with the *Herald*?

8 What is Hawaii's largest city?

9 In which city is Santa Monica Bay?

10 If it's noon in Boston, what time is it in New York?

11 Which two mid-Atlantic states have New in their names?

12 In which state are the Catskill Mountains?

13 The Horseshoe Falls are part of which famous Falls?

14 In which state is the Sun Studio famed for its Elvis recordings?

15 Which Gulf lies to the south of Florida?

16 Which city has an area called Haight Ashbury?

17 Which Mile Island is home to a nuclear power plant?

18 A museum in whose memory can be visited at Hyannis?

19 Which Island is the smallest state of the Union?

20 Which President had a summer retreat at Kennebunkport?

ANSWERS ON PAGE 285

61 GENERAL KNOWLEDGE

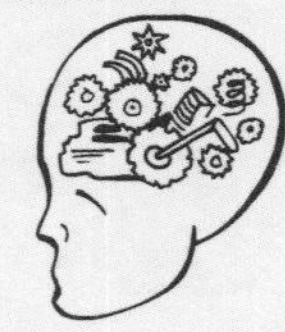
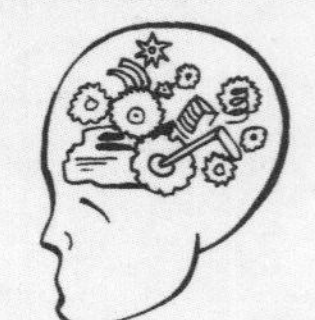
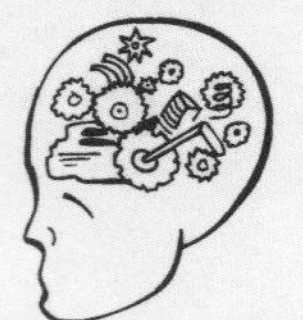

1 Most of The Three Tenors come from which country?

2 What did Dr Howard Carter discover?

3 In which decade of last century was the Cullinan diamond discovered?

4 Which Bond girl was played by Diana Rigg?

5 Whose last words were reputedly, "Either this wallpaper goes or I do"?

6 At which sport did Neil Adams win international success?

7 Who wrote the song *Mad Dogs And Englishmen*?

8 In which decade did the UK join the European Union?

9 Who wrote the children's classic *The Lion, The Witch And The Wardrobe*?

10 What's the link between boxing champion James Corbett and country singer Jim Reeves?

11 After a tennis match with Amelia Mauresmo who said, "I thought I was playing a guy"?

12 What post did Edward Shevardnadze hold in the USSR from 1985 to 1990?

13 In baseball where do the Braves come from?

14 Which musical featured the song *Wouldn't It Be Luvverly*?

15 Who did Clement Attlee replace as UK Prime Minister?

16 Who made No 1 in the UK with *Ready Or Not*?

17 De Efteling Theme Park is in which country?

18 According to the Monty Python team what does a lumberjack do all night?

19 Agno international airport is in which country?

20 Who said, "There will be no whitewash in the White House"?

ANSWERS ON PAGE 285

62 PICTURE QUIZ

What links these pictures?

ANSWERS ON PAGE 285

63 DOUBLE TAKE

In each case, the two-part quiz question leads to just one answer!

1 Which word means significant and is the name of an army officer?

2 Which word can mean a small crusty loaf and a male swan?

3 Which word means expensive as well as cherished?

4 Which word means the sea off Norfolk and to clean with soap?

5 Which word describes a busy phone line and being betrothed?

6 Which word means cooked under direct heat and interrogated?

7 Which word means a wine cellar and to jump?

8 Which word for a bargain also means to cut?

9 Which word for a fruit drink also means friendly?

10 Which word for whale fat also means to cry uncontrollably?

ANSWERS ON PAGE 285

64 RAILWAYS

1 In which century was the word railway first used?
☐ 17th ☐ 18th ☐ 19th

2 What was the name of Robert Stephenson's steam locomotive?
☐ Kettle ☐ Rocket ☐ Sidecar

3 Which was the first country to establish a railway?
☐ Germany ☐ UK ☐ USA

4 Which was the second country to establish a railway?
☐ France ☐ UK ☐ USA

5 Which Doctor's report led to closure of much of the UK rail system?
☐ Beeching ☐ Bolting ☐ Driver

6 When did the Trans-Siberian Railway open?
☐ 1904 ☐ 1914 ☐ 1924

7 Which Scottish railway bridge collapsed in 1879?
☐ Clyde ☐ Tay ☐ Forth

8 Which country has the longest rail network?
☐ Canada ☐ Russia ☐ USA

9 How were diesel-electric trains known?
☐ Deel ☐ Deltic ☐ Leccie

10 In which decade was air conditioning first installed on a train?
☐ 1850s ☐ 1880s
☐ 1920s

11 At which station was London Underground's worst rail disaster?
☐ King's Cross
☐ Moorgate ☐ Strand

12 In which year did the Channel Tunnel open?
☐ 1987 ☐ 1994 ☐ 1998

13 Mallard was what type of locomotive?
☐ Diesel ☐ Electric ☐ Steam

14 What colour were cabs of the Union Pacific?
☐ Blue ☐ Red ☐ Yellow

15 Which country developed the TGV?
☐ France ☐ Germany ☐ USA

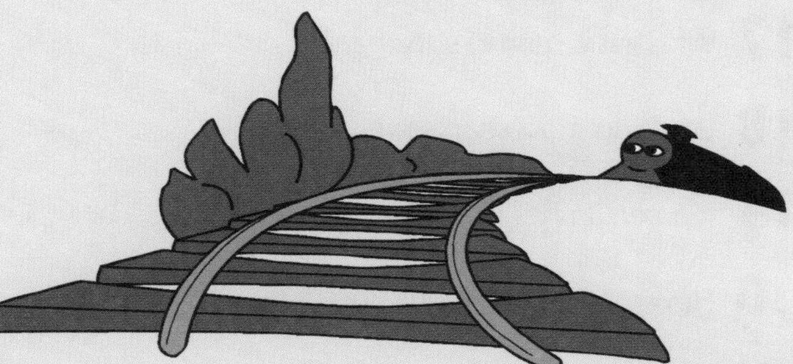

ANSWERS ON PAGE 285

65 NATURE

1 Tsunami is another name for what type of wave?

2 Where would a melanoma appear?

3 Which disease in humans has been linked to the cattle disease BSE?

4 What sort of creature is a fluke?

5 Which branch of medicine is concerned with disorders of the blood?

6 What name is given to an organism which is both male and female?

7 What sort of bird is a merlin?

8 Which part of the body might suffer from labyrinthitis?

9 What sort of creature is an abalone?

10 Where is a bird's patella?

11 Which racing creatures live in lofts?

12 What condition is caused by a shortage of haemoglobin?

13 What colour are the spots on a plaice?

14 What is a puffball?

15 Which part of the body does scabies affect?

16 Which digestive organ lies below the thorax in invertebrates?

17 Where is a human's scapula?

18 What do most sharks live on?

19 If a person has myopia what problem does he or she have?

20 How many pairs of ribs does a human have?

ANSWERS ON PAGE 285

66 TELEVISION CLASSICS

1 In *The Muppet Show* what colour was Kermit?

2 Who played Ricky Ricardo in *I Love Lucy*?

3 What was the name of the family in the *Beverly Hillbillies*?

4 Which Henry wrote the theme music to *The Pink Panther*?

5 What was Walter Cronkite's signing off catchphrase?

6 In 1970s/80s TV how was *The Hulk* described?

7 Which comedy classic promised, "And now for something completely different"?

8 Which star of *Police Woman* appeared in *Rio Bravo* with John Wayne in the 1950s?

9 What was Dr Kildare's first name?

10 Which team included Mr T?

11 Which creatures were the heroes of *Flipper*?

12 *The Case Of The Velvet Claw* was the first case for which attorney?

13 What is British TV's longest-running show?

14 Which children's TV classic asked, "Who was that masked man"?

15 What sort of creature was Mr Ed?

16 Who played the part of Sgt. Bilko?

17 In which sitcom was Tom married to Barbara?

18 In *Bewitched* what was Darrin's relation to Endora?

19 What was the female follow up to *The Man From U.N.C.L.E* called?

20 On which classic film was *The Wacky Races* based?

ANSWERS ON PAGE 285

67 LUCKY DIP

1. Which king had a round table?
2. Which US state, which joined the Union in 1912, has New and the name of a country in its name?
3. Who was the outgoing president when Bill Clinton took office?
4. Which town do the Flintstones live in?
5. What colour is produced by mixing blue and red?
6. Which river can be seen from the Houses Of Parliament?
7. How many of Henry VIII's wives were called Anne?
8. What is the symbol for Comic Relief?
9. Who in the Bible had a coat of many colours?
10. What type of creature was slain by Saint George?
11. What meat appears in a tradiitional Punch and Judy show?
12. In 2003, which large creature was the title of an album by The White Stripes?
13. Which London street is home to Sherlock Holmes?
14. Who was the tallest of Robin Hood's Men?
15. In the proverb, what should you do before you leap?
16. How many minutes are there in ten hours?
17. Is Sri Lanka north or south of the Equator?
18. Which cartoon character says, "What's up, doc?"?
19. Which feast was it when Good King Wenceslas looked out?
20. In your body where are your molars?

ANSWERS ON PAGE 286

68 MARILYN MONROE

1. What were her real first names?
2. The title of her 1953 movie was *How To Marry* who?
3. In which film which mentioned blondes did she play Lorelei Lee?
4. In the 1957 movie when Olivier played the Prince who was Monroe?
5. *Some Like It Hot*, about the aftermath of the St Valentine's Day massacre, is set in which decade?
6. Monroe had a minor role in which movie with Bette Davis, *All About* whom?
7. To which US President did she famously sing Happy Birthday?
8. Which Billy directed her in *The Seven Year Itch*?
9. Which classic Beatles album features Marilyn Monroe – among many others – on the cover?
10. In *Some Like It Hot* which stringed musical instrument does she play?
11. Which Ethel was her leading co star in *There's No Business Like Show Business*?
12. What was the official cause of her death?
13. What type of sportsman was her second husband?
14. Which playwright Arthur was her third and last husband?
15. In which decade did Marilyn Monroe die?
16. What was her first name as Miss Kane in *Some Like It Hot*?
17. Which brunette Jane was her co star in *Gentlemen Prefer Blondes*?
18. What sort of *Business* was the title of a 1952 movie?
19. Which 1953 movie took its name from some Canadian Falls?
20. With which King of Hollywood did she make her last completed film – which was also his final movie?

ANSWERS ON PAGE 286

69 GEOGRAPHY

1 Is the South Pole in the Arctic or the Antarctic?

2 What does each star on the flag of the United States stand for?

3 Which country does the holiday island of Ibiza belong to?

4 Which island would you visit to kiss the Blarney Stone?

5 Where would you be if you were visiting the Taj Mahal?

6 The south of which continent is closest to the Falkland Islands?

7 In which mountain range would you find Mount Everest?

8 Which country is Luxembourg the capital of?

9 What colour is the spot in the middle of the Japanese flag?

10 The island of Sicily is at the toe of which country?

11 Which European country has an area called Flanders?

12 In which country are Maoris the indigenous population?

13 In which Scandinavian country would you find fjords?

14 Which country's languages include English, Zulu and Afrikaans?

15 In which ocean is Fiji?

16 In which city is Vatican City?

17 What is K2 – a hurricane, a mountain or an underground cavern?

18 In which country is the Yellow River also known as Huang He?

19 Which country has four letters, the last one Q?

20 Which country, capital Bangkok, used to be called Siam?

ANSWERS ON PAGE 286

70 HISTORY

1 Which important ship canal was built by Ferdinand de Lesseps?

2 Which part of Captain Jenkins was cut off to start a war?

3 Who preferred "50000 rifles to 50000 votes"?

4 On which day in 1066 was William the Conqueror crowned King of England?

5 Who was Labour Prime Minister of Australia from 1983–1991?

6 In which year did Sir Winston Churchill die?

7 Which William was married to Mary II?

8 James I and Charles I were members of which royal dynasty?

9 On which island did King John set his seal to the Magna Carta?

10 Which Neville was British Prime Minister at the outbreak of World War II?

11 Who became Egyptian President after Sadat's assassination?

12 What was the name of the scandal over arms for hostages in which Oliver North was implicated?

13 Which Cabinet Minister was leader of Sheffield City Council for most of the 80s?

14 Who did Ronald Reagan defeat to become US President in 1980?

15 Which spin doctor did Neil Kinnock engage to run the 1987 election campaign?

16 In 1989 state schools were allowed to opt out of whose control?

17 Which woman became PM of Pakistan after the death of Zia in a plane crash?

18 Where did the parties of ZANU and ZAPU merge in 1987?

19 In 1986 the pass laws, concerning the carrying of identity documents, were repealed in which country?

20 Which Russian leader introduced the policy of perestroika?

ANSWERS ON PAGE 286

71 RIVER CITY

On which river do these capital cities stand?

1. AMMAN
2. LIMA
3. LISBON
4. BUENOS AIRES
5. DUBLIN
6. BAGHDAD
7. ZAGREB
8. WARSAW
9. SANTIAGO
10. BRUSSELS

ANSWERS ON PAGE 286

72 GUESS WHO . . . ?

1. Born in Cork in November 1969, she is Ireland's greatest-ever female athlete.
2. Born in Connecticut in 1907, she had an affair with Spencer Tracy and was played by Cate Blanchett in *The Aviator*.
3. Born in Connecticut in 1947, she had movie success with *Dangerous Liaisons* and *Fatal Attraction*, opposite Michael Douglas.
4. Born in Jamaica in 1960, she was still competing at the highest level in her forties, competing latterly for Slovenia.
5. She married Tom Cruise, starred opposite Ewan McGregor in *Moulin Rouge* and won an Oscar for *The Hours*.
6. Born in Dublin in 1940, she achieved fame with her first novel *Light a Penny Candle*.
7. Born in 1930 in Edinburgh, he was a body builder before becoming famous as secret agent 007.
8. Great niece of an Olympic swimmer of the 1920s, she held Marathon records but dropped out of the Athens race before the end.
9. Born in Jamaica with the first names Robert Nesta, he recorded *No Woman No Cry* and *I Shot the Sheriff*.
10. He is married to Laura, has twin daughters, the middle initial W and the same first name as his father.

ANSWERS ON PAGE 286

73 HOLIDAY RESORTS

1. Bali is how many degrees south of the Equator?
   ☐ Eight ☐ Twelve ☐ Twenty
2. If your resort was in the Vendée where would you be?
   ☐ France ☐ Italy ☐ Spain
3. Mellieha is on which island?
   ☐ Corfu ☐ Ibiza ☐ Malta
4. The beach of Mazzaro is on which island?
   ☐ Majorca ☐ Minorca ☐ Sicily
5. Which Lancashire resort has a famous Pleasure Beach?
   ☐ Blackpool ☐ Heysham
   ☐ Morecambe
6. In which county is Brighton?
   ☐ Dorset ☐ East Sussex ☐ Hampshire
7. How long is Australia's Great Ocean Road?
   ☐ 100 miles ☐ 250 miles ☐ 300 miles
8. What colour flag is awarded to quality beaches in Europe?
   ☐ Blue ☐ White ☐ Yellow
9. Where in Asia was the first Disneyland resort?
   ☐ Indonesia ☐ Japan ☐ Thailand
10. In which Florida resort are the Universal Studios?
    ☐ Miami ☐ Orlando ☐ Tampa
11. Majorca is part of which island group?
    ☐ Balearics ☐ Canaries ☐ Caribbean
12. Which Lancashire resort boasts a Frontierland?
    ☐ Blackpool ☐ Heysham
    ☐ Morecambe?
13. Where is Africa's single biggest game reserve?
    ☐ Kenya ☐ Mali ☐ Tanzania?
14. The resort of Kuta is on which island?
    ☐ Antigua ☐ Bali ☐ Vanuatu
15. Tenerife is part of which island group?
    ☐ Balearics ☐ Canaries
    ☐ Greek islands

ANSWERS ON PAGE 286

It's snow joke when the months are cold and the days are dark. Look on the bright side and think that spring is just around the corner. Here are 50 questions about the winter wonderland!

1 The Festival of St Lucia is celebrated in which country?

2 On which date is it celebrated?

3 Which island did St Lucia come from?

4 Which three star signs are the winter signs?

5 The play *The Lion In Winter* is about which English king?

6 Which Shakespeare play has Winter in the title?

7 Which plants, such as *Gaultheria procumbens*, have aromatic leaves used in medicine?

8 Which Royal family had a famous Winter Palace in St Petersburg?

9 In France, gateau des rois is eaten at which celebration?

10 Where did Torvill & Dean win their final Winter Olympics gold medal, earning a perfect score?

11 Chinese New Year can be held in either of which two winter months?

12 Away from the frozen Northern hemisphere, which South American country is famous for its Carnival?

13 What type of Carnival food is linguiça?

14 Which Commonwealth country's special day is January 26th?

15 In which month is St Nicholas's Day?

16 St Vincent, whose feast day is the 22nd January, is the patron saint of what?

17 What name is given to an animal's period of sleep during the winter?

18 In which country were the Nagano Winter Olympics held?

19 Which black rights leader has a special day in mid-January in the USA?

20 Diwali is the Hindu festival of what?

21 What colour clothes does St Nicholas wear?

22 For which winter sport is Alberto Tomba most famous?

23 Candlemas is a winter festival in which religion?

24 Which movie director was born in the winter of 1935 as Allen Stewart Konigsberg?

25 Which composer with the middle name Amadeus died in the winter of 1791?

26 Which band had a hit with *A Winter's Tale* in 1995?

27 In which decade of the 20th century were the Winter Olympics first held?

28 Which Shakespeare play includes the speech, "Now is the winter of our discontent . . ."?

29 Which American Tea Party took place in the winter of 1773?

30 In which winter sport did John Curry win Olympic gold?

31 Which winter festival is known as Weihnachten in German?

32 Which Winter Olympics sport was the movie *Cool Runnings* about?

33 What are the special Japanese cakes mochi made from?

34 The death of which Beatle took place in December 1980?

35 How many candles are lit in the candlestick used at Hannukah?

36 In which novel is Maxim de Winter the hero?

37 How many days are there usually in the winter months of December, January and February?

38 In which future state did the Pilgrim Fathers land in the winter of 1620?

39 What was Torvill & Dean's Olympic event?

40 What is the traditional colour for the dress worn by the girl who depicts St Lucia?

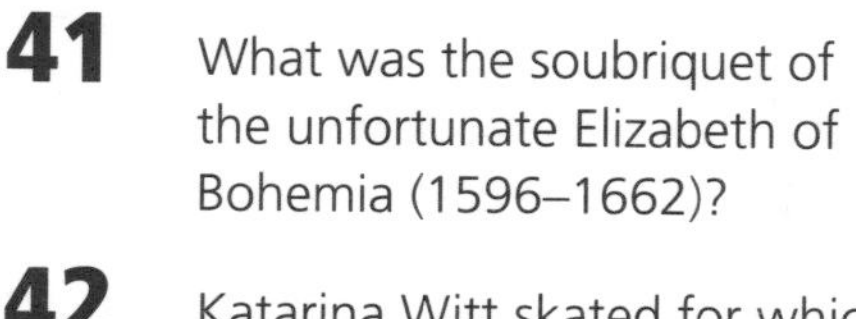

41 What was the soubriquet of the unfortunate Elizabeth of Bohemia (1596–1662)?

42 Katarina Witt skated for which country?

43 Which country celebrates Waitangi Day?

44 What name is given to skiing, bobsleigh and skating for example?

45 Where were the first Winter Olympics held?

46 Which dance is important in the colourful Brazilian carnival?

47 Hannukah is usually celebrated in which month of the Gregorian calendar?

48 What does a hannukiyah hold?

49 Which Shakespeare play is another name for Epiphany (6th January)?

50 Where were the first Winter Olympics of the new millennium held?

ANSWERS ON PAGE 286

75 ROCK & ROLL

1 At what time of year did Eddie Cochran get the blues?

2 Which group backed Buddy Holly?

3 Which creature comes next after "See you later, alligator"?

4 Who was known as "The Killer"?

5 Which Hill did Fats Domino sing about?

6 Which Elvis song has the line, "You ain't a never caught a rabbit"?

7 What comes before *Rattle And Roll* in a Bill Haley hit title?

8 Which Gene recorded *Be Bop A Lula*?

9 Which Big named vocalist died with Buddy Holly?

10 Which Tommy, who became an all-round entertainer, was billed as Britain's first rock'n'roll star?

11 What was Cliff Richard's first UK top ten hit?

12 In which US state was Elvis born?

13 Which instrument did Little Richard play on stage?

14 Which Carl penned and performed *Blue Suede Shoes*?

15 In which country did Eddie Cochran die?

16 What completes the lines, "cruising and playing the radio, With no particular place . . ."?

17 What was the colour of retro rocker Shakin' Stevens' "Door" in the 80s?

18 *Great Balls Of Fire* was the first UK No 1 for which artist?

19 Which British rock'n'roll singer Marty is the father of 80s hit maker Kim?

20 Which Johnny was backed by The Pirates?

ANSWERS ON PAGE 286

76 HALF CHANCE

½ ? ½ ? ½ ?

1 Which Frenchman gave his name to an item worn by ballet dancers – Leotard or Tutu?

2 Q is on which row of letters on a keyboard – middle or top?

3 Are Glen Cova and Malling Jewel types of blackcurrant or raspberry?

4 In which sport can there be a night watchman – cricket or ice hockey?

5 In Japan, is Hara-Kiri a hot rice dish or obligatory suicide?

6 In a limerick which line does the third line rhyme with – the second or the fourth?

7 Agatha Christie wrote about *The Murder of* which Roger – Roger Ackroyd or Roger Styles?

8 What was the nationality of fable writer Aesop – Egyptian or Greek?

9 Which subject was George Stubbs famous for painting – children or horse?

10 Do extracts from Jonathan Harker's diary appear in *Dracula* or *Treasure Island*?

11 Kayak, rotor and noon are all examples of what type of words – palindromes or synonyms?

12 Before *Titanic* was the last film to win 14 Oscar nominations *All About Eve* or *Ben Hur*?

13 The Golan Heights border Israel and which other country – Lebanon or Syria?

14 Which TV comedy series featured Miss Tibbs and Miss Gatsby – *Are You Being Served?* or *Fawlty Towers*?

15 Who was the youngest Beatle – George or Ringo?

16 Is the city of Salonika in Greece or Paraguay?

17 Did Tom Rowlands and Ed Simons became the Blues Brothers or the Chemical Brothers?

18 Does *Austin Powers Man Of Mystery* tackle Dr Evil or Dr Nasty?

19 Who had his statue removed from Russia's Red Square in 1991 – Lenin or Peter the Great?

20 Who did Caroline Quentin play in TV's *Jonathan Creek* – Joanna Creek or Maddy Magellan?

ANSWERS ON PAGE 286

77 SCIENCE

1 Which corporation developed the first MiniDisc, launched in 1992?

2 What was developed by Carlsson and Fuller in the late 1980s?

3 Who discovered the law of gravity?

4 What was the nationality of astronomer Galileo?

5 What dies the G stand for in GM crops?

6 What did Jean Nicot extract from tobacco?

7 Which "Effect" is associated with global warming?

8 Which layer of the Earth's atmosphere has been damaged above Antarctica?

9 What was the name of the first probe to send back pictures from Mars?

10 Who was the first woman to captain a space shuttle crew?.

11 In terms of Nobel prizes how did Marie Curie achieve two "firsts"?

12 Which physicist contributed to the development of Soviet nuclear weapons and was a civil rights campaigner?

13 Which rocket engineer played a major role in the US space programme?

14 Which aids to calculation did John Napier devise?

15 Which two elements did the Curies discover?

16 Leibnitz's calculating machine was the first able to do which function?

17 Which word was Candolle the first to use in the classification of plants?

18 For which measuring system did Joseph Louis Lagrange lay foundations?

19 On which Islands did Darwin's observations help him write *The Origin of Species*?

20 For which Soviet development was Igor Kurchatov team leader?

ANSWERS ON PAGE 286

78 LEADERS

1 Susilo Bambang Yudhoyono was President of which country devastated by the December 2004 tsunami?

2 Former dramatist Vaclav Havel became President of which Czech Republic?

3 Assassinated Prime Minister Olof Palme led which country?

4 Which US President called the USSR an "evil empire"?

5 Which Prime Minister of Australia wept on TV when he confessed to marital misdemeanours?

6 Which leader did John Hinckley Jr shoot?

7 Lord Carrington resigned as Foreign Secretary of the UK during which conflict?

8 Which personality became Mayor of Carmel, California in 1986?

9 Who did Nelson Mandela succeed as head of the ANC?

10 On which day of the week does the President of the USA give his weekly talk to the American people?

11 Which lady became Tony Blair's Secretary of State for Culture Media & Sport after the 2001 election?

12 Betty Boothroyd had which famous position of responsibility in Britain?

13 At the turn of the millennium which British queen – other than Victoria – had reigned longest?

14 How many years was Margaret Thatcher British Prime Minister?

15 Who did Jack Straw replace as Foreign Secretary?

16 In 1999 Ehud Barak became Prime Minister of which country?

17 Who was Bill Clinton's first Vice President?

18 Prince Rainier III ruled where for over 50 years?

19 Who did Gerhard Schroeder replace as German Chancellor?

20 Who was Mayor of New York at the time of the World Trade Center disaster?

ANSWERS ON PAGE 286

79 GENERAL KNOWLEDGE

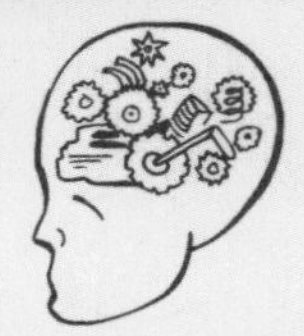

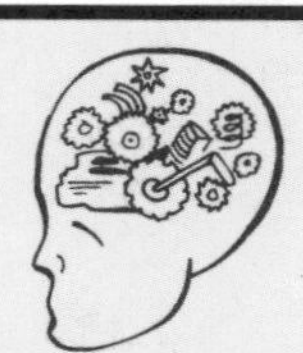

1 Opened in June 1999, Liverpool's Matthew Street Gallery was dedicated to whose works?

2 Neil Armstrong was a pilot in which war?

3 Which musical featured the song *Hello Young Lovers*?

4 Who wrote the *Scarlet Pimpernel*?

5 In which country was Mel Gibson born?

6 Which Spice Girl teamed with Bryan Adams on *When You're Gone*?

7 Which fraudster hid his debts in a secret account number 88888?

8 Louis Washkansky was the first recipient of what?

9 Which item of clothing cost Isadora Duncan her life?

10 How did William Cody become better known?

11 In which country was Ursula Andress born?

12 Early in the 20th century who wrote the novel *Nostromo*?

13 What part of Betty Grable was insured for over a million dollars?

14 In the summer 1999, Anna Kournikova signed a lucrative contract to model which item of clothing?

15 In which decade did Belgium join the European Union?

16 In which city did Man Utd win the 1999 European Champions' Cup Final?

17 On a computer keyboard which vowel is not on the top row of letters?

18 Louis Armstrong sang the title song for which Bond film?

19 What did Clarice Cliff create?

20 To the nearest million what is the population of London?

ANSWERS ON PAGE 286

80 COMEDY MOVIES

1 Which movie featured Jim Carrey as Truman Burbank?

2 Which comic star Ellen starred in *Doctor Doolittle* with Eddie Murphy?

3 Which Austin was the International *Man Of Mystery*?

4 Which Mr was the subject of the *Ultimate Disaster Movie*, with Rowan Atkinson?

5 In which 1997 movie did Jim Carrey promise to tell the truth for a whole day?

6 In which Yorkshire steel town was *The Full Monty* set?

7 Which zany Jerry made the 1960s version of *The Nutty Professor*?

8 Which cartoon family from Bedrock hit the big screen in 1994?

9 Who found fame as Charles in *Four Weddings And A Funeral*?

10 Which Day was the subject of a 1993 movie with Bill Murray and Andie MacDowell?

11 What job does Mrs Doubtfire take on to look after "her" own children?

12 Who received $8 million dollars for making the sequel to *Sister Act, Sister Act 2*?

13 In 1963 what sort of precious gem was *The Pink Panther*?

14 Whose World starred Mike Myers and Dana Carvey?

15 What sort of reptiles were Donatello and Leonardo?

16 Which trio took the *Road to Rio, Bali, Morocco* and *Utopia*?

17 Who were Chico, Gummo and Zeppo's two brothers?

18 Who was the baby's voice in *Look Who's Talking*?

19 Who played the title role in *Tootsie*?

20 Which star of *Cabaret* appeared with Dudley Moore in *Arthur*?

ANSWERS ON PAGE 286

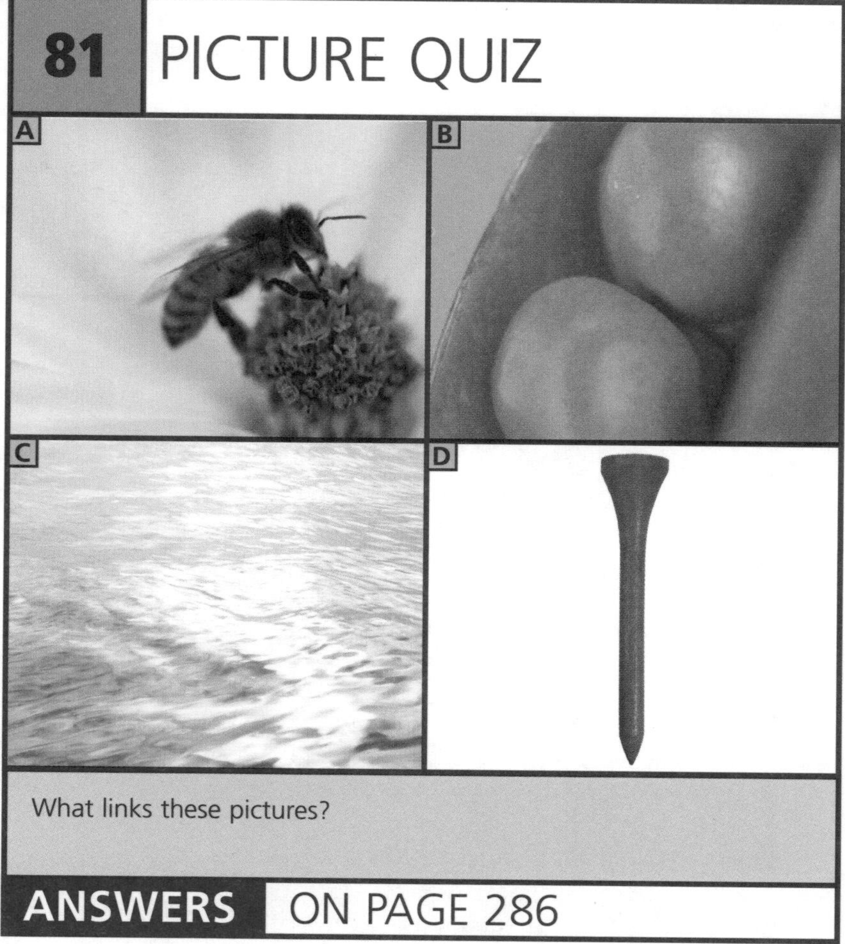

81 PICTURE QUIZ

A B C D

What links these pictures?

ANSWERS ON PAGE 286

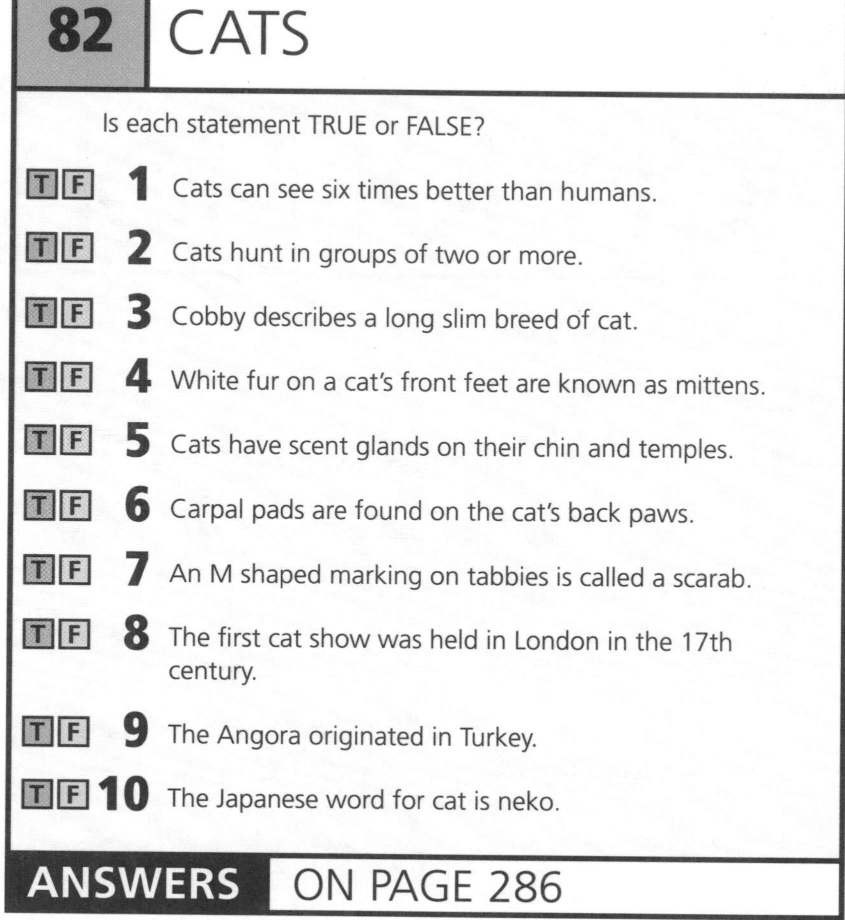

82 CATS

Is each statement TRUE or FALSE?

T F **1** Cats can see six times better than humans.

T F **2** Cats hunt in groups of two or more.

T F **3** Cobby describes a long slim breed of cat.

T F **4** White fur on a cat's front feet are known as mittens.

T F **5** Cats have scent glands on their chin and temples.

T F **6** Carpal pads are found on the cat's back paws.

T F **7** An M shaped marking on tabbies is called a scarab.

T F **8** The first cat show was held in London in the 17th century.

T F **9** The Angora originated in Turkey.

T F **10** The Japanese word for cat is neko.

ANSWERS ON PAGE 286

83 CASTLES

1 What was the central building of a castle called?
☐ Bailey ☐ Gatehouse ☐ Keep

2 What was the special feature of a drawbridge?
☐ Booby trapped ☐ Could move ☐ Fireproof

3 What were most castles built of?
☐ Concrete ☐ Stone ☐ Wood

4 A tower was built on a steep earth mound called a what?
☐ Bailey ☐ Gatehouse ☐ Motte

5 Ludwig II built a fairy-tale style castle in which German state?
☐ Alsace ☐ Bavaria ☐ Munich

6 What were gaps in battlements called?
☐ Bolts ☐ Crennels ☐ Storks

7 In which direction did a portcullis move?
☐ Diagonally ☐ Horizontally ☐ Vertically

8 In which country is Saumur Castle?
☐ France ☐ Germany ☐ Spain

9 What colour is the Tower of London known by?
☐ Black ☐ Red ☐ White

10 What would a moat usually be filled with?
☐ Rubbish ☐ Stones ☐ Water

11 What was the name for raised sections of battlements?
☐ Bolts ☐ Crennels ☐ Merlons

12 In which country is Conwy Castle?
☐ England ☐ Germany ☐ Wales

13 What was the walled area in front of the inner gatehouse called?
☐ Bailey ☐ Barbican ☐ Scullion

14 What was an assault on a castle known as?
☐ Check ☐ Rooking ☐ Siege

15 When did building begin on Beaumaris Castle in Wales?
☐ 11thC
☐ 13thC
☐ 15thC

ANSWERS ON PAGE 286

84 FOOD AND DRINK

1 What type of food is gravadlax?

2 Which type of brandy is made from cherries?

3 Which spirit is Pimm's No 1 based on?

4 Aspartame is an alternative to what when added to food?

5 In which month does Beaujolais Nouveau arrive?

6 Which powder includes turmeric, fenugreek, chillis and cumin?

7 Which country produces more than 70% of the world's olive oil?

8 What name is given to food prepared according to Muslim law?

9 How many standard wine bottles make up a Nebuchadnezzar?

10 Which fruit is also called the Chinese gooseberry?

11 Agar agar is a vegetarian alternative to what?

12 Which 1950s pop star's name is cockney rhyming slang for mild?

13 How is cook Isabella Mary Mayson better known?

14 What sort of food is a macadamia?

15 Atlanta is the headquarters of which drinks company?

16 Which pioneering cookery writer wrote *Mediterranean Food* and *French Country Cooking* in the 1950s?

17 What is ghee?

18 Caraway is related to which family of vegetables?

19 Which queen's nickname is the name of a cocktail?

20 Which drink did Sir Bob Geldof advertise on UK television?

ANSWERS ON PAGE 286

85 THE ARTS

1 What is the best-selling book of all time?

2 Who created the character of Miss Marple?

3 Which musical is the name of a US state?

4 In *Starlight Express* what do the performers wear on their feet?

5 What was Jesus Christ according to Tim Rice and Andrew Lloyd Webber?

6 According to the comedy title, There's a what In My Soup?

7 Where is the Fiddler in the musical which starred Topol?

8 Which London theatre's motto was, "We never close"?

9 Which New York street is famous for its theatres?

10 Which musical about Professor Higgins and Eliza Doolittle is based on *Pygmalion*?

11 Who wrote the music in the comic operas where Gilbert wrote the words?

13 What do the initials RSC stand for?

13 Which musical is based on T. S. Eliot's poems?

14 Who first played the title role in *Evita* in the West End?

15 What did Tolstoy write about along with War?

16 Which show includes *A Wand'rin' Star*?

17 Which bird of prey Has Landed, in the thriller war novel by Jack Higgins?

18 Which musical is about a circus impresario?

19 At which film festival is the prize the Golden Seashell awarded?

20 Which Boulevard is the title of a musical?

ANSWERS ON PAGE 286

86 PHOBIAS

What do you fear if you have the following PHOBIAS?

1 HYDROPHOBIA

2 PHAGOPHOBIA

3 APIPHOBIA

4 BRONTOPHOBIA

5 EREMOPHOBIA

6 AILUROPHOBIA

7 BASOPHOBIA

8 AGORAPHOBIA

9 PHOTOPHOBIA

10 CYNOPHOBIA

ANSWERS ON PAGE 286

87 DOUBLE TAKE

In each case, the two-part quiz question leads to just one answer!

1 Which lettuce shares a name with what collided with *Titanic*?

2 Which word for a trench also means to abandon?

3 Which word can be a tablet holder and a style of hat?

4 Which word for a money holder also means to pucker the lips?

5 Which Jellystone Park bear is also a word for a mystic?

6 Which word for twenty is also a tally or record?

7 Which word for oars also means to walk through water?

8 Which word for a set of rooms might also be a musical work?

9 Which name of a bird also means to gulp?

10 Which word for generally is also a protective garment?

ANSWERS ON PAGE 286

88 SEAS

1 What is the study of seas and oceans called?
☐ Merology ☐ Oceanography ☐ Sesimology

2 The Red Sea is in which ocean?
☐ Arctic ☐ Indian ☐ Pacific

3 What is the world's largest ocean?
☐ Arctic ☐ Indian ☐ Pacific

4 Egypt, Saudi Arabia and Ethiopia are on which sea's shore?
☐ Black Sea ☐ Dead Sea ☐ Red Sea

5 Salt water covers around what per cent of the Earth's surface?
☐ 50% ☐ 70% ☐ 90%

6 Which ocean contains most ice?
☐ Arctic ☐ Atlantic ☐ Indian

7 Brazil's coast borders which ocean?
☐ Atlantic ☐ Indian ☐ Pacific

8 What percentage of sea water is made up of common salt?
☐ 3% ☐ 6% ☐ 10%

9 What can be both spring or neap in the seas?
☐ Deposits ☐ Plankton ☐ Tides

10 What type of wave is caused by an underwater earthquake?
☐ Gyre ☐ Tsunami ☐ Trench

11 The Mariana Trench is in which ocean?
☐ Atlantic ☐ Indian ☐ Pacific

12 Which of these is not the name of a sea?
☐ Black ☐ Green ☐ Red

13 Which sea links with the seas of Azov and Marmara?
☐ Black ☐ China ☐ Coral

14 Which channel links the Hudson Bay to the Arctic Ocean?
☐ Catskill ☐ Foxe ☐ Rupert

15 Which Strait is between Siberia and Alaska?
☐ Arctic ☐ Bering ☐ Timor

ANSWERS ON PAGE 286

89 HORROR MOVIES

1 Who directed Kenneth Branagh in Mary Shelley's *Frankenstein*?

2 Who, according to the movie, fathered Rosemary's Baby?

3 In which *Dracula* movie did Anthony Hopkins play Professor van Helsing?

4 What was the sequel to *Scream* called?

5 Who wrote the screenplay of William Peter Blatty's *The Exorcist*?

6 What was the first name of Dracula actor Lugosi?

7 What sort of Man was Claude Rains in 1933?

8 Which Stephen's first novel *Carrie* was a successful 1970s movie?

9 Which screen Dracula played Saruman in *The Lord Of The Rings*?

10 Who directed and starred in *Psycho 3* in 1986?

11 Which creepy crawlies are the subject of *Arachnophobia*?

12 Which Stanley made *The Shining* with Jack Nicholson?

13 What part did Boris Karloff play in the pre-World War II *Frankenstein*?

14 Which 1978 movie shares its name with the spooky 31st October?

15 Which Sissy played the title role in *Carrie*?

16 On which Street was there a nightmare in the 1980s movie series?

17 In which decade was *The Exorcist* first released?

18 Which British studios were famous for their horror movies featuring stars such as Cushing and Lee?

19 Which British actor won an Oscar for *The Silence Of The Lambs*?

20 Which Hitchcock movie featured feathered attackers?

ANSWERS ON PAGE 286

90 LUCKY DIP

1 What is the maximum score with three darts?

2 What is the zodiac sign of Pisces?

3 Who has his statue at the top of a column in Trafalgar Square?

4 Who was No Angel accordiing to the title of a hit album?

5 If Jerry is the cartoon mouse, which cat chases him?

6 Which English king died at the Battle of Hastings?

7 In nursery rhyme, what did Tom, Tom the piper's son steal?

8 Who wrote most of The Beatles' songs along with Paul McCartney?

9 What did Delilah cut off to make Samson lose his strength?

10 According to proverb, what begins at home?

11 In the education sector, what does NUT stand for?

12 Who played Inspector Morse in the popular UK television series?

13 What did William Tell shoot off his son's head?

14 Who was the last queen of England before Elizabeth II?

15 What is the term for fear of enclosed spaces?

16 Name the consortium that runs the National Lottery?

17 What was the name of the Big River sung about by Jimmy Nail?

18 What is the name of the person who delivers the mail in Greendale?

19 What is the title of Edna Everage?

20 What tree does a date grow on?

ANSWERS ON PAGE 286

91 CRIME

1. Which US state tops the list for having most prisoners waiting on Death Row?
2. Who led The Family carrying out murders in Hollywood?
3. In which country did Thomas Hamilton carry out a shooting atrocity?
4. How was President Kennedy assassinated?
5. Myra Hindley and Ian Brady were known as which notorious murderers?
6. In which city did the Kray twins operate?
7. What did Tom Keating forge?
8. Which country has the highest proportion of prisoners to population?
9. What was his day job that allowed Harold Shipman to commit so many murders?
10. In what type of building did Eric Harris and Dylan Kiebold carry out mass murder?
11. Colombian underworld boss Pablo Escabor dealt in what commodity?
12. What type of bags were stolen in the Great Train Robbery?
13. Parker and Barrow were more usually known as what?
14. Which fictional caped crusader fought crime in Gotham City?
15. What was supposedly the profession of Sweeney Todd?
16. What did Burke and Hare snatch
17. Which English county was linked with the Ripper of the 70s and 80s?
18. What was the surname of Fred and Rosemary who operated the "House Of Horrors"?
19. Al Capone was finally nailed for what crime?
20. In which decade was the Hungerford Massacre carried out by Michael Ryan?

ANSWERS ON PAGE 286

92 GENERAL KNOWLEDGE

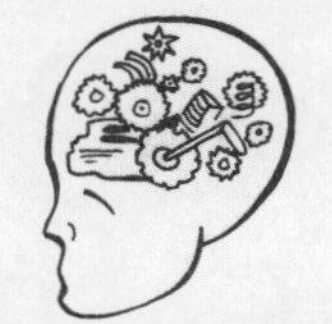
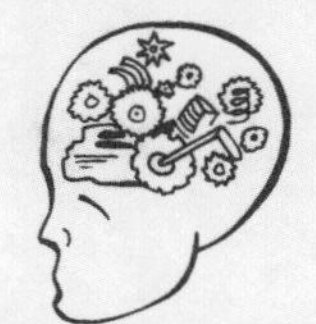

1. The River Ganges is a holy place for the followers of which religion?
2. What is the name for the home of an eagle?
3. Where was Robbie Burns born in Ayrshire?
4. Which Shakespearian play takes place in Illyria?
5. Which two leaders had a meeting in the Brenner Pass in the Second World War?
6. Tom Thumb, Tennis Ball and Winter Density are all types of what?
7. Which flower is particularly associated with Mary, the Madonna?
8. On which Yorkshire moor was a battle fought on July 2nd, 1644?
9. Which Music Hall comedian was known as the "Cheeky Chappie"?
10. In which industry was Lord Nuffield a pioneer?
11. Which word describes architecture dating from the time of James I?
12. What word describes the minimum number of members on a committee in attendance for it to reach valid decisions?
13. Who composed the "Thunder and Lightning" Polka?
14. Which war was fought in the Far East from 1950 to 1953?
15. What type of animal is a Kerry Blue?
16. In which year was the evacuation of Dunkirk?
17. Which German pianist took *A Walk In The Black Forest* in the 1960s?
18. What does an anemometer measure?
19. What is a filbert?
20. Which strait links the Black Sea and the Sea of Marmara?

ANSWERS ON PAGE 286

93 HALF CHANCE

½? ½? ½?

1. The soccer team Boca Juniors play in which country – Argentina or USA?
2. Was Pete Sampras born in New York or Washington DC?
3. Which country did athlete Said Aouita come from – Kenya or Morocco?
4. In what type of transport did Charles Lindbergh make history – a plane or a ship?
5. What is most of the Earth's surface covered by – desert or water?
6. What was Mrs Victor Meldrew's first name – Constance or Margaret?
7. What colour are most of the wines from France's Anjou region – rosé or white?
8. What was the name of the hotel chambermaid in *Fawlty Towers* – Lisa or Polly?
9. Which country has I as its international vehicle registration letter – India ir Italy?
10. In which country could you watch Alaves play a home soccer match – France or Spain?
11. What's the weather word linked to an *Absolutely Fabulous* character's surname – Monsoon or Showers?
12. Which former star actress Shirley became a US ambassador – MacLaine or Temple?
13. In which British city was Turnhouse airport built – Aberdeen or Edinburgh?
14. Are Desirée and Pentland Javelin types off computer language or potato?
15. Iran was at war with which neighbour for most of the 1980s – Egypt or Iraq?
16. In which Essex suburb is *Birds Of A Feathe*r set – Chigwell or Romford?
17. Did Colonel Oliver North feature in the Irangate or the Watergate affair?
18. Which Saint is commemorated at Lourdes – Bernadette or Patrick?
19. In which South American country is Casablanca Valley – Argentina or Chile?
20. What was John Lennon's youngest son called – Julian or Sean?

ANSWERS ON PAGE 286

94 THE BEATLES

1. Which Liverpool Club was associated with the early days of The Beatles?
2. What was the first Beatles film?
3. Who was the last member to join the band?
4. Which country was John's second wife Yoko Ono from?
5. What sort of Writer was the subject of a 1966 song?
6. It is credited to Lennon and McCartney, but who actually wrote *Yesterday*?
7. What is the name of Paul's designer daughter?
8. Which early album shared its name with a firearm?
9. Which fruit was the name of their own record label?
10. Which song introduced "yeah, yeah, yeah"?
11. Which Brian was their first manager?
12. In November 2003 which of the Fab Four was inducted into the Rock And Roll Hall of Fame?
13. What was the first of their singles to make the charts?
14. Who "picked up the rice in the church where the wedding had been"?
15. Who was the only Beatle to change his surname?
16. Which Scottish location was the title of a hit for Paul McCartney?
17. In which city was John Lennon murdered?
18. Which George produced the early Beatles' hits?
19. Which eastern musical instrument did George play on *Norwegian Wood*?
20. Which contemporary of The Beatles appears top right in the crowd on the *Sgt. Pepper's Lonely Hearts Club Band* album sleeve?

ANSWERS ON PAGE 286

95 PICTURE QUIZ

What links these pictures?

ANSWERS ON PAGE 286

96 WHO SAID . . . ?

1 "You cannot be serious!"

2 "The goal was scored by a little of the hand of God."

3 "If anyone sees me anywhere near a boat they have permission to shoot me."

4 "If you drink don't drive. Don't even putt."

5 "Diamonds are my best friends – it's the only way I can keep a hold on my wife."

6 "I was born for soccer as Beethoven was born for music."

7 "I think American women are treated by men as inferiors; probably in England women have a better deal."

8 "It's funny, but the more I practise the luckier I become."

ANSWERS ON PAGE 287

97 ISLANDS

1 Lanzarote is part of which island group?
☐ Balearics ☐ Canaries
☐ Greek islands

2 Which island's main resort is Kuta?
☐ Bali ☐ Crete ☐ Cuba

3 Sicily lies at the foot of which country?
☐ France ☐ Italy ☐ Spain

4 Which island gave its name to a wine a type of cake?
☐ Madeira ☐ Majorca ☐ Minorca

5 Malta is in which sea?
☐ Baltic ☐ Caribbean
☐ Mediterranean

6 On which island is the seaside resort of Sanur?
☐ Bali ☐ Crete ☐ Cyprus

7 Which island's capital is Havana?
☐ Bahamas ☐ Cuba ☐ Jamaica

8 Which island has the symbol of a three legged man?
☐ Gran Canaria ☐ Isle of Man
☐ Rhodes

9 Which island housed a notorious prison in South Africa?
☐ Pitt ☐ Reunion ☐ Robben

10 What is another name for Tonga?
☐ Friendly Islands ☐ Happy Islands
☐ Jolly Islands

11 Which Greek island was the home of the physician Hippocrates?
☐ Cos ☐ Crete ☐ Rhodes

12 On which island is Mount Etna?
☐ Corsica ☐ Cuba ☐ Sicily

13 Which Italian island has a Blue Grotto?
☐ Aeolian Islands ☐ Capri ☐ Sicily

14 Which is the smallest of the Great Sunda Islands?
☐ Borneo ☐ Java ☐ Sumatra

15 Salina Bay is on which island?
☐ Corfu ☐ Crete ☐ Malta

ANSWERS ON PAGE 287

98 ANIMALS

1. Which black and white creature sprays a foul-smelling liquid when attacked?
2. How does a boa constrictor kill its prey?
3. Why does a fish need gills?
4. What does a scorpion have at the end of its tail?
5. What does a chameleon change to camouflage itself?
6. What does an Isle of Man Manx cat not have?
7. What type of insect is a Red Admiral?
8. What is another name for an Alsatian dog?
9. What kind of animal is a Suffolk Punch?
10. A lynx is a member of which family group?
11. What is a koikoi?
12. What is the average life expectancy of the mayfly?
13. Which creature was named by Thomas Savage?
14. Which sense does the Old World vulture lack?
15. Why were Samoyeds originally bred?
16. Falabellas are native to where?
17. What is another name for the aye-aye?
18. Which animal has the longest tail?
19. What name is given to the smaller of a rhino's horns?
20. What does it mean if an animal is homoithermic?

ANSWERS ON PAGE 287

99 GOLF

1. Who is the most famous golfer to come from Cypress, California?
2. Who was the first man to win the US PGA and the US Open in the same year?
3. What was the world's first golf club called?
4. Who was Europe's captain in the 2004 Ryder Cup?
5. What was Payne Stewart's first victory in a major?
6. In 1986 Greg Norman equalled whose record low score of 63 in the US Masters?
7. Who did Tony Jacklin replace as Ryder Cup captain?
8. Tiger Woods first won the British Open in 2000, but on which course?
9. Who did Nick Faldo sensationally beat to win his third US Masters?
10. How old was Tiger Woods when he first won the US Masters?
11. In 1968 what became the longest course ever used for the British Open?
12. On which English course did Tom Lehman win his first major?
13. When Steve Jones first won the US Open he was the first qualifier to win a Major since who?
14. Where did the very first Ryder Cup take place?
15. Who won the first ever British Open?
16. Who is the President of Augusta National Golf Club?
17. Who did Nick Faldo sack as his coach at the same time as divorcing wife number two?
18. Which British Open winner was born in Shrewsbury in 1958?
19. Who was the first European to win the US Masters in the 1990s?
20. Who was the first US-born winner of the British Open?

ANSWERS ON PAGE 287

100 PEOPLE

1. Which person involved in world affairs was born on Nov 15th, 1954 in Birmingham, Alabama?
2. Which First Lady was nicknamed the Iron Butterfly?
3. Which American leader did Lee Harvey Oswald assassinate?
4. What was the first name of Mr Waite who was imprisoned in the Lebanon in the 1980s?
5. What was the cause of Franklin D Roosevelt's paralysis?
6. In 1995 O. J. Simpson was cleared of murdering which of his relatives?
7. Pol Pot led the Khmer Rouge on which continent?
8. Archbishop Desmond Tutu fought for civil rights in which country?
9. Who said, "The hardest thing to understand in the world is income tax"?
10. Simon Weston became famous after his courage following horrific injuries in which war?
11. What was the nationality of Brian Keenan, who was held hostage with John McCarthy?
12. Which nickname was given to Boston murderer Albert de Salvo?
13. Which Christian unveiled the "New Look" of the late 1940s?
14. Which media magnate mysteriously disappeared off his yacht in 1991?
15. John Glenn became the oldest man to travel where when he boarded the Discovery in 1998?
16. In which US city was Al Capone crime king during the Prohibition?
17. Which part of Evander Holyfield did Mike Tyson bite off during a professional fight?
18. Prosecutor Kenneth Starr was involved in impeachment proceedings against which US President?
19. What was the nationality of the driver of the car in which Princess Diana died?
20. Who teamed up with Benny, Bjorn and Anni-Frid to form Abba?

ANSWERS ON PAGE 287

101 THE HEADLINES

1. Tony Blair postponed the 2001 General Election because of which farming disaster?
2. The world's largest business merger joined AOL with which media corporation?
3. Who first provided the voice of the chimpanzees advertising PG Tips tea??
4. Nicolae Ceausescu led which country until 1989?
5. What did Gandhi's title Mahatma mean?
6. Who was George W Bush's first Attorney General?
7. How old was Steven Jobs when he developed the first Apple computer?
8. Who was the youngest of the Kennedy brothers, son of ex Ambassador Joseph Kennedy?
9. In the UK, who became the 1st Earl of Stockton?
10. Which spy left for the Soviet Union with Burgess and Maclean?
11. Richard Beeching is best remembered for his closure of what?
12. Which leader of Northern Ireland has the first names Ian Richard Kyle?
13. What was John Prescott's occupation before he entered politics?
14. Gitta Sereny caused controversy over her book about which child murderer?
15. Jane Couch became the first woman to be given a licence to do what?
16. George W Bush was Governor of which state before he became President?
17. What was the so-called Black day for the City in the late 1980s?
18. Which position did Tony Blair have in the Shadow Cabinet before he became leader of the Labour Party?
19. Zeng Jinlian of China holds which world record?
20. Who founded Amazon.com?

ANSWERS ON PAGE 287

102 LOVE STORIES

1 *West Side Story* was based on which classic love story by William Shakespeare?
2 Which Julia was the *Runaway Bride* in 1999?
3 Which romantic occasion follows *Muriel's* and *My Best Friend's* in movie titles?
4 Vivien Leigh, Scarlett O'Hara in *Gone With The Wind*, was from which country?
5 Which multi Oscar winning love story of the 1990s was set on a ship?
6 Which star of *Titanic* played opposite Claire Danes in *Romeo + Juliet* in the 1990s?
7 Does much of the action of *The English Patient* take place in the desert or the Arctic?
8 Who was Bonnie's partner in crime?
9 Colin Firth was Mark Darcy to Renée Zellweger's who?
10 Which actor, father of Tatum, played Oliver in the love story called *Love Story*?
11 Which Faye played opposite Steve McQueen in *The Thomas Crown Affair*?
12 Which Hill in London was the location for a Hugh Grant / Julia Roberts movie?
13 Which Tom played Sam in *Sleepless In Seattle* opposite Meg Ryan?
14 While making *Cleopatra*, Elizabeth Taylor fell in love with and later married which Richard?
15 Which Annie was a famous Woody Allen movie with Diane Keaton?
16 How many Weddings went with a Funeral in the Hugh Grant movie?
17 Was *Captain Corelli's Mandolin* set on a Greek island or a Caribbean one?
18 *Gone With The Wind* is a story with which American War as its background?
19 Which Gwyneth played opposite Joseph Fiennes in *Shakespeare In Love*?
20 *Brief Encounter* has a famous departure scene at a railway station or an airport?

ANSWERS ON PAGE 287

103 LUCKY DIP

1 Job, Judges, and Habakkuk are all examples of what?
2 Which device is used on a guitar fretboard to raise the strings' pitch?
3 The Lorelei rock is on which river?
4 In imperial measurement, how many yards are in a chain?
5 Martina Navratilova won most doubles trophies with which partner?
6 On television, "who was feared by the bad, loved by the good"?
7 With what do you play a vibraphone?
8 On a ship what are the scuppers?
9 With which sport is Peter Alliss associated?
10 Who became ruler of Spain after winning the Spanish Civil War?
11 In literature, how many Arabian Nights were there?
12 Which late singer once said, "You're not drunk if you can lie on the floor without holding on"?
13 Black, Italian, and Lombardy are all types of which tree?
14 In which war was the sea battle of Jutland?
15 What is the square root of 169?
16 Which Bruce Springsteen album topped the UK and US charts in 2002?
17 What is the lowest layer of the atmosphere?
18 Who took over as England cricket captain from Graham Gooch?
19 In London where is Poet's Corner?
20 In which art has Beryl Grey achieved fame?

ANSWERS ON PAGE 287

104 NAME GAME

How are these celebrities better known?

1 RICHARD STARKEY

2 EUNICE WAYMON

3 CAMILLE JAVEL

4 LOUIS FURBANK

5 VIRGINIA McMATH

6 CHESTER BURNETT

7 CARYN JOHNSON

8 DIANE EARLE

9 CHARLES CARTER

10 JOHN LYDON

ANSWERS ON PAGE 287

105 GUESS WHO . . . ?

1 Born in Notting Hill, London, he dominated the decathlon for 10 years, winning his second Olympic gold in 1984.

2 His wife is a lawyer, he has three sons and a daughter and became Prime Minister of his country in 1997.

3 Brother of James, he co starred in *The Blues Brothers* and died tragically in 1982.

4 Born in San Francisco and famous for starring in spaghetti westerns, he directed *Million Dollar Baby*.

5 Born in California in 1914, he was nicknamed the Yankee Clipper and married Marilyn Monroe in in 1954.

6 After working in newspapers and magazines this novelist achieved fame in 1979 with *A Woman of Substance*.

7 Born in Wales, and taking her middle name from her grandmother, she won an Oscar for *Chicago*.

8 Came to fame in the 1960s singing with Sonny, she had film success with *Moonstruck* and *Silkwood*.

9 Born in New York in 1963, he is one of the greatest basketball players of all time, winning Olympic gold in 1984 and 1992.

10 A singer/songwriter born in Canada, his song *Everything I Do* broke chart records.

ANSWERS ON PAGE 287

106 SIGNS AND SYMBOLS

1 What does a circle inside a square stand for in clothing labels?
☐ Iron ☐ Tumble drier
☐ Washing machine

2 What was the picture language of Ancient Egypt know as?
☐ Hieroglyphics ☐ Pictionairre
☐ Osiris

3 Depillon, Popham and Paisley all developed which system?
☐ Braille ☐ Morse Code
☐ Semaphore

4 What identifies a female in a sign for a ladies loo?
☐ Handbag ☐ High heels ☐ Skirt

5 In Morse Code which letter does a dot represent?
☐ A ☐ O ☐ E

6 How is 25 written in Roman numerals?
☐ DVD ☐ XXV ☐ XIX

7 What does a letter c enclosed in a circle stand for?
☐ Caution ☐ Copyright ☐ Registered

8 How many dots show on an iron to indicate warm?
☐ One ☐ Two ☐ Three

9 How is the letter T represented in Morse Code?
☐ Dash ☐ Dot ☐ Dash-Dot

10 In astronomy what is the sign for a new moon?
☐ Black circle ☐ Crescent
☐ White circle

11 Runes developed from which language?
☐ Danish ☐ German ☐ Hungarian

12 On a standard keyboard the £ sign shares a key with which number?
☐ 2 ☐ 3 ☐ 6

13 In playing cards, which suit symbol contains four angles?
☐ Clubs ☐ Diamonds ☐ Hearts

14 In meteorology what front is shown by triangles pointing up?
☐ Cold ☐ Occluded ☐ Warm

15 In Morse Code which letter does four dots represent?
☐ H ☐ O ☐ Y

ANSWERS ON PAGE 287

107 GENERAL KNOWLEDGE

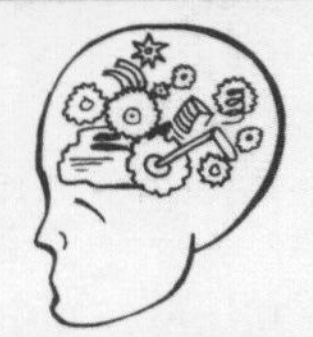

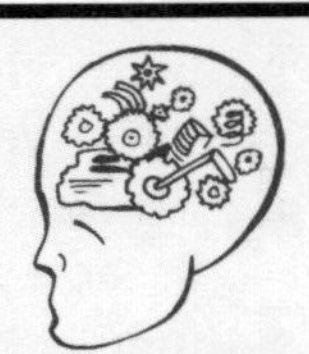

1. In Greek mythology, who is the god of love?
2. At night what colour light is shown on the starboard side of a ship?
3. Which day of the week is the Muslim holy day?
4. If you were using a spinnaker, what would you be doing?
5. What is the lightest weight in boxing?
6. What kind of animal is a merino?
7. Who was the first British Prime Minister to make use of Chequers?
8. In political scandal, who said, "Discretion is a polite word for hypocrisy"?
9. What sport would you practise if you were a toxophilite?
10. What colour jersey is worn by the leader in the Tour de France?
11. What other title is held by whoever is the First Lord of the Treasury?
12. What was the name of the mythical South American city of gold?
13. In *Dad's Army* what was Captain Mainwaring's day job?
14. On a London Underground map, what colour is the Piccadilly line?
15. What is the capital of Bolivia?
16. In which art did Barbara Hepworth become famous?
17. Of which country is Ajax a famous football team?
18. What sort of book was compiled by Moody and Sankey?
19. Which bird did Noah first send out of the ark?
20. Which river flows through the Grand Canyon in America?

ANSWERS ON PAGE 287

108 COUNTRY & WESTERN

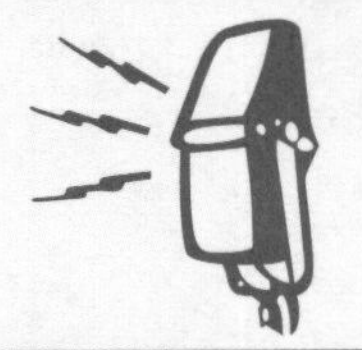
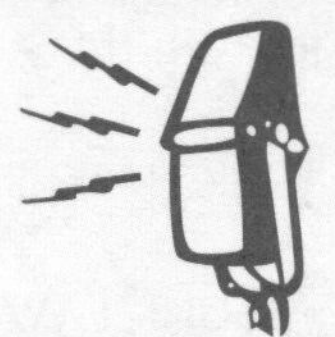

1. Which country boy recorded the albums *Ropin' The Wind* and *Scarecrow*?
2. Shania Twain featured on the soundtrack of which 1999 film with Hugh Grant?
3. How did Patsy Cline die?
4. What were the working hours of Dolly Parton in a movie title and a chart hit?
5. Who had huge chart success with *How Do I Live*?
6. What colour is Kenny Roger's beard?
7. To which lady did Dolly Parton plead, "I'm beggin' of you please don't take my man."?
8. How is Eileen Edwards better known?
9. Which huge Tammy Wynette hit was inspired by her split from husband George Jones?
10. Who wrote the country classic *Crazy*?
11. Johnny Cash recorded a number of live albums at what unusual institutions?
12. By what figure styling name is Otis Dewey Whitman known?
13. Shania Twain's first UK hit was *You're Still The* what?
14. According to his name, which state did Ernie Ford come from?
15. Who was dubbed "Gentleman Jim"?
16. Who had the hit *Stand By Your Man* which was also the name of her autobiography?
17. Crystal Gayle's eyes were made what colour in the title of her hit song?
18. What did Loretta Webb change her surname to?
19. In the 1980s Kenny Rogers sang about the "Coward of the" where?
20. Which Reba McEntire song shares its name with the Little capital of Arkansas?

ANSWERS ON PAGE 287

109 AT THE MOVIES

1 Which Danny directed *Trainspotting*?

2 In which decade of the 20th century was Kevin Costner born?

3 Which girl's first name completes the film title, ____ *Foyle*?

4 Which Peter played Inspector Clouseau?

5 Who got the lead in *Casablanca* after Hedy Lamarr turned it down?

6 Which actress links Bram Stoker's *Dracula* and *Beetlejuice*?

7 What according to Monroe *Are A Girl's Best Friend*?

8 Which ailment is mentioned in a movie title about King George III?

9 Janet Leigh played one of the most horrific scenes where in a motel?

10 Which female pop star featured in *Mad Max Beyond The Thunderdome*?

11 Scarlett O'Hara was heroine of which epic?

12 Which Gary starred in *The Fifth Element*?

13 Which political group is central to the plot of *The Sound Of Music*?

14 Which 1990s movie told of a group of stripping Sheffield steel workers?

15 Which blonde country star had a cameo role in *The Beverly Hillbillies*?

16 Which Audrey starred in *My Fair Lady*?

17 Who played the female lead in *Grease 2*?

18 In which movie did Meryl Streep play a Polish holocaust survivor?

19 Greta Garbo was born in which European capital city?

20 Martin Scorsese directed the video *Bad* for which pop superstar?

ANSWERS ON PAGE 287

110 HALF CHANCE

½? ½? ½?

1 Tortillas originate from which country – Greece or Mexico?

2 Which Apollo craft landed on the Moon – Apollo 11 or Apollo 13?

3 In which country is the Dalai Lama the spiritualist leader – Mongolia or Tibet?

4 Around which part of your body would you tie a cummerbund – ankle or waist?

5 What did the Romans keep in a catacomb – animals or dead bodies?

6 What did David Bowie call his first child – Ziggy or Zowie?

7 If the first of a month is a Thursday, what day will the 19th be – a Monday or a Tuesday?

8 Cassata is a type of which food – casserole or ice cream?

9 Is *The Deer Hunter* about the Vietnam War or the Gulf War?

10 In *The Simpsons* what colour is Mayor Quimby's suit – blue or brown?

11 What did *Monty Python's Flying Circus* use as theme music – *The Division Bell* or *The Liberty Bell*?

12 What does *tempus fugit* mean – time flies or time to fight?

13 A pipistrelle is what kind of creature – a bat or a snake?

14 Which wine can be fino or oloroso – port or sherry?

15 Which soccer side won four championships in a row with Johan Cruyff as boss – Barcelona or Real Madrid?

16 In France all motorways begin with which letter of the alphabet – an A or an X?

17 Where does a hydrophyte plant live – in sand or in water?

18 In music, which note is written on the bottom line of the treble clef – an E or an F?

19 In batik what is painted on to fabric along with dye – oil paint or wax?

20 Dermatology is concerned with the study of human what – behaviour or skin?

ANSWERS ON PAGE 287

111 CHARLES DICKENS

1. In *A Tale of Two Cities* what is the occupation of Sydney Carton?
2. In *Great Expectations* who is the lady who lives in the room where her wedding reception was to have taken place?
3. Which of his novels did Dickens say he liked the best?
4. How does Bill Sikes die?
5. Which historical events are the background to *Barnaby Rudge*?
6. Who are David Copperfield's two vastly different schoolfriends?
7. Which court case is at the heart of *Bleak House*?
8. In *Hard Times* who is Mr Bounderby's housekeeper?
9. In *Little Dorrit* who are Amy's brother and sister?
10. In *Great Expectations* what is Pip's full name?
11. In *Our Mutual Friend* who does Eugene Wrayburn marry?
12. In *A Tale of Two Cities* what is the name of the grave robber?
13. In *Oliver Twist* what is Rose's relation to Oliver discovered to be?
14. Who does David Copperfield's aunt Betsey Trotwood live with?
15. What is Little Nell's surname in *The Old Curiosity Shop*?
16. In *Edwin Drood*, at whose school at Cloisterham was Rosa brought up?
17. Which book remained unfinished on Dickens' death?
18. In *David Copperfield* how did Ham die?
19. What is the profession of Joe Gargery?
20. What are both Nip and Bullseye

ANSWERS ON PAGE 287

112 LUCKY DIP

1. In which country did the poets Keats and Shelley both die?
2. How many tusks does a wart hog have?
3. Alan Knott represented England at which sport?
4. Who wrote *Porgy and Bess*?
5. Who was King of France at the time of the French Revolution?
6. Which card game has two forms called auction and contract?
7. In which country does the Amazon rise?
8. Graphite is composed of which element?
9. Who was Pinocchio's father?
10. What can only be seen from earth every seventy-six years?
11. Where was the Mount Pinatubo eruption?
12. In finance what does the V stand for in VAT?
13. Which band released the successful album *Hail To The Thief*?
14. Who chronicled the cases of Lord Peter Wimsey?
15. In France what title was given to the eldest prince?
16. What does "m" stand for in Einstein's equation $E=MC^2$?
17. Which sign of the zodiac is represented as a man pouring water from a jug?
18. In which city are the Tivoli Gardens?
19. Who devised the modern system of naming organisms?
20. Whose fan did Oscar Wilde write of?

ANSWERS ON PAGE 287

113 PICTURE QUIZ

What links these pictures?

ANSWERS ON PAGE 287

114 NAME THE YEAR

1 King Camp Gillette patented the disposable safety razor blade. Daimler built the first Mercedes car. Sweden awarded the first Nobel prizes.

2 The hovercraft had its first public demonstration. Buddy Holly died. Castro took power in Cuba.

3 John Lennon married Yoko Ono. Golda Meir became Israel's first woman premier. Neil Armstrong landed on the Moon.

4 John Glenn, aged 77, became the oldest man to travel in space. The New York Yankees won the World Series for a 24th time. Frank Sinatra died.

5 Women gained the vote in Switzerland. Bangladesh became an independent state. The Best Picture Oscar went to *The French Connection*.

6 Madonna was born. Cardinal Roncalli became Pope John XXIII. Boris Pasternak won the Nobel Prize for *Dr Zhivago*.

ANSWERS ON PAGE 287

115 THE HEADLINES

1 The first shorn fleece of Dolly the cloned sheep was donated to which charity?

2 Who or what was *Mary Rose*, making an appearance after 500 years?

3 Results in which sunshine state held the result of the 2000 US Presidential election?

4 Which US President was linked with the "Star Wars" policy?

5 Why was 4th August 2000 a special date for Elizabeth, the Queen Mother?

6 Which Nobel Prize did Nelson Mandela win?

7 Who won the ladies' singles most times at Wimbledon in the 1980s?

8 Which letter is the symbol of the euro currency?

9 Where in America was George Michael arrested in 1998?

10 Sarah Ferguson became Duchess of where in the 1980s?

11 What kind of disaster claimed some 100,000 lives in Armenia in 1988?

12 Which US state was acquired from the Badsen Purchase?

13 In 1980 the SAS spectacularly freed hostages in which embassy in London?

14 "Don't Die Of Ignorance" was the message put out to combat which disease?

15 Where was the on-line bookstore Amazon first based?

16 The Prometheus was the first of which type of kitchen equipment?

17 In the 1980s who became the world's youngest-ever boxing heavyweight champion?

18 Which Scottish border town was the scene of a jumbo jet disaster in the 1980s?

19 Which country devastated by an earthquake in 1985 hosted the F.I.F.A. World Cup in 1986?

20 Tiananmen Square was a scene of conflict in which country?

ANSWERS ON PAGE 287

116 US PRESIDENTS

1 Who became the 43rd US President?
2 Which US President did Guiseppe Zangara attempt to assassinate?
3 Who used the line "Randy, where's the rest of me?" as the title of an early autobiography?
4 Which US President had the middle name Wilson?
5 What day of the week was President Kennedy assassinated?
6 Dean Acheson was US Secretary of State under which President?
7 In which year was George Bush Jnr first inaugurated as US President?
8 Which President is credited with the quote, "If you can't stand the heat get out of the kitchen"?
9 Who was the first assassin of a US President in the 20th century?
10 Who was the first US President to have been born in a hospital?
11 Which President conferred honorary US citizenship on Winston Churchill?
12 What did Ronald Reagan describe as a shining city on a hill?
13 Who said, "A radical is a man with both feet planted firmly in the air"?
14 In 1996 who was Bob Dole's Vice Presidential candidate?
15 Which US President was described as looking like "the guy in a science fiction movie who is first to see the Creature"?
16 Who described Ronald Reagan's policies as "Voodoo economics"?
17 What type of car was Kennedy traveling in when he was shot?
18 Which aristocratic title is one of Jimmy Carter's first names?
19 Which 20th century US President had the longest last name?
20 How old was John F Kennedy's assassin?

ANSWERS ON PAGE 287

117 GENERAL KNOWLEDGE

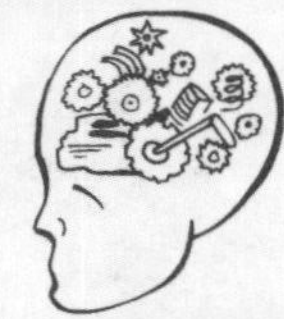
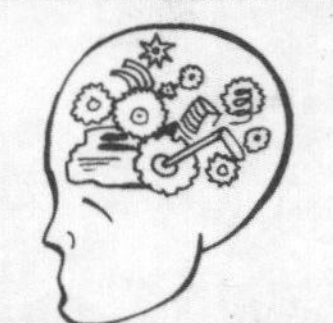

1 ICBM stands for Inter-Continental what?
2 What was a matchlock?
3 In which TV show did the Daleks cry "Exterminate!"?
4 What is the male equivalent of a ranee?
5 In chemistry, what is a substance which cannot be split into simpler substances?
6 According to the Germans, who were the "Ladies from Hell"?
7 Who created the television series *Till Death Us Do Part*?
8 In the song *Two Little Boys*, what did each boy have that was wooden?
9 Which American rodent builds dams and fells trees?
10 In which river was Jesus Christ baptized?
11 In which Shakespeare play does a forest move?
12 Of which country was John George Diefenbaker prime minister?
13 Which English soccer team has been landed with the nickname "The Pensioners"?
14 What was the name of the first nuclear-powered submarine?
15 Which country produces most wine in the world?
16 Which word can go after funny and before china?
17 In which language did Aristophanes write his plays?
18 Which English king died at the age of fifteen?
19 In which sport are stones and a broom used?
20 Which drink was promoted by *I'd Like To Teach The World To Sing*?

ANSWERS ON PAGE 287

118 CAPITALS

In which country would you find these capital cities?

1 LIMA

2 ANKARA

3 ACCRA

4 MANILA

5 OMAN

6 BRATISLAVA

7 DHAKA

8 ASUNCION

9 KIGALI

10 PORT-AU-PRINCE

ANSWERS ON PAGE 287

119 TENNIS

Is each statement TRUE or FALSE?

T F **1** The Wightman Cup was played between the USA and Australia.

T F **2** Venus Williams won the Olympic gold medal in Sydney.

T F **3** Paradorn Srichaphan is from Australia.

T F **4** Andy Roddick's first Grand Slam title was the French Open.

T F **5** Anna Kournikova won the Australian doubles with Martina Hingis.

T F **6** Thomas Muster was known as The King of Clay.

T F **7** Lleyton Hewitt was 18 when he won the US Open.

T F **8** Roger Federer beat Mark Philippoussis to win his first Wimbledon.

T F **9** Serena Williams played her first professional match at the age of 12.

T F **10** Kim Clijsters is younger than Justine Henin Hardenne.

ANSWERS ON PAGE 287

120 MOUNTAINS

1 In which continent are the highest mountains found?
☐ Asia ☐ America ☐ Australasia

2 Popocatepetl is located in which country?
☐ Chile ☐ Mexico ☐ Venezuela

3 What type of mountain are the Appalachians?
☐ Block ☐ Fold ☐ Volcanic

4 In song, where were Laurel & Hardy's Blue Ridge Mountains?
☐ Montanna ☐ Vermont ☐ Virginia

5 Mount Toubkal is the highest peak of which range?
☐ Andes ☐ Apennines ☐ Atlas

6 In which country are the Zagroz Mountains?
☐ India ☐ Iran ☐ Russia

7 Who was meant to live on Mount Olympus?
☐ Amazons ☐ Greek Gods ☐ Yeti

8 Which Edmund led the first trip to reach the top of Everest?
☐ Halley ☐ Hillary ☐ Tenzing

9 Which people of NE Nepal are famed for mountaineering skills?
☐ Gurkhas ☐ Sherpas ☐ Yaks

10 Which musical features the song *Climb Ev'ry Mountain*?
☐ *Cats* ☐ *Evita*
☐ *The Sound Of Music*

11 Cerro Aconcagua is in which country?
☐ Argentina ☐ Chile ☐ Peru

12 Who named Mount Everest?
☐ A surveyor ☐ British monarch
☐ The Pope

13 In which country is Mount Chimborazo?
☐ Chile ☐ Ecuador ☐ Spain

14 Which John sang about the *Colorado Rocky Mountain High*?
☐ Denver ☐ Lennon ☐ Travolta

15 Which term describes the formation or building of mountains?
☐ Faultism ☐ Orogenesis ☐ Platistism

ANSWERS ON PAGE 287

St Valentine's

Tackle these 50 questions about love, romance, and happy – and sometimes not so happy – couples. You will be in trouble with the other half if you can't remember the answer to the first question!

1 On what day of the year does St Valentine's Day fall?

2 What was the nationality of St Valentine?

3 Which Oscar Wilde play had its London premiere on 14th February, 1895?

4 In the movie *An Affair To Remember* Cary Grant and Deborah Kerr meet on a cruise to where?

5 Which Ben was a one-time co star and fiancé of Jennifer Lopez?

6 Which movie has the line, "I can't wait all my life waiting to catch you between husbands."?

7 Which Marilyn Monroe movie begins with the St Valentine's Day massacre?

8 Which heavyweight boxer was divorced on St Valentine's Day 1989?

9 Which classic film love story was based on the Noel Coward play *Still Life*?

10 In which century was the first Valentine sent?

11 Which musical, set in New York, was based on the classic love story of *Romeo and Juliet*?

12 Who played opposite Ewan McGregor in the period romantic comedy *Down With Love*?

13 Which British ice dancers won Olympic gold in Sarajevo in 1984?

14 Who played opposite heart throb Leonardo DiCaprio in *The Gangs Of New York*?

15 Which 20th century Prince announced both his engagements in Valentine's month?

16 Which Roman Emperor ordered the death of St Valentine?

17 Which French Canadian had a worldwide hit with the love theme from *Titanic*?

18 Who played opposite Nicole Kidman in *Moulin Rouge*?

19 Which Johnny came close to marriage with Winona Ryder?

20 Which gang was massacred on St Valentine's Day 1929?

21 Who wrote the novel *Love Story*?

22 According to the proverb, what makes the heart grow fonder?

23 In which city did the St Valentine's Day massacre take place?

24 Humphrey Bogart's affair with Lauren Bacall began on the set of which movie?

25 Which romantic hero did Colin Firth play in a TV drama opposite Jennifer Ehle?

26 Who was engaged to Brad Pitt before he married Jennifer Aniston?

27 Which Martin Scorsese film includes the affair between Howard Hughes and Ava Gardner?

28 In which year was the romantic movie *Gone With The Wind* first shown in Russia?

Day Quiz

29 Which popular children's writer wrote *Girls In Love*, a top seller at the end of the millennium?

30 Which romantic novelist was the step-grandmother of Diana, Princess of Wales?

31 Which partner of Sondra Locke starred with her in *The Outlaw Josey Wales*?

32 What follows in the proverb, "It is better to have loved and lost . . ."?

33 In which movie and stage play did Benjamin have an affair with Mrs Robinson?

34 How often did off-screen lovers Spencer Tracy and Katharine Hepburn star together on film?

35 Who wrote the *Bridget Jones* novels?

36 How long does the longest screen kiss last in *You're In the Army Now* (1941)?

37 Who wrote *Captain Corelli's Mandolin*, starring Nicolas Cage and Penelope Cruz in the film?

38 Which movie poster advertised, "They're young, they're in love and they kill people."?

39 Which world-famous lover's infamous memoirs were published between 1826 and 1838?

40 In which decade did the first movie screen kiss take place?

41 In which movie did Julia Roberts first play opposite Richard Gere?

42 According to the proverb, what goes with cold hands?

43 Which salad ingredient has also been known as the love apple?

44 Which film star married Prince Rainier of Monaco in 1956?

45 Which classic film love story was based on the play *Everyone Comes To Rick's*?

46 Warren Beatty's affair with Annette Bening began on the set of which movie?

47 Who is the romantic hero of Emily Brontë's *Wuthering Heights*?

48 Who played opposite Leonardo DiCaprio in the 1990s film remake of *Romeo and Juliet*?

49 Which famous screen lover died at the age of 31 in 1926?

50 According to the proverb, love makes what go round?

ANSWERS ON PAGE 287

122 TRAVEL

1 Mount Kilimanjaro is the highest point of which continent?

2 Which US state is the name of a musical by Rodgers & Hammerstein?

3 Which ocean lies to the east of South America?

4 Which New York borough is noted for its skyscraper skyline?

5 Where would you be if the Parliament was called The Althing?

6 Down which valley does the Mistral blow?

7 Inishmor is part of which island group?

8 Which European language is spoken in Chad?

9 Las Palmas is in which island group?

10 Where is the Magellan Strait?

11 Which Michigan town is famous for the production of motor vehicles?

12 Where is there a Parliament called the Knesset?

13 Sofia is the capital of which country?

14 Which capital of Tennessee is famous for its music?

15 What is the UK's chief Atlantic port?

16 Which US state's name has four letters, the first and last the same?

17 What is the Pacific terminus of the Trans Siberian Railway?

18 On which granite cliff are the faces of four Presidents carved?

19 What is the official residence of the French President?

20 Which country is known as the Land of the Long White Cloud?

ANSWERS ON PAGE 287

123 CHARLIE CHAPLIN

1 Chaplin said all he needed to make a movie was a park, a policeman and a pretty what?

2 In which British city was Chaplin born?

3 Which company famous for its crazy cops was Chaplin invited to join?

4 What was the first name of Mr Karno with whose troupe Chaplin first went to the USA?

5 What was Chaplin's middle name?

6 Which Mack first employed Chaplin in the movies?

7 Chaplin's debut movie was called *Making A* what?

8 Which United company did he found in 1919 with three other stars of the silent movie era?

9 Which *Rush* did he film in 1925?

10 Which actress Paulette did he marry in 1933?

11 Of his four wives how many were in their teens when he married them?

12 Where was Chaplin referring to when he said, "'I'll never go back there if Jesus Christ was President."?

13 Which Chaplin song proved a hit for Petula Clark and Harry Secombe?

14 *A Countess* from where was the title of a 1960s Chaplin movie?

15 Who wrote most of the musical score for *City Lights*?

16 *The Great Dictator* was made during which conflict?

17 Which Buster teamed up with Chaplin in *Limelight*?

18 What relation is actress Geraldine Chaplin to Charlie?

19 In which decade of the 20th century did Chaplin die at the age of 88?

20 Which film was a satire on the industrialisation of society?

ANSWERS ON PAGE 287

124 TELEVISION

1 Which actress plays Bobbi Adler in *Will And Grace*?

2 Shadrach, Marlon, Sam and Lisa are members of which soap family?

3 What is the middle name of *Sex And The City* actress Sarah Parker?

4 Which instrument does Lisa play in *The Simpsons*?

5 *Cutting It* is about what type of establishment?

6 Tara, Buffy and Willow featured in which series?

7 What colour is Phoebe's hair in *Friends*?

8 What type of workplace does David Brent operate in?

9 In which quiz show does a contestant call "Bank" to keep the accumulated cash?

10 Which Alan presented *How To Be A Gardener*?

11 Was Joanna Lumley born in the 1940s, 60s or 80s?

12 What is the first name of two satirists Bird and Fortune?

13 What was the first name of *New Baywatch* star Hasselhoff?

14 Holly the computer appeared on which TV sci fi comedy?

15 Rachel De Thame offers advice on what?

16 Who is the mate of spoof DJ Smashy?

17 In which decade was *Hollyoaks* first broadcast?

18 On which anarchic TV series did Neil, Mike, Rick and Vyvyan appear?

19 What was the first name of Wacky Racer Mr Dastardly?

20 What does the I stand for in ITV?

ANSWERS ON PAGE 287

125 CHILD STARS

1 Who found fame when he was left *Home Alone*?

2 Which O'Connor was a child star before being a huge success in *Singin' In The Rain*?

3 In which musical movie did Karen Dotrice appear as a child with a superhuman nanny?

4 Which child star later played Maria in the musical *West Side Story*?

5 Jack Wild played which cheeky role in *Oliver!*?

6 In which decade did Shirley Temple win a Special Oscar for her outstanding contribution to movies?

7 Which star of *E.T.* wrote an autobiography called *Little Girl Lost*?

8 Who sang *Long Haired Lover from Liverpool*?

9 Which Deanna was a contemporary of Judy Garland?

10 Anna Paquin won an Oscar with Holly Hunter for which movie?

11 What was the name of Henry Thomas's character in *E.T.*?

12 How many Von Trapp children were there in *The Sound of Music*?

13 Which movie based on a Louisa M Alcott novel starred a young Elizabeth Taylor?

14 Which Mary was the "world's sweetheart" and made her first movie aged 16 in 1909?

15 Who played the gangster's moll in *Bugsy Malone* before later becoming a multi Oscar winner?

16 Justin Henry was Oscar-nominated for which movie where his parents Meryl Streep and Dustin Hoffman are to divorce?

17 In which movie did Drew Barrymore find fame as Gertie?

18 Who was asked to Come Home in Elizabeth Taylor's 1943 movie?

19 In which decade of the 20th century was Drew Barrymore born?

20 Which Jackie was immortalised in Chaplin's *The Kid*?

ANSWERS ON PAGE 288

126 POP MUSIC

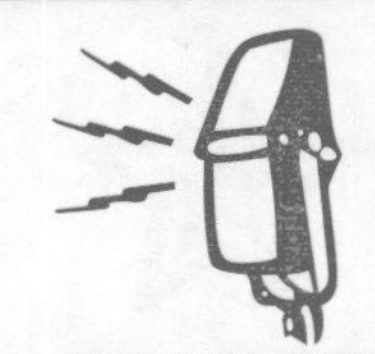
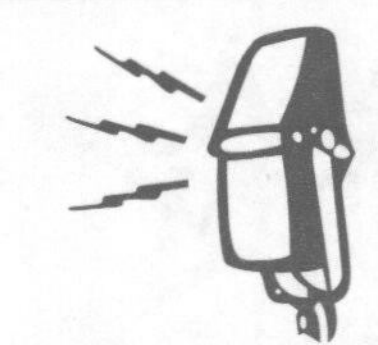
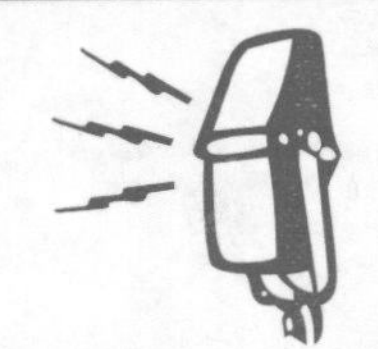

1. Who recorded the UK chart-topping album *Justified*?
2. Which boy band featured Nicky Byrne and Shane Filan?
3. Which Lionel sang with The Commodores?
4. In which US state was Elvis Presley's mansion?
5. Both Atomic Kitten and Blondie had UK No 1s with which song?
6. *I Will Always Love You* was an early 90s hit for which superstar?
7. Alan, Jay and Donny were part of which 1970s group?
8. Who sang with Robbie Williams on the 2001 version of *Somethin' Stupid*?
9. Which group is made up of Gibbs?
10. What instrument does Charlie Watts play in the Rolling Stones?
11. What was certainly the debut album by Oasis?
12. Who teamed up with Barbra Streisand for *Tell Him*?
13. Who was the original lead singer with The Supremes?
14. How many people were in the original Queen?
15. Who recorded the classic track *Riders On The Storm*?
16. Who is the only Bryan to have had a record at No 1 for 16 weeks?
17. Baker, Bruce and Clapton formed which 1960s supergroup?
18. In the mid 1990s Robert Hoskins was convicted of stalking which star?
19. Which supergroup contains "The Edge"?
20. Which band produced the mega selling album *Rumours*?

ANSWERS ON PAGE 288

127 SPORT

1. In which sport did Tampa Bay Lightning beat Calgary Flames in a 2004 Final?
2. How many attempts at the target does a player get in curling?
3. In which Spanish city were the 1992 Olympics held?
4. Eric Cantona joined Man Utd from which other English club?
5. The Vince Lombardi Trophy is awarded in which sport?
6. Gabriela Sabatini comes from which country?
7. What is "Magic" Johnson's first name?
8. English soccer international Graeme Le Saux was born in which group of islands?
9. What did Dionico Ceron win three years in a row in England's capital city?
10. What is Arnold Palmer's middle name?
11. In 1999 Ian McGeechan became coach of which international rugby team?
12. What word can follow American, Association or Gaelic to name a sport?
13. Which London-based soccer team plays at Craven Cottage?
14. Which country won cricket's 1996 World Cup?
15. Norman Whiteside was the youngest soccer player of the last century for which country?
16. In American Football where do the Colts come from?
17. What was athlete Florence Griffith-Joyner usually known as?
18. Rugby's William Henry Hare was better known by what nickname?
19. Which English city hosted the 2002 Commonwealth Games?
20. Micky Mantle became a legend in which sport?

ANSWERS ON PAGE 288

128 PICTURE QUIZ

A B C D

In what order were these buildings constructed starting with the first?

ANSWERS ON PAGE 288

129 DOUBLE TAKE

In each case, the two-part quiz question leads to just one answer!

1. Which word might be an assistant to Tiger Woods or a tea canister?
2. Which word for lightly cooked meat also means uncommon?
3. Which word for a weapon is also part of a piece of asparagus?
4. Which word for a frock also means to tend a wound?
5. Which spacecraft shares a name with a spool?
6. Which word for fullness of flavour can also mean a corpse?
7. Which prayer shares its name with a kind of style?
8. Which month shares a name with a word for could be?
9. Which word for stripes can also mean orchestras?
10. Which word for illumination can also mean not heavy?

ANSWERS ON PAGE 288

130 MONEY

1. Where in Europe could you spend a forint?
☐ Austria ☐ Estonia ☐ Hungary
2. What is the name of Bill Gates' wife?
☐ Melanie ☐ Melinda ☐ Millie
3. Which group sang about "money in the rich man's world"?
☐ Abba ☐ The Darkness ☐ The Jam
4. In proverb, money is the root of all what?
☐ Evil ☐ Happiness ☐ Sorrow
5. Which Joan kept a million-dollar advance for an unpublished novel?
☐ Baez ☐ Collins ☐ Rivers
6. In which US state did the first Wal-Mart store open?
☐ Arkansas ☐ Ohio ☐ Texas
7. Which country uses shekels as its currency?
☐ Israel ☐ Turkey ☐ Estonia
8. Ralph Lifshitz became seriously rich under what name?
☐ Bill Gates ☐ Puff Daddy
☐ Ralph Lauren
9. Which soccer club is the world's richest?
☐ Barcelona ☐ Man Utd
☐ Real Madrid
10. Which country has the world's richest royal family?
☐ Belgium ☐ United Kingdom
☐ Saudi Arabia
11. What do 100 dinars equal in Iran?
☐ Bhat ☐ Donor ☐ Rial
12. How was Judas paid for betraying Jesus?
☐ Gold ☐ Jewels ☐ Silver
13. In 1994 a bank error gave Howard Jenkins how many million dollars?
☐ 8 ☐ 18 ☐ 88
14. Which word links Armenian currency to drinking in Scotland?
☐ Chaser ☐ Dram ☐ Whisky
15. In which direction does Elizabeth II face on a UK coin?
☐ Straight out
☐ To her right
☐ To her left

ANSWERS ON PAGE 288

131 TOUGH GUYS

1. Which Reeves was Neo the computer wizard in *The Matrix*?
2. Which ex husband of Demi Moore was the psychiatrist in *The Sixth Sense*?
3. Which Harvey was in Quentin Tarantino's *Reservoir Dogs*?
4. Which Oliver died during the making of *Gladiator*?
5. Which Godfather star appeared with Colin Farrell in *The Recruit*?
6. Which music star had a "meaty" part in *Fight Club* in 1999?
7. How many were Dirty in the 1960s movie set during WWII?
8. Which star of *Friends* is the god daughter of TV and movie tough guy Telly Savalas?
9. Which Matt was the Private Ryan in the Spielberg war movie?
10. What is the first name of martial arts hero Van Damme?
11. Which two first names does actor Thornton of *Armageddon* fame have?
12. What is Samuel Jackson's middle initial?
13. In *Goodfellas*, Ray Liotta plays a member of which crime movement?
14. Which Charles was in *The Magnificent Seven* and *The Great Escape*?
15. Which Ben starred in *Pearl Harbor*?
16. Which real life tough guy Bill has been portrayed most often on screen?
17. Which first name is shared by Cusack and Malkovich of *Con Air* fame?
18. Which director of tough guy movies such as *Apocalypse Now* has the initials FFC?
19. Which *Titanic* director, James, also directed Schwarzenegger in *The Terminator*?
20. Which Sutherland's voice is heard in the movie *Phone Booth*?

ANSWERS ON PAGE 288

132 HALF CHANCE

½? ½? ½?

1. Ruby, Tawny and Vintage are styles of what – port or sherry?
2. What is contained or held in a creel – fish or snails?
3. On radio, Alistair Cooke broadcast his "Letter from" which country – America or Russia?
4. The name of which fish means a star in heraldry – guppy or mullet?
5. Do the letters PB by a runner's name indicate passed baton or personal best?
6. Harford, Hodgson and Souness have all managed which soccer club – Blackburn or Newcastle?
7. In which decade was Disney's *Pinocchio* released – 1940s or 1950s?
8. Which game was Abner Doubleday credited with creating – baseball or basketball?
9. Which Kennedy was involved in the Chappaquiddick Incident – Edward or Bobby?
10. Charlie Chaplin and Diana Princess of Wales shared which name – Jefferson or Spencer?
11. Which stewed item goes into a compote – fruit or vegetables?
12. Was Rubik's cube two-dimensional or three-dimensional?
13. Whose debut album was the highly acclaimed *Northern Soul* – M People or Pulp?
14. Are the Altamira cave paintings in Argentina or Spain?
15. What was the first name of Mr Ryder of Ryder Cup fame – Bobby or Samuel?
16. What was Lech Walesa's job before he became a Polish leader – carpenter or electrician?
17. Did Paul Hogan or Rolf Harris create the character Crocodile Dundee?
18. Which J was George Gershwin's original first name – Jacob or James?
19. John Ravenscroft broadcasted over 30 years under which name – John Peel or Kid Jensen?
20. Which red wine is drunk when young and called Nouveau – Beaujolais or Beaune?

ANSWERS ON PAGE 288

133 LUCKY DIP

1 Which Peter was the notorious Yorkshire Ripper?

2 In 2003, who had released the successful album *Simply Deep*?

3 In which decade did Channel 5 begin broadcasting in the UK?

4 What source of light is used in producing a hologram?

5 Which Bond movie provided a hit for Sheena Easton?

6 Both father and daughter of the Bhutto family have been Prime Minister of which country?

7 Where in Canada is the world's second-largest French speaking city?

8 Which character did Clark Gable play in *Gone With The Wind*?

9 Which Tsar conquered Kazan and Siberia in the 16th century?

10 What name is given to a plant which dies down at the end of the growing season?

11 Which Frank formed a long-standing comedy writing team with Denis Norden?

12 Which Italian artist included Halley's comet in a fresco of the Nativity?

13 Which object took almost seven hours to rise from the Solent in 1982?

14 Which *Dad's Army* star was married to Hattie Jacques?

15 What name is given to the genetic make-up of an individual?

16 Which English Queen has the same name as a type of plum?

17 What happened to the main character in Kafka's *Metamorphosis*?

18 What style of music was pioneered by jazzmen Charlie Parker and Dizzy Gillespie?

19 Which country did cricketer Daryll Cullinan play for?

20 Which John was MP for Huntingdon in the 90s?

ANSWERS ON PAGE 288

134 TV DRAMA

1 Which TV and movie actor played Dr Phillip Chandler in *St Elsewhere*?

2 Who was the cop hero of *Dragnet*?

3 Which series was set in the Alaskan town of Cicely?

4 What type of car did Frank Cannon drive?

5 What kind of house was The House of Eliott?

6 Who led *The A Team*?

7 What was the name of the detective agency in *Moonlighting*?

8 In which city was *Banacek* set?

9 How may thirtysomethings were there in the original drama series?

10 In the series name, Reilly was Ace of what?

11 What was the name of David Carradine's character in *Kung Fu*?

12 Who was the boss of Napoleon Solo and Ilya Kuryakin in *The Man From U.N.C.L.E.*?

13 Who played the character Ralph De Bricassart in *The Thornbirds*?

14 What was the first name of offbeat detective Columbo?

15 In which series did the character Hannibal Heyes appear?

16 What was special about Hopkirk in *Randall And Hopkirk*?

17 In *Hart To Hart* what was the name of Jonathan and Jennifer's dog?

18 In *Mike Hammer* who or what was Betsy?

19 Which MD practised at the Eastman Medical Center, LA?

20 What was the name of the FBI agent who had to find out who killed Laura Palmer?

ANSWERS ON PAGE 288

135 FOOD AND DRINK

1 What country is Pecorino cheese from?
2 What type of pastry are profiteroles made from?
3 Which fruits are usually served "belle hélène"?
4 What is the main flavour of aïoli?
5 Which vegetable can be oyster, chestnut or shitaki?
6 What is wiener schnitzel?
7 Which drink is Worcester sauce traditionally added to?
8 Which fish is the main ingredient of Scotch Woodcock?
9 How is steak tartare cooked?
10 Which area of England are Singing Hinnies from?
11 What is beef fillet cooked in puff pastry called?
12 What gives Windsor Red cheese its colour and flavour?
13 What is a Worcester Pearmain?
14 Which meat is used in Glamorgan sausages?
15 Which vegetables can be Pentland Crown or Maris Bard?
16 What type of food is basmati?
17 What is Roquefort cheese made from?
18 What are the two main ingredients of angels on horseback?
19 Which fruit is a cross between a blackberry and a raspberry?
20 Which type of pasta's name means "little worms"?

ANSWERS ON PAGE 288

136 NATURE

1 How is the maidenhair tree also known?
2 Which acid makes rhubarb leaves poisonous?
3 What is a tissue which forms on a damaged plant surface called?
4 Guano is used as fertiliser but what is it made from?
5 What makes the death cap mushroom so toxic?
6 Which European country produces more than half of Europe's rice?
7 Where would you find the home of the bristlecone pine?
8 The Venus flytrap is found naturally in which US states?
9 A meadow clary has flowers of what colour?
10 What sort of plants are cryptogams?
11 The world's tallest tree is native only to where?
12 If a leaf is sessile what is missing?
13 What is another name for the Saintpaulia?
14 How does a bladderwort receive its nourishment?
15 If a plant suffers from chlorosis what happens to it?
16 What is another name for the North American nightjar?
17 What is the only plant which can change its shape?
18 What does a mycologist study?
19 What type of plant is a saguaro?
20 To which family does the greater celandine belong?

ANSWERS ON PAGE 288

137 AIRPORTS

Can you name the countries where the listed airports are located?

1 LUXOR

2 BILLUND

3 ALMERIA

4 CALABAR

5 SPILVE

6 REJON

7 NORTH FRONT

8 MARCO POLO

9 VIGO

10 ADANA

ANSWERS ON PAGE 288

138 GUESS WHO . . . ?

1 Born Cassius Clay in Louisville, Kentucky he won his first world professional boxing title against Sonny Liston in 1964.

2 Born in Switzerland in 1936, she achieved fame in the first Bond movie *Dr No*.

3 Born in 1941, his real surname is Zimmerman and his songs include *Blowin' In the Wind* and *Mr Tambourine Man*.

4 The son-in-law of the late Arthur Miller, he starred in the double Oscar winning *My Left Foot,* and Miller's *The Crucible*.

5 Born in Dallas Texas in 1971, this cyclist overcame cancer and won his first Tour de France in 1999.

6 The Queen of Soul, she was born in Memphis, Tennessee and sang *Respect* and *Think*.

7 One of three successful literary sisters, she achieved fame with her novel about Heathcliff set in her native Yorkshire.

8 Son-in-law of Vanessa Redgrave, he starred in *Schindler's List* and *Kinsey*, for which he was nominated for a Golden Globe.

9 Born in Italy in 1967, "The Divine Pony Tail" missed a decisive penalty against Brazil in the 1994 World Cup.

10 Born in Richmond Virginia, brother of Shirley MacLaine, he starred in *Bonnie & Clyde* in 1967.

ANSWERS ON PAGE 288

139 BRIDGES

1 Which British bridge became the world's longest when completed in 1980?
☐ Forth Road ☐ Humber ☐ Severn

2 When did the Sydney Harbour Bridge open?
☐ 1932 ☐ 1942 ☐ 1952

3 What is the simplest form of bridge, with support at either end?
☐ Arch ☐ Beam ☐ Suspension

4 The Yangpu and Xupu bridges were built in which country?
☐ China ☐ Japan ☐ South Korea

5 What name is given to a temporary, floating bridge?
☐ Pontoon ☐ Rafter ☐ Suspension

6 What was the Golden Gate bridge designed to carry but never did?
☐ Animals ☐ Trains ☐ Water

7 In which decade was the Golden Gate Bridge completed?
☐ 1920s ☐ 1930s ☐ 1940s

8 In which US state did the original London Bridge end up?
☐ Arizona ☐ Utah ☐ Virginia

9 Who originally walked over the Bridge of Sighs?
☐ Poets ☐ Prisoners ☐ Soldiers

10 In which decade was the Pont de Normandie built in France?
☐ 1950s ☐ 1970s ☐ 1990s

11 In which country was the Skarnsundet Bridge built?
☐ China ☐ Japan ☐ Norway

12 What goes after "London Bridge is" in the old rhyme?
☐ Falling down ☐ Going round
☐ Upside down

13 The Akashi-Kaikyo bridge is built to withstand which Richter scale force?
☐ 7.5 ☐ 8.5 ☐ 9

14 What type of bridge can be opened and raised at the centre?
☐ Bascule ☐ Cantilever ☐ Trestle

15 *The Bridge On The River Kwai* was set in which country?
☐ Burma ☐ China ☐ Japan

ANSWERS ON PAGE 288

140 SCI-FI

1 Which actor Reeves starred in *The Matrix*?

2 What sort of creatures run amok in *Jurassic Park*?

3 E.T. arrived in a suburb of which Californian city?

4 Where were Gary Oldman and William Hurt lost in 1998?

5 Which Bruce faced *Armageddon* in 1998?

6 Which 1998 movie featured TV's Mulder and Scully?

7 What sort of giant reptile was Godzilla?

8 Which special day in the USA was the subject of a 1996 movie with Will Smith?

9 Which Judge was played by Sylvester Stallone in 1995?

10 Which Lois was played by Margot Kidder in *Superman*?

11 Close encounters of which kind were a 1977 Spielberg success?

12 What was the name of the Princess in *Star Wars*?

13 The planet of which creatures starred Charlton Heston in 1968?

14 The time-travelling hero of the *Highlander* movies came from which part of the UK?

15 *Aliens* was the sequel to which 1979 movie?

16 Which pop superstar David starred in *Labyrinth*?

17 In which decade was *Jurassic Park* released?

18 Which Matthew played Dr Niko Tatopoulos in *Godzilla*?

19 Which Runner starred Harrison Ford?

20 Tommy Lee Jones and Will Smith became The Men in what colour?

ANSWERS ON PAGE 288

141 GENERAL KNOWLEDGE

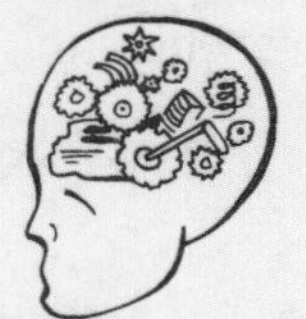
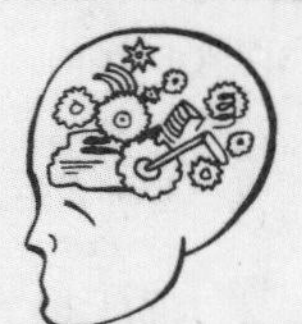

1 In aviation VTOL stands for what type of take-off and landing?

2 Which German prison camp did Pat Reid try to escape from?

3 How many lines are there in three limericks?

4 What measure is used for sound or noise?

5 Farouk was a king of which country?

6 Which county used to be divided into Ridings?

7 Who charted with *Virginia Plain*?

8 Which sport is played at Sunningdale?

9 Who composed the *1812 Overture*?

10 If a cricketer is out for 40, then 60 and then 80, what is the average?

11 Which royal residence is in Norfolk, UK?

12 In comics, by what other name is Bruce Wayne known?

13 Marrakesh is in which country?

14 In the traditional song, in which city did Molly Malone sell cockles and mussels?

15 What is the official residence of the French President?

16 How many square inches in a square foot?

17 In which sport are there wild water, sprint and slalom events?

18 In which month is the longest day in Britain?

19 Smack and sampan are types of what?

20 When is the Blue Peter flag raised on a ship?

ANSWERS ON PAGE 288

142 GEOGRAPHY

1 In which Swiss mountain range is the Jungfrau?
2 Which is the next largest island in the world after Australia?
3 Which English seaside resort has Super-Mare in its name?
4 On which continent is the Kariba Dam?
5 If the southern limit of the tropics is Capricorn what is the northern limit called?
6 What are Lakes Michigan, Superior, Huron, Erie and Ontario known as collectively?
7 Which island is to the south of Australia?
8 In the south of which country was Saigon?
9 If you were in Benidorm in which country would you be?
10 Which London palace is famous for its outdoor maze created by hedges?
11 Which isle off the west coast of England has three legs as its symbol?
12 Which country is connected to Wales by the Severn Bridge?
13 Which US state is a collection of islands in the Pacific?
14 Which language do natives of Hamburg speak?
15 What are the counties of Suffolk, Norfolk and parts of Essex and Cambridgeshire known as?
16 Which queen gave her name to the capital of Hong Kong?
17 Which Bank is made of sand in the North Sea?
18 In which English county is Penzance?
19 Which islands are Sark and Alderney part of?
20 Is Japan in the northern or the southern hemisphere?

ANSWERS ON PAGE 288

143 ELVIS PRESLEY

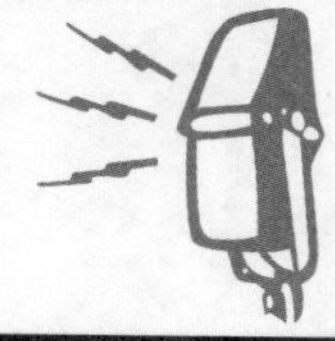
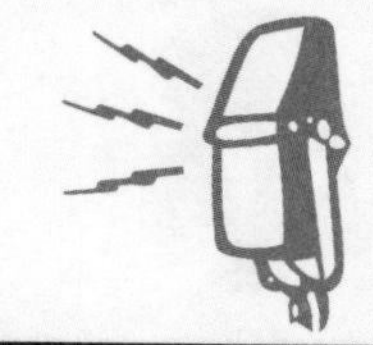
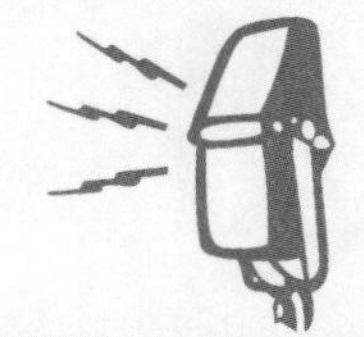

1 Elvis topped the UK singles charts in 2002, after a gap of how many years since his last No 1?
2 According to the movie title, where did Elvis have Fun in 1963?
3 What was Elvis's middle name?
4 Which screen tough guy co starred with him in *Kid Galahad*?
5 In which country was Elvis stationed to do his National Service?
6 What was the name of his private jet, named after a member of his family?
7 What was his first album which was a film soundtrack?
8 Which 1960s No 1 was based on the classic *O Sole Mio*?
9 In which state was Elvis born?
10 What was his first hit with Christmas in the title?
11 Which single shot to No 1 in the UK immediately after Elvis death?
12 What was his first No 1 on both sides of the Atlantic?
13 In a live recording of which Elvis classic does he stop singing because he is laughing so much?
14 What was the name of Priscilla Presley's book of her life with The King?
15 Which song did Elvis close his shows with during the 60s in his Las Vegas period?
16 *Elvis – That's The Way It Is* was a documentary about his concerts where?
17 Which medley included the *Battle Hymn Of The Republic*?
18 Where was Elvis Presley Boulevard, the location for his 1976 album?
19 What was his first million-seller single?
20 Which writing duo produced *Little Sister* and *His Latest Flame* for Elvis?

ANSWERS ON PAGE 288

144 HISTORY

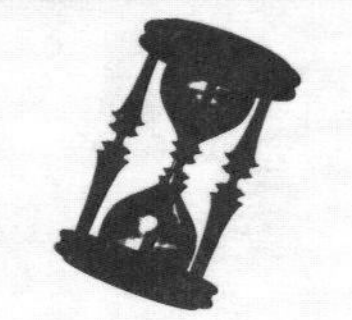

1 Bob Hawke and Paul Keating were Prime Ministers of which country?

2 In which country did Gadaffi seize power in the 1960s?

3 Who was British Prime Minister at the time of the 1990s Gulf War?

4 What was the last name of Ferdinand and Imelda, leaders of the Philippines?

5 Who was Prime Minister of the UK throughout the 80s?

6 Who seized power in Cuba in the late 1950s?

7 Which words did Winston Churchill use to describe the East and West divide in Europe?

8 Diana, Princess of Wales, led the campaign against the use of which explosive devices?

9 Haile Selassie ruled in which country?

10 How many general elections did Mrs Thatcher win in the UK?

11 Which 1990s leader said, "I did not have sexual relations with that woman"?

12 Who was the leader of the brutal Khmer Rouge government?

13 In which decade was Nelson Mandela sent to prison in South Africa?

14 What did the letter A stand for in Mandela's ANC?

15 Who was Britain's youngest Prime Minister of the 20th century?

16 The death of which General led to the restoration of the monarchy in Spain?

17 In the 90s Silvio Berlusconi won the general election in which country?

18 David Ben-Gurion was the first Prime Minister of which new state?

19 Nicholas II was the last person to hold which title in Russia?

20 Idi Amin became president of which country?

ANSWERS ON PAGE 288

145 SCIENCE

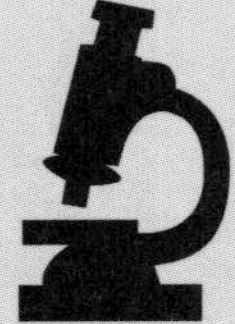

1 Which of the planets in our Solar System is last in alphabertical order?

2 Dry ice is solid or frozen what?

3 What is a defensive substance produced as a reaction to a foreign body called?

4 Sir Humphry Davy discovered that laughing gas has which effect?

5 Irish naval officer Sir Francis Beaufort gave his name to measurement of what?

6 What was the nationality of Archimedes?

7 Which spacecraft launched the Hubble telescope?

8 What does the letter d stand for in radar?

9 Pythagoras's most famous theorem is about which geometric shape?

10 Which part of London is associated with Mean Time?

11 Which German psychiatrist gave his name to a disease of senile dementia?

12 Famous for demonstrating TV, John Logie Baird also developed what type of sound?

13 The study of oncogenes is crucial in the treatment of which disease?

14 Who were the main opponents of Copernicus's assertion that the Sun was at the centre of the Universe?

15 How is the lady born Manya Sklodowska better known?

16 Which dog gave its name to Darwin's explorer ship?

17 What improvement did Edison make to Bell's telephone?

18 What did Geiger's counter measure?

19 In 1898 Marconi transmitted radio signals across where?

20 Which physician gave his name to the disease of paralysis agitans?

ANSWERS ON PAGE 288

146 PICTURE QUIZ

Starting with the oldest in which order were these celebrities born?

ANSWERS ON PAGE 288

147 INSECTS

Is each statement TRUE or FALSE?

T F **1** Dragonflies have long antennae.

T F **2** Grasshoppers have long hind legs.

T F **3** Cockroaches are largely nocturnal.

T F **4** Earwigs are herbivores.

T F **5** Stick insects are green or brown.

T F **6** The largest of all insect orders is the beetle.

T F **7** Flies have six small wings.

T F **8** Sawflies are part of the order of wasps.

T F **9** There are over a million known species of insects.

T F **10** The garden chafer is another name for the maybug.

ANSWERS ON PAGE 288

148 ANIMAL MOVIES

1 Who or what was Andre in the film of the same name?
☐ Gorilla ☐ Seal ☐ Tiger

2 What sort of whale was Willy?
☐ Blue ☐ Orca ☐ White

3 Which movie saw a creature threatening Amity off the Long Island coast?
☐ *Ants* ☐ *Jaws* ☐ *Them*

4 Beethoven was what type of family pet?
☐ Dog ☐ Parrot ☐ Snake

5 Dodie Smith's book became a film about which creatures?
☐ Dalmatians ☐ Dolphins
☐ Elephants

6 Which creatures predominate in *Deep Blue Sea*?
☐ Sharks ☐ Turtles ☐ Whales

7 Virginia McKenna starred in which classic wild animal movie?
☐ *Born Free* ☐ *The Birds*
☐ *Out Of Africa*

8 What sort of animal featured in *My Friend Flicka*?
☐ Goat ☐ Horse ☐ Sheep

9 Which Tom played opposite a dog in *Turner & Hooch*?
☐ Conti ☐ Cruise ☐ Hanks

10 Who joined Faye Wray on the Empire State Building?
☐ Godzilla ☐ King Kong ☐ Wolfman

11 How many horses did Gene Autry have called Champion?
☐ One ☐ Three ☐ Five

12 How many dogs made *The Incredible Journey* with the cat?
☐ One ☐ Two ☐ Three

13 Which animals were the stars of *Ring Of Bright Water*?
☐ Otters ☐ Seals ☐ Whales

14 What was Tom Mix's horse called?
☐ Palomino ☐ Silver ☐ Tony

15 What was the name of the first dog to play Lassie?
☐ Lassie
☐ Pal
☐ Petra

ANSWERS ON PAGE 288

149 FIFA WORLD CUP

1. How often is the FIFA World Cup held?
2. Which country did keeper Brad Friedel represent in the 2002 competition?
3. Who won the last World Cup of the 20th century?
4. What colour shirts were England wearing when they won in 1966?
5. Who was the manager of the 2002 winners Brazil?
6. Which England player was sent off against Argentina in the 1998 tournament?
7. Which country did Michael Ballack play for in 2002?
8. Who was England's No 1 keeper during the 2002 tournament?
9. Which club side was Michael Owen playing for at the time of the 2002 tournament?
10. In which year was the first World Cup final?
11. Dunga was captain of which World Cup winners?
12. Who were beaten finalists in the last World Cup of the 20th century?
13. Bulgaria, Italy and USA – which side has not hosted a World Cup tournament?
14. Which Gary was top scorer in the 1986 World Cup?
15. Antonio Carbajal played in five different tournaments for which country?
16. Which two countries co-hosted the 2002 tournament?
17. In France 98 which country did top marksman Suker play for?
18. Who was the first Englishman to lift the World Cup as winning captain?
19. Which country were the first to lose a Final on a penalty shoot out?
20. Did English legend Jimmy Greaves ever play in a World Cup Final?

ANSWERS ON PAGE 288

150 LUCKY DIP

1. Which Mick once married Jerry Hall?
2. Who created the three-dimensional cube in the 70s and 80s craze?
3. Which country does a car come from with the international registration letter D?
4. In UK politics, who came first as Labour leader, Callaghan or Wilson?
5. Which Mae said, "Is that a gun in your pocket or are you pleased to see me?"
6. In darts what is the highest score from three trebles?
7. C is the symbol of which chemical element?
8. Which cartoon character has Bluto as his arch rival?
9. Which two colours appear on the flag of Denmark?
10. What is the last month of the year to have exactly 30 days?
11. What was Norman Watts' nickname in *Coronation Street*?
12. Who recorded the best-selling album *Dark Side Of The Moon*?
13. What is the word for a group of elephants?
14. What is the largest organ in the human body?
15. Which group had a UK No 1 with *Belfast Child*?
16. How many players are in a Rugby League team?
17. In the UK what is the maximum number of years between General Elections?
18. What type of dance involves moving under a low horizontal pole?
19. Which high office has been held by Dr George Carey?
20. Which brothers, Jacob and Wilhelm, wrote and collected fairy tales?

ANSWERS ON PAGE 288

151 HALF CHANCE

½? ½? ½?

1. Dame Peggy Ashcroft became famous as what – an actress or a politician?
2. Would a French wine described as "doux" be medium sweet or medium dry?
3. Percy Blakeney was the alias of which hero – Captain America or The Scarlet Pimpernel?
4. In art cubism was founded in which country – Cuba or France?
5. Which movie sequel had the subtitle *Judgment Day* – *Lethal Weapon* or *Terminator II*?
6. Which animal shares its name with Samuel Crompton's spinning machine – horse or mule?
7. The Jewish day Yom Kippur is known as the Day of what – Atonement or Penitence?
8. Which Blue single came first – *If You Come Back* or *Too Close*?
9. What is Schindler's nationality in the movie *Schindler's List* – Austrian or Dutch?
10. The Hallé Orchestra is based in which English city – Manchester or Birmingham?
11. In horse racing where is the Lincoln Handicap held – at Ayr or Doncaster?
12. Still looking *Ab Fab*, was Joanna Lumley born in the 1940s or 1950s?
13. The M1 was originally constructed to link London to where – Birmingham or Leeds?
14. Is Harvey Keitel particularly known for his work with Scorsese or Stone?
15. *Seinfield* ran to how many episodes – 140 or 180?
16. Is pertussis more commonly known as influenza or whooping cough?
17. What S is added to pasta to make it green – sage or spinach?
18. Is The Althing the parliament of Estonia or Iceland?
19. In which western did John Wayne play The Ringo Kid – *The Alamo* or *Stagecoach*?
20. In drinks, what word goes with Moët – Chablis or Chandon?

ANSWERS ON PAGE 288

152 THE 1960s

60's? 60's? 60's?

1. Who founded the PLO?
2. Which Kennedy announced he was running for President in 1960?
3. Nikita Krushchev was head of state of which Union?
4. In which Italian city were the 1960 summer Olympics held?
5. Whose Lover was the subject of a court case in book form?
6. The USSR sent its first man where in April 1960?
7. Which Russian dancer Rudolph defected to the West?
8. Across which former European capital was a Wall built?
9. Which drug taken by pregnant mothers caused abnormalities in babies?
10. Which Harold became Labour leader in 1963 in the UK?
11. Of where did Neil Armstrong say, "The surface is like fine powder"?
12. What were mailbags containing over £1 million stolen from?
13. Caroline was the name of Britain's first off-shore pirate what?
14. Which British WWII leader died in 1965?
15. What sort of champion was Arkle?
16. Which communist country had its famous Red Guards?
17. Which knighted soccer star retired aged 50?
18. Who launched the *Queen Elizabeth II* – QE2 – on Clydebank?
19. Which model Jean was called "The Shrimp"?
20. If Mods rode scooters, who rode motorbikes?

ANSWERS ON PAGE 288

153 THE ARTS

1 Which musical is based on the story of Romeo and Juliet?

2 Who wrote the long-running play *The Mousetrap*?

3 Which words complete the title of the comedy, *No Sex Please* _____?

4 Which creator of Jeeves and Wooster is known by his initials P. G.?

5 At which film festival is the prize the Golden Swan awarded?

6 What was the profession of James Herriot?

7 What is the surname of romantic novelist Dame Barbara?

8 Which musical is the name of a fairground ride?

9 Whose Lover was the subject of a book by D. H. Lawrence?

10 Which sport are Dick Francis' novels about?

11 Which politician Jeffrey wrote *Kane and Abel*?

12 Which novelist Jackie has an actress sister called Joan?

13 Which Ruth created Inspector Wexford ?

14 Which Emily wrote *Wuthering Heights*?

15 What was on the Island Robert Louis Stevenson wrote about?

16 Flatford Mill is associated with which English landscape artist?

17 Which Peter took the Darling children to Never Never Land?

18 In which musical does Fagin appear?

19 What is the first name of novelist Miss Cookson?

20 Which detective novelist is known by her initials PD?

ANSWERS ON PAGE 288

154 ANIMALS

1 If a mammal has albinism what colour are its eyes?

2 What colour are dalmatians when they are born?

3 The tosa is a dog native to which country?

4 What is the reindeer of North America called?

5 What is a merino?

6 What colour is the coat of a samoyed?

7 What shaped mark does an adder have on its head?

8 What is another name for the wapiti?

9 What do alligators lay their eggs in?

10 Which dog do shepherds now most commonly use for herding sheep?

11 What type of animal is a beagle?

12 Where is a human's jugular vein?

13 What is the only truly amphibious member of the weasel family?

14 Are most animals vertebrates or invertebrates?

15 How many young does a kangaroo usually produce at any one time?

16 The bandicoot is a marsupial from which country?

17 Which bear is the largest meat-eating land animal?

18 What do all mammals feed their babies on?

19 Which part of a human includes loops and whorls?

20 In which hemisphere do penguins live in the wild?

ANSWERS ON PAGE 288

155 PICTURE QUIZ

Starting with the first in this group in which order did these actors first play James Bond?

ANSWERS ON PAGE 289

156 DOUBLE TAKE

In each case, the two-part quiz question leads to just one answer!

1 Which word for a bride's attendant is also part of a book?

2 Which word for a children's nurse is also a female goat?

3 Which herb shares a name with a money store?

4 Which insect shares a name with a listening device?

5 What can be a film award or the first name of playwright Wilde?

6 Which ocean shares a name with a word for conciliatory?

7 Which word for a long pillow can also mean to reinforce?

8 Which Venetian boat shares its name with a supermarket shelf unit?

9 Which crisp biscuit can also be a part of the Christmas festivities?

10 Which word can be a stick or the workforce?

ANSWERS ON PAGE 289

157 WORLD WAR II

1 Who made the "This was their finest hour" speech?
☐ Churchill ☐ Montgomery
☐ Roosevelt

2 What was the German airforce called?
☐ Doodlebug ☐ Luftwaffe ☐ Swastika

3 Which country declared war on Germany the same time as Britain?
☐ Belgium ☐ France ☐ Poland

4 An attack by which country saw the USA enter the war?
☐ Germany ☐ Italy ☐ Japan

5 Which German city was ferociously bombed in February 1945?
☐ Berlin ☐ Dresden ☐ Hamburg

6 The evacuation of Dunkirk was called Operation what?
☐ Dunkirk ☐ Dynamo ☐ Overlord

7 In the UK, how were the Local Defence Volunteers renamed?
☐ Home Guard ☐ Land Girls ☐ The Few

8 Where did Bevan Boys work?
☐ Coalmines ☐ Factories ☐ Farms

9 What kind of food was snoek?
☐ Fish ☐ Fruit ☐ Meat

10 Which 'Lord' was executed in 1946 for broadcasting Nazi propaganda?
☐ Haw-Haw ☐ Nelson ☐ Wodehouse?

11 What was the name given to the bomb that destroyed Hiroshima?
☐ Fat Boy ☐ Little Boy ☐ Lost Boy

12 In WWII who was in charge of the Afrika Korps?
☐ Hess ☐ Himmler ☐ Rommel

13 What number was the armoured division known as The Desert Rats?
☐ 4th ☐ 7th ☐ 9th

14 Which city was besieged by German troops for over 900 days?
☐ Moscow ☐ Leningrad ☐ Paris

15 How did Hitler die?
☐ Drowned ☐ Executed
☐ Shot himself

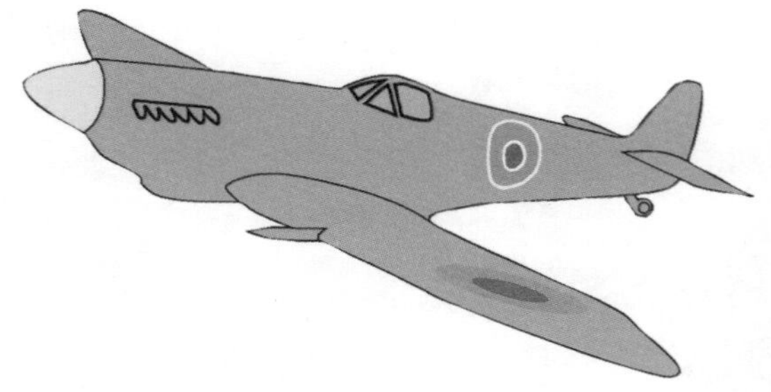

ANSWERS ON PAGE 289

158 TENNIS

1 Who was the first male tennis player to win 100 tournaments?
2 What is the surface of the courts at Roland Garros in Paris?
3 Who had the car number plate X CZECH?
4 Who won the first US Men's Championship in the "Open" era?
5 Who, in 1986, became the youngest woman semi finalist at Wimbledon for 99 years?
6 Which country does Roger Federer come from?
7 What was Monica Seles's first Grand Slam title?
8 Who was the first Australian woman to win the Wimbledon Singles?
9 Who did Boris Becker beat to become Wimbledon's youngest Men's Singles winner?
10 With whom did Billie Jean Moffitt win her first Wimbledon Doubles title?
11 Which US star was married to British player John Lloyd?
12 What is the score in tennis when the tie break is introduced?
13 Whose Wimbledon Men's Singles victory was sandwiched in between Sampras claiming seven titles?
14 What is the name of the venue of the Australian Open?
15 Which Grand Slam tournament did Sue Barker win?
16 Where is the final of the US Open played?
17 Who gave Virginia Wade her trophy when she won Wimbledon?
18 When were Women's Singles first played at Wimbledon – 1884, 1904 or 1924?
19 Which Grand Slam title has Boris Becker never won?
20 Which lady won two titles in a day at Wimbledon 96?

ANSWERS ON PAGE 289

159 GENERAL KNOWLEDGE

1 Of which country is Freetown the capital?
2 What is the term for a group of partridges?
3 What was the occupation of the legendary "Casey Jones"?
4 According to the proverb what is the mother of invention?
5 What is an area of water separated from the open sea by a coral reef?
6 In cricket how many balls are there in an over?
7 In the London theatre what is the longest-running play ever?
8 Which royal sport would you see at Cowdray Park and Hurlingham?
9 In astronomy what are falling stars properly called?
10 What are Hickling, Barton, and Breydon Water?
11 By population which is the largest city in the United States?
12 What is popularly meant by the Italian phrase "che sara sara"?
13 What was pioneered by the Austrian physician Dr. Mesmer?
14 Whom might you expect to see working in a dig?
15 In which city was there formerly a parliament building called the Reichstag?
16 Which is the smallest bird in the world?
17 Which saint's day falls on 30th November?
18 In fiction who lived in the stables at Birtwick Hall?
19 Who was Oberon?
20 What name was given to an airship that could be steered?

ANSWERS ON PAGE 289

160 SOUL & MOTOWN

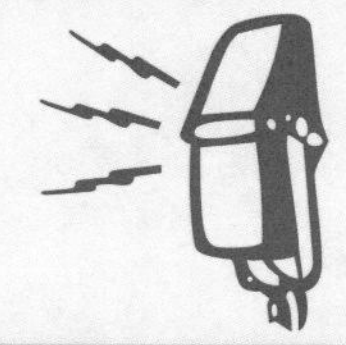 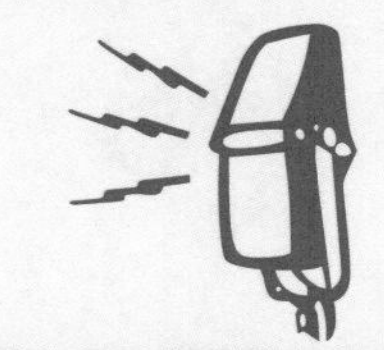 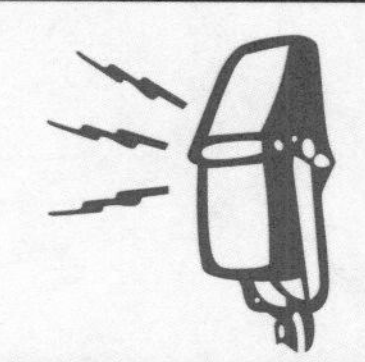

1. The Four Tops had only one UK No 1. – what was it?
2. Who was the boss of Tamla Motown?
3. Who sang with Sam on the hit *Soul Man*?
4. Which female soul star has recorded with Elton John, George Michael and George Benson?
5. Who made up the songwriting trio with Holland and Dozier?
6. Who was *Sitting On The Dock Of The Bay*?
7. Who according to Jimmy Ruffin "had love that has now departed"?
8. Which soul singer died in 1984 after lying in a coma for 8 years?
9. Rudolph, Ronald and O'Kelley were which singing Brothers?
10. Who is known as "The Godfather Of Soul"?
11. Which group featured Cindy Birdsong?
12. The Motown label was nearly called Tammy – after which Tammy?
13. Which Tamla song starts,"Set me free, why don't you babe"?
14. In the 1960s who was known as "The Wicked Pickett"?
15. Which group backed Martha Reeves?
16. Who recorded the soul classic *Sweet Soul Music*?
17. What was Diana Ross's first solo British No 1?
18. Which singer went solo after performing with the Commodores?
19. Who was backed by The Pips?
20. Which soul singer married Whitney Houston in 1992?

ANSWERS ON PAGE 289

161 AT THE MOVIES

1. Which Geena starred in *A League Of Their Own*?
2. In which country was Leslie Nielsen born?
3. Which Helen was the only American nominated for Best Actress Oscar in 1998?
4. Which actor links *Batman, A Few Good Men* and *Wolf*?
5. Steven Spielberg made *Close Encounters* of which *Kind*?
6. Which actress had an autobiography called *Goodness Had Nothing to Do With It?*
7. Which film whale was played by Keiko in which 90s movie?
8. *Top Gun* was about which of the armed services?
9. Was *Bambi* first released in the 1920s, 40s or 60s?
10. Which Frank starred in the 50s movie *From Here To Eternity*?
11. What is Nicolas Cage's real surname?
12. Real-life character Lee Harvey Oswald was in which Stone movie?
13. Which word completes the film title, *I Am A ____ From A Chain Gang*?
14. Which voice was that of Robin Williams in *Aladdin*?
15. Which James Bond actor has an actor son called Jason?
16. *Total Recall* and *Casino* featured which actress?
17. Who played opposite Ginger Rogers 10 times?
18. Which pop star Tina did Angela Bassett play in the 1993 biopic?
19. In which decade was *Batman Forever* released?
20. Who won the Best Actor Oscar for *The Godfather*?

ANSWERS ON PAGE 289

162 LUCKY DIP

1 Red, yellow and blue are all what type of colours?

2 In which television programme does Hyacinth Bucket appear?

3 In UK politics, which John was Labour leader before Tony Blair?

4 Which English soccer side has Alexandra in its name?

5 The Acol system is used in which game?

6 How many years are celebrated by a ruby anniversary?

7 Which peace protestor was dubbed "Hanoi Jane"?

8 Which Leo played the lead character in *Rumpole of the Bailey*?

9 What number does the Roman numeral C stand for?

10 What was the name of Miss Rigby in the song by the Beatles?

11 Stansted airport was built in which English county?

12 Which Ron created the role of Fagin on film?

13 Roberta Flack had a huge hit with a song called *The First Time I Saw Your* what?

14 What are the initials of the 20th century poet Mr Eliot?

15 According to rhyme, what did Polly Flinders sit in?

16 Which Frederick wrote *The Day Of the Jackal*?

17 Which term means related to the moon?

18 Which Roger has played James Bond?

19 Grandfather, cuckoo and carriage are types of what?

20 On what part of your body would you wear a muff?

ANSWERS ON PAGE 289

163 OLYMPICS

1 Which city hosted the summer Olympics of 2004?

2 Which country finished with second most gold medals, only three behind the US, in 2004?

3 How many gold medals did Mark Spitz win in Munich in 1972?

4 Which invasion caused a boycott of the Moscow Olympics in 1980?

5 In which country were the first Modern Olympics held in 1896?

6 In which two successive Olympics did Daley Thompson win gold?

7 Black, yellow, red, and green – which Olympic ring is missing?

8 Which country has won most summer Olympic medals since 1896?

9 Who set a world long jump record in the 1968 Games that lasted for 23 years?

10 Which creature went with Syd and Olly in the Sydney Olympics?

11 Which country did athletes with FRG after their names represent?

12 Who won silver at 100m in '88 and gold in the same event in '92?

13 Which singer performed the song *Oceania* at the opening ceremony in 2004?

14 Which gymnast scored the first perfect 10 in Olympic history?

15 Where were the 1964 Olympics held?

16 Who was disqualified after a drugs test in the men's 100m in 1988 and lost his gold?

17 Who collided with Zola Budd in the epic 3000 metres race in 1984?

18 Which American equalled Jesse Owens four golds in 1984?

19 At which sport was Katarina Witt an Olympic champion?

20 In which city were the Winter Olympics held when Torvill and Dean won gold in 1984?

ANSWERS ON PAGE 289

164 PICTURE QUIZ

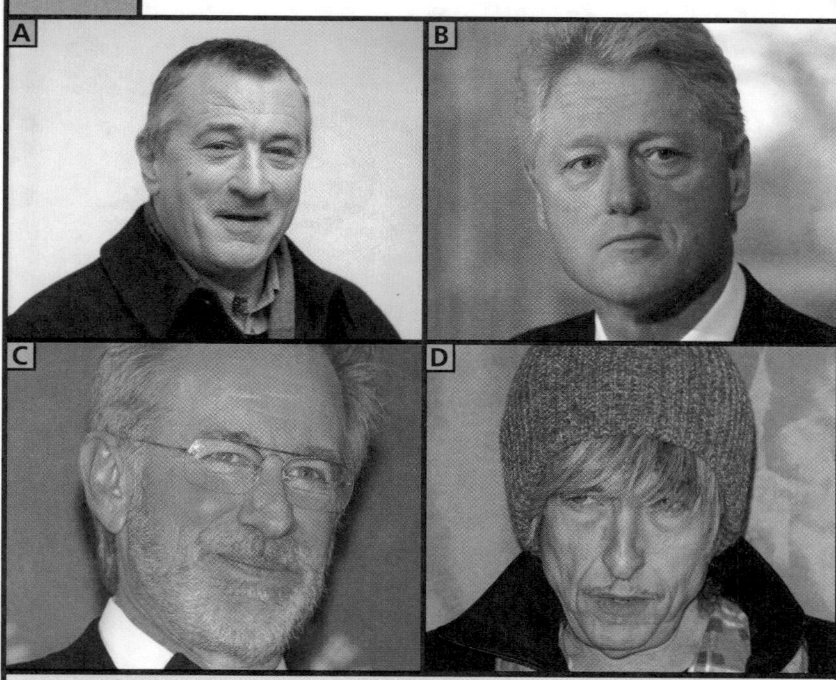

Starting with the oldest in which order were these celebrities born?

ANSWERS ON PAGE 289

165 NAME THE YEAR

1 Jimi Hendrix was born. Humphrey Bogart and Ingrid Bergman appeared in *Casablanca*. The Battle of El Alamein began.

2 Elton John was born as Reginald Dwight. Edwin Land's Polaroid camera produced photos in a few minutes. Gangster Al Capone died.

3 Construction of the Berlin wall began. J F Kennedy was sworn in as the youngest US President. Princess Diana was born.

4 The USA declared war on Germany. Mata Hari was executed in Paris for spying. Buffalo Bill died.

5 America launched the Space Shuttle. Jimmy Carter was inaugurated as President of the USA. Elvis Presley died.

6 England won the Rugby Union World Cup. Coldplay won a Grammy for *Clocks*. First solo crossing of the Atlantic in an open basket balloon.

ANSWERS ON PAGE 289

166 PEOPLE

1 Which British journalist was involved in the Michael Jackson trial of 2005?

2 Whose death at Chappaquiddick effectively stopped Edward Kennedy running for President?

3 What was Mother Teresa's real first name?

4 What was the name of Margaret Thatcher's husband?

5 What part of his body did Keith Richards insure for £1 million?

6 Betty Boothroyd became the first female Speaker where?

7 How was Elaine Bickerstaff better known on the West End stage?

8 Which chain of environmentally friendly shops did Anita Roddick found?

9 What did Nigel Kennedy change his name to, professionally, in the late 1990s?

10 Which Gordon was Tony Blair's first Chancellor of the Exchequer?

11 Which musical instrument was Dudley Moore famous for playing?

12 Who said in his autobiography, "I became one of the stately homos of England."?

13 Martina Navratilova changed nationality from Czech to what?

14 Why would you consult Nicky Clarke professionally?

15 Which two initials is crime novelist Baroness James known by?

16 Henry Cecil is a famous name in which sport?

17 Tesco founder Jack Cohen's business motto was, "Pile it high, sell it" how?

18 Which Spice nickname did Geri Halliwell have?

19 *The Aviator* was a biopic of which famous figure?

20 When Pamela Stephenson stood for Parliament which party did she represent?

ANSWERS ON PAGE 289

St Patrick's

Here are 50 questions celebrating St Patrick's Day on the 17th March and all things connected to Ireland, the Irish and a few other "Patricks".

1. What are the emblems of St Patrick?
2. Which work by St Patrick is the main history of his life?
3. County Kildare is famous for the breeding of which sporting creatures?
4. What is the only college of Dublin University?
5. Which fabric made from flax is Ireland famous for?
6. Which German engineer, famous for luxury cars, was born on this day 1834?
7. Which Australian tennis star had a surname associated with money?
8. What is the main river of Dublin?
9. Which Irish band recorded the worldwide best-selling album *The Joshua Tree*?
10. Belfast is on the border of which two counties?
11. Which of the notorious Kray twins died on St Patricks' Day 1995?
12. Which Patrick is a famous astronomer?
13. What does R stand for in the broadcasting company RTE?
14. Which city shares its name with a five-lined verse?
15. Which late US actress Grace had ancestors in Newport?
16. Which tennis champion had the forenames John Patrick?
17. In which Dublin Street is St Patrick's cathedral?
18. Which famous director of westerns was born Sean Aloysius O'Feeney?
19. Which traditional musical instrument was adopted as a logo by Guinness?
20. On which river does Galway stand?
21. Which city of four letters has St Finbarr's cathedral?
22. Who or what is a bodhran?
23. Which Patrick returned from the dead in an infamous shower scene in Dallas?
24. What is the name of Dublin's prison which begins with an M?

Day Quiz

25 In which county is Blarney castle?

26 What is Ireland's biggest Lough?

27 Which singer with the middle name King was born on this day in 1919?

28 What does the word whiskey mean?

29 Which holy place is regarded by many as the Lourdes of Ireland?

30 Which US car maker was born in Clonakilty?

31 For which musical instrument is James Galway most famous?

32 Which movie was based on Frank McCourt's Limerick childhood?

33 Which pub claims to be Ireland's oldest?

34 Where was the seat of the High Kings of Ireland?

35 Patrick Rafter played tennis for which country?

36 What is a drumlin?

37 In Dublin what is Eason's famous for?

38 What is Ireland's only inland city?

39 Which county is known as the Orchard County?

40 Two Irish woman presidents have shared which first name?

41 What would you do with Cashel Blue?

42 Which Russian dancer was born on St Patrick's Day 1938?

43 Which fabric is Donegal famous for?

44 Where was outlaw Ned Kelly transported to after being imprisoned in Tipperary jail?

45 What is the name of one of the world's largest breweries which is situated in Dublin?

46 What is the main ingredient of colcannon?

47 Which US President married Eleanor on St Patrick's Day 1905?

48 Which poet with the initials WB was born in County Sligo?

49 In which Dublin park is the HQ of the Garda?

50 Which channel is to the south east of Ireland?

ANSWERS ON PAGE 289

168 THE HEADLINES

1. What did Liam Gallagher lose in a bar brawl in Munich in 2002?
2. In 2001 whose car was found in Lake Coniston after an attempt on the water speed record over 30 years earlier?
3. Which city of the Ukraine was closest to Chernobyl?
4. Which crisis brought about the establishing of a hot line between the White House and the Kremlin?
5. Who was President of Argentina in the Falklands War?
6. Who replaced President Nixon after Watergate?
7. In the terrorist attacks on the US in 2001 in which state did the plane crash which did not crash into a building?
8. Who succeeded Ayatollah Khomeini as president of Iran?
9. Who, in 1979, became the first western rock star to visit the USSR?
10. Who succeeded JF Kennedy after his assassination?
11. In which year did Queen Elizabeth II celebrate her Golden Jubilee?
12. Which US city was the scene of a terrorist bomb in 1995?
13. In which country did Corazon Aquino become President after the death of her husband?
14. In which English county was Piltdown Man discovered in the early years of the 20th century?
15. Which Sinn Fein politician became Northern Ireland's Minister of Education after the Good Friday agreement?
16. Who was the first leader of the Scottish Parliament?
17. Which Japanese leader visited Britain amid great controversy in 1998?
18. Who preceded Putin as Russian leader?
19. Where in Greater Manchester did mass murderer Dr Harold Shipman practise?
20. Which drug was launched in the late 1990s as a cure for impotence?

ANSWERS ON PAGE 289

169 TRAVEL

1. What are the three Baltic states?
2. In which country does the Douro reach the Atlantic?
3. What is the capital of Catalonia?
4. Wall Street and Broadway lie on which island?
5. What do the Germans call Bavaria?
6. Which European capital stands on the river Liffey?
7. What is the Eiffel Tower made from?
8. How is the Danish region of Jylland known in English?
9. In which forest does the Danube rise?
10. Key West and Key Largo are off the coast of which state?
11. What covers most of Finland?
12. In which country is the world's highest dam?
13. What is the capital of the Ukraine?
14. What is a remarkable feature of the caves at Lascaux in SW France?
15. To the nearest thousand, how many islands does Indonesia have?
16. Where is France's Tomb of the Unknown Soldier?
17. Which area of the Rhône delta is famous for its nature reserve?
18. Which of the Low Countries is nearest the beginning of the alphabet?
19. What are the two official European languages of Luxembourg?
20. The Magyars are the largest ethnic group of which country?

ANSWERS ON PAGE 289

170 OLOGIES

What do you study if you pursue the following OLOGIES?

1 ONEIROLOGY

2 TIMBROLOGY

3 ZYMOLOGY

4 IRENOLOGY

5 OPHIOLOGY

6 DELTIOLOGY

7 PHYCOLOGY

8 CARCINOLOGY

9 AUTOLOGY

10 MYRMECOLOGY

ANSWERS ON PAGE 289

171 GUESS WHO . . . ?

1 This Pope from Poland succeeded John Paul I in 1978.

2 This novelist and playwright was born in New Orleans and wrote *Breakfast at Tiffany's* which was made into a film.

3 Born in Munich in 1945 he was the first man to captain and coach a football World Cup winning team.

4 Born in Washington DC this singer/songwriter recorded *I Heard It Through the Grapevine*, and was killed by his own father in 1984.

5 His middle name was Byron and he died in 1955 after making the movies *Giant* and *Rebel Without a Cause*.

6 He was a long jumper and broke the world record to win Olympic gold in Mexico in 1968.

7 He succeeded Canaan Banana as his country's president in 1987 in a country which used to be called Rhodesia.

8 This singer/songwriter recorded with the Comets with hits including *Rock Around the Clock*.

9 Born in London in 1961 he fought Mike Tyson in 1989 and won the WBC title in 1995.

10 Born in New York his films include *Taxi Driver, The Godfather Part II* and *Raging Bull*.

ANSWERS ON PAGE 289

172 PROVERBS

1 What makes the heart grow fonder?
☐ Absence ☐ Actions ☐ Attraction

2 Which fruit once a day keeps the doctor away?
☐ Apple ☐ Orange ☐ Pear

3 What can't you teach new tricks?
☐ Old dog ☐ Old man ☐ Old woman

4 Who finds work for idle hands?
☐ The boss ☐ The devil ☐ The family

5 What is the better part of valour?
☐ Discretion ☐ Honesty ☐ Integrity

6 Where does charity begin?
☐ At church ☐ At home ☐ At school

7 What is mightier than the sword?
☐ The character ☐ The pen
☐ The word

8 What goes before a fall?
☐ Confidence ☐ Isolation ☐ Pride

9 Which bird catches the worm?
☐ Eager ☐ Early ☐ Greedy

10 What is only skin deep?
☐ Beauty ☐ Honesty ☐ Sincerity

11 What is the best sauce?
☐ Hunger ☐ Need ☐ Poverty

12 What killed the cat?
☐ Celebrity ☐ Chicanery
☐ Curiosity

13 What doesn't change its spots?
☐ A dice ☐ A domino
☐ A leopard

14 Which city was not built in a day?
☐ London ☐ Paris ☐ Rome

15 What must you not throw out with the bathwater?
☐ The baby ☐ The soap ☐ The towel

ANSWERS ON PAGE 289

173 MUSICAL MOVIES

1. In which country does the action of *Evita* take place?
2. Which John starred in *Grease* in 1978?
3. Which Kelly directed *Hello Dolly*?
4. Which Antarctic creatures feature in *Mary Poppins*?
5. Which Diana played Dorothy in *The Wiz*?
6. In which movie based on *Romeo and Juliet* did Richard Beymer play Tony?
7. Which movie featured the song *Greased Lightning*?
8. In which *Picture Show* does Frank N Furter appear?
9. According to Irving Berlin's musical *There's No Business Like* what?
10. Which jazz trumpeter nicknamed Satchmo appeared in *High Society*?
11. Who played Tony Manero in *Saturday Night Fever*?
12. *The Sound Of Music* was set in which country?
13. Which 1968 film with Barbra Streisand was about Fanny Brice?
14. Which 1960s pop band's second movie was *Help!*?
15. *Secret Love* won best Oscar song from which Calamity film?
16. *Chim Chim Cheree* came from which movie about a super nanny?
17. Which pop brothers wrote the music for *Saturday Night Fever*?
18. *West Side Story* takes place on the West Side of which city?
19. Which Rex reprised his Broadway role as Professor Higgins in the movie *My Fair Lady*?
20. Which French star of musicals wrote an autobiography called *I Remember It Well*?

ANSWERS ON PAGE 289

174 HALF CHANCE

½? ½? ½?

1. Seal won a Grammy for *Kiss From A* what – a Grave or a Rose?
2. How did Jean Batten achieve fame – aviator or bandit?
3. In which country was Menachem Begin, a Prime Minister of Israel born – Germany or Poland?
4. With which sport is Bernard Hinault associated – boxing or cycling?
5. In the UK, what does the I stand for in CBI? – Industry or Information?
6. Actor Robert Carlyle was born in which part of the UK – Scotland or Wales?
7. Who did Daimler team up with to form a motor company – Benz or Rolls?
8. Who penned *Alexander's Ragtime Band* – Irving Berlin or Cole Porter?
9. Which Jane married Gerald Scarfe – Jane Asher or Jane Seymour?
10. Who was the first chemist to be Britain's Prime Minister – Thatcher or Wilson?
11. What are the international registration letters of a vehicle from Bulgaria – BG or BUG?
12. What was the first name of Dr Barnardo founder of Barnardo's Homes – Alfred or Thomas?
13. On which river was the Aswan High Dam built – Nile or Zambezi?
14. In African politics, does the letter C in ANC stand for Centre or Congress?
15. In which country is the deepwater port of Agadir – Algeria or Morocco?
16. What were the initials of the writer who created Bilbo Baggins – CS or JRR?
17. In *Rising Damp* what was the occupation of Rigsby – landlord or plumber?
18. What was the surname of pop duo Richard and Karen – Carpenter or Collins?
19. Was Julia Roberts born in the 1950s or 1960s?
20. The Wellington aircraft was built to carry what – bombs or passengers?

ANSWERS ON PAGE 289

175 W.W.W.

Can you identify the country in question from its internet code?

1 .br

2 .hu

3 .is

4 .pl

5 .tr

6 .ni

7 .lt

8 .mt

9 .am

10 .la

ANSWERS ON PAGE 289

176 FRIENDS

Is each statement TRUE or FALSE?

T F **1** *Friends* was first shown in the US in 1992.

T F **2** Chandler's surname was Bing.

T F **3** Phoebe's twin sister was Chloe.

T F **4** Monica was a chef in the early episodes of *Friends*.

T F **5** Jack Geller was played by Barbra Streisand's first husband.

T F **6** Joey's family were originally from Mexico.

T F **7** Ross's first wife was called Susan.

T F **8** Rachel's then real life husband appeared in *Friends*.

T F **9** The star of *Magnum PI* played Monica's older boyfriend.

T F **10** The first spin-off from *Friends* had Ross as its central character.

ANSWERS ON PAGE 289

177 THE BIBLE

1 Who received the Ten Commandments from God?
☐ Abraham ☐ Elijah ☐ Moses

2 Where was Jesus born?
☐ Bethlehem ☐ Jerusalem ☐ Nazareth

3 Which of the following was not one of the plagues of Egypt?
☐ Bees ☐ Boils ☐ Locusts

4 How did Jesus ride into Jerusalem on Palm Sunday?
☐ Chariot ☐ Donkey ☐ Horse

5 How many apostles did Jesus have?
☐ 10 ☐ 12 ☐ 21

6 Who was the wife of Abraham?
☐ Naomi ☐ Ruth ☐ Sarah

7 Which apostle was the brother of Peter?
☐ Andrew ☐ James ☐ John

8 Who wrote the first book of the New Testament?
☐ John ☐ Matthew ☐ Paul

9 In which garden did Adam and Eve live?
☐ Eden ☐ Gethsemane ☐ Olives

10 What was St Paul's previous name?
☐ Jonah ☐ Peter ☐ Saul

11 Who survived the Lions' Den?
☐ Daniel ☐ Darius ☐ David

12 What is the first book of the Old Testament?
☐ *Genesis* ☐ *Exodus* ☐ *Leviticus*

13 Which of the following was not one of the gifts of the Magi?
☐ Emeralds ☐ Gold ☐ Myrrh

14 Who asked for the head of John the Baptist?
☐ Delilah ☐ Esther ☐ Salome

15 What was Lot's wife turned into?
☐ Mountain of sand ☐ Pillar of salt
☐ Spitting snake

ANSWERS ON PAGE 289

178 GENERAL KNOWLEDGE

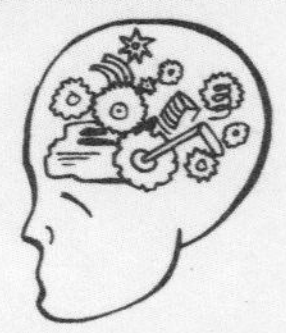
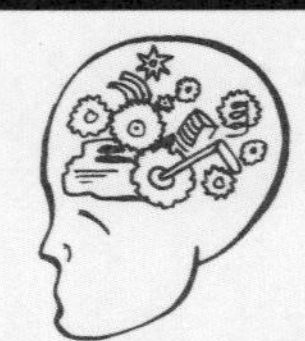
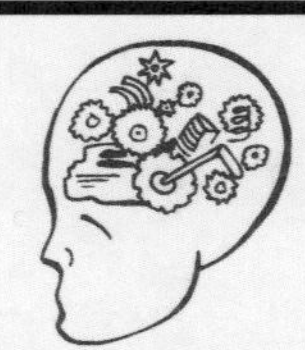

1 Who or what is Sweet William?

2 How did Princess Grace of Monaco die?

3 Which horror movie actor's real name was William Pratt?

4 Who "discovered" whom at Ujiji in 1871?

5 Which gas has the chemical symbol H?

6 In drama who says, "He is the very pineapple of politeness"?

7 Which breed of setter is named after a British duke?

8 Who wrote *Paradise Postponed*?

9 Which duo wrote and recorded *Mud, Mud, Glorious Mud*?

10 Which George did the Prince Regent become?

11 For which country did Denis Law play soccer?

12 How many atoms of oxygen are in one molecule of water?

13 Which "ologists'"study bumps on the human head?

14 Who wrote the book *William the Detective*?

15 Which Soviet city used to be called Leningrad?

16 How many faces did the Romans believe Janus to have?

17 kHz is an abbreviation for what?

18 What does a lexicographer write or make?

19 *Hedera helix* is better known as what?

20 If you are taking part in a Hamilton House or a Petronella what are you doing?

ANSWERS ON PAGE 289

179 AROUND OZ

1 Which city with 3 million inhabitants is Australia's largest by population?

2 What is the name of the world's longest reef?

3 Which Aborigine sacred rock is the world' s largest monolith?

4 Which state capital lies on the Swan River?

5 Which two oceans are to the east and west of Australia?

6 What is the name of the surfing beach on the outskirts of Sydney?

7 Darwin is the capital city of which state?

8 At which famous east coast bay did James Cook arrive in April 1770?

9 Which meandering river is Brisbane built around?

10 Which state is commonly called the Sunshine State?

11 Perth is the capital of which state?

12 Which mountain range to the west of Sydney was partly destroyed by bush fires in December 1993?

13 Which is the nearest major town to the south west of Ayers Rock?

14 What is the capital of the state of Victoria?

15 Which granite formation, formed by the wind, is to the east of Perth?

16 What is the coastline to the south of Brisbane called?

17 Which national park, known for aboriginal rock paintings and the wildlife, is to the east of Darwin?

18 Which Australian city hosted its final Formula 1 race in 1995?

19 What is the name of the world's largest sand island to the northeast of Brisbane?

20 What is Queensland's most northerly city, 2090 kms north of Brisbane?

ANSWERS ON PAGE 289

180 TELEVISION

1. Which comedy has episode titles starting "The One . . . "?
2. What colour clothes does Anne Robinson wear in *The Weakest Link*?
3. Teri Hatcher plays which character in *Desperate Housewives*?
4. Which programme looks at the love lives of Carrie, Samantha and Charlotte?
5. Which presenter Ian was a former goal-scoring legend with Arsenal soccer club?
6. Vernon Kaye hosted the game show called *Boys And* what?
7. Long-running game show *Countdown* is shown on which UK channel?
8. What are the first names of husband and wife presenters Madeley and Finnigan?
9. In which city do the Royle Family live – Exeter, Manchester or Newcastle?
10. What did *Flog It!* deal with – corporal punishment or auctions?
11. Victoria Wood has often teamed up with which Julie?
12. Hetty Wainthropp was an amateur what?
13. *One Man And His Dog* dealt with what type of trials?
14. Which vegetable was Popeye famous for eating?
15. In *Will And Grace* what is Grace's profession?
16. What is the first name of presenter Ms Feltz?
17. What was Compo's favourite item of footwear?
18. *Camberwick Green*, *Laramie* and *Maverick* – which was not a western?
19. What type of TV programmes are presented by Keith Floyd?
20. What was the name of Ned's shop in *The Simpsons*?

ANSWERS ON PAGE 289

181 POP MUSIC

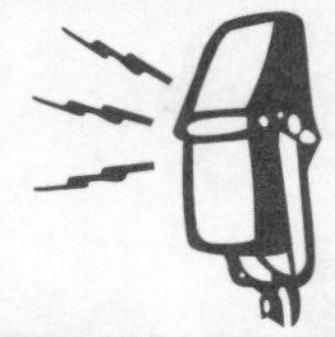
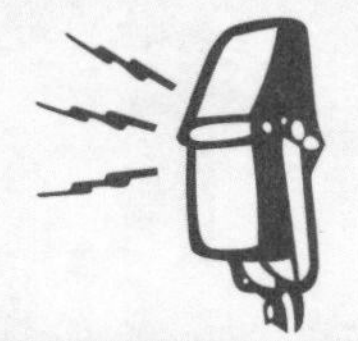
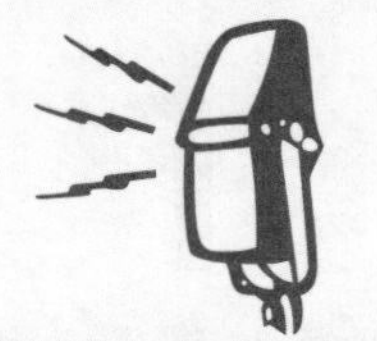

1. Whose best of album from 1988–2003 was called *In Time*?
2. Which US boy band featured three members of the Wilson family?
3. Which band recorded the album *Parallel Lines*?
4. In which decade was Jewel born?
5. The Sex Pistols were founders of which type of music?
6. Which female singer had an early 1990s hit with *Hero*?
7. Who sang in and starred in the movies *Grease* and *Xanadu*?
8. Andrew Ridgeley was the lesser known half of which chart-busting duo?
9. Which artist has had the most UK Top Ten hits in the 1990s
10. Who first charted with *Only The Lonely* back in 1960?
11. Which Spice Girl advertised Milky Bar as a small child?
12. *Do They Know It's Christmas?* was originally released to aid famine relief in which country?
13. Under what name did actor David Solberg have some big chart hits?
14. Pete Townshend and Keith Moon were members of which group?
15. In which London building was Elton John's first public performance of *Candle In The Wind* '97?
16. How many members were there in the Eurythmics?
17. Which country did Kraftwerk come from?
18. Who was backed by The Attractions?
19. Which 1960s London-based group featured two Davies brothers?
20. What sort of *Dancer* is Tina Turner on her first solo album?

ANSWERS ON PAGE 289

182 RELIGIONS

1 Whose birth shaped the calendar of the Western world?
2 Which country has the largest number of Roman Catholics?
3 Which movement promotes understanding between different branches of the Christian faith?
4 What are members of the Watchtower Movement better known as?
5 Whose newspaper is called *The Warcry*?
6 During which month do Muslims fast from before sunrise to sunset?
7 What do members of Jihad use to spread Islam?
8 Which religion is based on the teaching of Siddhartha Gautama?
9 Shintoism is the native religion of which country?
10 Which country has the largest Orthodox church?
11 What are members of the Society of Friends called?
12 In which religion are Shiva and Vishnu major gods?
13 Where should Muslims make a pilgrimage to once in their lifetime?
14 How is the International Society for Krishna Consciousness known?
15 What are members of the Unification church better known as?
16 In Judaism what is the Torah?
17 What nationality was Confucius?
18 What are members of the Church of Jesus Christ of Latter Day Saints better known as?
19 What does TM stand for in the movement founded by the Maharishi?
20 In Judaism what is the first day of the week?

ANSWERS ON PAGE 289

183 LUCKY DIP

1 In which country is JFK Airport?
2 Who had a worldwide hit with *Strangers In The Night*?
3 Which German childhood disease is also known as rubella?
4 Who topped the UK and US charts with the album *Survivor*?
5 Which Dennis was the first Australian cricketer to take 300 Test wickets?
6 Which King of England was called the Conqueror?
7 In rhyming slang what is meant by dickory dock?
8 Which Michael Caine film was about the Rorke's Drift battle?
9 Which word goes with hocus in magic?
10 In the Bible, who had a coat of many colours?
11 Which vegetable is also known as the egg plant?
12 Which country has most students in higher education?
13 Which comedy series featured the Boswell family?
14 What Egyptian obelisk stands on the Thames Embankment?
15 Which type of branch is used as a symbol of peace?
16 How many sides has an isosceles triangle?
17 What does a Geiger counter detect?
18 What is the ancient language of the Roman Empire?
19 Which major river flows through Newcastle?
20 Which actress links *Hannibal* and *Evolution*?

ANSWERS ON PAGE 289

184 PICTURE QUIZ

Which two of these celebrities were born on the same day?

ANSWERS ON PAGE 290

185 DOUBLE TAKE

In each case, the two-part quiz question leads to just one answer!

1 Which word for a group of schoolchildren is also a social category?

2 Which playing cards can also be winches?

3 Which part of a bird can also be the word for an invoice?

4 Which flat fish shares a name with part of the foot?

5 Which part of a cooked chicken might be used by a timpanist?

6 Which part of a castle can also be a word meaning to retain?

7 Which fish shares a name with a place for a bird to rest?

8 Which word for a gun cartridge can also be part of an egg?

9 Which kind of pâté shares a name with an adhesive?

10 Which word for lazy can also mean to tick over?

ANSWERS ON PAGE 290

186 GIRL POWER

1 How many of The Corrs are female?
☐ One ☐ Two ☐ Three

2 Where were Kylie's *Tears* in one of her early hits?
☐ *In Heaven* ☐ *In My Heart*
☐ *On My Pillow*

3 Which country did the Cheeky Girls come from?
☐ Greece ☐ Holland ☐ Romania

4 The album *Daydream* topped the charts for which female vocalist?
☐ Mariah Carey ☐ Celine Dion
☐ Sinead O'Connor

5 Whose second album was called *Chapter II*?
☐ Ashanti ☐ Madonna ☐ Norah Jones

6 Whose debut album on leaving a girl band was *Schizophonic*?
☐ Geri Halliwell ☐ Kelle Bryan
☐ Louise Nurding?

7 Which Cyndi recorded the famous *Girls Just Want to Have Fun*?
☐ Birdsong ☐ Lauper ☐ Smith

8 Whose real name is Susan Kay Quatrocchio?
☐ Dido ☐ Suzi Quatro
☐ Suzanne Vega

9 For which country did Celine Dion sing at a Eurovision Song Contest?
☐ Austria ☐ France ☐ Switzerland

10 Who released an album called *Jagged Little Pill*?
☐ Kate Bush ☐ Madonna
☐ Alanis Morissette

11 How many girls were in Abba?
☐ One ☐ Two ☐ Three

12 In which decade was the late vocalist Karen Carpenter born?
☐ 1950s ☐ 1960s ☐ 11970s

13 What was Marianne Faithfull's real surname?
☐ Faithfull ☐ Oldham ☐ Smith

14 Who had huge success with the album *The Kick Inside*?
☐ Kate Bush ☐ Dido
☐ Tina Turner

15 Who won a US Song of the Year Award for *Breathe Again*?
☐ Bjork
☐ Toni Braxton
☐ Celine Dion

ANSWERS ON PAGE 290

187 SPORT

1. Which team did Michael Schumacher race for in the 2004 Formula One Championship?
2. Susan Brown was the first woman to take part in which race?
3. Wentworth Golf Club is in which English county?
4. Which sporting ground has a Nursery End and a Pavilion End?
5. In which sport does the Fastnet Race take place?
6. What is the colour of the race leader's jersey in the Tour de France?
7. Who did England have to beat to stay in cricket's 1999 World Cup – and didn't?
8. In what year was soccer's World Cup last held in the 1980s?
9. Rugby is played at Ellis Park in which city?
10. Who was "The Crafty Cockney" – Eric Bristow, Frank Bruno or David Beckham?
11. Yapping Deng was a world champion in which sport?
12. Who captained South Africa in cricket's 1999 World Cup?
13. In which sport were Lonsdale Belts awarded?
14. Who was the first Footballer Of The Year in England to be an Italian?
15. Andy Caddick played for England at which sport?
16. In which decade did Man Utd players die in the Munich air disaster?
17. Which city's baseball team are the Giants?
18. The Fosbury Flop was developed in which athletics discipline?
19. The Australian Dawn Fraser was famous for which sport?
20. At which circuit does the San Marino Grand Prix take place?

ANSWERS ON PAGE 290

188 TREES

1. What do conifers have in their cones?
2. Which tree's leaves are the symbol of The National Trust?
3. What are Britain's three native coniferous trees?
4. Which garden tree with yellow flowers has poisonous seeds?
5. What colour are the flowers of the horse chestnut tree?
6. In which country did the bonsai technique develop?
7. Which tree do we get turpentine from?
8. On which continent did the monkey puzzle tree originate?
9. Which tree produces cobs and filberts?
10. Aspen is from which family of trees?
11. Is the wood of a coniferous tree hard or soft?
12. What is the more common name for the great maple?
13. What is the personalised name given to the world's most massive tree, a giant sequoia?
14. Which tree is cork obtained from?
15. In which county is England's largest forest, the Kielder Forest Park?
16. In which US state do the world's tallest trees grow?
17. Which beech tree has purplish leaves?
18. What is the Spanish chestnut also called?
19. Which tree can be English, American or Eurasian?
20. Bristlecone pines are the oldest living trees – are they around 1,000, 3,000 or 5,000 years old?

ANSWERS ON PAGE 290

189 GENERAL KNOWLEDGE

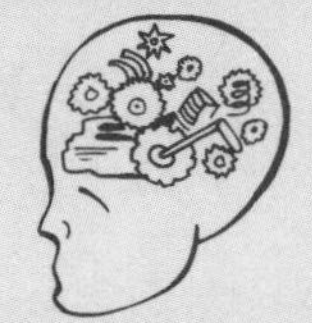 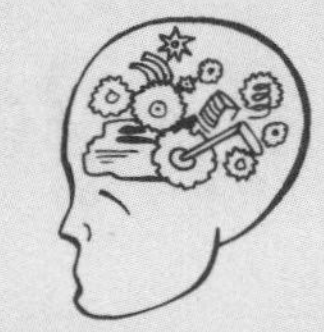 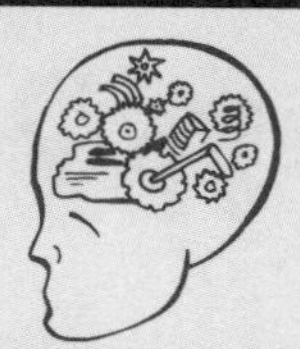

1 Which book of the Bible tells us about the creation of the world?

2 What is a lacuna?

3 Edible, blue, and hermit are all types of which creature?

4 Which Archbishop of Canterbury was murdered in his cathedral?

5 In which country is Waterloo, site of the Napoleonic battlefield?

6 Who wrote the play *The Importance of Being Earnest*?

7 Where is the metatarsal arch?

8 A lady would wear a mantilla in which country?

9 On a map, which places are joined by a contour?

10 In the song, which official is waiting "for me and my gal"?

11 What is pulchritude?

12 Which film comedians are associated with the phrase, "That's another fine mess you got me in"?

13 Which creature's song refers to a final speech or performance?

14 Which letter of the alphabet is used to describe a soft lead pencil?

15 Who was nicknamed the "Brown Bomber"?

16 In which country were there originally mandarins?

17 Who or what are Effingham, Grenville, Benbow and Collingwood?

18 For which sport is Gordon Pirie remembered?

19 What was Buddy Holly's real first name?

20 Which of Shakespeare's plays involves a pound of flesh?

ANSWERS ON PAGE 290

190 GEOGRAPHY

1 Which country can you easily walk to from Gibraltar?

2 In which US state is Miami?

3 Which is England's most northerly county?

4 What did Bejing used to be called?

5 Which is the Queen's London home?

6 In which European country is Salzburg?

7 Which county separates Cornwall from Somerset?

8 What "colour" is the Sea between Egypt and Saudi Arabia?

9 In which English county is the Peak District?

10 In which country is the resort of Rimini?

11 Madagascar is to the east of which continent?

12 Is California on the east or west coast of the USA?

13 Which is the nearest country to the Falkland Islands?

14 Near which French city is the Disney theme park?

15 In which country is the Algarve?

16 Which is further west – Algeria or Ethiopia?

17 Which country used to be called Siam?

18 In which country is the region of Tayside?

19 Which Scandinavian capital begins and ends with the same letter?

20 Chad is in which continent?

ANSWERS ON PAGE 290

191 SPACE

1 What would you find on a celestial map?

2 How is Ursa Major also known?

3 In which country are the headquarters of NASA?

4 Which TV programme called space "The Final Frontier"?

5 Were the first US Space Shuttle flights in the 1950s, 60s, or 80s?

6 What would Uranus have been called if it had been named after the reigning British monarch when first sighted, as had been planned?

7 What is a group of stars which make a recognisable pattern called?

8 What does the S stand for in NASA?

9 In which decade was the US's first satellite launched?

10 What is the English name for the lunar sea Mare Tranquillitas?

11 Castor and Pollux are two stars in which constellation?

12 John Young ate which item of fast food in space in 1968?

13 Was Apollo a US or USSR space programme?

14 Prior to being an astronaut was John Glenn in the Air Force or the Marines?

15 How long does it take the Earth to orbit the Sun?

16 Mishka, the 1980 Olympic mascot, was the first of which toy in space?

17 What were SCORE and Vanguard?

18 How many times did Gagarin orbit the Earth on his first space flight?

19 What travels at 186,272 miles per second?

20 Who was the first American to walk in space?

ANSWERS ON PAGE 290

192 HALF CHANCE

½? ½? ½?

1 As well as tennis Fred Perry was a champion at which other sport – golf or table tennis?

2 In which decade did the sitcom *Roseanne* begin – 1970s or 1980s?

3 What is the second word of *Imagine* – tomorrow or there's?

4 Princess Diana agreed to Prince Charles' request for a divorce in which year – 1994 or 1996?

5 Was Rowan Atkinson born in the 1950s or the 1960s?

6 Who declared, "The lady's not for turning" – Dolly Parton or Margaret Thatcher?

7 In the 1990s film was GI Jane played by Anna Friel or Demi Moore?

8 In which country was Pablo Picasso born – Mexico or Spain?

9 Who partnered Rowan in the classic 1960s comedy series *Laugh In* – Martin or Tree?

10 Who fronted Culture Club – Annie Lennox or Boy George?

11 Was Robert Mugabe the first Prime Minister of Nigeria or Zimbabwe?

12 In fiction what is the last name of the cannibal Dr Hannibal – Lecter or Starling?

13 *Brown-Eyed Handsome Man* was a hit for which singer after his death – Buddy Holly or Elvis Presley?

14 Chelmsford is the administrative centre of which English county – Essex or Surrey?

15 Which group sacked drummer Pete Best before they hit the big time – The Beatles or The Rolling Stones?

16 In medicine, does the D in CJD stand for Development or Disease?

17 What is the first name of best-selling sci-fi writer Pratchett – Terry or Ursula?

18 Which late comedian had "short, fat, hairy legs" – Eric Morecambe or Ernie Wise?

19 Which motorway links London to Cambridge – M11 or M8?

20 Timothy Dalton and Pierce Brosnan have both played which character – James Bond or Robin Hood?

ANSWERS ON PAGE 290

193 PICTURE QUIZ

Which two celebrities died on exactly the same day?

ANSWERS ON PAGE 290

194 WHO SAID . . . ?

1 "It's purely ugly. It looks like a sewer . . ." about the Diana memorial fountain.

2 "Our enemies are resourceful and so are we. They never stop thinking about new ways to harm our country and neither do we."

3 "My comedy is like emotional hang gliding."

4 "If you haven't cried your eyes can't be beautiful."

5 "You can't get spoiled if you do your own ironing."

6 "A man is a success if he gets up in the morning, goes to bed at night, and in between does what he wants."

7 "Money is like an arm or a leg – use it or lose it."

8 "There is only one difference between a madman and me. I am not mad."

ANSWERS ON PAGE 290

195 MEDICINE

1 Edward Jenner was a pioneer of what?
☐ Transplants ☐ Vaccination ☐ X rays

2 Which William discovered the mechanism of blood circulation?
☐ Harvey ☐ Hodgkin ☐ Jung

3 Hypertension is another name for what?
☐ Asthma ☐ High blood pressure
☐ Voice loss

4 Which disease is also called varicella?
☐ Chicken pox ☐ Measles ☐ Mumps

5 Oncology is the study of which disease?
☐ AIDS ☐ Cancer ☐ Heart disease

6 A hysterectomy involves removal of what?
☐ Kidney ☐ Lung ☐ Womb

7 Osteoporosis is a weakness and brittleness of what?
☐ Bones ☐ Nails ☐ Skin

8 What was the nationality of the founder of the Red Cross?
☐ French ☐ Swedish ☐ Swiss

9 Ebola is also known as which disease?
☐ Legionnaires' ☐ Crohn's ☐ Weil's?

10 Papworth hospital in Cambridgeshire is known for what type of surgery?
☐ Brain ☐ Eye ☐ Heart

11 In which country is Lassa, giving its name to Lassa fever?
☐ Algeria ☐ Ethiopria ☐ Nigeria

12 Which country was first to legalise voluntary euthanasia?
☐ Belgium ☐ Netherlands ☐ Sweden

13 Anabolic steroids are used to repair or build what?
☐ Bones ☐ Muscles ☐ Stamina

14 Shiatsu is a massage technique from which country?
☐ Indian ☐ Japan ☐ USA

15 If you suffer from photophobia what do you fear?
☐ Celebrities
☐ Chestnuts
☐ Light

ANSWERS ON PAGE 290

196 LUCKY DIP

1. The deepwater port of Valetta was developed on which island?
2. What is the zodiac sign of the Ram?
3. What is another name for "Old Glory", the USA flag?
4. Who had a No 1 hit with the song *I Just Called To Say I Love You*?
5. A dromedary is what type of creature?
6. Through which part of its body does a fish take in oxygen?
7. In the rhyme, how many fiddlers did Old King Cole have?
8. What was the name of the *Neighbours* character played by Kylie Minogue?
9. What word describes the permanent disappearance of a species?
10. According to proverb, what is thicker than water?
11. In the education sector, what does B.A. stand for?
12. In the human body, what has four chambers?
13. Which female singer topped the UK and US charts with the album *A New Day Has Come*?
14. Who was Helen of Troy's husband?
15. What is arachnophobia the fear of?
16. In opera, whose tiny hand was frozen?
17. How many cards of the same suit are needed for a flush in poker?
18. Which part of the body is described by the word labial?
19. What name is shared by composer Irving and a German city?
20. What type of food is Iceberg?

ANSWERS ON PAGE 290

197 HEAVY METAL

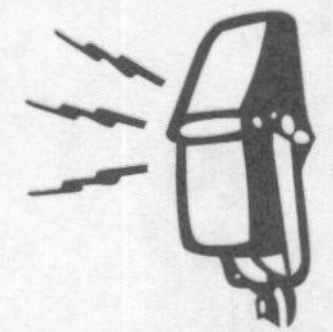

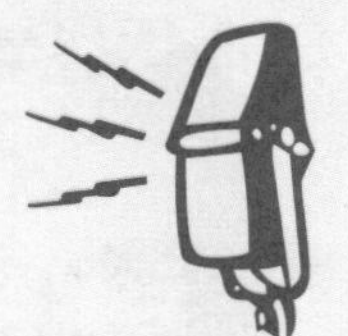

1. Which godfathers of heavy rock had No 1 US albums with *Get A Grip* and *Nine Lives*?
2. Which country do AC/DC come from?
3. Who recorded the metal classic *Paranoid*?
4. Slash was in which group?
5. Who were producing Holy Smoke in 1990?
6. Which 80s and 90s group has the name of a cattle and sheep disease?
7. Which sentimental head bangers asked *Is This Love* in 1987?
8. Who had the Hindenburg airship on the cover of their first album?
9. Metallica were in the charts with *Until It* what?
10. Def Leppard were formed in which country?
11. Deep Purple took a *Black* what into the singles charts?
12. *Hysteria* was a No 1 album for which band?
13. What instrument does veteran Jon Lord play?
14. What word goes before Fudge in the band name of the early heavies?
15. Who recorded the best-selling *The Number Of The Beast* album?
16. Which part of the guitar named a 1970s No 1 album from Deep Purple?
17. What physical defect did American guitarist Ted Nugent suffer after years of screaming solos?
18. Which group did Ritchie Blackmore form on leaving Deep Purple?
19. Who is Led Zeppelin's main vocals man?
20. What is Ozzy Ozbourne's actual first name?

ANSWERS ON PAGE 290

198 HISTORY

1 Who was known as the "father of the Soviet H-bomb"?
2 In which city's shipyards did Lech Walesa work before becoming Polish president?
3 Terry Waite was the envoy of which Archbishop of Canterbury when he was kidnapped?
4 The name of which UK PM was Ronald Reagan's middle name?
5 Who was the first US Ambassador in London?
6 Who recorded with the Hot Five and the Hot Seven in the 1920s?
7 Who became the youngest-ever member of the GLC in 1969?
8 Who was the 20th Prince of Wales?
9 Which Baron began a continental pigeon post in 1849 which developed into an international news agency?
10 What was Mikhail Gorbachev's wife called?
11 Which children's author was Russian correspondent for the *Daily News* during WWI and the Revolution?
12 Which prominent lawyer, film star and advocate of black rights left the US to live in England in the late 1950s?
13 Who was the last British monarch to refuse royal assent of a Bill through Parliament?
14 Who was German foreign minister during WWII?
15 Which UK PM was responsible for the purchase of US Polaris missiles?
16 Who did Douglas Hurd replace as Foreign Secretary in 1989?
17 Who became President of the ANC in 1997?
18 Which Chancellor of the Exchequer introduced old-age pensions into Britain?
19 Who founded Standard Oil in 1870?
20 Which invention by Davis Bostel improved on Alexander Cummings' invention a century earlier.

ANSWERS ON PAGE 290

199 SCIENCE

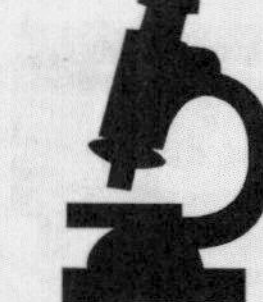
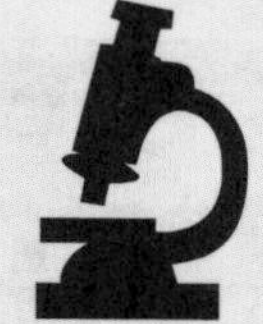
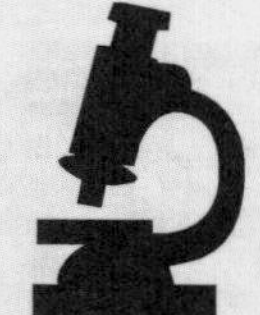

1 An abacus was an early type of what?
2 What did engineer Louis Renault manufacture?
3 Which needlework machine did Isaac Singer invent?
4 What provides solar power?
5 In which decade did Apple computers first appear?
6 In which decade did man first land on the Moon?
7 A stereo music system has how many speakers?
8 An aqueduct was constructed to carry what?
9 In CD-ROM what does the letter R stand for?
10 Which appeared first – camera, CD or modem?
11 What does H stand for in HTTP?
12 Which system of communication developed from ARPANET?
13 Astronomy is the study of what?
14 What's the name for the selection bar at the top of a computer screen?
15 What kind of code is scanned at a supermarket?
16 Which was developed last – space flight, telephone, television?
17 Which drug is Alexander Fleming famous for discovering?
18 Which rays for examining the inside of the body did Röntgen discover?
19 What did Robert Bunsen invent?
20 Who was the first scientist to split the atom?

ANSWERS ON PAGE 290

200 TELEVISION COMEDY

1 Which actress Ellen was the star of *Ellen*?

2 Which series was about a lawyer called Ally?

3 Who was Butt-Head's comedy partner?

4 Which British comic Benny created Fred Scuttle and Professor Marvel?

5 How many friends are there in *Friends*?

6 Where did Frasier live in the spin off from *Cheers*?

7 Where was *Thirtysomething* set?

8 In the 1970s, how were Mike, Carol, Greg, Marcia, Jan, Peter, Cindy and Bobby known?

9 What was the name of the father in the US sitcom *All In The Family*?

10 In what type of institution was *The Facts Of Life* set?

11 What became the most-watched TV show in history when it was screened in May 1993?

12 In which decade was *M*A*S*H* set?

13 In which show did Laverne and Shirley first appear?

14 In which Florida resort was *The Golden Girls* set?

15 Which sitcom, premiered in 1988, featured Dr Harry Weston?

16 Which spin-off from *The Cosby Show* premiered in 1987?

17 Who was head of *The Addams Family*?

18 Who was the neighbourhood police officer in *Top Cat*?

19 In *Cheers*, Sam was a former pitcher for which team?

20 In *The Cosby Show* which insect was the name of Theo's friend?

ANSWERS ON PAGE 290

201 THE ARTS

1 What sort of animals featured in the novel and animated film *Watership Down*?

2 Edward Elgar was from which country?

3 Which fictional detective is assisted by Captain Hastings?

4 How many Tenors were in concert at the World Cups in Italy, USA and France?

5 Charlotte Church came from which part of the UK?

6 Which insect follows Madame in the title of a Puccini opera?

7 In which city is La Scala opera house?

8 Which country does Kiri Te Kanawa come from?

9 Who played Che in the original stage production of *Evita*?

10 *Riverdance* was based on classic, traditional dance from which country?

11 Which Gothic horror story has the alternative title *The Modern Prometheus*?

12 For what types of book is Samuel Pepys famous?

13 Who wrote *The Female Eunuch* in 1970?

14 In which county were Jane Austen and Charles Dickens born?

15 At which film festival is the prize the Palme D'Or awarded?

16 In *Charlie And The Chocolate Factory*, what is Charlie's surname?

17 Which ex-jockey wrote a book of short stories called *Field Of Thirteen*?

18 Whose horror stories include *Carrie* and *The Shining*?

19 In which city is the Prado museum?

20 Who deisgned the Pompidou Centre in Paris?

ANSWERS ON PAGE 290

202 NAME GAME

How are these celebrities better known?

1 RUTH JONES
2 ALPHONSO JOSEPH d'ABRUZZO
3 STEVELAND JUDKINS
4 MARION MORRISON
5 VIRGINIA PUGH
6 ASA YOELSON
7 McKINLEY MORGANFIELD
8 SHIRLEY BEATTY
9 WILLIAM PERKS
10 FREDERICK AUSTERLITZ

ANSWERS ON PAGE 290

203 GUESS WHO . . . ?

1 This US President had the middle names Jefferson Blythe, his Vice President was called Albert and his daughter was Chelsea.
2 Born in 1942 in the US, he died in London in 1970 after having hits with *Purple Haze* and *Voodoo Chile*.
3 This English novelist created the characters Miss Marple and Hercule Poirot and wrote the long-running *The Mousetrap*.
4 Father of Michael, he was born in Amsterdam New York and is the father-in-law of Catherine Zeta Jones.
5 His first football club was Manchester United and he wrote the autobiography *My Side* before moving to Spain.
6 Born in Stirling, his first names are William Fisher Hunter and he was the first Scotsman to be champion jockey in the UK.
7 Born in Liverpool in 1943, he was part of the biggest Mersey band of all time and died after a long battle with cancer.
8 Married to outrageous Englishman Ozzy, she has homes on both sides of the Atlantic and appeared in the family's TV show.
9 One-time wife of Frank Sinatra and partner of Woody Allen, she starred in *Hannah and Her Sisters*.
10 Born in Las Vegas, he had won $19 million by 2000 and married fellow tennis star Steffi Graf.

ANSWERS ON PAGE 290

204 NEWSPAPERS

1 What is the world's best-selling English language daily paper?
☐ *Daily Mail* ☐ *Sun* ☐ *USA Today*

2 Which country has the daily paper with the highest circulation?
☐ China ☐ Japan ☐ USA

3 Which national newspaper was first published in London in 1785?
☐ *Guardian* ☐ *The Times* ☐ *Mirror*

4 In which country does *Le Figaro* appear?
☐ France ☐ Mexico ☐ Spain

5 The *Daily Herald* was revamped as which paper in the 1960s?
☐ *The Sun* ☐ *Today* ☐ *The Star*

6 Which Scottish city is home to D C Thomson?
☐ Dundee ☐ Edinburgh ☐ Glasgow

7 In which century did the first daily newspaper appear?
☐ 17thC ☐ 18thC ☐ 19thC

8 *Bild-Zeitung* was established in which city?
☐ Dresden ☐ Hamburg ☐ Berlin

9 Which country first took measures towards international copyright?
☐ Denmark ☐ France ☐ USA

10 Who worked with Bernstein to expose the Watergate Affair?
☐ Nixon ☐ Patson ☐ Woodward

11 Which European city published the newspaper *ABC*?
☐ Athens ☐ Madrid ☐ Vienna

12 In which country was the AAP press agency set up in 1935?
☐ Argentina ☐ Australia ☐ Austria

13 The first regular newspaper appeared in which city?
☐ Antwerp ☐ Paris ☐ Washington

14 Which was the first British paper to issue a colour supplement?
☐ *Observer* ☐ *Sunday Times*
☐ *Sunday Telegraph*

15 When was the *New York Post* founded?
☐ 1801 ☐ 1901 ☐ 1951

ANSWERS ON PAGE 290

205 GREAT BUILDINGS

1 Which is Britain's oldest cathedral?

2 Joern Utzon designed the Sydney Opera House as a result of what?

3 What is the Taj Mahal made from?

4 In which Parisian square is the Arc de Triomphe?

5 What is the cathedral of the diocese of London?

6 What was the highest building in the world until 1930?

7 Who ordered the building of St Basil's Cathedral in Moscow?

8 Whose Library in Venice was described as "the richest and most ornate building since antiquity"?

9 Who had Hampton Court Palace built?

10 Which Dukes does Chatsworth House in Derbyshire belong to?

11 Which stately home in Yorkshire was used for the filming of *Brideshead Revisited*?

12 Why is the Washington Memorial smaller now than when it was built?

13 The Empire State Building stands on which New York City avenue?

14 Other than Egypt, where were pyramids built?

15 Which French château has a Hall of Mirrors?

16 In which US city is the Sears Tower?

17 Where was Northern Europe's largest Gothic cathedral rebuilt after World War II?

18 Which chainstore proprietor commissioned the then tallest habitable building in the world in 1913?

19 Which famous Napoleonic war loot is still housed in the Louvre?

20 When was Blackpool Tower built?

ANSWERS ON PAGE 290

206 GENERAL KNOWLEDGE

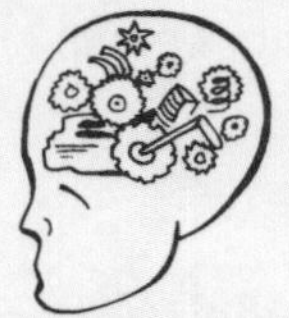
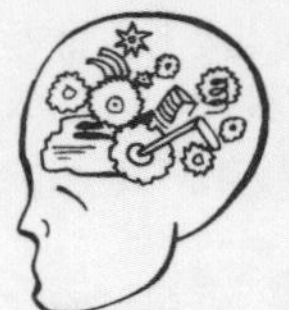

1 What is the coloured part of the eye called?

2 What is the special talent performed by Marcel Marceau?

3 Which city is linked with gangster Al Capone in the 1920s?

4 Who starred with Celia Johnson in *Brief Encounter?*

5 In which British city is the station Temple Meads?

6 What is a Stink Horn?

7 What was the name of John the Baptist's mother?

8 Which Tudor figure is the main character in *A Man For All Seasons*?

9 Stephane Grappelli became famous for playing which instrument?

10 In which country is Havana?

11 In legend, which bird rose from its own ashes?

12 Which brothers starred in the film *Duck Soup*?

13 What term describes a black and white horse?

14 Which animal does ermine come from?

15 If you have "mal de mer" what are you suffering from?

16 The Solidarity movement began in which country?

17 What type of angle is less than 90 degrees?

18 What type of farm did George Orwell write about?

19 In proverb, there is many a slip 'twixt what and what?

20 Which monkey possesses a blood factor that is shared with humans?

ANSWERS ON PAGE 290

207 PEOPLE

1 Who invented the Barbie doll?

2 How is writer Patricia Plangman better known?

3 Who was the first movie child to earn a million dollars?

4 Which diplomatic post did Joseph Kennedy hold at the outbreak of World War II in Europe?

5 Which colour precedes the name of Mr Adair, the firefighter who fought the Piper Alpha blaze?

6 Rebuilding the Globe Theatre in London was the brainchild of whom?

7 Which two members of The Goons had the same birthday?

8 Willie Park became the first winner of which sporting trophy?

9 Which country does Robert Pires play soccer for?

10 What was Britney Spears' second album called?

11 Which Spice Girl was the first to marry?

12 Fashion designer Donatella, sister of the murdered Gianni, has which surname?

13 Who owned the original yacht after whom The America's Cup was named?

14 Who is the smaller of the two comics who present *Little Britain*?

15 Peter Benenson, who died in 2005, founded which organisation in the 1960s?

16 Under whose administration did Joseph McCarthy carry out his "witch hunts"?

17 Where did Ferdinand Marcos live in exile?

18 Which terrorist group murdered Italian PM Aldo Moro?

19 Which American was nicknamed Old Blood and Guts?

20 Who referred to drawing "a line in the sand" referring to developments in the Gulf War?

ANSWERS ON PAGE 290

208 HOT WHEELS

1 Which F1 driver has scored most Grand Prix wins?

2 Who first had a record-breaking car and a boat called *Bluebird*?

3 How long is the Indianapolis track?

4 Which team did Jim Clark spend all his racing career with?

5 How many people are in the car in drag racing?

6 Which Belgian cyclist was known as "The Cannibal"?

7 How many times did Stirling Moss win the world championship?

8 In which country was the first organised car race?

9 Which Labour Party supporter is the head of Formula 1?

10 Where is the home of the French Grand Prix?

11 Who was the first British F1 Champion after James Hunt?

12 Which motor racing Park is east of Chester?

13 What type of racing is known in the US as demolition derbies?

14 How frequently does the Tour de France take place?

15 Who was the first man to be world champion on two and four wheels?

16 What relation was Emerson to Christian Fittipaldi?

17 Which Japanese team won its first F1 Grand Prix in 1967?

18 Who was the first man to win a Grand Prix in a car he designed?

19 Which was the first manufacturer to have over 100 Grand Prix wins?

20 In 1994 who was the first Austrian to win the German Grand Prix since Niki Lauda?

ANSWERS ON PAGE 290

209 LUCKY DIP

1. In which country is Phuket, a place devastated by the December 2004 tsunami?
2. Which country is Sean Connery from?
3. What word completes the title of the play, *Much Ado About*?
4. What is the name of Frank Sinatra's daughter?
5. How many times do you sing "Happy Birthday" if you sing two verses of the song?
6. What relation to you is your aunt's daughter?
7. What is the first name of Hollywood actress Ms Pfeiffer?
8. What type of entertainment is the musical *Barnum* about?
9. Which heavenly body does the word solar refer to?
10. Which game is played in an enclosed space with both players hitting the ball in the same direction?
11. Crystal Palace soccer club come from which city?
12. If a Frenchman drank café au lait would it be white or black coffee?
13. Which fruit is chiefly used in the dessert called Melba?
14. On which Street is the New York Stock Exchange?
15. What was the name of those hazardous good old boys Bo and Luke?
16. What is the first name of comedian Dee?
17. Which game with rackets shares its name with a fruit drink?
18. Which sport would you be watching if you were at Aintree?
19. What is the main ingredient of a risotto?
20. Which sewing tool is hidden in a haystack according to the saying?

ANSWERS ON PAGE 290

210 ELTON JOHN

1. Which song contains the repeated words, "I think it's going to be a long, long time."?
2. In which year did he become Sir Elton?
3. How many weeks did *Candle In The Wind 1997* spend at No 1 in Canada?
4. Elton John was chairman of which 1980s FA Cup finalists?
5. What was the name of the record label Elton John started?
6. Who was his co-writer on the classic *Your Song*?
7. Which opera star sang on *Live Like Horses*?
8. Which creature was described as being Honky in a 1972 hit?
9. Elton first made the UK No 1 spot duetting with Kiki Dee – how many US No 1 singles had he had by then?
10. Who did Elton team up with to have a UK No 1 with *Sorry Seems To Be The Hardest Word*?
11. Which duet gave writing credits to Ann Orson and Carte Blanche?
12. Which animal lent its name to a 1974 No 1 album?
13. From which singer did Elton get his surname?
14. Which album owes its name to where it was made at the Château d'Herouville?
15. What was the nationality of Elton's wife whom he married in 1984?
16. Which early song starts, "Turn me loose from your hands . . ."?
17. To two years, in what year did Elton's figure first appear at Madame Tussaud's?
18. Who duetted with him on *True Love* which featured on the album *Duets*?
19. Which 1995 single shared its title with a Cher hit?
20. Which Beatle's offspring is Elton's godchild?

ANSWERS ON PAGE 290

211 PICTURE QUIZ

Only one of these celebrities changed their name to become famous – which one?

ANSWERS ON PAGE 290

212 NAME THE YEAR

1 U2 won a Grammy for "Beautiful Day". The Best Film Oscar went to *Gladiator*. Pete Sampras won his record seventh Wimbledon singles title.

2 Leonid Brezhnev became General Secretary of the Soviet Union. England won the football World Cup. *Time* magazine dubbed England's capital "Swinging London".

3 Ernest Hemingway won the Pulitzer prize. Queen Elizabeth II was crowned. Hillary and Tensing scaled Everest.

4 Nicole Kidman won her first Oscar. The Queen Mother died. The Commonwealth Games were held in Manchester.

5 Tennis star Monica Seles was born. "Killing Me Softly with His Song" won the Grammy for Best Song. Tolkien, Picasso and Noel Coward all died.

6 Nelson Piquet beat Nigel Mansell to win the Formula 1 Championship. Black Monday saw shares crash on the international stock market. The United Kingdom was hit by a hurricane.

ANSWERS ON PAGE 290

213 HALF CHANCE

½? ½? ½?

1 Which Earl was the brother of Diana, Princess of Wales – Earl Grey or Earl Spencer?

2 In music who "just called to say I love you" – Donny Osmond or Stevie Wonder?

3 A Swedish car displays which international vehicle registration mark – S or SWE?

4 Was it Drew or Lionel Barrymore who featured in the film *Batman Forever*?

5 Does the B in SCUBA diving stand for Below or Breathing?

6 Strangeways prison is in which British city – Glasgow or Manchester?

7 Was Chubby Checker linked with the dance the Bossa Nova or the Twist?

8 What was the first name of ragtime pianist Joplin – Scott or Janis?

9 At the end of the 20th century how many UK monarchs had been called Walter – one or none?

10 *Trainspotting* was set in which country – Northern Ireland or Scotland?

11 Paul Newman promoted his own brand of which food – cookies or salad dressing?

12 Which Welsh city had a Millennium sports stadium built there – Cardiff or Swansea?

13 Is the deepwater port of Kagoshima in Japan or Korea?

14 What does the letter A stand for in AIDS – Actual or Acquired?

15 On which Isle was Ronaldsway airport built – Isle of Man or Isle of Wight?

16 Which Joseph was Hitler's minister of propaganda – Goebbels or Goering?

17 With which sport is Curtis Strange associated – golf or tennis?

18 Was General Pinochet a former ruler of Argetina or Chile?

19 BB King is associated with which musical instrument – drums or guitar?

20 Lord Mountbatten was the last viceroy of which country – Burma or India?

ANSWERS ON PAGE 290

Here's an eggs-tra special quiz about celebrations and all things connected with Easter. Be a good egg, and tackle all 50 questions.

1 Which 40-day fasting period precedes Easter?

2 What is the first day of Lent called?

3 Christians believe that Jesus spent a 40-day period of fasting where?

4 The word carnival comes from the Latin "carne vale" which means what?

5 Which buns are a traditional food on Good Friday?

6 On what date does the spring equinox fall?

7 What is the Friday before Easter called?

8 What is the Thursday before Easter called?

9 In which ocean is Easter Island?

10 What is the chief centre of Easter Island called?

11 Where did the Easter Rising begin on Easter Monday 1916?

12 What is the earliest date on which Easter Sunday can fall?

13 What is the latest date on which Easter Sunday can fall?

14 Which event in the Christian church does Easter Sunday commemorate?

15 Easter Island belongs to which South American country?

16 Easter usually takes place at a similar time to which Jewish festival?

17 Which event in the Christian church does Good Friday commemorate?

18 What name is given to the Sunday before Easter?

19 How many Bank Holidays precede Easter Monday in England and Wales?

20 Which dancer did Fred Astaire replace in the film musical *Easter Parade*?

21 Pâques is Easter in which language?

22 What is the day before the beginning of Lent called?

23 What does Mardi Gras literally mean?

24 On Palm Sunday Christ rode into Jerusalem by which mode of transport?

25 If you were born on Easter Sunday, you have been born under one of which two star signs?

26 Which flower is associated with St David's Day?

27 Which day falls 40 days after Easter Day?

28 What is another name for the Hindu Festival of Colour?

QUIZ

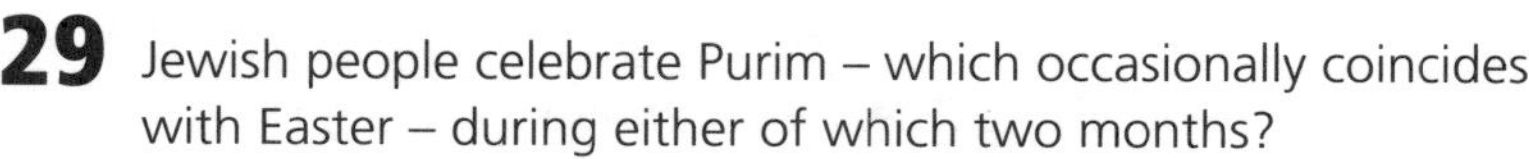

29 Jewish people celebrate Purim – which occasionally coincides with Easter – during either of which two months?

30 The story of Purim comes from which Book of the Bible, named after which woman?

31 What do people dance around to celebrate May Day?

32 Who is the most important person at a May Day festival?

33 Which mythical creature did St George traditionally slay?

34 Which Christian Spring festival is known as Fasika in Ethiopia?

35 What does the Muslim Spring festival of Eid celebrate the end of?

36 Which meat is part of the festivities on Easter Day?

37 On which day in April is a fish pinned on someone's back to make them look foolish?

38 Which of the following is not a moveable feast – Easter, Ascension Day or St Patrick's Day?

39 The god Krishna is associated with the festival of Holi in which religion?

40 Which festival is known as Vendredi Saint in France?

41 Is Hola Mohalla a Sikh or a Jewish festival?

42 Which festival, seven weeks after Easter, is also called Whit Sunday?

43 Who co starred with Fred Astaire in the film musical *Easter Parade*?

44 What is traditionally eaten in Western Europe on Shrove Tuesday?

45 Which vegetable is associated with St David's Day?

46 The Passover is a spring festival in which religion?

47 In the UK, which country does not have a saint's day in Spring?

48 Which of the following is not a spring flower – daffodil, narcissus or rose?

49 What is eaten on Easter Sunday to symbolise new life?

50 What name is given to the week before Easter?

ANSWERS ON PAGE 290

215 AT THE MOVIES

1 *Mrs Doubtfire* and *Jumanji* featured which actor?

2 Which Danny starred in *L.A. Confidential*?

3 The action of *The Killing Fields* takes place in which country?

4 Which Michael played Marty in *Back to the Future*?

5 Which musical set in gangland New York won 11 Oscars in the 1960s?

6 Which Henry produced the score for *The Pink Panther*?

7 Peter Lawford was the brother-in-law of which late US President?

8 Which word describes Clint Eastwood's character Harry?

9 Who wrote the musical score for *Star Wars*?

10 Which Oliver won the Best Director Oscar for *Platoon*?

11 The 1940s classic movie *The Outlaw* featured which Jane?

12 Which actress links *Ghost* and *The Juror*?

13 In which decade was *Some Like It Hot* released?

14 Which Nicolas starred in *Leaving Las Vegas*?

15 Who is Vincente Minnelli's famous daughter?

16 Which word completes the film title, *A Room With A* ____?

17 *Land Girls* starred which Anna?

18 Which Meg starred in *When Harry Met Sally*?

19 Madonna bought a burial plot next to where which blonde icon is buried?

20 In which decade of the 20th century was Al Pacino born?

ANSWERS ON PAGE 291

216 COPS & ROBBERS

1 In which city is Taggart set?

2 What was *The Bill*'s D.I. Burnside's first name?

3 What sort of literature does Commander Adam Dalgliesh write?

4 Which early British police series had the theme music *An Ordinary Copper*?

5 Who created the character of Chief Inspector Wexford?

6 Which detective called people "Pussycat"?

7 Which actor links *The Chief* and *The Professionals*?

8 What was Bergerac's first name?

9 Which crime takes place with great frequency in Midsomer?

10 Who played the title role in *Remington Steele*?

11 Who played the legendary Perry Mason?

12 In *Police Woman* what was Sgt Anderson's nickname?

13 Which series starred Patricia Hodge in the title role?

14 Who was Crockett's partner in *Miami Vice*?

15 Which breed of long-eared dog did Columbo have?

16 What were Starsky and Hutch's first names?

17 In which series did Steve Garrett say, "Book 'em Danno!"?

18 In which city did *Burke's Law* take place?

19 Which private investigator is known by the initials TS?

20 Which long-running crime series was a spin-off from a programme called *Police Surgeon*?

ANSWERS ON PAGE 291

217 NATURE

1 Glaucoma affects which part of the body?

2 Which flightless bird lays the world's largest egg?

3 What is a puffball?

4 What happens to a female butterfly after it has laid its eggs?

5 In what type of environment do most crustaceans live?

6 Which natural disaster is measured on the Richter scale?

7 What is the main ingredient of glass?

8 Does a millipede have more, less or exactly 1,000 feet?

9 An ore is a mineral which contains a what?

10 Is the whale shark a mammal, like the whale, or a fish, like the shark?

11 Which bird is the symbol of the USA?

12 Are butterflies more colourful in warmer or cooler countries?

13 What sort of rock is lava?

14 Which is larger, the dolphin or the porpoise?

15 The giant sequoia is the largest living what?

16 How many bones does a slug have?

17 Are worker ants male or female?

18 Altocumulus is a type of what?

19 What is the main source of energy in our ecosystem?

20 Which name for remains of plants and animals which lived on Earth means "dug up"?

ANSWERS ON PAGE 291

218 THE HEADLINES

1 In 2004, who or what were Charley, Frances, Ivan and Jeanne?

2 In which country were the Baader Meinhof gang based?

3 In which game did Nintendo's Mario character first appear?

4 The Bay of Pigs near which island was an area which triggered a missile crisis in 1961?

5 Black September were a terrorist group from which country?

6 In which year did the Battle of Britain begin?

7 Pinochet led a military coup in which country?

8 Who succeeded Mitterand as President of France?

9 Milton Friedman was policy adviser to which US President in the 1980s?

10 In which decade did Colonel Gaddafi seize power in Libya?

11 Where was there the "Great Leap Forward" in the 1950s?

12 Which site in Berkshire was the scene of anti-nuclear protests, mainly by women, in the 1980s?

13 Who was Soviet Foreign Minister for almost 30 years in the latter half of last century?

14 What was the former name of Harare?

15 Who was East German leader from 1976 to 1989

16 Which Irish family met George Bush on 17th March, 2005?

17 In which state did Martin Luther King lead the famous bus boycott?

18 Who led the sect which killed actress Sharon Tate?

19 Which Commission was set up to investigate the assassination of John F Kennedy?

20 Where in England was Princess Diana buried?

ANSWERS ON PAGE 291

219 COCKTAILS

1. What type of plant is Tequila made from?
2. What is the best-known type of Hollands called?
3. What is the Russian drink Kvass made from?
4. What is Drambuie made from?
5. What spice is used in a Whisky Sling?
6. What turns gin into a Pink Gin?
7. What are the traditional ingredients in a Daiquiri?
8. What is added to brandy to make a Sidecar?
9. What is the principal spirit in a Harvey Wallbanger?
10. What is a cocktail of rye whisky, vermouth and Angostura called?
11. Where is the brandy Birngeist made from?
12. Which drink was Prince Charles caught ordering while at Gordonstoun?
13. If a cocktail is served "in a mist" how is it served?
14. What is a dry Manhattan called?
15. What is the fruit in an Old Fashioned?
16. What makes a Whisky a Whisky Sour?
17. What are the two main ingredients of a Cuba Libre?
18. Which former PM do you get if you mix Cinzano, apricot brandy and Angostura bitters?
19. What savoury ingredient do you include in a Sputnik?
20. What does an Alexandra taste of?

ANSWERS ON PAGE 291

220 GENERAL KNOWLEDGE

 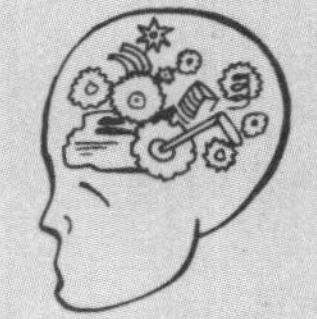 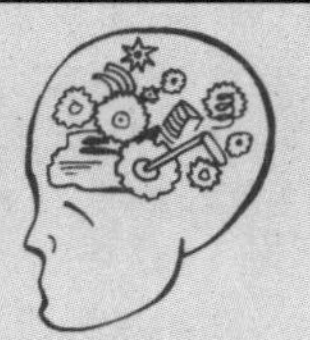

1. Which English boxer floored Muhammad Ali (Cassius Clay)?
2. Who bought Queen Elizabeth II her first corgi?
3. In 1915, which British liner was sunk by a German submarine?
4. What is the study and functioning of human societies called?
5. "Lay your head upon my pillow" appears in which Perry Como hit?
6. Which king and queen ruled Britain jointly from 1689 to 1694?
7. What nationality was detective writer Ngaio Marsh?
8. Which English city was once known as Eboracum?
9. Whom did Zeus seduce when he assumed the guise of a swan?
10. What does L.K. stand for in S.W.A.L.K.?
11. Which American told Madam Butterfly that he loved her?
12. What is the male reproductive organ of a plant called?
13. In the song, "I danced with a man, who danced with a girl who danced with . . ." who?
14. Which William was concerned with abolishing slavery?
15. Who commanded Prussian troops at the Battle of Waterloo?
16. Which school did Bily Bunter go to?
17. Whose real name is Bernard Schwarz?
18. What is xenophobia?
19. Who was the last British Prime Minister to be created an earl?
20. In the Bible, what book comes after Saint John?

ANSWERS ON PAGE 291

221 PICTURE QUIZ

What links these pictures?

ANSWERS ON PAGE 291

222 HORSES

Is each statement TRUE or FALSE?

T F **1** A horse's cannon bone is between the knee and the fetlock.

T F **2** A colt is a female horse under the age of four.

T F **3** Feathers are long hairs on a horse's legs.

T F **4** Camargue horses are grey.

T F **5** Dales ponies are always light in colour.

T F **6** Shetland ponies are measured in inches not hands.

T F **7** Pinto horses originated in Italy.

T F **8** Heavy horses are also known as coldbloods.

T F **9** Ireland does not have any indigenous ponies.

T F **10** The smallest horse in the world is the falabella.

ANSWERS ON PAGE 291

223 FLAGS

1 Which two colours do not touch on the Italian flag?
☐ Green/White ☐ Red/Green ☐ White/Red

2 What colour is the cross in the Cross of Saint George?
☐ Blue ☐ Red ☐ White

3 How many bands make up the Belgian flag?
☐ Two ☐ Three ☐ Four

4 What colour is the middle stripe on the Austrian flag?
☐ Blue ☐ Red ☐ White

5 Which colour goes with white and dark blue on the Estonian flag?
☐ Black ☐ Red ☐ White

6 Which country's flag has three horizontal stripes of black, red & gold?
☐ Denmark ☐ Germany ☐ Sweden

7 How many colours are on the Polish flag?
☐ One ☐ Two ☐ Three

8 Which flag depicts a cedar tree on a white background?
☐ Laos ☐ Lebanon ☐ Portugal

9 Which flag has the words Ordem & Progresso in a band on a globe?
☐ Algeria ☐ Brazil ☐ Peru

10 Which flag features a symbol based on the prayer shawl, the *tallit*?
☐ Israel ☐ Russia ☐ Turkey

11 What colour is the maple leaf on the Canadian flag?
☐ Green ☐ Red ☐ White

12 How many stars appear on the New Zealand flag?
☐ Three ☐ Four ☐ Seven

13 Which flag has a central red and blue yin-yang symbol?
☐ Laos ☐ Lebanon ☐ South Korea

14 Which two colours do not touch on the Bulgarian flag?
☐ Green/White ☐ Red/Green ☐ White/Red

15 What is the colour of the stars that appear on the flag of the USA?
☐ Blue ☐ Red ☐ White

ANSWERS ON PAGE 291

224 THE PERFORMING ARTS

1 Which opera venue is near Lewes?

2 Sir John Barbirolli was conductor of which orchestra at the time of his death?

3 If a sonata is for instruments what is a cantata written for?

4 Which London theatre was the home of Gilbert & Sullivan operas?

5 Sadler's Wells theatre is famous for which performing arts?

6 Who has written more plays, Shakespeare or Alan Ayckbourn?

7 Wayne Sleep was principal dancer with which ballet company?

8 What do you press with the right hand on an accordion?

9 Which of the Three Tenors played the title role in the film version of *Otello* in 1986?

10 How many strings are there on a double bass?

11 Richard Eyre replaced Peter Hall as artistic director at which London theatre?

12 What were all Joseph Grimaldi's clowns called?

13 What shape is the sound box on a balalaika?

14 Which male voice is between bass and tenor?

15 Which Scottish city holds an annual Fringe Festival?

16 In which US city was the Actors Studio founded?

17 What is the official name of London's Drury Lane theatre?

18 Miles Davis is famous for playing which musical instrument?

19 Which king did Handel write *The Water Music* for?

20 Whose 1986 recording of Vivaldi's *The Four Seasons* sold over a million copies?

ANSWERS ON PAGE 291

225 HALF CHANCE

½? ½? ½?

1 In the US, New York and which other city stage major marathons – Augusta or Boston?

2 How many Oscars for best director did Alfred Hitchcock win – one or none?

3 In music does the term largo mean heavily or slowly?

4 Who recorded the album *Electric Ladyland* – Jimi Hendrix or The Doors?

5 Is the city of Alexandria in Egypt or Greece?

6 After which Greek character was the drug morphine named – Morpheus or Slumbus?

7 In which year did Britain go decimal – 1971 or 1981?

8 Is the Tropical cockroach the world's fastest-moving or smelliest insect?

9 How is Robert Davies better known – Ray Davis or Jasper Carrott?

10 How many legs has a lobster – four or eight?

11 For what did the Swede Jenny Lind achieve fame – cycling or singing?

12 Which bird was selected in 1961 as the British national bird – the robin or the sparrow?

13 What did Georges Claude invent in 1911 – neon lights or nylon tights?

14 Which country was the first to insist upon car number plates – Canada or France ?

15 Who goes with Bess in George Gershwin's opera – Percy or Porgy?

16 Aconcagua is the highest peak in which country – Argentina or Paraguay?

17 Who is the magical spirit of the air in Shakespeare's *The Tempest* – Ariel or Puck?

18 Who wrote the lyrics to *A Whiter Shade Of Pale* – Gordon Lightfoot or Keith Reid ?

19 Which actress was jailed in 1982 for tax evasion – Julie Andrews or Sophia Loren?

20 In which country did the first Christmas stamp appear in 1898 – Canada or Sweden?

ANSWERS ON PAGE 291

226 LUCKY DIP

1 In tennis what is the name of a serve which isn't returned?

2 Who topped the UK and US charts with the album *Hot Shot*?

3 What carries blood around the body?

4 Kenny Sansom represented England at which sport?

5 In computer software what goes before XPress?

6 Which is the largest country in Great Britain?

7 Who was world professional billiards champion from 1968–80?

8 In Canada, of which province is St John's the capital?

9 Would a chilli dish normally be hot or mild?

10 In which country would a laird be a landowner?

11 Which beautiful youth did the Greek goddess Aphrodite love?

12 What is a surgeon's scalpel used for?

13 Which animal's name literally means "earth pig"?

14 If you were signalling using semaphore what would you be waving?

15 Which British ex PM took on the title the Earl of Stockton?

16 Which type of performer seems to make a dummy talk?

17 Who was the founder of the Christian Science movement?

18 If you were playing the bassoon would you strum it or blow it?

19 In which Tower are the Crown Jewels kept?

20 Which three South American countries cross the Equator?

ANSWERS ON PAGE 291

227 ROLLING STONES

1 What was the name of the 2003 tour?

2 What's the name of the real life Charlie in the group?

3 Who did Mick Jagger team up with for *Dancin' In The Street* at Live Aid?

4 How many UK Top Ten singles did the Stones have in the 1990s?

5 What colour was the Stones' *Little Rooster*?

6 Which two names are credited as writing most of the group's material?

7 Which long-time member of the group was born William Perks?

8 What word comes after *I Can't Get No* in a 1960s smash?

9 Which Ron joined the band in the 1970s?

10 What's the missing colour in the song song title *Paint It* ______?

11 What was the name of the 1994 album and the world tour to promote it?

12 In 1992 who decided to quit the Stones?

13 Which song mentions a "gin soaked queen in Memphis . . ."?

14 What instrument does Jagger blow on stage?

15 How did Brian Jones die?

16 Which 1960s girlfriend of Mick Jagger recorded their song *As Tears Go By*?

17 Keith Richards' daughter Angela was originally christened after what flowering weed?

18 What follows *Let It* in the title of the album released the year Brian Jones died?

19 Whose banquet was the title of an album from 1968?

20 What fastened and unfastened on the cover of the *Sticky Fingers* album?

ANSWERS ON PAGE 291

228 TRAVEL

1 Which New York street is famous for its fashion stores?
2 Tarom Airlines are based in which country?
3 What is the capital of the former Soviet state Georgia?
4 Which capital is further north – Budapest or Vienna?
5 Which Gulf is to the west of Estonia and Latvia?
6 Where is the news agency Centre d'Information Presse based?
7 In which country is Kranebitten International airport?
8 What is the chief port of Slovenia?
9 The Pelagian islands belong to which European country?
10 Bornholm is an island in which Sea?
11 Hoge Veluwe National Park is in which country?
12 Which US state used to be called the Sandwich Islands?
13 St Petersburg is at the head of which gulf?
14 What is the largest island in Europe?
15 Which two Italian volcanoes erupted in 1994?
16 What is the world's highest dam?
17 Which country is called Suomen Tasavalta in its own language?
18 Which capital is further north – Berlin or London?
19 Aero Lloyd Airlines are based in which country?
20 Which European country has the highest life expectancy for men and women?

ANSWERS ON PAGE 291

229 ANIMALS

1 How do the anaconda's victims die?
2 What is the badger's system of burrows called?
3 What is the skin on a deer's antlers called?
4 What colour face does a Suffolk sheep have?
5 Which small breed of dog has a German name meaning badger dog?
6 What is unusual about the sound of the dingo?
7 Aardvark means "earth pig" in which African language?
8 On which island was the dodo formerly found?
9 What is an impala?
10 What type of leopard is another name for the ounce?
11 Pit bull terriers were bred to do what?
12 To which family does the prairie dog belong?
13 Does the Indian rhinoceros have one or two horns?
14 Scrapie is a fatal disease of which animals?
15 Tinnitus affects which of the senses?
16 How many teeth do human adults have?
17 What is the most common colour of a Great Dane?
18 What does an ungulate animal have?
19 What do vampire bats feed on?
20 Lanolin is a by product of which domestic animal?

ANSWERS ON PAGE 291

230 ANIMAL LIKE

Each listed adjective relates to a type of animal. Can you name the creatures involved?

1 FELINE
2 OVINE
3 APIAN
4 URSINE
5 SIMIAN
6 AQUILINE
7 VULPINE
8 LUPINE
9 CERVINE
10 SAURIAN

ANSWERS ON PAGE 291

231 DOUBLE TAKE

In each case, the two-part quiz question leads to just one answer!

1 Which month shares its name with a military walk?
2 Which fortified building can also be a chess piece?
3 Which type of all-in holiday can also be a parcel?
4 Which restraint for a dog can also mean to go in front?
5 Which fictional detective shares his name with a code?
6 Which fruits might also be items found on a calendar?
7 Which cradle shares its name with a word meaning to copy?
8 Which type of fish shares a name with a deep voice?
9 Which fencing term is also a thin silver paper?
10 Which US President shared a name with a place to cross water?

ANSWERS ON PAGE 291

232 WITCHES

1 What is the colour of an evil witch's magic?
☐ Black ☐ Blue ☐ Green

2 The Pendle witches were based in which English county?
☐ Derbyshire ☐ Lancashire ☐ Yorkshire

3 Which animal is most closely linked to witches?
☐ Bat ☐ Cat ☐ Rat

4 How many witches appear in *Macbeth*?
☐ Two ☐ Three ☐ Thirteen

5 A witch was said to send her spirit into a creature known as a what?
☐ Familiar ☐ Grimbling ☐ Scullion

6 What is the colour of the magic performed by a good witch?
☐ Black ☐ Red ☐ White

7 Which group sang about a *Witchy Woman*?
☐ Eagles ☐ Iron Maiden ☐ Madness

8 Which Matthew was known as the Witch Finder General?
☐ Arnold ☐ Hopkins ☐ Proctor

9 What were suspected witches thrown into to test their innocence?
☐ Prison ☐ River ☐ Stocks

10 What happened to innocent people in the water "trial"?
☐ Drowned ☐ Escaped ☐ Pardoned

11 What was the name of television's Teenage Witch?
☐ Buffy ☐ Edwina ☐ Sabrina

12 What is the name for a group or sect of witches?
☐ Bevy ☐ Coven ☐ Cowling

13 In *The Crucible*, which slave woman dabbles in magic?
☐ Bessie ☐ Coral ☐ Tituba

14 Which word goes after witch to name a flowering shrub?
☐ Daisy ☐ Hazel ☐ Rose

15 In *The Wizard Of Oz* where does the wicked witch come from?
☐ East ☐ South ☐ West

ANSWERS ON PAGE 291

233 SCANDALS & DISASTERS

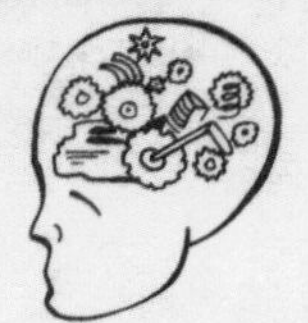
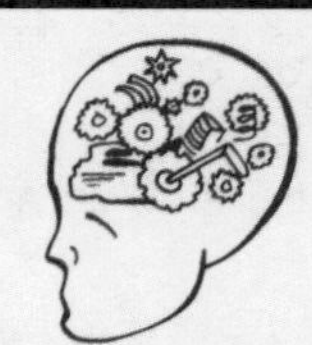
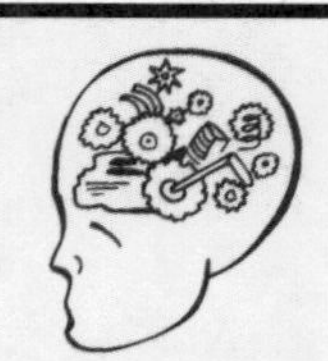

1 Which son of an ex Prime Minister was in trouble in 2005 for his involvement in a proposed coup?

2 Which Open Tennis tournament was John McEnroe expelled from for bad behaviour?

3 Shady tycoon Robert Maxwell drowned near which islands?

4 Which disaster took place in Kobe, Japan, in 1995?

5 Charles Rolls of Rolls-Royce fame was actually in what type of vehicle when he died?

6 In 1996 Stephen Cameron became the first UK fatality of which increasingly violent trend?

7 Famine in which country led to the Band Aid charity concert?

8 Bandleader Glenn Miller was last seen in an aircraft leaving which country?

9 In 1998 the Festina team was banned from what over drug allegations?

10 Where was the USA's worst nuclear accident, in 1979?

11 On which of the Canary Islands did a collision of two jumbo jets take place, making it one of the worst air disasters in history?

12 Who was the first US President to resign while in office?

13 Where in Wales was a school engulfed by a slag heap in 1966?

14 Which Olympic Games were the scene of a terrorist attack by Palestinian guerrillas?

15 Christine Keeler was involved in which Affair that involved British MPs?

16 What was the first name of the unfortunate wife of Dr Crippen?

17 Who was the lady involved in the Abdication Crisis in the UK?

18 Who were Liverpool's opposition when the Hillsborough FA Cup disaster took place?

19 The passenger ship *Herald of Free Enterprise* capsized outside which port?

20 Who made the marriage of Prince Charles and Diana, Princess of Wales, rather "crowded"?

ANSWERS ON PAGE 291

234 TELEVISION

1 At which number do the Kumars live?

2 Which soap featured the character Rick Alessi?

3 Andrew and Danielle are the children of which *Desperate Housewife*?

4 What is the name of the bar that Homer Simpson drinks in?

5 What was the name of Miranda's son in *Sex And The City*?

6 Which character replaced Oscar Blaketon as the sergeant in *Heartbeat*?

7 The drama series *This Life* was about what type of young professionals?

8 Which character was Gordon Brittas's wife in *The Brittas Empire*?

9 Which star of *Ballykissangel* appeared in *Goodnight Sweetheart*?

10 On *The Magic Roundabout* what kind of creature was Brian?

11 What is the name of Karen Walker's housekeeper in *Will And Grace*?

12 In which US city did *Cheers* take place?

13 Which Scottish doctor who kept a casebook was revived in a 1990s series?

14 What was the name of Edina's secretary in *Absolutely Fabulous*?

15 What was Mavis Wilton's maiden name in *Coronation Street*?

16 In *Neighbours*, Erinsborough is a suburb of which city?

17 Who played Elizabeth Darcy in the 1990s TV adaptation of *Pride And Prejudice*?

18 Who starred in *Knowing Me – Knowing You* – with Alan Partridge?

19 Which series featured Arkwright's corner shop?

20 What colour did the Incredible Hulk turn when angry?

ANSWERS ON PAGE 291

235 DICTATORS

1 In which country was Hitler born?

2 When did Saddam Hussein become President of Iraq?

3 Which Cambodian leader led the Khmer Rouge from the mountains after being deposed in 1979?

4 What name was given to the occasion in 1934 when Hitler had members of his own party murdered by the SS?

5 Chaplin played a Hitler-like figure in *The Great Dictator* but what else did they have in common?

6 What name was given to the link between Hitler's Germany and Mussolini's Italy?

7 Which organisation shot Mussolini?

8 Which civilian militia was established under Papa Doc Duvalier?

9 Which title did Napoleon take in 1799, instituting a military dictatorship?

10 Where was Napoleon given sovereignty of after his abdication in 1814?

11 What title did Stalin assume when he became war leader?

12 What does the word Stalin mean?

13 What was Spain's only legal party after the civil war?

14 When did Franco become absolute leader of Spain?

15 Who declared martial law in 1972 in the Philippines?

16 Which opposition leader in the Philippines was murdered in 1983?

17 Who was military leader of Argentina at the beginning of the Falklands War?

18 What does the name Ghengis Khan mean?

19 How old was Ghengis Khan when he succeeded his father?

20 Which leader launched his "Great Leap Forward" in 1958?

ANSWERS ON PAGE 291

236 GENERAL KNOWLEDGE

 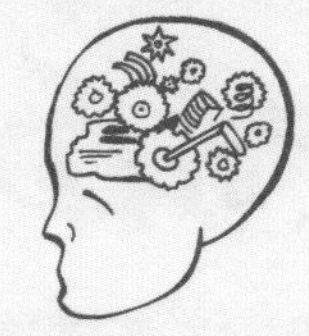 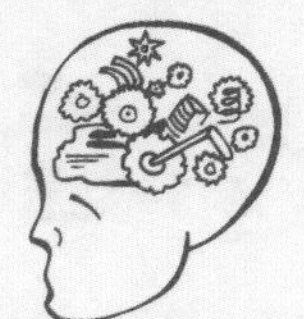

1 What is the main language spoken in Chile?

2 In which Shakespeare play do two grave diggers appear?

3 Which Eastern religion includes the caste system?

4 Who was king of England from 1413 to 1422?

5 What animal lives in a drey?

6 In which African country is the city of Bulawayo?

7 On which River do Rochester, Chatham and Gillingham stand in Kent?

8 What part of Cyrano de Bergerac's anatomy was particularly large?

9 In which sport was Sir Donald Bradman famous?

10 Who said, "I never had any problems with drugs, only with policemen"?

11 In the Bible, which son was Abraham asked to sacrifice?

12 Who was the last Roman Catholic king of England?

13 What sort of bird is a Cinnamon Norwich?

14 Winnipeg is the capital of which Canadian province?

15 Of which country was Aldo Moro formerly Prime Minister?

16 At which battle was Richard III killed?

17 Who wrote *Private Lives*?

18 What is the term for a group of bishops?

19 Which country does a car come from if it shows CDN as the International registration letter?

20 What part of the body would be affected if you suffered from myopia?

ANSWERS ON PAGE 291

237 VILLAINS

1 Which country does Osama Bin Laden come from?

2 In 1998 General Pinochet was arrested in the UK pending extradition to where?

3 Which Surveyor of the Queen's Pictures was stripped of his knighthood?

4 Michael Barratt was not the last person to be hanged in the UK but why was he a famous "last"?

5 Where was the murderer of 10 Rillington Place executed?

6 In which country did Martin Bryant go on a shooting spree?

7 How many patients was Harold Shipman originally convicted of killing?

8 Who was the first person to be executed by lethal injection in the USA?

9 Timothy McVeigh was executed for which bombing?

10 On what date did Lord Lucan disappear?

11 Which movie was about Derek Bentley who was hanged as a murderer but later pardoned?

12 Who did James Earl Ray shoot?

13 Where in the UK did Michael Ryan carry out his murders?

14 Who was the first woman to be executed in Texas in the 20th century?

15 Which group captured hostages John McCarthy, Brian Keenan and Frank Reed in Lebanon?

16 On TV what was the surname of the Weatherfield One?

17 In 1902 Harry Jackson was the first person convicted on the basis of what evidence?

18 How was Illich Ramirez Sanchez better known?

19 Marie Kelly is believed to be the final victim of which villain?

20 The book *Cried Unheard* was about which convicted killer?

ANSWERS ON PAGE 291

238 FOOD AND DRINK

1 Which wine comes from Worms?

2 How is sake usually drunk?

3 Which food shares its name with Latin American big band music?

4 What were angostura bitters originally used for?

5 If a dessert is served "a la mode" what is served with it?

6 Which "fruit" is passata made from?

7 What shape is a croissant?

8 What is chenin blanc wine known as in South Africa?

9 Which term describes the fermented grape juice added to wine that has lost its strength to perk it up?

10 If a wine is madeirized what has happened to it?

11 Where is Marsala, famed for its fortified wine?

12 In wine terms what is the difference between frizzante and spumante?

13 Which folded pizza dough dish takes its name from the Italian for trouser leg?

14 Which cereal is polenta made from?

15 How does Malaga wine achieve its dark colour?

16 Which Kensington restaurant was co founded by Mara Berni in 1963?

17 Where does Dao wine come from?

18 What is the study of wine called?

19 Where did balti cooking originate?

20 What is the main ingredient of a black pudding?

ANSWERS ON PAGE 291

239 PICTURE QUIZ

What links these pictures?

ANSWERS ON PAGE 291

240 NAME THE YEAR

1 Neil Diamond was born. Japanese attacked the US fleet at Pearl Harbor. *The Maltese Falcon* with Humphrey Bogart had its premiere.

2 George Bush was sworn in as 41st President of the USA. Democracy demonstrators in Peking were crushed by tanks. Boris Becker won the Wimbledon singles title for the third time.

3 Judi Dench won the Golden Globe award for her role in *Mrs Brown*. Geri Halliwell left The Spice Girls. France won the soccer World Cup.

4 Chris Evert won her third Wimbledon singles as Chris Evert-Lloyd. *Chariots Of Fire* won the Best Picture Oscar. President Reagan survived an assassination attempt.

5 The *Queen Elizabeth* caught fire and sank in Hong Kong harbour. US troops withdrew from Vietnam. Mark Spitz won seven Olympic gold medals.

6 Ronald Reagan became President of the USA. John Lennon was shot and killed in New York. The Olympic Games were held in Moscow.

ANSWERS ON PAGE 291

241 HALF CHANCE

½? ½? ½?

1 Which solo singer sang *Baby One More Time* in 1999 – Britney Spears or Madonna?

2 What sort of creature is a shrike – a bird or a reptile?

3 Edmund Hillary became the first man to reach the peak of which mountain – Everest or the Matterhorn?

4 Charles Holley became known as which entertainer Buddy – Greco or Holly?

5 Which clown shares his name with the Royal Family of Monaco – Coco or Grimaldi?

6 What does Blitzkrieg mean – lightning war or snowstorm?

7 Was the organisation Greenpeace founded in Australia or Canada?

8 Which zodiac sign links August and September – Leo or Virgo?

9 Is John McEnroe's middle name Liam or Patrick?

10 What was manufactured by the business set up by Harvey Firestone – ties or tyres?

11 Did Michael Douglas and Catherine Zeta Jones call their first baby son Dylan or Lennon?

12 Did Goran Ivanisevic play tennis for Austria or Croatia?

13 What does a hyacinth grow from – a bulb or a seed?

14 In *Dad's Army* who declared, "We're doomed" – Corporal Jones or Private Frazer?

15 The now extinct dodo was what type of creature – a bird or a fish?

16 Was Lesley Joseph's character in *Birds Of A Feather* called Camilla or Dorien?

17 A smolt is a young of which creature – eel or salmon?

18 Were Forty Niners searching for fossils or gold?

19 In the 1980s, were young upwardly mobile persons known as nimbys or yuppies?

20 Could you watch Nantes play a home soccer match in France or Portugal?

ANSWERS ON PAGE 291

242 AROUND ASIA

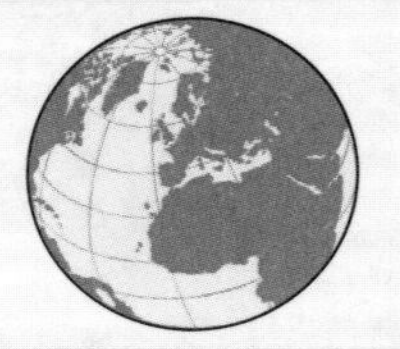

1 Which country has been officially called Myanmar since 1989?

2 Which country is made up of over 800 islands including Viti Levu?

3 Which desert covers part of China and Mongolia?

4 What title does the head of state of Nepal have?

5 Which 7000 island country lies in the Pacific, north east of the South China Sea?

6 How is The Republic of China better known?

7 To which country does East Timor belong?

8 Which neighbouring countries' currency is the Won?

9 What was the name of Bangladesh between 1847 and 1972?

10 In which country are the Cameron Highlands?

11 What are the majority of the islands of Micronesia made from?

12 Which country is bordered by Laos, Vietnam and Thailand?

13 Which sea lies to the north of Iran?

14 What is Japan's highest mountain?

15 How many vowels are there in Kyrgyzstan?

16 Which country's official name in Hindi is Bharat?

17 What are China's famous "warriors" made from?

18 Which country's capital is Ulan Bator?

19 In which two countries is the Thar desert?

20 Which social system is divided into brahmins, kshatriyas, vaishyas and shudras?

ANSWERS ON PAGE 291

243 LUCKY DIP

1 In the hymn, "All things bright" are also what?

2 How many minutes are there in half a day?

3 Which country is a car from with the international registration letter S?

4 Who came first, King Edward II or George II?

5 What is a small section of garlic called?

6 In Premiership soccer how many points are awarded for losing a game?

7 Ag is the symbol of which chemical element?

8 Who was Hollywood's first "Blonde Bombshell"?

9 What name is given to a book containing world maps?

10 What is the only month not to have the same number of days each year?

11 Bucks Fizz and Lulu have both won which Song Contest?

12 Who recorded the album *So Far So Good*?

13 Avian relates to which kind of creatures?

14 Which Bay housed the island prison Alcatraz?

15 Which creatures are said to desert a sinking ship?

16 Who sang with Frank Sinatra on the original version of *Somethin' Stupid*?

17 In the Bible, who was murdered by his brother Cain?

18 What was the name of the boy in the cartoon *The Jungle Book*?

19 What is the nickname of the New Zealand rugby team?

20 What did Siam change its name to?

ANSWERS ON PAGE 291

244 CAPITALS

In which country would you find these capital cities?

1 ABUJA
2 MAPUTO
3 ACCRA
4 MANILA
5 LUSAKA
6 BRIDGETOWN
7 JAKARTA
8 CARACAS
9 BOGOTA
10 DAKAR

ANSWERS ON PAGE 291

245 GUESS WHO . . . ?

1 His middle name was Fitzgerald and he was travelling by motorcade in Dallas when he was assassinated in 1963.
2 Born in Heidelberg, he was the youngest-ever Wimbledon Men's Singles Champion in 1985 when he was unseeded.
3 Front man of the Crickets, his hits included *Peggy Sue*, before his career was cut short due to a plane crash in 1959.
4 She married the heir to the British throne in 1981 and had two sons William and Harry before her early death in 1997.
5 Daughter of Debbie Reynolds, she starred in *Star Wars* and wrote *Postcards from the Edge*.
6 This English novelist wrote about conditions in Victorian England in novels such as *Oliver Twist* and *Great Expectations*.
7 Born in the US, she married a Beatle and one of her daughters became a world-famous dress designer.
8 Youngest sister in a famous singing family, she has the initials JJ and recorded *Doesn't Really Matter* in 2000.
9 Born in Brazil in 1972, he joined Ferrari in 2000 as the No 2 to Michael Schumacher.
10 Daughter of Henry and sister of Peter, she was an anti-Vietnam war demonstrator and later married Ted Turner.

ANSWERS ON PAGE 291

246 SUPERMODELS & CELEBS

1 Which Sarah was once married to Andrew Lloyd Webber?
☐ Brightman ☐ Kennedy ☐ Smith

2 Which Ms Dahl is famous in the modelling world?
☐ Sandie ☐ Sophie ☐ Susie

3 What is Jamie Oliver's wife called?
☐ Debs ☐ Jules ☐ Trace

4 Guy Ritchie married which US megastar in 2000?
☐ Cher ☐ Debbie Harry ☐ Madonna

5 Which Lawson was dubbed "a domestic goddess"?
☐ Leigh ☐ Jodie ☐ Nigella

6 From which part of the UK does Catherine Zeta Jones hail?
☐ Ireland ☐ Scotland ☐ Wales

7 Which Ford split with wife Melissa Mathison in 2001?
☐ Glenn ☐ Harrison ☐ John

8 Jemima Khan married what type of sportsman in Imran Khan?
☐ Boxer ☐ Cricketer ☐ Golfer

9 Which actor is ex beauty queen Shakira Caine married to?
☐ Michael ☐ Martin ☐ Melvyn

10 What is the surname of tabloid celeb Lady Victoria?
☐ Beckham ☐ Hervey ☐ Wood

11 Which Elizabeth ceased to be the main face of Estée Lauder in 2001?
☐ Dawn ☐ Hurley ☐ Taylor

12 Which country does Rachel Hunter come from?
☐ New Zealand ☐ South Africa ☐ USA

13 Which former model married actor Leigh Lawson?
☐ Barbara Bach ☐ Twiggy
☐ Mandy Smith

14 What was Elle McPherson known as on the catwalk?
☐ The Beauty ☐ The Best ☐ The Body

15 Naomi Campbell appeared in the flop movie Miami what?
☐ Models
☐ Rapture
☐ Vice

ANSWERS ON PAGE 292

247 WEATHER

1 Which country has the driest inhabited area in the world?

2 What does meteorological mean?

3 What name is given to an occasion when the Earth's Equator is furthest from the Sun?

4 Which county is England's wettest?

5 Which usually travels faster a cold front or a warm front?

6 Which sea area is immediately to the south of Eire?

7 Over which Mountains does the Chinook blow?

8 What are lines joining places of equal atmospheric pressure called?

9 The name of which type of cloud is Latin for lock of hair?

10 What is Fata Morgana and where would you see it?

11 What is the belt of light variable winds near the Equator called?

12 What number does the Beaufort Scale go up to in international use?

13 Where would you experience a Williwaw?

14 What colour are altostratus clouds?

15 What is the Buran?

16 What is the name of a front where a cold front has overtaken a warm front?

17 What is a hurricane called in the Pacific?

18 Where is the Tramontana?

19 Which sea area lies due east of Dogger and Humber?

20 Where does the Berg wind blow?

ANSWERS ON PAGE 292

248 POP MUSIC

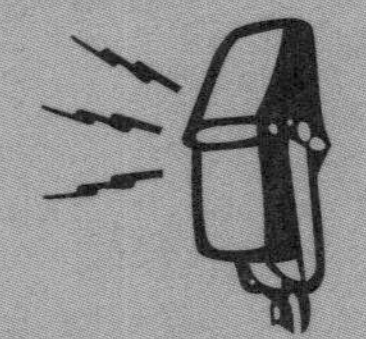
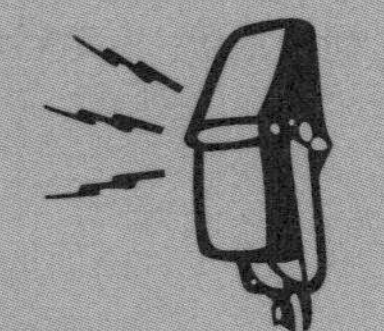
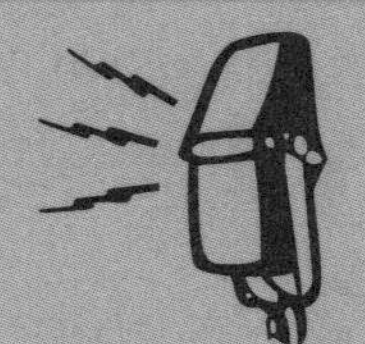

1 *World Of Our Own* was the tenth UK No 1 for which boy band?

2 Who recorded the UK chart-topping album *Permission To Land?*

3 Marti Pellow was the lead singer with which group?

4 What was Ashanti's second album called?

5 Who fronted the Boomtown Rats?

6 Which boy band had UK No 1s with *Babe* and *Sure*?

7 Dave Gilmore and Roger Waters were in which long-lasting group?

8 Which group became the first to have the word Pumpkins in their name?

9 Which group flew into the *Hotel California*?

10 Which Paul links the Style Council and The Jam?

11 How did Kurt Cobain end his life?

12 Whose *Nothing Compares 2 U* made No 1 in both the UK and the US?

13 What was the first single of The Spice Girls?

14 Which alternative dance group first charted with *Charly*?

15 Which all-girl group were first to sell more than a million copies of an album in the UK?

16 In the song, *When You Walk Through A Storm*, what do you hold up high?

17 *Mandy* was the first UK chart hit for which Barry?

18 Who sang with Olivia Newton-John on *You're The One That I Want*?

19 The Three Degrees came from which country?

20 Whose 1993 album was called *Bat Out of Hell II*?

ANSWERS ON PAGE 292

249 GENERAL KNOWLEDGE

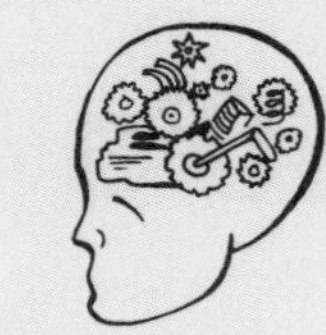
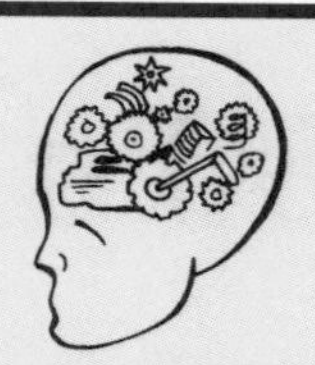

1 When a cow stands up, which legs does it get up on first?

2 Who sang the song *On The Good Ship Lollipop*?

3 According to the proverb, what is the better part of valour?

4 Which instrument did Stan Getz play?

5 Which sport did David Duckham play?

6 From which London railway station do trains normally leave for Bristol?

7 In which film is the *Harry Lime Theme*?

8 Which American city is named after a British Prime Minister?

9 Where would you find a dead man's handle?

10 Who wrote the musical *Oliver!*?

11 In Australia, Perth is the capital of which state?

12 Which country lies immediately east of Iraq?

13 Which London building was nicknamed "Ally Pally"?

14 Who claimed that, "History is Bunk"?

15 Who said, "Father, I cannot tell a lie"?

16 From which port was the bulk of the British Expeditionary Force evacuated in 1940?

17 Which architect designed New York's Guggenheim Museum?

18 Who wrote *Gulliver's Travels*?

19 In which city was General Gordon put to death?

20 What kind of animal is a pipistrelle?

ANSWERS ON PAGE 292

250 PLANET EARTH

1 In which US state is the Jewel cave system?

2 The largest man-made excavation in the world mines which element?

3 Which animal weighs the most – grizzly bear, polar bear or a walrus?

4 What is Europe's largest island which is not a country in its own right?

5 Which desert is on the US Mexico border?

6 What is the most common element in the earth's crust after oxygen?

7 Which Chinese landmark was viewed from space?

8 Acid rain results due to a pollution of the atmosphere with oxides of nitrogen and what?

9 Where was the meteorite High Possil found?

10 Where is the highest waterfall outside South America?

11 What is the world's highest island?

12 How many states does Lake Michigan cover?

13 Orogenesis is concerned with the formation of what?

14 What is the Great Barrier Reef made from?

15 Where was the meteorite Armanty found?

16 Actinobiology studies the effect of what on living organisms?

17 Cryogenics studies materials under what conditions?

18 Of the five largest glaciers in the world which is the only one not in Antarctica?

19 Which part of planet Earth would a pedologist observe?

20 How many countries does the Mekong river flow through?

ANSWERS ON PAGE 292

251 SPORT

1 Who was tennis star Martina Hingis named after?

2 Which player has played the most league games for Man Utd?

3 Which country does marathon man Abel Anton come from?

4 Who replaced Mike Atherton as England cricket captain?

5 What is the nickname of record-breaking sprinter Maurice Greene?

6 Which Robin was the first yachtsman to sail non-stop around the world?

7 Athlete Kelly Holmes was formerly a member of which armed service?

8 Which temperamental tennis player was dubbed Superbrat?

9 Which snooker world champion Ray was nicknamed "Dracula"?

10 What sort of eye accessory does Chris Eubank wear?

11 Where did the first Olympic women's basketball tournament take place?

12 Which Monica was stabbed in the back by a fanatical Graf supporter?

13 Baltusrol, Medinah and Oakmont are all types of what?

14 Who founded the Stewart motor racing team?

15 Who in 1996 became the first black manager of a Premiership club?

16 Which four-legged, three-times Grand National winner died in 1995?

17 Which Greg rejected a maple leaf for a Union Jack in the 1990s?

18 Who founded the book known as the cricketer's Bible?

19 How was Walker Smith Robinson better known?

20 Who was Ben Johnson running for when disqualified in Seoul?

ANSWERS ON PAGE 292

252 THE 1980s

80's? **80's?** **80's?**

1 The Hillsborough Agreement was between which two countries?

2 Where was there a major nuclear leak in the USSR in 1986?

3 Who was the last white President of South Africa, elected in 1989?

4 Which former liberal leader was made speaker of the national assembly of Czechoslovakia in 1989?

5 A fatwa calling for the death of which writer was made by Iran in '89?

6 Who succeeded Callaghan as Labour leader in the UK?

7 Who became France's first socialist President in 1981?

8 Who was Argentine President during the Falklands conflict?

9 Who made the album *Born In The USA*?

10 Michael Manley became leader of where in 1989?

11 Who owned *Rainbow Warrior*, sunk by the French in 1985?

12 Which drink did the Cocoa Cola Company launch in 1982?

13 How many times was Margaret Thatcher elected PM in the 1980s?

14 Which keeper was beaten by Maradona's "hand of God" 1986 FIFA World Cup goal?

15 Who was leader of the GLC from 1981–86?

16 What was the Black day of the week of the 1987 stockmarket crash?

17 Who moved from Transport House to Walworth Road in 1980?

18 In which hotel was the Brighton bomb in 1984?

19 Who became President of Serbia in 1986?

20 Most of which Caribbean island's buildings were destroyed by hurricane Hugo in 1989?

ANSWERS ON PAGE 292

253 PICTURE QUIZ

A B C D

What links these pictures?

ANSWERS ON PAGE 292

254 THE ORCHESTRA

Is each statement TRUE or FALSE?

T F **1** The modern orchestra is made up of four sections.

T F **2** The harp is part of the percussion section.

T F **3** The saxophone belongs to the woodwind section.

T F **4** A tam tam is a gong.

T F **5** The brass section usually sits on the back row of the orchestra.

T F **6** A side drum is bigger than a bass drum.

T F **7** Woodwind instruments can be made of metal or plastic.

T F **8** A vibraphone is used just for rhythm not for melody.

T F **9** The cor anglais is a type of horn.

T F **10** A tuba is smaller than a bassoon.

ANSWERS ON PAGE 292

255 PALACES AND BUILDINGS

1 The Elysée Palace is whose official residence?
☐ French President ☐ Pope ☐ Spanish King

2 When was Buckingham Palace originally built?
☐ 1703 ☐ 1803 ☐ 1903

3 Which city is closest to the Palace of Versailles?
☐ Paris ☐ Rheims ☐ Turin

4 Which William designed the Horse Guards Building, Whitehall, London?
☐ Essex ☐ Kent ☐ Surrey

5 Which Palace was built to house London's Great Exhibition of 1851?
☐ Crystal ☐ Ice ☐ Winter

6 In which English county was Blenheim Palace built?
☐ Kent ☐ Norfolk ☐ Oxfordshire

7 Which type of window is linked to the Early English or Gothic style?
☐ Lancet ☐ Oriel ☐ Rose

8 The Amalienborg Palace is the home of which Royal Family?
☐ Danish ☐ Spanish ☐ Dutch

9 What is a row of windows in the upper wall of a church called?
☐ Belvedere ☐ Clerestory ☐ Spandrel

10 Where were the Hanging Gardens built around the 7th century BC?
☐ Babylon ☐ Damascus ☐ Rhodes

11 Which country did architect Walter Gropius come from?
☐ Germany ☐ Switzerland ☐ USA

12 Where in England is King's College Chapel?
☐ Bath ☐ Cambridge ☐ London

13 Which John designed Brighton Pavilion?
☐ Jones ☐ Nash ☐ Vanbrugh

14 What is Venice's most noted cathedral?
☐ St Basil's ☐ St Mark's ☐ St Stephen's

15 Which Palace adjoins Kensington Gardens?
☐ Crystal ☐ Kensington ☐ Lambeth

ANSWERS ON PAGE 292

256 LUCKY DIP

1. Which word can go after salad and before gown?
2. What kind of animal is a Persian Blue?
3. Who composed the opera *Carmen*?
4. On a ship or boat what is a painter?
5. What kind of food is gazpacho?
6. Where in London is the statue of Peter Pan?
7. What does a chandler make?
8. In geometry, what is meant by concentric?
9. Which wooden puppet was first written about by Carlo Collodi?
10. In which of Dickens's novels does Sam Weller appear?
11. Which food, not rationed in the UK during World War II, was rationed after it?
12. Which religious writer was born in Elstow, near Bedford?
13. What is the name of the marmalade cat created by Kathleen Hale?
14. For what is the Médoc area of France famous?
15. Black, Whooper, and Bewick are all types of which bird?
16. Of which country was Field-Marshall Smuts a statesman?
17. Beau Brummel became known for his following of which subject?
18. What name was given to the mediaeval warlike expeditions to the Holy Land?
19. What do we call what the Italians call pesce?
20. In London, the Cambridge, the Lyric and the Adelphi are all what?

ANSWERS ON PAGE 292

257 GEOGRAPHY

1. What did Iran used to be called?
2. In which World are underdeveloped countries said to be?
3. Normandy is part of which country?
4. In which Sea is the island of Majorca?
5. Which country does the island of Rhodes belong to?
6. In which US state is Disney World?
7. Which English county is abbreviated to Oxon.?
8. In which country is the Costa del Sol?
9. Which is further south in England – Great Yarmouth or Brighton?
10. Is Torremolinos on the coast or inland?
11. Which sea lies between Italy and the former Yugoslavia?
12. On which coast of France are Cannes and St Tropez?
13. Which Falls are on the border between Zimbabwe and Zambia?
14. In which country is Buenos Aires?
15. In which continent is the holiday destination of Ibiza?
16. Where would you speak English and Maltese?
17. Which island lies at the eastern end of the Mediterranean?
18. Which group of islands does Tenerife belong to?
19. Which country does the Loire flow through?
20. In which Ocean is Greenland?

ANSWERS ON PAGE 292

258 GENERAL KNOWLEDGE

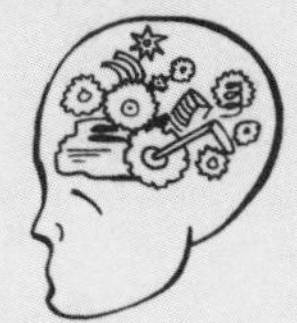
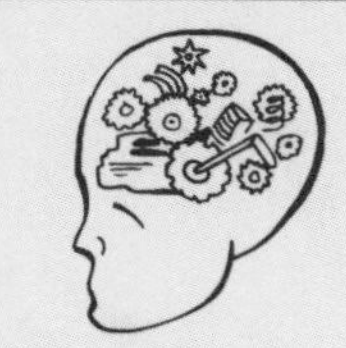
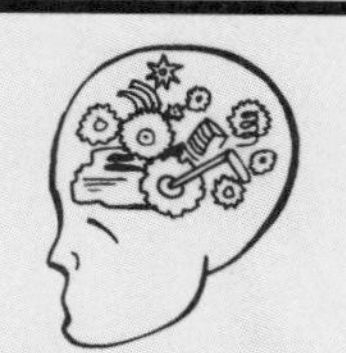

1 CIPS regulates which sport?
2 Which game was derived from baggataway?
3 Where is Rick Stein's famous seafood restaurant?
4 What is octopush?
5 Where did Gilley's Club open as the world's largest nightclub?
6 Who jointly opened La Gavroche in 1967?
7 Which amazing venue was designed by George London and Henry Wise?
8 What colour might your balls be in croquet?
9 What is the nearest town to the Lightwater Valley Theme Park?
10 Which game was originally called Lexico?
11 The Toucan Terribles are prolific champions at what?
12 What is a gricer?
13 Which UK town has the longest shopping mall?
14 Where was the Grand National run during WWI?
15 Who founded the London restaurants Quaglino's and Mezzo?
16 In judo which Dan grades are awarded a red belt?
17 How many points is the gold circle on an archery target worth?
18 In 1848 William Mitchell drew up the rules to which modern game?
19 In shinty what is the opponent's goal called?
20 Which musical instrument was the creation of Charles Wheatstone?

ANSWERS ON PAGE 292

259 HALF CHANCE

½? ½? ½?

1 What was Billie's follow up to *Because We Want To – Girlfriend* or *Honey To The Bee*?
2 In the comic opera *The Yeomen Of The Guard* is Jack Point an executioner or a jester?
3 In the 1990s did Macedonia declare its independence from Russia or Yugoslavia?
4 In which city did Prince Andrew marry Sarah Ferguson – London or New York?
5 What does a capo do to a guitar, raise the pitch or tune the strings?
6 What was Count Basie's actual first name – Thomas or William?
7 In cricket, how many bails are on the two sets of wickets – four or six?
8 She's still going strong but in which decade was Tina Turner born,1930s or1940s?
9 Rudyard Kipling was born in which country – Afghanistan or India?
10 Are Bonny Lad, Express and White Windsor varieties of broad beans or peas?
11 Which Stephen wrote the song *Send In The Clowns* – King or Sondheim?
12 Elk, Fox and Wolf can have which other animal added to their names – bison or hound?
13 In the award CBE does C stand for Commander or Creator?
14 In which US state is the resort of Orlando – Florida or Hawaii?
15 Did skater Kurt Browning come from Canada or New Zealand?
16 Monaco borders France and which other country – Italy or Spain?
17 Do the stripes on the American flag run horizontally or vertically?
18 Did Jim Henson create *The Muppets* or *The Simpsons*?
19 Ellen MacArthur became known for her solo what – sailing or singing?
20 In legend, was the giant horse delivered to the city of Troy made out of stone or wood?

ANSWERS ON PAGE 292

Mother's

Mother's Day is the one day when families look after mum, which seems scant reward as mum looks after the family for every other day of the year! These questions are in celebration of mothers.

1 Which mum plays mother to real-life daughter Joely Richardson in *Nip/Tuck*?

2 Who is the mother of Chelsea Clinton?

3 In the UK Mothering Sunday falls during which period of fasting?

4 Who was the mother of fashion designer Stella McCartney?

5 Which actress is the daughter of Janet Leigh who starred in the *Psycho* shower scene?

6 Which British-born Bond girl is the mother of twins?

7 Who wrote the "supermum" novel *I Don't Know How She Does It*?

8 In which month is the Fête des Mères celebrated in France?

9 Who starred with her daughter Rumer in the movie *Striptease* in 1996?

10 Who was Liza Minnelli's famous mother?

11 According to the proverb, what is the mother of invention?

12 Which UK Prime Minister was the mother of twins?

13 Which UK radio presenter is mother to Woody?

14 *Mommy Dearest* was a biopic about which Hollywood actress?

15 In France which flower is offered on Mother's Day?

16 Who is the famous mother of Brooklyn, Romeo and Cruz?

17 What does the expression "keep mum" mean?

18 Which popular pantomime has the word Mother in the title?

19 According to the proverb, what is the mother of invention?

20 What is George W Bush's mother called?

21 Which princess is the mother of Zara Phillips?

22 Which Japanese artist is the step-mother of Julian Lennon?

23 What is the lining of an oyster shell called?

24 Who is the mother of Liam Gallagher's son Lennon?

25 Which soul singer is the godmother of Whitney Houston?

26 Who wrote the play *Mother Courage* in 1941?

27 Which actress is the mother of playwright Amy Rosenthal?

28 Who sang about a Mother And Child Reunion in the 1970s?

29 Goldie Hawn is the mother of which famous actress?

30 Traditionally which cake did girls make to take home to their mothers?

31 Which star of *Moonlighting* is the mother of twins?

32 Who is the mother of Princesses Beatrice and Eugenie?

33 Carrie Fisher's mother Debbie Reynolds found fame in which movie with Gene Kelly?

34 Which band's music is used in the musical *Mamma Mia*?

35 What is the Italian word for mother?

36 What is the main flavour of the Mother's Day speciality simnel cake?

37 Who is the famous mother of Rocco and Lourdes?

38 What was the name of the mother of Jack, Robert and Edward Kennedy?

39 How many children did the Queen Mother have?

40 What is someone's native language also called?

41 Who is the mother-in-law of the former Sophie Rhys Jones?

42 Diane Cilento is the mother of which actor, whose dad once played 007?

43 Which actress, famous for *Fawlty Towers*, is the mother of actor Sam West?

44 Whose adopted daughter went on to marry her own former partner?

45 Which other famous mother had her funeral service on the same day as Mother Teresa of Calcutta in 1997?

46 Who is mother to Euan, Nicholas, Kathryn and Leo?

47 Which "mother" expression is another name for a nursery rhyme?

48 Which Oscar-winning Dame is the mother of Finty Williams?

49 Where was a "mummy" an embalmed body of an animal or person?

50 Which Oscar winning actress is the mother of Apple?

ANSWERS ON PAGE 292

261 GENERAL KNOWLEDGE

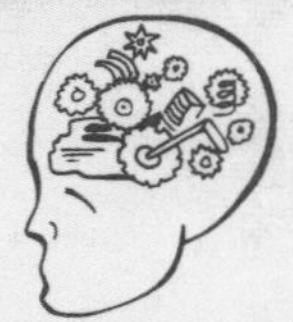  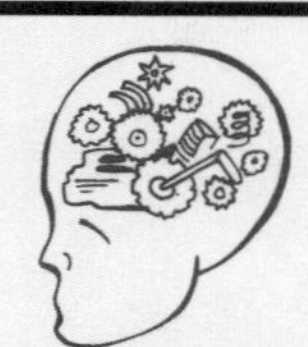

1 Who did Margaret Thatcher replace as leader of the Tory Party in Britain?

2 Who famously hit a golf shot on the moon?

3 Which dog show was first held in Islington in 1891?

4 What does "Honi soit qui mal y pense" mean?

5 In which "ology" were Freud and Jung active?

6 What acid gives nettles their sting?

7 Which British King was nicknamed "Farmer George"?

8 Who was the last Briton to win the Men's Singles at Wimbledon?

9 On which peninsula is the city of Sevastopol situated?

10 Which word goes after piece and before times to make new words?

11 What is nitrous oxide more commonly called?

12 Who was the Greek muse of dance?

13 Which rock guitarist prophetically said, "When you're dead you're made for life"?

14 Edward Gibbon wrote the *Decline And Fall Of* which empire?

15 UNICEF was established for the care of which group of people?

16 What colour of ballet shoes did Hans Christian Andersen write about?

17 What was Mrs Gaskell's first name?

18 Which British newspaper is nicknamed "The Thunderer"?

19 What according to Scott McKenzie did you wear in your hair in San Francisco?

20 Which "ology" is concerned with the human skin?

ANSWERS ON PAGE 292

262 FRANK SINATRA

1 In which decade was Sinatra born?

2 What is his nickname?

3 According to the lyrics, "Love And Marriage" go together like what?

4 What was his first UK No 1 in 1954?

5 What is Sinatra's middle name?

6 For which 1950s film did Sinatra win an Oscar?

7 What was Sinatra's own record label set up in 1961?

8 Which 1966 hit won a Grammy that year?

9 Which song was dedicated to his elder daughter?

10 Who wrote the English lyrics for Sinatra's signature tune *My Way*?

11 Which song did he take into the charts with Bono in 1993?

12 In which film did Sinatra sing his famous *The Lady Is A Tramp*?

13 Of which co star did he say on her death, "She was a princess from the day she was born"?

14 Which of Sinatra's wives went on to marry Andre Previn?

15 In which decade was *My Way* first released?

16 Which of Sinatra's children was kidnapped?

17 Which city gave Sinatra a 1950s hit?

18 Which city gave him a hit single 23 years later?

19 Who played the character loosely based on Sinatra in *The Godfather*?

20 In addition to *Sinatra-Basie* which album did he make with Count Basie in 1964?

ANSWERS ON PAGE 292

263 AT THE MOVIES

1 Which Woody starred in *Natural Born Killers*?

2 Which 007 starred in *The Lawnmower Man*?

3 What is the first name of FBI agent Starling in *The Silence Of The Lambs*?

4 In which country was Jean-Claude van Damme born?

5 Who sang *Fame* in *Fame*?

6 Johnny Weissmuller portrayed which jungle hero?

7 Which Diane played Steve Martin's wife in *Father Of The Bride*?

8 Which *Grease* star danced with Princess Diana at the White House?

9 Which Julie links *Darling* in the 1960s and *Afterglow* in the 90s?

10 In which decade of the 20th century did James Stewart die?

11 Which actor was tennis star John McEnroe's first father-in-law?

12 The character Harry Lime appears in which spy thriller?

13 What was Crocodile Dundee's homeland?

14 *The Sunshine Boys* starred which Walter?

15 Which western star John first acted as Duke Morrison?

16 In which decade was *Psycho* released?

17 In a movie title which word goes before *Of The Lost Ark*?

18 Which actress links *Se7en* and *Sliding Doors*?

19 Which Kim likened Hollywood to the Mafia?

20 Who played the villain Cruella in the 90s movie *101 Dalmatians*?

ANSWERS ON PAGE 292

264 BANDS

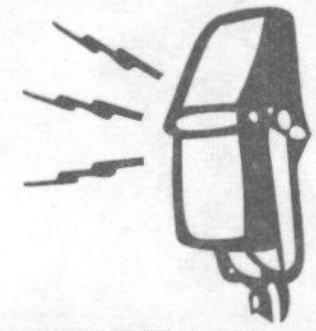

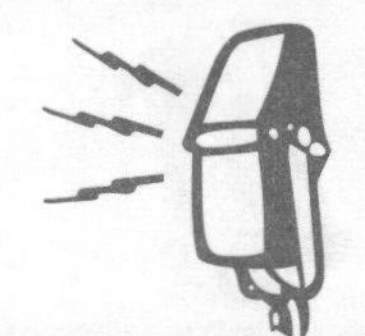

1 Which rock group managed to chart with unlikely sounding subjects such as *Clocks* and *The Scientist*?

2 Which band recorded the albums *Amnesiac* and *The Bends*?

3 Mickey Dolenz was in which 1960s sensation group?

4 In the 1970s who put *A Message In A Bottle*?

5 In which state did Chicago get together?

6 Which band had a big hit with *You Make Me Wanna*?

7 Which band produced the albums *The Division Bell* and *Pulse*?

8 *Money For Nothing* was an 1980s US No 1 for which band?

9 Whose hits include *Bad Moon Rising* and *Green River*?

10 Which Dimension had a 60s smash with *Aquarius*?

11 R.E.M. cut the No 1 album *Out Of* what?

12 Which US Boys band featured three members of the Wilson family?

13 Which band recorded the album *Parallel Lines*?

14 Which heavy metal group took the name of Dutch-born members guitarist Eddie and drummer Alex?

15 Which band sang *I Want To Know What Love Is*?

16 Who was backed by The Shondells?

17 How many brothers were in the original Jackson family line up?

18 Which 1960s icon was backed by The Band?

19 *Tusk* was a best-selling album for which band?

20 Who fronted The Heartbreakers?

ANSWERS ON PAGE 292

265 HISTORY

1 Which US President's father was a former Ambassador in the UK?

2 Edith Cresson was which country's PM from 1991–1992?

3 The Downing Street Declaration in 1993 involved the Prime Ministers of which two countries?

4 Which family died at Ekaterinburg in 1918?

5 Which school provided the UK with 19 Prime Ministers before 2000?

6 In which war did British soldiers first wear balaclava helmets?

7 Which mountaineer was the first person since Scott to reach the South Pole overland, in 1958?

8 The "Bomb Plot' of 1944 failed to assassinate whom?

9 What was the minimum age for joining the UK Home Guard in WWII?

10 Which former US President was a distant relative of Princess Diana?

11 Who was the first woman President of Ireland?

12 In which US state did Martin Luther King lead the 1955 bus boycott?

13 Who lost power in Germany in 1998 after 16 years?

14 Who became Secretary General of the UN in 1997?

15 Who was Bonnie Prince Charlie disguised as when he escaped to France with Flora MacDonald?

16 Who defected to the USSR with Guy Burgess in 1951?

17 Carlos Menem became President of which country in 1989?

18 Who was the first Governor General of India, until 1948?

19 What was the alliance between the Germans and the Italians in World War II called?

20 Where in the East End of London did Jack the Ripper operate?

ANSWERS ON PAGE 292

266 SCIENCE

1 Which company made the first PC?

2 What did the word astronaut originally mean?

3 An estimated how many people take the drug Prozac – 20 million, 40 million or 60 million?

4 What was the third planet to have been visited by a spacecraft?

5 Cohen and Boyer led developments into what in the 1960s and 70s?

6 Which company introduced Photo CD?

7 In which constellation is Rigel?

8 What is another name for slaked lime?

9 What was the third country to have a man in space?

10 Which bone is named after the Italian for flute?

11 What is emetophobia a fear of?

12 What is Saturn's biggest moon?

13 Willem Johan Kolff, a pioneer in medicine and health, devised which item of equipment?

14 How much faster does the strongest wind blow on Neptune than on Earth?

15 What is the term for organized energy of a moving body?

16 What is the next largest body in the Solar System after Uranus?

17 What is the next largest human organ after the brain?

18 Which company were involved in the cloning of Dolly the Sheep?

19 Asteroids usually appear between the orbits of Mars and which other planet?

20 In which decade were contact lenses first devised?

ANSWERS ON PAGE 292

267 PICTURE QUIZ

Which of these celebrities is not named in the title of a song?

ANSWERS ON PAGE 292

268 DOUBLE TAKE

In each case, the two-part quiz question leads to just one answer!

1 Which word describes a schoolchild as well as part of the eye?

2 Which spinning toy is also the word for the summit of a mountain?

3 Which horse is also a word meaning to scold or badger?

4 Which 90s pop band shares a name with flower arranging material?

5 Which word is a collar fastening and a horse-breeding farm?

6 Which bird is also a word meaning to bob down?

7 Which word is a chocolate sweet and also a fungus?

8 Which word describes something new as well as a work of fiction?

9 Which word for a young goat also means to fool or hoax?

10 Which citrus fruit is also the name of a type of porcelain?

ANSWERS ON PAGE 292

269 CLOCKS AND TIME

1 Which country developed the cuckoo clock?
☐ Austria ☐ Germany ☐ Switzerland

2 Which month is named after the Roman god of war?
☐ February ☐ March ☐ October

3 Which season ends with the vernal equinox?
☐ Spring ☐ Summer ☐ Winter

4 What is the first 31-day month to be followed by a 31-day month?
☐ March ☐ July ☐ October

5 If it's 9 am in Washington what time is it in Vermont?
☐ 9 am ☐ 10 am ☐ 12 noon

6 What follows Clockwork in the title of Anthony Burgess's book?
☐ Lemon ☐ Mouse ☐ Orange

7 Who or what is the month August named after?
☐ Herb ☐ God ☐ Roman Emperor

8 What does the D stand for in DST?
☐ Daylight ☐ Decimal ☐ Division

9 If the clock fingers show ten to nine in a mirror, what is the time?
☐ 3.10 ☐ 3.20 ☐ 9.10

10 In which century did Pope Gregory XIII evolve the Gregorian calendar?
☐ 15th ☐ 16th ☐ 17th

11 Which calendar did the Gregorian replace?
☐ Dominician ☐ Julian ☐ Syrian

12 What type of clock did the Dutch physicist Huygens invent?
☐ Pendulum ☐ Electric ☐ Radio

13 How many minutes are there in a day?
☐ 720 ☐ 1,200 ☐ 1,440

14 How is St Stephen's Day otherwise known?
☐ All Souls' Day ☐ Boxing Day
☐ Labour Day

15 Which calendar has the months Safar and Rajab?
☐ Chinese ☐ Jewish ☐ Muslim

ANSWERS ON PAGE 292

270 RECORD BREAKERS

1. Mark Spitz won seven Olympic golds at record speeds doing what?
2. Which South American soccer team has won most F.I.F.A.World Cups?
3. Was Tessa Sanderson competing in her second, fourth or sixth Olympics in 1996?
4. Lyn Davies broke the British record in which jump event?
5. In Rugby, David Campese was leading try scorer for which country?
6. Which Sally was a world record hurdler and a 1992 Olympic champion?
7. Who was made England's youngest-ever soccer coach in 1996?
8. Did Roger Bannister run the first four-minute mile in Oxford or Cambridge?
9. Was Martina Hingis 13, 15 or 17 when she first won Wimbledon doubles?
10. Which ice dancers won a record six successive British championships between 1978 and 1984?
11. Which Nigel was the first to win both F1 and Indy Car world championships?
12. Which record-breaker athlete Sebastian went on to become a Tory MP in Britain?
13. World record-breaker Kip Keino is from which continent?
14. Who won the 100m in Seoul in record time before being disqualified?
15. Which Steve was six times World Snooker Champion in the 1980s?
16. For which former Iron Curtain country did Marita Koch break records?
17. Alain Prost was the first to win the F1 world title for which country?
18. Who was the first player to score 100 goals in soccer's Premiership?
19. Which Pete equalled Borg's five Wimbledon singles wins in 1998?
20. Which Gareth became Wales' youngest-ever Rugby captain in 1968?

ANSWERS ON PAGE 292

271 LUCKY DIP

1. The first motorway was built in which country?
2. What is the zodiac sign of the Bull?
3. On a dart board, which number is bottom centre?
4. Who had a huge hit with the song *Dancing Queen*?
5. Born Arthur Jefferson in 1890, how was this comic better known?
6. What profession did Hillary Clinton practise before moving to the White House?
7. In the nursery rhyme, who went up a hill to fetch a pail of water?
8. In which sport are there madisons and pursuits?
9. Which Noel said, "Television is something you appear on: you don't watch it."
10. According to the proverb, what does the hand that rocks the cradle do?
11. In the communications sector, what did BT stand for in the UK?
12. Which stimulant is found in coffee?
13. In the fable, who was the town mouse's friend?
14. In which sport has Rob Andrew represented England?
15. What is hydrophobia the fear of?
16. In measurement, how many furlongs were in a mile?
17. In which town did Jesus grow up?
18. What was the name of the cross used as the Nazi emblem?
19. What type of animal is a Lhasa Apso?
20. What colours are on the flag of Argentina?

ANSWERS ON PAGE 292

272 AROUND AFRICA

1. Which two African countries begin with the letter Z?
2. What covers 85% of Algeria?
3. Famine in which country triggered the Band Aid Charity?
4. What do the initials OAU stand for?
5. In which country is Ouagadougou?
6. What is the Harmattan?
7. Which is further west Uganda or Kenya?
8. Which country used to be called South West Africa?
9. Which substance used to make a drink or sweet is Ghana's main export?
10. Which lake is between Kenya, Tanzania and Uganda?
11. What is Africa's highest mountain?
12. Which European language is an official language of Angola?
13. In which African country is El Alamein, scene of a WWII battle?
14. Which country is the main economic power in West Africa?
15. Which country's inhabitants were largely made up of Tutsi and Hutu tribes before civil war started in 1994?
16. Which language is Afrikaans derived from?
17. Near which major landmark is the Boiling Pot?
18. What is the area of savanna in West Africa called?
19. South Africa is the world's leading exporter of what?
20. The Kalahari desert is chiefly in which country?

ANSWERS ON PAGE 292

273 THE ARTS

1. Which Arthur Miller play features the character John Proctor?
2. Which Claude painted *Water Lillies*?
3. In *From One Charlie to Another*, who did Charlie Watts write about?
4. Which iconic singer wrote the book *Tarantula*?
5. What was the colour of the first Penguin paperback?
6. Which blonde wrote *The Constant Sinner*?
7. Which John Grisham book had a record initial print run of 2.8 million?
8. To be considered for the Booker Prize a book has to be published where first?
9. What according to Dickens was, "the best of times, the worst of times"?
10. Whose only novel won the Pulitzer Prize in 1937?
11. In which US city is the Guggenheim Museum?
12. For which novel did Tom Clancy receive an advance of $14 million?
13. Which joint 1992 Booker Prize winner had his book made into an Oscar-winning film?
14. Which Ian Fleming novel has the shortest title?
15. What was Hercule Poirot's last case called?
16. Who did J. M. Barrie give the royalties from *Peter Pan* to?
17. Who received a record-breaking advance of £17 million for three novels in 1992?
18. What was the sequel to D. H. Lawrence's *The Rainbow*?
19. Which French sculptor produced *The Thinker*?
20. Which festival is staged at Pilton in England?

ANSWERS ON PAGE 293

274 GENERAL KNOWLEDGE

 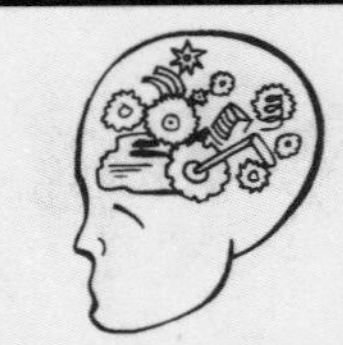 

1. Who made up the folk trio with Peter and Paul?
2. Which general of ancient Carthage is associated with elephants?
3. Who wrote the novel *The Seventh Scroll*?
4. In which London park is the Serpentine?
5. Of which country is Baffin Island a part?
6. Who wrote the novel *Lord Of The Flies*?
7. In South America, what is a gaucho?
8. What can cats do with their claws that dogs cannot do?
9. Which American writer created Tarzan?
10. Ipswich is the administrative headquarters of which English county?
11. What job is done by a concierge?
12. What is a peruke?
13. With what industry is the inventor Richard Arkwright associated?
14. What is the common name for calcium carbonate?
15. What do we call what the Germans call strumpfhose?
16. In chess, how many squares can the King move at a time?
17. With which industry is the Royal Smithfield Show concerned?
18. On what type of surface is the sport of curling played?
19. What are the main two political parties in the United States?
20. Which French King was husband to Marie Antoinette?

ANSWERS ON PAGE 293

275 WINE

1. Claret wine is produced in and around which French town?
2. What would be the term to describe a dry champagne?
3. In which country is the wine-growing Barossa Valley?
4. Which white wine grape variety is most widely planted in California?
5. In which country is the Marlborough wine region?
6. Retsina is native to which country?
7. Which wine has the varieties Malmsey and Sercial?
8. What is the normal capacity for a bottle of wine?
9. In which country is Rioja produced?
10. Along which river is most of France's Sauvignon Blanc cultivated?
11. What colour are most English wines?
12. What term do the Italians use for a dry wine?
13. What is a crate of twelve bottles of wine called?
14. Which country does Sukhindol wine come from?
15. In which part of the US is the Zinfandel grape chiefly cultivated?
16. What is the first name of wine writer Ms Robinson?
17. In which country is the wine-making area of Stellenbosch?
18. How many normal size wine bottles would you have in a Methuselah?
19. How are fizzy wines, other than champagnes, described?
20. In which area of Italy is Chianti Classico produced?

ANSWERS ON PAGE 293

276 PHOBIAS

What do you fear if you have the following PHOBIAS?

1 GYNOPHOBIA
2 AIGOPHOBIA
3 CANOPHOBIA
4 HAPHEPHOBIA
5 ACHLUOPHOBIA
6 NELOPHOBIA
7 CHIONOPHOBIA
8 SIDEROPHOBIA
9 HIPPOPHOBIA
10 BAROPHOBIA

ANSWERS ON PAGE 293

277 GUESS WHO . . . ?

1 Having the middle names Herbert Walker and married to Barbara, his Vice President was Dan Quayle.
2 Born in Scotland in 1971, he made his debut at Williams and moved to McLaren in 1996.
3 Born in New Jersey in 1963, she married Bobby Brown and starred in *The Bodyguard*.
4 This Chicago-born actor found fame in *Star Wars* and the *Indiana Jones* series of movies.
5 Born in England in 1929, he went to Oxford University to study medicine and broke the four-minute mile in 1954.
6 Former fiancé of J Lo, he co wrote the movie *Good Will Hunting* with Matt Damon.
7 Famous for *Uptown Girl* and *Just The Way You Are,* he writes, sings and plays the piano.
8 Born in Edinburgh in 1859, he created the famous detective Sherlock Holmes of Baker Street London.
9 Star of *Butch Cassidy and the Sundance Kid* and *The Sting,* he founded the Sundance film festival in Utah, USA.
10 He won five successive gold medals in successive Olympics and wrote his autobiography *A Golden Age* in 2000.

ANSWERS ON PAGE 293

278 COMPUTERS

1 In which decade were the first Apple Macs produced?
☐ 1960s ☐ 1970s ☐ 1980s

2 How many lines of keys do the letters take up on a keyboard?
☐ Two ☐ Three ☐ Five

3 What goes with black, yellow and cyan in colour printing?
☐ Blue ☐ Magenta ☐ Purple

4 What does the I stand for in RSI?
☐ Injury ☐ Interface ☐ Internet

5 What is type size measured in?
☐ Blocks ☐ Pints ☐ Points

6 Cascade and Jerusalem were both types of what?
☐ Drive ☐ Software ☐ Virus

7 What is a single box in a spreadsheet called?
☐ Cell ☐ Glitch ☐ Label

8 What does the M stand for in MIDI?
☐ Manipulated ☐ Mini ☐ Musical

9 What does a degauss button get rid of on a monitor?
☐ Colour ☐ Lines ☐ Static

10 Which worldwide virus was detected in Hong Kong in May 2000?
☐ Crash ☐ I Love You ☐ Meltdown

11 Which letter is between a C and a B on a keyboard?
☐ J ☐ N ☐ V

12 What word is given to text lined up on the left and right?
☐ Aligned ☐ Justified ☐ Tabulated

13 What does the L stand for in ALU?
☐ Located ☐ Logged ☐ Logic

14 If you change one film image into another what are you doing?
☐ Filtering ☐ Morphing ☐ Wrapping

15 Which side of the apple has a piece missing in an Apple Mac logo?
☐ Left
☐ Right
☐ Top

ANSWERS ON PAGE 293

279 PEOPLE

1 What is David Bailey famous for?

2 How many days after Princess Diana's death was the death of Mother Teresa announced?

3 Max Clifford became famous in which line of activity?

4 What do kd lang's initials stand for?

5 Which larger than life opera star launched a perfume for men named after him?

6 What is the name of Joan Collins' novelist sister?

7 Which part of his body did soccer goalkeeper David Seaman insure for £1 million?

8 Which actor Kenneth was Emma Thompson's first husband?

9 What did Michael Jackson say instead of "I do" when he married Lisa Marie Presley?

10 Brooklyn Beckham is the son of which Spice Girl ?

11 What is Hillary Clinton's daughter called?

12 Richard Gere won a scholarship to the University of Massachusetts in which sport?

13 How did US Ambassador Shirley Temple Black earn fame and fortune as a child?

14 Which singer Cleo is married to Johnny Dankworth?

15 After his defection in 1961 Rudolf Nureyev took citizenship of which country in 1982?

16 Which Peter co-founded the Aldeburgh Festival in East Anglia?

17 Child expert Dr Spock won an Olympic gold medal in what event?

18 Which school was founded by Kurt Hahn in 1934?

19 What were pilot Bomber Harris's real first names?

20 Which veteran actor owned the restaurant Langan's Brasserie?

ANSWERS ON PAGE 293

280 THE HEADLINES

1 How long were Britney Spears and Jason Allen Alexander married?

2 In which city did the ill-fated Millennium Dome open?

3 Who was the first cartoon character to appear on a US postage stamp?

4 Which Prime Minister declared war on Germany in 1939?

5 In which decade of the 20th century was the Boy Scout movement founded?

6 How was the Geheime Staatspolizei better known?

7 According to the wartime slogan, careless talk does what?

8 In which year was the Easter Rising in Dublin?

9 Lord Nuffield founded which car company which originally bore his name?

10 What type of clinic did Marie Stopes open?

11 Which Russian leader died in 1924?

12 In which decade did the Wall Street Crash take place?

13 In which German city was the Nazi party founded?

14 Which "Queen" left on her maiden voyage across the Atlantic in 1946?

15 Which British Duke and Duchess famously visited Hitler in Berlin in 1937?

16 Which island received a medal for gallantry after WWII?

17 Which city called the German Florence was heavily bombed in 1945?

18 Which now annual arts Festival opened for the first time in Scotland in 1947?

19 Where was the first gold rush in Western Australia in 1885?

20 Which actor who had been involved in Hary Potter movies died aged 72 in October 2002?

ANSWERS ON PAGE 293

281 MUSICALS

1 If Sky and Nathan were Guys, what were Sarah and Miss Adelaide?

2 Which Sweet musical had the show-stopper *Rhythm of Life*?

3 Which show was based on the autobiography of Gypsy Rose Lee?

4 *South Pacific* was set during which war?

5 Which musical was based on the life of Annie Oakley?

6 What was the name of the first hippie musical?

7 The King in the *King And I* is ruler of where?

8 Which show, which opened in the 1940s, takes its name from a fairground attraction?

9 What was *Jesus Christ* according to the Rice/Lloyd Webber show?

10 What did the Little Shop hold in the movie which premiered in 1982?

11 In which country is *My Fair Lady* set?

12 Which Line was the longest-running musical in Broadway history?

13 Where was the Fiddler in the musical's title?

14 In which decade did *Godspell* open on Broadway?

15 Which circus musical starred Glenn Close as the hero's wife on Broadway?

16 Where was the *Best Little Whorehouse* according to the musical title?

17 Which Count appears in *The Woman In White*?

18 Which revival hit shares its name with a gangster city?

19 *Annie Warbucks* was the sequel to which one-word titled musical?

20 Which George wrote *Crazy For You*?

ANSWERS ON PAGE 293

282 HALF CHANCE

½? ½? ½?

1 Hilary Swank appeared in *Million Dollar* what – Baby or Man?

2 Which country was first to have ten kings all called Rameses – China or Egypt?

3 In which decade did the Mini car first appear on British roads – 1950s or 1960s?

4 In the human skeleton, is the fibula above or below the patella?

5 Did the character Charlie Hungerford appear in *Bergerac* or *The Sopranos*?

6 Was it in the 1920s or 1930s that Jesse Owens set a long-standing long jump record?

7 The Disney animation about Moses was called *Prince Of* where – Egypt or Israel?

8 In *Bewitched* what did Samantha twitch to cast a spell – her ear or her nose?

9 In which London street did Sweeney Todd operate – Bond Street or Fleet Street?

10 What do people usually do with a Stradivarius – play it or wear it?

11 Yassir Arafat led which organisation known by its initials – FBI or PLO?

12 What does foodie Rick Stein specialise in – fish or wine?

13 What is the second highest mountain in the world called – K2 or K10?

14 Which month was named after Mars, the god of war – March or May?

15 Which item is now the biggest cause of seabird death – hunting or oil pollution?

16 The UAE stands for which United Emirates – Arab or Asian?

17 A praying mantis is a type of what – an insect or religious hermit?

18 What does the first A stand for in NASA – Aeronautics or American?

19 Which UK TV show coined the catchphrase "Pass" – *Mastermind* or *The Weakest Link*?

20 Which John made a comeback in the movie *Pulp Fiction* – Belushi or Travolta?

ANSWERS ON PAGE 293

283 MANCHESTER UNITED

1 Which United manager signed Eric Cantona?

2 How old was Ryan Giggs when he made his first team debut?

3 Who wrote the autobiography *The Good, The Bad And The Bubbly*?

4 Which player went to Newcastle as part of the deal that bought Andy Cole?

5 In which country was Sir Matt Busby born?

6 Which club was Paul Ince bought from?

7 Mark Hughes has moved from Man Utd twice. Which clubs did he join?

8 Which team were the opponents in the Cantona Kung-Fu spectator attack in January 1995?

9 Alex Ferguson sold his son Darren to which club?

10 Who is the elder of the Neville brothers?

11 What was Denis Law's usual shirt number?

12 What infamous first went to Kevin Moran in the 1985 FA Cup Final?

13 What is the surname of 1970s brothers Brian and Jimmy?

14 Which Utd manager signed Bryan Robson?

15 Who was the scoring skipper in the 1996 FA Cup Final?

16 Which country did Peter Schmeichel play for?

17 Ruud Van Nistelrooy joined Man Utd from which club?

18 Which name links former United players Beckham, May and Saddler?

19 Which two United players were members of England's World Cup winning team?

20 Who was the first Man Utd player to hit five goals in a Premier League match?

ANSWERS ON PAGE 293

284 LUCKY DIP

1 Which country is Aeroflot from?

2 What was the currency of Germany before adopting the Euro?

3 Which instrument measures a plane's height above sea level?

4 Who recorded the album *Listen Without Prejudice*?

5 Who played the Bandit in *Smokey and The Bandit*?

6 Which King of England abdicated?

7 In rhyming slang what is meant by rabbit and pork?

8 Which Ronnie Barker comedy was set inside a prison?

9 In pop music, who took their name from characters in the Tintin cartoons?

10 In the Bible, what is the first book of the Old Testament?

11 What is the common name for the complaint bursitis?

12 In which country is La Scala opera house?

13 In the British army which rank comes between Lieutenant and Major?

14 What colour is the gem jet?

15 In which sport might you see a Chinaman and a maiden?

16 How many sides has a heptagon?

17 What type of creature is used for the dish Bombay duck?

18 Where on your body is your olfactory organ?

19 Which major river flows through Liverpool?

20 Who topped the UK and US charts with the album *Kid A*?

ANSWERS ON PAGE 293

285 PICTURE QUIZ

What links these four pictures?

ANSWERS ON PAGE 293

286 THE 2004 OLYMPICS

Is each statement TRUE or FALSE?

T F **1** Greece entered the stadium first at the opening ceremony.

T F **2** The first gold medal of the games was won by the USA.

T F **3** Cian O'Connor won Ireland's only medal.

T F **4** Michael Phelps won seven gold medals.

T F **5** The last gold medal of the games was won by Italy.

T F **6** The Olympics were held in the month of July.

T F **7** The top European country in the medals table was Germany.

T F **8** The top Asian country was Russia.

T F **9** Chile and Israel won gold medals for the first time.

T F **10** China won 643 medals in all.

ANSWERS ON PAGE 293

287 RIVERS

1 Which great river has its source in the mountains of Burundi?
☐ Amazon ☐ Nile ☐ Yangtze

2 What is the longest river in the UK?
☐ Severn ☐ Thames ☐ Tyne

3 Which river runs through Belgrade, Budapest and Vienna?
☐ Danube ☐ Rhine ☐ Rhone

4 Which country has the rivers Douro, Tagus and Guadiana?
☐ Italy ☐ Portugal ☐ Spain

5 Holy Loch is an inlet of which river?
☐ Don ☐ Clyde ☐ Tyne

6 On which river are the Niagara Falls?
☐ Niagara ☐ Victoria ☐ Zambesi

7 Where does the River Loire flow into the Atlantic?
☐ Brest ☐ La Rochelle ☐ Nantes

8 In Russian folklore what name is often applied to the Volga?
☐ Father ☐ Mother ☐ Sister

9 On which river does the city of Florence stand?
☐ Arno ☐ Basento ☐ Po

10 On which long river is the Aswan Dam?
☐ Amazon ☐ Nile ☐ Yangtze

11 What is the location of the Orinoco in America?
☐ Central ☐ North
☐ South

12 How many tributaries does the Amazon have?
☐ 5,000 ☐ 10,000
☐ 15,000

13 Which famous Falls are on the Zambesi?
☐ Angel ☐ Niagara ☐ Victoria

14 The Oise and the Marne are tributaries of which river?
☐ Danube ☐ Rhine ☐ Seine

15 Which Sir George gave his name to an Australian river?
☐ Darling ☐ Murray ☐ Thomson

ANSWERS ON PAGE 293

288 GENERAL KNOWLEDGE

  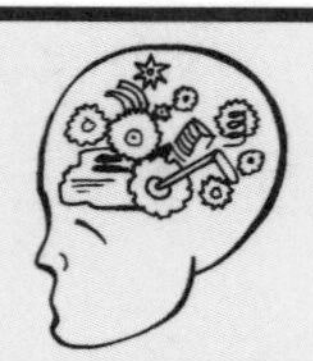

1 Which Ancient British priests were linked with mistletoe?

2 What does a theodolite measure?

3 Which poisonous gas is given off from a car exhaust?

4 In Scotland, what are Eigg, Muck and Rhum?

5 What is ornithology?

6 Robert Menzies was a Prime Minister of which country?

7 What is the currency of Poland?

8 What colour are the flowers of St. John's Wort?

9 In maths, what is meant by three dots in a triangular formation?

10 Traditionally, what does a cooper make?

11 Which motorway goes east to west across the Pennines in England?

12 What are workers and drones types of?

13 What is the middle name of Winston S. Churchill?

14 On what calendar date is Burns' Night?

15 What is the home of a beaver called?

16 How many stations are there on a Monopoly board?

17 Which spaceman appeared on the front page of the original 1950s *Eagle* comic?

18 What has the body of a lion and the head of a human?

19 Who invented the method by which the blind can read by touch?

20 Segovia is associated with which musical instrument?

ANSWERS ON PAGE 293

289 FOOD AND DRINK

1 What colour is the flesh of a cantaloupe melon?

2 Simnel cake was traditionally eaten on which Sunday?

3 What type of oven is traditionally used for a tandoori?

4 What is a champignon?

5 What type of milk was first processed in 1899?

6 Which expensive vinegar is aged in wooden barrels?

7 What is added to pasta to make it green?

8 Which drink is grown in the Douro basin and exported from Oporto?

9 Which cooking pot boils food at a higher temperature than boiling point?

10 What is another name for dietary fibre?

11 What is bisque – a dessert, a sauce or a soup?

12 Where did satsumas originate?

13 What are cornichons?

14 Puerto Rico and Jamaica are the main producers of which spirit?

15 What colour is cayenne pepper?

16 What type of pastry is used to make a steak and kidney pudding?

17 Which drink is served in a schooner?

18 What is a Laxton's Superb?

19 Which seafood, usually fried in breadcrumbs, is the Italian name for shrimps?

20 Tofu and TVP come from which bean?

ANSWERS ON PAGE 293

290 OPERA

1. Which country is Kiri Te Kanawa from?
2. What are the Christian names of the three tenors?
3. Which German composer's only opera was *Fidelio*?
4. Which Gilbert and Sullivan operetta is set in the Tower of London?
5. Which composer from East Anglia wrote the opera *Peter Grimes*?
6. What was the nationality of composer Aaron Copland?
7. What was the name of Gounod's opera based on *Doctor Faustus*?
8. How did Lehar describe the Widow in his operetta?
9. Who wrote *Madame Butterfly* and *La Boheme*?
10. Which opera does *Nessun Dorma* come from?
11. Which work did The Who call a rock opera?
12. Where was the barber from in the title of Rossini's opera?
13. How is Kurt Weill's *Die Dreigroschenoper* better known?
14. What does an operetta have which an opera usually doesn't?
15. Which Russian-born composer wrote *The Rite of Spring*?
16. What is Lesley Garrett's home county in England?
17. Which surname is shared by composers Johann and Richard?
18. Which Italian composer's English name would be Joseph Green?
19. For which sporting event did *Nessun Dorma* become a TV theme tune?
20. What is the religious equivalent of opera without costumes and scenery?

ANSWERS ON PAGE 293

291 TRAVEL

1. What is the currency of Bolivia?
2. Between which two rivers does Manhattan lie?
3. What is the most northeastern US state?
4. In which country is the city of Curitiba?
5. What is the capital of Brunei?
6. In which country is the deepwater port of Lobito?
7. The islands of of Taipa and Coloane are part of which possession?
8. Pluna Airlines are based in which country?
9. Which capital is further north – Khartoum or Addis Ababa?
10. What is the official language of Bhutan?
11. In which country is Kakadu National Park?
12. Which country is due north of Uruguay?
13. Which two countries border Morocco?
14. Which desert lies between the Kalahari and the Atlantic Ocean?
15. Where is the news agency Colprensa based?
16. What is Madison Square Garden situated over?
17. On which island is Nassau, the capital of the Bahamas?
18. In which US state was the first National Park?
19. How is Denali in Alaska also known?
20. The Negev desert tapers to which port?

ANSWERS ON PAGE 293

292 THE 1970s

70's? 70's? 70's?

1. What did Ceylon change its name to?
2. What was the name of the mansion where Elvis Presley died?
3. Pol Pot overran which country in 1970?
4. A revolution in which country led to the overthrow of the Shah?
5. Who did Captain Mark Phillips marry at Westminster Abbey?
6. Which company developed the Walkman?
7. What was the name of the fashionable short pants worn by women?
8. Which supersonic transatlantic commercial aircraft came into service?
9. Which French Film Festival celebrated its 25th anniversary in 1971?
10. Which country, capital Beirut, saw civil war?
11. Who was Satchmo who passed away in 1971?
12. The monarchy was restored to power in which European country?
13. Who or what was Chia Chia?
14. What type of *Fields* were linked with Cambodia?
15. The Aswan High Dam was opened in which country?
16. Which daughter of Judy Garland found success with the movie *Cabaret*?
17. In 1979 the Shah was forced to flee from which country?
18. Who became the first US President to resign from office?
19. In which African country did Steve Biko die?
20. Which Czechoslovakian-born sportswoman Martina defected to America?

ANSWERS ON PAGE 293

293 TELEVISION

1. What was the name of Charlotte's first husband in *Sex And The City*?
2. Who plays Grace in *Will And Grace*?
3. What was the surname of *The Beverly Hillbillies*?
4. Which character in *Desperate Housewives* was a model before her marriage?
5. Who is Bart Simpson's teacher?
6. At which city hospital did Charlie Fairhead used to work?
7. In *Dad's Army*, Lance Corporal Jones ran what type of shop?
8. Who or what was Worzel Gummidge?
9. *Prisoner Cell Block H* was made in which country?
10. Which Alan portrayed the character Jonathan Creek?
11. Which drama series set in the Edwardian era featured the wealthy Bellamy family?
12. Which comedian played Edmund Blackadder?
13. Which creepy family had a butler called Lurch?
14. Which sitcom featured Bill and Ben Porter?
15. How did Alan Bradley die in *Coronation Street*?
16. Which series featured the character Jessica Fletcher?
17. In *Sex And The City* what is Samantha Jones' job?
18. What type of cartoon creature was Mr Jinks?
19. *I Could Be So Good For You* was the theme tune to which comedy drama?
20. Who was Peter Cook's partner?

ANSWERS ON PAGE 293

294 NAME GAME

How are these celebrities better known?

1 CHRISTIAN HAWKINS

2 KRISHNA BHANJI

3 ELAINE BICKERSTAFF

4 ARTHUR JEFFERSON

5 ERIC CLAPP

6 IVO LIVI

7 WILLIAM BAILEY

8 JOYCE FRANKENBURG

9 DORIS KAPELHOFF

10 NICHOLAS COPPOLA

ANSWERS ON PAGE 293

295 WHO SAID . . . ?

1 "How can anyone believe I won't win? Don't I look more beautiful than ever?"

2 "I may look like a Bedford truck but somehow I give the promise of having a V8 engine."

3 "Art is a lie that makes us realise the truth."

4 "To be the mother of a great man is far more important than to produce a great work of art."

5 "All the art in the world isn't worth a good potato pie."

6 "Intellectually I'm a caveman."

7 "First I lost my weight, then I lost my voice, now I've lost Onassis."

8 "If only men go into space there will be no order there at all."

ANSWERS ON PAGE 293

296 THE BLUES

1 What is Eric Clapton's nickname?
☐ Handy Man ☐ Slider ☐ Slowhand

2 Which Birds featured Eric Clapton and Jimmy Page?
☐ Caged birds ☐ Jailbirds ☐ Yardbirds

3 Which 1920s singer recorded *Down Hearted Blues*?
☐ Sara Martin ☐ Bessie Smith ☐ Ma Rainie

4 The urban blues of the 1920s centred on which US city?
☐ Chicago ☐ New Orleans ☐ New York

5 What was John Mayall's group known as?
☐ Blue Boys ☐ Bluesbreakers ☐ Blues Brothers

6 Who did Diana Ross play in *Lady Sings The Blues*?
☐ Herself ☐ Billie Holliday ☐ Bessie Smith

7 Which veteran John Lee recorded *The Healer*?
☐ Clapton ☐ Hooker ☐ Waters

8 Which instrument did Little Walter play?
☐ Guitar ☐ Harmonica ☐ Piano

9 Who recorded *Hoochie Coochie Man* and *Got My Mojo Working*?
☐ Son House ☐ Muddy Waters ☐ Howlin' Wolf

10 In which country was Alexis Korner born?
☐ France ☐ South Africa ☐ USA

11 Which bluesman Long John sang *Let The Heartaches Begin*?
☐ Baldry ☐ Elton ☐ McTell

12 Which guitarist made the album *Ballads And Blues*?
☐ Hank Marvin ☐ Brian May ☐ Gary Moore

13 Who joined Bruce and Clapton in Cream?
☐ Cook ☐ Cooper ☐ Baker

14 Who had a hit with *I Guess That's Why They Call It The Blues*?
☐ Elton John ☐ R.E.M. ☐ Dire Straits

15 Which word goes with Lemon Jefferson?
☐ Blind ☐ Howling ☐ Tall

ANSWERS ON PAGE 293

297 LUCKY DIP

1 Who wrote the music for the *The Threepenny Opera*?

2 Which botanist gave his name to fuchsias?

3 What nationality was ballet star Rudolf Nureyev?

4 Who is known as "The Big Yin"?

5 Which two states battled for victory during the Punic Wars?

6 Who left an unfinished novel called *Sanditon*?

7 On a computer keyboard what letter is far left on the lowest row of letters?

8 Who was LB in *Dynasty*?

9 Who carried the spirits of dead warriors to Valhalla?

10 The Soviet secret police are known by their initials – what are they?

11 Which actor appeared in drag in the movie *Tootsie*?

12 In Bryan Adams' mega hit which three words come before, *I Do It For You*?

13 The album *One By One* was a chart sucess for which Fighters?

14 Who said, "To err is human but it feels divine"?

15 Which precinct does Ed McBain write about?

16 Which fruit is dried to make prunes?

17 If an elderly couple are happily married who are they likened to?

18 Which city has given its name to a wheelchair and to a bun?

19 Which sport is played at Rosslyn Park?

20 What is the term for a period of play in polo?

ANSWERS ON PAGE 293

298 INVENTIONS

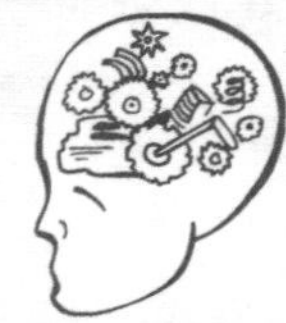
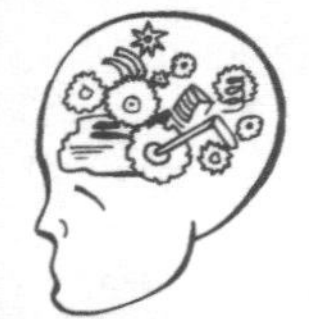

1 Which method of fast writing did Pitman develop?

2 Which two major electronics companies developed the CD in 1979?

3 What was invented by US students using aluminium flan cases?

4 In which country was the first modern motorway created?

5 Who registered the first patents for the rail sleeping car?

6 Which Swiss company developed the first widely used instant coffee?

7 Which rubber-based product was patented in the US in 1869?

8 Why was the invention of the electric iron useless in the US in 1882?

9 What was American Mr Bissel's dust-collecting invention?

10 What was the surname of King Camp who invented the safety razor?

11 What was the occupation of Dom Pierre Perignon who developed the champagne process?

12 What type of pens did Pentel invent?

13 Which building toy was designed by Dane, Ole Kirk Christiansen?

14 What is unusual about Mark Button's invention the Koosh ball?

15 Which Kimberley Clark Co invention was first called Celluwipes?

16 Which form of precautionary medicine was discovered by Jenner?

17 What was the nationality of saxophone inventor Adolphe Sax?

18 Which type of transport did John Outram invent in 1775?

19 Which sauce did Henry Heinz invent in 1876?

20 Which company produced the iPod?

ANSWERS ON PAGE 293

299 POP MUSIC

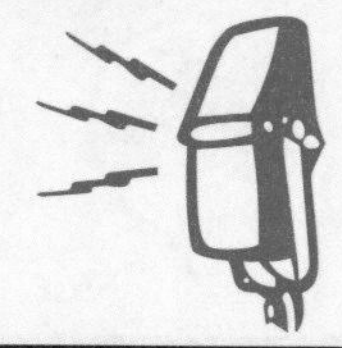
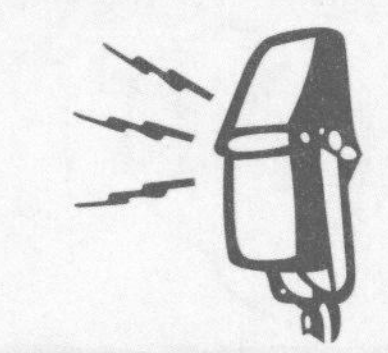
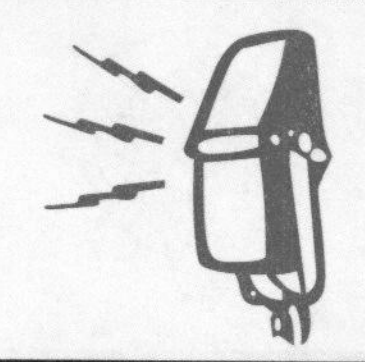

1 Which Daniel recorded the UK chart topping album *Gotta Get Thru This*?

2 Which Michael fronted R.E.M?

3 Which group launched their career with *The Sultans Of Swing*?

4 Which Australian singer inspired INXS's *Suicide Blonde*?

5 Which song from the movie *Bridget Jones's Diary* gave Geri Halliwell a hit in 2001?

6 What was Elton John's first solo No 1 in the US?

7 Which nickname did The Verve's Richard Ashcroft have?

8 What was the most famous song on Queen's album *A Night At The Opera*?

9 With which music legend did U2's Bono sing *I've Got You Under My Skin*?

10 How many members did the Manic Street Preachers originally have?

11 What was Billie's first UK No 1?

12 Which port provided a hit for The Beautiful South?

13 What's the only battle to have been the one-word title of a UK No 1?

14 What colour was the wine that UB40 sang about?

15 Which chart-smashing group featured Adams, Brown and Chisholm?

16 Which UK No 1 of 1999 featured a 50+ female choir on vocals?

17 Which band released the hit album *New Jersey*?

18 Who had her first UK No 1 with *Wuthering Heights*?

19 Who did Chrissie Hynde guest with for *I Got You Babe*?

20 Which group, whose name is a repeated word, played a US gig in 2003 after an 18-year break?

ANSWERS ON PAGE 293

300 NATURE

1 Where is water stored in a cactus plant?

2 Are most conifers evergreen or deciduous?

3 Ceps and chanterelles are types of what?

4 Flax is grown to produce which fabric?

5 Which drug is obtained from the coca plant?

6 Bamboo is the tallest type of what?

7 Which Mexican drink comes from the agave plant?

8 Is it true or false that laurel has poisonous leaves?

9 The petiole is which part of a plant?

10 What colour is cuckoo spit?

11 Juniper is the flavouring in which drink?

12 What colour are oil seed rape flowers?

13 What goes before lavender and holly to make another plant's name ?

14 What can be obtained from the cassava plant which would have gone in a typical school dinner pudding?

15 What are tulips grown from?

16 Does a polyanthus have a single or several blooms?

17 Which ingredient in tonic water comes from the bark of the cinchona?

18 Which plants would a viticulturist grow?

19 Wild cornflowers are usually what colour?

20 Which paintbrush cleaner is found in the resin of a conifer?

ANSWERS ON PAGE 293

301 ARTISTS

1 Who painted *The Blue Boy* and *Mr & Mrs Andrews*?

2 Which Pierre-Auguste painted *Umbrellas* and *The Bathers*?

3 What is Leonardo Da Vinci's *La Gioconda* also known as?

4 In which century did Vincent Van Gogh live?

5 Whose *Progress* did William Hogarth paint?

6 What is arguably the most famous painting by Dutchman Frans Hals?

7 Which Egyptian sculpture is more than 73m long?

8 Which 1960s art vogue was based on optical illusion?

9 What is paint applied to in a fresco?

10 Which sculpture did Auguste Bartholdi give to the USA?

11 What is notable about the woman in Ingres' *Valpinçon Bather*?

12 What type of work is Albrecht Dürer famous for?

13 Of which school of painting was Claude Monet a leading exponent?

14 What type of art form is a Japanese netsuke?

15 Who painted *Bubbles*, which has been used in a soap ad?

16 Which English sculptor produced rounded forms such as *Reclining Figure*?

17 Which Spaniard is known for his hallucinatory paintings?

18 What is the binding medium in gouache technique?

19 Who painted Campbell soup cans?

20 What type of paintings is Joshua Reynolds famous for?

ANSWERS ON PAGE 293

302 GENERAL KNOWLEDGE

1 What is the name of the singing bear in Disney's *Jungle Book*?

2 What is the capital city of Malta?

3 Where in the body is the thyroid gland?

4 In politics what is the opposite of a dove?

5 What is another name for the Northern Lights?

6 What is the main language spoken in Mexico?

7 Who wrote *Paradise Lost*?

8 A coney is what sort of animal?

9 When Jesus was crucified, which Roman was governor of Jerusalem?

10 What name was given to a seller of illegal alcohol?

11 Which Scottish Isle became linked to the mainland by a bridge in 1995?

12 Which British Prime Minister was known as "Dizzy"?

13 Henry Cotton became famous in which sport?

14 What name is given to a vertical divide in a window?

15 In the song *I Believe*, what happens for every drop of rain that falls?

16 Which word of four letters can go after beach and before gown to make new words?

17 What colour is the Northern Line on a London Underground map?

18 Astrakhan comes from which creature?

19 What is the practice of favouring your own relatives?

20 Which British Prime Minister spoke of "peace in our time"?

ANSWERS ON PAGE 293

303 PICTURE QUIZ

A B C D

Which of these was developed first?

ANSWERS ON PAGE 294

304 NAME THE YEAR

1 A Pan Am jet exploded over Lockerbie. South Korea hosted the Olympic Games. An earthquake caused devastation in Armenia.

2 Jesse Owens won four Olympic gold medals. *The Queen Mary* left Southampton on its maiden voyage to New York. Charlie Chaplin made his final silent movie.

3 Sharon Stone starred in the controversial *Basic Instinct*. Andre Agassi won his first Wimbledon Singles title. The USA celebrated the 500th anniversary of Columbus's arrival.

4 The satellite Telstar was launched. Marilyn Monroe died. John Glenn became the first American to orbit the Earth.

5 President Marcos was overthrown in the Philippines. US *Challenger* space shuttle exploded killing its crew. Chernobyl power station caught fire.

6 Edison announced the invention of the electric battery. A major exhibition of El Greco's work was held in Madrid. Beatrix Potter's *Peter Rabbit* made his literary debut.

ANSWERS ON PAGE 294

305 SPORT

1 Which city has a team of Bulls and a team of Bears?

2 Who has managed both Monaco and Arsenal?

3 Which golfer said in 1998, "The ball doesn't know how old you are"?

4 Which post-war cricketer played his first England game aged 18 and his last aged 45?

5 In which sport in 90s Britain did Leopards overcome Sharks in a final?

6 Terry Mancini played soccer for which country?

7 In which decade did Alex Higgins first become snooker world champion?

8 What has been won by *Australia II* and *America³*?

9 Who won golf's US Open in 1994 and 1997 and the British Open in 2002?

10 Which player who was with Arsenal scored for France in the 1998 World Cup Final?

11 Colin Jackson was a world record-holder in which event?

12 Did Nadia Comaneci first score a perfect Olympic 10 at the age of 14, 16 or 18?

13 In which US state is the Masters golf tournament played?

14 Brian Boitano won Olympic gold wearing what on his feet?

15 In which shport are there Cardinals in St Louis and Royals in Kansas City?

16 In 1994 which golfer won the US Amateur Championship for the first time?

17 In which sport did Steve Baddeley win 143 caps in the 1980s?

18 Who did Damon Hill join after he was dropped by Williams?

19 Golf star Vijay Singh comes from where?

20 The early days of which sport featured the Renshaw twins and the Baddeley twins?

ANSWERS ON PAGE 294

SUMMER

Get out the deckchair, and have a relax as you tackle these 50 questions about the crazy, lazy, hazy days of summer.

1 In which month is Midsummer Day in the Northern Hemisphere?

2 When is St Swithin's Day?

3 If it rains on St Swithin's Day how many days of rain are supposedly likely to follow?

4 In 852 AD Swithin was appointed Bishop of where?

5 Which three star signs are the summer signs?

6 What name is given to the hot days between 3rd July and 11th August?

7 From which musical does the song *Summer Nights* come from?

8 Which Shakespeare play has Summer in the title?

9 What are the two main ingredients of a summer pudding?

10 At the festival of Kodomono-Hi the Japanese fly flags shaped like which fish?

11 Which summer month is named after Roman queen of the gods?

12 Çocuk Bayrami is a children's festival in which country?

13 Eid ul Fitr is the breaking of what in the Muslim calendar?

14 In which country is an Eisteddfod celebrated?

15 Where were the summer Olympics of 2000 held?

16 Which festival was initiated by the UN General Assembly in 1972?

17 Where were the last Summer Olympics to be held in Europe staged?

18 Who wrote the music for *Don't Let the Sun Go Down on Me*?

19 Which US state is called the Sunflower state?

20 Which American playwright wrote the screenplay and play of *The Sunshine Boys*?

21 What Summer is a late calm period, or a period of fine weather in autumn?

QUIZ

22 What was Canada Day originally called?

23 At which Summer Olympics was the Marathon first established?

24 Which French monarch was called the "Sun King"?

25 Which summer sport is played with bat, ball, pads and wickets?

26 Which Sixties band sang about *Summer In The City*?

27 Where was the F.I.F.A. World Cup held in the summer of 1998?

28 How many million miles is the Sun from the Earth?

29 Is it Prince William or Prince Harry who has a summer birthday in June?

30 Which film and stage musical is about some friends taking a bus to Europe for a vacation?

31 In which country did Princess Diana tragically die in the summer of 1997?

32 Where will be the Summer Olympic Asian venue of 2008?

33 Which President celebrated his 80th birthday on 19th July 1998 in Johannesburg?

34 In which summer month do the Wimbledon tennis championships begin?

35 If you were born on 4th July what would your star sign be?

36 What did the Greeks call their sun god?

37 In the summer of 1990 did Martina Navratilova win her 7th, 8th or 9th Wimbledon Singles title?

38 In the 1956 Summer Olympics, why were equestrian events held in Sweden?

39 Canada Day falls on which date (unless it happens to be a Sunday)?

40 Which leaf appears on the Canadian flag?

41 Which martyr shares his saint's day with Midsummer's Day?

42 Who wrote *Summertime* (and the livin' is easy)?

43 Esala Perahera is a Sri Lankan festival of which religion?

44 The ninth month of the Muslim calendar is which holy month?

45 Which animal is an important part of the Sri Lankan Esala Perahera?

46 What do scouts in Turkey plant to celebrate Çocuk Bayrami?

47 At which ancient site on Salisbury Plain do people meet to celebrate the summer solstice?

48 In which decade of the 20th century was Donna Summer born?

49 Which family members celebrate their love for each other in the festival Raksha Bandhan?

50 Which US state is called the Sunshine state?

ANSWERS ON PAGE 294

307 AMERICAN LITERATURE

1 Against which background is Hemingway's *For Whom The Bell Tolls* told?

2 Which American-born novelist lived in France and became a British citizen in 1915?

3 Who wrote *Who's Afraid Of Virginia Woolf?*?

4 In which Arthur Miller play do you meet Willy Loman?

5 Which title is a work of literature by Herman Melville and an opera by Benjamin Britten?

6 Where are most of Pearl S. Buck's novels set?

7 Who wrote the short story *I Robot* in 1950?

8 Who died at the age of 44 with his novel *The Last Tycoon* unfinished?

9 Who wrote the *Leatherstocking* tales on frontier life with their hero Natty Bumpo?

10 *A Farewell To Arms* is based on Hemingway's own experience as what in World War I?

11 Where were Robert Frost's poems first published?

12 Which character appears in all nine of Raymond Chandler's novels?

13 Who wrote *The Maltese Falcon*?

14 Louisa May Alcott's saga *Little Women* is about which sisters?

15 Which Norman Mailer novel is based on a protest march on the Pentagon?

16 Whose novels are about social and economic conditions especially of farmers in his native California?

17 Which dramatist wrote *A Long Day's Journey Into Night*?

18 Where is the setting for Hemingway's *The Old Man And The Sea*?

19 What is Frank L. Baum's most famous story?

20 Which US poet married Ted Hughes, later Poet Laureate?

ANSWERS ON PAGE 294

308 HALF CHANCE

½? ½? ½?

1 Where were thousands of Kurds killed in the 1980s – Iraq or Syria?

2 Was the perambulator an early type of baby buggy or zimmer frame?

3 Other than English, which language is spoken in Canada – French or Spanish?

4 Who went with Butt Head in the TV series – Bean Bag or Beavis?

5 Which is the first name to have been used by eight Kings of England – Edward or Henry?

6 Is a banshee a type of ghost or an illegal spirit?

7 What colour was Tin Tin's dog – black or white?

8 When were you born if your birthdate occcurs only once in four years – 29th February or 1st April?

9 In the saying, what will the mice do when the cat's away – make hay or play?

10 Which country along with Brazil in South America begins with a B – Bolivia or Botswana?

11 Was the first personal stereo called a Soundabout or a Walkman?

12 Which European country beginnings with an S is landlocked – Sweden or Switzerland?

13 What sort of Hat was the title of an elegant Fred Astaire movie – *Baseball* or *Top*?

14 Anna Edson Taylor was the first person to travel Niagara Falls in what – a barrel or a canoe?

15 What is the traditional colour of the headwear known as a fez – red or white?

16 Ford cars were originally made in which country – UK or USA?

17 What title does the vampire have in the story *Dracula* – Baron or Count?

18 What would you do with a deerstalker – fire it or wear it on the head?

19 In the UK, what special day follows Shrove Tuesday – Ash Wednesday or St Swithin's Day?

20 What colour is the Taj Mahal – yellow or white?

ANSWERS ON PAGE 294

309 RICH AND FAMOUS

£$ £$ £$

1 Who had a cabinet known as the Tycoon's Club, with 13 of the 16 core members being millionaires?

2 Who founded Standard Oil?

3 Fitness trainer Carlos Leon was the father of which singer/actress's child?

4 What was the name of Frank Sinatra's last wife?

5 In which North African country was Mohammed Al-Fayed born?

6 Which of the founders of United Artists had the last name nearest the beginning of the alphabet?

7 What is Madonna's first daughter called?

8 Who presented the first Oscars?

9 Which movie star married jockey Robyn Smith in 1980?

10 In which US state was Wallis Warfield Simpson born?

11 In 1996 who did The Spice Girls say was their Girl Power role model?

12 What is Frankie Dettori's real first name?

13 How did Sir Ranulph Twisleton-Wykeham-Fiennes achieve fame?

14 Madeleine Gurdon is the third wife of which millionaire?

15 What relation was Henry Ford II to Henry Ford?

16 What is the first name of Charles' brother of Saatchi & Saatchi?

17 In which country was Earl Spencer's acrimonious divorce settlement heard?

18 Who did Stella McCartney dedicate her first collection for Chloe to?

19 In which North African country was Yves St Laurent born as Henri Donat Mathieu?

20 What is Caprice's last name?

ANSWERS ON PAGE 294

310 ANIMALS

1 Which land mammal has the largest ears?

2 Which wild animal is the domesticated dog descended from?

3 Are mammals warm-blooded or cold-blooded?

4 Which part of the body has a crown and a root?

5 What is another name for the larynx?

6 Do tigers hunt in packs or alone?

7 Which group of animals shares its name with an archbishop?

8 What type of creature is an Aylesbury?

9 What was the first animal to be domesticated?

10 Cheviot and Suffolk are both types of what?

11 Shrews have acute sense of smell and hearing to compensate for which weak sense?

12 The opossum and the skunk are famous for what?

13 What colour is a grizzly bear?

14 The llama is native to which continent?

15 Which part of a human's body has a cornea?

16 A leveret is a young what?

17 What part of a Basset Hound is particularly long?

18 Which northerly US state is famous for the brown bear?

19 Does the moose live in a warm or cold climate?

20 Are crocodiles carnivores or herbivores?

ANSWERS ON PAGE 294

311 AT THE MOVIES

1 Who in the movie title is the *International Man Of Mystery*?

2 Who directed *Forrest Gump*?

3 Which song won Best Song Oscar for *Breakfast At Tiffany's*?

4 Which Tom won the Best Actor Oscar for *Philadelphia* in 1993?

5 Which Jane starred in *Barbarella*?

6 Which British movie is about the 1924 Olympics?

7 What's the name of the chief villain of *The Lion King*?

8 Which Emma wrote the screenplay for *Sense And Sensibility*?

9 Which boxing legend played himself in *The Greatest*?

10 *Love Me Tender* was the first film for which rock'n'roll star?

11 Which actor links *True Lies, Total Recall* and *Twins*?

12 The character Richard Hannay is in a film about how many steps?

13 Who played Dolly in the 60s movie *Hello Dolly*?

14 Which creatures were In *The Mist* in the Sigourney Weaver movie?

15 Was *Ghostbusters* first released in the 1960s, 70s or 80s?

16 Which epic movie ends with, "Tomorrow is another day"?

17 In which decade of the 20th century was Dennis Quaid born?

18 Which wife of Kenneth Branagh has also been Oscar nominated?

19 Who did Timothy Dalton play in *Licence To Kill*?

20 Who created the accident-prone *Mr Bean*?

ANSWERS ON PAGE 294

312 BEER

1 What does beer contain which ale traditionally didn't?

2 What does CAMRA stand for?

3 What nationality is the lager giant Grolsch?

4 Who did Tolly Cobbold name their Tollyshooter after?

5 Which brewers sponsored the England Test cricket team in 1995?

6 Which beer was said to be "good for you"?

7 In which northern city was Boddington's brewery established?

8 Which beer is made in Southwold in Suffolk?

9 Which has more hops, bitter or mild?

10 Which company has sponsored a pre-Wimbledon tennis tournament?

11 In the USA what is the difference between cider and hard cider?

12 What is advertised as "probably the best lager in the world"?

13 On which brewer's site in Chiswick, London, has there been a brewery for more than 300 years?

14 What colour is porter?

15 Which lager "reached the parts other beers couldn't reach"?

16 Where are lambic and faro beers made?

17 What expected ingredient is missing from lambic and faro beers?

18 Which East Anglian brewery developed Abbot Ale?

19 Which West Country drink can be sweet, dry or rough?

20 Thwaites' and Young's were famous for what type of delivery vehicles?

ANSWERS ON PAGE 294

313 PICTURE QUIZ

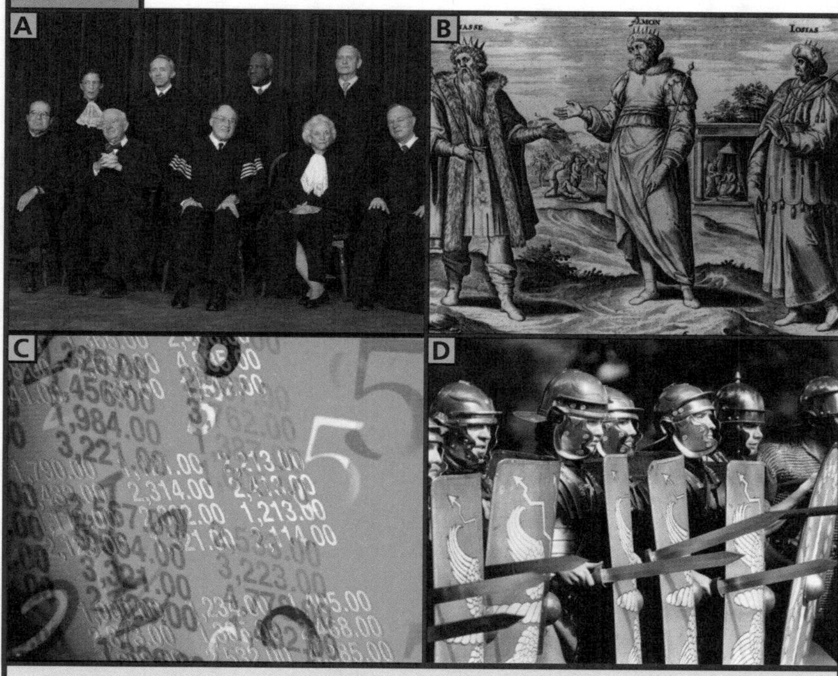

What links these four pictures?

ANSWERS ON PAGE 294

314 DOUBLE TAKE

In each case, the two-part quiz question leads to just one answer!

1 Which word can be a chess piece or a cleric?

2 Which word can be part of a doorway or a dance move?

3 Which word for a criminal is also the name of a shepherd's stick?

4 Which type of music is also the word for a sharp blow?

5 Which word describes where someone lives as well as a speech?

6 Which word can be a musical instrument or a part of the body?

7 Which word for a main performer can also mean a heavenly body?

8 Which word describes a sports field as well as tar?

9 Which word for a coal container also means to scurry or dash?

10 Which word for germs also means records something secretly?

ANSWERS ON PAGE 294

315 FAST FOOD

1 If you had *allium cepa* with your burger what would you have?
☐ Cheese ☐ Fries ☐ Onions

2 Which is the most popular vegetable used to make chips?
☐ Celery ☐ Parsnips ☐ Potatoes

3 When were pressure cookers first manufactured?
☐ 1883 ☐ 1905 ☐ 1921

4 What are the small creamy seeds on top of a burger bun?
☐ Grape ☐ Poppy ☐ Sesame

5 In Chinese cooking what are wooden ears?
☐ Beansprouts ☐ Chopsticks
☐ Fungus

6 What shape is cannelloni pasta?
☐ Flat ☐ Spiral ☐ Tube

7 Charles Strite invented which fast food maker?
☐ Microwave ☐ Teasmade ☐ Toaster

8 What is the topping for a pizza Quattro Formaggio?
☐ Cheeses ☐ Herbs ☐ Tomatoes

9 What is the main ingredient of sushi?
☐ Cheese ☐ Pasta ☐ Rice

10 What is a croque monsieur?
☐ Omelette ☐ Thin pizza
☐ Toasted sandwich

11 If pasta is "all'uovo" what is added?
☐ Cheese ☐ Eggs ☐ Spinach

12 Which dessert was invented as the popsicle?
☐ Fruit fool ☐ Ice cream ☐ Ice lolly

13 Which milk is pizza's Mozzarella cheese made from?
☐ Buffalo ☐ Goat ☐ Sheep

14 Who invented the Mars Bar?
☐ Cadbury ☐ Mars ☐ Rowntree

15 Which sauce is "pickled fish brine" in Chinese?
☐ Chilli ☐ Hoi Sin ☐ Ketchup

ANSWERS ON PAGE 294

316 LUCKY DIP

1 Which name is shared by writer Agatha and athlete Linford?
2 Which sport awards the Harmsworth Trophy?
3 Which country has the international car registration letters DK?
4 Which ruled first in the United Kingdom, the Royal House of Windsor or the House of Hanover?
5 In 2003, who released the highly successful album *Think Tank*?
6 In snooker what is the score for potting a red?
7 O is the symbol of which chemical element?
8 *Myosotis* is more commonly known as which flower?
9 Which Tropic is further north, Capricorn or Cancer?
10 What does the second H stand for in HRH?
11 Which orange seller became mistress of Charles II?
12 What is the Paris underground called?
13 What is the word for a group of hounds?
14 Which sport is a mixture of map reading and cross country running?
15 Which Alfred mapped out moorland routes in northern England?
16 What name is given to an adult male seal?
17 In music, what is the name of the horizontal lines around which notes are written?
18 Which Harold said, "Most of our people have never had it so good."
19 Which group backed Bill Haley in the 50s?
20 Who made his last stand at Little Bighorn?

ANSWERS ON PAGE 294

317 GEOGRAPHY

1 Which language other than English is an official language of the Channel Islands?
2 Which Tsar changed Russia's capital from Moscow to St Petersburg?
3 You would find Palermo on a map of which country?
4 Is Moldova in Europe or Africa?
5 Which continent has an Ivory Coast?
6 On which island is the Giant's Causeway?
7 If you were on a French autoroute what type of road would you be on?
8 Which Gulf lies between Saudi Arabia and Iran?
9 Lake Superior is on the border of the USA and which other country?
10 Which tiny European landlocked state is a Grand Duchy?
11 Macedonia was formerly a part of which communist republic?
12 Which Himalayan kingdom has been called the world's highest rubbish dump because of waste left behind by climbers?
13 Which capital shares its name with a Duke and a boot?
14 Which river which flows through Germany is Europe's dirtiest?
15 Where would you be if you saw Nippon on the map?
16 The Ural Mountains mark the eastern frontier to which continent?
17 Which country has Lakes Garda, Maggiore and Como?
18 Is Madagascar an island or is it an African peninsula?
19 The Home Counties surround which English city?
20 Malta is to the south of which island to the south of Italy?

ANSWERS ON PAGE 294

318 AMERICAN SPORT

1. In American football what does NFL stand for?
2. Which sport do the Buffalo Sabres play?
3. Which club was the first to win the Super Bowl two years in succession on two occasions?
4. Which sport has a Hall of Fame at Cooperstown, New York?
5. Who won the Baseball World Series in 1994?
6. In which sport is the Stanley Cup awarded?
7. Where are the Astros baseball team from?
8. Which city do the Redskins American football team come from?
9. What was "Babe" Ruth's actual name?
10. Which lady sang before the 2005 Super Bowl?
11. Philadelphia 76ers won the 1967 NBA Championship. Which team won every other year in the 1960s?
12. Which basketball team did Magic Johnson play for?
13. The Princeton College rules drawn up in 1867 affect which sport?
14. Which city had two NFL teams in the 1990s but none in 2004?
15. In American football in which year did the AFL and the NFL merge?
16. How many members of an ice hockey team can be on the ice at once?
17. What sport is played by the Detroit Pistons?
18. What was the nickname of baseball's Lawrence Peter Berra?
19. Which city has had Super Bowl-winning Giants and Jets?
20. The invention of which sport is credited to Dr J A Naismith?

ANSWERS ON PAGE 294

319 GENERAL KNOWLEDGE

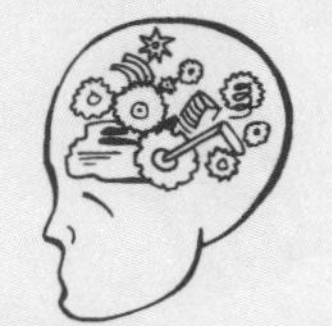
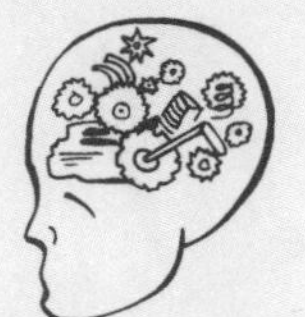

1. Who said, "Anyone who hates children and dogs can't be all bad"?
2. In our solar system which planet takes the least time to orbit the sun?
3. In London, which road runs from Charing Cross to Fleet Street?
4. Whose cave inspired Mendelssohn to compose his *Hebrides Overture*?
5. Who wrote the *Waverley* novels?
6. Which word can go after blue and before neck?
7. What tragedy occurred in Skopje in 1963?
8. Is an okapi an animal, a vegetable or mineral?
9. Which is the home state of former US President Jimmy Carter?
10. On which country's stamps would you find the words Magyar Posta?
11. EasyEverything is the name of a type of what sort of establishment?
12. Cornice and Bon Chretin are types of which fruit?
13. In which part of New York was Barry Manilow born?
14. What did Antonio Stradivari specialise in making?
15. Whose real name is Steveland Judkins?
16. By what English name is the mountain Yr Wyddfa known?
17. Is the suburb of Southgate in the north, south, east or west of London?
18. Which famous British film company is associated with the symbol of a man striking a gong?
19. In Greek tragedy, which king married his own mother?
20. Which star sign is shared by Pat Cash and Steffi Graf?

ANSWERS ON PAGE 294

320 HISTORY

1 Who became US President in 1992 when Governor of Arkansas?

2 Which religious Army was founded by Catherine and William Booth?

3 Which scientist gave his name to the process of pasteurization?

4 Who left $9 million to give prizes in five different fields?

5 Which King of England provided his children with most stepmothers?

6 Who lit the fuse for the 1605 Gunpowder Plot?

7 Was it John Ford or Henry Ford who manufactured cars?

8 During which war did Anne Frank write her diary?

9 Indira Gandhi was Prime Minister of which country?

10 John Paul Getty made his millions from which commodity?

11 Who is Labour leader Neil Kinnock's wife who became an MEP?

12 Who was the first 20th century Prince of Wales to be divorced?

13 How was Argentinian Ernesto Guevara de la Serna better known?

14 William Gladstone was Prime Minister under which monarch?

15 What was suffragette leader Emmeline Goulden's married name?

16 Who became President of Iraq in 1979?

17 How many English kings have been called Stephen?

18 What was the nationality of the Duchess of Windsor?

19 Which legendary cricketer had the first names William Gilbert?

20 How old was Hitler when he died – 46, 56 or 66?

ANSWERS ON PAGE 294

321 QUEEN

 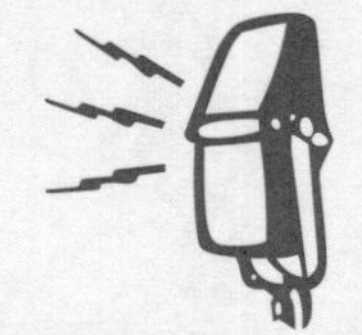 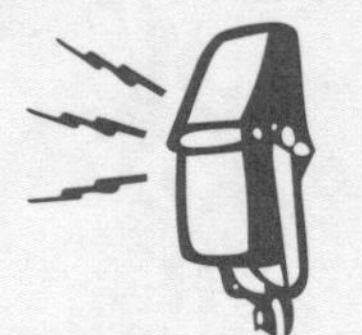

1 Who did Queen team up with for the 2000 version of *We Will Rock You*?

2 Who is Queen's bass player?

3 Who was the oldest member of the original line up of Queen?

4 Who did Freddie Mercury record *Barcelona* with to tie in with the Spanish Olympic Games?

5 Which song famously mentions Moet et Chandon?

6 Which 1970s album shared its name with a newspaper?

7 Which hit with David Bowie featured on the album *Hot Space*?

8 Which album in 1991 was also the name of a UK No 1 single?

9 Which album first featured *Killer Queen*?

10 What was Freddie's only solo UK No 1 single?

11 Which member of the band recorded the solo album *Back To The Light*?

12 Which 1995 album was dedicated to the "immortal spirit of Freddie Mercury"?

13 Where did Queen play a legendary free concert in London in 1976?

14 Which stately home was the scene of their final live concert with Freddie Mercury?

15 Which member of the band was born outside the UK?

16 What was the first track on *A Night At The Opera*?

17 Which decade's hits featured on the album *Live Killers*?

18 What sort of race was on the other side of *Fat Bottomed Girls*?

19 What was the follow-up album to *A Night At The Opera*?

20 Who scripted the stage musical *We Will Rock You*?

ANSWERS ON PAGE 294

322 WORLD SOCCER

Can you give the country that each of these international soccer stars has represented?

1. GABRIEL BATISTUTA
2. EIDUR GUDJOHNSEN
3. HUGO SANCHEZ
4. MIKE ENGLAND
5. DAVOR SUKER
6. JUNICHI INAMOTO
7. PAOLO MALDINI
8. HENRIK LARSSON
9. BRIAN McBRIDE
10. TEOFILO CUBILLAS

ANSWERS ON PAGE 294

323 GUESS WHO . . . ?

1. Former lover of Kylie Minogue and Paula Yates, the lead singer of INXS, he died in Sydney in 1997.
2. A singer/songwriter for 40 years, he has raised millions of pounds and dollars for his Aids Foundation.
3. Born Norma Delores Egstrom in 1920, this jazz singer's hits include *Fever* and *Manana*.
4. Born in France in 1824, his most famous creations are the Three Musketeers.
5. Born in the Bronx, New York, her real first name is Alicia and she starred in *The Silence of the Lambs*.
6. Born in Oregon, this high jumper changed his event for ever by creating a "flop" which won him Olympic gold in 1968.
7. Former singing partner of Cher in the 1960s he died in a skiing accident in 1998.
8. She has the middle names Louise Veronica, starred in the movie *Evita* and has two children Rocco and Lourdes.
9. Born in 1895, this boxer was known as the Manassa Mauler and fought the first million-dollar fight in 1921.
10. This Canadian uses the middle initial J and appeared in *Back to the Future* before being diagnosed with Parkinson's disease.

ANSWERS ON PAGE 294

324 PARIS

1 Which fictional figure is linked to Notre Dame?
☐ Hunchback ☐ Little Prince
☐ Phantom

2 What was the Louvre originally built as?
☐ Fortress ☐ Palace ☐ Prison

3 What is the main feature in the Place de la Concorde?
☐ Obelisk ☐ Statue ☐ Tower

4 Which day is the Bastille Day celebration?
☐ June 30th ☐ July 14th ☐ July 31st

5 What sport is played at Roland Garros?
☐ Boules ☐ Soccer ☐ Tennis

6 Which of the following is south of the Seine?
☐ Champs Elysées ☐ Eiffel Tower
☐ Montmartre

7 Who commissioned the building of the Arc de Triomphe?
☐ de Gaulle ☐ Louis XV ☐ Napoleon

8 When did the Opera House open?
☐ 1785 ☐ 1815 ☐ 1875

9 Which stadium hosted the 1998 F.I.F.A. World Cup Final?
☐ St Denis ☐ St Mark
☐ Hugo Stadium

10 Which US President has a Metro station named after him?
☐ Carter ☐ Roosevelt ☐ Truman

11 What did the architect Chalgrin design?
☐ Arc de Triomphe ☐ Louvre
☐ The Dome Church

12 Which bridge is closest to the Eiffel Tower?
☐ Alma ☐ Léna ☐ Neuf

13 In which year did the Paris Metro open?
☐ 1900 ☐ 1910 ☐ 1920

14 Chaillot Palace stands in which gardens?
☐ Botanical ☐ Tuileries ☐ Trocadero

15 Which area is known as the "Butte" by Parisians?
☐ Opera Quarter
☐ Montmartre
☐ Passy

ANSWERS ON PAGE 294

325 HALF CHANCE

½? ½? ½?

1 Which major river flows through New Orleans – the Ohio or the Mississippi?

2 In the UK and the USA what is the most common surname for people – Brown or Smith?

3 Did William Tell shoot an apple off his son's head using a crossbow or a longbow?

4 The Aztecs came from which part of the world – Australia or Mexico?

5 In a calendar year which is the first month to have exactly 30 days – March or April?

6 Which letter along with H appears on pencils – A or B?

7 How many kings are there in two packs of playing cards – four or eight?

8 What colour are the stars on the American flag – blue or white?

9 Sherlock Holmes lived in a street named after which type of worker – Baker or Cook?

10 The composer Sibelius is associated with which country – Finland or Norway?

11 Where is the Sea of Showers – America or on the Moon?

12 Did Susanna Hoffs front The Bangles or Black Box?

13 In which decade was the movie *Gone With the Wind* made – the 1930s or 1940s?

14 What did the J stand for in the name of Rugby legend JPR Williams – John or Joseph?

15 The words of William Blake appear in which stirring song – *Jerusalem* or *Rule Britannia*?

16 Which country was formerly known as Portuguese West Africa – Angola or Namibia?

17 In Shakespeare's play which King does Macbeth murder – King Donald or King Duncan?

18 Did Alan Shearer first play league soccer for Blackburn or Southampton?

19 What did Ben Travers specialise in writing – farces or film scores?

20 Was Joaquin Rodrigo's famous 1930s concerto written for a guitar or a violin?

ANSWERS ON PAGE 294

326 SCIENCE

1 What was invented by Lazlo and Georg Biro?

2 Which fashion item is Oscar Levi Strauss responsible for?

3 What nationality was motor vehicle pioneer Gottlieb Daimler?

4 What was developed by André and Edouard Michelin?

5 What type of pen did Lewis Waterman invent?

6 Which air cushion vehicle was invented by Christopher Cockerell?

7 Which engine used in aircraft was invented by Sir Frank Whittle?

8 What did John Logie Baird invent, first called "seeing by wireless"?

9 Which communication system is Alexander Graham Bell famous for?

10 Who invented a code made up of dots and dashes?

11 For whom did Louis Braille develop his writing system?

12 Which method of food preservation did Clarence Birdseye invent?

13 What type of lamp is Humphry Davy famous for?

14 Which predecessor of the CD player was invented by Thomas Edison?

15 Which breakfast food was developed by Will Keith Kellogg in 1898?

16 Which invention is Marconi known for?

17 Which company, whose motto "Small is beautiful", was founded in the late 1940s and developed the Walkman?

18 Which explosive was invented by Alfred Nobel?

19 What type of milk did Louis Pasteur give his name to, because of the treatment it undergoes?

20 In which source of power were Volta and Ampère pioneers?

ANSWERS ON PAGE 294

327 MURDER MOST FOUL

1. Who was murdered along with O J Simpson's estranged wife Nicole?
2. Who was nicknamed the Vampire of Dusseldorf because of his taste for human blood?
3. Which English major road is linked to the James Hanratty murder trial?
4. *The Sicilian Specialist* by Norman Lewis is a thinly disguised fictional account of which assassination plot?
5. Where was Martin Luther King assassinated?
6. What was the real name of Butch Cassidy?
7. What was the name of the rally which Yitzhak Rabin had attended just before his assassination?
8. Which famous name was killed by Kenneth Halliwell?
9. Under what name did Dr Crippen leave the country after the murder of his wife?
10. In which Lake did Peter Hogg dump the body of his wife in 1976 although it was 11 years before he was jailed?
11. PC Keith Blakelock was killed in riots where in London?
12. Who did the Boston Strangler say he worked for in order to gain his victims' confidence?
13. How many men did Dennis Nilsen admit to killing between 1978 and 1983?
14. Where did John Christie live?
15. Which monarch did Gaetano Bresci assassinate?
16. What was gangster Lucky Luciano's real first name?
17. What was the name of Ruth Ellis's lover whom she murdered?
18. How was murderer Pedro Alonzo Lopez nicknamed?
19. How old was the Yorkshire Ripper when he was captured, after a five-year killing campaign?
20. How did 1940s murderer John Haigh dispose of his victims' bodies?

ANSWERS ON PAGE 294

328 LUCKY DIP

1. What is the name of the most famous computer game hedgehog?
2. What is the zodiac sign of the Crab?
3. On television do Will and Grace share a flat, a house or a houseboat?
4. What does the N stand for in NATO?
5. In golf what is the term for two over par?
6. The initials TC stand for which cartoon character?
7. George Eastman invented what type of equipment?
8. Which country's national flag is a green rectangle?
9. Who topped the UK and US charts with the album *Break The Cycle*?
10. According to the proverb, what can't you teach an old dog?
11. The failure to produce enough insulin leads to which medical condition?
12. Magician David Kotkin managed to change his name to what?
13. Which Scottish soccer team are known as The Dons?
14. In which month is Royal Ascot horse-racing season?
15. What is agoraphobia a fear of?
16. What do the initials RAM stand for in computing?
17. Which Beatrix created Peter Rabbit?
18. How many kilogrammes make one ton?
19. What was the name given to the "Ripper" in Victorian London?
20. What type of plant is dill?

ANSWERS ON PAGE 294

329 THE ARTS

1 Which James Bond actor was in the chorus in *South Pacific* in London?

2 Which musical star was Andrew Lloyd Webber's second wife?

3 Who wrote the novels introducing the detective Jack Frost?

4 Which was Elaine Paige's first musical on Broadway?

5 Which musical does the song *I Am What I Am* come from?

6 In which musical is Maria Von Trapp the heroine?

7 Which theatre award is named after actress Antoinette Perry?

8 Who played C. S. Lewis in *Shadowlands* on stage?

9 Which musical is based on *The Taming of the Shrew*?

10 What is the name of the most famous theatre in London's Drury Lane?

11 Who originally played the role of Alex in *Aspects Of Love*?

12 Who wrote the lyrics for *Tell Me On A Sunday* and *Sunset Boulevard*?

13 Who co-produced the revival of *Anything Goes* with Elaine Paige?

14 Which musical is the song *Ol' Man River* from?

15 Which song from *South Pacific* was recorded by Captain Sensible?

16 In which country is *The King And I* set?

17 Which musical are the songs *Tonight* and *Somewhere* from?

18 What was the profession of the heroine in the musical *Gypsy*?

19 Who wrote *Into the Woods* and *A Little Night Music*?

20 In which musical does *You'll Never Walk Alone* appear?

ANSWERS ON PAGE 294

330 SPORTING LEGENDS

1 Which was the only Grand Slam title Pete Sampras did not win?

2 Which former Scottish jockey has the first names William Hunter Fisher?

3 Which music did Torvill & Dean use for a full hand of perfect scores at the 1984 Olympics?

4 Which sport did Hank Aaron play?

5 What did Muhammad Ali refuse to do that saw him stripped of his World Heavyweight tile in 1967?

6 Which Spaniard became the youngest golfer of the 20th century to win the British Open?

7 Which soccer club side did George Best join immediately after leaving school?

8 In which decade did Ian Botham make his Test debut?

9 Who was the first man to hold the world record at 200m and 400m simultaneously?

10 Anatoli Karpov was world champion in what?

11 Who broke Fred Perry's record of three consecutive Wimbledon titles?

12 Which sport did Jahangir Khan play?

13 How many Wimbledon titles did Billie Jean King win?

14 For which English soccer side did Jimmy Greaves make his debut as a striker?

15 In which decade did Wayne Gretzky make his professional debut?

16 What was Sally Gunnell's Olympic gold medal winning event?

17 Who was non-playing captain of the European Ryder Cup team between 1983 and 1989?

18 Which Rugby player scored a record 90 points for Wales between 1966 and 1972?

19 Which side did Alex Ferguson manage before he went to Man Utd?

20 Which golfer replaced Tiger Woods as world No 1 at the end of 2004?

ANSWERS ON PAGE 294

331 PICTURE QUIZ

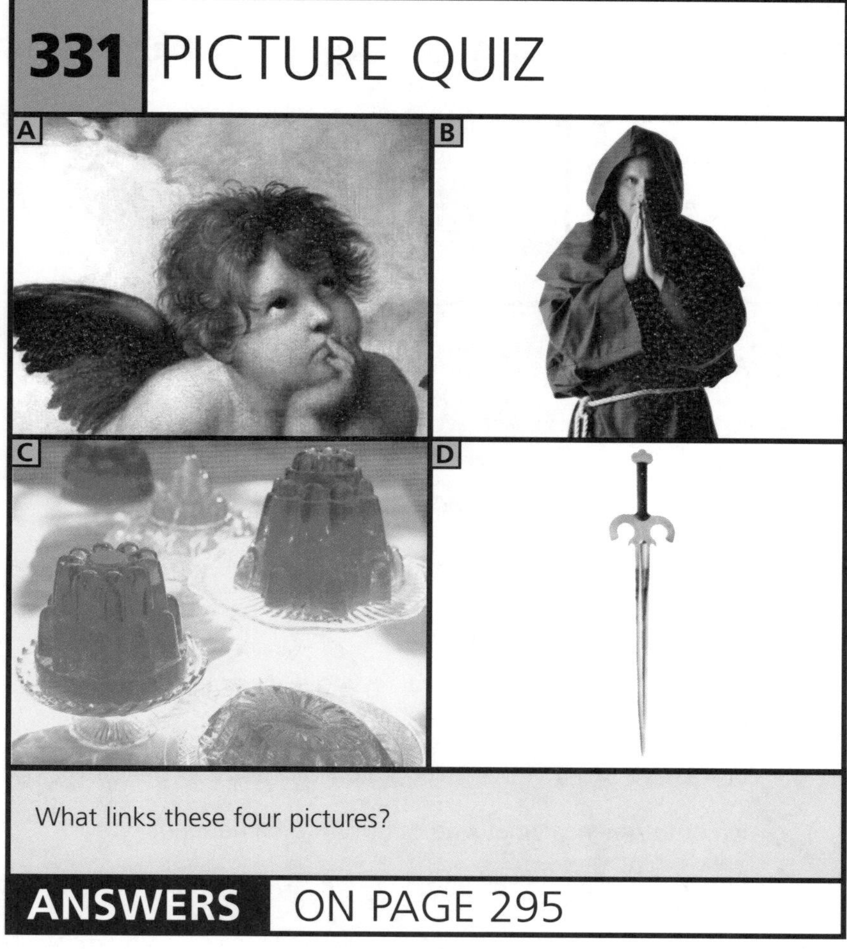

A B C D

What links these four pictures?

ANSWERS ON PAGE 295

332 BIRDS

Is each statement TRUE or FALSE?

T F **1** Fulmars are oceanic seabirds.

T F **2** All swans, geese and ducks are carnivorous.

T F **3** Birds of prey are sometimes called raptors.

T F **4** Pigeons are vegetarian.

T F **5** Cuckoos have extremely short tails.

T F **6** Young flamingos are grey.

T F **7** The puffin is part of the auk family.

T F **8** The tawny owl is the least rare.

T F **9** The female pheasant has green and gold plumage.

T F **10** Cormorants feed on fish.

ANSWERS ON PAGE 295

333 GARDENING

1 What is the most common colour for a daffodil?
☐ Pink ☐ White ☐ Yellow

2 Hybrid tea and floribunda are types of what?
☐ Rose ☐ Daffodil ☐ Poppies

3 Which vegetables can be globe or Jerusalem?
☐ Artichokes ☐ Cabbages ☐ Peas

4 Antirrhinums are also known as what?
☐ Begonias ☐ Phlox ☐ Snapdragons

5 What are lilies grown from?
☐ Bulbs ☐ Seeds ☐ Pellets

6 What do secateurs do?
☐ Cut ☐ Dig ☐ Sieve

7 What are culinary herbs used for?
☐ Aromas ☐ Cooking ☐ Decoration

8 Althaea is more commonly known as what?
☐ Foxglove ☐ Hollyhock ☐ Larkspur

9 If you grew a box in your garden what would it be?
☐ Flower ☐ Shrub ☐ Vegetable

10 Which plant's name is from the Latin lavo, meaning I wash?
☐ Laburnum ☐ Lavender ☐ Lovage

11 What is significant about bonsai plants?
☐ Colourful ☐ Large ☐ Small

12 What sort of fruit is a Cox's Orange Pippin?
☐ Apple ☐ Orange ☐ Peach

13 Which princely name follows Sweet in a cottage garden plant?
☐ Charles ☐ Harry ☐ William

14 What is the depth of the head of a spade known as?
☐ Ditch ☐ Spit ☐ Tilth

15 Which fruits follow elderflowers?
☐ Elder currants
☐ Elderberries
☐ Elder fruit

ANSWERS ON PAGE 295

334 PEOPLE

1 Jamie Foxx won an Oscar in 2005 for portraying which singer?

2 In which silent film did Harold Lloyd hang from the clockface in a memorable sequence?

3 Habitat was founded by which Terence?

4 What was the profession of Margaret Thatcher's father?

5 Which Princess was the youngest daughter of Mrs Frances Shand Kydd?

6 Which Rupert launched the satellite TV station which became Sky?

7 To the nearest five years, how old would Marilyn Monroe have been in 2000?

8 Who was John McEnroe's best man when he married Tatum O'Neal?

9 Who was the first Beatle to be knighted?

10 Which singing star turned out as a transvestite in *Little Britain*'s special show for Comic Relief?

11 Who created Bugs Bunny?

12 The ship *Queen Elizabeth* was named after who?

13 Which 1990s Wimbledon champion married actress Brooke Shields?

14 Whose funeral made Sam Goldwyn say, "The only reason ... people showed up . . . was . . . to make sure he was dead"?

15 Which Spice Girl sang *Happy Birthday* to Prince Charles at his 50th birthday party?

16 Who lost out on Best Director Oscar for both *The Aviator* and *Gangs Of New York*?

17 Who was the fiancée of Michael Hutchence of INXS at the time of his suicide?

18 What was Camilla Shand's surname after her first marriage?

19 In which country did Princess Anne marry for the second time?

20 Which skinny Sixties model married actor Leigh Lawson?

ANSWERS ON PAGE 295

335 GENERAL KNOWLEDGE

 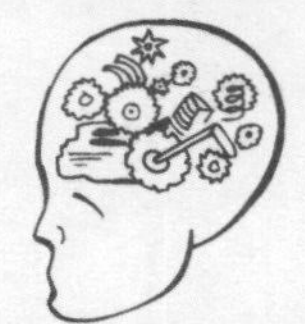 

1 Who composed the opera *The Tales of Hoffman*?

2 In the classic movie, why were Bob Hope and Bing Crosby "*Like Webster's Dictionary*"?

3 For what is Frank Lloyd Wright famous?

4 Who wrote a novel about Kenilworth in Warkwickshire?

5 What are the Howard League concerned with?

6 Mount Ararat is the traditional resting place of which ship or boat?

7 In *Treasure Island* which sailor dreamed of toasted cheese?

8 In South America what kind of building is a hacienda?

9 Which country won the Battle of Flodden?

10 In a fairy story a queen had to guess the name of a little man, or lose her baby. What was the mysterious name?

11 In which book would you find Mrs Do-as-you-would-be-done-by?

12 What did the M stand for in the name of writer Louisa M. Alcott?

13 What is a mazurka?

14 What term is given to the making of patterns by inlaying different coloured pieces of wood?

15 In which art did John and Ethel Barrymore achieve fame?

16 What new denomination of coin was isssued in the UK in 1983?

17 With which composer is the German town of Bayreuth associated?

18 Who wrote the *Inspector Morse* novels?

19 Which of these is not a freshwater fish – cod, pike, carp, roach?

20 Which chocolate bar was supposed to help you work, rest and play?

ANSWERS ON PAGE 295

336 CELEBRITIES

1. Who was born first – Ronald Reagan or Frank Sinatra?
2. Jerry Hall hails from which oil state?
3. Which actress is Carrie Fisher's mother?
4. Who accompanied Hugh Grant to the premiere of *Four Weddings and a Funeral* in a dress held together with safety pins?
5. Who did Jacqueline Bouvier marry in September 1953?
6. Reports of a relationship with which model ended the presidential campaign of Senator Gary Hart?
7. Twiggy was the most famous model of which decade?
8. Which 1980s US President survived an assassination attempt?
9. Which Richard did Elizabeth Taylor marry twice?
10. Which Italian actress launched her own perfume Sophia?
11. Which Mia is the daughter of Maureen O'Sullivan?
12. Where was Sean Lennon's mother born?
13. Who is older, Jay or Donny Osmond?
14. Which Spice Girl was the first to marry?
15. In which year were Madonna, Michael Jackson and Prince all born?
16. How old was Lady Diana Spencer when she became engaged?
17. Which supermodel Naomi wrote a novel called *Swan*?
18. Which Bob who founded Band Aid received an honorary knighthood in 1986?
19. Giorgio Armani is famous in which field?
20. Fashion designer Donatella, sister of the murdered Gianni, has which last name?

ANSWERS ON PAGE 295

337 FOOD AND DRINK

1. What is hanepoot?
2. Who or what was Buck's Fizz named after?
3. Which snack's name comes from the Turkish for rotating?
4. In which country is the yeastless beer faro made?
5. Where was Anton Mosimann's first position as chef in the UK?
6. Kummel is a Russian liqueur extracted from what?
7. The macadamia is native to where?
8. What is the main ingredient of a brandade?
9. Who opened the Miller Howe restaurant in 1971?
10. In his diary what did Pepys call jucalette?
11. Where in a dish would you put gremolata?
12. Which country has a wine-growing area called O'Higgins?
13. Which term indicates the amount of wine by which a container falls short of being full?
14. What did Madame Harel, a French farmer's wife, create in about 1790?
15. What is the base of a florentine biscuit made from?
16. Where did malmsey wine originate?
17. Balti is the Indian word for what?
18. Which abbreviation indicates wine between the qualities of vin de pays and appellation controlée?
19. What is a mesclun?
20. What is cocose?

ANSWERS ON PAGE 295

338 THE HEADLINES

1 In 2004, which actor ended his 18-year marriage to Melissa Mathison ?

2 Whose breast made a brief and unscheduled appearance at the 2004 Super Bowl?

3 In which decade did Queen Elizabeth II come to the throne?

4 Rasputin hit the headlines for activities in which country?

5 In 2004, Simon Mann was linked with a coup involving which son of a former Prime Minister?

6 Which Princess did the future Lord Snowdon marry in 1960?

7 Which Maxwell disappeared off his yacht in 1991 before news about misappropriation of pension funds?

8 BSE was also called mad what disease?

9 Which African country had rebel cricket tours because of its policy on apartheid?

10 Ken Russell was a controversial name in which area of the arts?

11 The 1990 round the world yacht *Maiden* had a crew made up entirely of who or what?

12 Sir Ranulph Fiennes hit the headlines in what capacity?

13 At which British organization did Mark Thompson take over from Greg Dyke in 2004?

14 Which O in Northern Ireland was the scene of an horrific bomb in 1998?

15 Which sculpture of the North was erected near Gateshead?

16 Which meat did the government ban from being eaten on the bone during the BSE crisis?

17 In which decade did Hillary climb Everest?

18 Salman Rushdie hit the headlines with a controversial what?

19 The Good Friday Agreement was drawn up to help solve problems in which part of the UK?

20 2004's first election saw Dr Mikhail Saakashvili becoming President of where?

ANSWERS ON PAGE 295

339 HEALTH

1 What are the initials for the human form of BSE?

2 Oncology is the study of which disease?

3 A hysterectomy involves removal of what?

4 Osteoporosis is a weakness and brittleness of what?

5 In which decade did a report first appear in the US saying smoking could damage health?

6 What was the nationality of the founder of the Red Cross?

7 Penicillin was the first what?

8 Ebola is also known as which disease?

9 What does S stand for in AIDS?

10 Appendicitis causes pain where?

11 Which insects cause bubonic plague?

12 Which disease – more common in children – is also called varicella?

13 Where was the first ambulance used?

14 Which part of the body is affected by conjunctivitis?

15 The infection of wounds by what can bring on tetanus?

16 Which of the following is not a blood group – AB, O or T?

17 What sort of flies transmit sleeping sickness?

18 Reflexologists massage which part of the body?

19 Shiatsu is a massage technique from which country?

20 What does an analgesic drug do?

ANSWERS ON PAGE 295

340 RIVER CITY

On which river do these capital cities stand?

1 BUDAPEST
2 KIEV
3 TOKYO
4 CANBERRA
5 BRATISLAVA
6 MADRID
7 VILNIUS
8 RIGA
9 PRAGUE
10 SEOUL

ANSWERS ON PAGE 295

341 DOUBLE TAKE

In each case, the two-part quiz question leads to just one answer!

1 Which part of a needle is also an organ of the body?
2 Which part of a church organ is a word which means to halt?
3 Which word for a bus is also a word for a sports teacher?
4 Which word means funny and is also a type of magazine?
5 Which type of cotton or linen is also the name of a tool?
6 Which river of north-east England shares a name with golf pegs?
7 Which word for a cutting tool also means observed?
8 Which plant juice is also a word meaning to undermine?
9 Which type of artichoke can also be a map of the world?
10 Which shade of blue is also a military service?

ANSWERS ON PAGE 295

342 AROUND IRELAND

1 Which river flows through Dublin?
☐ Foyle ☐ Lee ☐ Liffey

2 What is lough the Irish word for?
☐ Bog ☐ Castle ☐ Lake

3 O'Connell Street is which city's main thoroughfare?
☐ Belfast ☐ Cork ☐ Dublin

4 Which city is known as the Maiden City?
☐ Belfast ☐ Cork ☐ Derry

5 What sort of jewelled Isle is Ireland often called?
☐ Emerald ☐ Pearl ☐ Ruby

6 In which county are the Mountains of Mourne?
☐ Cork ☐ Down ☐ Kerry

7 Which famous 9th century book is in Trinity College?
☐ Blarney ☐ Kells ☐ Wells

8 Cork city is on which river?
☐ Foyle ☐ Lee ☐ Liffey

9 Which Irish place gives its name to a short rhyme?
☐ Drogheda ☐ Limerick ☐ Sligo

10 What is Ireland's biggest lough?
☐ Conn ☐ Gur ☐ Neagh

11 Which water is to the west of Ireland?
☐ Atlantic ☐ Irish Sea ☐ North Sea

12 In which city is Queens University?
☐ Belfast ☐ Cork ☐ Dublin

13 Which type of glass is Waterford famous for?
☐ Crystal ☐ Plate ☐ Stained

14 How many main railway stations are there in Dublin?
☐ One ☐ Two ☐ Three

15 Which stone is kissed to receive the gift of smooth talking?
☐ Blarney
☐ Limerick
☐ Touch

ANSWERS ON PAGE 295

343 LUCKY DIP

1 Which country's national airline is Lufthansa?

2 What does the H stand for in VHF?

3 What is another word for nacre?

4 Who recorded the album *Stars*?

5 Which mountain was said to be home of the Greek gods?

6 From which fish is caviare obtained?

7 In which European city are the Bardini Museum and the Bargello Museum?

8 How is Frances Gumm better known?

9 Which bear was created by A. A. Milne?

10 What colour is the dye obtained from the plant woad?

11 In which branch of the arts is the metronome used?

12 Churchill, Sherman and Panzer were all developed as types of what?

13 What type of whale is the largest?

14 What colour is vermilion?

15 Which Desmond wrote *The Naked Ape*?

16 How many sides has a decagon?

17 What is the fourth book of the Old Testament?

18 Which Spike said, "Money can't buy friends, but you can get a better class of enemy"?

19 Which major river flows through Glasgow?

20 A cob is a male of which creature?

ANSWERS ON PAGE 295

344 TRAVEL

1 Which was the first European city to open an underground railway system in the 20th century?

2 Which is the USA's largest state?

3 In which part of London is the Natural History Museum?

4 Which natural disaster is the San Andreas Fault prone to?

5 What does D.C. stand for in Washington D.C.?

6 What is Switzerland's largest city?

7 In which state is the Grand Canyon?

8 Which seaside resort has Lanes and a nudist beach?

9 What is the second largest of the Ionian Islands??

10 Which was the first of the original 13 states of the USA?

11 Where is the main space exploration centre in Florida?

12 Where would you spend stotinki?

13 Which other city lies entirely within Rome?

14 Which American city is famous for its jazz music?

15 What is the longest river in Portugal, and the fifth longest in Europe?

16 In which English county is Sizewell nuclear power station situated?

17 Where is New York's financial centre?

18 Which US state has the highest population?

19 Which city did Truman Capote describe as like "eating an entire box of chocolate liqueurs in one go"?

20 Which two New York boroughs begin with B?

ANSWERS ON PAGE 295

345 JAMES BOND

1 Who described James Bond as "a blunt instrument wielded by a government department"?

2 Which 007 movie did Sean Connery make prior to *Marnie*?

3 Which Bond film did Deborah Kerr appear in?

4 How many Bond films were released during Ian Fleming's lifetime?

5 Where is the first hour of *Tomorrow Never Dies* set?

6 Which movie's villain was Xenia Onatopp?

7 Which movie first had the toothpaste with plastic explosives?

8 What is the only Bond movie not to have an action sequence before the credits?

9 In which movie did Rowan Atkinson make his big screen debut?

10 Which Bond girl married a Beatle?

11 Which 007 backed the restaurant chain the Spy House?

12 Which movie had the electro magnetic watch with the spinning blade?

13 To fifteen minutes, how long does *You Only Live Twice* last?

14 Which golf course featured in Goldfinger?

15 What was the most successful Bond film of the 1970s and 80s in terms of cinema admissions?

16 What was the final Bond movie as far as Ian Fleming was concerned?

17 May Day was the Bond girl in which film?

18 In the films what replaced the Soviet organisation Smersh which existed in the books?

19 What was Goldfinger's first name?

20 In which movie did Blofeld kidnap US and USSR spaceships to try and gain planetary control?

ANSWERS ON PAGE 295

346 GENERAL KNOWLEDGE

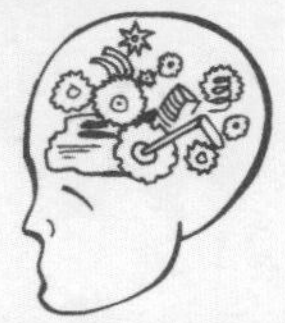 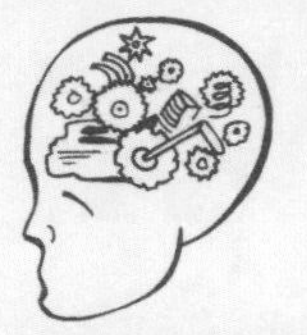 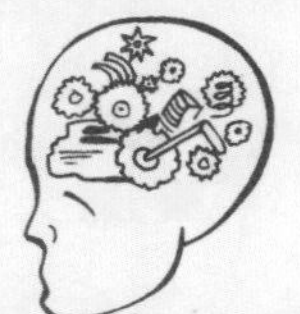

1 On which Isle is Osborne House?

2 Who composed the piece known as the *Moonlight Sonata*?

3 What name is given in law to a person who makes a will?

4 What colour were the shirts of Mussolini's Italian Fascists?

5 What is the green colouring matter in plants known as?

6 What is the official residence of the Chancellor of the Exchequer?

7 What is another name for mercury?

8 Where are your clavicles?

9 In area, which is the world's largest desert?

10 What do your olfactory organs help you do?

11 Who or what live in a holt?

12 What is the name of the medical oath taken by doctors?

13 Which religion observes the Passover?

14 Anzac troops come from which two countries?

15 How many years is the term of office of the American President?

16 In which part of the body is the cornea located?

17 Which film star gave her name to a life jacket?

18 Which English city was once known as Sarum?

19 What is H_2SO_4?

20 Who wrote the novel *The Glass Lake*?

ANSWERS ON PAGE 295

347 MOTOR SPORTS

1 Which Grand Prix has been held at Mosport and Mont Tremblant?

2 In which decade of the 20th century was the Indianapolis 500 inaugurated?

3 At the beginning of the new millennium which country had the most Grand Prix wins?

4 How many times was a Finn F1 World Champion in the 1990s?

5 In which decade was Barry Sheene world 500cc champion twice?

6 During which Grand Prix did Ayrton Senna meet his death?

7 Which race is run on the Circuit de la Sarthe?

8 Who was the head of F1 at the end of the 20th century?

9 Which motor sport has the governing body the AMA?

10 In which country is the Suzuka circuit?

11 In which month does the Indianapolis 500 take place?

12 Who did Damon Hill race for when he was World Champion in 1996?

13 What is the first rally of the World Rally Championship?

14 Where is the Francorchamps circuit?

15 Which country was Nelson Piquet from?

16 When Michael Schumacher first became Formula 1 champ he was with which team?

17 On which race track was Jim Clark killed?

18 In which US state is the Daytona Beach circuit?

19 In which decade was the Le Mans 24-hour race first held?

20 Who was the first person to clock up over 250 Grand Prix starts?

ANSWERS ON PAGE 295

348 HALF CHANCE

½? ½? ½?

1 In the Bible which infant was hidden in bulrushes for his own safety – Jesus or Moses?

2 Which famous composer had the first names Wolfgang Amadeus – Bach or Mozart?

3 How many fortnights are there in two years – 26 or 52?

4 What is the shape of a pie chart – circular or oblong?

5 Which was the second country to send a man into space – Russia or USA?

6 What colour is platinum – black or greyish white?

7 If a number is squared what is it multiplied by – half or itself?

8 Which bone is the longest bone in the human body – the rib or the thigh?

9 What does U stand for in VDU – unit or user?

10 Hr is the abbreviation for what – horsepower or hour?

11 What would you own if you possessed a Canaletto – a small river boat or a painting?

12 What is a fox's tail known as – a broom or a brush?

13 Was Queen Elizabeth II crowned in an Abbey or a Castle?

14 Which side of a ship is starboard – left or right?

15 Which shredded vegetable goes into sauerkraut – cabbage or onion?

16 In 1997 Hong Kong was returned to the rule of which country – China or Japan?

17 Which Scotsman gave his name to a type of raincoat – Cagoule or Mackintosh?

18 Which Mel voiced Rooster in *Chicken Run* – Brooks or Gibson?

19 Is a great bustard a bird or a long-winded politician?

20 What does the P stand for in PTA – parents or pupils?

ANSWERS ON PAGE 295

349 PICTURE QUIZ

Starting with the first, in which order were these items invented?

ANSWERS ON PAGE 295

350 GUESS WHO . . . ?

1 Born in 1908, his middle name was Lancaster and he wrote the James Bond novels.

2 Born in Kent in 1970, she left an army career, won two gold medals in Athens in 2004 and was made a Dame.

3 Born in Melbourne in 1968, she found fame in *Neighbours* prior to chart success and a cameo role in *Moulin Rouge*.

4 Born in Liverpool, this left-handed guitarist was married to Linda then to Heather.

5 Born in Oxford, he became England's highest ranked tennis player in 1996 and reached the Wimbledon semi finals in 1998.

6 Born in New Brunswick, his films include *Wall Street* and *Fatal Attraction*. His second wife is from Wales.

7 Former leader of the Khmer Rouge, his party ruled Cambodia between 1975 and 1979 during the "Killing Fields".

8 Raised in landlocked Derbyshire she made a record breaking solo trip around the world in 2005 and was made a Dame.

9 A former student of astronomy, he was part of Queen and played guitar on the roof of Buckingham Palace in 2002.

10 Born in Cardiff in 1967, he became world record-holder in the 110 metres hurdles in 1993 but failed to win an Olympic gold.

ANSWERS ON PAGE 295

351 SAILORS

1 Which of the following is a patron saint of sailors?
☐ Erasmus ☐ Gabriel ☐ Stephen

2 Who won the first solo transatlantic yacht race?
☐ Chichester ☐ Drake
☐ Knox-Johnston

3 Where was Christopher Columbus born?
☐ America ☐ Italy ☐ Spain

4 "Sail under false colours" referred to whose ships?
☐ Fishermen ☐ Pirates ☐ Yachtsmen

5 Which English Prime Minister was an accomplished sailor?
☐ Callaghan ☐ Heath ☐ Wilson

6 Which admiral had a ship called *HMS Victory*?
☐ Jervis ☐ Mountbatten ☐ Nelson

7 In which century were galleons first used?
☐ 16th ☐ 17th ☐ 18th

8 What is the sailing trophy the America's Cup named after?
☐ A liner ☐ A schooner ☐ A warship

9 Which English king was called the sailor king?
☐ George III ☐ Henry VIII ☐ William IV

10 Who was the first Englishman to circumnavigate the globe?
☐ Drake ☐ Nelson ☐ Percival

11 How many ships did Columbus cross the Atlantic with in 1492?
☐ Three ☐ Six ☐ Eight

12 What was the name of the yacht in which Ellen MacArthur's sailed in 2005?
☐ B & Q ☐ PDQ ☐ P & O

13 The strait named after Magellan is to the south of which continent?
☐ Africa ☐ America ☐ Europe

14 In which London square is there a monument to Nelson?
☐ Eaton ☐ Soho ☐ Trafalgar

15 Who led the first expedition round the Cape of Good Hope?
☐ Da Gama
☐ Drake
☐ Nelson

ANSWERS ON PAGE 295

Wedding

For better or for worse, here are 50 questions about tying the marriage knot, and some of the couples who have tried to live happily hereafter.

1 Which precious metal celebrates a 60th wedding anniversary?

2 According to the proverb, if you marry in haste, what must you then do?

3 How many years have you been married to celebrate a pearl wedding?

4 Which Felix wrote a famous wedding march?

5 In which country did David Beckham marry Victoria?

6 What follows, something old, something new, something borrowed, in the rhyme?

7 A French wedding cake is traditionally made from which type of pastry?

8 What was Cherie Blair's surname before her wedding to Tony?

9 Which star of *ET* starred in *The Wedding Singer*?

10 Which actor said, "Monogamy requires genius."

11 What colour dress did Paula Yates wear at her wedding to Bob Geldof?

12 Which jockey did Catherine Allen marry in the late 1990s?

13 Which tough guy actor did Ali McGraw marry in 1973?

14 Which word completes the movie *My Big Fat ____ Wedding*?

15 How many weddings did Judy Garland have?

16 Who did Dawn French marry in 1984?

17 Which of her *Scream* co-star's names did Courtney Cox add to her own after her marriage?

18 Who was the first US President to have been divorced?

19 Which member of the Kennedy clan married Arnold Schwarzenegger?

20 Who did Paul McCartney marry in Ireland?

21 Which international cricketer turned politician did socialite Jemima Goldsmith marry?

22 Who did actor Don Johnson marry twice?

23 What was Victoria Beckham's surname before her marriage to David?

24 Which Welsh actress became the second Mrs Michael Douglas?

25 Which two ex-Wimbledon and US champions of the 1990s subsequently married each other?

26 Whose second marriage was to director Sam Mendes?

27 Who was the last Beatle to marry twice?

28 Who was Elizabeth Taylor's husband when they were both nominated for an Oscar?

29 Which actor, real surname Coppola, married Elvis Presley's daughter?

30 Who was the bride at Andrew Lloyd Webber's second wedding?

31 Which Oscar-winning actress was once married to Tom Cruise?

32 How many years have you been married to celebrate a ruby wedding?

33 Who was married to Ava Gardner when husband and wife were both Oscar nominated?

34 Which tennis star did actress Tatum O'Neal marry?

35 Which film director did Jamie Lee Curtis marry?

36 Which actor/director said, "Marriages are made in heaven but so is thunder and lightning."?

37 In how many of Henry VIII's weddings was the bride called Catherine?

38 According to the 17th century proverb you hear of a marriage if what has happened?

39 Which tough guy actor said, "I was married by a judge. I should have asked for a jury."

40 Who did Jennifer Aniston marry in real life when she was starring in *Friends*?

41 Which TV personality said, "Marriage is grand. Divorce is twenty grand."

42 Which director did Madonna marry in Scotland?

43 Which is the first wedding anniversary which merits a royal wish from the Queen?

44 What was Hillary Clinton's surname before she married Bill?

45 Who played Michael Douglas's wife in the movie *A Perfect Murder*?

46 How many years have you been married to celebrate a silver wedding?

47 What does the word wed actually mean?

48 Ava Gardner married three times, but how many wives did her husbands have between them?

49 Arthur Miller, who died in 2005, was married to which 20th-century screen icon?

50 Who was married to Madonna when they made *Shanghai Surprise* in 1986?

ANSWERS ON PAGE 295

353 TELEVISION

1 Which show had the catchphrase, "Suits you sir!"?

2 Where is *Sex And The City* set?

3 Which delivery man had a cat named Jess?

4 Who introduced *Shooting Stars* along with Vic Reeves?

5 Which character committed suicide at the beginning of *Desperate Housewives*?

6 In which country was the short-lived soap *Eldorado* set?

7 Which Renault advertising character frequently found her father in compromising situations?

8 What race is Dr Spock from *Star Trek*?

9 *News At Ten* was a long-running programme on which UK channel?

10 Which cop show featured Frank Furillo?

11 Who can you phone on *Who Wants To Be A Millionaire?*?

12 Which Mary played Laura in *The Dick Van Dyke Show*?

13 Which character did Joan Collins play in *Dynasty* – Alexis, Crystal or Sparkler?

14 Who is Bart Simpson's older sister?

15 Which British soap star recorded *Anyone Can Fall In Love*?

16 What was the name of the Teenage Witch?

17 Which sitcom couple had Pippa and Patrick as next door neighbours?

18 Which UK soap featured a map of Chester in its opening credits?

19 What was Grace's last name in *Will And Grace*?

20 What type of driver was Don Brennan in *Corrie*?

ANSWERS ON PAGE 295

354 STATESMEN

1 Who was described by his foreign minister as having "a nice smile, but he has got iron teeth"?

2 Which world figure has the middle name Rolihlahla?

3 Who was did Ariel Sharon take over from as Prime Minister of Israel?

4 Who was Nigeria's first President and has been described as the father of modern Nigeria?

5 Who was born Karl Herbert Frahm?

6 Who was chairman of the Organisation of African Unity from 1975–76?

7 Errol Flynn's last film was a documentary tribute to which world leader?

8 Gorbachev introduced the expression "perestroika" but what does it mean?

9 Who was the first PM of South Africa?

10 Which newspaper originally coined the term "Iron Lady" about Margaret Thatcher?

11 In what year did Hussein become King of Jordan?

12 How was Francois Duvalier more commonly known?

13 Which leader did Churchill say was like a "female llama surprised in her bath"?

14 Who was the last leader of Communist East Germany?

15 Who did Lionel Jospin replace as French PM?

16 What name was given to the period of rule of Emperor Hirohito?

17 Which part of Lenin was preserved after his death?

18 Who said, "We are not at war with Egypt. We are in armed conflict"?

19 In what year was the world's first woman Prime Minister elected?

20 Who was the leader of ZAPU?

ANSWERS ON PAGE 295

355 W.W.W.

Can you identify the country in question from its internet code? Some may be obvious . . . some may not!

1 .ad
2 .pe
3 .tn
4 .pt
5 .es
6 .bw
7 .cn
8 .at
9 .tg
10 .uy

ANSWERS ON PAGE 295

356 CAKES

Is each statement TRUE or FALSE?

T F **1** Dundee cake has a creamy topping.
T F **2** Macaroons are flavoured with strawberry.
T F **3** A jalousie is made with flaky pastry.
T F **4** Tarte tatin is made with apples.
T F **5** Simnel cake was originally made at Christmas.
T F **6** A Black Forest Gateau contains caraway seeds.
T F **7** Battenberg cake is wrapped in almond paste.
T F **8** A Gâteau St Honoré is a type of cheesecake.
T F **9** A meringue is made with egg whites and sugar.
T F **10** Sachetorte is a rich chocolate cake.

ANSWERS ON PAGE 295

357 WEAPONS

1 Which bomber dropped the first atom bomb?
☐ Enola Gay ☐ Eole I ☐ Hawk III

2 In 1915 Germans first used poison gas against whom?
☐ British ☐ French ☐ Russians

3 What is a Kalashnikov?
☐ Assault rifle ☐ Machine gun ☐ Revolver

4 In Roman times what was a gladius?
☐ Shield ☐ Spear ☐ Sword

5 Which was invented first?
☐ Dynamite ☐ Gelignite ☐ Nitro glycerine

6 Which Russian Minister gave his name to an explosive device?
☐ Andropov ☐ Gromyko ☐ Molotov

7 When was the bullet-proof vest developed?
☐ 1940s ☐ 1960s ☐ 1980s

8 What was a Mill's bomb?
☐ Hand grenade ☐ Machine gun ☐ Torpedo?

9 What was the two edged French sword of the 14th century?
☐ Epée ☐ Katana ☐ Rapier

10 In German V2 rockets what (in English) does V stand for?
☐ Valour ☐ Vengeance ☐ Victory

11 What did the Chinese call "huo phao"?
☐ Bayonet ☐ Gunpowder ☐ Hand grenade

12 Who invented the revolver?
☐ Colt ☐ Deringer ☐ Lewis

13 Which WWII jacket was used for protection?
☐ Bomber ☐ Flak ☐ Smoking

14 In which month was the first atomic bomb dropped?
☐ May ☐ August ☐ October

15 What was the code name of the first atomic bomb?
☐ Little Boy ☐ Mighty Atom ☐ Pacific Pride

ANSWERS ON PAGE 295

358 LUCKY DIP

1 If it rains on St Swithin's Day how many more days is it supposed to rain?

2 Henry Ford claimed that, "History is . . ." what?

3 Which John starred in *Fawlty Towers*?

4 Which composer wrote *The Marriage Of Figaro*?

5 What is a low, shallow basket used by gardeners called?

6 How many years are celebrated by a golden anniversary?

7 In *David Copperfield* what was the surname of Uriah?

8 Over which country did the Ptolemies once rule?

9 What number does the Roman numeral M stand for?

10 What sort of creature is a capercaillie?

11 In which month is Remembrance Day?

12 What name is given to a prayer before meals?

13 What was the first name of Elizabethan explorer Drake?

14 What are the initials of *Lady Chatterley* writer Lawrence?

15 What name is given to a litter of piglets?

16 What type of dancing is associated with Margot Fonteyn?

17 In what game do you peg, and score for pairs and fifteens?

18 Which number formed the title of The Beatles top-selling album of 2000?

19 Which motorway forms the Edinburgh to Glasgow route?

20 What is the Bourse in Paris?

ANSWERS ON PAGE 295

359 POP MUSIC

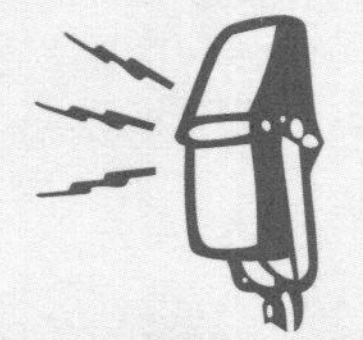

1 Who recorded the hit album *Life For Rent*?

2 What was Victoria Beckham's maiden name?

3 Which single finally saw Ozzy Osbourne at No 1 in the UK single charts?

4 Which Phil won awards for his songs for the movie *Tarzan*?

5 Which country does Celine Dion come from?

6 R.E.M. played live at which US President's inauguration in 1992?

7 Which *Pie* did Madonna sing about – American, Apple or Pumpkin?

8 Which sporting event did Kylie Minogue close in 2000?

9 Whose memory was celebrated at the 1992 *Concert For Life*?

10 Which band named after a US state were In *Demand* in 2000?

11 Which female singer went straight to No 1 in the US with *Fantasy*?

12 What went with *Beauty* in the title of Celine Dion's first UK chart success?

13 T Boz, Left Eye and Chilli made up which band?

14 Which Beatles single was their first No 1 in the US?

15 Which band had their first seven singles become UK No 1s?

16 What was Michael Jackson's last UK No 1 of the 20th century?

17 Which film did *You're The One That I Want* come from?

18 How were sisters June, Anita, Ruth and Bonnie known collectively?

19 Which Leo had a UK and US No 1 with *When I Need You*?

20 How many times is Annie's name mentioned in John Denver's *Annie's Song*?

ANSWERS ON PAGE 295

360 1990s SPORT

1 How many goals were scored in the 1998 World Cup Final?
2 Rugby's man mountain Jonah Lomu plays for which country?
3 Albertville and Lillehammer were the two of the three 1990s venues for which event?
4 Who did Man Utd defeat in the 1999 European Champions' Cup Final?
5 Dallas won the 1993 and 1994 Super Bowl finals – who lost both games?
6 Which racing team dropped Damon Hill the season he became world champion?
7 In which sport was Bob Nudd a world champion?
8 In English soccer, which was the first team not called United to win the Premiership?
9 Which best-on-the-planet trophy did Francois Pienaar collect in 1995?
10 In cricket, which team inflicted W Indies' first home Test series defeat in over 20 years?
11 Which man managed victory in all the tennis Grand Slam titles?
12 What did Miguel Indurain win each year from 1991 to 1995?
13 Which team bought out the Stewart motor racing team?
14 Jonathan Edwards was a world champion in 1995 in which athletic event?
15 Where did the Super Bowl XXXI winning Packers come from?
16 England soccer manager Graham Taylor was likened to which vegetable by the press?
17 Which flat racing jockey rode over 200 winners in both 1997 and 1998?
18 Who won a record ninth Wimbledon Singles title in 1991?
19 In 1995 Man Utd set a record Premiership score by beating which team 9-0?
20 In motor racing who was the only Canadian to be F1 champion?

ANSWERS ON PAGE 295

361 GENERAL KNOWLEDGE

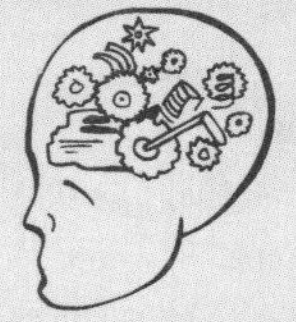
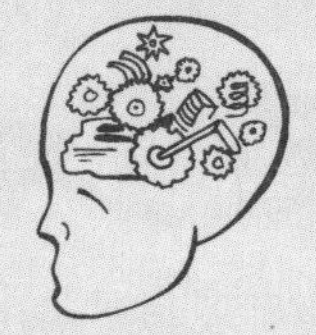
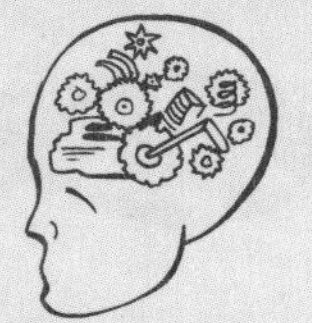

1 Which planet is known as the Red Planet?
2 What name links Hastings, New Romney, Hythe, Dover, and Sandwich?
3 If you are sinistral, what are you?
4 According to Napoleon, what does an army march on?
5 Which American President was assassinated in a theatre?
6 Which city is a holy one for three religions?
7 In Scotland what style of cloth was illegal from 1745 to 1782?
8 In land area which is the world's largest continent?
9 Of which country is Jutland a part?
10 In what kind of theatre did Vesta Tilley become famous?
11 Who in 1984 scored the first nine-dart 501 finish in a major event?
12 In the Wild West, for what was Annie Oakley famous?
13 Which word is used for a group of quails?
14 On television, whose boss was Dr Gillespie?
15 What would be the state of a person in "Carey Street"?
16 From which London station would you leave if travelling to Carlisle?
17 In a Shakespeare play who kills Desdemona?
18 Which was the last year which looked the same when the figures were looked at upside down?
19 What do Roman Catholics call the state or place where souls are purified after death?
20 What was the title of Dick Francis's first horse-racing thriller?

ANSWERS ON PAGE 295

362 SEA LIFE

1 The whale shark is the largest what?

2 Which fish shares its name with a sports boot?

3 What is the name of the heaviest mammal which lives in the sea?

4 A mollusc's body is covered in what?

5 What is a baby whale called?

6 Great white and hammerhead are types of what?

7 Which one of these creature has pincers – jellyfish, plaice or scorpion?

8 Which nationality Man o' War is a sea creature?

9 Which of the following is not a type of whale Blue, Gold or White?

10 Where would you find plankton?

11 How many legs does a seahorse have?

12 A fish breathes through what?

13 A sardine is a young what?

14 How many tentacles does a squid have?

15 Nurse and tiger are both types of what?

16 Blue, fin and humpback are all types of what?

17 What do marine mammals feed their babies on?

18 What is the name for a whale's layer of fat?

19 How good is the eyesight of a whale – outstandingly good or poor?

20 The skeleton of a shark is made up from what?

ANSWERS ON PAGE 296

363 AT THE MOVIES

1 What was the last movie made by director Stanley Kubrick?

2 Which Ethan starred in the 1998 *Great Expectations*?

3 What rank is Benjamin according to the film title?

4 Who replaced Timothy Dalton as James Bond?

5 Did *Toy Story* last 45, 80 or 240 minutes?

6 In which country was 1990s James Bond Pierce Brosnan born?

7 Which Richard won the Best Director Oscar for *Gandhi*?

8 In which decade of the 20th century was Kirstie Alley born?

9 Robin Williams played which cartoon sailor?

10 *The Avengers* and *Dangerous Liaisons* featured which actress?

11 *The Deer Hunter* was about which war?

12 Which Bruce starred in *The Jackal*?

13 Who did Kramer take to court?

14 Which 1970s film had the ad line, "Love means never having to say you're sorry"?

15 Is Gromit a person, a dog or a sheep?

16 Which Sir Alec starred in *Star Wars*?

17 Which zany comedian often co-starred with Dean Martin in the 1950s?

18 Who played a lead role in *Bonnie And Clyde* after Jane Fonda turned it down?

19 Which John won the Best Actor Oscar for *True Grit*?

20 "In Space no one can hear you scream" was the cinema poster line for which Sigourney Weaver movie?

ANSWERS ON PAGE 296

364 PICTURE QUIZ

Starting with the first, in which order did these actors win their first Best Actor Oscars?

ANSWERS ON PAGE 296

365 DOUBLE TAKE

In each case, the two-part quiz question leads to just one answer!

1 Which word can be a paved area and a legal arena?

2 Which word can be part of a hearth or can mean to shred?

3 Which word can be a stick or a place to drink?

4 Which word can be a piece of sporting equipment or a dance?

5 Which word can mean to hit or be the victor in a contest?

6 Which word can mean to drill and to be tiresome and dull?

7 Which word can be something to fire an arrow or a piece of tied ribbon?

8 Which word can be a dish or it can mean to throw a ball in cricket?

9 Which word can mean strength or the expression could do?

10 Which word can be an electric charge or mean up to date?

ANSWERS ON PAGE 296

366 WEDDINGS

1 What follows wedding to describe the post-wedding meal?
☐ Breakfast ☐ Lunch ☐ Dinner

2 On which finger of the left hand is the ring worn?
☐ First ☐ Second ☐ Third

3 Which fabric marks the 12th anniversary?
☐ Cotton ☐ Silk ☐ Wool

4 In which of these countries did penny weddings take place?
☐ Ireland ☐ USA ☐ Wales

5 Which food signifies the 6th anniversary?
☐ Cakes ☐ Fruit ☐ Sugar

6 In the royal family where does the wedding ring gold come from?
☐ France ☐ Norway ☐ Wales

7 How many years does a platinum anniversary signify?
☐ 60 ☐ 65 ☐ 70

8 Which gem marks the 40th anniversary?
☐ Emerald ☐ Ruby ☐ Sapphire

9 What is the maximum carat usually used in a wedding ring?
☐ 9 ☐ 18 ☐ 22

10 What is the traditional colour for horses at a wedding?
☐ Black ☐ Brown ☐ Grey

11 Which blue stone signifies 45 years married?
☐ Amethyst ☐ Sapphire ☐ Turquoise

12 What name is given to a wedding forced upon the couple?
☐ Bow & arrow ☐ Shotgun
☐ Torpedo

13 Which is the first of these anniversaries?
☐ China ☐ Crystal ☐ Pearl

14 In which country is a silver wreath given at 25 years?
☐ Germany ☐ UK ☐ USA

15 Which fine fabric signifies the 13th anniversary?
☐ Lace
☐ Ribbon
☐ Silk

ANSWERS ON PAGE 296

367 HALF CHANCE

½? ½? ½?

1 Northern Territory is a state in which country Australia or New Zealand?

2 Which Ford was *The Fugitive* on the big screen – Harrison or Glenn?

3 How many letters are there in the English alphabet before Y – 23 or 24?

4 What sort of transport is a clipper – an aircraft or a ship?

5 In Monopoly, do you pass Free Parking or Go to start another round of the board?

6 Is the mark on precious metals to denote their purity the benchmark or the hallmark?

7 King Hussein was ruler of which Middle East country – Egypt or Jordan?

8 Irving Berlin was famous for writing what – plays or songs?

9 What does P stand for in the initials ISP – printer or provider?

10 What did the Russians call their first spacemen – cosmonauts or vostoks?

11 Michael Jordan featured in the movie *Space* what – *Jam* or *Station*?

12 In London, does Nelson's Column stand in a Crescent or a Square?

13 How many people usually play a game of chess – one or two?

14 Which part of the body can go before the words ache and muff – ear or leg?

15 Was Francis Drake an explorer in the reign of Queen Anne or Queen Elizabeth I?

16 In which Story was Woody a hero – *Love Story* or *Toy Story*?

17 Does a coracle travel in the air or on water?

18 How many letters are there in the English alphabet between E and T – 12 or 15?

19 What did Galileo invent as an aid to study the stars – binoculars or telescope?

20 What name is given to a world map presented in spherical form – globe or orb?

ANSWERS ON PAGE 296

368 CLASSICAL MUSIC

1 Who wrote *The Hallelujah Chorus*?

2 From which work does the piece *Nimrod* come from?

3 Who wrote the concerto called *The Emperor*?

4 Which work by Sibelius represented the defiance of the Finns?

5 What is the name of Bizet's duet in the depth of the Holy Temple?

6 In which Gilbert and Sullivan opera do fairies take over Parliament?

7 Which US newspaper shares its name with a march by Sousa?

8 Which work by Bach became famous for being used in a cigar advertisement?

9 What was the first name of baroque organist and composer of *Canon in D*, Pachelbel?

10 What is Dvorak's *9th Symphony* written in the US often called?

11 Which Vivaldi composition did Nigel Kennedy recently popularise?

12 Which Englishman wrote *On Hearing the First Cuckoo In Spring*?

13 For which instrument is Joaquin Rodrigo most famous?

14 Which Old Testament prophet was the subject of an oratorio by Mendelssohn?

15 Which Mozart composition's title was translated by Sondheim into the name of a musical?

16 Who wrote the *Bolero* Torvill and Dean danced to?

17 What was in the *Carnival* in the Saint-Saens composition?

18 The 300th anniversary of the death of which English composer took place in 1995?

19 What is the English title of *La Gazza Ladra* by Rossini?

20 Which suite by Gustav Holst's features *Mars* and *Jupiter*?

ANSWERS ON PAGE 296

369 LUCKY DIP

1 What animal-linked name describes someone who always gets blamed?

2 How many seconds in five minutes?

3 Which country has the international car registration letter I?

4 Who ruled first, Queen Victoria or Queen Anne?

5 What was the former name of Sellafield?

6 In snooker what is the score for potting a black?

7 Pb is the symbol of which chemical element?

8 Who recorded the seasonal favourite *Merry Xmas Everybody*?

9 Which term means to die without making a will?

10 In which country is Sondica International airport?

11 In which novel does Jim Hawkins meet Long John Silver?

12 Who recorded the album *Bat Out Of Hell*?

13 What is the word for a group of bees?

14 Which musical instrument is associated with Acker Bilk?

15 What is another name for the prairie wolf?

16 How many colours are there in the rainbow?

17 In music, what is a note if it is neither sharp nor flat?

18 Which English city is famed for its annual Goose Fair?

19 How many inches in two yards?

20 What type of fruit is dried to produce a sultana?

ANSWERS ON PAGE 296

370 SPORT

1 Which "veteran" tennis player won the Australian Open in 2000, 2001 and 2003?

2 If you "put" a shot what do you do actually do with it?

3 How frequently are the Paralympics held?

4 The racecourse at Aintree is near which northern city?

5 Who was the first driver to be sacked by Benetton twice?

6 In which city is the US Tennis Open held?

7 Which famous jockey was born on Bonfire Night 1935?

8 Michael Jordan played basketball for the Chicago Bulls and which other team?

9 Who won swimming gold in the 100m freestyle at the 1956, '60 and '64 Olympics?

10 Who was the first Briton to be British and US Open golf champion at the same time?

11 Walter Swinburne won his first Derby on which legendary horse?

12 Motor Racing's Juan Manuel Fangio came from which country?

13 What did the G stand for in W G Grace's name?

14 Who was the first Scottish soccer player to gain 100 caps?

15 Apart from sprinting, in which event did Carl Lewis twice take Olympic gold?

16 Which England soccer World Cup winner of 1966 was knighted in 1998?

17 Which country did long-distance runner Emil Zatopek come from?

18 Who was the first batsman to hit over 500 in a first-class cricket game?

19 Who was UK champion jockey on the flat most times last century?

20 How many legs or sections are there in a relay race?

ANSWERS ON PAGE 296

371 RAP

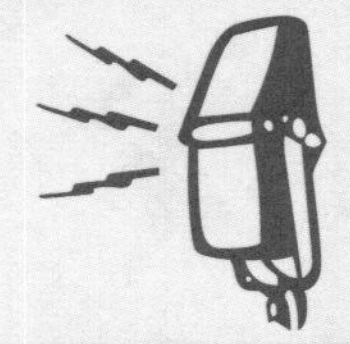
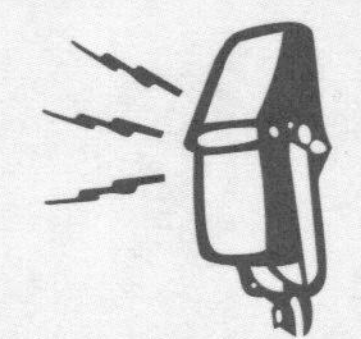
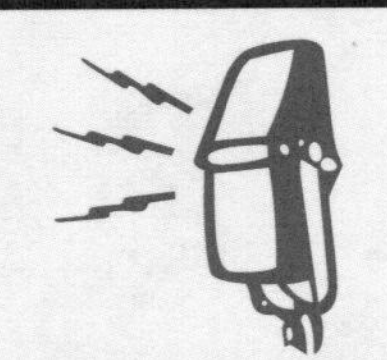

1 Which controversial rapper's No 1s include *The Real Slim Shady* and *Stan*?

2 How is rapper Durron Butler of Snap! fame better known?

3 *Gangsta's Paradise* is based on a record by which artist?

4 Vanilla Ice had won three national championships in which sport?

5 The first No 1 for The Outhere Brothers was released on which record label?

6 Who had hits with *Men In Black* and *Black Suits Comin'*?

7 What was the name of the first Rap album ever to enter the US charts at No 1?

8 Which female provided vocals on Puff Daddy's *I'll Be Missing You*?

9 Where was Dr Dre born?

10 In 2002, who was *Cleanin' Out My Closet*?

11 Who had a 1990s hit with *Another Boy Murdered*?

12 How was Christopher Wallace better known?

13 Who joined Keith Murray on the chart single which shared its name with a film with Macaulay Culkin?

14 What was Public Enemy's follow-up album to *It Takes A Nation Of Millions To Hold Us Back*?

15 Who was born Sean Combs in New York in 1970?

16 How was Makaveli also known?

17 *What's My Name?* was the first chart hit for which top rapper?

18 Who set up No Limit Records?

19 What was the first rap record to enter the UK chart at No 1....?

20 ... and who recorded it?

ANSWERS ON PAGE 296

372 GENERAL KNOWLEDGE

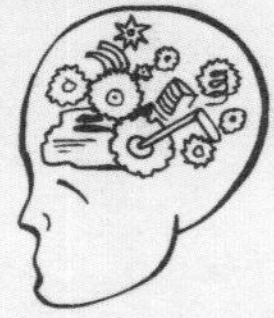
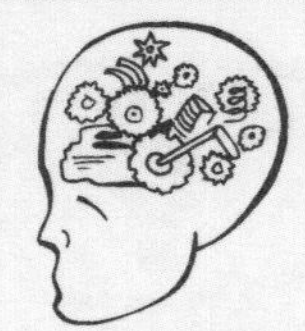
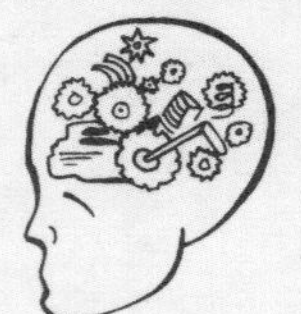

1 When made in Europe, what are the three main ingredients of a kedgeree?

2 If a violinist is playing pizzicato, what is he doing?

3 For what kind of building is Rievaulx in North Yorkshire famous?

4 Which alcoholic drink is flavoured with juniper?

5 What is the legal term for telling lies under oath?

6 In which town in 1914 was an archduke assassinated?

7 What was a Sopwith Camel?

8 In which London Park is Birdcage Walk?

9 What was the trade of the famous Russian Fabergé?

10 Who composed *Finlandia*?

11 In adverts, which drink could be taken, "Anytime, any place anywhere"?

12 What is a dactylogram?

13 Which group of islands are you going to if you are sailing to Skye?

14 If you betray your country what crime do you commit?

15 In which country did the Bengali language originate?

16 From the fibres of which plant is linen made?

17 In a book, what is a frontispiece?

18 Which English King was responsible for building the Tower of London?

19 What instrument is Larry Adler famed for?

20 How many equal angles are there in an isosceles triangle?

ANSWERS ON PAGE 296

373 NAME GAME

How are these celebrities better known?

1 ROBIN McMILLAN

2 WILLIAM BROAD

3 MICHAEL DUMBLE-SMITH

4 DEMITRIA GUYNES

5 FRANCES GUMM

6 JOSEPH SADDLER

7 MARGARITA CANSINO

8 ELEANOR GOW

9 RICHARD ESTERHUYSEN

10 THOMAS WOODWARD

ANSWERS ON PAGE 296

374 GUESS WHO . . . ?

1 Born in Philadelphia, he converted to Buddhism and starred with Jennifer Lopez in *Shall We Dance?*.

2 Born in 1967, he became the first male runner to win Olympic gold in the 200m and 400m sprints.

3 His middle name was Milhous, he was involved in the Watergate scandal.

4 Born in 1957, she was the daughter of Tippi Hedren and husbands include Don Johnson (twice) and Antonio Banderas.

5 He was born in Zanzibar in 1946, fronted supergroup Queen and died in 1991.

6 Born in 1975 and a former college basketball champion, she won three gold medals at the Sydney Olympics.

7 Born in Texas in 1921, she wrote the novel on which *The Talented Mr Ripley* was based.

8 Star of the 1972 movie *Cabaret*, her marriage to David Gest foundered in 2004, nearly 35 years after her mother Judy died.

9 He was part of a duo with Art Garfunkel, married Carrie Fisher and recorded *Graceland*.

10 Born in Alabama in 1913, he won four gold medals at the Berlin Olympics in 1936.

ANSWERS ON PAGE 296

375 CLASSICAL LINKS

1 In which country did the Three Tenors first come together?
☐ Belgium ☐ France ☐ Italy

2 Who duetted with Pavarotti on *Live Like Horses*?
☐ Bono ☐ Elton John ☐ Phil Collins

3 *Rock Me Amadeus* was about which classical composer?
☐ Beethoven ☐ Chopin ☐ Mozart

4 Which Light Orchestra took *Rockaria* into the 70s charts?
☐ Berlin ☐ Boston ☐ Electric

5 Which instrument does Einaudi play?
☐ Flute ☐ Guitar ☐ Piano

6 Who did Chuck Berry tell to Roll Over?
☐ Beethoven ☐ Mozart ☐ Purcell

7 Which musical does *America* come from?
☐ *Cats* ☐ *Chicago* ☐ *West Side Story*

8 What type of voice does Russell Watson have?
☐ Baritone ☐ Bass ☐ Tenor

9 Whose Song – minus lyrics – gave James Galway a hit?
☐ Anitra's ☐ Annie's ☐ Rusalka's

10 Which Barry borrowed some Chopin for *Could It Be Magic*?
☐ Gibb ☐ Manilow ☐ White

11 Which country is the tenor Carreras from?
☐ Argentina ☐ Italy ☐ Spain

12 On TV who was the detective who loved opera?
☐ Campion ☐ Frost ☐ Morse

13 Soccer's Euro 96 competition used which composer's music?
☐ Beethoven ☐ Elgar ☐ Wagner

14 The album *Chant* was a hit for monks of which order?
☐ Benedictine ☐ Franciscan
☐ Greyfriars

15 Kiri Te Kanawa sang an anthem in which world sporting event?
☐ Rugby Union
☐ Soccer
☐ Tennis

ANSWERS ON PAGE 296

376 PLANTS

1. In which US state is the Tongass National Forest?
2. Which herb reputedly travels seven times to the devil before it will emerge?
3. What does a saphrophyte feed on?
4. Urtica ferox is a deadly tree nettle native to where?
5. Is the agapanthus native to South Africa or South America?
6. Which of the following originated in the Middle East – barley, maize or millet?
7. What is another name for the blade of a plant?
8. What name is given to a plant whose seed is not enclosed in an ovary?
9. Which of the following are in the Aquilfoliacae group – hollies, ivies or conifers?
10. What name is given to a plant which grows on another without damaging it?
11. The Whistler Tree is what type of tree?
12. What is another name for Myosotis?
13. What is a funicle?
14. What is the world's fastest-growing plant?
15. How is lunaria biennis better known?
16. What type of plant is a Silver Slipper?
17. What colour are the blooms of the Zephirine Drouhin?
18. What is another name for the meadow saffron?
19. What is the Rose of Lancaster also called?
20. What are Alice Forbes and Bailey's Delight?

ANSWERS ON PAGE 296

377 GEOGRAPHY

1. Which South American city has a famous Copacabana beach?
2. The Bass Strait divides which two islands?
3. Which Middle East capital is known locally as El Qahira?
4. Where is the official country home of US Presidents?
5. Whose Vineyard is an island off Cape Cod?
6. Which river cuts through the Grand Canyon?
7. Which US state has a "pan handle" separating the Atlantic from the Gulf of Mexico?
8. In which two countries is the Dead Sea?
9. The site of ancient Babylon is now in which country?
10. On which river is the Aswan Dam?
11. Which continent produces almost 50% of the world's cars?
12. In England, The Fens were formerly a bay of which Sea?
13. What is Japan's highest peak?
14. To which country do the Galapagos Islands belong?
15. Aconcagua is an extinct volcano in which mountain range?
16. Where in California is the lowest point of the western hemisphere?
17. In which London Square is the US Embassy?
18. Ellis Island is in which harbour?
19. Which city is known to Afrikaaners as Kaapstad?
20. On which Sea is the Gaza Strip?

ANSWERS ON PAGE 296

378 LUCKY DIP

1 What takes just over 365 days to move once around the Sun?
2 What is the zodiac sign of the Twins?
3 In which part of the body is the patella?
4 Who recorded the album *From The Cradle*?
5 What is the second letter of the Greek alphabet?
6 Which town of Lombardy gave its name to a bright reddish mauve dye?
7 Which island is situated between Sumatra and Bali?
8 In which month of the year is Queen Elizabeth II's official birthday?
9 Which Bamber originally introduced UK television's *University Challenge*?
10 According to the proverb, what does a stitch in time save?
11 Dr Stephen Hawking wrote a brief history of what?
12 Which board game involves moving through rooms to solve a murder?
13 Which day of the week is named after the god Woden?
14 What type of jewels are traditionally associated with Amsterdam?
15 What is zoophobia a fear of?
16 Who came first as US President, Ford or Kennedy?
17 Which early screen comedian's real name was Louis Cristillo?
18 Which Edith sang, "Je ne regrette rien" (No Regrets)?
19 What colour is the Central Line on a London Underground map?
20 In the 1990s which UK Home Secretary had his son named in a drugs case?

ANSWERS ON PAGE 296

379 BOOKS

1 Whose Diary was written by Helen Fielding?
2 What was the initial print run for *Harry Potter & The Goblet Of Fire*?
3 Which leading actress wrote an anthology of critics' anecdotes called *No Turn Unstoned*?
4 Whose first novel was *The Rachel Papers* in 1974?
5 Who wrote the best seller of 2004–05 *The Da Vinci Code*?
6 Which pop celebrity wrote *Be My Baby*?
7 How many *Barchester Chronicles* are there?
8 Who wrote the novel on which the movie *Prince of Tides* was based?
9 Who went from *Deceit and Betrayal* to *A Dark Devotion*?
10 Whose book *Sex*, coincided with a dance album *Erotica*?
11 Which science fiction writer wrote the *Foundation* trilogy?
12 Which 1957 Evelyn Waugh novel is largely autobiographical?
13 Who or what was the *Empress of Blandings*?
14 Whose 19th-century dictionary standardised US English?
15 Which comedian wrote *Families and How to Survive Them*?
16 Which sports stars' autobiography was called *Facing the Music*?
17 Rider Haggard's colonial service where influenced his books?
18 Who publishes *Hansard*?
19 Whose 1998 best seller argued that our universe is a part of a super universe?
20 Which novelist's great-great-grandfather founded the *Yorkshire Post*?

ANSWERS ON PAGE 296

380 HISTORY

1. Who was the youngest queen of Henry VIII to be beheaded?
2. Which nation introduced chocolate to Europe?
3. Which American was known as Ike?
4. Which future President organized the Free French Forces in WWII?
5. What was Indira Gandhi's maiden name?
6. Who became US Vice President in 1993?
7. Which title did Hitler take as Nazi leader?
8. Who was the last Tsarina of Russia?
9. Who was Soviet Foreign Minister from 1957 to 1985?
10. Whose resignation on 1st November 1990 began Thatcher's downfall?
11. Whose 1963 Report led to the closure of many railway stations?
12. What was the religion of a French Huguenot?
13. Who was British Prime Minister during the abdication crisis?
14. For how long were Hitler and Eva Braun married?
15. Which US evangelist asked his flock to make a "decision for Christ"?
16. Which ex-athlete became MP for Falmouth and Camborne in 1992?
17. Which world leader celebrated his 80th birthday in July 1998?
18. Who was the first Archbishop of Canterbury?
19. Which US President publicly pardoned ex-President Nixon?
20. In which category did Einstein win his Nobel prize in 1921?

ANSWERS ON PAGE 296

381 SCIENCE

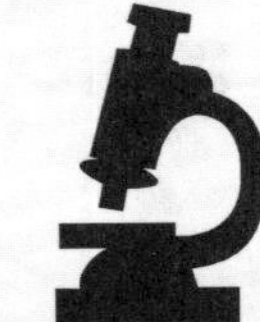

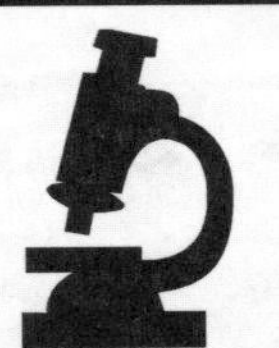

1. In 2001 Kevin Sanderson announced the invention of self-cleaning what?
2. What type of company can be found in Silicon Glen in Scotland?
3. Which scale measures the hardness of substances?
4. Was the first modern cassette made in the 1940s, 60s or 70s?
5. Which type of transport has rubber skirts?
6. What is another name for noble gases?
7. Did early TV have 405 or 625 lines?
8. The Manhattan Project in the early 1940s was developing what?
9. Which substance, recently found to be dangerous, is called "woolly rock"?
10. What is the lowest number on the Beaufort Scale?
11. Which metal is used in thermometers?
12. Is coal obtained from decayed animal or plant matter?
13. What produces bubbles in the making of champagne?
14. Which aptly named Chicago-based Laboratories developed the mobile?
15. William Morris, Lord Nuffield, was the first UK manufacturer of mass-produced what?
16. What is the most common element in the universe after hydrogen?
17. What name is given to a human being's complete set of genes?
18. What sort of invention was Sinclair's C5?
19. Which letter is farthest left on a computer keyboard?
20. Nylon took its name from which two cities?

ANSWERS ON PAGE 296

382 PICTURE QUIZ

Which of these actresses was the first in this group to win the first Best Actress Oscar?

ANSWERS ON PAGE 296

383 CHEERS

Is each statement TRUE or FALSE?

T F **1** *Cheers* was originally shown in the US in 1988.

T F **2** The Cheers bar was in New York state.

T F **3** Sam Malone used to play for the Boston Red Sox.

T F **4** Diane's surname was Charles.

T F **5** Cliff Claven was a postman.

T F **6** Frasier Crane was a psychologist.

T F **7** Norm's wife was called Vera.

T F **8** 150 million people watched the final US episode of *Cheers* in 1993.

T F **9** The spin-off from *Cheers* was called *Friends*.

T F **10** The pub where *Cheers* was set was called the Finch and Bull.

ANSWERS ON PAGE 296

384 FISH

1 What does a fish take oxygen through?
☐ Ears ☐ Gills ☐ Mouth

2 What colour are the spots on a plaice?
☐ Black ☐ Red/orange ☐ White

3 What sort of fish is a skipjack?
☐ Eel ☐ Salmon ☐ Tuna

4 Which fish has the varieties brown, sea or rainbow?
☐ Bass ☐ Herring ☐ Trout

5 Caviare is which part of the sturgeon?
☐ Fins ☐ Roe ☐ Tail

6 *Tinca tinca* is the Latin name of which fish?
☐ Tench ☐ Trout ☐ Tuna

7 Alevin and parr are stages in the development of which fish?
☐ Bream ☐ Haddock ☐ Salmon

8 Where is a fish's dorsal fin?
☐ Back ☐ Gills ☐ Tail

9 What is a young pilchard called?
☐ Pilch ☐ Sardine ☐ Smelten

10 What colour is a live lobster?
☐ Blue/black ☐ Red/orange ☐ White

11 From which part of the cod is a beneficial oil produced?
☐ Heart ☐ Liver ☐ Tail

12 The minnow is the smallest member of which family?
☐ Carp ☐ Flatfish ☐ Herring

13 Where would you find barbels on a fish?
☐ On its back ☐ On the tail
☐ Round its mouth

14 What is another name for the common European sole?
☐ Dover sole ☐ Brighton sole
☐ Red sole

15 What is a buckie another name for?
☐ Prawn ☐ Muscle ☐ Whelk

ANSWERS ON PAGE 296

385 LEISURE

1 What is the range of numbers on a European roulette wheel?

2 Which form of flying was perfected by Francis Rogallo in the 70s?

3 FIDE is the governing body of which game?

4 If you were watching the Queen's horse race, what colour sleeves would the jockey have?

5 In the 1970s the NBA and the ABA merged in which sport?

6 John Tomlinson is credited with starting which hobby?

7 In abseiling what are karabiners?

8 In cyclocross what do you do with your bike when you're not riding it?

9 Which UK tourist attraction is on the site of an 8th-century fortress?

10 Where in Normandy would you visit Monet's garden?

11 If you collected Bizarre pottery whose work would you have?

12 Paintball is a simulation of what?

13 How many zones does an archery target have?

14 In which London street was the first artificial ice rink opened?

15 In shinty what is the curved stick called?

16 In which activity do you "dive for the horizon"?

17 In which sport does a match last for a certain number of heads?

18 John Gold was the owner of which night club for over 30 years?

19 Which activity has two main types, tomiki and uyeshiba?

20 How many more people are there in an outdoor handball team than there are in an indoor one?

ANSWERS ON PAGE 296

386 GENERAL KNOWLEDGE

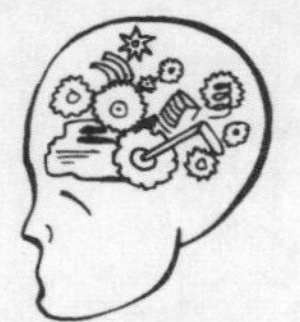
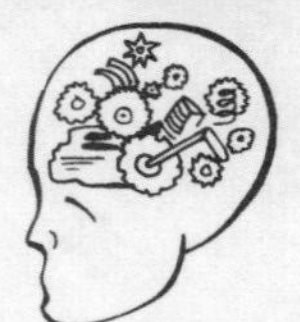

1 Under what name did Dino Crocetti achieve fame?

2 Tsar Kolokol is the biggest what in the world?

3 On how many tablets of stone were the Ten Commandments carved?

4 Which politician's memoirs appeared in the book *Upwardly Mobile*?

5 From the Victorian age, what did Mary Ann Cotton gain notoriety as?

6 What instrument did Nat "King" Cole play?

7 Cleopatra supposedly bathed in the milk of which animal?

8 Who was the first Eliza Doolittle in the stage play of *My Fair Lady*?

9 What was tested at Bikini Atoll in 1954?

10 The Boat Race course is situated between Putney and where?

11 Charles II gives his name to which type of animal?

12 Which horror great played the monster in the 1931 version of *Frankenstein*?

13 Who sang about Mr Woo?

14 Who had a flagship called *Victory*?

15 What toy is named after US President Theodore Roosevelt?

16 How is Michael Barrett better known in the pop world?

17 Which famous person did John Wilkes Booth shoot?

18 What is the pigment inside red blood cells?

19 In broadcasting what does CNN stand for?

20 Who is the patron saint of mountaineers?

ANSWERS ON PAGE 296

387 FOOD AND DRINK

1 Which batter mix is an accompaniment to roast beef?

2 Which can be French, runner or baked?

3 What colour wine is Beaujolais Nouveau?

4 What colour is the flesh of an avocado?

5 What colour is Double Gloucester cheese?

6 Would you eat or drink a Sally Lunn?

7 What type of egg is covered in sausage meat?

8 Scrumpy is a rough form of what?

9 Which mashed vegetable tops a shepherd's pie?

10 Which food has given its name to a road network near Birmingham?

11 What is the usual shape of a Camembert cheese?

12 Which fruit is associated with tennis at Wimbledon?

13 Which Mexican drink is distilled from the agave plant?

14 Is a Melton Mowbray pie sweet or savoury?

15 In Swiss cooking what is a leckerli?

16 What is added to an omelette to make an omelette Argenteuil?

17 Which herbs are put in a bearnaise sauce?

18 Which fruit is used to make slivovitz?

19 Foie gras is the liver of which creatures?

20 In ceviche raw fish is marinaded in what?

ANSWERS ON PAGE 296

388 BOXING

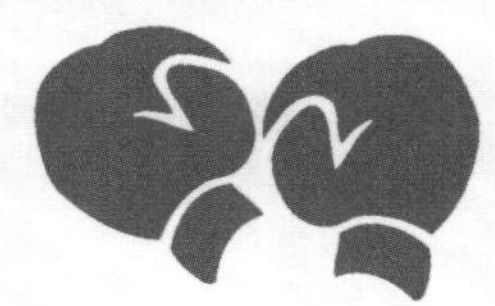

1 How many of his 61 fights did Muhammad Ali lose?

2 Who fought George Foreman in the *Rumble In The Jungle*?

3 Which country did boxer Lennox Lewis represent at the Olympics?

4 Which boxer used to enter the ring to Tina Turner's *Simply The Best*?

5 Which former world heavyweight champion was awarded a belt despite never winning a world title fight?

6 Who was the first boxer to twice regain the World Heavyweight title?

7 Which country does boxer Vitali Klitschko come from?

8 Who was known as The Manassa Mauler?

9 Boxer Naseem Hamed was brought up in which English city?

10 Whose ear did Mike Tyson take a bite at during a boxing match in 1997?

11 In which gambling venue did Evander Holyfield become World Boxing Champion in 1997?

12 Which British boxer did Mike Tyson beat to become champion in 1996?

13 Who did Mike Tyson beat to win the World Heavyweight Championship for the third time?

14 Who did Evander Holyfield beat in his first win by a knock out in the 1990s?

15 Which American state renewed Mike Tyson's boxing licence in 1998?

16 Back in the 1930s, Tony Canzoneri was world light-welterweight champ for only how many days?

17 Which boxer was ordained at the Church of the Lord Jesus Christ, Houston, Texas?

18 Which nickname was given to Shannon Briggs?

19 In which country was Joe Bugner born?

20 How did Rocky Marciano die?

ANSWERS ON PAGE 296

389 NATURE

1 Which cereal can survive in the widest range of climatic conditions?

2 Which purple aromatic plant takes its name from the Latin Lavo, meaning I wash?

3 What colour are edelweiss flowers?

4 Which plant is St Patrick said to have used to illustrate the Holy Trinity?

5 Succulents live in areas lacking in what?

6 How many points does a sycamore leaf have?

7 What is the ornamental shaping of trees and shrubs called?

8 What is an alternative name for the narcotic and analgesic aconite?

9 What colour are laburnum flowers?

10 What is another name for a yam?

11 What shape are flowers which include the name campanula?

12 What is a frond on a plant?

13 Which climbing plant is also called hedera helix?

14 Agronomy is the study of what?

15 What is a Sturmer?

16 Which fruit is called "earth berry" in German?

17 What is another name for belladonna?

18 What is the effect on the nervous system of taking hemlock?

19 Are the male, female or either hop plants used to make beer?

20 What is the most common plant grown in Assam in India?

ANSWERS ON PAGE 296

390 LUCKY DIP

1 Which country are All Nippon Airways from?

2 What is the currency of India?

3 Who released the album *A New Day At Midnight*?

4 How many squares are there on a chess board?

5 In which film did a character named Rod Tidwell appear?

6 Which king of England was called the Lionheart?

7 In rhyming slang what are plates of meat?

8 How is Gordon Sumner better known?

9 Which Thomas wrote *The Silence Of The Lambs*?

10 In the Bible, who was famous for his wisdom?

11 What was the state police of Nazi Germany called?

12 In which country is Schiphol airport?

13 Iraq invaded which neighbouring state to start the 90s Gulf War?

14 What colour is heliotrope?

15 Which tree family includes the sycamore and maple?

16 How many sides has a dodecagon?

17 Which flightless bird hides by burying its head in the sand?

18 What is the home of a beaver called?

19 Which short-legged dog is named after the 18th century parson who bred them?

20 What name is given to an extension of a stage in front of a curtain?

ANSWERS ON PAGE 296

391 AIRPORTS

Can you name the countries where the listed airports are located?

1 MAXGLAN
2 KOMAKI
3 JACKSONVILLE
4 IZMIR
5 FREJORGUES
6 EL DORADO
7 PORT HARCOURT
8 TACOMA
9 OREBRO
10 LINATE

ANSWERS ON PAGE 296

392 DOUBLE TAKE

In each case, the two-part quiz question leads to just one answer!

1 Which word can be food or payment for a journey?
2 Which word can be a corner or an old European nation?
3 Which word can mean to support and is also the word for the spine?
4 Which word can mean putting clothes on or a sauce for salad?
5 Which word can be a container or can mean to fight?
6 Which word can be something to keep you cool or an avid supporter?
7 Which word can be a number and the outline of the body?
8 Which word can be reading matter or can mean to reserve a seat?
9 Which word can be an apartment or a punctured tyre?
10 Which word can be a brick or can mean to obstruct?

ANSWERS ON PAGE 296

393 HUMAN BODY

1 What is a phalanx?
☐ Bone ☐ Muscle ☐ Nerve

2 What is another word for the eye socket?
☐ Fontanelle ☐ Maxilla ☐ Orbit

3 Which is bigger, the ulna or the radius?
☐ Radius ☐ Same size ☐ Ulna

4 Where is the thoracic curve?
☐ Backbone ☐ Ribcage ☐ Skull

5 Where are the metatarsals located?
☐ Arm ☐ Skull ☐ Foot

6 In what part of the body is the brachialis?
☐ Arm ☐ Back ☐ Leg

7 There are approximately how many muscles in the human body?
☐ 500 ☐ 650 ☐ 900

8 Appendicitis causes pain where?
☐ Abdomen ☐ Back ☐ Throat

9 Cranial osteopathy involves the manipulation of which bones?
☐ Knee ☐ Ribs ☐ Skull

10 Where is the malleus located?
☐ Foot ☐ Inner ear ☐ Nose

11 Which part of the brain deals with voluntary movement?
☐ Cerebellum ☐ Forebrain ☐ Stem

12 What is the term for the complete set of genes in a body?
☐ Genome ☐ Katyotype ☐ Mendel

13 How many bones are there in the human body?
☐ 206 ☐ 360 ☐ 602

14 What is the longest muscle in the body?
☐ Brachialis ☐ Pronator ☐ Sartorius

15 Which bone in the throat supports the tongue?
☐ Hyoid ☐ Ilium ☐ Sacrum

ANSWERS ON PAGE 297

394 SOLOISTS

1 What was Alanis Morissette's follow up to *Jagged Little Pill*?

2 Who did Morrissey leave behind when he went solo?

3 How is Florian Cloud de Bounevialle Armstrong better known?

4 Whose death moved Don McLean to write *American Pie*?

5 Which Robinson went solo after singing with the Miracles?

6 Which No 1 singer was born Arnold George Dorsey in Madras?

7 What does the R stand for in R Kelly's name?

8 Who was the biggest-selling country artist of the 90s worldwide?

9 Who had hits with *Hollywood* and *American Life*?

10 Who has recorded singles with Paul McCartney, Julio Iglesias and Diana Ross?

11 Whose Army provided Elvis Costello with an early hit?

12 Which singer's real name is Michael Bolotin?

13 Who released an album of *The Globe Sessions*?

14 Whose most famous hit was *Lady in Red*?

15 Which chart topper started life at Leigh, Lancashire as Clive Powell?

16 Where was Peter Andre brought up?

17 Which 1960s artist was the first British-born artist with three No 1 hits?

18 How is James Michael Aloysious Bradford better known?

19 Whose debut solo album was *Shepherd Moons*?

20 Who joined the Beatles on their first hit to enter the charts at No 1?

ANSWERS ON PAGE 297

395 THE ARTS

1 In which US state is the Sundance Film Festival held?

2 In which Dickens novel did Uriah Heap appear?

3 *Old Possum's Book Of Practical Cats* is composed of what?

4 What is Ripley's first name in Patricia Highsmith's *The Talented Mr Ripley*?

5 In which book did John Braine introduce Joe Lampton?

6 What type of book is the OED?

7 What is the subject of Desmond Morris's *The Naked Ape*?

8 What type of books did Patricia Highsmith write?

9 Which detective first appeared in *A Study In Scarlet* in 1887?

10 In which Holy Book other than the Bible is there the Garden of Eden?

11 What is Beethoven's 9th Symphony known as?

12 For which instrument did Paganini chiefly compose?

13 Which famous piece by Prokofiev is for orchestra and narrator?

14 What type of performance was *The Rite Of Spring* written for?

15 What is the Wagner opera cycle which includes *Siegfried* and *Die Walküre*?

16 What are Iannis Xenakis pieces written with the aid of?

17 How is the *Pomp And Circumstance March* sung at the Proms better known?

18 Which river is celebrated in Strauss's most famous waltz?

19 Which line follows "Rule Britannia" in the chorus of the song?

20 Who are Russia's opponents in the campaign commemorated in the *1812 Overture*?

ANSWERS ON PAGE 297

396 GENERAL KNOWLEDGE

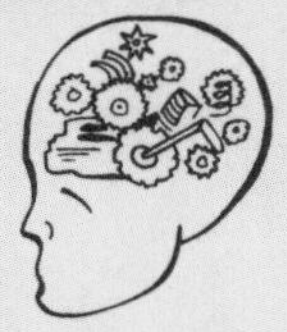
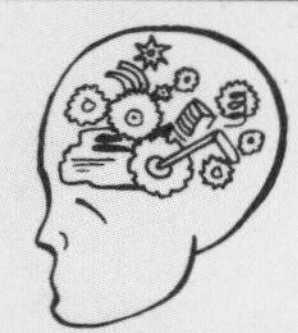
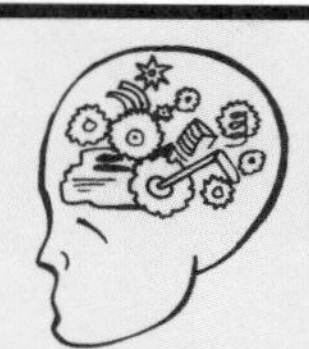

1 Which group backed singer Gary Puckett?

2 If two straight lines are always the same distance apart what are they said to be?

3 Who wrote *The Great Gatsby*?

4 Nat Lofthouse was famous in which sport?

5 In the 14th century what was the bubonic plague called in England?

6 What is another word for a sleepwalker?

7 What would the initials WO stand for in the army?

8 Which city was painted by Canaletto?

9 Who composed the *Enigma Variations*?

10 In politics, how many readings does a bill have in the Commons in the UK?

11 Yum Yum and Ko-Ko appear in which opera?

12 In which war was the Victoria Cross first awarded?

13 An ampersand is a sign for which word?

14 In Spanish, which word is used to address a young, or unmarried, lady?

15 The Suez Canal connects the Red Sea to which other Sea?

16 Which country did composer Aaron Copland come from?

17 Where did the Norse Gods live?

18 In financial terms, what is the IMF?

19 By what name is musician Raymond O'Sullivan better known?

20 Who composed the music for *West Side Story*?

ANSWERS ON PAGE 297

397 KINGS AND QUEENS

1 At which address was Elizabeth II born?

2 Where were George V and Queen Mary crowned Emperor and Empress of India?

3 Who was the only British monarch from the House of Wettin?

4 Who was William IV's Queen?

5 Which monarch's mother was Sophia of Bohemia?

6 How did George II's eldest son die?

7 Who was the first British monarch to make a Christmas Day broadcast?

8 Which English King's wife was a former wife of Louis VII of France?

9 Which British monarch produced the most legitimate children?

10 What was notable about Henry VI's coronation in 1470?

11 Who made Henry VIII "Fidei Defensor"?

12 Where was Charles I born?

13 What shape was Queen Anne's coffin and why?

14 Which English King is reputed to have invented the handkerchief?

15 Where were Richard III's bones thrown when his grave was desecrated?

16 Why was Henry VIII's execution of Richard Empson and Edmund Dudley a popular move?

17 Who was threatened by the Rye House Plot?

18 Where is William the Conqueror buried?

19 Which King founded the first English zoo?

20 Who was the penultimate Emperor of India?

ANSWERS ON PAGE 297

Independence Day

Here's a 50 question quiz celebrating American Independence Day and all things American!

1 Independence Day celebrates America's independence from whom?

2 In which year did America's Declaration of Independence take place?

3 What was rung to accompany the first reading of the Declaration of Independence?

4 Who won the Pulitzer Prize for *Independence Day* in 1996?

5 Which tennis star was born on 4th July?

6 Which US city was named after its first President?

7 How many colonies won their independence in the American Revolution?

8 Which founder of homes for destitute children was born on 4th July 1845?

9 Who was the first Irish American to be US President?

10 Which Peace recognised US independence in 1783?

11 In which century did Pennsylvania join the Union?

12 Who was the first grandson of a President to become President?

13 Which US President was born on Independence Day 1872?

14 Work began on which canal on 4th July 1904?

15 Which surname was shared by two of the first six US Presidents?

16 Which 19th century Great Famine meant many immigrants flocked to the US?

17 In 1898 the US waged war against which European country?

18 Was cotton grown in the Northern or Southern states?

19 Which early US President shared a surname with a 20th century blonde movie star?

20 In what year did Columbus "discover" America?

21 Which state was founded by Lord Baltimore in 1632?

22 For how much did Dutch settlers buy Manhattan from native American Indians?

23 What was the first European name for New York?

24 The early settlers in America were from Britain, Spain and which other European country?

25 In which city did George Washington take his oath as US President?

26 Dedicated in 1886, what does the Statue of Liberty hold in her left hand?

27 On which Cape did the Pilgrim Fathers land in 1620?

Quiz

28 Which state was the first to be a member of the Union?

29 Which President who was assassinated had a Vice President called Hannibal?

30 Who or what was New York named after?

31 What happened to the Liberty Bell when it was rung for Washington's birthday in 1846?

32 Who killed, 4,280 buffalo in eight months to feed Union Pacific railroad workers?

33 Which US playwright was born on Independence Day?

34 In which century did Texas join the Union?

35 *Annie Get Your Gun* was based on the life of which 19th century American?

36 What was the most important thing to be discovered in California in 1848?

37 Why was Utah not allowed to be a US state until 1896?

38 Which state originally acquired from Mexico now has the largest Native American population?

39 Which founder of movie studio MGM was born on 4th July?

40 Was the American Civil War won by the Northern or the Southern states?

41 Which group of islands did the US acquire in 1898?

42 Who delivered the Gettysburg address in 1863?

43 How many US Presidents died on US Independence Day in the 19th century?

44 Which US jazz trumpeter was born on 4th July 1900?

45 Bill Clinton's middle name is the same as the surname of which early US President?

46 Independence Day traditionally falls during which Grand Slam tennis tournament?

47 Which of the original states of the US is still the smallest?

48 At which siege was Davy Crockett killed?

49 Who of Barnum & Bailey was born on 4th July?

50 In which century did New Mexico join the Union?

ANSWERS ON PAGE 297

399 PEOPLE

1 Who is the famous mother of Elijah Blue?

2 Marina Mowatt is the daughter of which British Princess?

3 Fitness trainer Carlos Leon was the father of which singer/actress's child?

4 Who won an Oscar for playing female boxer Maggie Fitzgerald?

5 In which North African country was Mohammed Al–Fayed born?

6 Longleat is the stately home of which Marquess?

7 What is Madonna's first daughter called?

8 Who created Popeye?

9 Who was Axl Rose's famous singer father-in-law?

10 Which multi million pound sport is Bernie Ecclestone associated with?

11 In 1996 who did The Spice Girls say was their Girl Power role model?

12 What is Frankie Dettori's real first name?

13 How did Sir Ranulph Twistleton-Wykeham-Fiennes achieve fame?

14 Madeleine Gurdon is the third wife of which millionaire?

15 What is the much played creation of Alfred Butts?

16 What is the first name of Charles' brother of Saatchi & Saatchi?

17 In which country was Earl Spencer's acrimonious divorce settlement heard?

18 Who did Stella McCartney dedicate her first collection for Chloe to?

19 In which North African country was Yves St Laurent born as Henri Donat Mathieu?

20 Who was the first man to win 13 tennis Grand Slam titles?

ANSWERS ON PAGE 297

400 BLOCKBUSTER MOVIES

1 Which Bond movie was shown in Japan as *No Need For A Doctor*?

2 Which star of *Titanic* was King Louis XIV in *The Man in the Iron Mask*?

3 Which Ralph starred as Steed in *The Avengers*?

4 Which comic book character was played by George Clooney of *ER* fame in 1997?

5 Which Jonathan, a star of *Evita*, played villain Elliott Carver in *Tomorrow Never Dies*?

6 Who starred as Harry Dalton in *Dante's Peak*?

7 What type of natural disaster is the setting for *Twister*?

8 In which decade did the action of *Apollo 13* take place?

9 Which Mrs Cruise, Nicole starred in *Batman Forever*?

10 Which 1995 Mel Gibson movie told the story of Scot William Wallace?

11 Which daughter of Tony Curtis played Arnold Schwarzenegger's wife in *True Lies*?

12 In which movie – from the classic TV series of the same name – did Harrison Ford play Richard Kimble?

13 Which British-born Jane was Roger Moore's first Bond girl in *Live And Let Die*?

14 Which Landings make up the action of *Saving Private Ryan*?

15 In which decade was *The Lost World: Jurassic Park* released?

16 Which role did Timothy Dalton play in *The Living Daylights*?

17 Who played the Bond girl in *Dr No*?

18 Which comedian Eddie appeared in *The Avengers*?

19 *The Great Escape* was an escape from what?

20 Which Richard starred in *Where Eagles Dare*?

ANSWERS ON PAGE 297

401 GUESS WHO . . . ?

1 Born in Denmark in 1805, he wrote *The Ugly Duckling* and *The Emperor's New Clothes*.

2 Born in 1905. this French couturier designed the New Look of the 1940s.

3 This Spanish tenor studied in Mexico City and sang with Carreras and Pavarotti.

4 He commanded the *Apollo 11* moon landing, becoming the first man to walk on the moon.

5 Born Margaret Hookham. she was one of the finest ballerinas of the 20th century.

6 His brother is a zoologist; he is an actor and director whose 1982 film won eight Oscars.

7 This German-born Dutch Jewish girl left a moving diary of family life in occupied Amsterdam.

8 Born in 1934, he was the first man to orbit the earth and died in a plane crash in 1968.

9 The daughter of Nehru, she was Indian PM from 1966–77 and was assassinated in 1984.

10 Born in 1929, he became chairman of the PLO in 1968 and died in Paris in 2004.

ANSWERS ON PAGE 297

402 WHO SAID . . . ?

1 "He (Yasser Arafat) was like a surrealistic painting. He was complex, deep, superficial, rational, irrational, cold, warm."

2 "There are many vampires in the world today – you only have to think of the film business."

3 "There were three people in this marriage so it was a bit crowded."

4 "To err is human – but it feels divine."

5 "I squint because I can't take too much light."

6 "Kissing Marilyn (Monroe) was like kissing Hitler."

7 "Man is the only animal that blushes – or needs to."

8 "I'm sort of the boy next door – if that boy has a good script writer."

ANSWERS ON PAGE 297

403 TV TRIVIA

1 What follows *Brideshead* in the series featuring Jeremy Irons?
☐ Alone ☐ Lost ☐ Revisited

2 Where did Mavis go when she left *Coronation Street*?
☐ Cornwall ☐ Lake District ☐ Scotland

3 Vince and Penny were Just Good what?
☐ Buddies ☐ Friends ☐ Guys

4 What was Mrs Fforbes Hamilton's first name in *To The Manor Born*?
☐ Amy ☐ Audrey ☐ Emma

5 Which folk hero was played by Richard Greene?
☐ Robin Hood ☐ Lone Ranger
☐ William Tell

6 In which area of England was Nick Berry's *Harbour Lights* set?
☐ East ☐ North ☐ West

7 Which John played writer Peter Mayle in *A Year In Provence*?
☐ Alderton ☐ Major ☐ Thaw

8 In which relationship comedy did Jack Davenport play Steve?
☐ *Cold Feet* ☐ *Coupling* ☐ *This Life*

9 Singer Adam Rickitt found fame in which soap?
☐ *Coronation Street* ☐ *EastEnders*
☐ *Emmerdale*

10 In *Countdown*, how many people occupy Dictionary Corner?
☐ One ☐ Two ☐ Four

11 In *Bargain Hunt*, what sort of bargains are being hunted?
☐ Antiques ☐ Cars ☐ Houses

12 What is the postcode of Albert Square, Walford?
☐ E1 ☐ E15 ☐ E20

13 Which Doctor returned to UK TV in 2005?
☐ Finlay ☐ Kildare ☐ Who

14 Which Arms featured in *Where The Heart Is*?
☐ Skeldale ☐ Skelthwaite
☐ Waterside

15 Which comedy show was famous for its "Fork handles" sketch?
☐ *Two Ronnies* ☐ *Monty Python*
☐ *The Good Life?*

ANSWERS ON PAGE 297

404 ANIMALS

1 What is a common name for the Asteroidea which have five arms?

2 At what stage of development is the imago stage of an insect?

3 What is the aquatic larva of an amphibian more commonly called?

4 What is chameleon capable of changing?

5 What does a reptile shed in the process of sloughing?

6 What is another name for snake poison?

7 The aardvark is a native of which continent?

8 Which is the only mammal able to fly?

9 Which type of dark-coloured bear is the largest?

10 What do Americans call reindeer?

11 Man has seven vertebrae in his neck. How many does a giraffe have?

12 What is the main diet of hedgehogs?

13 Which two colours are wolves?

14 What is the fastest land animal?

15 From which border do Border collies originate?

16 What colour is a Chow Chow's tongue?

17 What is the mammal *homo sapiens* better known as?

18 Where does an arboreal animal live?

19 What is the smallest breed of dog?

20 Do dolphins have teeth?

ANSWERS ON PAGE 297

405 THE HEADLINES

1 Who did George W. Bush defeat when elected as President for the second time?

2 Yves St Laurent found fame designing what?

3 Oskar Schindler, whose story was told in a Spielberg movie, was from which country?

4 Which former English King did Wallis Simpson marry?

5 How many children did Tony Blair have when he became Prime Minister?

6 Lenin was a key figure in which revolution?

7 In which country did a Pan Am jumbo jet explode over Lockerbie in 1988?

8 Francois Mitterand was a Socialist head of state in which country?

9 The Battle of El Alamein was during which war?

10 The suffragettes campaigned for votes for whom?

11 Mao Tse Tung led the Long March in which country?

12 In which decade of the 20th century did Nelson Mandela become South African President?

13 Which bandleader Miller disappeared over the English Channel during WWII?

14 The tragedy of Aberfan took place in which part of the UK?

15 Mussolini led which country in WWII?

16 After WWII Germany was divided into West Germany and Communist what?

17 In the UK, the NUM was the National Union of what?

18 How many UK Prime Ministers were there in the 1990s?

19 What outbreak delayed the 2001 British General Election?

20 In which seaside location did an IRA bomb explode at a Tory Party Conference in 1984?

ANSWERS ON PAGE 297

406 FRENCH CUISINE

1 If a steak is cooked "bleu" is it well done or very lightly done?

2 In the dish crème brulée, what does brulée actually mean?

3 What is a crêpe Suzette?

4 Pears belle Hélène are coated with what type of sauce?

5 What does the word fondue mean?

6 If a dish is made à la Niçoise it is in the style of which chic French town?

7 Are Provençal dishes from the North or the South of the country?

8 Crudités are vegetables served in which way?

9 Baguette is the French word for what?

10 Which vegetables are used in a gratin dauphinois?

11 If a dish is cooked in the style Du Barry which vegetable is included?

12 Aïoli is a mayonnaise flavoured with what?

13 Which shellfish are an important part of a French Christmas Eve meal?

14 Which type of food is cooked à la meunière?

15 Which vegetable is included in food cooked à la Lyonnais as well as potatoes?

16 Which meat is bought from a charcuterie?

17 Which herbs are most frequently included in a bouquet garni?

18 Roquefort is made from which type of milk?

19 What is a bouillon?

20 What type of sauce is a béchamel?

ANSWERS ON PAGE 297

407 HALF CHANCE

1 The zodiac sign Pisces covers which two months – February/March or April/May?

2 Who won the first soccer FA Cup Final played in Cardiff – Arsenal or Liverpool?

3 Is the coast of Belgium on the Mediterranean Sea or the North Sea?

4 Which item of swimwear is named after an atoll in the Pacific – bikini or snorkel?

5 Which initials are linked with genetic fingerprinting – DNA or FBI?

6 Divali is an important feast in which religion – Hindu or Jewish?

7 What type of weapon is a kukri – a knife or a rifle?

8 What kind of Day gave U2 a No 1 hit – *Beautiful Day* or *Rainy Day*?

9 How many legs do a group of twelve seahorses have between them – 12 or none?

10 Hermit and spider are types of what – bee or crab?

11 The game of boules comes from which country – Bulgaria or France?

12 Which Queen reputedly said, "We are not amused" – Cleopatra or Victoria?

13 In place names what can go before England, Hampshire and York – New or Old?

14 Is the part of a parachute jump before the parachute opens called downtime or freefall?

15 Which type of lines on a map run north to south – latitude or longitude?

16 Macaulay Culkin sacked his dad from which job – his manager or his accountant?

17 Out of his six wives, how many did Henry VIII have beheaded – two or three?

18 Which language was spoken by the ancient Romans – Latin or Romany?

19 Did the Vikings come from Scandinavia or South East Asia?

20 How many letters are not vowels in the word queen – two or three?

ANSWERS ON PAGE 297

408 LUCKY DIP

1 Whose albums include *Body Language* and *Fever*?
2 What was suspended from 1996 to 1999 after an accident involving Alberto Puig?
3 Catherine Parr outlived which monarch who was her husband?
4 Which English club did soccer TV pundit Alan Hansen play for?
5 What spirit is made from fermented sugar cane?
6 How many years are celebrated by a silver anniversary?
7 What does the letter C stand for in RSPCA?
8 What is the capital of the Isle of Man?
9 What number does the Roman numeral I stand for?
10 Which Tom starred in *Magnum*?
11 Which word, meaning "letter", is in titles of books of the Bible?
12 Who wrote the play *The Caretaker*?
13 What paper is used to test acid and alkali?
14 What are the initials of English writer Priestley?
15 What does the letter W stand for in POW?
16 How many seconds in quarter of an hour?
17 Which special day follows Shrove Tuesday?
18 Who came first as US President, Washington or Lincoln?
19 Diana Ross, Florence Ballard and Mary Wilson formed what?
20 On what part of your body would you wear plus fours?

ANSWERS ON PAGE 297

409 20th CENTURY

20C? 20C? 20C?

1 Where in the USA was there a total eclipse in 1991?
2 Which David headed the Cult which staged a 1993 mass suicide in Waco?
3 What type of vehicle was O J Simpson driving when he tried to avoid police after his wife's death?
4 Lee Teng-Hui won the first democratic Presidential election in which country?
5 In 1910 Paul Ehrlich developed a cure for which disease?
6 Who founded the American Institution of Public Opinion in 1935?
7 Who was Hitler's Prime Minister in Prussia?
8 Who was British PM when independence was granted to India and Pakistan?
9 In 1939 who described the actions of Russia as, "a riddle wrapped in a mystery inside an enigma"?
10 At which overseas Embassy did Kim Philby work with Guy Burgess after WWII?
11 In which country did Torvill and Dean win Olympic gold with their Bolero routine?
12 Where did the US side of the Band Aid concert take place?
13 Virgin Atlantic flights first went to New York, but which UK airport did they fly from?
14 Which oil tanker disastrously ran aground off Brittany in 1987?
15 In which year did the £1 note cease to be legal tender in England?
16 How were the balls at Wimbledon different in 1986 from previous years?
17 In which country was the first permanent bungee-jumping site situated?
18 Which capital city was the scene of a major summit between Reagan and Gorbachev in 1986?
19 Proceedings in which British House were televised for the first time in January 1985?
20 Who co-wrote the Band Aid song *Feed The World* with Bob Geldof?

ANSWERS ON PAGE 297

410 PICTURE QUIZ

Who are the celebrity parents of these children?

ANSWERS ON PAGE 297

411 GUESS WHO . . . ?

1 Released from jail in 1990 and a co winner of the Nobel Peace Prize, he was South Africa's first black President.

2 Known as The Boss, he recorded *Born in the USA* and the single *Streets of Philadelphia*.

3 He fought Muhammad Ali in the Rumble in the Jungle in Zaire in 1970 and was ordained in Texas in 1978.

4 He was the first male rapper to have two No 1s in the UK but not under his real name of Marshall Mathers.

5 Born in France in 1802, he wrote the novel on which the record-breaking musical *Les Miserables* was based.

6 Her real name is Geraldine, she was famous for a Union Jack dress and was the first Spice Girl to leave the group.

7 She began writing at the age of 44, earning over £14 million from her books which were translated into 17 languages.

8 Born in Belfast in 1946, he began his career at Manchester United. He had a liver transplant in 2002.

9 He became a heavyweight boxing champion, had wives called Robin and Monica and bit off part of Evander Holyfield's ear.

10 Born in New York in 1960, he was the first to be champion jockey on both sides of the Atlantic.

ANSWERS ON PAGE 297

412 MOTOR SPORT

1 Which cars have won more Grand Prix than any other car?
☐ Benetton ☐ Ferrari ☐ Williams

2 What does the A stand for in FIA?
America ☐ Association ☐ Automobile

3 At the beginning of the new millennium which country had the most Grand Prix wins?
☐ Brazil ☐ France ☐ Great Britain

4 How many times was a Finn F1 World Champion in the 1990s?
☐ Once ☐ Twice ☐ Three times

5 Which Grand Prix was held at the Nurburgring in 1998?
☐ Belgian ☐ German ☐ Luxembourg

6 How old was James Hunt when he became World Champion?
☐ 24 ☐ 29 ☐ 33

7 During which Grand Prix did Ayrton Senna meet his death?
☐ French ☐ German ☐ San Marino

8 In which month does the Isle of Man TT race take place?
☐ April ☐ June ☐ September

9 Who did Damon Hill race for when he was 1996 Champion?
☐ Arrows ☐ Benetton ☐ Williams

10 Where is the Francorchamps circuit?
☐ Belgium ☐ France ☐ Luxembourg

11 Where is the Suzuka circuit?
☐ Japan ☐ Spain ☐ USA

12 In which month does the Indianapolis 500 take place?
☐ May ☐ April ☐ September

13 Which Grand Prix is held at Imola?
☐ Belgian ☐ German ☐ San Marino

14 How many times was a Briton F1 World Champion in the 1990s?
☐ Once ☐ Twice ☐ Three times

15 In which decade of the 20th century was the first Indianapolis 500m?
☐ First ☐ Second ☐ Third

ANSWERS ON PAGE 297

413 AT THE MOVIES

1 *Lady and the Tramp* were what type of animals?

2 *Shakespeare In Love* and *A Perfect Murder* featured which actress?

3 According to a movie title, *Only Angels Have* what?

4 Which word follows *Never Say Never* in a Sean Connery movie title?

5 What is the name of Michael Douglas's actor father?

6 Which star actor was in *Apollo 13, Sleepless In Seattle* and *Big*?

7 Who sang the theme song for *Titanic*?

8 Which word follows *Dirty Rotten* in a Steve Martin movie title?

9 War veteran Ron Kovic featured in which movie?

10 Which Barbra starred with Nick Nolte in *The Prince Of Tides*?

11 Who sang the title song of *Help!*?

12 Which famous Carole tested for the role of Scarlett O'Hara?

13 In *Mary Poppins*, what job does Mary take?

14 Which Melanie starred in *Working Girl*?

15 According to the film title how many *Degrees of Separation* are there?

16 Which Elliott featured in *M*A*S*H*?

17 Which director had a long custody battle for his children with Mia Farrow?

18 *The Empire Strikes Back* was a sequel to which blockbuster?

19 Which actor Martin was assigned to assassinate Brando in *Apocalypse Now*?

20 Which actress links *Pretty Woman* and *Hook*?

ANSWERS ON PAGE 297

414 TRAVEL

1 Which country do Greenland and the Faeroe Islands belong to?

2 What is France's highest point?

3 Which country's currency is the Lev?

4 What are the two official languages of Finland?

5 On which continent is the Kalahari desert?

6 Which country has the international registration letter M?

7 In terms of tonnes of cargo handled, which is Europe's busiest port?

8 The M8 motorway goes to which major European city?

9 On which side of the road do the Japanese drive?

10 In which city is Lime St Station?

11 The river Nile is found in which continent?

12 Which Portuguese province borders Spain and the Atlantic Ocean?

13 Which is Europe's largest country after Russia?

14 What colour is the District Line on a London Underground map?

15 Where was Checkpoint Charlie?

16 Which country owns the southernmost part of South America?

17 Most of the Lake District is in which county?

18 Which continents are separated by the Dardanelles?

19 What is the distance between two rails on a track called?

20 Which French city is Europe's largest?

ANSWERS ON PAGE 297

415 DUOS

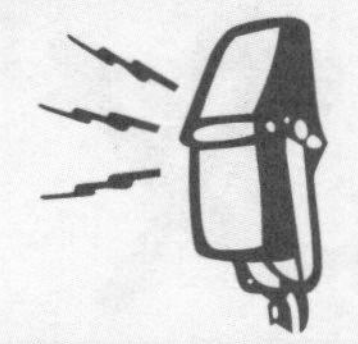
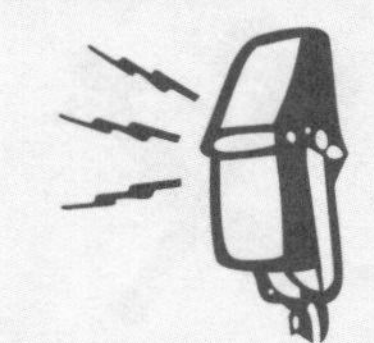

1. Who produced Ike and Tina Turner's *River Deep Mountain High*?
2. "It's four o'clock and we're in trouble deep" comes from which Everly Brothers song?
3. What relation was Sonny to Cher in their single-making days?
4. Which teen-dream duo had a transatlantic No 1 with *Last Christmas*?
5. Who was the male half of the Eurythmics?
6. What little animal did Nina and Frederick sing about?
7. Which duo were made up of Paul and Art?
8. Who did Diano Ross duo with on *Endless Love*?
9. Which Simon and Garfunkel song starts "I'm sitting in a railway station"?
10. Who did Elton John sing with on his first British No 1?
11. What were the first names of the Ofarims?
12. Which artist did Brian and Michael sing about in a surprise UK No 1?
13. Who did John Travolta duet with in the hits from *Grease*?
14. According to Peter and Gordon, to know you is to do what?
15. *It Takes Two* featured Tammi Terrell and who else?
16. How are Christopher Lowe and Neil Tennant better known?
17. Who were Respectable in 1987?
18. How many of duo Miki and Griff were female?
19. Which duo had a No 1 with *Would I Lie To You*?
20. Which duo comprised Marc Almond and David Ball?

ANSWERS ON PAGE 297

416 GENERAL KNOWLEDGE

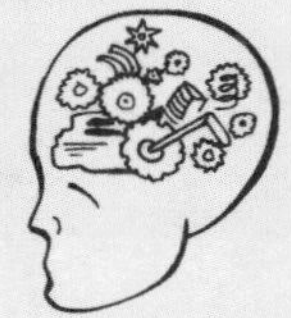
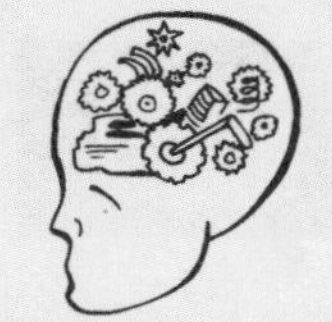
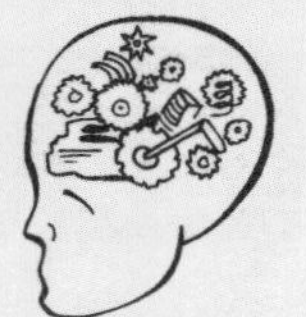

1. How many players are there in a British lacrosse team?
2. St Stephen's Day is better known as which day?
3. Who recorded the original of *Love Is All Around*?
4. Which year forms the title of a George Orwell novel?
5. What word in music means to gradually get louder and louder?
6. Which watch is 8pm to midnight at sea?
7. Who was the god of war in Roman mythology?
8. Which Derbyshire town is noted for a church with a crooked spire?
9. In cartoons, which song does Huckleberry Hound sing?
10. What type of stone is the Koh-i-noor?
11. What is the study of family history called?
12. Which creature sends down share values on the stock exchange?
13. Which sport has its headquarters in St John's Wood, London?
14. Which language was invented for international use?
15. What was climbed, "Because it is there"?
16. The Lutine Bell is in which London institution?
17. Which film was about Eric Liddell and Harold Abrahams?
18. Which drug is obtained from foxglove leaves?
19. In which English county is Romney Marsh?
20. Who directed Michael Jackson's best-selling albums?

ANSWERS ON PAGE 297

417 TELEVISION

1. Which is the female half of Mulder and Scully?
2. Was the first *Who Wants To Be A Millionaire?* UK millionaire a man or a woman?
3. In *Desperate Housewives* Susan Mayer is the mother of which character?
4. Who founded Springfield in *The Simpsons*?
5. *Sex And The City* is the name of Carrie Bradshaw's column in which newspaper?
6. Which Ally is a zany US TV lawyer?
7. What is Homer's favourite food?
8. *Ground Force* offered a viewer a makeover in which part of the home?
9. Which Australian co-presented *Animal Hospital*?
10. Which part of England is served by Anglia Television?
11. Kermit, Gonzo and Miss Piggy all belong to which group of characters?
12. Which letters does TV's Kavanagh have after his name?
13. What sex was the audience of Chris Tarrant's show *Man O Man*?
14. Who first presented the celebrity version of *Ready Steady Cook*?
15. Which TV presenter is Johnny Ball's daughter?
16. Which Mary founded the Clean Up TV campaign in 1964?
17. Which world famous female pop quintet launched Channel 5 in the UK?
18. In 2005 the Brian Clark play *Whose Life Is It Anyway* marked the West End debut of which *Sex And The City* actress?
19. Which Jerry hosts a controversial talk show that became the subject of a musical?
20. In which work location was the series *The Hello Girls* set?

ANSWERS ON PAGE 297

418 BATTLES

1. In which war did the Battle of Ebro take place?
2. Where was the peace treaty signed after the Korean War?
3. What name was given to that part of France not occupied by the Germans until 1942?
4. Which dams were destroyed by bouncing bombs in 1943?
5. Which Norwegian leader aided the 1940 invasion of his country through non resistance?
6. Which part of his body did Lord Raglan lose at Waterloo?
7. Who was commander of the US forces in the Pacific from March 1942?
8. In which city did the German High Command formally surrender to General Eisenhower?
9. What was the German 11th Chasing Squadron known as in WWI?
10. Who assassinated Archduke Franz Ferdinand in 1914 thus precipitating WWI?
11. What was the last of the treaties which ended WWI?
12. Which countries were on either end of the Maginot Line?
13. Which birthplace of Nero was the site of an Allied beachhead invasion in WWII?
14. How is the battle at St Quentin in 1918 also known?
15. Who led the military coup in Sierra Leone's Civil War in 1997?
16. How many countries made up the coalition v Iraq in the Gulf War?
17. In the Nicaraguan Civil War which faction had US support?
18. Which navy was defeated at the Battle of Midway Island in 1942?
19. Hitler's plan "Watch on the Rhine" was aimed at which troops?
20. In which area of Belgium/Luxembourg was the Battle of the Bulge?

ANSWERS ON PAGE 297

419 ART GALLERY

Who created the following famous works of art?

1 At The Moulin Rouge
2 David
3 The Fighting Temeraire
4 Haystacks
5 The Scream
6 The Night Watch
7 The Last Supper
8 The Hay Wain
9 The Persistence Of Memory
10 The Starry Night

ANSWERS ON PAGE 297

420 TROPHIES

Is each statement TRUE or FALSE?

T F 1 The America's Cup is competed for in golf.
T F 2 Women golfers compete for the Curtis Cup.
T F 3 The Gordon Bennett Trophy was an early motor racing trophy.
T F 4 The Lapham Trophy is a prize for baseball teams.
T F 5 The Leonard Trophy is awarded in the bowling world.
T F 6 The Vince Lombardi Trophy is a prize in American football.
T F 7 The Sam MacGuire Trophy is awarded to champion jockeys.
T F 8 The Prince Rainier Cup is awarded in fencing.
T F 9 The Seawanhaka Cup is awarded in sailing.
T F 10 The Thomas Cup is competed for in table tennis.

ANSWERS ON PAGE 297

421 GUITAR STARS

1 Which University awarded Mark Knopfler an honorary music doctorate?
☐ Bristol ☐ London ☐ Newcastle

2 Ted Nugent said, "if it's too loud you're too . . ." what?
☐ Drunk ☐ Old ☐ Soft

3 What did Brian May study at university?
☐ Astronomy ☐ Greek ☐ Music

4 Who recorded *From The Cradle*?
☐ Eric Clapton ☐ Jon Bon Jovi ☐ Pete Townshend

5 Which guitarist's first two names were Brian Robson?
☐ Hank Marvin ☐ Jimi Hendrix ☐ Ken Downing

6 Which album featured Mark Knopfler and Chet Atkins?
☐ *Licks* ☐ *Neck And Neck* ☐ *Picks*

7 What was Bruce Springsteen's first group called?
☐ Castille ☐ The Rogues ☐ Springers

8 Which Roy guested on Pink Floyd's *Wish You Were Here*?
☐ Harper ☐ Orbison ☐ Wood

9 In which city did Hendrix die?
☐ London ☐ New York ☐ Seattle

10 What was Jeff Beck's debut solo album called?
☐ *Beckham* ☐ *Beck-ola* ☐ *Beck Tracks*

11 Which group was included guitarists John Williams and Kevin Peek?
☐ Cream ☐ Sky ☐ Yes

12 Peter Buck is in which mega rock band?
☐ Free ☐ Judas Priest ☐ R.E.M

13 Jimi Hendrix used which guitar to make *Are You Experienced?*
☐ Fender ☐ Gibson ☐ Stratocaster

14 The guitar piece *Cavatina* came from which movie?
☐ *Alien* ☐ *The Deer Hunter* ☐ *E.T.*

15 What was the name of BB King's beloved Gibson guitar?
☐ Claudette ☐ Lucille ☐ Miss Molly

ANSWERS ON PAGE 297

422 HALF CHANCE

½? ½? ½?

1. Who had a hit single with *Independent Woman* – Destiny's Child or The Honeyz?
2. The movie and stage show *Grease* is set in which decade – 1950s or 1960s?
3. Is a flexible diving board called a downboard or a springboard?
4. What are the minimum number of notes needed to produce a chord – two or three?
5. What did George Everest give his name to – Georgia or Mount Everest?
6. In the traditional song, is the *House Of The Rising Sun* in New Orleans or New York?
7. Would a mural be painted on a floor or a wall?
8. Nero was the Emperor when which ancient city was destroyed – Cairo or Rome?
9. What was the *Streetcar Named* in the Brando movie – Desire or Passion?
10. Were Honda cars originally manufactured in Honduras or Japan?
11. Was Little John or Will Scarlet the tallest person in Robin Hood's Merry Men?
12. How many pairs of ribs does a human have – 12 or 24?
13. Which gas is believed to be encouraging global warming – carbon dioxide or hydrogen?
14. What is a clavichord – a bone in the ear or a musical instrument?
15. What is the day job of the characters in *Baywatch* – customs officers or lifeguards?
16. How many letters appear in the English alphabet before Q – 14 or 16?
17. What is the French word meaning yellow – jaune or oriel?
18. How is Uluru also known – Ayers Rock or Easter Island?
19. Who is head of the family in the fiendishly funny *Addams Family* – Gomez or Homer?
20. What colour is the cheapest property on a London Monopoly board – brown or green?

ANSWERS ON PAGE 298

423 BIRDS

1. What is the term for someone who studies or watches birds?
2. What species of kite breeds in Britain?
3. What is the study of birds' eggs?
4. An exaltation is a group of which birds?
5. What would you see if there was a Turdus on your window sill?
6. What colour are wild budgerigars?
7. A scapular on a bird is a type of what?
8. Which extinct bird was last sighted in Mauritius?
9. Which bird is sacred in Peru?
10. What type of wren is the smallest British bird?
11. What type of birds are ratites?
12. Which birds group to mate and are shot in braces?
13. What name is given to a flock or gathering of crows?
14. What is special about the bones of most birds?
15. Which family of birds does the robin belong to?
16. Golden and argus are varieties of which bird?
17. Which of the senses is poorly developed in most birds?
18. What is special about a palmiped?
19. Which bird lays the largest egg?
20. What is the oldest known fossil bird?

ANSWERS ON PAGE 298

424 PICTURE QUIZ

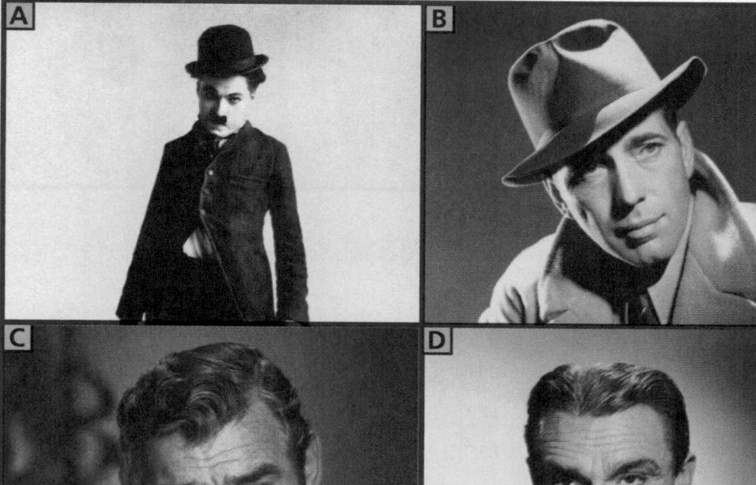

Who was the youngest of these Hollywood greats?

ANSWERS ON PAGE 298

425 NAME THE YEAR

1 The Wright brothers make the first powered aircraft flight. The Ford Motor Company was formed. Marie Curie became the first woman to win a Nobel prize

2 Sean Connery was born. The first Oscars were presented. The first colour TV image was demonstrated in New York.

3 Gene Kelly was born. Captain Scott reached the South Pole. The *Titanic* sank on its maiden voyage.

4 John F Kennedy was assassinated. Martin Luther King delivered his "I have a dream" speech. The American Express card was launched in the UK.

5 Philips and Sony introduced compact discs. Argentine forces invaded the Falkland Islands. Prince William, son of Prince Charles and Princess Diana, was born.

6 Tom Hanks won an Oscar for *Forrest Gump*. Andre Agassi won his first US Open Championship. *Streets Of Philadelphia* was the Grammy Song of the Year.

ANSWERS ON PAGE 298

426 POP MUSIC QUIZ

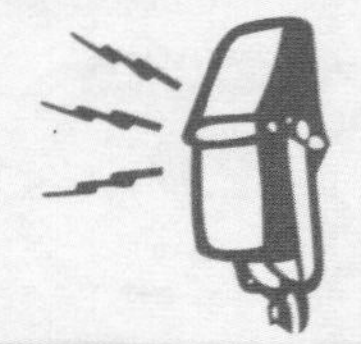
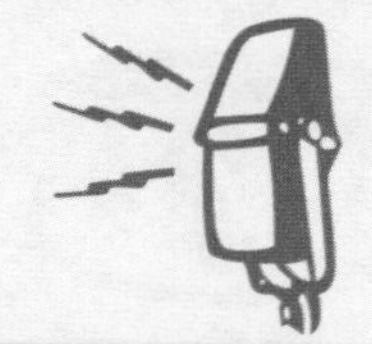

1 What was R Kelly's first UK No 1 of this millennium?

2 Which group made the albums *Turnaround* and *Coast To Coast*?

3 Which one word is shared by hits for Shaggy, Madonna and Rod Stewart?

4 Which seabird took Fleetwood Mac to No 1 in the UK?

5 Who recorded the *Immaculate Collection*?

6 Which Lonnie was the first UK male to have two US Top Ten hits?

7 Damon Albarn was lead singer with which Britpop band?

8 What word was replaced by the letter T in T. Rex?

9 How many brothers were in the original Jackson line up?

10 Which insects were Adam backed by?

11 Which supergroup recorded *Seven Seas Of Rhye* back in the 1970s?

12 What was Robert Palmer *Addicted To* according vto a song title?

13 Who had a hit with *Orinoco Flow*?

14 What line comes before "Why, why, why, Delilah?"?

15 Under what name had the late Mary O'Brien been famous?

16 Which song was a No 1 for Nilsson and Mariah Carey?

17 Who had a singer Roger Daltrey and a drummer Keith Moon?

18 Which country does Bjork come from?

19 Who has been both *Bad* and *Dangerous*?

20 Who linked up with Aitken and Waterman to make a chart-busting UK production trio?

ANSWERS ON PAGE 298

427 LUCKY DIP

1 The Rio Grande separates which two countries?

2 In the 14th century, which two countries fought at Poitiers?

3 In music, a flat sign lowers a note but what sign raises a note?

4 What are the two main colours on the Vatican flag?

5 Chemically pure gold contains how many carats?

6 In chess, which piece always moves diagonally?

7 Are sea-urchins animal, vegetable or mineral?

8 Dexter and May have captained England in which sport?

9 Which artist painted *Sunflowers*?

10 In which county is Windsor Castle?

11 What term is given to the distance from the centre of a circle to the outer edge?

12 What is the highest mountain in the Alps?

13 Who wrote the story *The Invisible Man*?

14 Wayne Rooney was first capped for England while he was at which league club?

15 Which writer created Philip Marlowe the private eye?

16 How many degrees are there in a right angle?

17 Which Derbyshire town gives its name to a Tart?

18 Jonquil is a shade of which colour?

19 Who or what is halitosis?

20 Who created the character Kiki the parrot?

ANSWERS ON PAGE 298

428 PERFORMING ARTS

1 What is the first name of conductor Rattle?

2 What was the name of opera singer Callas?

3 What was the nationality of Tchaikovsky?

4 What do you do to a tambourine to get a noise out of it?

5 Which musical features the character Grizabella?

6 Which musical instrument did Yehudi Menuhin play?

7 Which play features in the musical *Kiss Me Kate*?

8 What night of the week is the last *Night of the Proms* in the UK?

9 Which is the lowest male voice?

10 Who is Gertie in the musical *Noel And Gertie*?

11 Which Arthur Miller play is a comment on McCarthyism?

12 Which screenplay did Miller write for his wife Marilyn Monroe?

13 Who wrote plays with a political theme such as *The Little Foxes* and *The Searching Wind*?

14 Which poet spent time in an American mental hospital after supporting Mussolini and the Fascists in World War II?

15 Whose real name was Samuel Langhorne Clemens?

16 Which Hemingway novel is an account of life in an expatriate American community in Paris in the 20s?

17 In which Tennessee Williams play do you meet Big Daddy?

18 Who wrote the stories of Rip Van Winkle?

19 What type of writing is Paul Theroux associated with other than novels?

20 Which musical does *Tell Me It's Not True* come from?

ANSWERS ON PAGE 298

429 WHAT COLOUR IS . . .?

1 the middle stripe of the French flag?

2 Delft Dutch earthenware?

3 rosé wine?

4 the leader's jersey in the Tour de France?

5 the rind of Edam cheese?

6 the eight of diamonds?

7 the cross outside a French chemist's shop?

8 the background on the European Union flag?

9 the shirt worn by a Cambridge rower in the university boat race?

10 the flag of surrender?

ANSWERS ON PAGE 298

430 DOUBLE TAKE

In each case, the two-part quiz question leads to just one answer!

1 Which word can be slang for a US dollar or a male rabbit?

2 Which word can be a body joint or an expression meaning fashionable?

3 Which word can be earth or a description of pulverised coffee?

4 Which word is the first letter of a proper noun or a country's chief city?

5 What can be a pet or an old-fashioned whip?

6 Which word can be part of the body or another word for audacity?

7 Which word means to retrieve something thrown or a snag?

8 Which word can be a group of animals or to load a suitcase?

9 Which word describes longing for something and also names a tree?

10 Which word is a slang term for cowardly or is a young hen?

ANSWERS ON PAGE 298

431 GOSSIP AND SCANDAL

1 In which city did Hugh Hefner open his first Playboy Club?
☐ Chicago ☐ New York ☐ Washington

2 Which Miss was Lindi St Clair dubbed?
☐ Backlash ☐ Eyelash ☐ Whiplash

3 Which Bruce has a South American wife called Wilnelia?
☐ Forsyth ☐ Springsteen ☐ Willis

4 How many times was Elizabeth Taylor married last century?
☐ Five ☐ Six ☐ Eight

5 What is the name of Sir Michael Caine's daughter?
☐ Natasha ☐ Shania ☐ Victoria

6 What is the first name of Lady Archer, wife of the disgraced peer?
☐ Martha ☐ Mary ☐ Monica

7 Which Robbie's name was linked with Geri Halliwell?
☐ Coltrane ☐ Fowler ☐ Williams

8 Which Ms Mills did Paul McCartney marry?
☐ Hayley ☐ Heather ☐ Helen

9 Which Ms Kidd was one of the faces of the 1990s?
☐ Jodie ☐ Naomi ☐ Sophie

10 What is the nickname of Ms Legge Bourke?
☐ Tiffi ☐ Tiggy ☐ Twiggy

11 Which emblem did Patsy Kensit have tattooed on her ankle?
☐ Angel ☐ Shamrock ☐ Vulture

12 In which country was Mariella Frostrup born?
☐ Norway ☐ UK ☐ USA

13 What is Frank Sinatra's widow's first name?
☐ Ava ☐ Barbara ☐ Nancy

14 Which Catherine did Michael Douglas marry?
☐ Deneuve ☐ Walker ☐ Zeta Jones

15 Which Marquess is the brother of "It Girl" Victoria Hervey?
☐ Bath ☐ Bristol ☐ Buckingham

ANSWERS ON PAGE 298

432 SPORT

1 Which team won the first Super Bowl?

2 How many players are there in a baseball team's batting lineup?

3 In which decade was Tiger Woods born?

4 Which event on ice is the fastest team sport in the world?

5 In which sport do players compete for the Davis Cup?

6 Who went from Leeds to Manchester Utd for a reputed record transfer fee of £30 million?

7 Which country has won most Olympic golds for judo?

8 In cricket. which English bowler took a 1990s hat trick against the West Indies?

9 In which US state were the last summer Olympics of the 20th century held?

10 Who was the first golfer to be No 1 when the official rankings appeared in the 1980s?

11 Which American beat Tim Henman in his first Wimbledon Singles semi-final?

12 Who inflicted Nigel Benn's first defeat as a professional?

13 Who was the last team to be relegated from the Premiership in the 20th century?

14 Yuan Yuan was caught carrying drugs for which Chinese team?

15 In 1998 Tegla Loroupe set a new world record in the women's section of which event?

16 Which soccer team moved to Pride Park in the 1990s?

17 In which sport did Andy Thomson become a world champion?

18 Which legendary American golfer played his last British Open in 1995?

19 In tennis how many events make up the Grand Slam?

20 How often is the Epsom Derby held?

ANSWERS ON PAGE 298

433 POP LYRICS

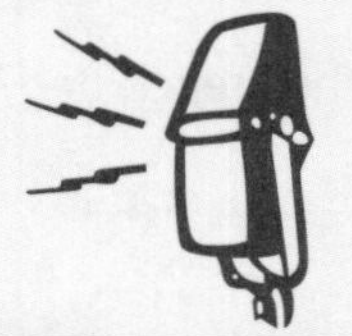
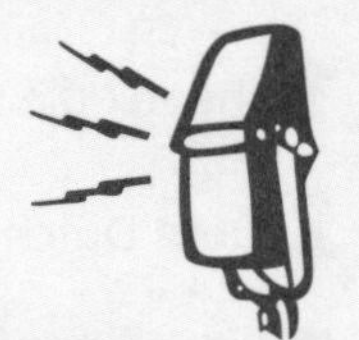

1 What line comes after, "Her name was Lola"?

2 Where are you if you want to "wake up in a city that never sleeps"?

3 "The answer, my friend, is blowing . . ." where?

4 What did he paint apart from "Matchstalk Men"?

5 What line comes before "I feel it in my toes"?

6 How many time do you sing "Yeah" in the chorus of *She Loves You*?

7 To whom did Dolly Parton beg please don't take my man?

8 If tonight is the night how is Whitney Houston feeling?

9 According to Pink Floyd, "We don't need no education, We don't need no . . ." what?

10 What word comes before, "Not a sound from the pavement"?

11 Finish the line: "You never close your eyes anymore when I kiss . . ."

12 Which Elton John line follows "It's a little bit funny"?

13 Which two herbs go with "parsley, sage"?

14 In *Sultans Of Swing* who "knows all the chords"?

15 In *Grease*, what line comes before "Did she put up a fight?"?

16 Finish the Roy Orbison line: "You're not the truth, No-one could look as . . ."?

17 What four words go after, "Do I love you, My oh my"?

18 Who was "wearing a face that she keeps in a jar by the door"?

19 "Do you really want to hurt me? Do you really want to" do what?

20 "Her face at first just ghostly turned" what colour?

ANSWERS ON PAGE 298

434 GEOGRAPHY

1. The Golan Heights are on the border of which two countries?
2. What is the largest country of South America?
3. Mont Blanc is on the border between Italy and which country?
4. In which country is Cologne?
5. Does London or Rome have the higher population?
6. Which strait separates Australia from Tasmania?
7. Which landlocked country is divided into cantons?
8. Where might you receive the honour of Nederlandsche Leeuw?
9. Bohemia is part of which Republic, formerly part of Czechoslovakia?
10. Is Schiphol an airport or a river in the Netherlands?
11. Antwerp is a province and city in which country?
12. Which country is known as the Bundesrepublik Deutschland?
13. Which is further north, Switzerland or Italy?
14. Andorra lies between France and which other country?
15. Which country was formerly the Dutch East Indies?
16. Belarus and Ukraine were formerly part of which huge republic?
17. What is the English name for the city known to Italians as Venezia?
18. Is Sweden a kingdom or a republic?
19. Vienna lies on which river?
20. Is Ibiza part of the Canaries or the Balearics?

ANSWERS ON PAGE 298

435 HISTORY

1. In which World War was the Home Guard founded in the UK?
2. In which country were the Borgias a powerful family?
3. Which nurse is famous for her work during the Crimean War?
4. Which Al was crime boss of Chicago during Prohibition?
5. Which South African shared the Nobel Peace Prize with FW de Klerk in 1993?
6. What was President John F Kennedy's wife called?
7. Which English Quaker founded the colony of Pennsylvania?
8. What was Argentinian vice president Eva Duarte's married name?
9. Roman Emperor Hadrian gave his name to what in Britain?
10. Which animals did Hannibal use to frighten the Romans?
11. Hirohito was Emperor of which country during WWII?
12. Which Russian word for Caesar was used by Russian monarchs?
13. Where was T. E. Lawrence involved in an independence struggle?
14. Which Russian revolutionary took his name from the River Lena?
15. In which country was the policy of glasnost launched?
16. Which 11th century Scottish king was the subject of a Shakespeare play?
17. In which country of the UK was David Livingstone born?
18. Which British admiral Horatio was born in Norfolk?
19. Whose Royal Family were buried in 1998 after their murder in 1918?
20. Which country put the first woman in space?

ANSWERS ON PAGE 298

436 ACTION MOVIES

1 In which movie did Robert Duvall say, "I love the smell of napalm in the morning"?

2 In *Tomorrow Never Dies*, who played M?

3 Which singer appeared in *Mad Max Beyond Thunderdome*?

4 What was the third *Die Hard* movie called?

5 Which French city was the location for *French Connection II*?

6 What was the name of Sean Connery's villain in *The Avengers*?

7 Who was Harrison Ford's male co-star in *The Devil's Own*?

8 Which tunnel is the location for a helicopter pursuit in *Mission Impossible*?

9 What was Serpico's first name, as played by Al Pacino?

10 Ian Fleming's Jamaican home gave its name to which Bond movie?

11 Which actor plays the head of the crew in *Armageddon*?

12 Which 007 starred in *Dante's Peak*?

13 What came number three in Oliver Stone's Vietnam trilogy?

14 Which 1970s movie with Jack Lemmon was about a cover up over a nuclear accident?

15 In *Day Of The Jackal* who was the leader who was to be assassinated?

16 What was the name of Eddie Murphy's character in *48 Hours*?

17 *Courage Under Fire* was about which conflict?

18 Who was the star of *Last Action Hero*?

19 Who sang the Bond theme from *For Your Eyes Only*?

20 What was Leonardo DiCaprio's first film after *Titanic*?

ANSWERS ON PAGE 298

437 GENERAL KNOWLEDGE

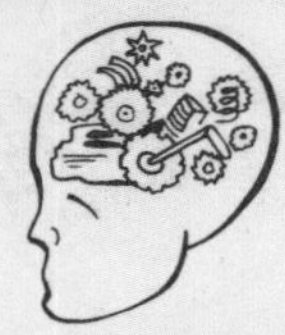 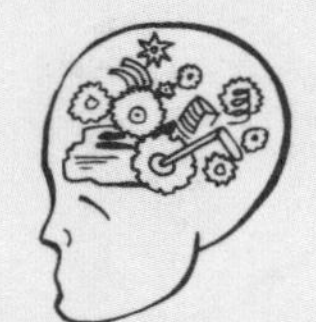 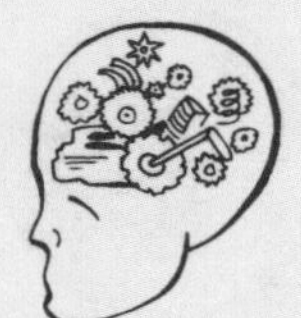

1 In which capital city was Alexander Graham Bell born?

2 Whose first book was called *Child Whispers*?

3 Which breed of dog is named after a character in a novel by Sir Walter Scott?

4 On which river does Moscow stand?

5 Where do the Greek gods live?

6 Mount Parnassus is in which country?

7 What were the names of Wendy Darling's brothers in *Peter Pan*?

8 Which Willkie Collins book is said to be the first detective story written in English?

9 Ena Sharples and Elizabeth of Glamis are types of what?

10 In British government who sits on The Woolsack?

11 Which planet did Herschel discover in 1781?

12 What is the nearest planet to the sun?

13 In which war was The Charge of the Light Brigade?

14 Who was Henry VIII's last wife?

15 Which William led a gang called the Outlaws?

16 If you were awarded an OBE what would you be?

17 Who led the Argonauts in their quest for the Golden Fleece?

18 Who is Queen Elizabeth II's eldest grandchild?

19 What nationality was composer Richard Wagner?

20 By what name did the late singer/actor Terrence Nelhams become better known?

ANSWERS ON PAGE 298

438 PICTURE QUIZ

Which star was born in the 19th century?

ANSWERS ON PAGE 298

439 GUESS WHO . . . ?

1 Born in Russia, he became French then American and wrote *The Rite of Spring*.

2 Born in London, her most famous novels are *Rebecca* and *My Cousin Rachel*.

3 Known as "The Ice Man", he won 11 Grand Slam Singles titles before retiring aged 26 in 1983.

4 Born in Dublin in 1882, his most famous novels are *Dubliners* and *Ulysses*.

5 Born in New York with the real first name Alfredo, he starred in *The Godfather* and *Scent of a Woman*.

6 Born in Nottinghamshire in the 19th century, *Sons & Lovers* and *Lady Chatterley's Lover* caused great scandals.

7 Born in New Zealand, she sang at the wedding of Prince Charles and Lady Diana Spencer and was made a Dame.

8 Father of driver Damon, he was World Champion in 1962 and died in a plane crash in 1975.

9 Born in London, he co wrote *Evita* and *Jesus Christ Superstar* with Tim Rice and was made a Lord.

10 Born in Cincinnati in 1947, his films range from *Jaws* to *The Color Purple* to *Saving Private Ryan*.

ANSWERS ON PAGE 298

440 CARTOONS

1 What is the name of the dinosaur in *Toy Story*?
☐ Dino ☐ Rex ☐ Steggi

2 Who was Pongo's partner in *101 Dalmatians*?
☐ Paula ☐ Penelope ☐ Perdita

3 What type of animal was Dumbo?
☐ Donkey ☐ Elephant ☐ Vulture

4 Who did Minnie Driver provide the voice for in *Tarzan*?
☐ Jane ☐ Parrot ☐ Tarzan

5 What type of creature was Felix, an early animation character?
☐ Cat ☐ Dog ☐ Rabbit

6 Anne Bancroft did a voice-over in which 1998 insect movie?
☐ *Antz* ☐ *A Bugs Life* ☐ *Spiders*

7 *The Return Of Jafar* was the sequel to which movie?
☐ *Aladdin* ☐ *Toy Story* ☐ *Nemo*

8 In which movie was there a Twilight Bark?
☐ *Antz* ☐ *101 Dalmatians*
☐ *Jungle Book*

9 Which two colours does Donald Duck usually wear?
☐ Blue & red ☐ Blue & white
☐ Red & white

10 In which decade was *Snow White* released?
☐ 1930s ☐ 1940s ☐ 1950s

11 Who did Nick Park create as Wallace's faithful hound?
☐ Dawson ☐ Gromit ☐ Preston

12 What was the name of the rabbit in *Bambi*?
☐ Dumper ☐ Shenzi ☐ Thumper

13 Which film featured the song *The Bare Necessities*?
☐ *Jungle Book* ☐ *Pocahontas*
☐ *Space Jam*

14 Which Mel was the voice of Captain Smith in *Pocahontas*?
☐ Brooks ☐ Gibson ☐ Smith

15 Which film featured Buzz Lightyear and Mr Potato Head?
☐ *Aladdin*
☐ *Jungle Book*
☐ *Toy Story*

ANSWERS ON PAGE 298

441 HALF CHANCE

½? ½? ½?

1 Which university is the oldest in the USA – Harvard or Yale?
2 At Royal Ascot which day is Ladies' Day – third day or final day?
3 In Spanish, what is the number cuatro – four of five?
4 Which name for a long race comes from a battle in the years BC – Derby or Marathon?
5 The *Titanic* sank while travelling across which ocean – Atlantic or Pacific?
6 How many colours appear on the Australian flag – three or four?
7 What is the line across the middle of a circle called – diameter or radius?
8 Who set up a communications system that used dots and dashes – Caxton or Morse?
9 Josiah Wedgwood found fame making what – pottery or trains?
10 What does the middle w in www stand for – wide or web?
11 What is the next prime number after 7 – 11 or 17?
12 In cards is the Queen of Spades known as The Black Lady or The Dark Damsel?
13 What is a baked Alaska's outer layer made from – ice cream or meringue?
14 Bryan Ferry named his son after which musical hero – John Lennon or Otis Redding?
15 Which actress has been President of the Dyslexia Institute – Joanna Lumley or Susan Hampshire?
16 Who created the character George Smiley – John Le Carré or Colin Dexter?
17 In the English alphabet, how many letters are there before J – nine or ten?
18 The Roman God Janus gives his name to which month – January or August?
19 Michael Balcon was involved with which comedies – Ealing Comedies or *Carry On*?
20 What was the 1990s operation to eject Iraqis from Kuwait codenamed – Desert Storm or Sandblast?

ANSWERS ON PAGE 298

442 LATE GREATS

1 Which member of T Rex died exactly the same day as Maria Callas?
2 Which part of the brilliant Albert Einstein was preserved after his death?
3 Which Princess and former film star died in a car crash near Monte Carlo in 1982?
4 How many times did Greta (I want to be alone) Garbo marry?
5 Linda McCartney launched a range of what type of food?
6 Which opera singer's real name was Maria Kalogeropoulos?
7 Yitzhak Rabin was Prime Minister of which country when he was assassinated in 1995?
8 Which Yuri made the first human journey into space?
9 Which fuel made millions for J. Paul Getty?
10 How was Argentinian revolutionary Ernesto Guevara de la Serna better known?
11 Charles de Gaulle was President of which European country?
12 Who was the youngest US President to die in office?
13 T. E. Lawrence's name is mostly associated with which country?
14 Yehudi Menuhin was famous for playing which musical instrument?
15 Glenn Miller's plane disappeared during which war?
16 Which blonde icon made her name in *Gentlemen Prefer Blondes*?
17 Fans visit Graceland in the USA to pay tribute to which rock legend?
18 In which country did Mother Theresa found her mission to help the destitute?
19 Who was the first Queen of England in the 20th century?
20 What was the name of the musical about rock legend Buddy Holly?

ANSWERS ON PAGE 298

443 LUCKY DIP

1. Who is the father of Rosanna Davison, the 2003 Miss World?
2. What is the zodiac sign of the Lion?
3. Although they were over 30 years apart, who recorded the albums *Abraxus* and *Shaman*?
4. Which bell was named after Benjamin Hall?
5. In the Bible, what part of John the Baptist's anatomy did Salome demand as a reward for her dancing?
6. Which UK comedian talked about "Loadsamoney"?
7. The Basque region surrounds which mountains?
8. Which sport in the Olympics includes pikes, tucks and twists?
9. Who did Tony Robinson play in the *Blackadder* series?
10. According to the proverb, how do still waters run?
11. Whose official residence is the Mansion House in London?
12. Which exotic bird stands on one leg?
13. Who directed *Lethal Weapon*?
14. Which actor played the title role in the television series *Lovejoy*?
15. What is hippophobia a fear of?
16. What is the name given to squarish parcels of pasta filled with meat, vegetables and/or cheese?
17. Which Great breed of dog sounds like it comes from Scandinavia?
18. Which fictional girl met a Mad Hatter and a Cheshire cat?
19. Which Alexander Graham patented the telephone?
20. Which singer with Vinegar Joe and Power Station passed away in September 2003?

ANSWERS ON PAGE 298

444 FOOD AND DRINK

1. Tikka is a dish in which country's cookery?
2. A strudel is usually mainly filled with which fruit?
3. What relation is Albert to fellow chef and restaurateur Michel Roux?
4. Which pasta sauce originated in Bologna in Italy?
5. What is a frankfurter?
6. How are eggs usually cooked in the breakfast dish bacon and eggs?
7. What is fromage frais a soft type of?
8. Does an Italian risotto contain rice or pasta?
9. Over what would you normally pour a vinaigrette dressing?
10. Rick Stein's restaurant and cooking specialises in what?
11. What colour wine is a Valpolicella?
12. In which country did Chianti originate?
13. What is the main filling ingredient of a quiche?
14. Is a poppadum crisp or soft?
15. What type of meat is found in a cock-a-leekie soup?
16. Is brioche a type of bread or a fruit?
17. What shape is the pasta used to make lasagne?
18. What is mozzarella?
19. What colour is fudge?
20. Which north of England county is famous for its hotpot?

ANSWERS ON PAGE 298

445 SHAKESPEARE

1 In what year was Shakespeare born?

2 What was Juliet's last name in *Romeo and Juliet*?

3 Which play is often known as The Scottish Play?

4 Which forest provides the setting for *As You Like It*?

5 How many gentlemen come from Verona in the title of a play?

6 Which musical features the song *Brush Up Your Shakespeare*?

7 In *Hamlet*, who is the sister of Laertes?

8 Who became Mrs Shakespeare?

9 Which character is the villain of *Othello*?

10 How many plays did Shakespeare write?

11 Which play includes the famous "To be, or not to be" speech?

12 Who appears before *Macbeth* as a spectre that no-one else can see?

13 Which King appears in *The Tempest*?

14 What is the name of the clown in *As You Like It*?

15 Which play features the characters Priam, Hector and Paris?

16 Which character says, "Nothing will come of nothing: speak again."?

17 Who performs the marriage ceremony in *Romeo and Juliet*?

18 What was his last play?

19 What title does Cymbeline hold in the play bearing his name?

20 In what year did Shakespeare die?

ANSWERS ON PAGE 298

446 GENERAL KNOWLEDGE

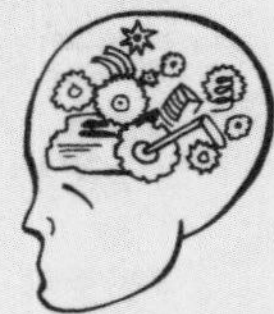
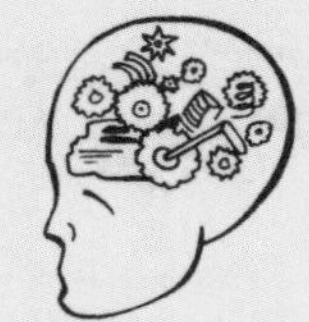
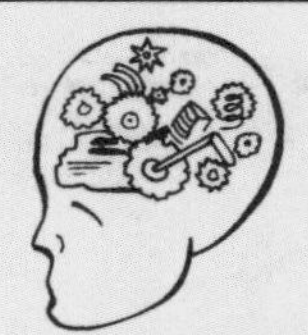

1 In Japan what name is given to ritual suicide?

2 What is the first name of songwriter Sondheim?

3 Of the seven wonders of the world, where was the Colossus?

4 What did Leo Fender make?

5 Which gorge is crossed by the Clifton Suspension Bridge?

6 What is the name of the bone in your thigh?

7 In which ocean are the Azores?

8 What type of heavenly body is named after Edmund Halley?

9 Which Australian bird is famous for laughing?

10 Of which country was Archbishop Makarios Prime Minister?

11 Which German brothers collected such stories as "Hansel & Gretel"?

12 What nationality was Hans Christian Andersen?

13 Who said, "A Scout smiles and whistles under all circumstances"?

14 Who first urged Beethoven to "roll over" in 1956?

15 What name was given to the practice which tried to turn lead into silver and gold?

16 Who shared a Nobel Prize for physics with his son?

17 A chinook is what type of vehicle?

18 In which country was Rudyard Kipling born?

19 Which poet drowned while sailing off the coast of Italy in 1822?

20 What did the Italian soldier Garibaldi give his name to?

ANSWERS ON PAGE 298

447 NAME GAME

How are these celebrities better known?

1 JENNIFER MORROW
2 MAURICE MICKLEWHITE
3 DAVID JONES
4 CHARLES BUCHINSKI
5 LESLIE CHARLES
6 CHRISTOPHER DAVIDSON
7 DONNA GAINES
8 SHAHNOUR AZNOURIAN
9 JANE PETERS
10 GORDON SUMNER

ANSWERS ON PAGE 298

448 SAUCES

Is each statement TRUE or FALSE?

T F **1** Worcestershire sauce contains anchovies.
T F **2** Bechamel is a rich white sauce.
T F **3** Apple sauce is an accompaniment to beef.
T F **4** A Melba sauce contains blackcurrants.
T F **5** Thai fish sauce is white in colour.
T F **6** Mornay sauce is flavoured with cheese.
T F **7** Aurore sauce has chocolate or cocoa in it.
T F **8** Mayonnaise contains raw eggs.
T F **9** Cumberland sauce is always served piping hot.
T F **10** A sabayon sauce is sweet.

ANSWERS ON PAGE 298

449 CAR REGISTRATION

1 Which country has the international vehicle registration code A?
☐ Albania ☐ Austria ☐ Australia

2 What is the registration for Bulgaria?
☐ B ☐ BG ☐ BUG

3 How many letters are there in the registration for Syria?
☐ One ☐ Two ☐ Three

4 Which of the choices has a registration that does not start with a J?
☐ Jamaica ☐ Japan ☐ Jordan

5 Which country has the registration code PA?
☐ Panama ☐ Pakistan ☐ Portugal

6 EAT is the tasty sounding code for which country?
☐ Estonia ☐ Kenya ☐ Tanzania

7 Which country has South Africa's code in reverse?
☐ Australia ☐ Azerbaijan ☐ Zimbabwe

8 Where has a car come from if it carries the letters PL?
☐ Panama ☐ Poland ☐ Portugal

9 No codes begin with an X and which other letter?
☐ O ☐ Q ☐ V

10 A car from where can display the letters WAG?
☐ The Gambia ☐ Vietnam ☐ Zambia

11 Which country has the registration code T?
☐ Thailand ☐ Togo ☐ Turkey

12 How many letters are there in the registration for Honduras?
☐ One ☐ Two ☐ Three

13 Which country not starting with H has the code HR?
☐ Chad ☐ Croatia ☐ Uganda

14 What is the registration for Venezuela?
☐ EV ☐ YV ☐ ZA

15 Which country has the registration code ET?
☐ Egypt ☐ Estonia ☐ Ethiopia

A2D45C
S6B22A
D35E62
R45T67

ANSWERS ON PAGE 298

For those of you who like dressing up as ghosts and ghouls or munching your way through enormous quantities of chocolate and nuts to mark the onset of winter, here are 50 questions to test your knowledge of all things sepulchral.

1 Which Celtic new year festival was the pre-Christian forerunner of Halloween?

2 Which traditional Halloween pastime is thought to derive from the symbol of the Pomona, the Roman goddess of fruit and gardens?

3 Which composer wrote the *Funeral March of a Marionette*?

4 When the Romans invaded Celtic Britain in the first century AD, which autumn festival of their own did they merge with Samhain?

5 Which seventh-century Vatican leader designated November 1st as All Saints' Day?

6 What is the name of the eighteenth-century gothic novel by Horace Walpole featuring a haunted building?

7 When French explorer Jacques Cartier explored the St Lawrence region of North American in 1584 he reported finding "gros melons". What were they?

8 Which three early Christian celebrations come together to form the festival period of Hallowmas?

9 Are pumpkins fruits or vegetables?

10 What Halloween prop is derived from an Irish myth about a man named "Stingy Jack"?

11 In England what alternative autumnal celebration was adopted when the Puritan church abandoned the worshipping of saints.

12 It is traditional in Ireland to eat barnbrack at Halloween. What is it?

13 Where is Dracula's castle located?

14 The name Halloween is Scottish in origin. What is it short for?

15 What is the name of Jane Austen's spoof gothic novel?

16 What were the Celtic priests called who danced around sacrificial fires in the forest to mark the end of the season of the sun.

17 Who played Laurie Strode in John Carpenter's classic horror movie *Halloween* (1978)?

18 Who wrote a short story entitled *The Black Cat* in 1843?

19 What is Wicca?

20 What is arachnophobia?

21 Which composer wrote *The Sorcerer's Apprentice*?

22 The ghost of which English queen has been spotted on many occasions, sometimes carrying her head, in the Tower of London?

23 Who played the eponymous role in *Buffy the Vampire Slayer*?

24 *"Eye of newt and toe of frog,*
Wool of bat and tongue of dog,
Adder's fork and blind-worm's sting,
Lizard's leg, and howlet's wing …
Where does the recipe for this particular charmed pot come from?

25 What is the name of Harry Potter's evil adversary?

26 Who wrote the novel *Dracula*?

27 How do the superstitious country folk of parts of the West Indies protect themselves against the predatory desires of the local supernatural blood-suckers?

28 In Mexico and parts of the United States, on November 2 people hold picnics at the graves of dead relatives and eat skulls made of sugar with the names of the departed on the forehead. What is this festival called?

29 On which day do Catholics believe that the living may intercede on behalf of the dead through prayer?

30 Who played Dr Samuel "Sam" J. Loomis in the horror movie *Halloween*?

31 According to folklore, what is the preferred method of transport for witches?

32 Who is the self-styled Queen of Narnia?

33 Where does Harry Potter go to school?

34 According to voodoo belief, the body of a dead person can be given the semblance of life, by the intervention of a supernatural force or spell, usually for some evil purpose. By what name are the living dead known?

35 Where are the world's only three species of vampire bats to be found?

36 What company started producing "a palatable confection and most nourishing food" in Lancaster, Pennsylvania in 1894?

37 In the 1740s, Horace Walpole purchased an estate on the River Thames near London and set about remodelling it in what he called "Gothick" style, adding towers, battlements, arched doors and windows with a spurious medieval architectural flavour. What was the name of the house?

38 Who secretly created an eight-foot-tall monster out of separate body parts collected from a charnel house?

39 In the *Wizard of Oz*, which evildoer does Dorothy have to contend with?

40 Who was the Ancient Egyptian god of the underworld, with associations with funerary rights and the physiological processes of death and decay?

41 Which former US President is said to haunt the White House?

42 Which medieval German magician was a prolific author of books on witchcraft and was reputed to be the greatest necromancer of his age?

43 Which actresses played the title roles in *The Witches of Eastwick*?

44 In which horror movie are the Freeling family terrorized by ghosts?

45 What was weird about Marilyn to Herman, Lily, Eddie and Grandpa?

46 Who was lured into incarceration by a wicked witch who lived in a forest in a house made of bread and covered in cakes?

47 Which contemporary Halloween custom is derived from the early celebrations of All Souls' Day when the poor would go begging and the housewives would give them special pastries called "soul cakes"?

48 In the Middle Ages, what creatures were renowned as witches' familiars?

49 Which major food source for the Native Americans is now a very popular comestible Halloween gift?

50 In which poem did a skeleton ship engender horror in the watching crew that sailed past it?

ANSWERS ON PAGE 298

451 SCIENCE

1 What does the G stand for in WYSIWYG?

2 In which decade was the Sony Walkman stereo launched?

3 In the UK what was Oftel set up to regulate?

4 What powered James Watt's engine in 1765?

5 Which country launched the first space probe in 1959?

6 What kind of codes did American supermarkets introduce in the mid 1970s?

7 What does the B stand for in IBM?

8 The Three Mile Island nuclear leak in the 70s was in which country?

9 Which Bill formed Microsoft?

10 Which Clarence pioneered quick freezing in the food industry?

11 Modulator-Demodulator is usually shortened to what?

12 Foods will not brown in what type of oven?

13 What used to go round at 33⅓ r.p.m.?

14 In which decade was the Channel Tunnel first opened?

15 Which word did Ernest Starling add to the language after his studies of the human body?

16 The Sony company originated in which country?

17 Which popular small car was introduced by Austin Morris at the end of the 50s?

18 Which country combined with Britain in building Concorde?

19 What touches the surface of a CD when playing?

20 What does the F stand for in FM?

ANSWERS ON PAGE 299

452 WORLD HISTORY

1 What was the last ruling dynasty of China?

2 Slovenia, Macedonia and Croatia were the first three states to break away from which country in 1991?

3 Where did the Hundred Flowers Movement encourage government criticism in the 1950s?

4 How did the former Princess Alix of of Hessen meet her death?

5 Who did not seek re-election as Austrian President in 1991 after revelations about his activities in WWII?

6 Who was the first President of Israel?

7 How many days after Waterloo did Napoleon resign?

8 Which Governor of Sumatra was responsible for the founding of Singapore?

9 Which city has the oldest university in the world?

10 What does Rasputin mean, as a name given to Grigory Efimovich?

11 Where were all but six French Kings crowned?

12 Which country had a secret police force called the securitate which was replaced in 1990?

13 Which President Roosevelt was Republican?

14 What name was given to the incorporation of Austria into the Third Reich?

15 What did Haile Selassie's title Ras Tafari mean?

16 Who was Nazi minister of eastern occupied territories from 1941–44?

17 Who was Secretary of State to Kennedy and Johnson?

18 Who was the first president of an independent Mozambique?

19 In which country was the Rosetta Stone found in in 1799?

20 What name was given to the socialist movement which carried out the Nicaraguan Revolution?

ANSWERS ON PAGE 299

453 THE ARTS

1. In which languages did Irishman Samuel Beckett write his plays?
2. Who performed his one-man show EFX in Las Vegas?
3. Princess Diana was patron of which ballet company?
4. Which type of singing means "in the style of the chapel"?
5. Which play did Stephen Fry walk out of in the mid-1990s?
6. Who went on a Red Hot world tour in 1996?
7. Who founded the American Academy of Motion Picture Arts and Sciences?
8. Who won the 1962 Tchaikovsky competition with Ashkenazy?
9. At which film festival is the prize the Golden Pyramid awarded?
10. Grappelli and Reinhardt were leaders of which Quintet?
11. What was the name of Wayne Sleep's 1980 dance company?
12. Tennessee Williams was born in which US state?
13. Which opera singer sang with Sarah Brightman in *Requiem*?
14. Who played the Artful Dodger in the first stage production of *Oliver!*?
15. Which Ben Elton novel was the first to be adapted into a West End play?
16. Who had a one-woman show called *Live And Kidding*?
17. Who shared management of the Old Vic between 1944 and 1950?
18. Double bass, viola and violin – which is the largest of these?
19. In which city is the Uffizi Gallery?
20. Who choreographed *West Side Story* and *Fiddler On The Roof*?

ANSWERS ON PAGE 299

454 LUCKY DIP

1. A pilgrimage to which city is stipulated in the five pillars of Islam?
2. Which of the seven deadly sins begins with G?
3. What was Ghana's former name?
4. The Dutch Royal Family gained its name from which French town?
5. Is the corncrake a bird, mammal or reptile?
6. What name is given to animals which do not hunt or eat meat?
7. Over which continent did the ozone hole form?
8. Which tanker suffered a severe oil spill in Alaska in 1989?
9. What name is given to thousands of small bodies which orbit the sun?
10. Which structural tissue is found in between the vertebral discs
11. Which two colours appear on the U.N. flag?
12. Which building is used for the election of a Pope?
13. In which country would you find polders?
14. In which country are the Angel Falls?
15. Which actress's real name is Julia Wells?
16. In which two cities would you find Cleopatra's Needles?
17. In which African country is Timbuktu?
18. Who said, "Marriage is a wonderful invention – but so is the bicycle repair kit"?
19. Which English Prime Minister was known as the "Great Commoner"?
20. Who was the first person to notice the Sun had spots?

ANSWERS ON PAGE 299

455 FURNITURE

1 What name is given to the material made from paper, often soaked in glue before shaping?

2 How does a butler's tray differ from an ordinary tray?

3 What is or was a what not?

4 What is a long bench in a church called?

5 What is the more colloquial name for a long case clock?

6 What is parquetry?

7 Robert Gillow had a shop in London's Oxford Street, but where was he from?

8 What is the literal translation of chaise longue?

9 A Canterbury was used for storing what?

10 What is a Davenport?

11 What name is given to walnut from the knotty gnarled area at the base of the tree trunk?

12 What name is given to the use of different woods to give a decorative effect?

13 Dressers originated in which part of the UK?

14 Sheraton furniture dates from which century?

15 What is an étagère?

16 Gesso is a form of what type of decoration?

17 What is a cheval mirror?

18 What is a credenza?

19 Which style of furniture of the 1740s contained scrolls and flowers?

20 What was a bureau plat?

ANSWERS ON PAGE 299

456 HALF CHANCE

½? ½? ½?

1 How many women in total travelled to the Moon in the 20th century – one or none?

2 What was the wife of a tsar called – Tsardine or Tsarina?

3 *Heartbreak High* is set in which city – New York or Sydney?

4 Was the great plague of the 14th century known as The Creeping Death or The Black Death?

5 Acupuncture is a form of what – medicine or tattooing?

6 What was spaceman Yuri Gagarin's home town renamed after his death – Gagarin or Sputnik?

7 Does Robe or Stone go after *Harry Potter And The Philosopher's*?

8 What is the name of the stick used in croquet – croquette or mallet?

9 Puri is a bread that originally came from which country – India or Greece?

10 Is a pagoda a type of card game or a type of temple?

11 What is the top colour on a rainbow – orange or red?

12 Where in the body is the smallest bone – in the ear or in the foot?

13 Which English county is part of Superman's secret alias – Kent or Surrey?

14 What is the playing area called in a basketball match – the court or the pitch?

15 Which part of a car did John Dunlop develop – tyres or windscreen?

16 Chicago is known as what type of city – dirty or windy?

17 What does Costa Blanca mean – Blank Cheque or White Coast?

18 What did Billy Elliott want to be – a ballet dancer or a dress designer?

19 Which sport did Hank Aaron play – American Football or baseball?

20 What type of institution was named after John Harvard – a church or a university?

ANSWERS ON PAGE 299

457 PICTURE QUIZ

A

B

C

D

What links these four pictures?

ANSWERS ON PAGE 299

458 DOUBLE TAKE

In each case, the two-part quiz question leads to just one answer!

1 Which word can be a store or can mean to betray?

2 Which word can be a playground toy or a hair grip?

3 Which word means someone who is bright and someone who is well dressed?

4 Which word can be a ghost or a strong drink?

5 Which word can be a season or a coil of metal?

6 Which word can be an animal and can also mean to nag or pester?

7 Which word can be a piece of furniture or a chart?

8 Which word can be something to wear or another word for storing?

9 Which word can be a military vehicle or a container for fish?

10 Which word means to remove clothes and can be a narrow section?

ANSWERS ON PAGE 299

459 PHOTOGRAPHERS

1 Which nationality was the inventor of photography?
☐ French ☐ German ☐ Swiss

2 What was Daguerre's original occupation?
☐ Actor ☐ Physicist ☐ Scene painter

3 Who was the first woman photographer at Magnum Photos?
☐ Arnold ☐ Arbus ☐ Cameron

4 What is Francis Smythe famous for photographing?
☐ Dogs ☐ Mountains ☐ Ships

5 Who married the sister of Queen Elizabeth II?
☐ Bailey ☐ Lichfield ☐ Snowdon

6 Whose was the first book with photographic illustrations?
☐ Fox Talbot ☐ Sheeler ☐ Sutcliffe

7 Annie Leibovitz was chief photographer on what in the 80s?
☐ *Time* ☐ *Vanity Fair* ☐ *Vogue*

8 Who epitomised the Swinging Sixties?
☐ Cecil Beaton ☐ David Bailey
☐ Norman Parkinson

9 What did Thomas Dallmeyer invent?
☐ Box camera ☐ Flash gun
☐ Telephoto lens

10 Who wrote *Self Portrait* in 1963?
☐ Arthur Rothstein ☐ Dorothea Lange
☐ Man Ray

11 What is the Earl of Lichfield's first name?
☐ Andrew ☐ George ☐ Patrick

12 Complete the Kodak motto, You press the button . . .
☐ Say cheese ☐ Wait
☐ We do the rest

13 Eve Arnold was famous for photographing which subjects?
☐ Children ☐ War zones ☐ Women

14 Who photographed for *Vogue* before and after WWII?
☐ Diane Arbus ☐ Eve Arnold
☐ Lee Miller

15 Angus McBean was famous for which photography?
☐ Fashion ☐ Royalty ☐ Theatrical

ANSWERS ON PAGE 299

460 GENERAL KNOWLEDGE

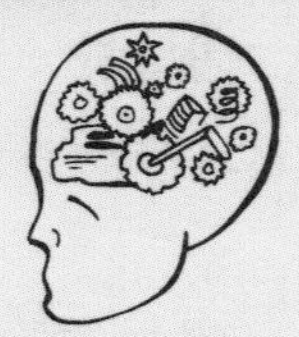
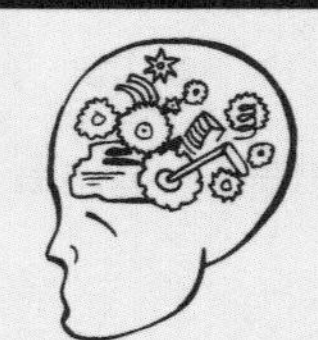
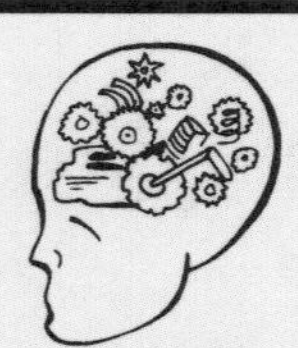

1 What are Steadman triples, Plain Bob Caters, and Gransire triples?

2 What kind of animal is a chamois?

3 In which African country is the city of Ibadan?

4 Which part of the body would be affected by astigmatism?

5 What nationality was the playwright Ibsen?

6 Which city is the administrative headquarters of Cumbria?

7 Which dancer's real name was Virginia McMath?

8 Where in your body is the frontal bone?

9 On which day does the Christian Church celebrate Jesus entering Jerusalem?

10 Which Berlin hit was used in the movie *Top Gun*?

11 Who wrote the musicals *The Dancing Years* and *King's Rhapsody*?

12 What is the collective noun to describe a number of nightingales?

13 With which holy city is the name Zion associated?

14 Which Scandinavian animals are famous for running over cliff tops?

15 Before he became a disciple of Jesus, what was Matthew's job?

16 Which city has or had the nickname Auld Reekie?

17 Boswell wrote the biography of which famous writer?

18 Ophelia appears in which Shakespeare play?

19 To what does the adjective crepuscular refer?

20 In Australia, what animal is a jumbuck?

ANSWERS ON PAGE 299

461 LADY WRITERS

1 What was the occupation of Jane Austen's father?

2 Which Austen novel was originally called "First Impressions"?

3 Which pretty but foolish girl does Emma take under her wing in the novel of the same name?

4 Which Austen novel was first called *Elinor and Marianne*?

5 Who played Elizabeth Bennett in the famous BBC 1995 production of *Pride And Prejudice*?

6 Who are Sir Walter Elliot's three daughters in *Persuasion*?

7 In *Mansfield Park* what is the name of Mrs Price's daughter taken in by Sir Thomas Bertram and his family?

8 In which Austen novel do we meet Catherine Morland?

9 Who wrote the screenplay for *Sense and Sensibility* in the film of the mid 1990s?

10 Of the three Bronte sisters who survived to adulthood who was the eldest?

11 Which pseudonym did the Bronte sisters use when they published a collection of poems in in 1846?

12 Which two novels did Anne Bronte write?

13 Where did Charlotte and Emily go to study languages in 1842?

14 Which member of the Bronte family died in the same year as Emily?

15 What was Charlotte's married name?

16 In *Jane Eyre* who cares for Jane after she flees Thornfield Hall?

17 In *Jane Eyre* what is the name of the Asylum based on Cowan Bridge where her sisters contracted the consumption from which they died?

18 Which novel by Charlotte reflects her life as a governess abroad?

19 Who is the character of Shirley Keeldar based on in *Shirley*?

20 Which author of *Cranford* wrote the definitive *Life of Charlotte Bronte* in 1857?

ANSWERS ON PAGE 299

462 PEOPLE

1. Which famous daughter was made chief designer at Chloe in 1997?
2. Paul Keating was a controversial Prime Minister of which country?
3. Nelson Mandela was born in which decade of the 20th century?
4. Which Royal sold her autobiography for $1.3 million to Simon & Schuster?
5. How many golfing majors did Jack Nicklaus win?
6. Which French chef is famed for his Manoir aux Quat'Saisons restaurant?
7. Which movie gave Hilary Swank her first Oscar?
8. Which Italian fashion designer was murdered on the orders of his ex-wife?
9. Michael Flatley shot to fame during an interval filler on which programme?
10. Which perfume house did Helena Bonham-Carter advertise?
11. Chevy Chase was a professional in which sport?
12. Whose 50th birthday party did Prince Charles host at Highgrove in the summer of 1997?
13. Which pop star did model Iman marry in 1992?
14. Which crimper to the famous launched his Hairomatherapy products in the 1990s?
15. Who is Gwyneth Paltrow's mother?
16. Who has been the husband of Catherine Deneuve, Marie Helvin and Catherine Dyer?
17. Whose marriage was headlined in *Variety* magazine as "Egghead weds Hourglass"?
18. Who did Princess Diana's make up before her wedding in 1981?
19. In which country was Ivana Trump born and brought up?
20. In basketball, who smashed Magic Johnson's career assists record?

ANSWERS ON PAGE 299

463 THE HEADLINES

1. Going into 2005 how many countries made up the EU?
2. What freak event struck Boscastle, Cornwall, in August 2004?
3. In which building was Princess Diana's funeral service held?
4. In which month did JFK die?
5. Jacqueline Cochrane was the first woman to break what?
6. Who or what were Able and Baker, the first pair of their kind to return safely from space?
7. In which hospital was the world's first test tube baby born?
8. Which Superman actor passed away in 2004?
9. Cricketer Allan Lamb changed nationality from South African to what?
10. Which former actor and US President received an honorary British knighthood?
11. Which UK Foreign Secretary did Gaynor Regan marry in 1998?
12. Which nanny Louise was tried on TV in the US over the death of a baby in her care?
13. What was the first name of Miss Lewinsky whose White House activities almost brought down Bill Clinton?
14. Who stormed off court at the end of the 1999 French Open and had to have her mother coax her back?
15. In which country were banknotes first used?
16. In 1995 Michael Foale was the first Briton to walk where?
17. Which weapon did Samuel Colt develop and popularise?
18. What was the name of Nelson Mandela's wife when he was released from prison?
19. Which Prime Minister was known as "The Iron Lady"?
20. Matthew Simmons hit the headlines after he was kicked by which then Man Utd French footballer?

ANSWERS ON PAGE 299

464 SCREEN PARTNERS

1 Which on and off screen partner of Mia Farrow starred with her in *Hannah And Her Sisters*?
2 Which star of musicals has her husband Blake Edwards written for and directed?
3 Who starred with husband Paul Newman in *Mr & Mrs Bridge*?
4 Which legendary screen couple met on the set of *Cleopatra* in the 1960s?
5 Which *Full Monty* star played opposite Emily Watson in *Angela's Ashes*?
6 Who played Lord Wessex opposite Gwyneth Paltrow in *Shakespeare In Love*?
7 Which widow of Laurence Olivier appeared in *Tea With Mussolini*?
8 Who plays the gentleman thief to Catherine Zeta Jones's insurance investigator in *Entrapment*?
9 Who was Julianne Moore's co-star in *Hannibal*?
10 Which star of *The Banger Sisters* met partner Tim Robbins on the set of *Bull Durham*?
11 Who met Diane Keaton on the set of *Reds* and later married Annette Bening?
12 Which daughter of Vanessa Redgrave starred with husband Liam Neeson in *Nell*?
13 Which star of *Evita* married Melanie Griffith?
14 What did Joanne Whalley add to her name during her marriage then dropped it again?
15 Who co-starred with Jim Carrey in *Bruce Almighty*?
16 Which Davis was Mrs Renny Harlin when he directed her in *Cutthroat Island*?
17 Who was Clint Eastwood's partner when they worked together on *Every Which Way You Can*?
18 Which Kate Winslet/Dougray Scott film was about a wartime code breaking team?
19 Which on and off screen partner did Woody Allen direct in *Annie Hall* and *Manhattan*?
20 Which *Good Will Hunting* actress co starred with Colin Firth in *Hope Springs*?

ANSWERS ON PAGE 299

465 NATURE

1 What is the common name for the Antirrhinum?
2 Which hanging basket favourite is also called Pelargonium?
3 The adrenal gland is above which organ?
4 The pilchard is a member of which fish family?
5 What type of Bell is a Campanula?
6 Which famous yellow pink-flushed rose was bred by Meilland in 1945?
7 Which wild flower is also known as the Knapweed?
8 What distinction does Kitti's hog-nosed bat hold?
9 What would you find in an anther on a stamen?
10 What is the common name for the plant Impatiens?
11 Pulmonary refers to which part of the body?
12 Which skin disorder is caused by inflammation of the sebaceous glands?
13 What is the popular name for mouth to mouth recussitation?
14 A BCG is a vaccination against which disease?
15 Where is the pituitary gland?
16 Which tendon pins the calf muscle to the heel bone?
17 Hepatic refers to which organ of the body?
18 What colour head does a male mallard usually have?
19 Which flower gets its name from a Persian or Turkish word for turban?
20 Which plant is grown not for its flowers but for its silvery seed pods?

ANSWERS ON PAGE 299

466 WHAT COLOUR IS . . . ?

1. the matter used to describe someone's intelligence?
2. the flower on a forsythia bush?
3. the traditional colour worn by tennis players at Wimbledon?
4. ball with highest value in snooker?
5. associated with the exclusive London store Harrods?
6. the flower which is the national emblem of Wales?
7. a fully grown flamingo?
8. the salad ingredient radicchio?
9. the flesh of a water melon?
10. the left-hand stripe of the French flag?

ANSWERS ON PAGE 299

467 GUESS WHO . . . ?

1. He was the first American to orbit the Earth in 1962 and made a return trip in 1998 at the age of 77.
2. Born in 1945 in London and married to *Ray* director Taylor Hackford, she starred in *The Madness of King George*.
3. Born in 1956, she competed at five Olympic Games, winning gold in the javelin in 1984.
4. Born in Oxford she uses her initials PD and created detective Adam Dalgliesh.
5. She won her first Grand Slam in 2003 beating compatriot Kim Clijsters and won the Australian Open in 2004.
6. The god daughter of Kojak aka Telly Savalas, she married Brad Pitt while playing Rachel in *Friends*.
7. She played a Bond girl opposite Piers Brosnan and won an Oscar for *Monster's Ball*.
8. Educated at Eton and Oxford, he won his fourth gold medal at the Athens Olympics and became a knight in the New Years Honours.
9. He appeared on the original poster for *The Graduate* and also starred in *Rain Man* and *Tootsie*.
10. Born in Massachusetts in 1957, she starred in the successful *Thelma and Louise* with Susan Sarandon.

ANSWERS ON PAGE 299

468 THE USA

1. Golden Gate Park is the biggest park in which city?
   ☐ Kansas ☐ San Francisco ☐ St Paul
2. What is California's state capital?
   ☐ Denver ☐ Hartford ☐ Sacramento
3. What is the famous produce of the Napa Valley?
   ☐ Cars ☐ Computers ☐ Grapes/Wine
4. What is the favourite sport of the area around Lake Tahoe?
   ☐ Angling ☐ Skiing ☐ Surfing
5. What is Ohio's largest city?
   ☐ Columbus ☐ Pierre ☐ Raleigh
6. Which state lies due east of Alabama?
   ☐ Georgia ☐ South Carolina ☐ Texas
7. Which lake provides Chicago with 20 miles of lake shore?
   ☐ Erie ☐ Michigan ☐ Superior
8. New York City is divided into how many boroughs?
   ☐ Five ☐ Seven ☐ Ten
9. Which Avenue links the Capitol to the White House?
   ☐ Big Apple ☐ Kennedy ☐ Pennsylvania
10. Which city has an area named after Jonas Bronck?
    ☐ New York ☐ San Francisco ☐ Seattle
11. What colour are Dakota's hills said to be?
    ☐ Black ☐ Blue ☐ Green
12. Which President is Austin's Library and Museum dedicated to?
    ☐ Ford ☐ Johnson ☐ Kennedy
13. Which river rises at Lake Itasca, Minnesota?
    ☐ Colarado ☐ Mississippi ☐ Savannah
14. Which Tennessee city was home to Sun Records?
    ☐ Memphis ☐ Nashville ☐ Oxford
15. Which Frank designed New York's Guggenheim Museum?
    ☐ Garfunkel ☐ Ifield ☐ Lloyd Wright

ANSWERS ON PAGE 299

469 LUCKY DIP

1 In the UK, on which day of the week does the Chancellor of the Exchequer usually deliver the Budget?

2 In which UK television programme did Del Boy and Rodney appear?

3 Which fictional bear is named after a London station?

4 Putter, iron and niblick are types of what?

5 What is the largest state of the USA?

6 How many years are celebrated by a pearl anniversary?

7 Which curly-leaved salad plant is a member of the chicory family?

8 Which armoured combat vehicle was first used in World War I?

9 What number does the Roman numeral V stand for?

10 Which two British comics said, "It's goodnight from me . . . And it's goodnight from him!"?

11 In which month is the shortest day?

12 What became Glenn Miller's signature tune?

13 In which quiz board game do the players collect coloured wedges?

14 Which Nazi died in jail after being imprisoned for 46 years?

15 Which group had a UK No 1 with *See My Baby Jive*?

16 What name describes a paved, open air area adjoining a house?

17 How is Russian revolutionary Vladimir Ilyich Ulyanov better known?

18 Who played Cruella de Vil's sidekick Jasper in *101 Dalmatians*?

19 Which group comprised, among others, Marc Bolan and Micky Finn?

20 On what part of your body would you wear a sneaker?

ANSWERS ON PAGE 299

470 BOB DYLAN

1 Which Bob Dylan composition was a US hit for Peter, Paul and Mary and Stevie Wonder?

2 What was his first UK hit single?

3 What was the first chart-topping composition by Dylan?

4 Which album includes the lengthy *Sad Eyed Lady of the Lowlands*?

5 Why was Dylan booed off stage in 1965 and 1966?

6 Which Dylan song was a hit for Manfred Mann in 1968?

7 Which album did he record with the help of Johnny Cash?

8 To the nearest £1,000 how much did Dylan receive for a one hour session at the Isle of Wight festival in 1969?

9 What was the name of the novel he published in 1970?

10 Which album was said to have been due to the end of his marriage?

11 Which Dylan song was a hit for Eric Clapton and Guns N'Roses?

12 Which film did he act in and provide the music for in Mexico?

13 When asked what were the most overrated and underrated books of the last 75 years, what did he reply?

14 What was the name of his own record label?

15 Which UK guitarist co produced *Infidels*?

16 Which religion did he embrace in the late 1970s?

17 Which Dylan song was a hit for Jimi Hendrix in 1968?

18 For which film did he write *Lay Lady Lay* – though it was not chosen?

19 Which Dylan band also included George Harrison and Roy Orbison?

20 Which cricketer added Dylan to his first names?

ANSWERS ON PAGE 299

471 HALF CHANCE

½? ½? ½?

1 Was Linda Tripp the confidante of Monica Lewinsky or Princess Diana?
2 A lippizaner is what type of animal – goat or horse?
3 A pollex is another name for which part of the body – shin or thumb?
4 Hitler was born in which country – Austria or Poland?
5 In sport what can go after Cotton, Orange and Sugar – Ball or Bowl?
6 Did Thomas Turner or Thomas Tallis introduce Willow pattern pottery?
7 Agatha Christie wrote romantic novels under the pseudonym of Mary who – Shelley or Westmacott?
8 Artists Manet and Monet both came from which city – Lyons or Paris?
9 Copacabana beach is in which South American city – Buenos Aires or Rio de Janeiro?
10 Which name is in a Beatles song title and a Thomas Hardy novel title – Eleanor or Jude?
11 Who was first to wear white boots in an English FA Cup Final – John Barnes or Eric Cantona?
12 Which Jeff played a mathematician in *Jurassic Park* – Bridges or Goldblum?
13 In *Coronation Street* was Mavis's pet Beauty a budgie or a gerbil?
14 How many states were in the original union of the United States – 13 or 15?
15 R.E.M. sang about *Shiny Happy* what – People or Places?
16 What would a palaeontologist study – fossils or plates?
17 What do the words post mortem mean – after death or final report?
18 Who played Lord Alfred Douglas in the movie *Wilde* – Matt Damon or Jude Law?
19 Who was John F Kennedy's brother who predeceased him – Joseph Jr or Edward Snr?
20 How many Best Actor Oscars did Sean Connery get for playing James Bond – two or none?

ANSWERS ON PAGE 299

472 ANIMALS

1 What is the only mammal to live as a parasite?
2 How is a Sibbald's rorqual also known?
3 For how many hours in a period of 24 does a giraffe sleep?
4 What is the world's largest rodent?
5 What gives the sloth its greenish appearance?
6 Which mammal lives at the highest altitude?
7 Which animals are famously sold at Bampton Fair?
8 The mammal which can live at the greatest depth is a species of what?
9 From which part of a sperm whale is ambergris obtained?
10 Where does a cane toad squirt poison from?
11 What is the longest type of worm?
12 Where would you find a shark's denticles?
13 What does the male mouse deer have that no other deer has?
14 Where does a browser find food?
15 What is the only bird which can fly backwards?
16 A Clydesdale was originally a cross between a Scottish draught horse and a what?
17 What colour is a mandrill's beard?
18 The wisent is native to where?
19 Lemurs are only found in their natural habitat – where?
20 What is the oldest indigenous breed of cat in the US?

ANSWERS ON PAGE 299

473 IRISH HISTORY

1. In 1846 which famine seriously affected Ireland?
2. Which Rule movement was led by Parnell?
3. What was Parnell's first name?
4. Where did most people emigrate to after the famine of the 1840s?
5. What was the first name of O'Connell known as The Liberator?
6. The Phoenix Park murders of 1882 took place in which city?
7. Which British PM (initials W.E.) supported Home Rule?
8. Who travelled on "coffin ships"?
9. The Fenians were active in Ireland and which country where much immigration had taken place'?
10. Was it Pitt the Younger or the Elder who oversaw the Act of Union?
11. Was Catholic emancipation seen in the former or latter half of the century?
12. What population count took place in 1851, 1861 and 1871?
13. Was Gaelic or English the main language in Ireland in the 19th century?
14. The English Pale surrounded which city?
15. In which century was the Battle of the Boyne?
16. Which people from the British mainland came to Ireland when James I was on the British throne?
17. Which saint developed Christianity in Ireland?
18. Which Oliver came to Ireland in the mid 17th century?
19. Which Scandinavians invaded Ireland in the 9th and 10th centuries?
20. What was the first name of 18th century politician Grattan?

ANSWERS ON PAGE 299

474 GENERAL KNOWLEDGE

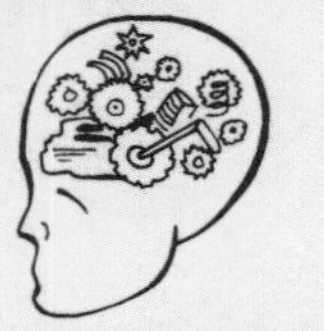
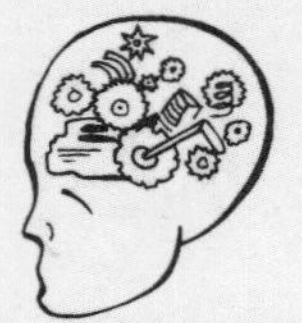

1. From which wood were longbows made?
2. In which country is the Corinth Canal?
3. Which month has the least number of days?
4. Of which European country are Madeira and the Azores a part?
5. What did people do with Oxford bags?
6. In a poem by Edward Lear, what was peculiar about the "Pobble"?
7. Pascal, Cobol, and Basic are all types of what?
8. In yards, how long was a rod, pole, or perch?
9. What is UXB?
10. What is or was Tin Lizzie?
11. Which comedian's catch phrase was, "Now there's a funny thing"?
12. What name is given to the unit of electrical power?
13. According to the proverb what do drowning men clutch?
14. What is a copper's nark?
15. What is the modern equivalent for the word behest?
16. Back, Blanket, and Buttonhole are all types of what?
17. In which Shakespeare play is Shylock introduced?
18. Which folk singer also recorded as Lucky (or Boo) Wilbury?
19. In the Old Testament which son of David was famous for his wisdom?
20. How does a grasshopper produce its distinctive sound?

ANSWERS ON PAGE 299

475 PICTURE QUIZ

A B C D

Which name links these four famous faces?

ANSWERS ON PAGE 299

476 CARTOONS

Is each statement TRUE or FALSE?

T F **1** Mel Blanc was the voice of Bugs Bunny.

T F **2** Elton John wrote the music for *The Lion King*.

T F **3** *Pokemon* is a Norwegian animation.

T F **4** In *South Park*, Stan's dog was called Sparky.

T F **5** Gromit is a cat.

T F **6** Tom, in *Tom and Jerry,* was originally to have been called Jasper.

T F **7** Bruce, in *Finding Nemo,* was a goldfish.

T F **8** There are seven brands of Duff beer in *The Simpsons*.

T F **9** Wilma Flintstone's maiden name was McBricker.

T F **10** Pumba in *The Lion King* was a warthog.

ANSWERS ON PAGE 299

477 DANCE

1 How many dancers feature in a pas de deux?
☐ Two ☐ Four ☐ Six

2 Which Jennifer starred opposite Richard Gere in *Shall We Dance?*
☐ Aniston ☐ Grey ☐ Lopez

3 Who was Ginger Rogers' famous partner?
☐ Astaire ☐ Kelly ☐ O'Connor

4 What colour ballet shoes did Hans Christian Andersen write about?
☐ Blue ☐ Red ☐ White

5 In 2005 a controversial ballet was staged about which princess?
☐ Caroline ☐ Diana ☐ Eugenie

6 Siegfried is the hero in which ballet?
☐ *Coppelia* ☐ *Nutcracker*
☐ *Swan Lake*

7 What type of dance appears in the show *Stepping Out*?
☐ Ballet ☐ Ballroom ☐ Tap

8 Who wrote the music for *The Nutcracker*?
☐ Stravinsky ☐ Strindberg
☐ Tchaikovsky

9 Where is the home of the Bolshoi Ballet?
☐ Austria ☐ Hungary ☐ Russia

10 Sadler's Wells ballet became known as what?
☐ English ☐ London ☐ Royal

11 Where was Rudolf Nureyev born?
☐ On a boat ☐ On a plane
☐ On a train

12 Who founded the Ballet Russes?
☐ Balanchine ☐ Diaghilev ☐ Nijinsky

13 In 1972 Bob Fosse won a dance Oscar for what?
☐ *All That Jazz* ☐ *Cabaret*
☐ *Sweet Charity*

14 Which musical has a song called *Shall We Dance?*
☐ *Cats* ☐ *The King and I*
☐ *South Pacific*

15 In what colour raincoat does Gene Kelly sing *Singin in the Rain*?
☐ Blue
☐ Red
☐ Yellow

ANSWERS ON PAGE 299

478 TRAVEL

1 In which Irish city is the Abbey Theatre?

2 What is the official language of Denmark?

3 The Philippines are in which Ocean?

4 Rhodes is an island belonging to which country?

5 The Riviera is on the French/Italian coast on which sea?

6 St Moritz is famous for what type of sports?

7 St Peter's Basilica is in which Italian city?

8 What are a group of six states on the NE American coast known as collectively?

9 Which ocean lies between Europe and America?

10 Which Rock is on the south coast of Spain

11 In which continent is Slovenia?

12 Faro, or the Algarve, is in which country?

13 In which French city is the university called the Sorbonne?

14 County Sligo is on which coast of Ireland?

15 What is traditionally easily available in Reno?

16 In which European country could you once spend pesetas?

17 In which country are baguettes and brioches traditional breads?

18 The Shannon is which country's chief river?

19 Which language is the first language of around 6% of the population of America?

20 In which part of Europe is the Baltic Sea?

ANSWERS ON PAGE 299

479 US POLITICS

1 Which name of a US President is Bill Clinton's middle name?

2 Which US statesman won the Nobel Peace Prize in 1973 although the man he shared it with declined his award?

3 Which two journalists broke the Watergate break in story?

4 Under whose Presidency was racial discrimination in the US made illegal?

5 Which US President was born Leslie Lynch King?

6 Who is the only US President to have been divorced?

7 Who was the first US President to resign office?

8 Which First Lady was nicknamed the Steel Magnolia?

9 Which President initiated his "Great Society" programme?

10 Who was John F Kennedy's Attorney General?

11 Which founder of "Democrats for the 80s" and widow of an eminent US Democrat is the mother of Winston Churchill MP?

12 Other than John F Kennedy which President was assassinated last century?

13 Which Secretary of State announced to the world he was in charge after the assassination attempt on Ronald Reagan?

14 What is Al Gore's wife called?

15 Which President ordered the dropping of the atomic bombs on Hiroshima and Nagasaki?

16 Which US President's foreign policy was to "speak softly with a big stick"?

17 Which President's memoirs were called "Mandate for Change" and "Waging Peace"?

18 Which President was a former director of the CIA?

19 Which Democrat founded what he called his "Rainbow Coalition"?

20 What was the official name of Reagan's so called "Star Wars" programme ?

ANSWERS ON PAGE 300

480 TELEVISION

1 How many children does Lynette Scavo have in *Desperate Housewives*?

2 James Garner starred in which classic *Files*?

3 *Absolutely Fabulous* started life as a sketch on which comedy duo's show?

4 In *The Simpsons*, what is Chief Wiggum's first name?

5 What was "dropped" in the comedy about the Globelink newsroom?

6 Which *Street* teaches about letters and numbers?

7 In which US city was Cagney and Lacey set?

8 How was Ken Hutchinson known in the 1970s series with David Soul and Paul Michael Glaser?

9 Which actress Anna found fame as Beth Jordache in *Brookside*?

10 Which Engine's friends were Terence the Tractor and Bertie the Bus?

11 *Jewel In The Crown* was set in 1940s where?

12 In which English county was *All Creatures Great And Small* set?

13 Which David said, "what a bobbydazzler!"?

14 Which Ricky starred in *The Office*?

15 Which sitcom was based in a French cafe in occupied France?

16 Which character converted to Judaism in *Sex And The City*?

17 Does Tom or Jerry have the furrier coat?

18 Which hero was "Riding through the glen, With his band of Men."?

19 Are Smurfs blue or orange?

20 Who was Dalziel's detective partner, from the novels by Reginald Hill?

ANSWERS ON PAGE 300

481 POP MUSIC QUIZ

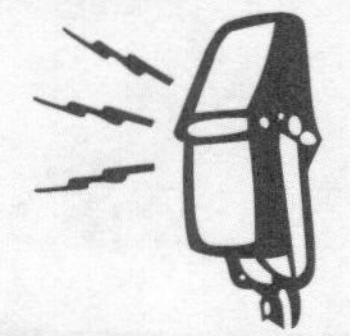
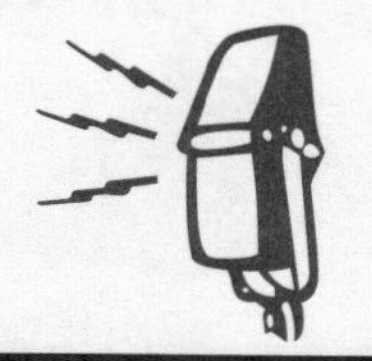
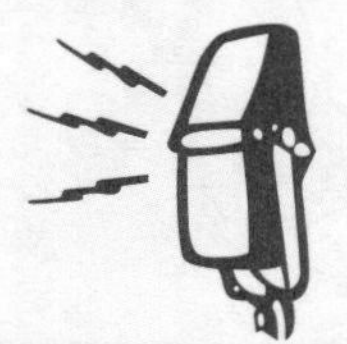

1 *You Said No* and *Crashed The Wedding* were UK No 1s for which band?

2 Who made the US chart-topping album *Chocolate Factory*?

3 Who was the first female to top the UK singles chart with a self-composed song?

4 Whose album *Fat Of The Land* debuted at No 1 in more than 20 countries?

5 "Time goes by so slowly, And time can do so much," comes from which song?

6 Under which name has Orville Burrell topped the charts?

7 Who had a best-selling 1980s album *No Jacket Required*?

8 What nationality were Rednex?

9 Who linked up with Aitken and Waterman to make a chart busting UK production trio?

10 *Pictures Of Matchstick Men* was the first UK hit for which veteran rockers?

11 Vincent Furnier became better known as whom?

12 In which country did INXS's Michael Hutchence tragically lose his life?

13 *What Don't Work* according to the Verve's UK chart topper?

14 Which singer linked to *Lord Of The Ring*s made the album *Watermark*?

15 Who won a Grammy for *Tears In Heaven*?

16 Who made the album *Don't Shoot Me I'm Only The Piano Player*?

17 How many boys were there in the Pet Shop Boys?

18 What did the letter O stand for in ELO?

19 "And so I face the final curtain" comes from which song?

20 Which female vocalist topped the US charts with *Always On Time*?

ANSWERS ON PAGE 300

482 ANCIENT EGYPT

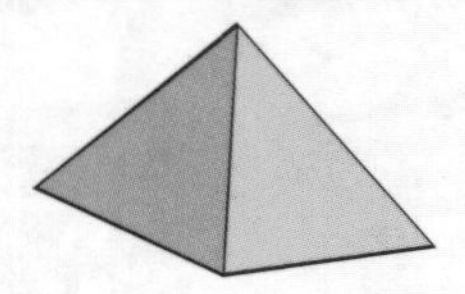
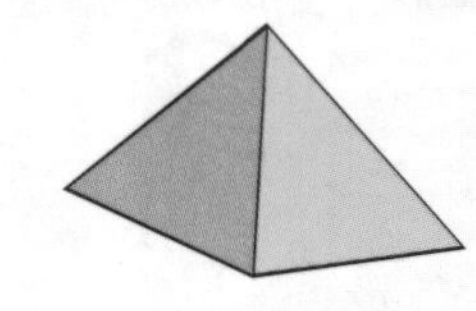
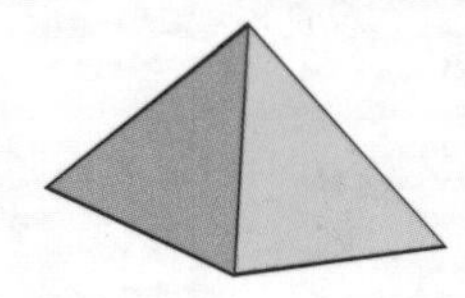

1 What were Egyptians kings called?

2 What was the process called for preserving or mummifying a dead body?

3 Who was the Egyptian god of the dead?

4 In which decade of the last century was Tutankhamun's tomb discovered?

5 Which insect did the Egyptians adopt as a symbol of good fortune?

6 Which place name links with modern-day Tennessee?

7 What was the name of the material on which the Egyptians used to write?

8 What is the Great Sphinx of Giza made out of?

9 What was the name for the sacred carved signs found on temple walls?

10 Which god was thought to be the king of the afterworld?

11 The sphinx had the body of which creature?

12 Which king built The Great Pyramid?

13 The god Horus has the head of which animal?

14 How old was Tutankhamun when he became King?

15 What did children wear in Ancient Egypt?

16 What was the name of the green eye make up used as protection from the sun?

17 What was Tutankhamun's funeral mask made out of?

18 Where in Egypt is the Valley Of The Kings located?

19 How is the area of Nubia known today?

20 What was the name of the tiny model servants left in a tomb

ANSWERS ON PAGE 300

483 LUCKY DIP

1 Which London Street used to be the home of newspapers?

2 Which term describes arranging text on screen to fit round a picture?

3 Which country is a car from with the international registration letter F?

4 Who came first as Prime Minister, Attlee or Gladstone?

5 In which field of work did Gilbert White become an expert?

6 In snooker, how many points are scored for potting the green ball?

7 S is the symbol of which chemical element?

8 Who recorded the album *Music Box*?

9 Picardy is in the north east of which country?

10 What is the second month of the year to have exactly 31 days?

11 In the Bible, who led the children of Israel to the Promised Land?

12 What goes before mantle, slipper and smock in flower names?

13 Which Greek city contains the hill citadel of the Acropolis?

14 In comics, who is "the boy wonder"?

15 Hamlet was prince of which country?

16 Timperley Early and Cawood Castle are types of what?

17 In the solar system what is the third planet from the sun?

18 What has subdivisions comprising 12, 52 and 365 units?

19 To what type of meeting was Mahatma Gandhi going when he was assasinated?

20 According to proverb, a little what is a dangerous thing?

ANSWERS ON PAGE 300

484 PICTURE QUIZ

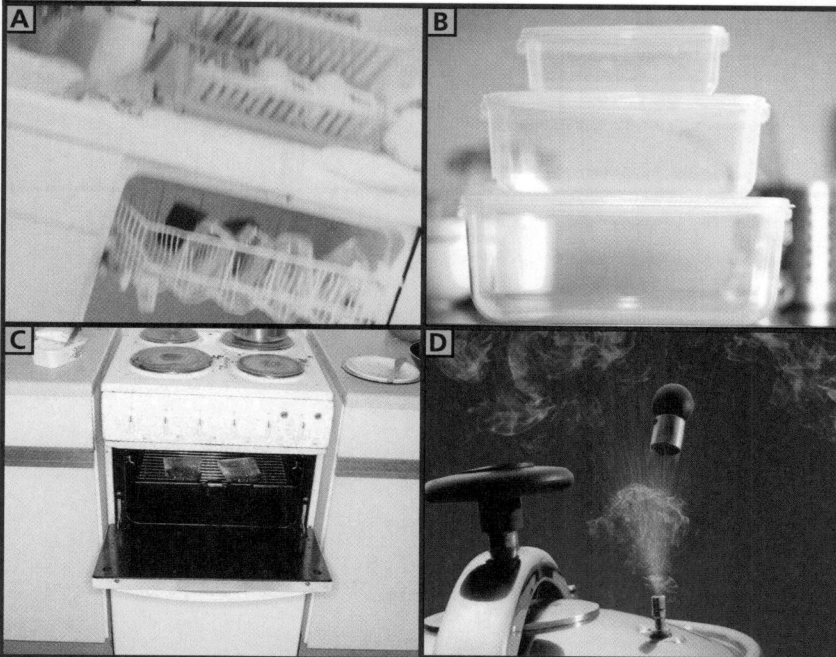

Starting with the first, in which order would these items have appeared in domestic kitchens?

ANSWERS ON PAGE 300

485 NAME THE YEAR

1 Mary Brush patented the first corset in the US. Humphry Davy invented the miner's safety lamp. Napoleon was defeated at the Battle of Waterloo.

2 Amy Johnson completed her solo flight from Britain to Australia. Sherlock Holmes' creator, Sir Arthur Conan Doyle, died. Uruguay won the first F.I.F.A.World Cup in Montevideo.

3 Indira Gandhi was assassinated by one of her bodyguards. Ronald Reagan won a second term as US President. Carl Lewis won four Olympic golds in Los Angeles.

4 Pope John Paul I was pope for only 33 days. Muhammad Ali won his third World Heavyweight championship. The world's first test tube baby was born.

5 Elizabeth Taylor married Richard Burton for the first time.The Beatles toured the USA for the first time. Kruschev was deposed in the USSR.

6 Tracy Austin became the youngest winner of the US Open. Sebastian Coe broke three world records in six weeks. John Wayne died.

ANSWERS ON PAGE 300

486 HALF CHANCE

½? ½? ½?

1 Who was the first President to live in the White House – Adams or Jefferson?

2 What was the colouring of the great race horse Arkle – bay or black?

3 In which American state is De Paul University – Chicago or Montana?

4 How many tiles are there in a game of mah-jong – 99 or 144?

5 *Perfect Day* first appeared on which Lou Reed album – *Berlin* or *Transformer*?

6 Was Cary Grant's middle name Alexander or Alfred?

7 Which sport follows FINA rules – fencing or swimming?

8 In silent movies, how long would a "two reeler" last – 20 mins or 30 mins?

9 Serigraphy is what type of printing – block foil or silk screen?

10 Dr Niko Tatopoulos appeared in which creature movie – *Godzilla* or *King Kong*?

11 Who was thought to have murdered his family nanny Sandra Rivett – Dr Crippen or Lord Lucan?

12 Which female singer performed with the Miami Sound Machine – Gloria Estefan or Neneh Cherry?

13 Which President of the USA had Walter Mondale as Vice President – Carter or Ford?

14 Which board game features a racing car, a top hat and a dog – Cluedo or Monopoly?

15 The *General Belgrano* was sunk in which conflict – Falklands War or Gulf War?

16 Aged 80, who won an Oscar for *The Sunshine Boys* – Fred Astaire or George Burns?

17 Whose first single had the title of a Bronte novel – Kate Bush or Diana Ross?

18 What was US President Lyndon Johnson's middle name – Baines or Beans?

19 If you were an LLD, what subject would you have studied – Law or Logistics?

20 Which actress played the ex-wife in *Mrs Doubtfire* – Sally Field or Meryl Streep?

ANSWERS ON PAGE 300

487 WALT DISNEY

1 Who said, "Disney has the best casting. If he doesn't like an actor he just tears him up."?

2 In which 1932 film did he experiment with colour?

3 Where did he first meet Ub Iwerks?

4 Which movies were made as a result of a government goodwill tour of South America?

5 What was the first of the *Silly Symphonies* called?

6 A meeting with which photographers brought about the True Life nature films?

7 What was Disney's job during WWII?

8 What did Disney and Iwerks call their first cartoons?

9 Which actress won an Oscar for the last major film he made before his death?

10 What was Disney's star sign?

11 Which special Oscar award did he receive for *Snow White And The Seven Dwarfs*?

12 Which animated film was he working on at the time of his death?

13 Who with Disney received a special Oscar for *Fantasia*?

14 What was the first of his all live action movies?

15 What were the first two silent Mickey Mouse cartoons called?

16 What was Goofy originally called?

17 Which morale boosting movie did Disney make in 1943?

18 In 1923 what was the name of the animated live action cartoons he produced with his brother Roy and Ub Iwerks?

19 What was the last film in the series which began with *Seal Island*?

20 How many Oscars did Disney win in his lifetime – 19, 23 or 29?

ANSWERS ON PAGE 300

488 GENERAL KNOWLEDGE

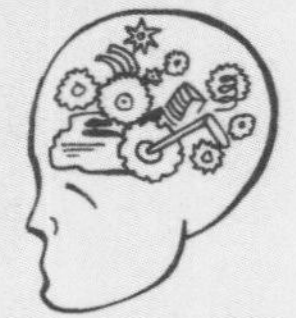 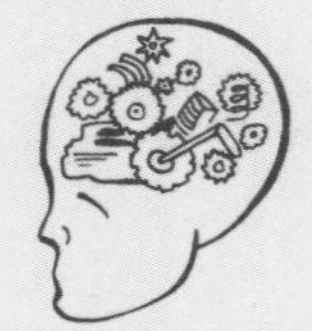 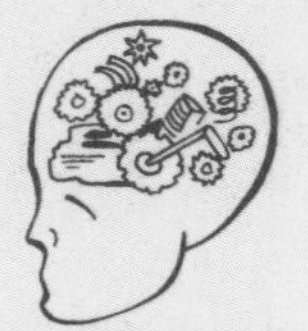

1 Coal is composed of which element?

2 The Bronte sisters had a brother what was his name?

3 Who was chief of the Greek gods?

4 What is the longest river in Russia?

5 Who formulated the law of gravity?

6 Which 1930s American criminal was known as "Public Enemy No 1"?

7 The blueberry or the whortleberry is also known as what?

8 In which opera does the heroine work in a cigarette factory?

9 Who succeeded Winston Churchill as British Prime Minister?

10 In which London dormitory town was *The Good Life* set?

11 Who was Ginger Rogers' most famous dancing partner?

12 Two Japanese cities were hit by atomic bombs in World War II Hiroshima was one what was the other?

13 William of where won the Battle of Hastings?

14 What musical word is an anagram of cart-horse?

15 What is the colour of the live wire in a British three-prong plug?

16 In which century did Queen Victoria die?

17 Which word goes after lime and before house to make new words?

18 What sea lies between Turkey and Russia?

19 Who said, "Well he would say that, wouldn't he?"

20 In Disney's *The Lion King* who is king at the end of the film?

ANSWERS ON PAGE 300

489 FOOD AND DRINK

1 Which term coined in the 70s describes food which does not have rich sauces?

2 What are most beer and soft drinks cans made from?

3 What ingredient is included in food in a florentine style?

4 What sort of food is a rollmop?

5 What colour are fully ripened olives?

6 What type of food is Cullen Skink?

7 Why do cashew nuts have to be roasted to be eaten?

8 A morel is a type of what?

9 What is pancetta?

10 Which herb is in pesto sauce?

11 In Indian cookery what is naan?

12 What type of fish is in an omelette Arnold Bennett?

13 What shape is the pasta called rigatoni?

14 What is couscous made from?

15 Which food is also called the vegetable oyster?

16 Which chef created the Bombe Nero and the Pêche Melba?

17 Which sweet rice wine is used in Japanese cookery?

18 Tartrazine colours food which colour?

19 Which classic French sauce was named after a courtier of Louis XIV?

20 Vermouth is wine flavoured with what?

ANSWERS ON PAGE 300

490 SAINTS

1 Who is the patron saint of children?

2 Which gospel writer is the patron saint of tax collectors?

3 What is the name of *The Saint* created by Leslie Charteris?

4 Which river of North America runs from Lake Ontario to the Atlantic?

5 Which saint gave her name to a firework?

6 Which saint reputedly rid Ireland of snakes?

7 Where does a saint have his or her halo?

8 Whose saint's day is the 26th December?

9 Which fictional girls' school was created by cartoonist Ronald Searle?

10 Who is a patron saint of Greece and the patron saint of Scotland?

11 Which London station shares its name with England's first consecrated church?

12 Which large breed of dog shares its name with a saint?

13 Who is the patron saint of lovers?

14 Which London cathedral on Ludgate Hill was designed by Wren?

15 The Spirit of which "saint" made an early flight across the Atlantic?

16 St Joseph Cupertino is the patron saint of which group of 20th century travellers?

17 Which church is also called the Church of Latter Day Saints?

18 Which church, the largest in the world, is in the Vatican?

19 On which date does All Saints Day fall?

20 Which gospel writer is the patron saint of surgeons?

ANSWERS ON PAGE 300

491 SPORT

1 Thierry Henry joined Arsenal from which soccer club?

2 Who has been the UK's champion National Hunt jockey from 1995 to 2004?

3 In which sport would someone perform a kip?

4 What position does American football's record-breaking Jerry Rice play?

5 Who was France's last Wimbledon Men's Singles winner of the 20th century?

6 In which events did Gert Frederiksson win six Olympic Golds?

7 Which sporting first is held by the New Zealander E J "Murt" O'Donoghue?

8 Which team were Super Bowl runners-up four years in a row in the 1990s?

9 Who was Man Utd's captain in the 1999 European Champions' Cup Final?

10 In which decade were the Badminton Horse Trials first held?

11 What nickname was given to basketball's Wilt Chamberlain?

12 Who was Edson Arantes do Nascimento?

13 Who is France's most successful motor racing driver of all time?

14 Who was the youngest Wimbledon Women's Champion of last century?

15 Who was the Joe who first defeated Muhammad Ali?

16 Who was the first soccer manager to have taken charge of both Australia and England?

17 In the 1996 Olympics which Michael won both 200 and 400m sprint races?

18 What name was shared by motor racing's brothers Emerson and Wilson?

19 Which tennis player had a father named Peter who was jailed for tax irregularities?

20 Alfredo di Stefano played soccer for three countries – Argentina, Spain and who else?

ANSWERS ON PAGE 300

492 GEOGRAPHY

1 Which country's capital is Tirana?

2 Where is a passion play staged every ten years?

3 Which state was Macedonia part of from 1945 to 1991?

4 Which conflict-torn country has Grozny as its capital?

5 Which country's highest mountain is the Grossglockner?

6 Which is the most easterly of the Windward Islands in the Caribbean?

7 Where is The Netherlands' seat of government and administration?

8 What are the Dardanelles and where are they?

9 Which southern German city is famous for its October beer festival?

10 Which country is called Elleniki Dimokratia or Hellenic Republic?

11 Whose principal river is the Po?

12 Which country capital Vaduz has no armed forces?

13 Which sea lies to the north of Poland?

14 The Alps stretch into Austria, France, Switzerland and which other country?

15 Which country covers 10% of the globe's land surface?

16 By what English name is Köln known?

17 Which country's landscape is made up of volcanoes and geysers?

18 Between which countries does the Skagerrak lie?

19 What is Bessarabia, Moldavia and part of the USSR now known as?

20 Which country is between Nicaragua and Panama?

ANSWERS ON PAGE 300

493 GUESS WHO . . . ?

1 The subject of the movie *Finding Neverland* this Scottish dramatist wrote *Peter Pan*.

2 Born in 1939, he wrote the screenplay for Patton and directed *The Godfather*.

3 This American composer and conductor wrote the music for *West Side Story*.

4 This French violinist founded the Quintette du Hot Club de France and was a jazz legend in his lifetime.

5 This Argentinian revolutionary was killed in Bolivia in the 1960s and then became a famous face on posters.

6 Born in Italy in 1899, this gangster, nicknamed "Scarface", found fame in Chicago, USA.

7 Based in Hollywood from 1940, this British movie director made *Notorious* and *Psycho*.

8 With the middle name Maria, born in Barcelona, he defeated leukaemia and became one of the Three Tenors.

9 This English author of Norwegian parentage wrote children's books such as *Matilda*.

10 This English composer of Swedish descent was born in 1874, and wrote *The Planets*.

ANSWERS ON PAGE 300

494 DOUBLE TAKE

In each case, the two-part quiz question leads to just one answer!

1 Which word means young cows and parts of the legs?

2 Which word can be a noise or a strait of water?

3 Which word can be a piece of computer equipment or a rodent?

4 Which word means to swerve or veer and also a profession or vocation?

5 Which word describes something of high quality and is also a financial penalty?

6 Which word can be a sport or an insect?

7 What can be a standard used as a country's emblem or a word meaning to lose energy?

8 Which word means a musical instrument and an ice cream biscuit?

9 What can be a piece of fabric used to wash the face or a slang term for flattery?

10 Which word can be an item of ladies' underwear or loaves of bread?

ANSWERS ON PAGE 300

495 FOOD FOR THOUGHT

1 How is a ragout cooked?
☐ Fried ☐ Poached ☐ Stewed

2 What is usually served Thermidor?
☐ Crab ☐ Lobster ☐ Squid

3 Which meat is cooked "blanquette"?
☐ Beef ☐ Chicken ☐ Venison

4 Koftas form part of which country's cuisine?
☐ Greece ☐ India ☐ Turkey

5 Al dente usually refers to what?
☐ Cheese ☐ Fruit ☐ Pasta

6 Which meat is cooked in a navarin?
☐ Beef ☐ Lamb ☐ Pork

7 Balti is Indian-style cooking which originated where?
☐ Britain ☐ India ☐ Sri Lanka

8 What does doner mean in doner kebab?
☐ Frying ☐ Rotating ☐ Stirring

9 What is a bourgignon cooked in?
☐ Champagne ☐ Red wine ☐ White

10 If something is cooked jardinière what accompanies it?
☐ Pastry ☐ Sauce ☐ Vegetables

11 Au gratin means topped with cheese or what?
☐ Breadcrumbs ☐ Herbs ☐ Onion

12 Which vegetable is included in a florentine dish?
☐ Cauliflower ☐ Mushroom
☐ Spinach

13 Which sauce has a name meaning hunter?
☐ Bearnaise ☐ Bechamel ☐ Chasseur

14 What does fondue mean?
☐ Cheesy ☐ Hot ☐ Melted

15 If something is served sauté how is it cooked?
☐ Not at all ☐ Quickly ☐ Slowly

ANSWERS ON PAGE 300

496 NUMBERS

1. Which Dollar Baby was an Oscar winner in 2005?
2. What name is given to the coloured sugar strands used in cake decorating?
3. Alphabetically, which is the first of the Seven Dwarfs?
4. Which number is represented as M in Roman numerals?
5. Which Shakespeare play shares its name with the feast of Epiphany?
6. How many little maids from school were there in *The Mikado*?
7. Who was the first man to run a four-minute mile?
8. Which star of the TV show *ER* starred in *Oceans Eleven* and its sequel?
9. How many people did Jesus feed in the parable of the loaves and fishes?
10. From which musical does the song *One* come?
11. How many hills of Rome are there?
12. Which animal is said to have nine lives?
13. Who is the four-legged member of the *Famous Five*?
14. The three-day eventing is a contest in which sport?
15. Which actress wrote the autobiography *The Two of Us*?
16. What name was given to those who took part in the California gold rush?
17. Which sense is intuition or clairvoyance?
18. Who wrote *The Nine Tailors*?
19. Who in England was the "Nine Days Queen"?
20. How many winks is a short sleep?

ANSWERS ON PAGE 300

497 LUCKY DIP

1. How many packs of cards are needed for a game of Canasta?
2. What is the zodiac sign of the Virgin?
3. Gillian Gilks played for England at which sport?
4. In the 90s which European country had a King Albert?
5. Bill Gates founded which computer corporation?
6. Which Clark was a journalist on *The Daily Planet*?
7. If I stands for Intelligence what does Q stand for in IQ?
8. Who was known as the "Forces Sweetheart" in the Second World War?
9. What is the first name of television cook Stein?
10. According to proverb, what should you do before you leap?
11. In the medical sector, what does GP stand for?
12. Which Sea is to the west of Denmark?
13. In which decade did Croatia appoint their first President?
14. In song, what did Tony Bennett leave in San Francisco?
15. What are the two main ingredients of a Bloody Mary?
16. In the rhyme, who killed Cock Robin?
17. What is a world sport, an American vegetable and a British soft drink?
18. Who recorded the album *The Colour Of My Love*?
19. Which game is played with a plastic saucer-shaped disc?
20. On which Common could you discover The Wombles?

ANSWERS ON PAGE 300

498 HISTORY

1 In what month was the Japanese attack on Pearl Harbor?

2 In which European city did the SAS storm the Iranian embassy in the 1980s?

3 The Rotary Club was founded in 1905 in which American city?

4 Which Ben was disqualified from the Seoul Olympics for drug taking?

5 In which Sea did the oil rig Piper Alpha catch fire?

6 Which famous Indian monument was built by Shah Jahan?

7 Where did the Gang of Four seize power in 1976?

8 Which US president was the victim of an unsuccessful assassination attempt in the 1980s?

9 Whose epitaph reads, "Hereabouts died a very gallant gentleman"?

10 President Marcos was ousted in a rebellion in which island country?

11 Desmond Tutu became an Archbishop in which country?

12 Who was the second of Queen Elizabeth II's sons to marry?

13 In Nazi Germany what was *Endlöslung*?

14 At which UK stadium was the Live Aid concert held?

15 Who was awarded a Nobel Peace Prize for her work with the poor in India?

16 Who did Flora Macdonald rescue?

17 Which war in the south Atlantic was Britain involved in during the 1980s?

18 In which country was a monarchy restored in 1975?

19 Sally Ride became the USA's first woman where?

20 At which place of work was Lady Diana Spencer famously photographed in a seemingly see-through skirt?

ANSWERS ON PAGE 300

499 SCIENCE

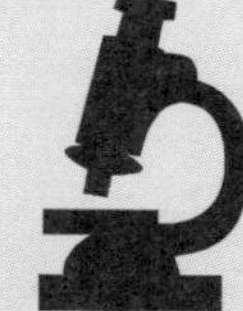

1 REM stands for rapid movement of what?

2 Which Charles wrote *The Origin Of Species*?

3 What metallic element is mixed with tin to form the alloy bronze?

4 Who discovered that the universe is expanding?

5 Which metal is made from bauxite?

6 What scale is used to measure wind velocity?

7 Au is the symbol of which chemical element?

8 What is the chief ingredient in the production of glass?

9 Who discovered the neutron?

10 What is the most common element in the human body after oxygen?

11 What name is given to the animal and plant life which lives at the bottom of the sea?

12 What does a limnologist study?

13 Claudie Andre-Deshays was the first woman in space from which country?

14 What does a space shuttle land on when it returns to Earth?

15 Which space station is named after the Russian word for "peace"?

16 What name is given to a site for watching astronomical phenomena?

17 Which Italian painter drew early ideas for a helicopter?

18 Which scientist discovered alpha, beta and gamma rays?

19 Which American developed the light bulb?

20 Where is the International Robot Exhibition held every two years?

ANSWERS ON PAGE 300

Thanksgiving

The harvest is over and all is safely gathered in . . . it's time to tackle our Thanksgiving Day Quiz.

1 On which ship did the Pilgrim Fathers sail to the Americas?

2 What is another word for the horn of plenty which is a symbol of Thanksgiving?

3 Who set the date of Thanksgiving as the final Thursday in November?

4 Pongal is the Hindu festival for which harvested crop?

5 Shavuot is a Jewish harvest festival and also celebrates God giving the Torah to whom?

6 Which bird is traditionally eaten at Thanksgiving in the USA?

7 In which months is corn harvested in New Zealand?

8 What name did the Pilgrim Fathers first give their home in the New World?

9 Which Jewish festival was originally known as the Feast of the Harvest?

10 In which season does the Jewish festival Sukkot take place?

11 Which plants are used in the celebrations of Sukkot?

12 To which animals do Hindus devote the third day of Pongal?

13 Mihr Jashan is a harvest festival celebrated by people from which religion?

14 On which Rock did the Pilgrim Fathers arrive in 1620?

15 What is the French word for thank you?

16 If you harvested a Pitmaston Pineapple what would you have picked?

17 Is a potato an annual or a perennial crop?

18 Which country produces the most rubber, Thailand or the Philippines?

19 The avocado is a native of which continent?

20 The wheat harvest festival in India is called what?

21 When is Thanksgiving Day celebrated in Canada?

22 Trung Thus is a Moon festival in which country?

23 The festival of N'cwala is held to celebrate the harvest in which African country?

24 Which is the hottest chilli pepper you might harvest, a Scotch bonnet or a Jalapeno?

25 Which country has the largest coffee harvest?

26 Which plant can grow faster than any other?

27 What is another name for corn meal?

28 Which cereal which can grow in cold climates is used in Europe to make black bread?

Day Quiz

29 What is a Blenheim Orange?

30 Which is the larger crop worldwide, cotton or linen?

31 If you made pumpernickel from rye what would you have made?

32 Which cereal is used to make porridge?

33 What name is given to the fungus which can grow so large it covers several hectares?

34 What is another name for the cereal Avena?

35 Where did turkeys originate?

36 Which country is the leading producer of rice in Europe?

37 Is hard wheat richer in gluten or richer in starch?

38 What colour is the flesh of a pumpkin?

39 Which cereal is used to make the Russian drink Kvass?

40 Which fruit's Latin name is *prunus perica*?

41 Is a pea a legume or a succulent?

42 Which country produces the most rice, Vietnam or China?

43 Which cereal beginning with B is malted and used in brewing beer and distilling whisky?

44 Is a carrot an annual or a biennial crop?

45 What is the German expression for thank you?

46 What is another name for India's Holi festival?

47 Which Pie is traditionally eaten on Thanksgiving Day in the USA?

48 Japan's Lantern festival celebrates the harvest of which crop?

49 Onam is a harvest festival celebrated by people from which religion?

50 Custard powder, cornflour and polenta are all produced from which cereal?

ANSWERS ON PAGE 300

501 FASHION

1 What is Jimmy Choo most famous for?

3 Which designer made clothes for younger people under the Emporio label?

3 Which former partner of Malcolm McLaren was at the forefront of punk fashion?

4 Who is noted for her exotic designs and pink hair?

5 Who took over the house of Dior on Dior's death?

6 Which designer is the daughter of a Beatle?

7 Which Gibraltan-born designer left Givenchy for Dior in 1996?

8 What is the name of Terence and Shirley Conran's dress designer son?

9 Which Welsh designer was famous for designing small patterns in natural fabrics?

10 Which designer known as Coco is famous for a perfume range?

11 Which label is famous for sweaters – notably for golfers!?

12 Which Versace took over the fashion house after her brother's murder?

13 Which Bond Street label is famous for its raincoat with checked lining?

14 Which designer epitomised the Swinging London of the Sixties?

15 Which Bruce worked for Saint Laurent and designed for Bendel's store in New York?

16 Who designed Kelly Holmes' outfit when she became a "Dame"?

17 Who was famous for the New Look, the A line and The Sack?

18 Which Ralph's original surname was Lipschitz?

19 Which London designer was Designer of the Year, London Fashion Awards in 1996?

20 Which American is credited with the development of "designer" jeans?

ANSWERS ON PAGE 300

502 GENERAL KNOWLEDGE

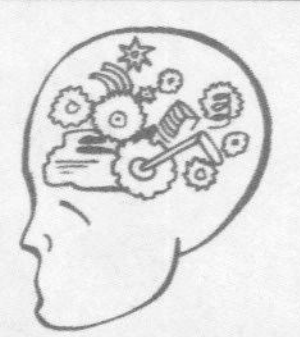

1 What was Captain Kirk's first name in *Star Trek*?

2 Canaan Banana was the first president of which country?

3 What was the name of the Queen of Faeries in *A Midsummer Night's Dream*?

4 Who was divorced from Mark Phillips?

5 What was the name of the girl who visited *The Wizard of Oz*?

6 Who came directly after Pope John-Paul I?

7 Which product was advertised by Supermodel Eva Herzagovia using the slogan, "Hello Boys"?

8 What does a Frenchman mean when he says, "Quel dommage"?

9 Which stretch of water separates Alaska from the Russian mainland?

10 In which city is Sauchiehall Street?

11 Who was the last chemist to be Britain's Prime Minister?

12 Which principality lies between France and Spain in the Pyrenees?

13 Gerald Scarfe was a famous what?

14 How many letters are there in the Greek alphabet?

15 Which elephants have the bigger ears, Indian or African?

16 *If I Were A Rich Man* comes from which stage show?

17 What word follows paper and goes before gammon to make new words?

18 Who was lead singer with The Boomtown Rats?

19 In *Thunderbirds*, who was Lady Penelope's puppet chauffeur?

20 In the Bible, what was St Luke's profession?

ANSWERS ON PAGE 300

503 PICTURE QUIZ

What links these four pictures?

ANSWERS ON PAGE 300

504 GUESS WHO . . . ?

1 He was born in 1949, the son of a famous novelist. His first novel was *The Rachel Papers* and he also writes short stories.
2 Born in Belfast, he acts, directs and writes and founded a theatre company. He was once married to Emma Thompson.
3 Born in the Irish Republic, he starred in the TV series *Remington Steele* before becoming agent 007.
4 The youngest person to have a stand-up show in the West End, he wrote *Blackadder*.
5 He appeared in the original stage production of *Oliver!*, joined Genesis but also made albums under his own name.
6 Born in December 1962, he shot to fame in the movie *Schindler's List* and starred in *The English Patient*.
7 Born in Tiger Bay, Cardiff in 1937, she has sung all over the world – including recording several Bond movie theme songs.
8 Born in 1950, he founded a record shop in 1971 and his own label. Launched a transatlantic airline and a radio station.
9 Born in 1938 and brought up in Kent, his first novel was *The Day of the Jackal* which became a successful movie.
10 His plays include *Absurd Person Singular*. He has had five plays running simultaneously in London's West End.

ANSWERS ON PAGE 300

505 MOVIE DIRECTORS

1 Which film got Clint Eastwood his first Best Director Oscar?
☐ *Loser* ☐ *Pale Rider* ☐ *Unforgiven*

2 What was the first name of Italian director Fellini?
☐ Carlo ☐ Federico ☐ Oscar

3 What is the first name of Minghella, who made *The English Patient*?
☐ Alan ☐ Anthony ☐ Archie

4 Which *Dirty* film led Robert Aldrich to found his own studio?
☐ Dames ☐ Dancing ☐ Dozen

5 What is Blake Edwards' real last name?
☐ Blake ☐ Edworthy ☐ McEdwards

6 Which Oliver directed *Platoon*?
☐ Sands ☐ Slate ☐ Stone

7 In which country was Milos Forman born?
☐ Czechoslovakia ☐ Mexico
☐ Sweden

8 Who won the Best Director Oscar for *Braveheart*?
☐ Clint Eastwood ☐ Mel Gibson
☐ Ridley Scott

9 Which director Roger did Brigitte Bardot marry?
☐ Moore ☐ Rodgers ☐ Vadim

10 Which Frank won an Oscar for *It Happened One Night*?
☐ Capra ☐ Gatsby ☐ Stein

11 Which John directed *The Treasure of The Sierra Madre*?
☐ Ford ☐ Huston ☐ Wayne

12 Who directed and starred in *The Great Dictator* in 1940?
☐ Bogart ☐ Chaplin ☐ Heston

13 How was Albert Broccoli better known?
☐ Bubbly ☐ Cubby ☐ Curly

14 Which Robert directed *M*A*S*H*?
☐ Altman ☐ Redford ☐ Hoskins

15 Whose *Baby* was the Hollywood debut for Roman Polanski?
☐ Jane's ☐ Mia's ☐ Rosemary's

ANSWERS ON PAGE 300

506 HALF CHANCE

½? ½? ½?

1 On which day are US elections (except Presidential) always held – Tuesday or Wednesday?
2 What did Charles Lewis Tiffany trade in – jewels or stocks?
3 What is the next white note on a keyboard below G – A or F?
4 TV drama *The West Wing* was about life where – in the White House or in an asylum?
5 What can be cardinal, ordinal or prime – a cut of beef or a number?
6 Which game is played at Roland Garros – Rugby or lawn tennis?
7 Who or what swims on the cover of Nirvana's album *Nevermind* – a baby or a shark?
8 In which mountain range is Mount Elbert the highest peak – The Rockies or The Andes?
9 What is the traditional colour of an Indian wedding sari – scarlet or white?
10 Which country, outside Spain, has a famous Spanish Riding School – Austria or Russia?
11 What is the real first name of Jay Kay of Jamiroquai fame – Jake or Jason?
12 Ingemar Johansson became Sweden's first champion in which sport – boxing or judo?
13 The first kindergarten was established in which country – Holland or Switzerland?
14 Which was the "Black" day of the 1929 Wall Street Crash – Monday or Thursday?
15 Australia's first PM shared the surname of which fictional detective – Barton or Holmes?
16 Which country has the longest coastline in the world – Canada or Japan?
17 If the 12th January is a Friday what day is the 12th February – Monday or Sunday?
18 How many hurdles are there in total in a six-lane 400 metre hurdle race – 60 or 72?
19 Did mulligatawny soup originate from – China or India?
20 The first heart transplant patient lived how long after the operation – 18 hours or 18 days?

ANSWERS ON PAGE 300

507 THE SIMPSONS

1 What was Marge Simpson's maiden name?
2 Homer Simpson works in which sector of the Springfield Nuclear Power Plant?
3 In the *Itchy and Scratchy* cartoons which character is the mouse?
4 Where do Patty and Selma Bouvier work?
5 What colour is Krusty the Clown's hair?
6 Who drives the bus to Springfield Elementary School?
7 "Thank you. Come again", is the catchphrase of which character?
8 Which character can play the lute?
9 What colour are Bart's shorts?
10 What is Grampa's first name?
11 Who does Principal Seymour Skinner live with?
12 What is the name of Mr. Burns' loyal assistant?
13 Miss Hoover teaches which member of the Simpson family?
14 Rod and Todd are the sons of which character?
15 Which grade is Bart in at Springfield Elementary?
16 Who is Homer's best friend?
17 Which brand of beer is drunk by the characters in The Simpsons?
18 Herschel Krustofski is the real name of which character?
19 Bobo is the long-lost teddy bear of which character?
20 Who is the bully in Bart's class?

ANSWERS ON PAGE 301

508 THE ARTS

1 At which film festival is the prize the Golden Bear awarded?

3 Which Austrian city is home of Mozart?

3 Who wrote the lyrics for Lloyd Webber's *Whistle Down the Wind*?

4 Which is the highest female singing voice?

5 How is adventure and spy writer David Cornwell better known?

6 Thornton Wilder's novel *The Matchmaker* was made into which musical?

7 Which musical term means "like a harp"?

8 Who wrote the songs for *Doctor Dolittle*?

9 In which Stephen King novel and play does the character Annie Wilkes feature?

10 Who founded the RSC aged 30?

11 How many lines are there in a limerick?

12 Which writer and politician bought poet Rupert Brooke's house?

13 Which fictional barrister was created by John Mortimer?

14 Whose first novel, *A Woman Of Substance* became a best seller?

15 Which best-selling late lady novelist wrote some 700 romantic novels?

16 The novel *The Day Of The Jackal* is about an assassination plot on whom?

17 For which Salman Rushdie book did Ayatollah Khomeni impose a fatwa?

18 In which city is the Ashmolean Museum of Art and Archaeology?

19 To five years, how old was Mary Wesley when her first bestseller was published?

20 Award-winning novelist Ben Okri hails from which country?

ANSWERS ON PAGE 301

509 LUCKY DIP

1 Which country are Qantas airlines from?

2 What is the currency of Russia?

3 What type of plant grows from seed, flowers and dies in a year?

4 Helen Sharman was the first Britain to go where?

5 What is Roget's word book known as?

6 Which English king was the husband of Queen Elizabeth the Queen Mother?

7 In rhyming slang what is Barnet Fair?

8 How is Declan McManus better known?

9 What animal is shown in the painting *The Monarch Of The Glen*?

10 In the Bible, what sort of den did Daniel enter?

11 Who recorded the album *Made In England*?

12 In which game are words made from letter tiles of different values?

13 What is the first name of Polish film director Polanski?

14 What colour is saffron?

15 What began in Pudding Lane and spread through London?

16 How many sides has a trapezium?

17 Which breed of dog is a favourite of Queen Elizabeth II?

18 Which metal is an alloy of copper and zinc?

19 Who won the Best Director Oscar for *Forrest Gump*?

20 What is a Blenheim Orange?

ANSWERS ON PAGE 301

510 HORSE RACING

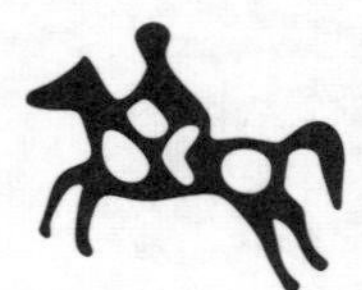

1. Which horse gave jockey Jim Culloty a hat-trick of Cheltenham Gold Cup victories?
2. Which jockey rode Sakhee in 2001 and Marienbard in 2002 to Prix de l'Arc de Triomphe wins?
3. Which star jockey returned to racing in 1990 when aged over 50?
4. Which horse was first to win the Grand National three times?
5. Where is the William Hill Lincoln Handicap held?
6. In which country was Shergar captured?
7. In which month is the Melbourne Cup held?
8. Which horse Benny won the 1997 Derby?
9. Which English classic is held at Doncaster?
10. Formed in 1750, can you say to 10 years, when were women allowed to join The Jockey Club?
11. Which horse race was abandoned in 1997 after a bomb scare?
12. The Prix du Jockey-Club is held at which race course?
13. Which horse had the nickname Corky?
14. Which Gordon, a trainer of over 2000 winners, died in September 1998?
15. Which country hosts the Belmont and Preakness Stakes?
16. The Curragh is in which Irish county?
17. Which race meeting is described as Glorious?
18. The 12th Earl of where gave his name to a famous race?
19. Which horse was the first to win Horse of the Year four times?
20. Who was Champion flat jockey from 2001 to 2003 in the UK and Ireland?

ANSWERS ON PAGE 301

511 PEOPLE

1. In 1968 The Oscars ceremony was postponed for 48 hours because of whose death?
2. In the 1960s the Queen dedicated an acre of ground in the UK to the memory of whom?
3. Who created Fantasyland, Adventureland and Frontierland?
4. Who led so-called witch hunts against communists in the USA after WWII?
5. Which two astronomers discovered the comet Hale-Bopp?
6. Which Russian leader was buried in 1998 in his family's vault?
7. Aung San Suu Kyi is a controversial leader in which country?
8. Where did Henry Stanley say, "Dr Livingstone I presume."?
9. Who became President of the European Commission in 1995?
10. What was Marilyn Monroe's only line of dialogue in the scene which took 59 takes in *Some Like It Hot*?
11. Who once described his paintings as "hand-painted dream photographs"?
12. Where was Ronnie Biggs arrested in 1974 after over eight years on the run?
13. Which French PM's funeral was attended by his wife and his mistress in 1996?
14. Which world leader married Graca Machel in 1998?
15. Whose last words were reputedly, "Thank God I have done my duty"?
16. Whose TV roles have included Arkwright and Fletcher?
17. Who opened The Royal Albert Hall in London?
18. Which type of building did Louis XIV have built at Versailles?
19. Who wrote *Nessun Dorma*, now regarded as Pavarotti's theme tune?
20. Which US First Lady is credited as being the first to use the name?

ANSWERS ON PAGE 301

512 W.W.W.

Can you identify the country in question from its internet code? Some may be obvious . . . some may not!

1 .al

2 .ua

3 .za

4 .se

5 .ml

6 .dz

7 .bo

8 .gl

9 .mc

10 .ee

ANSWERS ON PAGE 301

513 WHO SAID . . . ?

1 "Experience is the name everyone gives to their mistakes."

2 On receiving an Oscar, who said, "I deserve this."

3 "Plastic surgeons are always making mountains out of molehills."

4 "Winning isn't everything but wanting to win is."

5 "Send two dozen roses to room 424 and put 'I love you Emily' on the back of the bill."

6 "No woman can be too rich or too thin."

7 "As long as my picture is on the front page I don't care what they say about me on page 96."

8 "I've been on a calendar but never on time."

ANSWERS ON PAGE 301

514 GEMS AND JEWELS

1 What shape is the diamond Star of South Africa?
☐ Pear shaped ☐ Spherical ☐ Square

2 Which stone is said to aid weak eyesight?
☐ Emerald ☐ Topaz ☐ Zircon

3 Which gem is found in an oyster shell?
☐ Garnet ☐ Pearl ☐ Turquoise

4 Who was the first British queen to wear the Koh i Noor diamond?
☐ Elizabeth ☐ Mary ☐ Victoria

5 What does Koh i Noor mean?
☐ Brightest star ☐ Light of the world
☐ Mountain of light

6 What is the largest known diamond?
☐ Culdees ☐ Cullinan ☐ Culloden?

7 Which gem did the ancients consider an antidote to poison?
☐ Diamond ☐ Ruby ☐ Sapphire

8 Who wore the Sancy diamond at his coronation?
☐ Francis I ☐ Henry VIII ☐ Louis XV

9 In heraldry which planet does the ruby represent?
☐ Earth ☐ Mars ☐ Pluto

10 What colour is the Hope Diamond?
☐ Blue ☐ Pink ☐ White

11 Which was the purest material for the Chinese?
☐ Emerald ☐ Jade ☐ Jet

12 Mercury is represented by which jewel in heraldry?
☐ Amethyst ☐ Pearl ☐ Topaz

13 Which gems are said to be a girl's best friend?
☐ Diamonds ☐ Emeralds ☐ Peridots

14 Which European city is famous for its diamond-cutting trade?
☐ Amsterdam ☐ Paris ☐ Barcelona

15 Which diamond brings good luck to women and bad to men?
☐ Hope ☐ Koh i Noor ☐ Sancy

ANSWERS ON PAGE 301

515 GENERAL KNOWLEDGE

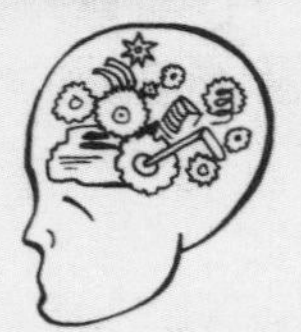 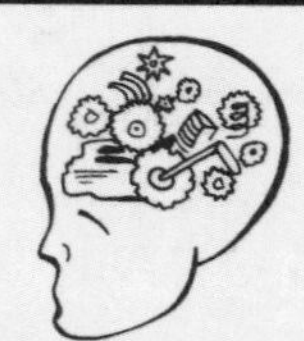 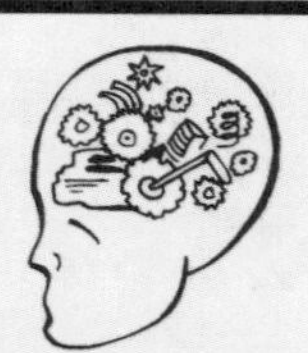

1 Which gas shares its name with Superman's home planet?

2 To whom does the expression "Father of the House" refer?

3 On which island is Wall Street?

4 Which Harry won a Lifetime Achievement Grammy in 2000?

5 What is the study of fluids moving in pipes?

6 What type of person studies the relationship between living organisms and their environment?

7 What was George Washington's wife's first name?

8 Which English place is an anagram of ancestral?

9 Where, in Baker Street, did Sherlock Holmes live?

10 What does the word Bolshoi mean?

11 In mythology, who was banished by his son Jupiter?

12 What London suburb is the G in GMT?

13 Which "ology" is the art of ringing bells?

14 What is Eric Clapton's middle name?

15 How many dancers feature in a pas de deux?

16 Which William wrote a poem about daffodils?

17 What was the name of the World War I ace, nicknamed "The Red Baron"?

18 In which country were fireworks invented?

19 Who is credited with inventing frozen food?

20 What unit is used to measure the gas we use in our homes?

ANSWERS ON PAGE 301

516 LEISURE

1 Ellem in Scotland is the oldest club of what type?

2 Which eating house did Ruthie Rogers found?

3 If you spent your leisure time in a sulky where would you be?

4 1949 saw what innovation in the game of badminton?

5 Who founded the Harlem Globetrotters?

6 How many tiles are there in a game of mah-jong?

7 Where is the Liseberg theme park?

8 What type of art was known as Jugenstil in Germany?

9 Which British country pursuit became illegal in 2005?

10 In the early days of cinema how long would a two reeler last?

11 Serigraphy is also known as what?

12 What name is given to the style of skiing on a single broad ski?

13 Which type of outdoor spectacular was created by Paul Houdin and first shown at the Château de Chambord in 1952?

14 Which craft takes its name from the Arabic for striped cloth?

15 Where did canasta originate?

16 What are the two winning numbers made with two dice in craps?

17 Wing chun is the best known form of which sport?

18 If you follow FINA rules which sport do you practise?

19 How many dominoes are there in a double six set?

20 Southampton boasts of having the first sports area of what type in the country?

ANSWERS ON PAGE 301

517 AT THE MOVIES

1 Which US comic star Gary featured in the 1990s *Doctor Doolittle*?

2 Which country links *Town* and *Syndrome* in movie titles?

3 Which Debbie starred in the classic musical movie *Singin' In The Rain*?

4 Which Mike starred in *Wayne's World*?

5 *Shine* was about a musician playing which instrument?

6 *There's Something About Mary* featured which Cameron?

7 Which actor links *Jurassic Park* and *Coming To America*?

8 In *Some Like It Hot* what disguise do Curtis and Lemmon adopt?

9 Which actress appeared on the cinema poster for *Titanic*?

10 Which Kevin featured in *A Fish Called Wanda*?

11 In which 1980 movie did Robert De Niro play a boxer?

12 What did George C. Scott refuse to do about his Oscar for *Patton*?

13 The song *A Whole New World* comes from which animated movie?

14 What did John Wayne wear on his face in *True Grit*?

15 Which Kevin won Best Director for *Dances With Wolves*?

16 Which direction completes the film title *Once Upon A Time In The* ____?

17 How many times did Greta Garbo marry?

18 Which Nick won an Oscar for *The Wrong Trousers*?

19 Which Bo Derek film had a number as the title?

20 Which Mr Jones was a character in *Raiders Of The Lost Ark*?

ANSWERS ON PAGE 301

518 THE HEADLINES

1 Fleur Lombard was the first woman to die on duty in which profession?

2 Robert McCartney was murdered after a confrontation in which Belfast bar?

3 Who was the most famous person to have a tracheotomy at Rome's Gemelli hospital in Feb 2005?

4 Who did Princess Diana leave most of her money to?

5 Barzan and Watban were half brothers of which ousted leader?

6 Which was the first country in the world to have a postcode made up of letters and numbers?

7 What was the occupation of Philip Lawrence who was killed outside his place of work in 1995?

8 Nicoletta Mantovani made the news through her relationship with which big figure in the entertainment world?

9 Released on June 22nd 1999, Patrick Magee was known as which Bomber?

10 Which supersonic aircraft was grounded in 2000 after crashing outside Paris?

11 Timothy McVeigh was convicted for which bombing?

12 Which American First Lady had to give evidence over the Whitewater scandal?

13 Which company owned the pesticide plant in Bhopal which saw a tragic chemical leak?

14 Who was the youngest winner of the Nobel Peace Prize when a winner in 1964?

15 Which woman space traveller published *The Space Place* in 1997?

16 Marc Dutroux hit the headlines over a "house of horrors" in which country?

17 Che Guevara was killed while training guerrillas against which government?

18 About which British politician did Francois Mitterand say, "She has the mouth of Marilyn Monroe and the eyes of Caligula?"

19 In 1992 Don Hollister and Don Pelazzo were responsible for developing a high tech what?

20 Who was the last British Wimbledon Singles Champion of the 20th century?

ANSWERS ON PAGE 301

519 COMPUTERS

1 What does the first w stand for in www?

2 What computer problem was feared, seemingly unnecessarily, for 2000?

3 Which page of a Web site is called a Home Page?

4 In addition to the computer what else must a modem be plugged into?

5 What does Q mean in FAQ?

6 What does S mean in ISP?

7 In which country did the Internet start?

8 A small "a" in a circle (@) is pronounced how?

9 What name is given to the software program needed to access the Web?

10 What goes after Netscape in the name of a popular Internet browser?

11 A 2001 computer virus was called after which tennis star?

12 What is the opposite of downloading?

13 What is freeware?

14 If you log off what do you do?

15 What is netiquette?

16 What is the minimum number of computers which can be networked?

17 What letter appears on screen when you are using Microsoft Internet Explorer?

18 What name is given to a program designed to cause damage by attaching itself to other programs?

19 Where does bounced email return to?

20 Which was the first full-length feature film designed completely on computer?

ANSWERS ON PAGE 301

520 LUCKY DIP

1 Who recorded the album *The Violin Player*?

2 In what year was the 50th anniversary of VE Day?

3 In 1979, Brighton Council decided to allow what type of beach?

4 Which David told his life story in *The Moon's A Balloon*?

5 Rocks are broken down by the elements by what gradual process?

6 Who sang *Happy Birthday* to Prince Charles on his 50th bash?

7 The word lupine relates to which animals?

8 In which country is the volcano Popocatepetl?

9 What number does the Roman numeral D stand for?

10 Which cookery term means to bring to the boil and bubble gently?

11 In which month is the first day of Spring?

12 Where does the rattlesnake have its rattle?

13 Which stage direction means to go off stage?

14 What are the two initials of Narnia creator Lewis?

15 What was the name of the Spanish waiter in *Fawlty Towers*?

16 Which British dessert is made from sponge topped with custard and cream?

17 Which element is found in bones, shells and teeth?

18 Which monarch followed directly after George I?

19 What part of a garment is a raglan?

20 In which country is the Table Mountain?

ANSWERS ON PAGE 301

521 PICTURE QUIZ

A

B

C

D

What links these four people?

ANSWERS ON PAGE 301

522 DRINKS

Is each statement TRUE or FALSE?

T F **1** Angostura bitters were named after a town in Venezuela.

T F **2** Tokay is a sweet Japanese wine.

T F **3** Pilsener is a German beer.

T F **4** The main spirit in a Manhattan is rum.

T F **5** Hock is named after a town of the same name in Germany.

T F **6** Calvados is made in Normandy in France.

T F **7** Bourbon is a US whisky made from corn with malt and rye.

T F **8** Marsala originated on the island of Corsica.

T F **9** Chartreuse was originally green in colour.

T F **10** Sherry comes from the port of Jerez near Cadiz.

ANSWERS ON PAGE 301

523 THE ELEMENTS

1 What is copper named after?
☐ Copenhagen ☐ Copernicus
☐ Cyprus

2 What colour is zinc?
☐ Bluish white ☐ Brown ☐ Dark red

3 What is the chemical symbol for iron?
☐ Fe ☐ Ir ☐ Me

4 Which element has the highest electrical conductivity known?
☐ Copper ☐ Gold ☐ Silver

5 Ancient alchemists believed silver represented what?
☐ Moon ☐ Rain ☐ Sun

6 Who or what was Strontium named after?
☐ Its discoverer ☐ Roman soldier
☐ Scottish village

7 Which element are diamonds made from?
☐ Carbon ☐ Nickel ☐ Sodium

8 When was neon discovered?
☐ 1765 ☐ 1898 ☐ 1910

9 What colour is produced when sodium is added to flames?
☐ Blue ☐ Green ☐ Yellow

10 What is gold called in heraldry?
☐ Argent ☐ Azure ☐ Or

11 Which married couple discovered radium?
☐ Curie ☐ Davy ☐ Raeburn

12 Which element occurs naturally in limestone?
☐ Calcium ☐ Iron ☐ Radon

13 What is the lead in a pencil made from?
☐ Lead ☐ Graphite ☐ Nickel

14 Which metallic element is used in thermometers?
☐ Iron ☐ Mercury ☐ Tin

15 What alloys with copper to make bronze?
☐ Aluminium
☐ Tin
☐ Zinc

ANSWERS ON PAGE 301

524 HALF CHANCE

½? ½? ½?

1. Which Howard discovered Tutankhamun's tomb – Howard Carter or Howard Hawkes?
2. Was Southern Rhodesia renamed in the 1980s – Sri Lanka or Zimbabwe?
3. What is the most number of letters in the name of any one calendar month – nine or ten?
4. Which Scandinavian act had most success in the 1990s US singles chart – Ace of Base or Roxette?
5. A sea containing many islands is called what – an archipelago or an isthmus?
6. In which country is the city of Panshan – China or India?
7. Who was the first US President to visit the USSR – Clinton or Nixon?
8. Who was named along with Alvin and Theodore in The Chipmunks – Martin or Simon?
9. Who or what was the Cullinan diamond after – the mine owner or the discoverer?
10. The first solo transatlantic flight went from New York to where – London or Paris?
11. In which century was Robbie Burns born – 17th or 18th?
12. How many members of the Righteous Brothers were actual brothers – two or none?
13. In India what was Suttee – a fertility dance or widow sacrifice?
14. Constantine, Liberius and Sissinius are names of what – popes or stars?
15. Was Abba's only US No 1 single *Dancing Queen* or *Waterloo*?
16. Is it the absence of G or I that prevents F to L appearing in alphabetical order on a keyboard?
17. Who left a chart-topping group to record *All Things Must Pass* – George Harrison or Robbie Williams?
18. Which first name is derived from Greek for rock or stone – Paul or Peter?
19. Which country were the first to retain soccer's F.I.F.A. World Cup – Brazil or Italy?
20. Which early pop classic begins, "I'm so young and you're so old" – *Diana* or *Too Young*?

ANSWERS ON PAGE 301

525 THEATRES

1. Which is London's oldest theatre?
2. In which city is the world's largest opera house?
3. At which West End theatre did *The Woman In White* open?
4. Who wrote *Tosca*?
5. Including intervals, approximately how long does Wagner's *Götterdämmerung* last?
6. Where is the *Ballet Rambert* based?
7. In which city is Europe's largest opera house?
8. Which theatre was the National's temporary home from 1963?
9. Who wrote the ballet *The Nutcracker*?
10. In which street is London's Savoy Theatre?
11. Which Czech-born playwright wrote *Jumpers and Arcadia*?
12. Which London theatre was gutted by fire in 1990?
13. Who first produced *Les Misérables* in London?
14. In 1984 The Society of West End Theatre Awards were renamed in honour of whom?
15. In which town is the largest stage in the UK?
16. How is *The Marriage of Figaro* known in Italian?
17. What is Shakespeare's longest play?
18. Which former UK PM's wife shares her name with a Bellini opera?
19. The Olivier Theatre is part of which London venue?
20. Which US director was the impetus behind the new Globe Theatre in London?

ANSWERS ON PAGE 301

526 GENERAL KNOWLEDGE

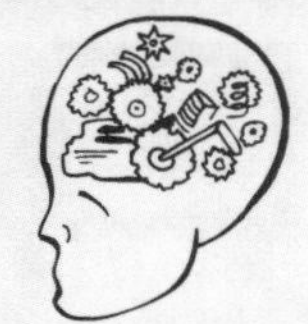
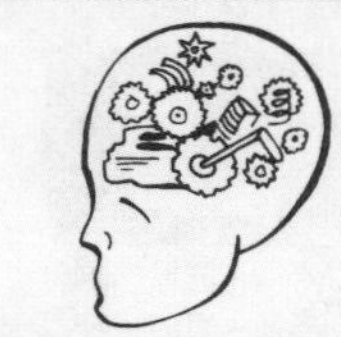
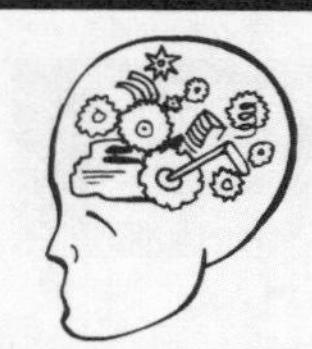

1. Troglodytes lived alone in what particular type of dwelling?
2. Who created a garden at Sissinghurst in Kent?
3. Which famous brothers made a movie called *A Night At The Opera*?
4. What is Prince William's second name?
5. What chicken dish is named after a battle of the Napoleonic Wars?
6. Who wrote the 1988 novel *Prime Time*?
7. During which war were concentration camps introduced?
8. Which famous writer was married to archaeologist Sir Max Mallowan?
9. Who invented the Flying Shuttle in 1733?
10. "The City of Dreaming Spires" is which English city?
11. What is a tine?
12. Which Sondheim musical tells the story of a murdering barber?
13. What breed of retriever takes its name from a North American bay?
14. What does a Geiger Counter measure?
15. In which "ology", founded in the early 1950s, is self-awareness paramount?
16. In 1997 Britain's lease on which country came to an end?
17. Who defeated Richard III at Bosworth in 1485?
18. Which Hollywood actress's real name was Lucille Le Seur?
19. Beaumaris, Conway and Harlech are famous for what type of building?
20. Whom did Thugs worship?

ANSWERS ON PAGE 301

527 IRISH LITERATURE

1. Whose *Ashes* were the title of a best seller by Frank McCourt?
2. Which Oscar wrote *The Importance of Being Earnest*?
3. Which initials did poet Yeats have?
4. What was the first name of playwright Beckett?
5. Which horror character is Bram Stoker most famous for?
6. Which Seamus became Ireland's fourth Nobel literary laureate in 1995?
7. Which Daniel played poet Christopher Nolan on the big screen in *My Left Foot*?
8. What followed *Paddy Clarke* in the title of Roddy Doyle's Booker Prize winner?
9. James Joyce's first novel shares its name with which inhabitants of an Irish city?
10. Which G B wrote the play *Pygmalion* that was adapted into *My Fair Lady*?
11. Who was being "Waited For" in the Samuel Beckett play?
12. What is best-selling novelist Ms Binch's first name?
13. What went with *Juno* in the title of Sean O'Casey's work?
14. Which English gaol did Oscar Wilde write a *Ballad of*?
15. Roddy Doyle wrote of *The Woman Who Walked Into* what?
16. In which French city did Oscar Wilde die?
17. Writer Neil Jordan went on to find fame as what?
18. Which Edna wrote *The Country Girls*?
19. Which Saint was a play by Bernard Shaw?
20. About whose famous Travels did Jonathan Swift write?

ANSWERS ON PAGE 301

528 TRAVEL

1 Baffin Island is between Baffin Bay and which island?

2 Bali is a mountainous island off which country?

3 The Falkland Islands are off which country?

4 Which US state is dubbed the Golden State?

5 Which city, also the name of a film, has the world's largest mosque?

6 How many islands make up Fiji?

7 Baku is the capital of which country on the Caspian Sea?

8 What is Europe's highest capital city?

9 The Barbary Coast is the Mediterranean coast of where?

10 Which Egyptian city is Africa's largest city?

11 Greenwich Village is in which part of New York?

12 On which river is Ho Chi Minh City?

13 Where is Waikiki Beach?

14 Baghdad is on which river?

15 In which part of New York is Coney island?

16 Who or what was London's Liverpool Street station named after?

17 Where are the Roaring Forties?

18 Which city gave its name to a type of riding breeches?

19 What is South Africa's largest city?

20 In which ocean are the Bahamas?

ANSWERS ON PAGE 301

529 TELEVISION

1 Which Teletubby's name is first alphabetically?

2 The last episode of which series was compulsive viewing in the US when broadcast in May 1998?

3 In *Sex And The City* which character was the lawyer?

4 Which Australian entertainer and TV presenter had a chart hit with *Stairway To Heaven*?

5 In which fictional suburb is *Desperate Housewives* set?

6 Who narrated *The Wombles*?

7 *Unchained Melody* turned which two TV actors into pop stars?

8 Which televized pop concert raised money for famine relief in Ethiopia?

9 Which Denis is a long standing presenter of *It'll Be All Right On the Night*?

10 Back in the 1950s, which Hughie presented the original *Opportunity Knocks*?

11 In *Dallas*, who did Miss Ellie marry after Jock died?

12 In which US state was *Sweet Valley High* set?

13 What colour is Marge's hair in *The Simpsons*?

14 In the US Jim Bakker and Jimmy Swaggart are famous for what type of show?

15 Which character did Ted Danson play in *Cheers*?

16 Which Mr Kelly presented *Stars In Their Eyes*?

17 Who presented *The Full Wax*?

18 How many Monkees were there in the classic 1960s television shows?

19 Which clerical sitcom was set on Craggy Island – *Father Ted* or *The Vicar of Dibley*?

20 Which TV astronomer was born Patrick Caldwell-Moore?

ANSWERS ON PAGE 301

530 AIRPORTS

Can you name the countries where the listed airports are located?

1 HELLENIKON

2 HOPKINS

3 LINATE

4 FORNEBU

5 PAPHOS

6 REGINA

7 SANTANDER

8 VAASA

9 PERETOLA

10 KALMAR

ANSWERS ON PAGE 301

531 DOUBLE TAKE

In each case, the two-part quiz question leads to just one answer!

1 Which word can be a squall of wind or an imperfection?

2 Which word can be the body of a ship and also means to remove the core from strawberries?

3 Which word means to squeeze or wedge into a space and also is a sweet preserve?

4 Which word describes a Scottish dance or can mean to throw?

5 Which word describes a series of bars used to climb and a snag or flaw in fabric?

6 Which word describes a large pond or reddish pigment?

7 Which word describes a sheepskin and can also mean to swindle?

8 Which word describes a dry throat and a breed of dog used in the Arctic?

9 Which word can be a long, flat slave ship or a tray for type in printing?

10 Which word describes a creamy fruit dessert and can be a stupid person?

ANSWERS ON PAGE 301

532 WEIRD WEATHER

1 What caused red snow to fall in Switzerland in 1755?
☐ Lichen ☐ Dead birds ☐ Red dust

2 The word tsunami comes from which language?
☐ Chinese ☐ Japanese ☐ Thai

3 What caused the death of 1.5 million people in India in 1943–44?
☐ Drought ☐ Flood ☐ Smog

4 Which Chinese river has flooded over 1500 times?
☐ Henan ☐ Huang He ☐ Yangtze

5 Which animals were part of a rain shower in England in 1939?
☐ Frogs ☐ Mice ☐ Tortoises

6 On which December date did the Asian tsunami strike at the end of 2004?
☐ 24th ☐ 25th ☐ 26th

7 Which is the hottest, driest place in the USA?
☐ Arizona ☐ Death Valley ☐ Nevada

8 Which place is the coldest?
☐ Alaska ☐ Siberia ☐ Yukon

9 Which weather caused the death of 21 people in Zimbabwe in 1975?
☐ Flood ☐ Hail ☐ Lightning

10 Where did snow fall for the first time in September 1981?
☐ Kilimanjaro ☐ Kalahari ☐ Okovango

11 Prior to the disaster in 2004 where was the previous worst tsunami?
☐ Chile ☐ Japan ☐ Morocco

12 Which type of weather disaster is considered most costly?
☐ Avalanche ☐ Drought ☐ Flood

13 Which place is the cloudiest?
☐ Ben Nevis ☐ Everest
☐ Mount Olympus

14 What was part of a rain shower in the USSR in 1940?
☐ Balls ☐ Coins ☐ Road signs

15 What caused the death of nearly 3000 people in London in 1952?
☐ Hail
☐ Hurricane
☐ Smog

ANSWERS ON PAGE 301

533 DAVID BECKHAM

1. Where was David Beckham born?
2. Which middle name does he share with his eldest son?
3. He was on loan to which side in 1995?
4. David Beckham's first son was named after an area of which city?
5. In which country were Victoria and David Beckham married?
6. Prior to the match where he was sent off in France 98 Beckham scored against whom?
7. What was his transfer fee in 2003 when he went to Spain?
8. Against whom did he make the longest strike in the Premiership in the 1996–97 season?
9. What was his autobiography called?
10. Which honour did he receive from the Queen in 2003?
11. Against which side did he make his England debut?
12. Which was the first of Beckham's children to be born in Spain?
13. Who were England playing when he was sent off in the 1998 World Cup?
14. What colour shirt was he wearing when he was sent off in France 98?
15. Against which European country did he gain his 50th England cap?
16. In what year did he first win the Premiership with Man Utd?
17. What was the first Spanish side he played for?
18. How many times did he win the Charity Shield with Man Utd?
19. In which Games did he play a part in the opening ceremony in 2002?
20. Against which side did David Beckham score his first pro own goal?

ANSWERS ON PAGE 301

534 POP MUSIC QUIZ

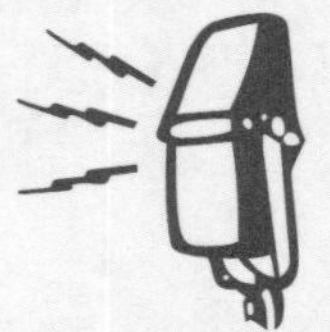
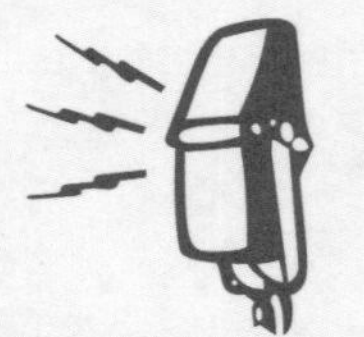

1. Which lady was *Beautiful* at the top of the UK charts?
2. Which musician is the father of Norah Jones?
3. What line follows, "Is this the real life"?
4. Which Irish group has a name which means family?
5. Which former Beatle was the first to have a solo No 1 in the US?
6. Siobhan Fahey and Marcella Detroit were in which band in the 1990s?
7. How many members were in the the original line up of Boyz II Men?
8. Which American city links songs by Bruce Springsteen and Elton John?
9. What type of creature was Michael Jackson's pet Muscles?
10. How old was Elvis Presley when he died – 32, 42 or 48?
11. What is in brackets in the title of Cher's *The Shoop Shoop Song*?
12. Falco's *Rock Me Amadeus* was sung in which language?
13. Who had an insect-sounding hit with *The Fly*?
14. Who released a mid 1990s album called *A Different Beat*?
15. Who created the character Ziggy Stardust?
16. Which group's music featured in the frock horror film *Priscilla Queen Of The Desert*?
17. Which veteran singer had his first UK No 1 in the 1970s with *Maggie May*?
18. Who was "The Boss"?
19. Which band actually had a Noddy as lead singer?
20. After seven No 1s in a row, which Westlife single only made No 2 in the UK charts?

ANSWERS ON PAGE 301

535 LUCKY DIP

1 Which extra title was given to Catherine II of Russia?

2 What type of pattern is on a raccoon's tail?

3 Which country is a car from with the international registration letter H?

4 Which came first, The House of Tudor or The House of Stuart?

5 What do you fear if you have bibliophobia?

6 In Premiership soccer how many points are awarded for a draw?

7 Zn is the symbol of which chemical element?

8 Which is not the name of a sea – Black, North or West?

9 According to proverb, one man's meat is another man's what?

10 What colour pottery is Josiah Wedgwood noted for?

11 William and Conference are types of what?

12 Who recorded the album *Medusa*?

13 Feline relates to which kind of animals?

14 What is the capital of Afghanistan?

15 Who was the magician at King Arthur's court?

16 Who fell in love with Juliet Capulet?

17 If you are watching the Grand National, which race course are you at?

18 What was the name of the Ewing ranch in Dallas?

19 How many yards in a mile?

20 Which Jules wrote *Around The World In Eighty Days*?

ANSWERS ON PAGE 301

536 KNIGHTS

1 How many knights are there 0n a chess board at the start of a game?

2 Which is the oldest British Order of Knighthood?

3 The word knight comes from an old English word meaning what?

4 What did a knight use his lance for?

5 What did the Knights Hospitaller do?

6 What did chivalry originally mean?

7 At aged seven a future knight lived with another family as a what?

8 What did a future knight become at 14?

9 What was the ceremony of tapping the new knight on the shoulder with a sword called?

10 What was a hauberk made from?

11 What protected a knight's hand and wrist?

12 What title does the wife of a modern knight take?

13 Plate armour, made from silvery steel, was also called what?

14 What did a cuisse protect?

15 What is the system of knights using special shields and badges called?

16 What did knights do in a tiltyard?

17 Which part of the leg did the greave protect?

18 What was the designer of a knight's coat of arms called?

19 Where was a sabaton worn?

20 What did the Knights Templar do?

ANSWERS ON PAGE 301

537 SPORT

1 Who were the beaten finalists in soccer's Euro 2004?
2 In men's badminton, what is the number of points a player must gain to win a single game?
3 In which year were women allowed to enter the Olympics?
4 In which country were the rules for modern ice hockey formulated?
5 Seb Coe broke existing world records in the 800m, 1500m and what other distance?
6 Who is the only player to score a hat-trick in a F.I.F.A. World Cup Final?
7 Who told a Wimbledon umpire, "You are the pits of the world"?
8 Which soccer side did Jose Mourinho leave when he came to manage Chelsea?
9 Which American tennis player was undefeated on clay between 1973 and 1979?
10 In baseball, which team bats first?
11 Which Scot broke Juan Fangio's record 24 Grand Prix wins?
12 What was the 1992 men's US Olympic basketball team dubbed?
13 Which golfer was responsible for founding the US Masters in Augusta?
14 Which Peter was John McEnroe's partner in most of his Grand Slam doubles titles?
15 Ed Moses won Olympic gold in 1976 and 1984 – what prevented him from winning in 1980?
16 Which Open was Jack Nicklaus' first win?
17 Where did Steve Redgrave win the fourth of his Olympic gold medals?
18 Which Willie was the first jockey to ride more than 8,000 winners?
19 How many times was Steve Davis World Snooker Champion in the 1980s?
20 In 1934 what were women players allowed to wear at Wimbledon?

ANSWERS ON PAGE 302

538 GEOGRAPHY

1 The Sargasso Sea is part of which ocean?
2 Which US city's name means The Fields?
3 Alberta is a province of which country?
4 Which two countries does the Khyber Pass separate?
5 Which Cape was originally called the Cape of Storms?
6 In America what type of natural phenomenon is a chinook?
7 What is the principal island of Japan?
8 Where is the town of Kurri Kurri?
9 What is Africa's highest volcano?
10 By which abbreviation is the mountain Chogori known?
11 What is the only permanent river in the Kalahari desert?
12 Which Ocean's deepest point is the Java Trench?
13 Where would you be if someone put a lei round your neck?
14 Where is the world's longest canal?
15 Afrikaans is the official language of which country in addition to South Africa?
16 In which desert is the Bactrian camel found?
17 What is the largest city of Nevada?
18 Is Namibia in northern or southern Africa?
19 Which is the only Great Lake wholly in the USA?
20 The Kariba Dam is on the border of which two countries?

ANSWERS ON PAGE 302

539 PICTURE QUIZ

Which name links these four famous people?

ANSWERS ON PAGE 302

540 GUESS WHO . . . ?

1 A former teacher, she married Lenny Henry in 1984 and starred in *Murder Most Horrid* and *The Vicar of Dibley*.
2 Born on the Texas border, her daughter is a model, she starred in a *Batman* movie and was partner of a Rolling Stone.
3 Born in 1965, he was brought up in Leeds and is famous for exhibiting carcasses of sheep and cows preserved in formaldehyde.
4 The son of a Methodist minister, he read English at Cambridge and has made many TV interviews.
5 He was the only British Best Actor Oscar winner of the 1990s, he appeared on Broadway and at the RSC.
6 He shot to fame in *Four Weddings and a Funeral* and starred opposite Renée Zellweger in the *Bridget Jones* movies.
7 He has red hair, an older brother called William and is the youngest grandson of the Queen.
8 This fashion designer worked for Dior and Givenchy. Madonna wore his designs in *Evita*.
9 Born in Yorkshire, he has exhibited around the world, designed for theatre and opera and lives in California.
10 His brother Julian is a cellist, he wrote *Cats* and *The Woman in White* and has a famous art collection.

ANSWERS ON PAGE 302

541 FICTIONAL DECTECTIVES

1 Which instrument did Sherlock Holmes play?
☐ Cello ☐ Piano ☐ Violin

2 Who lived at Whitehaven Mansions?
☐ Dalgleish ☐ Holmes ☐ Poirot

3 In which city did Morse operate?
☐ Boston ☐ Cambridge ☐ Oxford

4 Who solved *The Body In The Library* murder?
☐ Miss Marple ☐ Morse ☐ Poirot

5 Which series centred on Townsend Investigations?
☐ *Charlie's Angels* ☐ *Moonlighting*
☐ *The Informer*

6 Who created off beat sleuth Jonathan Creek?
☐ Colin Dexter ☐ Lynda LaPlante
☐ David Renwick

7 Which series began with an answering machine message?
☐ *LA Law* ☐ *Law And Order*
☐ *The Rockford Files*

8 In which series was Slade assisted by Holly?
☐ *Crime Traveller* ☐ *Longstreet*
☐ *Madigan*

9 Who investigated at a monastery in Shrewsbury?
☐ Cadfael ☐ Shoestring
☐ The Equalizer

10 Who played mini-skirted detective Anna Lee?
☐ Imogen Stubbs ☐ Emma Thompson
☐ Kate Winslet

11 Which series began with a pilot called *Killer* in 1983?
☐ *Bergerac* ☐ *Morse* ☐ *Taggart*

12 What was the first name of TV's *Van der Valk*?
☐ Jan ☐ Piet ☐ Ruud

13 Who had a Rolls Royce called *The Grey Panther*?
☐ Sexton Blake ☐ Hercule Poirot
☐ Lord Peter Wimsey

14 Chief Inspector Keen was in which 1960s TV series?
☐ *Gideon's Way*
☐ *Perry Mason*
☐ *Z Cars*

15 Which Ms Gray was in *An Unsuitable Job For A Woman*?
☐ Agnes
☐ Cordelia
☐ Penelope

ANSWERS ON PAGE 302

542 TV SOAPS

1 In *Coronation Street* who was Gail's murderous husband?

2 Who was Pauline Fowler's younger son, Mark or Martin?

3 Which Shane played Albert Square's Alfie Moon?

4 Which heavenly name did Jane Asher have in the revamped *Crossroads*?

5 In which county is *Emmerdale* set?

6 In which Liverpool-based soap was the body of a wife-beater buried under the patio?

7 Which chocolate-makers first sponsored *Coronation Street* in 1996?

8 Which doomed BBC soap was set in Spain?

9 *The Colbys* was a spin off from which US soap?

10 What was *Emmerdale* called when it was first screened in the UK in the afternoon?

11 *Knots Landing* was a spin off from which oil-based soap?

12 As opposed to oil, *Falcon Crest* was about which commodity California is famous for?

13 Which Ken is the only original member of the *Coronation Street* cast?

14 In which *Ward* was the *Emergency* in TV's first medical soap?

15 In 1993 *Emmerdale* suffered an air disaster similar to which real-life tragedy?

16 In which soap did Roy Hudd play Archie the undertaker?

17 Which soap launched the pop careers of Kylie Minogue and Jason Donovan?

18 Which soap ran the classic cliff hanger, "Who shot J.R.?"?

19 Which soap from Down Under was created to rival *Neighbours*?

20 In *Coronation Street* what does Mike Baldwin's factory make?

ANSWERS ON PAGE 302

543 GENERAL KNOWLEDGE

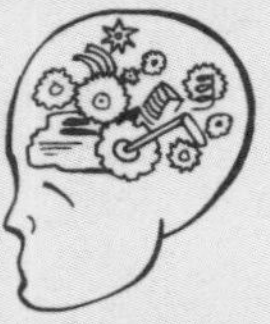
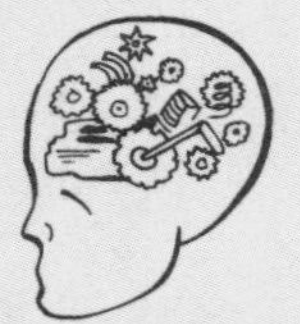
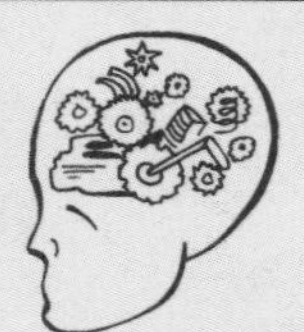

1 What was Bill Bojangles noted for doing?

2 In geometry, how many degrees are there in a complete circle?

3 Where did William III defeat a French and Irish army in 1690?

4 Which is the main language spoken in Hungary?

5 What was American inventor Thomas Edison's middle name?

6 What does hydrogen combine with to form water?

7 Who asked for the head of John the Baptist?

8 What is the northern-most point of the British mainland?

9 Which cartoon cat is the creation of Jim Davis?

10 What is the process by which plants use light to make food?

11 Which branch of medical science is concerned with muscle?

12 Which late actor's real name was Reginald Varey?

13 Prince George of Denmark was which English queen's husband?

14 What was the true vocation of the detective whose cases were written about by G. K. Chesterton?

15 Which alloy of tin and lead is used for making tankards and mugs?

16 Whom did Orpheus attempt to rescue from the Underworld?

17 Which group wanted, "To take it to the limit one more time."?

18 In music what does ENO stand for?

19 A plant produced by crossing different species is known as what?

20 Which cartoon sailor has a tattoo of an anchor on his arm?

ANSWERS ON PAGE 302

544 GILBERT & SULLIVAN

1 Frederick and Mabel are the romantic leads in which operetta?
2 Which operetta is set at the Tower of London?
3 In *The Mikado* who is the son of The Mikado?
4 John Wellington-Wells is a dealer of what?
5 Which work has the alternative title *The King of Barataria*?
6 Which character founds a university for ladies only?
7 What was Ko-ko's trade before becoming the Lord High Executioner?
8 In *Iolanthe*, Strephon is the unfortunate position of being half mortal, half what?
9 Who claimed he possessed, "information vegetable, animal and mineral"?
10 Who is the strolling jester in *The Yeomen Of The Guard*?
11 Which operetta poked fun at the aesthetic movement as personified by Oscar Wilde?
12 Which operetta opens with the line, "We sail the ocean blue . . ."?
13 Which flowers are the ladies singing to at the opening of *The Gondoliers*?
14 Who is Ralph Rackstraw's romantic interest?
15 Which operetta features Celia, Leila and Fleta?
16 Who makes up the three little maids along with Yum-Yum and Pitti-Sing?
17 Which character tackles the fiendishly tongue-twisting *Nightmare Song*?
18 In which Cornish village does the action take place in *Ruddigore*?
19 Captain Corcoran appears in *H.M.S. Pinafore* and which other operetta?
20 What is the final word that is sung in *The Mikado*?

ANSWERS ON PAGE 302

545 HALF CHANCE

½? ½? ½?

1 Kim Campbell was the first woman PM of which country – Canada or New Zealand?
2 Which paper did Superman work on – Daily Globe or Daily Planet?
3 In popular music, who was Bacharach's long-time writing partner – David or Greenway?
4 When was the Panama Canal opened – 1914 or 1924?
5 Did Dolly Parton or Madonna say, "It costs a lot to make me look so cheap"?
6 What did George Williams found in 1844 – Alcoholics Anonymous or YMCA?
7 Was daredevil stuntman Jean Francois Gravelet known as Blondin or Houdini?
8 Which film soundtrack topped the first UK album chart – *Oklahoma!* or *South Pacific*?
9 John Sell Cotman became famous for doing what – painting or singing?
10 Which Harris had a huge hit with *Macarthur Park* – Richard Harris or Rolf Harris?
11 What nationality was the first team to reach the South Pole – Norwegian or Polish?
12 Where could you watch Jazz Pori play a home soccer match – Finland or Italy?
13 Elizabeth Garrett Anderson was the first British woman what – doctor or firefighter?
14 According to Henry Kissinger what was "the ultimate aphrodisiac" – money or power?
15 What was singer songwriter Hoagy Carmichael's real first name – Charlie or Hoagland?
16 Joseph Merlin invented what kind of sporting footwear – roller skate or trainer?
17 In which country is the city of Sorocaba – Brazil or Venezuela?
18 Ed Koch is a former mayor of which city – Atlanta or New York?
19 Which country became the first to legalise abortion – Holland or Iceland?
20 Who wrote Blondie's comeback hit *Maria* – Jimmy Destri or John "Mutt" Lange?

ANSWERS ON PAGE 302

546 LUCKY DIP

1 Who was top scorer in the 2002 F.I.F.A World Cup?
2 What is the zodiac sign of the Balance?
3 Which animal is supposed to go mad in March?
4 The borders of Turkey make up most of the land around which sea?
5 What type of horse racing does not include fences and obstacles?
6 *Somewhere My Love* was the theme tune of which film?
7 Which season does the word vernal relate to?
8 Which device produces the mix of air and petrol in internal combustion engines?
9 What is a butterfly's proboscis?
10 According to proverb, what is a change as good as?
11 What does GMT stand for?
12 What was built in Hyde Park for the Great Exhibition of 1851?
13 What letter is used for numbers relating to food additives?
14 Hawthorn traditionally blooms in which month?
15 Which game is played with rackets and shuttlecocks?
16 What part of his anatomy did Van Gogh cut off?
17 Who played King Arthur in the film musical *Camelot*?
18 Napster is known for downloading what?
19 Which city of central England gave its name to a shade of green?
20 In which century was tea first brought to Europe?

ANSWERS ON PAGE 302

547 SPEED STARS

1 Which American cyclist became the first to win the Tour de France six successive times?
2 What was the name of Gordon Richards' first winning horse?
3 Which great athlete died at Tuscon, Arizona in 1980?
4 In which decade did Brooklands stage its first F1 GP?
5 Armin Hary and Harry Jerome set world records in what?
6 Who was driving for McLaren when they won their first F1 race?
7 Which UK lady won the first two London Marathons?
8 Who was the first person to officially run 100 metres in 9.90 seconds?
9 Which country does sprinter Donovan Bailey come from?
10 In 1995 on which horse did Walter Swinburn set a Derby record time?
11 Chloe Ronaldson was a speed star of the 1960, 70s and 80s, but at what?
12 Which lady won gold at Sydney in the 100m, 200m and 4 x 400m relay?
13 Frankie Dettori won the Ascot Gold Cup in 1992 and 1993 on which horse?
14 Who was the first Irishman to win the Tour de France?
15 Driving for which team did Jim Clark win his World Championships in 1963 and 1965?
16 Who won the Derby on the unseasonably named Santa Claus?
17 In which sport did the American Eric Heiden excel?
18 Who won the first F1 World Championship San Marino GP in 1981?
19 Who was the first British motor cycle rider to be World 125cc Champ?
20 What was the sport of Stirling Moss's sister Pat?

ANSWERS ON PAGE 302

548 PICTURE QUIZ

Starting with the first, put these these ladies in the order they lived in The White House?

ANSWERS ON PAGE 302

549 FABRICS

Is each statement TRUE or FALSE?

T F **1** Muslin was originally made in the town of Mosul in Iraq.

T F **2** Harris tweed was named after Robert Harris who first wove it.

T F **3** Worsted is named after a village where Flemish weavers settled.

T F **4** Damask is named after the Syrian city of Damascus.

T F **5** Angora comes from the long hair of a camel.

T F **6** Cashmere is so called because it is expensive to produce.

T F **7** Lawn is a fine linen named after Larne in Ireland.

T F **8** Shantung is a silk fabric originally from China.

T F **9** Silk is made by worms.

T F **10** Denim was first made in the USA by North American Indians.

ANSWERS ON PAGE 302

550 FOLK MUSIC

1 What happened to the dog on the ship the *Irish Rover*?
☐ Captured ☐ Drowned ☐ Escaped

2 What is a bodhran?
☐ Drum ☐ Flute ☐ Guitar

3 What was Woody Guthrie's middle name?
☐ Hoover ☐ Truman ☐ Wilson

4 Who penned the folk club favourite *Streets Of London*?
☐ Bob Dylan ☐ Phil Ochs
☐ Ralph McTell

5 Who was Fairport Convention's original female singer?
☐ Judy Collins ☐ Sandy Denny
☐ Judy Dyble

6 Uillean pipes are a type of what?
☐ Bagpipes ☐ Church organ
☐ Penny whistle

7 Who wrote *The Last Thing On My Mind*?
☐ Bob Dylan ☐ Tom Paxton
☐ Paul Simon

8 Which five-piece group recorded *Light Flight*?
☐ Fivepenny Piece ☐ Pentangle
☐ Strawbs

9 Which band did Dave Cousins lead?
☐ Highwaymen ☐ Steeleye Span
☐ Strawbs

10 Who featured with Bob Dylan on *Nashville Skyline*?
☐ Joan Baez ☐ Johnny Cash
☐ Paul Simon

11 Which Brothers backed Tommy Makem in the 1960s?
☐ Bellamy ☐ Blues ☐ Clancy

12 Which Christy was a major player with Planxty?
☐ O'Connor ☐ Moore ☐ Reed

13 Billy Connolly and Gerry Rafferty formed which group?
☐ Humblebums ☐ Yins ☐ Yaks

14 What produces the sound in an Irish bouzouki?
☐ Keys ☐ Strings ☐ Sticks

15 In song, what goes with parsley, sage and rosemary?
☐ Dill
☐ Mint
☐ Thyme

ANSWERS ON PAGE 302

Some of these questions may be gifts and some may need the knowledge of the Wise Men to answer them ... but they are all about that most magical time of year, Christmas!

1 Which event in the Christian church does Christmas Day commemorate?

2 What is the name of the Bank Holiday which follows Christmas Day in the UK?

3 Which parasite with white berries is used as a Christmas decoration?

4 In which country do children receive presents from the witch Befana on 6th January?

5 What is the first word of the chorus of the Christmas classic *White Christmas*?

6 Which object, which is part of the Christmas activities, was introduced by St Boniface?

7 Where do children repeatedly hit a clay pot until it breaks and showers them with sweets?

8 Which patron saint, and the subject of a carol, has his saint's day on 28th December?

9 Which period precedes Christmas in the Christian calendar?

10 On which date does Christmas end and Epiphany begin?

11 In which town do Christians believe Christ was born?

12 Where is there a legend of Baboushka, who was said to have accompanied the Wise Men?

13 Who played the title role in the movie *Bad Santa*?

14 In which movie was *White Christmas* first sung?

15 Which Christmas plant is of the genus Ilex?

16 In western Europe, what do children leave out so St Nicholas can fill it with presents?

17 If children haven't been good, what does St Nicholas leave for them?

18 What is the name of the miser in Dickens's *A Christmas Carol*?

19 Which province of South Africa was discovered by Vasco da Gama on Christmas Day 1497?

20 In the Christmas story, what was used as a crib for the baby Jesus?

21 What is Christmas called in France?

22 In the Netherlands what is added to pastry to make a special cake called Letterbanket?

23 Who sang about a *Blue Christmas* in 1964?

24 Which star of the silent screen died on Christmas Day 1977?

25 Which famous puppets made a movie based loosely on *A Christmas Carol*?

26 Which ex-wife of Frank Sinatra was born on Christmas Eve 1922?

27 What would you do with a wassail?

28 Who was married to Jesus's mother Mary?

29 What is a Christingle?

30 What did "my true love" send to me on the Fifth Day of Christmas?

31 Which husband and wife team discovered radium on 26th December 1898?

32 What is a Bûche de Noel, eaten in France as part of the Christmas meal?

33 What name is given to a form of comic family show presented around Christmas time?

34 Who visited the Christ child at the feast of Epiphany?

35 Which creatures pull Santa Claus's sleigh?

36 Which song begins, "Long time ago in Bethlehem, So the holy Bible say"?

37 What type of calendars are popular with children in the weeks leading up to Christmas?

38 Who, with his young friend, went to visit Father Christmas in the tale by Raymond Briggs?

39 Which word for a biscuit shares its name with a Christmas novelty which goes with a bang?

40 What name is given to a song about the story of the nativity?

41 On what date near Christmas is the Feast of St Stephen?

42 Which industrialist, whose biopic was called *The Aviator*, was born on Christmas Eve 1905?

43 The practice of decorating a Christmas tree originated in which European country?

44 The Christmas rose is from which family of plants?

45 Which Christmas plant, mentioned in a famous carol, is of the genus Hedera?

46 Which saint is also called Santa Claus?

47 When is the feast day of St Nicholas?

48 From which country does the story of the poinsettia come?

49 Which star of the classic movie *Casablanca* was born on Christmas Day 1899?

50 What is the emblem of St Nicholas?

ANSWERS ON PAGE 302

552 NATURE

1. The world's largest spider is named after which Biblical character?
2. Which animal can be field or harvest?
3. Where would an insect have its antenna?
4. What name is given to small hardy plants ideal for rockeries, such as saxifraga?
5. The name tulip is derived from a Turkish word meaning what type of headgear?
6. What type of soil is vital for growing rhododendrons?
7. What is the most common colour of primula vulgaris or common primrose?
8. What colour are natural sponges?
9. What sort of feet do antelopes have?
10. What do carnivorous plants eat?
11. Which flowers are said to symbolise the Crucifixion?
12. Which flower also called Chalk Plant or Baby's Breath is a favourite with flower arrangers?
13. Bachelor's Buttons are a variety of which yellow wild flower?
14. Which flower's seeds are pickled to make capers?
15. Which animals love Nepeta giving it its common name?
16. What sort of hyacinth is a Muscari?
17. Which flower – Lychnis – shares its name with a fictional detective?
18. Which two flowers would you find in an orchestra?
19. An urodele is another name for which reptile?
20. Found in Papua New Guinea, the Queen Alexandra's Birdwing is the largest known what?

ANSWERS ON PAGE 302

553 HISTORY

1. In which country did black activist Steve Biko die in 1977?
2. Which US President was brought down by the Watergate scandal?
3. Who said, "There cannot be a crisis next week, my schedule is already full"?
4. Who succeeded John Paul I as Pope?
5. Which tree population was decimated by a Dutch disease in the 20th century?
6. Detectors at a nuclear plant in which country led to awareness of the Chernobyl disaster?
7. Christa McAuliffe tragically perished in an accident in what type of vehicle in 1986?
8. The New English version of which Book was published in 1970?
9. Which country celebrated its bicentenary in 1988?
10. In which country did Pol Pot conduct a reign of terror?
11. Germany's Red Army Faction was popularly called what after its two founders?
12. Which James succeeded Harold Wilson as Prime Minister?
13. Tora tora tora was the signal to attack Pearl Harbor but what does tora mean?
14. Which country did the USSR invade in 1979?
15. Which Lord disappeared after his nanny was murdered?
16. In the UK, who beat four male candidates to become Tory leader in 1975?
17. Which war ended with the fall of Saigon in 1975?
18. Athletes from which country were murdered at the 1972 Olympics?
19. Which country was the first to make lead-free catalytic convertors compulsory?
20. Who succeeded Brezhnev as Soviet Premier?

ANSWERS ON PAGE 302

554 PICTURE QUIZ

What do these four famous people have in common?

ANSWERS ON PAGE 302

555 DOUBLE TAKE

In each case, the two-part quiz question leads to just one answer!

1 Which word describes something covered thinly with gold and can be a young sow?

2 Which word describes being situated at the back, and is the name of a female deer?

3 Which word describes a skin irritation and is also the name of homes of bees?

4 Which word can be a game bird and a word meaning to complain?

5 Which word describes a whip-like movement and is a hair on the edge of the eyelid?

6 Which word describes a monk's robe and can be a practice that is hard to give up?

7 Which word describes a flat-bottomed boat and a device for igniting?

8 Which word can mean a man, or a rope to secure a tent?

9 Which word means to grasp firmly and is the cavity below the deck of a ship?

10 Which word describes a Caribbean dance and an intermediate state or condition?

ANSWERS ON PAGE 302

556 ANIMAL GROUPS

1 Which birds gather in musters?
☐ Magpies ☐ Pheasants ☐ Peacocks

2 Nightingales congregate in what?
☐ A darkness ☐ A melody
☐ A watch

3 What is a group of ducks called?
☐ Gaggling ☐ Paddling ☐ Waddling

4 Lots of monkeys gather in a what?
☐ Battalion ☐ Platoon ☐ Troop

5 A host is a group of which garden visitors?
☐ Robins ☐ Sparrows ☐ Starlings

6 What is a group of moles called?
☐ Labour ☐ Lethargy ☐ Link

7 Which birds collect in a gaggle?
☐ Ducks ☐ Geese ☐ Grouse

8 What is a group of mules called?
☐ A barren ☐ A muffin ☐ A warren

9 In a shrewdness you find what?
☐ Aardvarks ☐ Alligators ☐ Apes

10 Which animals congregate in a sleuth?
☐ Bears ☐ Beavers ☐ Bobcats

11 Which pets collect in clowders?
☐ Cats ☐ Gerbils ☐ Goldfish

12 What would you find in an unkindness?
☐ Cuckoos
☐ Ravens
☐ Vultures

13 What is a group of foxes called?
☐ Poach ☐ Shadow ☐ Skulk?

14 Which creatures collect in prides?
☐ Anteaters ☐ Lions ☐ Peacocks

15 Which birds meet in exaltations?
☐ Eagles ☐ Housemartins ☐ Larks

ANSWERS ON PAGE 302

557 IRISH AMERICANS

1 Which actress Grace who became Princess had ancestors in Newport?

2 Which Kennedy became US President?

3 Which tennis player John Patrick was dubbed Superbrat?

4 John Ford (born Sean Aloysius O'Feeney) directed what type of movies?

5 Ed Sullivan had a famous chat show on TV or radio?

6 How was journalist Edward Murrow better known?

7 What was the first name of silent movie actor Keaton?

8 By which first name was singer/actor Harry Crosby better known?

9 Did F. Scott Fitzgerald write novels or TV scripts?

10 What was the first name of actor Peck?

11 Did Henry Ford manufacture cars or boats?

12 Playwright Eugene O'Neill was the father-in-law of which English comedy film star Charlie?

13 Was John F Kennedy's father called Joseph or Bobby?

14 William Randolph Hearst found fame in which industry, newspapers or shipping?

15 Was Joseph McCarthy in US politics in the 19th or 20th century?

16 Which US President married Nancy?

17 Did John F Kennedy Jr die in a plane or car crash?

18 Grace Kelly became Princess Grace of where?

19 Which comic Kops did Canadian-born Mack Sennet establish?

20 Which dancer Gene starred in the movie *Singin' In the Rain*?

ANSWERS ON PAGE 302

558 GENERAL KNOWLEDGE

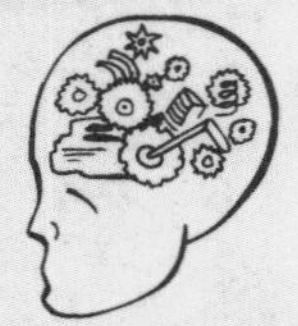
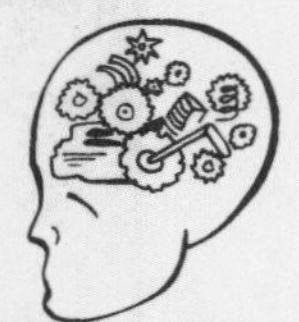

1 How many games did Arsenal lose in winning the Premiership in 2003–04?

2 Which composer had a Broadway hit with *Song And Dance*?

3 Who did Neil Kinnock succeed as leader of the Labour Party?

4 What relation was Mary I to Elizabeth I?

5 Which city features in television's long-running series *Taggart*?

6 Which ocean lies to the north of Russia?

7 In which mythology does Yggdrasil feature?

8 What did the S stand for in Harry S. Truman?

9 On which Shakespeare play did Verdi base his opera *Othello*?

10 What is *cortaderia selloana* better known as?

11 Of which ballet is Prince Siegfried hero?

12 What was William Gladstone's middle name?

13 Who led the British forces during the Siege of Mafeking?

14 Who wrote the novel *The Thorn Birds*?

15 In which decade did John Logie Baird invent television?

16 Which European country has the longest border with Russia?

17 What was landscape gardener "Capability" Brown's first name?

18 Which theory is concerned with the sums of the squares of right-angled triangles

19 From which part of France do German Shepherd dogs take their familiar name?

20 What is the boiling point of water on the Fahrenheit Scale?

ANSWERS ON PAGE 302

559 FRENCH WORDS

1 What is an idée fixe?
2 If you cherchez la femme who are you in pursuit of?
3 Is the pièce de résistance the climax or the lowest point of something?
4 If noblesse oblige what does privilege bring?
5 Which French expression describes a badly behaved or embarrassing child or person?
6 What does en passant mean?
7 What is the most appropriate word?
8 Would you like or dislike your bête noir?
9 Where would you suffer le mal de mer?
10 What sort of letter is a billet doux?
11 Which expression describes a friendship between France and the UK?
12 If food is cooked au gratin which ingredient is used?
13 Which expression alludes to something with a double meaning?
14 Which town is known as Douvres in France?
15 What would you do with a pamplemousse, eat it, wear it or sit on it?
16 Would you like to be involved in a mêlée?
17 If you are told to tenez la droite in France what must you do?
18 Which French expression means a pseudonym, or writer's assumed name?
19 What do the French call London?
20 If a sign says défense de stationner what must you not do?

ANSWERS ON PAGE 302

560 SCIENCE

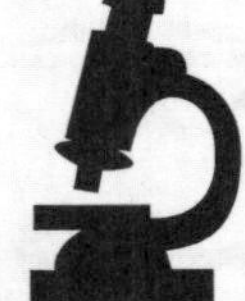
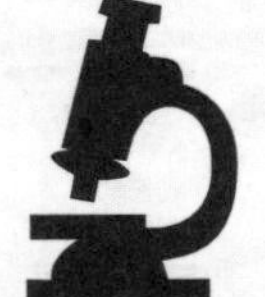

1 Which hormone makes the heart pound in times of stress?
2 In computing, what does P refer to in PCs?
3 What process did pasteurization entail in order to kill bacteria, as researched by Pasteur?
4 Seismologist Charles Richter studied what?
5 What makes acid rain acid?
6 In what type of atmosphere do algae live?
7 Carbohydrates are made up of carbon, hydrogen and what?
8 If a disease is congenital when does it date from?
9 What is the minimum number of species in a hybrid?
10 What does the V stand for in the fertility treatment IVF?
11 Who discovered radio waves?
12 Who gave his name to a unit of radioactivity?
13 Which 15th-century scientist proposed that the Earth orbited the Sun?
14 Who is best known for his theory of black holes?
15 On what did Otto Hahn, Lise Meitner and Fritz Strassman work?
16 In which branch of mathematics was Hipparchus a pioneer?
17 Which Baron of Largs gave his name to the degrees on the absolute scale?
18 What does Hans Geiger's Geiger Counter detect?
19 What did Frank Clarke invent in 1902?
20 Which tracking device did Sir Robert Watson-Watt develop?

ANSWERS ON PAGE 302

561 LUCKY DIP

1 Who recorded the album *Meteora*?

2 What is the currency of South Africa?

3 What is usually the first word of a fairy tale?

4 What was the first name of *King And I* actor Brynner?

5 What was the first name of Burgess, the spy who defected to Russia?

6 Which English king was beheaded?

7 In rhyming slang what is dog and bone?

8 What type of drift net fishing caused the deaths of hundreds of dolphins in the 1980s?

9 What was created in the Big Bang theory?

10 In the Bible, which book follows Matthew?

11 When do nocturnal creatures sleep?

12 In which country is the Matterhorn?

13 What kind of cat appears in *Alice In Wonderland*?

14 What colour is associated with an Oxford or Cambridge sports award?

15 Which rock forms the greater part of the White Cliffs of Dover?

16 Mount Toubkal is the highest peak of which mountain range?

17 Who played Doug Roberts in *The Towering Inferno*?

18 Who was Perry Mason's secretary?

19 Which major river flows through Gloucester?

20 What colour was the road Dorothy had to follow in Oz?

ANSWERS ON PAGE 302

562 WIMBLEDON

1 Who was the first unseeded man to win Wimbledon?

2 Who was first to win Women's Singles at Wimbledon, Serena or Venus Williams?

3 How many times did Martina Navratilova win the Wimbledon Singles?

4 What was Evonne Goolagong's married name on her second Wimbledon triumph?

5 What nickname did Ilie Nastase gain for his Wimbledon antics?

6 Who was the first black American to have won the Men's Singles at Wimbledon?

7 Why did Catherine McTavish make Wimbledon history on No1 court in 1979?

8 Which year did Ivan Lendl win Wimbledon?

9 Who partnered Jerremy Bates when the British pair won the 1987 Wimbledon Mixed Doubles?

10 Who sobbed on the Duchess of Kent's shoulder when she lost her Wimbledon final to Steffi Graf?

11 What did line judge Dorothy Cavis Brown do in a 1964 Wimbledon match?

12 Who did Virginia Wade beat in the final to win Wimbledon in 1977?

13 Which German won the Wimbledon Men's Singles in 1991?

14 Who was the last amateur to become the Men's Singles champion?

15 Who was the last Englishman before Tim Henman to reach the Men's quarter finals?

16 Who won seven Men's Singles titles in eight years, starting in 1993?

17 Which two ladies competed in the all-British Wimbledon final in 1961?

18 Which British player had a hat-trick of Men's Singles victories back in the 1930s?

19 What are the colours of the All England Lawn Tennis Club?

20 How many successive Men's Singles titles did Bjorn Borg win?

ANSWERS ON PAGE 302

563 NAME GAME

How are these celebrities better known?

1 ANNA ITALIANO

2 VINCENT FURNIER

3 CATHLEEN COLLINS

4 CATHERINE DORLEAC

5 CALVIN BROADUS

6 PAULINE MATTHEWS

7 STANLEY BURRELL

8 EMANUEL GOLDENBERG

9 DONALD WAYNE

10 MICHAEL DOUGLAS

ANSWERS ON PAGE 302

564 GUESS WHO . . . ?

1 Born in 1965, he directed for the RSC, won an Oscar for *American Beauty* and married Kate Winslet.

2 He used the stage name David Barron when working as an actor but is more famous for writing *The Caretaker*.

3 He had TV roles in *Maverick* and *The Saint* in the 1960s, starred as 007 and then became a UNICEF ambassador.

4 Liverpool-born, he made his professional debut at 19 and has since conducted orchestras from Berlin to Birmingham.

5 She was born Anita Perilli, is known as an environmental campaigner and the founder of the Body Shop chain.

6 Born in England in 1974, known for her slender frame,this model has appeared on the covers of *Elle* and *Vogue*.

7 She has starred opposite Tom Cruise, Hugh Grant and Ralph Fiennes on screen and has a younger sister called Serena.

8 Her surname is Nicholson, she played violin around the world from the age of 12 and has crossed the pop/classic divide.

9 She has been referred to as the new Mrs Beeton and is a major shareholder of Norwich City FC.

10 Her father narrated the original *Magic Roundabout* on TV, she has an actress sister called Sophie and is an Oscar winner.

ANSWERS ON PAGE 302

565 GREAT LAKES

1 What is the largest of the Great Lakes?
☐ Huron ☐ Michigan ☐ Superior

2 What is the world's biggest freshwater lake?
☐ Lagonda ☐ Baikal ☐ Neagh

3 What is Africa's largest lake?
☐ Victoria ☐ Tanganyika ☐ Chad

4 In which country is Lake Disappointment?
☐ Australia ☐ Canada ☐ New Zealand

5 What is the largest freshwater lake in the British Isles?
☐ Loch Ness ☐ Loch Lomond ☐ Lough Neagh

6 Which British Poet Laureate came from the Lake District?
☐ Betjemin ☐ Keats ☐ Wordsworth

7 What is the world's oldest lake?
☐ Baikal ☐ Eyre ☐ Geneva

8 What is the farthest north of the Great Lakes?
☐ Huron ☐ Ontario ☐ Superior

9 In which country is the Great Slave Lake?
☐ Canada ☐ Russia ☐ USA

10 Approximately how much of Sweden is covered by water?
☐ 4% ☐ 9% ☐ 14%

11 In which US state is Lake Crater?
☐ California ☐ Idaho ☐ Oregon

12 Lake Michigan is in how many US states?
☐ Two ☐ Three ☐ Four

13 Lake Titicaca straggles the borders of Peru and where?
☐ Argentina ☐ Bolivia ☐ Chile

14 In which country is Lake Matana?
☐ Indonesia ☐ Malawi ☐ Norway

15 Which country has the greatest area of inland water?
☐ Canada ☐ India ☐ China

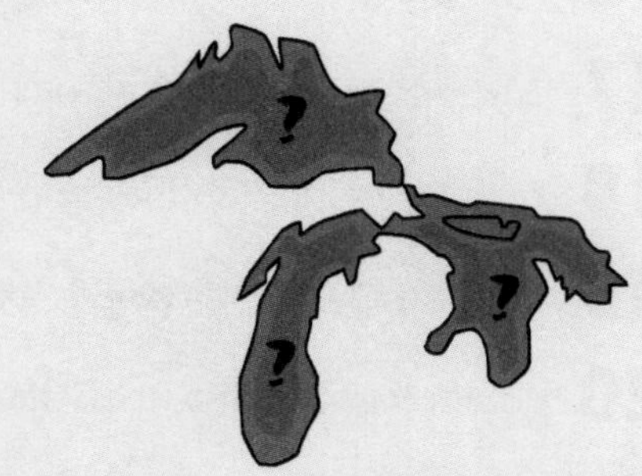

ANSWERS ON PAGE 302

566 THE ARTS

1 Who played the title role in *Barnum* and *Billy*?

2 Which actress was Maureen Lipman's show *Re Joyce* about ?

3 Which novel is *Heathcliff* based on?

4 Which character sings *I Don't Know How to Love Him*?

5 Which musical is *I Know Him So Well* from?

6 Which former Saint turned down a musical role in *Aspects Of Love*?

7 Who replaced Elaine Paige as Norma Desmond in the London production of *Sunset Boulevard*?

8 Which novelist once owned a Rolls registration number ANY 1?

9 Which musical hailed the dawning of the age of Aquarius?

10 Which musical is the song *One* from?

11 Who wrote *The House Of Stairs* under a pseudonym?

12 Which detective novelist wrote the screenplay for *Strangers On A Train*?

13 What was Charles Dickens' second novel, after *Pickwick Papers*?

14 Who wrote *The Exorcist* which was made into a successful film?

15 How were Patrick Dannay and Manfred B Lee better known?

16 Who produced *The Truth That Leads to Eternal Life*?

17 Who wrote the historical romance *Micah Clarke*?

18 In which musical do they sing about a Jellicle Ball?

19 Whose early novels were *Bella, Harriet* and *Prudence*?

20 How is the wife of author Eric Siepmann better known?

ANSWERS ON PAGE 302

567 PEOPLE

1 Who won an Oscar for portraying Katherine Hepburn in *The Aviator*?

2 Dr Condolezza Rice was Provost at which American university?

3 For how long were Napoleon and Josephine married?

4 How many weekly radio addresses did Ronald Reagan make to the American people?

5 Who said on 10th March 1876, "Come here, Watson, I want you."?

6 Who was the first person to hit a golf ball on the Moon?

7 In which hotel did John Lennon and Yoko Ono have their famous "bed in"?

8 Who was the first First Lady of the USA – before the actual phrase had been coined?

9 Which film director married Alma Reville?

10 Who was the first American to be buried in the Kremlin?

11 What was the actress born Anne Frances Robbins most famous married name?

12 Which member of the Monty Python team wrote *The Rutland Dirty Weekend Book*?

13 Which novelist investigated the Fatty Arbuckle assault case when working for the Pinkerton Detective Agency?

14 Who was the youngest Pope of the 20th century?

15 Which country did Audrey Hepburn visit as a UNICEF Ambassador shortly before her death?

16 To which film score musician did Martin Scorsese dedicate *Taxi Driver*?

17 What did Giorgio Armani study at university?

18 On what date did Marilyn Monroe famously sing "Happy Birthday" to John F Kennedy?

19 David Marks and Julia Barfield designed which London landmark ?

20 How is cosmetics queen Florence Nightingale Graham better known?

ANSWERS ON PAGE 303

568 SPIELBERG

1 Which studio did he make his first professional movies with?

2 What was Amblin's logo?

3 Who gave Spielberg his first professional contract?

4 With whom did he found Dreamworks?

5 Who was Mrs Spielberg after Amy Irving?

6 What was the name of the police chief in his first blockbuster *Jaws*?

7 Who was his wife when he made *Always*?

8 Under what star sign was he born?

9 Who does he say he is always thinking of when he is directing?

10 In which 1980 movie did he have a cameo role?

11 On whose eyes were E.T.'s eyes based?

12 Who wrote the book on which his first Oscar winner as director was based?

13 Which movie did he re-issue as *The Special Edition* because he was initially dissatisfied with it?

14 Which *Indiana Jones* movie did Mrs Spielberg star in?

15 With which movie did he win an amateur contest aged 13?

16 On whose novel was his 1987 movie based?

17 What was his first film after *Close Encounters Of The Third Kind*?

18 Which company did he form in 1984?

19 What was his 1970s debut as a feature film director?

20 Which animated features did he make prior to *Who Framed Roger Rabbit?*?

ANSWERS ON PAGE 303

569 FOOD AND DRINK

1 Which herb is used in gremolata?

2 When were pressure cookers invented – 1870, 1905 or 1930?

3 All citrus fruit are rich in which vitamin?

4 Cherry, orange, plum – which is not a type of tomato?

5 Mozzarella was originally made from which type of milk?

6 What is the most common colour of an aubergine?

7 Which pulses are used to make hummus?

8 Other than tomatoes and onions which is the main vegetable used in moussaka?

9 In which country is the famous wine-growing area of the Barossa valley?

10 What flavour do ratafia biscuits have?

11 Which size of wine bottle is the equivalent of 12 standard bottles?

12 Enchiladas were originally part of which country's cooking?

13 Which "nuts" are usually used in a pesto sauce?

14 Which food item comes from the Hindi meaning pounded meat?

15 Which food comes from the Tamil word meaning pepper water?

16 Dom Bernardo Vincelli devised which drink?

17 Which Japanese dish is made from rice, seaweed and raw fish?

18 Which Earl gave his name to a type of mild tea?

19 What would you be eating if you were served calamari?

20 Fitou is made from which grape?

ANSWERS ON PAGE 303

570 GENERAL KNOWLEDGE

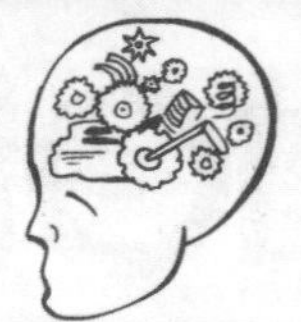
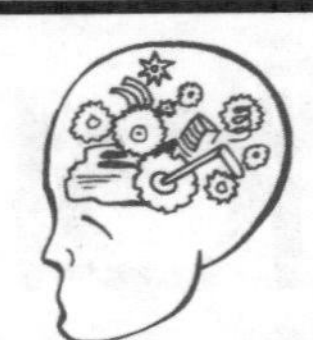

1 What was the first national park established in the USA in 1872?

2 What popular drink was known in China as early as 2737 BC?

3 What is the other name for the star Polaris?

4 On how many stone tablets were the Ten Commandments engraved?

5 Who wrote *The Three Sisters*?

6 What was the nickname of Edward Prince of Wales, son of Edward III?

7 Which insects communicate to each other by dancing?

8 Which disease was deliberately introduced to rabbits in the UK?

9 Where are the semicircular canals in the body?

10 What part of a cola tree is used to flavour drinks?

11 Which is the largest Greek island?

12 What was the original purpose of the Leaning Tower of Pisa?

13 Who married Josephine de Beauharnais and Princess Marie Louise?

14 Lack of iron in the diet may cause which disease?

15 Which George Orwell novel showed the dangers of excessive state control?

16 Riyadh is the capital of which country?

17 In which far eastern country was the Unification Church (Moonies) founded in 1954?

18 Which Minister of Health inaugurated the National Health Service?

19 Which strait links San Francisco Bay with the Pacific?

20 Which famous gardener helped landscape Blenheim and Stowe?

ANSWERS ON PAGE 303

571 BELGIANS

1 Who was the first Belgian to win a tennis Grand Slam tournament?

2 What did Adolphe Sax invent?

3 What was the name of Agatha Christie's Belgian detective?

4 Which multiple Tour de France-winning cyclist was known as "The Cannibal"?

5 Which actor was known as "the Muscles from Brussles"?

6 Which soccer player made a record international 96 appearances between the 1970s and 1990s?

7 By what name did Jeanne Deckers have a 1960s hit with *Dominique*?

8 Cartoonist Peyu devised which race of small blue creatures?

9 Who was the King of the Belgians at the start of the 21st century?

10 What was the family name of the brewers at the Den Horen Brewery who created Stella Pils?

11 Which 16th century Flemish painter painted *The Blind Leading The Blind*?

12 Who invented the stroboscope?

13 What was the screen name of actress Edda van Heemstra?

14 Which Belgian tennis player was ranked No 1 without having won a Grand Slam tournament?

15 Sandra Kim became the youngest winner of what?

16 Which footballer won the case that changed the whole transfer market?

17 Which name was jazz guitarist Jean Baptiste Reinhardt known by?

18 What did Charles van Depoele invent?

19 Who was the first King of the Belgians?

20 Georges Rimi adopted which name when he created *TinTin*?

ANSWERS ON PAGE 303

572 PICTURE QUIZ

Starting with the tallest, put these buildings in order of height?

ANSWERS ON PAGE 303

573 NAME THE YEAR

1. First space tourist visits the International Space Station. Tiger Woods won his second US Masters. New York's Twin Towers were attacked in September.
2. Tennis star Kim Clijsters was born. The first American woman travels in space. Mrs Jane Walton of Liverpool gave birth to sextuplets – all girls.
3. Television is invented by John Logie Baird. Hirohito became Emperor of Japan. Escapologist Harry Houdini died aged 52.
4. First video recorder invented. Actress Grace Kelly married Prince Rainier of Monaco. The Hungarian uprising began.
5. Cassius Clay (later Muhammad Ali) became a professional boxer. Clark Gable died. Theodore Maiman built the world's first laser.
6. Singer/songwriter Sting was born as Gordon Sumner. Miss Sweden won the first Miss World contest. Randolf Turpin won the World Middleweight Boxing title.

ANSWERS ON PAGE 303

574 LUCKY DIP

1. Which knockabout Kops were created by Mack Sennett?
2. In which TV programme did the staff of Grace Brothers originally appear?
3. Which war started with the capture of Fort Sumter?
4. What is the name of the Irish Parliament?
5. Which game has queens, bishops and knights as movable pieces?
6. What city is the capital of Kuwait?
7. Which Julie had a No 1 hit with *Don't Cry For Me Argentina*?
8. What name is given to the most used table of the elements?
9. What number does the Roman numeral XI stand for?
10. In the children's party game, what is passed around and unwrapped?
11. Which rock group's name is the Latin for existing state of things?
12. Who was the Egyptian god of the underworld?
13. What word taken from the French describes an afternoon show?
14. What are the initials of Irish poet Yeats?
15. Which moorland shrub is said to bring good luck?
16. Which organ of the body secretes insulin?
17. Which club side did Michael Owen play for when he was first capped for England?
18. The Pompidou Centre was built in which European city?
19. What are Hank Marvin, Brian Bennett and Bruce Welch better known as?
20. On what part of your body would you wear a homburg?

ANSWERS ON PAGE 303

575 HALF CHANCE

½? ½? ½?

1 Which Shakespeare play is in three parts – *Henry VI* or *Richard III*?
2 In song, who regrets she is unable to lunch today – Miss Havisham or Miss Otis?
3 Which breed of dog comes from Kerry in south-west Ireland – Kerry blue or Kerry terrier?
4 Is Europe the second-largest or the second-smallest continent?
5 Which security item did Joseph Glidden's patent in 1873 – barbed wire or distress flare?
6 Robben Island is a prison in which Bay – Biscay or Table?
7 Which castle is at the west end of the Royal Mile – Edinburgh or Glamis?
8 Which bird is also the name of a play by Chekhov – Falcon or Seagull?
9 Which Tony featured on Dawn's *Tie A Yellow Ribbon* – Braxton or Orlando?
10 Which country originally produced Volvo cars – Belgium or Sweden?
11 Syracuse is part of New York, but where does it exist in Europe – Malta or Sicily?
12 In which US state was John Travolta born – New Jersey or Vermont?
13 Spaghetti Junction is on which UK motorway – M1 or M6?
14 Roger Moore played 007 in how many films – five or seven?
15 How many steps are there to the top of the Eiffel Tower – 1789 or 1812?
16 Which country marks the most westerly point of mainland Europe – France or Portugal?
17 In which US state was the first drilling for oil – Pennsylvania or Texas?
18 Which Mike broke Bob Beaman's long jump record in 1991 – Peters or Powell?
19 In which country was escapologist Houdini born – Hungary or Poland?
20 Did Johann Christophe Denner invent the clarinet or the flute?

ANSWERS ON PAGE 304

576 FAMOUS FIRSTS

1st? 1st? 1st?

1 Which type of transport was designed by Christopher Cockerell in the 1950s?
3 C-Curity was the name of the first type of what?
3 Who was the first man to set foot on the moon?
4 Ruud Gullit became the Premiership's first black manager at which club?
5 Golda Meir was the first female Prime Minister of which country?
6 In which country did the Grunge movement first begin?
7 Helen Sharman was the first British woman to go where?
8 The Bates Motel first appeared in which film?
9 Christiaan Barnard carried out which medical first?
10 Who was the first Spanish golfer to win the British Open?
11 In which decade did the first wheel clamps arrive in Britain?
12 Which Charles first flew non-stop across the Atlantic?
13 Which famous first is claimed by Hillary and Tenzing?
14 In 1975, which Arthur became the first black champion in the Men's Singles at Wimbledon?
15 Who starred in the first talkie movie?
16 The first successful cloning of an adult took place with what type of animal?
17 Which major sporting contest first took place in 1930?
18 Which Alexander discovered the first antibiotic?
19 Who was the leader of the first successful expedition to the South Pole?
20 Who was the only British monarch to abdicate in the 20th century?

ANSWERS ON PAGE 303

577 GENERAL KNOWLEDGE

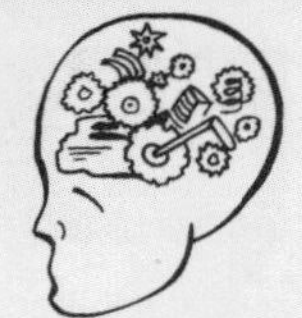 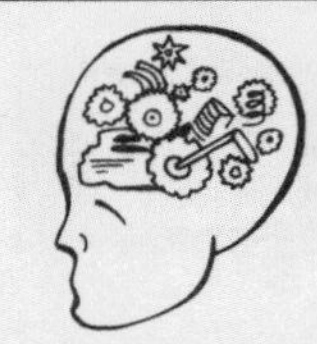 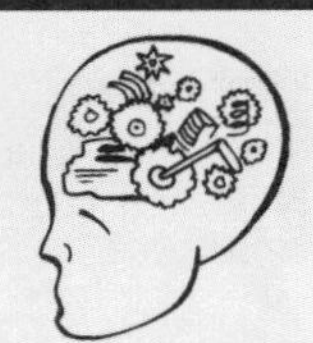

1 Which instrument did Franz Liszt play?

2 By what name is Betty Jean Perske better known?

3 In which republic of the former USSR is Chernobyl?

4 In which year were East and West Germany unified?

5 Where was the treaty signed that established the EEC?

6 Who won the first Rugby Union World Cup, held in 1987?

7 On which circuit is motor racing's Grand Prix d'Endurance run?

8 Which two South American countries produce the most coffee?

9 What is the capital of Ecuador?

10 Helium belongs to which group of elements?

11 Where in the cell is DNA stored?

12 Who was the author of *Spycatcher* in 1987?

13 Which French fashion designer created the "little black dress"?

14 Which Australian city is named after William IV's Queen?

15 Which Greenpeace ship was sunk in Auckland Harbour in 1985?

16 How many carats is pure gold?

17 What is Del Boy's local?

18 Who was the first director of Britain's National Theatre Company?

19 Which English ballet dancer was born Margaret Hookham in 1919?

20 Who painted *The Nightwatch*?

ANSWERS ON PAGE 303

578 MUSICALS

1 Who wrote the novel on which Lloyd Webber's *The Woman In White* was based?

2 Who wrote the words for *My Fair Lady* and *Camelot*?

3 Which city saw the premiere of *Les Misérables*?

4 In which country was *A Little Night Music* set?

5 What type of shop was the *Little Shop Of Horrors*?

6 Which show does *I Don't Know How To Love Him* come from?

7 Who wrote the music for *The Lion King*?

8 Which American city saw the premiere of *Sunset Boulevard*?

9 Which Lloyd Webber musical was billed as Now And Forever?

10 On whose fable was *Guys And Dolls* based on?

11 Which musical featured the songs *A Secretary is Not A Toy*, and *The Company Way*?

12 In *La Cage Aux Folles*, what was La Cage Aux Folles?

13 Who was the musical *Mack And Mabel* about?

14 *I'm Gonna Wash That Man Right Out Of My Hair* came from which show?

15 Which musical was a reworking of Puccini's *Madame Butterfly*?

16 In which country was Frederick Loewe born?

17 Which musical featured the song *I Remember It Well*?

18 Which show was based on Miguel de Cervantes' *Don Quixote*?

19 Which show, starring Robert Preston and Barbara Cook on Broadway, was about River City, Iowa?

20 Which ground-breaking American musical was based on the book *Green Grow The Lilacs*?

ANSWERS ON PAGE 303

579 TRAVEL

1 Which famous London House has an Egyptian Hall for banqueting?

2 In which County is Bantry Bay in the south of Ireland?

3 What is Italy's Capodimonte famous for?

4 In which city is the Pompidou Centre?

5 From which resort at the foot of Mont Blanc does the highest cable car in the world rise?

6 Who said, "Concorde is great. It gives you three extra hours to find your luggage"?

7 Whose tomb was opened to the public in Egypt for the first time in 1996?

8 Which Scandinavian country is called Suomi in its own language?

9 In which city did the first car hire company start, in 1918?

10 In which American city would you go to see the Frick Collection?

11 What was St Petersburg called for much of the 20th century?

12 What is the chief city of Catalonia, and Spain's second largest?

13 In which American state is the Rockefeller Folk Art Collection?

14 Where is the park called the Bois de Boulogne?

15 What was the name by which Lesotho used to be known?

16 In which city is the Prado art gallery?

17 Which is the farthest north – Estonia, Latvia or Lithuania?

18 During which marathon do runners cross the Verrazano Bridge?

19 Which Palace was once the site of a famous coronation stone?

20 In what year did the first McDonald's open in Moscow – 1980, 1990 or 2000?

ANSWERS ON PAGE 303

580 TELEVISION

1 In *Desperate Housewives* what is the name of Carlos and Gabrielle Solis' teenage gardener?

2 In which country was *The Sullivans* set?

3 Who was Butt-Head's comedy partner?

4 Which actress played Charlotte York in *Sex And The City*?

5 Who launched the first Pay TV system?

6 Jub-Jub the Iguana belongs to which character in *The Simpsons*?

7 Which *Coronation Street* character had the names Fairclough and Sullivan?

8 Alvin Hall's programmes told people how to handle what – money or love?

9 *Dangerfield* dealt with what type of police personnel?

10 Who did the creator of Ally McBeal model his main character on?

11 Which Robert played Ben in *My Family*?

12 What was the name of the bar manager played by Kirstie Alley in *Cheers*?

13 Michael Gambon played which French detective in the 1990s?

14 Which David presented *Bargain Hunt*?

15 Which 1980s hit was set on the island of Jersey?

16 Which soap sparked the campaign to "Free the Weatherfield 1"?

17 Who was Bobby married to in *Dallas*?

18 What was the first, unsuccessful, spin off of *Baywatch*?

19 *Never Mind The Buzzcocks* asks questions about which subject?

20 Which female duo first found fame on *The Comic Strip Presents*?

ANSWERS ON PAGE 303

581 WORLD SOCCER

Can you give the country that each of these international soccer stars has represented?

1 ROBERTO CARLOS
2 MATT HOLLAND
3 TEBOHO MOKOENA
4 BRAD FRIEDEL
5 LILIAN THURAM
6 GERMAN BURGOS
7 MICHAEL BALLACK
8 MARK VIDUKA
9 EBBE SAND
10 JULIUS AGHAHOWA

ANSWERS ON PAGE 303

582 CARS

Is each statement TRUE or FALSE?

T F 1 The first road vehicle powered by an engine was built in 1770.
T F 2 The inventor of the internal combustion engine was Belgian.
T F 3 Mercedes was the name of a car manufacturer.
T F 4 Henry Ford was a car manufacturer from Detroit.
T F 5 The first mass-produced car was the Model H.
T F 6 The VW Beetle was originally called the KdF Wagen.
T F 7 The name Volkswagen means "versatile car".
T F 8 The first cars produced on a production line were all blue.
T F 9 The VW Beetle was developed by Ferdinand Porsche.
T F 10 By 1920 half the cars in the world were Model T Fords.

ANSWERS ON PAGE 303

583 OSCAR ACTRESSES

1 Who played Viola in *Shakespeare in Love*?
☐ Angelina Jolie ☐ Gwyneth Paltrow
☐ Judi Dench

2 For what did Hilary Swank win her first Oscar?
☐ *Boys Don't Cry* ☐ *Buffy*
☐ *The Next Karate Kid*

3 For what did 11-year-old Anna Paquin win a 1993 Oscar?
☐ *Jane Eyre* ☐ *Philadelphia*
☐ *The Piano*

4 Who won for *Erin Brokovich*?
☐ Annette Bening ☐ Helen Hunt
☐ Julia Roberts

5 Which winner was Miss USA 1987?
☐ Gwyneth Paltrow ☐ Halle Berry
☐ Kate Hudson

6 Cher won for what in a most outrageous dress?
☐ *Mermaids* ☐ *Moonstruck* ☐ *Silkwood*

7 Who said "I deserve this" on winning in 1983?
☐ Ellen Burstyn ☐ Jane Fonda
☐ Shirley MacLaine

8 Who won the year after Glenda Jackson's first win?
☐ Ellen Burstyn ☐ Jane Fonda ☐ Sally Field

9 Which English actress won as a child in 1960?
☐ Hayley Mills ☐ Jane Asher
☐ Patsy Kensit

10 Who is the daughter of Blythe Danner?
☐ Gwyneth Paltrow ☐ Minnie Driver
☐ Uma Thurman

11 Who said "You like me you really like me" in her Oscar speech?
☐ Cher ☐ Halle Berry ☐ Sally Field

12 Goldie Hawn's first nomination was for which of her films?
☐ First ☐ Second ☐ Third

13 Who was nominated for *Shirley Valentine*?
☐ Anne Bancroft ☐ Kathleen Turner
☐ Pauline Collins

14 What did Nicole Kidman win for?
☐ *Eyes Wide Shut* ☐ *Moulin Rouge*
☐ *The Hours*

15 Catherine Zeta Jones won the Supporting Oscar for which film?
☐ *Chicago*
☐ *Entrapment* ☐ *Zorro*

ANSWERS ON PAGE 303

584 OSCAR TRIVIA

1 Which movie earned Steven Spielberg Best Director Oscar following *Schindler's List*?

2 Who composed the Oscar-winning song for *Three Coins In The Fountain*?

3 Where did Hannibal Lecter escape to after his Oscar-winning outing?

4 Which actor co-produced the first movie since *It Happened One Night* to win five Oscars?

5 Who hosted the Oscar ceremony when Russell Crowe received his first award?

6 Which 1970s film had 11 nominations but won nothing?

7 Who was the first Best Actress to be British born and of British parents?

8 Which future Mrs Janusz Kaminski won an Oscar the same night he did in 1993?

9 *Only Angels Have Wings* was the first film to be nominated for what?

10 Which movie had seven nominations but lost out to *Forrest Gump*?

11 In *Midnight Cowboy* Dustin Hoffman was nominated for playing which character?

12 Who was nominated for Pasha in the 60s movie with Julie Christie and Omar Sharif?

13 Who was the first actress to win in consecutive years?

14 Which movie broke all records by winning in all categories for which it was nominated in 1988?

15 How many Oscars did Tim Rice win in the 1990s?

16 Who was the first British actor to win Best Actor?

17 At which British university did Anthony Minghella teach before winning an Oscar?

18 Who was the first President of the Academy which presents the Oscars?

19 Which Coppola won an Oscar for *The Godfather Part II*?

20 Who was Oscar-nominated for music for *American Beauty*?

ANSWERS ON PAGE 303

585 LUCKY DIP

1 Which sex chromosomes are possessed by a human male?

2 Who came first as British Prime Minister, Churchill or Disraeli?

3 What does a barometer measure?

4 Which country is a car from with the international registration letter J?

5 What is the third letter of the Greek alphabet?

6 What flavour is Grand Marnier?

7 Whose national airline is called Garuda?

8 How many counters are on a backgammon board at start of play?

9 What was the last book written by Aldous Huxley?

10 In the 1950s whose quintet did John Coltrane play with?

11 In darts, what is the lowest score from three different trebles?

12 Who were the beaten finalists in the 2002 F.I.F.A World Cup?

13 What word can go after soap and before house?

14 What name is given to the vast grassy plains of Eastern Europe?

15 Which Oscar said, "I have nothing to declare except my genius!"?

16 In the nursery rhyme who was married on a Wednesday?

17 Which Bond movie features the partially dressed Ursula Andress?

18 Which British rock band had Syd Barrett among its founders?

19 Which number code system is based on the digits 1 and 0?

20 Ermine is the fur from which animal?

ANSWERS ON PAGE 303

586 PICTURE QUIZ

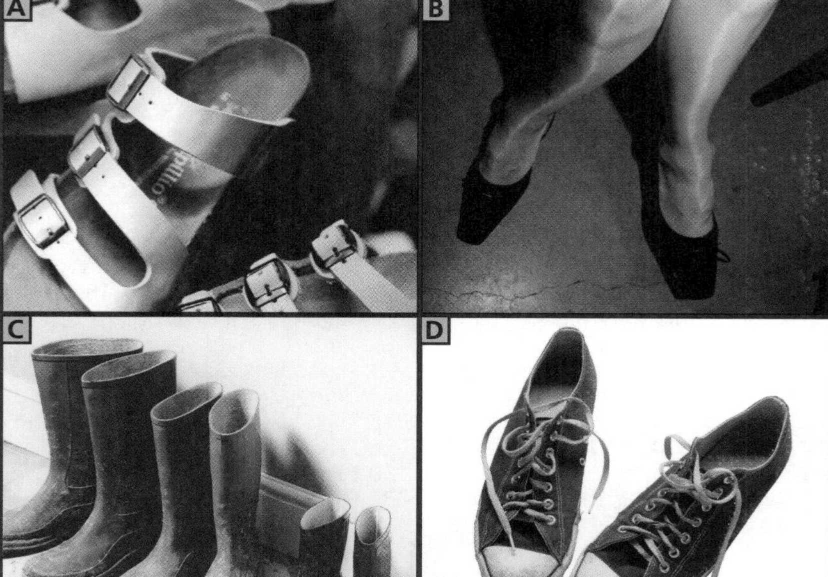

Starting with the first, in which order were these items of foot and legwear developed?

ANSWERS ON PAGE 303

587 DOUBLE TAKE

In each case, the two-part quiz question leads to just one answer!

1 Which word describes a picnic basket and can mean to hinder or obstruct?

2 Which word names the fruit of the tree citrus medica, and is another name for calcium oxide?

3 Which word describes a piece of hair a section of a canal or river with sluice gates?

4 Which word describes a measurement for horses and a selection of playing cards?

5 Which word describes a long, straight mark, and means to cover the inside of a garment?

6 Which word means principal, and is a channel for gas or sewage?

7 Which word names a bird of prey and means to carry items around to offer for sale?

8 Which word means even more angry, and is also a red dye obtained from a plant?

9 Which word describes a quantity of bread or can mean to laze around?

10 Which word describes a boundary of shrubs and can mean avoiding a decision?

ANSWERS ON PAGE 303

588 PORTS

1 On which coast of Cuba is Havana?
☐ NE ☐ NW ☐ SE

2 Which French port's name means the haven?
☐ Le Havre ☐ La Rochelle
☐ Le Touquet

3 Which is Canada's largest Pacific port and railhead?
☐ Halifax ☐ Montreal ☐ Vancouver

4 On which river is Liverpool?
☐ Irwell ☐ Mersey ☐ Tees

5 Which port is in Guanabara Bay?
☐ Buenos Aires ☐ Rio de Janeiro
☐ Santos

6 Which German port was the birthplace of Brahms?
☐ Bremen ☐ Hamburg ☐ Kiel

7 On which estuary is Shanghai?
☐ Huang He ☐ Xi Jiang ☐ Yangtze

8 Pearl Harbor is part of which island group?
☐ Fiji ☐ Hawaii ☐ Philippines

9 Which port is the capital of Corsica?
☐ Ajaccio ☐ Bastia ☐ Bonifacio

10 Which Moroccan port shares its name with a famous film?
☐ Alexandria ☐ Casablanca
☐ Tangier

11 Which Japanese port suffered a major earthquake in 1995?
☐ Kobe ☐ Kochi ☐ Osaka

12 On which ocean is the port of Valparaiso?
☐ Atlantic ☐ Indian ☐ Pacific

13 Which US port gave its name to a dance?
☐ Baltimore ☐ Charleston
☐ Galveston

14 Which port boasts the Topkapi Palace?
☐ Istanbul ☐ Izmir ☐ Smyrna

15 Which port is Australia's oldest and largest city?
☐ Adelaide ☐ Melbourne ☐ Sydney

ANSWERS ON PAGE 303

QUIZ 1. AT THE MOVIES
1 India. 2 Thompson. 3 3 hours. 4 Ridley Scott. 5 *The Boxer*. 6 Marlon Brando. 7 1930s. 8 Cage. 9 Boxing. 10 Julia Roberts. 11 *The Godfather.* 12 Oldman. 13 Quentin. 14 Brad Pitt. 15 Mike Newell. 16 Tony Curtis. 17 Mitty. 18 *Jaws*. 19 Winona. 20 Stone.

QUIZ 2. POP MUSIC
1 Eminem. 2 Queen. 3 Alicia Keyes. 4 *Spice*. 5 Shania Twain. 6 George Michael. 7 Dublin. 8 Paul McCartney. 9 The Police. 10 Pill.11 Abba. 12 The Sheriff. 13 Motown Spinners. 14 *Billie Jean*. 15 Stevie Wonder. 16 Every. 17 Aretha Franklin.18 His father. 19 *Candle In the Wind*. 20 Art Garfunkel.

QUIZ 3. FAMOUS FIRSTS
1 Margaret Thatcher (UK). 2 1950s. 3 Naomi James. 4 The typewriter. 5 Sweden. 6 Parking meter. 7 A streaker. 8 Marie Curie. 9 Australia/ UK. 10 USA.11 *Never Say Die*. 12 Barclays. 13 Erling Kagge. 14 Alcoholics Anonymous.15 *Genie In A Bottle*. 16 Thames Estuary. 17 Reinforced concrete. 18 Ralph Bunche. 19 Fuchs. 20 Chicago.

QUIZ 4. GENERAL KNOWLEDGE
1 72. 2 Hurricane. 3 4th July. 4 Jefferson. 5 Texas. 6 Dolly Parton. 7 Desk. 8 Atlanta. 9 Eric Clapton. 10 *Snow White And The Seven Dwarfs*. 11 1920s. 12 *Evita*. 13 Phoenix. 14 Elvis Presley. 15 1930s. 16 Cancer Research. 17 Blue. 18 Jack Nicklaus. 19 George Bush (Snr). 20 Garth Brooks.

QUIZ 5. PICTURE QUIZ
All link to *Penny Lane*. A) Barber. B) Queen. C) A pretty nurse. D) Fireman.

QUIZ 6. WHO SAID . . . ?
1 Tony Blair. 2 Charles Darwin. 3 Kingsley Amis. 4 Noel Coward. 5 Beethoven. 6 Dylan Thomas. 7 Mark Twain. 8 Neil Armstrong.

QUIZ 7. CLEVER ANIMALS
1 Orang-utan. 2 Monkeys. 3 Chimpanzee. 4 Laughter. 5 Dolphin. 6 Seal. 7 Owl. 8 Silver. 9 Cat. 10 Paddington. 11 Orwell. 12 Turtles. 13 Paddington. 14 Macavity. 15 Human.

QUIZ 8. GEOGRAPHY
1 Nile. 2 Pope. 3 West. 4 Canada. 5 Bombay. 6 Abominable. 7 Australia. 8 Southern. 9 India. 10 Peru. 11 Caribbean. 12 Zimbabwe. 13 Suez. 14 Coast. 15 Pacific. 16 Lake. 17 Abraham Lincoln. 18 Arizona. 19 Australia. 20 Sahara.

QUIZ 9. BRITISH ROYALS
1 February. 2 Edward. 3 Henry. 4 Prince Charles. 5 Princess Margaret. 6 Highgrove. 7 Camilla Parker Bowles. 8 Philip. 9 Gordonstoun. 10 Anne. 11 Two. 12 St Paul's. 13 Princess Anne. 14 Nazi. 15 Red. 16 Althorp. 17 Falklands. 18 Duchess of York. 19 Cambridge. 20 Eton.

QUIZ 10. PICTURE QUIZ
Phonetic alphabet. A) Golf. B) Hotel. C) Oscar. D) Tango.

QUIZ 11. NAME THE YEAR
1 2004. 2 1990. 3 1997. 4 1950. 5 1918. 6 1945.

QUIZ 12. SPORT
1 Washington. 2 Belmont. 3 American Football League. 4 Darts. 5 Paris. 6 Real Madrid. 7 Speed skating. 8 Japan. 9 Czechoslovakia & USA. 10 Pole vault. 11 Al Joyner. 12 Chelsea. 13 10. 14 Long jump. 15 Golf. 16 California. 17 Middleweight. 18 Cycling. 19 Central Park. 20 Women golfers.

QUIZ 13. ANIMALS
1 In a pouch. 2 Panda. 3 Australia. 4 Six. 5 Spider. 6 Camel. 7 King Charles. 8 Jellyfish. 9 Cobra. 10 Meat. 11 Monkey. 12 Brush. 13 St Bernard. 14 It doesn't have one. 15 Trotters. 16 Indian. 17 Caviar. 18 Hibernation. 19 400. 20 Chick.

QUIZ 14. HISTORY
1 Buster Keaton. 2 Nelson Mandela. 3 Mao Tse Tung. 4 Groucho. 5 Mary. 6 Miller. 7 Mussolini. 8 Italian. 9 Tony Blair. 10 John F Kennedy. 11 The French. 12 Israel. 13 John F Kennedy. 14 Myanmar. 15 Noriega. 16 Little St Bernard. 17 Mary McAleese. 18 My Lai. 19 Madeleine Albright. 10 Hong Kong.

QUIZ 15. NAME GAME
1 Mel Brooks. 2 Tony Bennett. 3 Lauren Bacall. 4 Bono. 5 Natalie Wood. 6 Marilyn Manson. 7 Sam Shepard. 8 Elvis Costello. 9 Julianne Moore. 10 Eminem.

QUIZ 16. GUESS WHO?
1 Carl Lewis. 2 Kingsley Amis. 3 Jamie Lee Curtis. 4 Zola Budd. 5 Luciano Pavarotti. 6 Ronald Reagan. 7 Chuck Berry. 8 Sergey Bubka. 9 Kate Winslet. 10 Ray Charles.

QUIZ 17. PIRATES
1 Crossbones. 2 Roger. 3 Spanish Main. 4 Blackbeard. 5 15. 6 Cutlass. 7 Pew. 8 Women.9 Flintlock. 10 Captain Hook. 11 1718. 12 Penzance. 13 Vitamin C. 14 Gentleman. 15 Marooned.

QUIZ 18. MADONNA
1 Ciccone. 2 Britney Spears (*Me Against The Music*). 3 Susan. 4 Virgin. 5 The Groove. 6 Papa. 7 Sean Penn. 8 Blonde. 9 *Dick Tracy*. 10 Immaculate. 11 *Sex*. 12 Material. 13 Pyjamas. 14 *American Pie*. 15 Blue. 16 *Vogue*. 17 Stalking. 18 Daughter. 19 *The Look Of Love*. 20 Pepsi Cola.

QUIZ 19. LUCKY DIP
1 Avril Lavigne. 2 A stamp. 3 Drat. 4 Butterfly. 5 Bill Clinton. 6 Feet. 7 Windsor Castle. 8 Saint David. 9 Doe. 10 Pumpkin. 11 Jersey. 12 Hands. 13 Italy. 14 India. 15 America. 16 Ten. 17 Maple Leaf. 18 Cecil Beaton. 19 Flock together. 20 The gold standard.

QUIZ 20. FANTASY ON FILM
1 *The Fellowship Of The Ring*. 2 New Zealand. 3 *Beauty And The Beast*. 4 Hermione. 5 Zemeckis. 6 Myers. 7 Ian McKellen. 8 *The Nutcracker Suite*. 9 Chris Columbus. 10 Elijah Wood. 11 *Harry Potter & The Sorcerer's Stone* 12 1940s. 13 JRR Tolkien. 14 Grimm. 15 Cameron Diaz. 16 California. 17 Hagrid. 18 Rupert Grint. 19 Mickey Mouse. 20 Dumbledore.

QUIZ 21. HALF CHANCE
1 Superman. 2 Peach. 3 Eiffel Tower. 4 Wales. 5 Hexagon. 6 Electronic. 7 Winnie the Pooh. 8 Beans. 9 Turkey. 10 Texas. 11 Gemini. 12 Wright Brothers. 13 1970s. 14 Ships. 15 Blow into it. 16 Area. 17 1000. 18 Cat. 19 48. 20 Train.

QUIZ 22. EUROPEAN TOUR
1 Maine et Loire. 2 Wind. 3 Belgium. 4 Bosnia Herzegovina. 5 Norway. 6 Ancona. 7 Nine. 8 Poland. 9 Tolar. 10 Belarus. 11 Badajoz. 12 Casablanca. 13 Orne. 14 Hungary. 15 Basle. 16 Tarifa Point. 17 Belarus. 18 Baltic. 19 Caen. 20 Valira.

QUIZ 23. SCIENCE
1 Bonnie. 2 Sewing. 3 Kitchen. 4 Tupperware. 5 Choc ice. 6 Sandwich. 7 Waterproof. 8 Traveller's cheque. 9 Box camera. 10 Helicopters. 11 DNA. 12 Ampere. 13 Descartes. 14 Davy. 15 HIV. 16 Chadwick. 17 Hydrogen bomb. 18 Cathode ray tube. 19 Boyle. 20 Faraday.

QUIZ 24. PICTURE QUIZ
All are computer items. A) A key. B) A ram. C) A mouse. D) Chips.

QUIZ 25. NAME THE YEAR
1 1938. 2 1957. 3 1961. 4 1974. 5 1968. 6 1991.

QUIZ 26. THE ARTS
1 Alice. 2 Three. 3 Crusoe. 4 The Willows. 5 Scrooge. 6 Venice. 7 Daffodils. 8 Poetry. 9 Belgian. 10 Monk. 11 South. 12 High. 13 Calcutta. 14 Earnest. 15 Dolls. 16 Rita. 17 *Miss Saigon*. 18 *Les Misérables*. 19 Hello. 20 Love.

QUIZ 27. NEW YEAR'S DAY
1 Capricorn. 2 Janus. 3 Chicken (or Rooster). 4 15. 5 Ben Kingsley. 6 March/April. 7 Albania. 8 Aswan Dam. 9 Turquoise. 10 13th. 11 12. 12 Scotland. 13 Baisakhi Mela. 14 Chicken (or Rooster). 15 World War I. 16 Fidel Castro. 17 The Pentagon. 18 Snowdrop. 19 Louis Braille. 20 Ronald Reagan. 21 Sugababes. 22 Samuel Pepys. 23 China. 24 Rat. 25 The Terrible. 26 *The Times*. 27 *Auld Lang Syne*. 28 Jack Nicklaus. 29 March. 30 J Edgar Hoover. 31 George Bush. 32 Farthings. 33 U2. 34 Concorde. 35 Donna Summer. 36 31. 37 JRR Tolkien. 38 South Africa. 39 Capricorn. 40 Pierre de Coubertin. 41 Rosh Hashanah. 42 Harlem Globetrotters. 43 Garnet. 44 20th Century Fox. 45 Japan. 46 Serpent. 47 Ellis Island. 48 Anthony Hopkins. 49 Alaska. 50 Narcissus.

QUIZ 28. GENERAL KNOWLEDGE
1 1970s. 2 "The Jackal". 3 Lisa Marie Presley. 4 1920s. 5 AK. 6 Bolton. 7 Henry. 8 To go. 9 Sri Lanka. 10 Leary. 11 Code. 12 Florida. 13 Jackson. 14 USA. 15 Detroit. 16 Seattle. 17 San Francisco. 18 Devil. 19 Guitar. 20 Madonna.

QUIZ 29. KARAOKE
1 *Your Song*. 2 *That Don't Impress Me Much*. 3 *She*. 4 *Love Is All Around*. 5 *We Don't Talk Anymore*. 6 *Brothers In Arms*. 7 Village People. 8 *Frozen*. 9 Heart. 10 Rainbow. 11 The Tough. 12 *Bohemian Rhapsody*. 13 Rose. 14 "Your heart away". 15 10. 16 Major Tom. 17 "Miss Molly". 18 "In a while, crocodile". 19 *Stand By Your Man*. 20 *Goodbye Yellow Brick Road*.

QUIZ 30. OLOGIES
1 Grasses. 2 Lying. 3 Weapons. 4 Mosses. 5 Flags. 6 Codes. 7 Feet. 8 Wines. 9 Sleep. 10 Handwriting.

QUIZ 31. DOGS
1 True. 2 False. 3 False. 4 False. 5 True. 6 False. 7 True. 8 False. 9 False. 10 True.

QUIZ 32. THE PLANETS
1 Nine. 2 Mercury. 3 Larger. 4 Oxygen. 5 The Sun. 6 Uranus. 7 Atmosphere. 8 The Sun. 9 Holst. 10 Jupiter. 11 Uranus. 12 Red. 13 Mars. 14 Earth. 15 Pluto.

QUIZ 33. FOOD AND DRINK
1 Spears. 2 Deer. 3 Mint. 4 Potatoes. 5 Pancakes. 6 Yellow. 7 Truffle. 8 Italy. 9 Smoked. 10 Potato. 11 Holland. 12 Oats. 13 Rice. 14 Spiral. 15 Colourless. 16 Spain. 17 Apples. 18 Almonds. 19 Hot. 20 Chartreuse.

QUIZ 34. PEOPLE
1 Morgan Freeman. 2 Saddam Hussein. 3 James Lovell. 4 Brian Epstein. 5 Gorbachev. 6 Danforth. 7 Princess Diana. 8 Frank Lloyd Wright. 9 Gerald Ford. 10 Juan Carlos. 11 Shaw. 12 Tutankhamun. 13 Jimmy Carter. 14 Milhous. 15 Mother Theresa. 16 McCarthy. 17 Jim Henson. 18 Harlem. 19 Andy Warhol. 20 Paul McCartney.

QUIZ 35. PICTURE QUIZ
They can all go after the word RED. A Coat. B) Cross. C Herring. D) Tape.

QUIZ 36. DOUBLE TAKE
1 Salts. 2 Broom. 3 Passage. 4 Solvent. 5 Nirvana. 6 Cos. 7 Knight. 8 Venus. 9 Note. 10 Chat.

QUIZ 37. SPIES
1 Fleming. 2 Code. 3 Ring. 4 Mole. 5 Morse. 6 George. 7 Julius Caesar. 8 Oddjob. 9 Kim Philby. 10 Cylinder. 11 Enigma. 12 Square. 13 Dutch. 14 MI5. 15 Pig pen.

QUIZ 38. THE OSCARS
1 American. 2 Russia. 3 Binoche. 4 Las Vegas. 5 Affleck. 6 Aniston. 7 New York. 8 80s. 9 Christie. 10 Hollywood. 11 Gwyneth Paltrow. 12 Gladiator. 13 Scottish. 14 Swank. 15 *Titanic*. 16 *Million Dollar Baby*. 17 1970s. 18 Olympics. 19 Wayne. 20 Sarandon.

QUIZ 39. THE HEADLINES
1 Adopted over the internet. 2 East Pakistan. 3 Hitler. 4 Callaghan. 5 Health. 6 Zaire. 7 Al Gore. 8 Monetary. 9 Swedish. 10 Army. 11 Rabin. 12 Italy. 13 Kipling. 14 McCarthy. 15 Literature. 16 Russia. 17 Martin Bashir. 18 Saddleworth. 19 Nepal. 20 1920s.

QUIZ 40. LUCKY DIP
1 Hoover. 2 Airports. 3 Coldplay. 4 Leaves. 5 Golf. 6 Three. 7 Suffolk. 8 Strings. 9 5 pence. 10 Leek. 11 West End. 12 Egypt. 13 1940s. 14 Make light work. 15 Spades. 16 Snakes and ladders. 17 Pig. 18 Fire. 19 Three. 20 Dartboard.

QUIZ 41. CLINT EASTWOOD
1 Spaghetti westerns. 2 Orang-utan. 3 John F Kennedy. 4 He did!. 5 Dollars. 6 Madison. 7 Costner. 8 *Alcatraz*. 9 1930s. 10 *Every Which Way But Loose*. 11 *Coogan's*. 12 *Rawhide*. 13 *The Ugly*. 14 Best Director. 15 Locke. 16 Daly. 17 Wales. 18 Mayor. 19 *Paint Your Wagon*. 20 Jazz.

QUIZ 42. TRAVEL
1 Cotton. 2 Albania & Yugoslavia. 3 China & Russia. 4 Aotearoa. 5 Hyde Park. 6 Ringgit. 7 Wales. 8 Bath. 9 Mount Redoubt. 10 Azores. 11 Rome. 12 Charlotte Town. 13 Rondonia. 14 Jordan. 15 Luzon. 16 Australia. 17 West Point. 18 Salt Lake City. 19 Djibouti. 20 Hainburg in Austria.

QUIZ 43. TELEVISION
1 Paul Young. 2 Karen Walker. 3 *Miami Vice*. 4 *Baywatch*. 5 *Cheers*. 6 Hospital. 7 Ralph. 8 Colorado. 9 1970s. 10 Manhattan. 11 Orbit City. 12 Vietnam. 13 The Addams Family. 14 Helicopter. 15 New York. 16 Wonder Woman. 17 *The Partridge Family*. 18 Six. 19 Curtis. 20 Hawkeye.

QUIZ 44. NAME GAME
1 Elton John. 2 Helen Mirren. 3 George Michael. 4 Kirk Douglas. 5 Tina Turner. 6 Ava Gardner. 7 Iggy Pop. 8 Julie Andrews. 9 Jelly Roll Morton. 10 Tony Curtis.

QUIZ 45. GUESS WHO . . . ?
1 Sebastian Coe. 2 Leonardo DiCaprio. 3 Kevin Costner. 4 Neil Diamond. 5 Florence Griffith-Joyner. 6 Jane Austen. 7 Hillary Clinton. 8 Jim Morrison. 9 Ben Johnson. 10 Tom Cruise.

QUIZ 46. EXTINCT CREATURES
1 99.9. 2 Lizard. 3 65 million. 4 China. 5 Martha. 6 Stupid. 7 Mauritius. 8 Mermaid. 9 Aurochs. 10 Brain. 11 20th. 12 Bird. 13 Tyrannosaurus Rex. 14 Mesozoic. 15 Plants.

QUIZ 47. WAR ZONES
1 Powell. 2 Afghanistan. 3 Six Days. 4 Jane Fonda. 5 Chechnya. 6 Czechoslovakia. 7 Cuba. 8 France. 9 Hiroshima. 10 Belgium. 11 Japan. 12 Italians. 13 Mustard gas. 14 Overlord. 15 Tank. 16 Sri Lanka. 17 Vietnam. 18 Nigeria. 19 Scotland. 20 Cyprus.

QUIZ 48. GENERAL KNOWLEDGE
1 Dolly. 2 Fitzgerald. 3 Da Nang. 4 Doris Day. 5 Camp David. 6 New York. 7 Argentina. 8 Miami. 9 Cruise. 10 Dog. 11 Coca-Cola. 12 50s. 13 Oasis. 14 Q. 15 Opera. 16 Italy. 17 Australia. 18 Vietnam. 19 Sweden. 20 Italy.

QUIZ 49. LEADING LADIES
1 Cameron Diaz. 2 Catherine Zeta Jones. 3 Julia. 4 *(The) Hours*. 5 Lopez. 6 Halle. 7 Julianne. 8 Dog. 9 Hair colour. 10 Beautiful. 11 Bergman. 12 Walters. 13 Drew. 14 Kate Winslet. 15 Meg. 16 Julie Andrews. 17 Emily. 18 Fonda. 19 Kylie Minogue. 20 Scott Thomas.

QUIZ 50. HALF CHANCE
1 Sweetcorn. 2 Wales. 3 Flying. 4 East. 5 Pierce Brosnan. 6 Madonna. 7 Invention. 8 Air. 9 Autobahn. 10 Needles. 11 57. 12 Pink. 13 Fat. 14 April. 15 Athens. 16 West. 17 The Alps. 18 Big. 19 Riding trousers. 20 19th.

QUIZ 51. POP MUSIC
1 Norah Jones. 2 Christina Aguilera. 3 Mariah Carey. 4 New Kids On The Block. 5 Phil Collins. 6 Ashanti. 7 One. 8 Nirvana. 9 Willie Nelson. 10 Freddie Mercury. 11 Sting. 12 Albert Hall. 13 Cliff Richard. 14 Whitney Houston. 15 Diana Ross. 16 *Goldeneye*. 17 Lou Reed. 18 Andrew Lloyd Webber. 19 U2. 20 Kylie Minogue.

QUIZ 52. UK TOUR
1 East. 2 Aberdonian. 3 East. 4 Loch Ness. 5 Cheddar. 6 Bedfordshire. 7 Blackpool. 8 Balmoral. 9 Scotland. 10 Hospital. 11 Red. 12 Glasgow. 13 Battersea. 14 Isle of Wight 15 England. 16 Norfolk. 17 Liverpool. 18 M4. 19 Medical profession. 20 Heathrow.

QUIZ 53. PICTURE QUIZ
They all names of cocktails. A) Gimlet. B Manhattan. C) Screwdriver. D) Sidecar.

QUIZ 54. BONES
1 True. 2 True. 3 False. 4 False. 5 True. 6 True. 7 False. 8 False. 9 True. 10 False.

QUIZ 55. BEST ACTOR OSCAR
1 *Ray*. 2 Harrison. 3 Tom Hanks. 4 *Gladiator*. 5 Gary Cooper. 6 *Training Day*. 7 Duvall. 8 Priest. 9 Musician. 10 18 years. 11 France. 12 None. 13 Michael. 14 Malloy. 15 *Rain Man*.

QUIZ 56. LUCKY DIP
1 Royal. 2 Citrus. 3 Mr Hyde. 4 The Broth. 5 Greece. 6 Elephants. 7 Crossword. 8 Tug of War. 9 Green. 10 Four. 11 The Umpire. 12 Beauty. 13 Clay. 14 Stalactite. 15 X. 16 Hard. 17 Italian. 18 13. 19 St Martins. 20 *Today*.

QUIZ 57. WESTERNS
1 Kilmer. 2 Civil War. 3 Clint Eastwood. 4 *The Shootist*. 5 Cooper. 6 Marvin. 7 Mitchum. 8 Bob Dylan. 9 *Paint Your Wagon*. 10 1960s. 11 Horse operas. 12 Autry. 13 Hackman. 14 *True Grit*. 15 *The Magnificent Seven*. 16 Stanwyck. 17 Freeman. 18 Newman. 19 1950s. 20 *Shane*.

QUIZ 58. AT THE MOVIES
1 Meg Ryan. 2 *Pulp Fiction*. 3 Sarandon. 4 Demi Moore. 5 1990s. 6 Leonardo DiCaprio. 7 D Day. 8 Orson Welles. 9 Dillon. 10 Sea. 11 Mia Farrow. 12 1980s. 13 Sigourney Weaver. 14 Claude Rains. 15 Jodie Foster. 16 Batman. 17 Mel Gibson. 18 1980s. 19 Grapes. 20 Lee Curtis.

QUIZ 59. SPORT
1 New England Patriots. 2 Peter Shilton. 3 24 years. 4 Ice skating. 5 Jenny Pitman. 6 American. 7 Blue (five points, brown is four). 8 Cotton. 9 Rugby League. 10 Number 10. 11 Fencing and skiing. 12 San Marino, Italy. 13 Adrian Moorhouse in 1987. 14 American Football. 15 Daytona. 16 Monaco. 17 Yes. 18 Yes. 19 David Campese. 20 Four.

QUIZ 60. AROUND AMERICA
1 Florida. 2 Pacific. 3 New Orleans. 4 New York. 5 Massachusetts. 6 Connecticut. 7 *Globe*. 8 Honolulu. 9 Los Angeles. 10 Noon. 11 New York and New Jersey. 12 New York. 13 Niagara. 14 Tennessee. 15 Mexico. 16 San Francisco. 17 Three Mile Island. 18 John F Kennedy. 19 Rhode Island. 20 George Bush Snr.

QUIZ 61. GENERAL KNOWLEDGE
1 Spain. 2 Tutankhamen's tomb. 3 First decade. 4 Tracy Vincenzo. 5 Oscar Wilde. 6 Judo. 7 Noel Coward. 8 1970s. 9 C S Lewis. 10 Both known as Gentleman Jim. 11 Lindsay Davenport. 12 Minister of Foreign Affairs. 13 Atlanta. 14 My Fair Lady. 15 Winston Churchill. 16 Fugees.17 The Netherlands. 18 Sleep. 19 Switzerland. 20 Richard Nixon.

QUIZ 62. PICTURE QUIZ
They are palindromes (read the same forwards and back). A) Abba. B) Ewe. C) Kayak. D) Minim.

QUIZ 63. DOUBLE TAKE
1 Major. 2 Cob. 3 Dear. 4 Wash. 5 Engaged. 6 Grilled. 7 Vault. 8 Snip. 9 Cordial. 10 Blubber.

QUIZ 64. RAILWAYS
1 17th century. 2 Rocket. 3 UK. 4 France. 5 Beeching. 6 1904. 7 Tay. 8 USA. 9 Deltic. 10 1850s. 11 Moorgate. 12 1994. 13 Steam. 14 Yellow. 15 France.

QUIZ 65. NATURE
1 Tidal wave. 2 On the skin. 3 CJD. 4 Worm. 5 Haematology. 6 Hermaphrodite. 7 Falcon. 8 Ear. 9 Marine snail. 10 Knee. 11 Pigeons. 12 Anaemia. 13 Orange. 14 Fungus. 15 Skin. 16 Abdomen. 17 Shoulder blade. 18 Fish. 19 Short sighted. 20 12.

QUIZ 66. TELEVISION CLASSICS
1 Green. 2 Desi Arnaz. 3 Clampett. 4 Mancini. 5 "That's the way it is". 6 Incredible. 7 *Monty Python's Flying Circus*. 8 Angie Dickinson.

9 James (Jim). 10 *The A Team*. 11 Dolphins. 12 Perry Mason. 13 *Blue Peter*. 14 *The Lone Ranger*. 15 Horse (who could talk). 16 Phil Silvers. 17 *The Good Life*. 18 Son-in-law. 19 *The Girl From U.N.C.L.E.* 20 *The Great Race*.

QUIZ 67. LUCKY DIP
1 Arthur. 2 New Mexico. 3 George Bush (Snr). 4 Bedrock. 5 Purple. 6 The Thames. 7 Two. 8 Red Nose. 9 Joseph. 10 Dragon. 11 Sausages. 12 Elephant. 13 Baker Street. 14 Little John. 15 Look. 16 600. 17 North. 18 Bugs Bunny. 19 Stephen. 20 Mouth.

QUIZ 68. MARILYN ONROE
1 Norma Jean. 2 *A Millionaire*. 3 *Gentlemen Prefer Blondes*. 4 *The Showgirl*. 5 1920s. 6 Eve. 7 Kennedy. 8 Wilder. 9 *Sergeant Pepper's Lonely Hearts Club Band*. 10 Ukelele. 11 Merman. 12 Drugs overdose. 13 Baseball player. 14 Miller. 15 1960s. 16 Sugar. 17 Russell. 18 *Monkey Business*. 19 *Niagara*. 20 Clark Gable in *The Misfits*.

QUIZ 69. GEOGRAPHY
1 Antarctic. 2 A state. 3 Spain. 4 Ireland. 5 India. 6 America. 7 Himalayas. 8 Luxembourg. 9 Red. 10 Italy. 11 Belgium. 12 New Zealand. 13 Norway. 14 South Africa. 15 Pacific. 16 Rome. 17 Mountain. 18 China. 19 Iraq. 20 Thailand.

QUIZ 70. HISTORY
1 Suez Canal. 2 His ear. 3 Benito Mussolini. 4 Christmas Day. 5 Bob Hawke. 6 1965. 7 William III. 8 Stuarts. 9 Runnymede. 10 Chamberlain. 11 Mubarak. 12 Irangate. 13 David Blunkett. 14 Jimmy Carter. 15 Peter Mandelson. 16 Local authority. 17 Benazir Bhutto. 18 Zimbabwe. 19 South Africa. 20 Mikhail Gorbachev.

QUIZ 71. RIVER CITY
1 Zarqa. 2 Rimac. 3 Tagus. 4 Plate. 5 Liffey. 6 Tigris. 7 Sava. 8 Vistula. 9 Mapocho. 10 Senne.

QUIZ 72. GUESS WHO . . . ?
1 Sonia O'Sullivan. 2 Katharine Hepburn. 3 Glenn Close. 4 Merlene Ottey. 5 Nicole Kidman. 6 Maeve Binchy. 7 Sean Connery. 8 Paula Radcliffe. 9 Bob Marley. 10 George W Bush.

QUIZ 73. HOLIDAY RESORTS
1 Eight. 2 France. 3 Malta. 4 Sicily. 5 Blackpool. 6 East Sussex. 7 250 miles. 8 Blue. 9 Japan. 10 Orlando. 11 Balearics. 12 Morecambe. 13 Tanzania. 14 Bali. 15 Canaries.

QUIZ 74. WINTER QUIZ
1 Sweden. 2 December 13th. 3 Sicily. 4 Capricorn, Aquarius, Pisces. 5 Henry II. 6 *A Winter's Tale*. 7 Wintergreen. 8 Russian. 9 Epiphany (Twelfth Night). 10 Sarajevo, Yugoslavia. 11 January or February. 12 Brazil. 13 Sausage on a stick. 14 Australia. 15 December. 16 Vine growers. 17 Hibernation. 18 Japan. 19 Martin Luther King. 20 Light. 21 Red. 22 Skiing. 23 Christian. 24 Woody Allen. 25 Mozart. 26 Queen. 27 1920s (1924). 28 Richard III. 29 Boston Tea Party. 30 Ice skating. 31 Christmas. 32 Dolls. 33 Pink rice. 34 John Lennon. 35 Eight. 36 Rebecca. 37 90. 38 Massachusetts. 39 Ice dancing. 40 White. 41 "The Winter Queen". 42 (East) Germany. 43 New Zealand. 44 Winter sports. 45 Chamonix, France. 46 Samba. 47 December. 48 Candles. 49 Twelfth Night. 50 Salt Lake City, USA.

QUIZ 75. ROCK & ROLL
1 Summertime. 2 The Crickets. 3 Crocodile. 4 Jerry Lee Lewis. 5 *Blueberry Hill*. 6 *Hound Dog*. 7 Shake. 8 Vincent. 9 Bopper. 10 Steele.11 *Move It*. 12 Mississippi. 13 Piano. 14 Perkins. 15 England. 16 To go. 17 "Green". 18 Jerry Lee Lewis. 19 Wilde. 20 Johnny Kidd.

QUIZ 76. HALF CHANCE
1 Leotard. 2 Top. 3 Raspberry. 4 Cricket. 5 Obligatory suicide. 6 The fourth. 7 Roger Ackroyd. 8 Greek. 9 Horses. 10 *Dracula*. 11 Palindromes. 12 *All About Eve*.13 Syria. 14 *Fawlty Towers*. 15 George. 16 Greece. 17 Chemical Brothers. 18 Dr Evil. 19 Lenin. 20 Maddy Magellan.

QUIZ 77. SCIENCE
1 Sony Corporation. 2 Prozac. 3 Isaac Newton. 4 Italian. 5 Genetically. 6 Nicotine. 7 Greenhouse. 8 Ozone layer. 9 Viking. 10 Eileen Collins. 11 First woman winner and first ever to receive the award twice. 12 Andrei Sakharov. 13 Werner Von Braun. 14 Logarithms. 15 Polonium, radium. 16 Multiply. 17 Taxonomy. 18 Metric. 19 Galapagos. 20 Explosion of the atomic bomb.

QUIZ 78. LEADERS
1 Indonesia. 2 Czech Republic. 3 Sweden. 4 Ronald Reagan. 5 Bob Hawke. 6 Ronald Reagan. 7 Falklands War. 8 Clint Eastwood. 9 Oliver Tambo. 10 Saturday. 11 Tessa Jowell. 12 Speaker of the House of Commons. 13 Elizabeth II. 14 11 years. 15 Robin Cook. 16 Israel. 17 Al Gore. 18 Monaco. 19 Helmut Kohl. 20 Rudy Giuliani.

QUIZ 79. GENERAL KNOWLEDGE
1 John Lennon. 2 Korean. 3 *The King And I*. 4 Baroness Orczy. 5 USA. 6 Mel C. 7 Nick Leeson. 8 Heart transplant 9 Scarf – it was caught in a moving car wheel. 10 Buffalo Bill. 11 Switzerland. 12 Joseph Conrad. 13 Legs. 14 Bra. 15 1950s. 16 Barcelona. 17 A. 18 *On Her Majesty's Secret Service*. 19 Pottery. 20 Seven million.

QUIZ 80. COMEDY MOVIES
1 *The Truman Show*. 2 DeGeneres. 3 Powers. 4 Bean. 5 Liar Liar. 6 Sheffield. 7 Lewis. 8 The Flintstones. 9 Hugh Grant. 10 *Groundhog Day*. 11 Nanny. 12 Whoopi Goldberg. 13 Diamond. 14 *Wayne's World*. 15 Turtles. 16 Bob Hope, Bing Crosby, Dorothy Lamour. 17 Harpo and Groucho (Marx). 18 Bruce Willis. 19 Dustin Hoffman. 20 Liza Minnelli.

QUIZ 81. PICTURE QUIZ
They all sound like letters of the alphabet. A) Bee. B) Pea. C) Sea. D Tee.

QUIZ 82. CATS
1 True. 2 False. 3 False. 4 True. 5 True. 6 False. 7 True. 8 False. 9 True. 10 True.

QUIZ 83. CASTLES
1 Keep. 2 Could move. 3 Stone. 4 Motte. 5 Bavaria. 6 Crennels. 7 Vertically. 8 France. 9 White. 10 Water. 11 Merlons. 12 Wales. 13 Barbican. 14 Siege. 15 13thC.

QUIZ 84. FOOD AND DRINK
1 Fish. 2 Kirschwasser. 3 Gin. 4 Sugar. 5 November. 6 Curry powder. 7 Greece. 8 Halal. 9 20. 10 Kiwi fruit. 11 Gelatin. 12 Marty Wilde. 13 Mrs Beeton. 14 Nut. 15 Coca Cola. 16 Elizabeth David. 17 Clarified butter. 18 Carrot. 19 Bloody Mary. 20 Milk.

QUIZ 85. THE ARTS
1 The Bible. 2 Agatha Christie. 3 *Oklahoma*. 4 Skates. 5 Superstar. 6 Girl. 7 On The Roof. 8 The Windmill. 9 Broadway. 10 *My Fair Lady*.11 Sullivan. 12 Royal Shakespeare Company. 13 *Cats*. 14 Elaine Paige. 15 Peace. 16 *Paint Your Wagon*. 17 Eagle. 18 *Barnum*. 19 San Sebastian, Spain. 20 Sunset.

QUIZ 86. PHOBIAS
1 Water. 2 Eating. 3 Bees. 4 Thunder. 5 Solitude. 6 Cats. 7 Walking. 8 Open spaces. 9 Light. 10 Dogs.

QUIZ 87. DOUBLE TAKE
1 Iceberg. 2 Ditch. 3 Pill box. 4 Purse. 5 Yogi. 6 Score. 7 Paddles. 8 Suite. 9 Swallow. 10 Overall.

QUIZ 88. SEAS
1 Oceanography. 2 Pacific. 3 Pacific. 4 Red Sea. 5 70%. 6 Arctic. 7 Atlantic. 8 3%. 9 Tides. 10 Tsunami. 11 Pacific. 12 Green. 13 Black. 14 Foxe. 15 Bering.

QUIZ 89. HORROR MOVIES
1 Kenneth Branagh. 2 The Devil. 3 *Bram Stoker's Dracula*. 4 *Scream 2*. 5 William Peter Blatty. 6 Bela. 7 Invisible. 8 Stephen King. 9 Christopher Lee. 10 Anthony Perkins. 11 Spiders. 12 Kubrick. 13 The creature. 14 *Halloween*. 15 Spacek. 16 Elm Street. 17 1970s. 18 Hammer. 19 Anthony Hopkins. 20 *The Birds*.

QUIZ 90. LUCKY DIP
1 180. 2 Fish. 3 Lord Nelson. 4 Dido. 5 Tom. 6 King Harold. 7 A pig. 8 John Lennon. 9 His hair. 10 Charity. 11 National Union of Teachers. 12 John Thaw. 13 Apple. 14 Queen Victoria. 15 Claustrophobia. 16 Camelot. 17 Tyne. 18 Postman Pat. 19 Dame. 20 Palm.

QUIZ 91. CRIME
1 California. 2 Charles Manson. 3 Scotland. 4 Shot. 5 Moors murderers. 6 London. 7 Paintings. 8 USA. 9 Doctor. 10 School. 11 Drugs. 12 Mailbags. 13 Bonnie and Clyde. 14 Batman. 15 Barber. 16 Bodies. 17 Yorkshire. 18 West. 19 Not paying taxes. 20 1980s.

QUIZ 92. GENERAL KNOWLEDGE
1 Hinduism. 2 Eyrie. 3 Alloway. 4 *Twelfth Night*. 5 Hitler and Mussolini. 6 Lettuce. 7 Lilies. 8 Marston Moor. 9 Max Miller. 10 Motor car manufacturing. 11 Jacobean. 12 Quorum. 13 Johann Strauss the Younger. 14 Korean War. 15 Dog. 16 1940. 17 Horst Jankowski. 18 Wind speed. 19 A hazelnut. 20 The Bosphorous.

QUIZ 93. HALF CHANCE
1 Argentina. 2 Washington DC. 3 Morocco. 4 Plane. 5 Water. 6 Margaret. 7 Rose. 8 Polly. 9 Italy. 10 Spain. 11 Monsoon. 12 Temple. 13 Edinburgh. 14 Potato. 15 Iraq. 16 Chigwell. 17 Irangate. 18 Bernadette. 19 Chile. 20 Sean.

QUIZ 94. THE BEATLES
1 Cavern. 2 *A Hard Day's Night*. 3 Ringo. 4 Japan. 5 *Paperback Writer*. 6 McCartney. 7 Stella. 8 *Revolver*. 9 Apple. 10 *She Loves You*. 11 Brian Epstein. 12 George Harrison. 13 *Love Me Do*. 14 Eleanor Rigby. 15 Ringo Starkey. 16 Mull of Kintyre. 17 New York. 18 George Martin. 19 Sitar. 20 Bob Dylan.

QUIZ 95. PICTURE QUIZ
They can all follow the word SAND. A) Bank. B) Castle. C) Paper. D) Stone.

QUIZ 96. WHO SAID . . . ?
1 John McEnroe. 2 Diego Maradona. 3 Steve Redgrave. 4 Dean Martin. 5 Richard Burton. 6 Pele. 7 Katharine Hepburn. 8 Gary Player.

QUIZ 97. ISLANDS
1 Canaries. 2 Bali. 3 Italy. 4 Madeira. 5 Mediterranean. 6 Bali. 7 Cuba. 8 Isle of Man. 9 Robben. 10 Friendly Islands. 11 Cos. 12 Sicily. 13 Capri. 14 Java. 15 Malta.

QUIZ 98. ANIMALS
1 Skunk. 2 Squeezing. 3 To breathe. 4 Sting. 5 Colour. 6 A tail. 7 Butterfly. 8 German Shepherd. 9 Horse. 10 Cats. 11 Poisonous frog. 12 Couple of hours. 13 Gorilla. 14 Smell. 15. To herd reindeer. 16 Argentina. 17 Lemur. 18 Asian elephant. 19 Forehead horn. 20 Warm blooded.

QUIZ 99. GOLF
1 Tiger Woods. 2 Gene Sarazen. 3 Gentleman Golfers of Edinburgh. 4 Bernhard Langer. 5 1989 PGA. 6 Nick Price. 7 John Jacobs. 8 Royal Lytham. 9 Greg Norman. 10 21. 11 Carnoustie. 12 Royal Lytham. 13 John Daly in 1991. 14 Worcester, Massachusetts. 15 Willie Park. 16 Bobby Jones (in perpetuity). 17 David Leadbetter. 18 Sandy Lyle. 19 Nick Faldo. 20 Walter Hagen.

QUIZ 100. PEOPLE
1 Condoleezza Rice. 2 Nancy Reagan. 3 John F Kennedy. 4 Terry. 5 Polio. 6 His wife.7 Asia. 8 South Africa. 9 Albert Einstein. 10 Falklands. 11 Irish. 12 Strangler. 13 Dior. 14 Robert Maxwell. 15 Space. 16 Chicago. 17 Ear. 18 Clinton. 19 French. 20 Agnetha.

QUIZ 101. THE HEADLINES
1 Foot & mouth. 2 Time Warner. 3 Peter Sellers. 4 Romania. 5 "Great Soul". 6 John Ashcroft. 7 21. 8 Edward. 9 Macmillan. 10 Philby. 11 Railways. 12 Paisley. 13 Seaman. 14 Mary Bell. 15 Box. 16 Texas. 17 Monday. 18 Home Secretary. 19 Tallest woman ever. 20 Jeff Bezos.

QUIZ 102. LOVE STORIES
1 *Romeo And Juliet*. 2 Roberts. 3 Wedding. 4 UK. 5 *Titanic*. 6 Leonardo DiCaprio. 7 Desert. 8 Clyde. 9 Bridget Jones. 10 Ryan O'Neal. 11 Dunaway. 12 Notting Hill. 13 Hanks. 14 Burton. 15 Hall. 16 Four. 17 Greek. 18 American Civil War. 19 Paltrow. 20 Railway station.

QUIZ 103. LUCKY DIP
1 Books of the Old Testament. 2 Capo. 3 Rhine. 4 22. 5 Pam Shriver. 6 Robin Hood. 7 With small hammers. 8 Holes to allow water to run off the deck. 9 Golf. 10 General Franco. 11 1001. 12 Dean Martin. 13 Poplar. 14 World War I. 15 13. 16 *By The Way*. 17 The troposphere. 18 Mike Atherton. 19 Westminster Abbey. 20 Ballet.

Quiz 104. NAME GAME
1 Ringo Starr. 2 Nina Simone. 3 Brigitte Bardot. 4 Lou Reed. 5 Ginger Rogers. 6 Howlin' Wolf. 7 Whoopi Goldberg. 8 Diana Ross. 9 Charlton Heston. 10 Johnny Rotten.

QUIZ 105. GUESS WHO . . . ?
1 Daley Thompson. 2 Tony Blair. 3 John Belushi. 4 Clint Eastwood. 5 Joe Di Maggio. 6 Barbara Taylor Bradford. 7 Catherine Zeta Jones. 8 Cher. 9 Michael Jordan. 10 Bryan Adams.

QUIZ 106. SYMBOLS
1 Tumble drier. 2 Hieroglyphics. 3 Semaphore. 4 Skirt. 5 E. 6 XXV. 7 Copyright. 8 Two. 9 Dash. 10 Black circle. 11 German. 12 3. 13 Diamonds. 14 Cold. 15 H.

QUIZ 107. GENERAL KNOWLEDGE
1 Eros. 2 Green. 3 Friday. 4 Sailing/Yachting. 5 Flyweight. 6 Sheep. 7 David Lloyd George. 8 Christine Keeler. 9 Archery. 10 Yellow. 11 Prime Minister. 12 Eldorado. 13 Bank manager. 14 Dark Blue. 15 La Paz. 16 Sculpture. 17 Holland. 18 Hymn book. 19 Raven. 20 Colorado River.

QUIZ 108. COUNTRY & WESTERN
1 Garth Brooks. 2 *Notting Hill*. 3 In a plane crash. 4 *9 to 5*. 5 LeAnn Rimes. 6 White. 7 Jolene. 8 Shania Twain. 9 *D.I.V.O.R.C.E.* 10 Willie Nelson. 11 Prisons. 12 Slim. 13 One. 14 Tennessee. 15 Jim Reeves. 16 Tammy Wynette. 17 Blue. 18 Lynn. 19 The County. 20 Little Rock.

QUIZ 109. AT THE MOVIES
1 Danny Boyle. 2 50s. 3 Kitty. 4 Sellers. 5 Ingrid Bergman. 6 Winona Ryder. 7 Diamonds. 8 Madness. 9 Shower. 10 Tina Turner. 11 *Gone With The Wind*. 12 Oldman. 13 Nazis. 14 *The Full Monty.* 15 Dolly Parton. 16 Hepburn. 17 Michelle Pfeiffer. 18 *Sophie's Choice*. 19 Stockholm. 20 Michael Jackson.

QUIZ 110. HALF CHANCE
1 Mexico. 2 Apollo 11. 3 Tibet. 4 Waist. 5 Dead bodies. 6 Zowie. 7 Monday. 8 Ice cream. 9 Vietnam War. 10 Blue. 11 The Liberty Bell. 12 Time flies. 13 Bat. 14 Sherry. 15 Barcelona. 16 A. 17 In water. 18 E. 19 Wax. 20 Skin.

QUIZ 111. CHARLES DICKENS
1 Barrister. 2 Miss Havisham. 3 David Copperfield. 4 Accidentally hangs himself. 5 Gordon riots. 6 Steerforth and Traddles. 7 Jarndyce v Jarndyce. 8 Mrs Sparsit. 9 Fanny and Tip. 10 Philip Pirrip. 11 Lizzy Hexam. 12 Jerry Cruncher. 13 Aunt. 14 Mr Dick. 15 Trent. 16 Miss Twinkleton's. 17 *The Mystery Of Edwin Drood*. 18 Drowns. 19 Blacksmith. 20 Dogs.

QUIZ 112. LUCKY DIP
1 Italy. 2 Four. 3 Cricket. 4 George Gershwin. 5 Louis XVI. 6 Bridge. 7 Peru. 8 Carbon. 9 Geppetto. 10 Halley's Comet. 11 The Philippines. 12 Value. 13 Radiohead. 14 Dorothy L Sayers. 15 Dauphin. 16 Mass. 17 Aquarius. 18 Copenhagen. 19 Linnaeus. 20 Lady Windermere's.

QUIZ 113. PICTURE QUIZ
They are all types of knife. A) Bowie. B) Bread. C) Fish. D) Pen.

QUIZ 114. NAME THE YEAR
1 1901. 2 1959. 3 1969. 4 1998. 5 1971. 6 1958.

QUIZ 115. THE HEADLINES
1 Cystic Fibrosis Fund. 2 Ship. 3 Florida. 4 Ronald Reagan. 5 It was her 100th birthday. 6 Peace. 7 Martina Navratilova. 8 E. 9 Beverly Hills. 10 York. 11 Earthquake. 12 Arizona. 13 Iranian. 14 AIDS. 15 Seattle. 16 Electric kettle. 17 Mike Tyson. 18 Lockerbie. 19 Mexico. 20 China.

QUIZ 116. US PRESIDENTS
1 George W. Bush. 2 Roosevelt. 3 Ronald Reagan. 4 Reagan. 5 Friday. 6 Truman. 7 2001. 8 Harry S Truman. 9 Leon Czolgosz. 10 Jimmy Carter. 11 Kennedy. 12 USA. 13 Roosevelt. 14 Jack Kemp. 15 Gerald Ford. 16 George Bush Snr. 17 Lincoln. 18 Earl. 19 Eisenhower. 20 24.

QUIZ 117. GENERAL KNOWLEDGE
1 Ballistic Missile. 2 Gun. 3 *Dr. Who*. 4 Rajah. 5 Element. 6 Highland soldiers in kilts. 7 Johnny Speight. 8 Horse. 9 Beaver. 10 The Jordan. 11 *Macbeth*. 12 Canada. 13 Chelsea. 14 Nautilus (in 1955). 15 France. 16 Bone. 17 Greek. 18 Edward VI. 19 Curling. 20 Coca Cola.

QUIZ 118. CAPITALS
1 Peru. 2 Turkey. 3 Ghana. 4 Philippines. 5 Muscat. 6 Slovakia. 7 Bangladesh. 8 Paraguay. 9 Rwanda. 10 Haiti.

QUIZ 119. TENNIS
1 False. 2 True. 3 False. 4 False. 5 True. 6 True. 7 False. 8 True. 9 False. 10 False.

QUIZ 120. MOUNTAINS
1 Asia. 2 Mexico. 3 Fold. 4 Virginia. 5 Atlas. 6 Iran. 7 Greek Gods. 8 Hillary. 9 Sherpas. 10 *The Sound Of Music*. 11 Argentina. 12 A surveyor. 13 Ecuador. 14 Denver. 15 Orogenesis.

QUIZ 121. ST VALENTINE'S DAY QUIZ
1 14th February. 2 Italian. 3 *The Importance of Being Earnest*. 4 New York. 5 Affleck. 6 *Gone With The Wind*. 7 *Some Like It Hot*. 8 Mike Tyson. 9 *Brief Encounter*. 10 15th. 11 *West Side Story*. 12 Renée Zellweger. 13 Torvill & Dean. 14 Cameron Diaz. 15 Prince Charles. 16 Claudius II. 17 Celine Dion. 18 Ewan McGregor. 19 Depp. 20 Bugs Moran's. 21 Erich Segal. 22 Absence. 23 Chicago. 24 *To Have And Have Not*. 25 Mr Darcy. 26 Gwyneth Paltrow. 27 *The Aviator.* 28 1989. 29 Jacqueline Wilson. 30 Barbara Cartland. 31 Clint Eastwood. 32 "Than never to have loved at all". 33 *The Graduate*. 34 10. 35 Helen Fielding. 36 Three minutes 15 seconds. 37 Louis de Bernières. 38 *Bonnie & Clyde*. 39 Casanova. 40 1890s. 41 *Pretty Woman*. 42 A warm heart. 43 Tomato. 44 Grace Kelly. 45 *Casablanca*. 46 *Bugsy*. 47 Heathcliff. 48 Claire Danes. 49 Rudolf Valentino. 50 The world.

QUIZ 122. TRAVEL
1 Africa. 2 Oklahoma. 3 Atlantic. 4 Manhattan. 5 Iceland. 6 Rhone. 7 Aran. 8 French. 9 Canaries. 10 Tip of South America. 11 Detroit. 12 Israel. 13 Bulgaria. 14 Nashville. 15 Liverpool. 16 Ohio. 17 Vladivostok. 18 Mount Rushmore. 19 Elysée Palace. 20 New Zealand.

QUIZ 123. CHARLIE CHAPLIN
1 Girl. 2 London. 3 Keystone. 4 Fred. 5 Spencer. 6 Sennett. 7 *Making A Living*. 8 United Artists. 9 *The Gold Rush*. 10 Goddard. 11 All four. 12 America. 13 *This Is My Song*. 14 *Hong Kong*. 15 Chaplin himself. 16 World War II. 17 Keaton. 18 Daughter. 19 1970s. 20 *Modern Times*.

QUIZ 124. TELEVISION
1 Debbie Reynolds. 2 Dingle. 3 Jessica. 4 Saxophone. 5 Hair salon. 6 *Buffy The Vampire Slayer*. 7 Blonde. 8 Office. 9 *The Weakest Link*. 10 Titchmarsh. 11 1940s. 12 John. 13 David. 14 *Red Dwarf*. 15 Gardening. 16 Nicey. 17 1990s 18 *The Young Ones*. 19 Dick. 20 Independent.

QUIZ 125. CHILD STARS
1 Macaulay Culkin. 2 Donald. 3 *Mary Poppins*. 4 Natalie Wood. 5 The Artful Dodger. 6 1930s. 7 Drew Barrymore. 8 Little Jimmy Osmond. 9 Durbin. 10 *The Piano*. 11 Elliott. 12 Seven. 13 *Little Women*. 14 Pickford. 15 Jodie Foster. 16 *Kramer vs. Kramer*. 17 *E.T.*. 18 Lassie. 19 1970s. 20 Coogan.

QUIZ 126. POP MUSIC
1 Justin Timberlake. 2 Westlife. 3 Richie. 4 Tennessee. 5 *The Tide Is High*. 6 Whitney Houston. 7 The Osmonds. 8 Nicole Kidman. 9 The Bee Gees. 10 Drums. 11 *Definitely Maybe*. 12 Celine Dion. 13 Diana Ross. 14 Four. 15 The Doors. 16 Bryan Adams. 17 Cream. 18 Madonna. 19 U2. 20 Fleetwood Mac.

QUIZ 127. SPORT
1 Ice Hockey. 2 Two. 3 Barcelona. 4 Leeds. 5 American Football. 6 Argentina. 7 Earvin. 8 Channel Islands. 9 Marathon. 10 Daniel. 11 Scotland. 12 Football. 13 Fulham. 14 Sri Lanka. 15 Northern Ireland. 16 Baltimore. 17 Flo-Jo. 18 Dusty. 19 Manchester. 20 Baseball.

QUIZ 128. PICTURE QUIZ
B) The Taj Mahal 1630–53.
D) The White House 1792–99.
A) The Eiffel Tower 1899.
C) The Empire State Building 1931.

QUIZ 129. DOUBLE TAKE
1 Caddy. 2 Rare. 3 Spear. 4 Dress. 5 Shuttle. 6 Body. 7 Grace. 8 May. 9 Bands. 10 Light.

QUIZ 130. MONEY
1 Hungary. 2 Melinda. 3 Abba. 4 Evil. 5 Collins. 6 Arkansas. 7 Israel. 8 Ralph Lauren. 9 Man Utd. 10 Saudi Arabia. 11 Rial. 12 Silver. 13 88 million. 14 Dram. 15 To her right.

QUIZ 131. TOUGH GUYS
1 Keanu. 2 Bruce Willis. 3 Keitel. 4 Reed. 5 Al Pacino. 6 Meat Loaf. 7 Dozen. 8 Jennifer Aniston. 9 Damon. 10 Jean Claude. 11 Billy Bob. 12 L. 13 Mafia. 14 Bronson. 15 Affleck. 16 Buffalo Bill. 17 John. 18 Francis Ford Coppola. 19 Cameron. 20 Kiefer.

QUIZ 132. HALF CHANCE
1 Port. 2 Fish. 3 America. 4 Mullet. 5 Personal best. 6 Blackburn. 7 1940s. 8 Baseball. 9 Edward. 10 Spencer. 11 Fruit. 12 Three-dimensional. 13 M People. 14 Spain. 15 Samuel. 16 Electrician. 17 Paul Hogan. 18 Jacob. 19 John Peel. 20 Beaujolais.

QUIZ 133. LUCKY DIP
1 Sutcliffe. 2 Kelly Rowland. 3 1990s. 4 Laser. 5 *For Your Eyes Only*. 6 Pakistan. 7 Montreal. 8 Rhett Butler. 9 Ivan the Terrible. 10 Herbaceous. 11 Muir. 12 Giotto. 13 The Mary Rose. 14 John Le Mesurier. 15 Genotype. 16 Victoria. 17 Turned into an insect. 18 Bebop. 19 South Africa. 20 Major.

QUIZ 134. TV DRAMA
1 Denzel Washington. 2 Joe Friday. 3 *Northern Exposure*. 4 Lincoln Continental. 5 A fashion house. 6 Hannibal Smith. 7 Blue Moon. 8 Boston. 9 Seven. 10 *Ace of Spies*. 11 Kwai Chang Caine. 12 Mr Waverly. 13 Richard Chamberlain. 14 Philip. 15 *Alias Smith & Jones*. 16 He was deceased. 17 Freeway. 18 His pistol. 19 Doogie Howser. 20 Dale Cooper.

QUIZ 135. FOOD AND DRINK
1 Italy. 2 Choux pastry. 3 Pears. 4 Garlic. 5 Mushroom. 6 Veal. 7 Tomato juice. 8 Anchovy. 9 It's served raw. 10 North East. 11 Beef Wellington. 12 Red wine. 13 Apple. 14 None, they are made from cheese. 15 Potatoes. 16 Rice. 17 Ewe's milk. 18 Oysters and bacon. 19 Tayberry. 20 Vermicelli.

QUIZ 136. NATURE
1 Ginkgo. 2 Oxalic. 3 Callus. 4 Bird droppings. 5 It dissolves blood corpuscles. 6 Italy. 7 Rockies. 8 North & South Carolina. 9 Blue. 10 Ferns and mosses (don't have flowers). 11 Pacific coast of North America. 12 Stalk. 13 African violet. 14 From insects. 15 It loses its green colour. 16 Whippoorwill. 17 Rose of Jericho. 18 Fungi. 19 Cactus. 20 Poppy.

QUIZ137. AIRPORTS
1 Egypt. 2 Denmark. 3 Spain. 4 Nigeria. 5 Latvia. 6 Mexico. 7 Gibraltar. 8 Venice. 9 Spain. 10 Turkey.

QUIZ 138. GUESS WHO . . . ?
1 Muhammad Ali. 2 Ursula Andress. 3 Bob Dylan. 4 Daniel Day-Lewis. 5 Lance Armstrong. 6 Aretha Franklin. 7 Emily Brontë. 8 Liam Neeson. 9 Roberto Baggio. 10 Warren Beatty.

QUIZ 139. BRIDGES
1 Humber. 2 1932. 3 Beam. 4 China. 5 Pontoon. 6 Trains. 7 1930s. 8 Arizona. 9 Prisoners (on the way to their execution). 10 1990s. 11 Norway. 12 Falling down. 13 8.5. 14 Bascule. 15 Burma.

QUIZ 140. SCI-FI
1 Keanu. 2 Dinosaurs. 3 Los Angeles. 4 *Lost In Space*. 5 Willis. 6 *The X Files*. 7 Lizard. 8 *Independence Day*. 9 *Judge Dredd*. 10 Lois Lane. 11 *Close Encounters Of The Third Kind*. 12 Leia. 13 The Apes. 14 Scotland. 15 *Alien*. 16 Bowie. 17 1990s. 18 Broderick. 19 *Blade Runner*. 20 Black.

QUIZ 141. GENERAL KNOWLEDGE
1 Vertical. 2 Colditz. 3 15. 4 Decibels. 5 Egypt. 6 Yorkshire. 7 Roxy Music. 8 Golf. 9 Tchaikovsky. 10 60. 11 Sandringham House. 12 Batman. 13 Morocco. 14 Dublin. 15 Elysée Palace. 16 144. 17 Canoeing. 18 June. 19 Boats. 20 When about to leave port.

QUIZ 142. GEOGRAPHY
1 Alps. 2 Greenland. 3 Weston Super-Mare. 4 Africa. 5 Tropic of Cancer. 6 Great Lakes. 7 Tasmania. 8 Vietnam. 9 Spain. 10 Hampton Court. 11 Isle of Man. 12 England. 13 Hawaii. 14 German. 15 East Anglia. 16 Victoria. 17 Dogger Bank. 18 Cornwall. 19 Channel Islands. 20 Northern.

QUIZ 143. ELVIS
1 25 years. 2 Acapulco. 3 Aaron. 4 Charles Bronson. 5 Germany. 6 Lisa Marie. 7 *King Creole*. 8 *It's Now Or Never*. 9 Mississippi. 10 *Blue Christmas*. 11 *Way Down*. 12 *Jailhouse Rock*. 13 *Are You Lonesome Tonight?* 14 *Elvis And Me*. 15 *Can't Help Falling In Love*. 16 Las Vegas. 17 *American Trilogy*. 18 Memphis. 19 *Heartbreak Hotel*. 20 Pomus and Shuman.

QUIZ 144. HISTORY
1 Australia. 2 Libya. 3 John Major. 4 Marcos. 5 Margaret Thatcher. 6 Castro. 7 Iron Curtain. 8 Land mines. 9 Ethiopia. 10 Three. 11 Bill Clinton. 12 Pol Pot. 13 1960s. 14 African. 15 Tony Blair. 16 Franco. 17 Italy. 18 Israel. 19 Tsar. 20 Uganda.

QUIZ 145. SCIENCE
1 Venus. 2 Carbon dioxide. 3 Antibody. 4 Anaesthetic. 5 Wind. 6 Greek. 7 *Discovery*. 8 Detection. 9 Triangle. 10 Greenwich. 11 Alzheimer. 12 Stereo. 13 Cancer. 14 The Church. 15 Marie Curie.16 *HMS Beagle*. 17 Better microphone. 18 Radioactivity. 19 English Channel. 20 Parkinson.

QUIZ 146. PICTURE QUIZ
A) John Travolta, 1954.
D) Martina Navratilova, 1956.
C) Madonna, 1958.
B) Carl Lewis, 1961.

QUIZ 147. INSECTS
1 False. 2 True. 3 True. 4 False. 5 True. 6 True. 7 False. 8 True. 9 True. 10 False.

QUIZ 148. ANIMAL MOVIES
1 Seal. 2 Orca. 3 *Jaws*. 4 Dog. 5 Dalmatians. 6 Sharks. 7 *Born Free*. 8 Horse. 9 Hanks. 10 King Kong. 11 Three. 12 Two. 13 Otters. 14 Tony. 15 Pal.

QUIZ 149. FIFA WORLD CUP
1 Every four years. 2 USA. 3 France. 4 Red. 5 Luis Felipe Scolari. 6 David Beckham. 7 Germany. 8 David Seaman. 9 Liverpool. 10 1930. 11 Brazil 1994. 12 Brazil. 13 Bulgaria. 14 Gary Lineker. 15 Mexico. 16 Japan and Korea. 17 Croatia. 18 Bobby Moore. 19 Italy. 20 No.

QUIZ 150. LUCKY DIP
1 Mick Jagger. 2 Rubik. 3 Germany. 4 Wilson. 5 West. 6 180. 7 Carbon. 8 Popeye. 9 Red and white. 10 November. 11 Curly. 12 Pink Floyd. 13 Herd. 14 Liver. 15 Simple Minds. 16 13. 17 Five. 18 Limbo. 19 Archbishop of Canterbury 20 Grimm.

QUIZ 151. HALF CHANCE
1 Actress. 2 Medium sweet. 3 The Scarlet Pimpernel. 4 France. 5 *Terminator II*. 6 Mule. 7 Atonement. 8 *Too Close*. 9 Austrian. 10 Manchester. 11 Doncaster. 12 1940s. 13 Birmingham. 14 Scorsese. 15 180 episodes. 16 Whooping cough. 17 Spinach. 18 Iceland. 19 Stagecoach. 20 Chandon.

QUIZ 152. 1960s
1 Yasser Arafat. 2 John. 3 Soviet. 4 Rome. 5 Lady Chatterley's. 6 Space. 7 Nureyev. 8 Berlin. 9 Thalidomide. 10 Wilson. 11 The Moon. 12 Train. 13 Radio station. 14 Churchill. 15 Horse. 16 China. 17 Sir Stanley Matthews. 18 Queen Elizabeth II. 19 Jean Shrimpton. 20 Rockers.

QUIZ 153. ARTS
1 *West Side Story*. 2 Agatha Christie. 3 We're British. 4 Wodehouse. 5 Copenhagen Film Festival. 6 Vet. 7 Cartland. 8 *Carousel*. 9 Lady Chatterley. 10 Horse racing. 11 Archer. 12 Collins. 13 Rendell. 14 Brontë. 15 Treasure. 16 John Constable. 17 Pan. 18 *Oliver!*. 19 Catherine. 20 James.

QUIZ 154. ANIMALS
1 Pink. 2 White. 3 Japan. 4 Caribou. 5 Sheep. 6 White or cream. 7 V shape. 8 Elk. 9 Sand. 10 Border collie. 11 Dog. 12 Neck. 13 Otter. 14 Invertebrates. 15 One. 16 Australia. 17 Polar bear. 18 Milk. 19 Fingerprints. 20 Southern.

QUIZ 155. PICTURE QUIZ
D) Sean Connery. C) Roger Moore. B) Timothy Dalton. A) Pierce Brosnan.

QUIZ 156. DOUBLE TAKE
1 Page. 2 Nanny. 3 Mint. 4 Bug. 5 Oscar. 6 Pacific. 7 Bolster. 8 Gondola. 9 Cracker. 10 Staff.

QUIZ 157. WORLD WAR II
1 Churchill. 2 Luftwaffe. 3 France. 4 Japan. 5 Dresden. 6 Dynamo. 7 Home Guard. 8 Coalmines. 9 Fish. 10 Lord Haw-Haw. 11 Little Boy. 12 Rommel. 13 9th. 14 Leningrad. 15 Shot himself.

QUIZ 158. TENNIS
1 Jimmy Connors. 2 Clay. 3 Martina Navratilova. 4 Arthur Ashe. 5 Gabriela Sabatini. 6 Switzerland. 7 French Open. 8 Margaret Smith. 9 Kevin Curren. 10 Karen Hantze. 11 Chris Evert. 12 Six games all. 13 Richard Krajicek. 14 Melbourne Park. 15 French Open. 16 Flushing Meadow. 17 The Queen. 18 1884. 19 French. 20 Helena Sukova.

QUIZ 159. GENERAL KNOWLEDGE
1 Sierra Leone. 2 A covey. 3 Railroad engineer. 4 Necessity. 5 Lagoon. 6 Six. 7 *The Mousetrap*. 8 Polo. 9 Meteors. 10 Norfolk Broads. 11 San Francisco. 12 What ever will be, will be. 13 Hypnotism or mesmerism. 14 An archaeologist. 15 Berlin. 16 Humming bird. 17 St. Andrew. 18 Black Beauty. 19 King of the Fairies. 20 Dirigible.

QUIZ 160. SOUL AND MOTOWN
1 *Reach Out, I'll Be There*. 2 Berry Gordy. 3 Dave. 4 Aretha Franklin. 5 Holland. 6 Otis Redding. 7 "The Broken Hearted". 8 Jackie Wilson. 9 The Isley Brothers. 10 James Brown. 11 The Supremes. 12 After the song *Tammy* by Debbie Reynolds. 13 *You Keep Me Hangin' On*. 14 Wilson Pickett. 15 The Vandellas. 16 Arthur Conley. 17 *I'm Still Waiting*. 18 Lionel Richie. 19 Gladys Knight. 20 Bobby Brown.

QUIZ 161. AT THE MOVIES
1 Davis. 2 Canada. 3 Hunt. 4 Jack Nicholson. 5 The Third Kind. 6 Mae West. 7 Willy. 8 Air Force. 9 1940s. 10 Sinatra. 11 Coppola. 12 *JFK*. 13 Fugitive. 14 The Genie. 15 Sean Connery. 16 Sharon Stone. 17 Fred Astaire. 18 Turner. 19 1990s. 20 Marlon Brando.

QUIZ 162. LUCKY DIP
1 Primary. 2 *Keeping Up Appearances*. 3 Smith. 4 Crewe 5 Bridge. 6 40. 7 Jane Fonda. 8 McKern. 9 100. 10 Eleanor. 11 Essex. 12 Moody. 13 Face. 14 TS. 15 The cinders. 16 Forsyth. 17 Lunar. 18 Moore. 19 Clock. 20 Hands.

QUIZ 163. OLYMPICS
1 Athens. 2 China. 3 Seven. 4 Afghanistan. 5 Greece. 6 1980 and 1984. 7 Blue. 8 USA. 9 Bob Beamon. 10 Millie. 11 West Germany. 12 Linford Christie. 13 Bjork. 14 Nadia Comaneci. 15 Tokyo. 16 Ben Johnson. 17 Mary Decker. 18 Carl Lewis. 19 Ice skating. 20 Sarajevo.

QUIZ 164. PICTURE QUIZ
D) Bob Dylan, 1941. A) Robert De Niro, 1943. B) Bill Clinton, 1946. C) Steven Spielberg1947.

QUIZ 165. NAME THE YEAR
1 1942. 2 1947. 3 1961. 4 1917. 5 1977. 6 2003.

QUIZ 166. PEOPLE
1 Martin Bashir. 2 Mary Jo Kopechne. 3 Agnes. 4 Denis. 5 Third finger, left hand. 6 House of Commons, UK. 7 Elaine Paige. 8 Body Shop. 9 Kennedy. 10 Brown. 11 Piano. 12 Quentin Crisp. 13 American. 14 To do your hair. 15 PD. 16 Horse racing. 17 Cheap. 18 Ginger. 19 Howard Hughes. 20 Blancmange Thrower.

QUIZ 167. ST PATRICK'S DAY
1 Snakes & a shamrock. 2 Confession. 3 Horses. 4 Trinity. 5 Linen. 6 Daimler. 7 Pat Cash. 8 Liffey. 9 U2. 10 Antrim & Down. 11 Ronnie. 12 Moore. 13 Radio. 14 Limerick. 15 Grace Kelly. 16 McEnroe. 17 Patrick Street. 18 John Ford. 19 Harp. 20 Corrib. 21 Cork. 22 Drum. 23 Duffy. 24 Mountjoy. 25 Cork. 26 Neagh. 27 Nat King Cole. 28 Water of life. 29 Knock. 30 Henry Ford. 31 Flute. 32 *Angela's Ashes*. 33 Brazen Head. 34 Tara. 35 Australia. 36 Small hill. 37 Books. 38 Kilkenny. 39 Armagh. 40 Mary. 41 Eat it (it's a cheese). 42 Rudolf Nureyev. 43 Tweed. 44 Australia. 45 Guinness. 46 Potatoes. 47 Franklin D Roosevelt. 48 Yeats. 49 Phoenix Park. 50 St George's.

QUIZ 168. THE HEADLINES
1 His front teeth. 2 Donald Campbell. 3 Kiev. 4 Cuban Missile. 5 Galtieri. 6 Ford. 7 Pennsylvania. 8 Rafsanjani. 9 Elton John. 10 Johnson. 11 2002. 12 Oklahoma. 13 The Philippines. 14 East Sussex. 15 Martin McGuinness. 16 Donald Dewar. 17 Akihito. 18 Yeltsin. 19 Hyde. 20 Viagra.

QUIZ 169. TRAVEL
1 Estonia, Latvia and Lithuania. 2 Portugal. 3 Barcelona. 4 Manhattan. 5 Bayern. 6 Dublin. 7 Iron. 8 Jutland. 9 Black Forest. 10 Florida. 11 Trees. 12 Switzerland. 13 Kiev. 14 Cave paintings. 15 13,000. 16 Under the Arc de Triomphe. 17 Camargue. 18 Belgium. 19 French & German. 20 Hungary.

QUIZ 170. OLOGIES
1 Dreams. 2 Stamp collecting. 3 Science of fermentation. 4 Peace. 5 Snakes. 6 Picture postcards. 7 Algae. 8 Crustaceans. 9 Oneself. 10 Ants.

QUIZ 171. GUESS WHO . . . ?
1 John Paul II. 2 Truman Capote. 3 Franz Beckenbauer. 4 Marvin Gaye. 5 James Dean. 6 Bob Beamon. 7 Robert Mugabe. 8 Bill Haley. 9 Frank Bruno. 10 Robert De Niro.

QUIZ 172. PROVERBS
1 Absence. 2 Apple. 3 Old dog. 4 The devil. 5 Discretion. 6 At home. 7 The pen. 8 Pride. 9 Early. 10 Beauty. 11 Hunger. 12 Curiosity. 13 A leopard. 14 Rome. 15 The baby.

QUIZ 173. MUSICAL MOVIES
1 Argentina. 2 Travolta. 3 Gene. 4 Penguins. 5 Diana Ross. 6 *West Side Story*. 7 *Grease*. 8 *The Rocky Horror Show*. 9 Show Business. 10 Louis Armstrong. 11 John Travolta. 12 Austria 13 *Funny Girl*. 14 The Beatles. 15 *Calamity Jane*. 16 *Mary Poppins*. 17 Bee Gees. 18 New York. 19 Harrison. 20 Maurice Chevalier.

QUIZ 174. HALF CHANCE
1 Rose. 2 Aviator. 3 Poland. 4 Cycling.5 Industry. 6 Scotland. 7 Benz. 8 Irving Berlin. 9 Jane Asher. 10 Thatcher. 11 BG. 12 Thomas. 13 Nile. 14 Congress. 15 Morocco. 16 J R R (Tolkein). 17 Landlord. 18 Carpenter. 19 1960s. 20 Bombs.

QUIZ 175. w.w.w.
1 Brazil. 2 Hungary. 3 Iceland. 4 Poland. 5 Turkey. 6 Nicaragua. 7 Lithuania. 8 Malta. 9 Armenia. 10 Laos.

QUIZ 176. FRIENDS
1 False. 2 True. 3 False. 4 True. 5 True. 6 False. 7 False. 8 True. 9 True. 10 False.

QUIZ 177. THE BIBLE
1 Moses. 2 Bethlehem. 3 Bees. 4 Donkey. 5 12. 6 Sarah. 7 Andrew. 8 Matthew. 9 Eden. 10 Saul. 11 Daniel. 12 Genesis. 13 Emeralds. 14 Salome. 15 Pillar of salt.

QUIZ 178. GENERAL KNOWLEDGE
1. A flowering plant. 2 Car crash. 3 Boris Karloff. 4 Henry Morton Stanley discovered David Livingstone. 5 Hydrogen. 6 Mrs Malaprop in Sheridan's *The Rivals*. 7 The Gordon Setter (after the Duke of Richmond and Gordon). 8 John Mortimer. 9 Flanders and Swann. 10 George IV. 11 Scotland. 12 One. 13 Phrenologists. 14 Richmal Crompton. 15 St. Petersburg. 16 Two. 17 Kilohertz. 18 Dictionaries. 19 Ivy. 20 Scottish country dancing.

QUIZ 179. AROUND OZ
1 Sydney. 2 Great Barrier Reef. 3 Ayers Rock or Uluru. 4 Perth. 5 Pacific and Indian. 6 Bondi Beach. 7 The Northern Territory. 8 Botany Bay. 9 Brisbane River. 10 Queensland. 11 Western Australia. 12 The Blue Mountains. 13 Alice Springs. 14 Melbourne. 15 Wave Rock. 16 The Gold Coast. 17 Kakadu National Park. 18 Adelaide. 19 Fraser Island. 20 Cairns.

QUIZ 180. TELEVISION
1 *Friends*. 2 Black. 3 Susan Mayer. 4 *Sex And The City*. 5 Ian Wright. 6 Girls. 7 Channel 4. 8 Richard and Judy. 9 Manchester. 10 Auctions. 11 Walters. 12 Detective. 13 Sheepdog trials. 14 Spinach. 15 Interior Designer. 16 Vanessa. 17 Wellies. 18 *Camberwick Green*. 19 Food programmes. 20 The Leftorium.

QUIZ 181. POP MUSIC
1 R.E.M. 2 The Beach Boys. 3 Blondie. 4 1970s. 5 Punk. 6 Mariah Carey. 7 Olivia Newton-John. 8 Wham!. 9 Madonna. 10 Roy Orbison. 11 Emma Bunton. 12 Ethiopia. 13 David Soul. 14 The Who. 15 Westminster Abbey. 16 Two. 17 Germany. 18 Elvis Costello. 19 The Kinks. 20 Private.

QUIZ 182. RELIGIONS
1 Jesus Christ. 2 Brazil. 3 Ecumenical Movement. 4 Jehovah's Witnesses. 5 The Salvation Army. 6 Ramadan. 7 Holy Wars. 8 Buddhism. 9 Japan. 10 Russia. 11 Quakers. 12 Hinduism. 13 Mecca. 14 Hare Krishna. 15 Moonies. 16 Book. 17 Chinese. 18 Mormons. 19 Transcendental Meditation. 20 Sunday.

QUIZ 183. LUCKY DIP
1 USA. 2 Frank Sinatra. 3 Measles. 4 Destiny's Child. 5 Dennis Lillee. 6 William. 7 Clock. 8 *Zulu*. 9 Pocus. 10 Joseph. 11 Aubergine. 12 USA. 13 Bread. 14 Cleopatra's Needle. 15 Olive. 16 Three. 17 Radioactivity. 18 Latin. 19 Tyne. 20 Julianne Moore.

QUIZ 184. PICTURE QUIZ
B) Doris Day and C) Marlon Brando.

QUIZ 185. DOUBLE TAKE
1 Class. 2 Jacks. 3 Bill. 4 Sole. 5 Drumsticks. 6 Keep. 7 Perch. 8 Shell. 9 Paste. 10 Idle.

QUIZ 186. GIRL POWER
1 Three. 2 *On My Pillow*. 3 Romania. 4 Mariah Carey. 5 Ashanti. 6 Geri Halliwell. 7 Lauper. 8 Suzi Quatro. 9 Switzerland. 10 Alanis Morissette. 11 Two. 12 1950s. 13 Faithfull. 14 Kate Bush. 15 Toni Braxton.

QUIZ 187. SPORT
1 Ferrari. 2 The Boat Race. 3 Surrey. 4 Lord's. 5 Yachting. 6 Yellow. 7 India. 8 1986. 9 Johannesburg. 10 Eric Bristow. 11 Table tennis. 12 Hanse Cronje. 13 Boxing. 14 Gianfranco Zola. 15 Cricket. 16 1950s. 17 San Francisco. 18 High jump. 19 Swimming. 20 Imola.

QUIZ 188. TREES
1 Seeds. 2 Oak. 3 Yew, Scots Pine, Juniper. 4 Laburnum. 5 White/ cream. 6 Japan. 7 Pine. 8 America. 9 Hazel. 10 Poplar. 11 Soft. 12 Sycamore. 13 General Sherman. 14 Cork oak. 15 Northumberland. 16 California. 17 Copper beech. 18 Sweet chestnut. 19 Elm. 20 5,000 years old.

QUIZ 189. GENERAL KNOWLEDGE
1 Genesis. 2 A gap or space, where something is missing. 3 Crab. 4 Thomas A Becket. 5 Belgium. 6 Oscar Wilde. 7 In your foot. 8 Spain. 9 Places of the same height. 10 The parson. 11 Beauty. 12 Laurel and Hardy. 13 Swan. 14 B. 15 Joe Louis. 16 China. 17 British admirals. 18 Long distance running. 19 Charles. 20 *The Merchant Of Venice*.

QUIZ 190. GEOGRAPHY
1 Spain. 2 Florida. 3 Northumberland. 4 Peking. 5 Buckingham Palace. 6 Austria. 7 Devon. 8 Red. 9 Derbyshire. 10 Italy. 11 Africa. 12 West. 13 Argentina. 14 Paris. 15 Portugal. 16 Algeria. 17 Thailand. 18 Scotland. 19 Oslo. 20 Africa.

QUIZ 191. SPACE
1 Stars. 2 Great Bear. 3 USA. 4 *Star Trek*. 5 1980s. 6 George. 7 Constellation. 8 Space. 9 1950s. 10 Sea of Tranquillity. 11 Gemini. 22 Burger. 13 US. 14 Marines. 15 A year. 16 Teddy bear. 17 Artificial satellites. 18 Once. 19 Light. 20 Edward White.

QUIZ 192. HALF CHANCE
1 Table tennis. 2 1980s. 3 There's. 4 1996. 5 1950s. 6 Margaret Thatcher. 7 Demi Moore. 8 Spain. 9 Martin. 10 Boy George. 11 Zimbabwe. 12 Lecter. 13 Buddy Holly. 14 Essex. 15 The Beatles. 16 Disease. 17 Terry. 18 Ernie Wise. 19 M11. 20 James Bond.

QUIZ 193. PICTURE QUIZ
A) Yul Brynner and D) Orson Welles

QUIZ 194. WHO SAID . . . ?
1 Elton John. 2 George W Bush. 3 Robin Williams. 4 Sophia Loren. 5 Meryl Streep. 6 Bob Dylan. 7 Henry Ford. 8 Salvador Dali.

QUIZ 195. MEDICINE
1 Vaccination. 2 Harvey. 3 High blood pressure. 4 Chicken pox. 5 Cancer. 6 Womb. 7 Bones. 8 Swiss. 9 Legionnaires'. 10 Heart. 11 Nigeria. 12 Netherlands. 13 Muscles. 14 Japan. 15 Light.

QUIZ 196. LUCKY DIP
1 Malta. 2 Aries. 3 The Stars And Stripes. 4 Stevie Wonder. 5 Camel. 6 Gills. 7 Three. 8 Charlene. 9 Extinction. 10 Blood. 11 Bachelor of Arts. 12 The heart. 13 Celine Dion. 14 Menelaus. 15 Spiders. 16 Mimi's (in La Bohème). 17 Five. 18 The lips. 19 Berlin. 20 Lettuce.

QUIZ 197. HEAVY METAL
1 Aerosmith. 2 Australia. 3 Black Sabbath. 4 Guns 'N' Roses. 5 Iron Maiden. 6 Anthrax. 7 Whitesnake. 8 Led Zeppelin. 9 Sleeps. 10 UK. 11 Night. 12 Def Leppard. 13 Keyboards. 14 Vanilla. 15 Iron Maiden. 16 Machine Head. 17 Went partly deaf. 18 Rainbow. 19 Robert Plant. 20 John.

QUIZ 198. HISTORY
1 Andrei Sakharov. 2 Gdansk. 3 Robert Runcie. 4 Wilson. 5 John Adams (later 2nd US President). 6 Louis Armstrong. 7 Jeffrey Archer. 8 The future Edward VIII. 9 (Paul Julius) Reuter. 10 Raisa. 11 Arthur Ransome. 12 Paul Robeson. 13 Queen Anne. 14 Joachim von Ribbentrop. 15 Macmillan. 16 John Major. 17 Thabo Mbeki. 18 Asquith. 19 John D Rockefeller. 20 Flushing toilet.

QUIZ 199. SCIENCE
1 Calculator. 2 Cars. 3 Sewing machine. 4 Sun. 5 1970s. 6 1960s. 7 Two. 8 Water. 9 Read. 10 Camera. 11 Hyper. 12 Internet. 13 Stars. 14 Menu. 15 Bar. 16 Space flight. 17 Penicillin. 18 X-rays. 19 Bunsen burner. 20 Ernest Rutherford.

QUIZ 200. TELEVISION COMEDY
1 Ellen DeGeneres. 2 *Ally McBeal*. 3 Beavis. 4 Hill. 5 Six. 6 Seattle. 7 Philadelphia. 8 *The Brady Bunch*. 9 Archie Bunker. 10 Girls' boarding school. 11 Final episode of *Cheers*. 12 1950s. 13 *Happy Days*. 14 Miami. 15 *Empty Nest*. 16 *A Different World*. 17 Gomez. 18 Officer Dibble. 19 Boston Red Sox. 20 Cockroach.

QUIZ 201. THE ARTS
1 Rabbits. 2 England. 3 Hercule Poirot. 4 Three. 5 Wales. 6 Butterfly. 7 Milan. 8 New Zealand. 9 David Essex. 10 Ireland. 11 *Frankenstein*. 12 Diary. 13 Germaine Greer. 14 Hampshire. 15 Cannes Film Festival. 16 Buckett. 17 Dick Francis. 18 Stephen King. 19 Madrid. 20 Richard Rogers.

QUIZ 202. NAME GAME
1 Dinah Washington. 2 Alan Alda. 3 Stevie Wonder. 4 John Wayne. 5 Tammy Wynette. 6 Al Jolson. 7 Muddy Waters. 8 Shirley MacLaine. 9 Bill Wyman. 10 Fred Astaire.

QUIZ 203. GUESS WHO . . . ?
1 Bill Clinton. 2 Jimi Hendrix. 3 Agatha Christie. 4 Kirk Douglas. 5 David Beckham. 6 Willie Carson. 7 George Harrison. 8 Sharon Osbourne. 9 Mia Farrow. 10 Andre Agassi.

QUIZ 204. NEWSPAPERS
1 *The Sun*. 2 Japan. 3 *The Times*. 4 France. 5 *The Sun*. 6 Dundee. 7 17th. 8 Hamburg. 9 Denmark. 10 Woodward. 11 Madrid. 12 Australia. 13 Antwerp. 14 *The Sunday Times*. 15 1801.

QUIZ 205. GREAT BUILDINGS
1 Canterbury. 2 International competition. 3 Marble. 4 Etoile. 5 St. Paul's. 6 Eiffel Tower. 7 Ivan the Terrible. 8 San Marco. 9 Cardinal Wolsey. 10 Devonshire. 11 Castle Howard. 12 It has sunk into the ground. 13 Fifth Avenue. 14 Mexico. 15 Versailles. 16 Chicago. 17 Cologne. 18 F.W. Woolworth. 19 Venus de Milo. 20 1894.

QUIZ 206. GENERAL KNOWLEDGE
1 Iris. 2 Mime. 3 Chicago. 4 Trevor Howard. 5 Bristol. 6 Fungus. 7 Elizabeth. 8 Thomas More. 9 Violin. 10 Cuba. 11 Phoenix. 12 Marx Brothers. 13 Piebald. 14 Stoat. 15 Sea sickness. 16 Poland. 17 Acute. 18 *Animal Farm*. 19 Cup and lip. 20 Rhesus.

QUIZ 207. PEOPLE
1 Jack Ryan. 2 Patricia Highsmith. 3 Jackie Coogan. 4 Ambassador to Britain. 5 Red. 6 Sam Wanamaker. 7 Harry Secombe & Peter Sellers. 8 Golf's British Open. 9 France. 10 *Oops I Did It Again*! 11 Mel B. 12 Versace. 13 Stevens. 14 Matt Lucas. 15 Amnesty International. 16 Truman. 17 Hawaii. 18 Red Brigade. 19 Patton. 20 George Bush (Snr).

QUIZ 208. HOT WHEELS
1 Micharl Schumacher. 2 Malcolm Campbell. 3 2.5 miles. 4 Lotus. 5 One. 6 Eddie Merckx. 7 Never. 8 France. 9 Bernie Ecclestone. 10 Magny Cours. 11 Nigel Mansell. 12 Oulton Park. 13 Stock car racing. 14 Annually. 15 John Surtees. 16 Uncle. 17 Honda. 18 Jack Brabham. 19 Ferrari. 20 Gerhard Berger.

QUIZ 209. LUCKY DIP
1 Thailand 2 Scotland. 3 Nothing. 4 Nancy. 5 Eight. 6 Cousin. 7 Michelle. 8 Circus. 9 The sun. 10 Squash. 11 London. 12 White. 13 Peach. 14 Wall Street. 15 Duke. 16 Jack. 17 Squash. 18 Horse racing. 19 Rice. 20 Needle.

QUIZ 210. ELTON JOHN
1 *Rocket Man*. 2 1998. 3 45 weeks. 4 Watford. 5 Rocket. 6 September. 7 Pavarotti. 8 Cat. 9 Four. 10 Blue. 11 *Don't Go Breaking My Heart*. 12 *Caribou*. 13 Long John Baldry. 14 *Honky Chateau*. 15 German. 16 *Skyline Pigeon*. 17 1976. 18 Kiki Dee. 19 *Believe*. 20 Sean Lennon.

QUIZ 211. PICTURE QUIZ
A) Tammy Wynette born Virginia Pugh. Others are B) Art Garfunkel. C) Clint Eastwood. D) Goldie Hawn.

QUIZ 212. NAME THE YEAR
1 2000. 2 1966. 3 1953. 4 2002. 5 1973. 6 1987.

QUIZ 213. HALF CHANCE
1 Earl Spencer. 2 Stevie Wonder. 3 S. 4 Drew. 5 Breathing. 6 Manchester. 7 Twist. 8 Scott. 9 None. 10 Scotland. 11 Salad dressing. 12 Cardiff. 13 Japan. 14 Acquired. 15 Isle of Man. 16 Goebbels. 17 Golf. 18 Chile. 19 Guitar. 20 India.

QUIZ 214. EASTER QUIZ
1 Lent. 2 Ash Wednesday. 3 The wilderness. 4 Without meat. 5 Hot Cross Buns. 6 21st March. 7 Good Friday. 8 Maundy Thursday. 9 Pacific. 10 Hanga-Roa. 11 Dublin. 12 22nd March. 13 25th April. 14 The Resurrection of Christ. 15 Chile. 16 Passover. 17 Christ's crucifixion. 18 Palm Sunday. 19 Two. 20 Gene Kelly. 21 French. 22 Shrove Tuesday. 23 Fat Tuesday. 24 On a donkey. 25 Aries or Taurus. 26 Daffodil. 27 Ascension Day. 28 Holi. 29 February or March. 30 Esther. 31 May Pole. 32 The May Queen. 33 Dragon. 34 Easter. 35 Ramadan. 36 Lamb. 37 1st April.

38 St Patrick's Day. 39 Hinduism. 40 Good Friday. 41 Sikh. 42 Pentecost. 43 Judy Garland. 44 Pancakes. 45 Leek. 46 Jewish. 47 Scotland (St Andrew's Day). 48 Rose. 49 Eggs. 50 Holy Week.

QUIZ 215. AT THE MOVIES
1 Robin Williams. 2 DeVito. 3 Cambodia. 4 Michael J Fox. 5 *West Side Story*. 6 Mancini. 7 John F Kennedy. 8 Dirty. 9 John Williams. 10 Stone. 11 Russell. 12 Demi Moore. 13 1950s. 14 Cage. 15 Liza Minnelli. 16 View. 17 Friel. 18 Ryan. 19 Marilyn Monroe. 20 1940s.

QUIZ 216. COPS AND ROBBERS
1 Glasgow. 2 Frank. 3 Poetry. 4 *Dixon of Dock Green*. 5 Ruth Rendell. 6 Kojak. 7 Martin Shaw. 8 Jim. 9 Murders. 10 Pierce Brosnan. 11 Raymond Burr. 12 Pepper. 13 Jemima Shore. 14 Tubbs. 15 Basset hound. 16 Dave & Ken. 17 *Hawaii Five-O*. 18 Los Angeles. 19 Magnum. 20 *The Avengers*.

QUIZ 217. NATURE
1 Eyes. 2 Ostrich. 3 Fungus. 4 It dies. 5 Water. 6 Earthquake. 7 Sand. 8 Less. 9 Metal. 10 Fish. 11 Eagle. 12 Warmer. 13 Volcanic rock. 14 Dolphin. 15 Tree. 16 None. 17 Female. 18 Cloud. 19 Sun. 20 Fossil.

QUIZ 218. THE HEADLINES
1 Hurricanes (that hit Florida). 2 Germany. 3 Donkey Kong. 4 Cuba. 5 Palestine. 6 1940. 7 Chile. 8 Chirac. 9 Reagan. 10 1960s. 11 China. 12 Greenham Common. 13 Gromyko. 14 Salisbury. 15 Honecker. 16 McCartney. 17 Alabama. 18 Charles Manson. 19 Warren. 20 Althorp.

QUIZ 219. SPIRITS AND COCKTAILS
1 Cactus. 2 Schnapps. 3 Rye. 4 Scotch whisky and heather honey. 5 Nutmeg. 6 Angostura bitters. 7 Bacardi and lime juice. 8 Cointreau. 9 Vodka. 10 Manhattan. 11 Pears. 12 Cherry brandy. 13 On crushed ice. 14 Bronx. 15 Cherries. 16 Orange and lemon. 17 Rum and Coca Cola. 18 Mr Callaghan. 19 Cocktail onion. 20 Chocolate.

QUIZ 220. GENERAL KNOWLEDGE
1 Henry Cooper. 2 Her father, King George VI. 3 *Lusitania*. 4 Sociology. 5 *For The Good Times*. 6 William III and Mary II. 7 New Zealander. 8 York. 9 Leda. 10 Loving Kiss. 11 Lieutenant Pinkerton. 12 The stamen. 13 The Prince of Wales. 14 William Wilberforce. 15 Blucher. 16 Greyfriars. 17 Tony Curtis. 18 Hatred of foreigners. 19 Harold Macmillan. 20 The Acts of the Apostles 1.

QUIZ 221. PICTURE QUIZ
They are all nicknames of US states. A) Badger. B) Bear. C) Beaver. D) Sunflower.

QUIZ 222. HORSES
1 True. 2 False. 3 True. 4 True. 5 False. 6 True. 7 False. 8 True. 9 False. 10 True.

QUIZ 223. FLAGS
1 Red/Green. 2 Red. 3 Three. 4 White. 5 Black. 6 Germany. 7 Two. 8 Lebanon. 9 Brazil. 10 Israel. 11 Red. 12 Four. 13 South Korea. 14 White/Red. 15 White.

QUIZ 224. PERFORMING ARTS
1 Glyndebourne. 2 Halle. 3 Voices. 4 Savoy. 5 Opera and ballet. 6 Alan Ayckbourn. 7 Royal Ballet. 8 Piano-style keyboard. 9 Placido Domingo. 10 Four. 11 National. 12 Joey. 13 Triangular. 14 Baritone. 15 Edinburgh. 16 New York. 17 Theatre Royal. 18 Trumpet. 19 George I. 20 Nigel Kennedy.

QUIZ 225. HALF CHANCE
1 Boston. 2 None. 3 Slowly. 4 Jimi Hendrix. 5 Egypt. 6 Morpheus. 7 1971. 8 Fastest moving. 9 Jasper Carrott. 10 Eight. 11 Singing. 12 The robin. 13 Neon lights. 14 France. 15 Porgy. 16 Argentina. 17 Puck. 18 Keith Reid. 19 Sophia Loren. 20 Canada.

QUIZ 226. LUCKY DIP
1 Ace. 2 Shaggy. 3 Veins. 4 Soccer. 5 Quark. 6 England. 7 Rex Williams. 8 Newfoundland. 9 Hot. 10 Scotland. 11 Adonis. 12 Cutting. 13 Aardvark. 14 Flags. 15 Harold Macmillan. 16 Ventriloquist. 17 Mary Baker Eddy. 18 Blow it. 19 Tower of London. 20 Brazil, Colombia and Ecuador.

QUIZ 227. ROLLING STONES
1 40 Licks. 2 Watts. 3 David Bowie. 4 None. 5 Red. 6 Jagger & Richards. 7 Bill Wyman. 8 Satisfaction. 9 Wood. 10 Black.11 *Voodoo Lounge*. 12 Bill Wyman. 13 *Honky Tonk Women*. 14 Harmonica. 15 Drowned. 16 Marianne Faithfull. 17 Dandelion. 18 Bleed. 19 *Beggar's Banquet*. 20 Zip.

QUIZ 228. TRAVEL
1 Fifth Avenue. 2 Romania. 3 Tbilisi. 4 Vienna. 5 Gulf of Riga. 6 Brussels. 7 Austria. 8 Koper. 9 Italy. 10 Baltic. 11 Netherlands. 12 Hawaii. 13 Gulf of Finland. 14 Great Britain. 15 Mount Etna and Stromboli. 16 Grande Dizence in Switzerland. 17 Finland. 18 London. 19 Germany. 20 Liechtenstein.

QUIZ 229. ANIMALS
1 Suffocation. 2 Sett. 3 Velvet. 4 Black. 5 Dachshund. 6 It cannot bark. 7 Afrikaans. 8 Mauritius. 9 Antelope. 10 Snow leopard. 11 Fight. 12 Squirrel. 13 One. 14 Sheep & goats. 15 Hearing. 16 32. 17 Fawn. 18 Hooves. 19 Blood of birds and mammals. 20 Sheep

QUIZ 230. ANIMAL LIKE
1 Cat. 2 Sheep. 3 Bee. 4 Bear. 5 Monkey. 6 Eagle. 7 Fox. 8 Wolf. 9 Deer. 10 Lizard.

QUIZ 231. DOUBLE TAKE
1 March. 2 Castle. 3 Package. 4 Lead. 5 Morse. 6 Dates. 7 Crib. 8 Bass. 9 Foil. 10 Ford.

QUIZ 232.WITCHES
1 Black. 2 Lancashire. 3 Cat. 4 Three. 5 Familiar. 6 White. 7 Eagles. 8 Hopkins. 9 River. 10 Drowned. 11 Sabrina. 12 Coven. 13 Tituba. 14 Hazel. 15 West.

QUIZ 233. SCANDALS & DISASTERS
1 Mark Thatcher. 2 Australian. 3 Canary Islands. 4 Earthquake. 5 Aeroplane. 6 Road rage. 7 Ethiopia. 8 England. 9 Tour de France. 10 Three Mile Island. 11 Tenerife. 12 Richard Nixon. 13 Aberfan. 14 Munich. 15 Profumo Affair. 16 Cora. 17 Wallis Simpson. 18 Nottingham Forest. 19 Zeebrugge. 20 Camilla Parker Bowles.

QUIZ 234. TELEVISION
1 No 42. 2 *Neighbours*. 3 Bree van de Kamp. 4 Moe's Tavern. 5 Brady Hobbes. 6 Raymond Craddock. 7 Lawyers. 8 Helen. 9 Dervla Kirwan. 10 Snail. 11 Rosario. 12 Boston. 13 Dr Finlay. 14 Bubble. 15 Riley. 16 Melbourne. 17 Jennifer Ehle. 18 Steve Coogan. 19 *Open All Hours*. 20 Green.

QUIZ 235. DICTATORS
1 Austria. 2 1979. 3 Pol Pot. 4 Night of the Long Knives. 5 Born the same year. 6 Axis. 7 Italian Resistance. 8 Tonton Macoute. 9 First Consul. 10 Elba. 11 Generalissimus. 12 Man of steel. 13 National Movement. 14 1939. 15 Marcos. 16 Begnino Aquino. 17 Galtieri. 18 Very Mighty Ruler. 19 13 years old. 20 Mao Tse Tung.

QUIZ 236. GENERAL KNOWLEDGE
1 Spanish. 2 *Hamlet*. 3 Hindu. 4 Henry V. 5 Squirrel. 6 Zimbabwe. 7 The Medway. 8 His nose. 9 Cricket. 10 Keith Richard. 11 Isaac. 12 James II. 13 Canary. 14 Manitoba. 15 Italy. 16 Battle of Bosworth. 17 Noel Coward. 18 Bench. 19 Canada. 20 Eyes.

QUIZ 237. VILLAINS
1 Saudi Arabia. 2 Spain. 3 Anthony Blunt. 4 Hanged publicly. 5 Pentonville. 6 Australia. 7 15 victims. 8 Charles Brooks. 9 Oklahoma. 10 7th November. 11 *Let Him Have It*. 12 Martin Luther King. 13 Hungerford. 14 Karla Faye Tucker. 15 Hezbollah. 16 Rachid. 17 Fingerprints. 18 Carlos the Jackal. 19 Jack the Ripper. 20 Mary Bell.

QUIZ 238. FOOD AND DRINK
1 Liebfraumilch. 2 Warm. 3 Salsa. 4 Stomach remedy. 5 Ice cream. 6 Tomatoes. 7 Crescent shaped (roll). 8 Steen. 9 Stum. 10 Browned at the edges due to age. 11 Sicily. 12 Semi-sparkling, fully sparkling. 13 Calzone. 14 Maize. 15 Grapes are partly sun-dried before use. 16 San Lorenzo. 17 Portugal. 18 Oenology. 19 Britain. 20 Blood.

QUIZ 239. PICTURE QUIZ
They are all names of parts of the body. A) Ear (of corn). B) (Chewing) gum. C (Electric) organ. D (Elephant's) trunk.

QUIZ 240. NAME THE YEAR
1 1941. 2 1989. 3 1998. 4 1981. 5 1972. 6 1980.

QUIZ 241. HALF CHANCE
1 Britney Spears. 2 Bird. 3 Everest. 4 Holly. 5 Grimaldi. 6 Snowstorm. 7 Canada. 8 Virgo. 9 Patrick. 10 Tyres. 11 Dylan. 12 Croatia. 13 Bulb. 14 Private Frazer. 15 A bird. 16 Dorien. 17 Salmon. 18 Gold. 19 Yuppies. 20 France.

QUIZ 242. AROUND ASIA
1 Burma. 2 Fiji. 3 Gobi. 4 King. 5 Philippines. 6 Taiwan. 7 Indonesia. 8 North & South Korea. 9 East Pakistan. 10 Malaysia. 11 Coral. 12 Cambodia. 13 Caspian. 14 Mount Fujiyama. 15 One. 16 India. 17 Terracotta. 18 Mongolia's. 19 India & Pakistan. 20 Caste system.

QUIZ 243. LUCKY DIP
1 Beautiful. 2 720. 3 Sweden. 4 Edward II. 5 Clove. 6 None. 7 Silver. 8 Jean Harlow. 9 Atlas. 10 February. 11 Eurovision. 12 Bryan Adams. 13 Birds. 14 San Francisco Bay. 15 Rats. 16 Nancy Sinatra. 17 Abel. 18 Mowgli. 19 All Blacks. 20 Thailand.

QUIZ 244. CAPITALS
1 Nigeria. 2 Mozambique. 3 Ghana. 4 Philippines. 5 Zambia. 6 Barbados. 7 Indonesia. 8 Venezuela. 9 Colombia. 10 Senegal.

QUIZ 245. GUESS WHO . . . ?
1 John F Kennedy. 2 Boris Becker.

3 Buddy Holly. 4 Princess Diana. 5 Carrie Fisher. 6 Charles Dickens. 7 Linda McCartney. 8 Janet Jackson. 9 Rubens Barrichello. 10 Jane Fonda.

QUIZ 246. SUPERMODELS & CELEBS
1 Brightman. 2 Sophie. 3 Jules. 4 Madonna. 5 Nigella. 6 Wales. 7 Harrison. 8 Cricketer. 9 Michael. 10 Hervey. 11 Hurley. 12 New Zealand. 13 Twiggy. 14 "The Body". 15 Rapture.

QUIZ 247. WEATHER
1 Egypt. 2 Matters of the atmosphere. 3 Solstice. 4 Cumbria. 5 Cold front. 6 Fastnet. 7 Rockies. 8 Isobars. 9 Cirrus. 10 Mirage, Strait of Messina, Italy. 11 Doldrums. 12 12. 13 Alaska (wind). 14 Grey. 15 Russian wind. 16 Occluded front. 17 Typhoon. 18 Spain. 19 German Bight. 20 South Africa.

QUIZ 248. POP MUSIC
1 Westlife. 2 The Darkness. 3 Wet Wet Wet. 4 *Chapter II*. 5 Bob Geldof. 6 Take That. 7 Pink Floyd. 8 Smashing Pumpkins. 9 The Eagles. 10 Weller. 11 He shot himself. 12 Sinead O'Connor. 13 *Wannabe*. 14 Prodigy. 15 Eternal. 16 Your head. 17 Manilow. 18 John Travolta. 19 USA. 20 Meat Loaf.

QUIZ 249. GENERAL KNOWLEDGE
1 Back (hind). 2 Shirley Temple. 3 Discretion. 4 Saxophone. 5 Rubgy Union. 6 Paddington. 7 *The Third Man*. 8 Pittsburgh. 9 In an electric train, tube train. 10 Lionel Bart. 11 Western Australia. 12 Iran. 13 Alexandra Palace. 14 Henry Ford. 15 George Washington. 16 Dunkirk. 17 Frank Lloyd Wright. 18 Jonathan Swift. 19 Khartoum. 20 A bat.

QUIZ 250. PLANET EARTH
1 South Dakota. 2 Copper. 3 Walrus. 4 West Spitsbergen. 5 Sonoran. 6 Silicon. 7 Great Wall of China. 8 Sulphur. 9 Strathclyde. 10 South Africa. 11 New Guinea. 12 Four. 13 Mountain chains. 14 Coral. 15 Western Mongolia. 16 Radiation. 17 Low temperatures. 18 Novaya. 19 Soil. 20 Six.

QUIZ. 251. SPORT
1 Martina Navratilova. 2 Bobby Charlton. 3 Spain. 4 Alec Stewart. 5 Kansas Cannonball. 6 Robin Knox-Johnson. 7 Army. 8 John McEnroe. 9 Reardon. 10 Monocle. 11 Montreal. 12 Seles. 13 American golf course. 14 Jackie Stewart. 15 Ruud Gullit. 16 Red Rum. 17 Rusedski. 18 Wisden. 19 Sugar Ray Robinson. 20 Canada.

QUIZ 252. THE 1980s
1 UK and Eire. 2 Chernobyl. 3 FW de Klerk. 4 Dubcek. 5 Salman Rushdie. 6 Michael Foot. 7 Francois Mitterrand. 8 Galtieri. 9 Bruce Springsteen. 10 Jamaica. 11 Greenpeace. 12 Diet Coke. 13 Twice. 14 Peter Shilton. 15 Ken Livingstone. 16 Monday. 17 The Labour Party. 18 Grand Hotel. 19 Slobodan Milosevic. 20 Montserrat.

QUIZ 253. PICTURE QUIZ
All have things named after them. A) Anna Pavlova. B) Mae West. C) Nellie Melba. D) Teddy Roosevelt.

QUIZ 254. THE ORCHESTRA
1 True. 2 False. 3 True. 4 True. 5 False. 6 False. 7 True. 8 False. 9 False. 10 False.

QUIZ 255. PALACES AND BUILDINGS
1 French President. 2 1703. 3 Paris. 4 Kent. 5 Crystal Palace. 6 Oxfordshire. 7 Lancet. 8 Danish. 9 Clerestory. 10 Damascus. 11 Germany. 12 Cambridge. 13 Nash. 14 St Mark's. 15 Kensington.

QUIZ 256. LUCKY DIP
1 Dressing. 2 Cat. 3 Bizet. 4 Rope. 5 Soup. 6 Kensington Gardens. 7 Candles. 8 Having the same centre. 9 Pinocchio 10 *The Pickwick Papers*. 11 Bread. 12 John Bunyan. 13 Orlando. 14 Wines. 15 Swan. 16 South Africa 17 Fashion 18 The Crusades. 19 Fish. 20 Theatres.

QUIZ 257. GEOGRAPHY
1 Persia. 2 Third World. 3 France. 4 Mediterranean. 5 Greece. 6 Florida. 7 Oxfordshire. 8 Spain. 9 Brighton. 10 On the coast. 11 Adriatic. 12 South. 13 Victoria. 14 Argentina. 15 Europe. 16 Malta. 17 Cyprus. 18 Canary Islands. 19 France. 20 Arctic.

QUIZ 258. HOBBIES
1 Angling. 2 Lacrosse. 3 Padstow, Cornwall. 4 Underwater hockey. 5 Houston, Texas. 6 The Roux Brothers. 7 Hampton Court maze. 8 Blue, red, yellow or black. 9 Ripon. 10 Scrabble. 11 Marbles. 12 Trainspotter. 13 Milton Keynes. 14 Gatwick. 15 Terence Conran. 16 9th to 11th. 17 10 points. 18 Bowls. 19 Hail. 20 Harmonica.

QUIZ 259. HALF CHANCE
1 *Girlfriend*. 2 Jester. 3 Yugoslavia. 4 London. 5 Raise the pitch. 6 William 7 Four. 8 1930s. 9 India. 10 Broad beans. 11 Sondheim. 12 Hound. 13 Commander. 14 Florida. 15 Canada. 16 Italy. 17 Horizontally. 18 *The Muppets*. 19 Sailing. 20 Wood.

QUIZ 260. MOTHER'S DAY QUIZ
1 Vanessa Redgrave. 2 Hillary. 3 Lent. 4 Linda McCartney. 5 Jamie Lee Curtis. 6 Jane Seymour. 7 Allison Pearson. 8 May. 9 Demi Moore. 10 Judy Garland. 11 Necessity. 12 Margaret Thatcher. 13 Zoe Ball. 14 Joan Crawford. 15 Lily of the Valley. 16 Victoria Beckham. 17 Keep quiet. 18 Mother Goose. 19 Necessity. 20 Barbara. 21 Anne. 22 Yoko Ono. 23 Mother of pearl. 24 Patsy Kensit. 25 Aretha Franklin. 26 Brecht. 27 Maureen Lipman. 28 Paul Simon. 29 Kate Hudson. 30 Simnel cake. 31 Cybill Shepherd. 32 Duchess of York (Sarah Ferguson). 33 *Singin' In the Rain*. 34 Abba. 35 Madre. 36 Marzipan/almonds. 37 Madonna. 38 Rose. 39 Two. 40 Mother tongue. 41 Queen Elizabeth II. 42 Jason Connery. 43 Prunella Scales. 44 Mia Farrow's adopted daughter married Woody Allen. 45 Diana Princess of Wales. 46 Cherie Blair. 47 Mother Goose rhyme. 48 Dame Judi Dench. 49 Egypt. 50 Gwyneth Paltrow.

QUIZ 261. GENERAL KNOWLEDGE
1 Edward Heath. 2 Alan Shepard. 3 Crufts. 4 Evil to him who evil thinks it. 5 Psychology. 6 Formic acid. 7 George III. 8 Fred Perry. 9 The Crimea. 10 Meal. 11 Laughing gas. 12 Terpsichore. 13 Jimi Hendrix. 14 Roman Empire. 15 Children. 16 Red. 17 Elizabeth. 18 *The Times*. 19 Flowers. 20 Dermatology.

QUIZ 262. FRANK SINATRA
1 1910s (1915). 2 Ole Blue Eyes. 3 A Horse And Carriage. 4 *Three Coins in the Fountain*. 5 Albert. 6 *From Here To Eternity*. 7 Reprise 8 *Strangers in the Night*. 9 *Nancy (With the Laughing Face)*. 10 Paul Anka. 11 *I've Got You Under My Skin*. 12 *Pal Joey*. 13 Grace Kelly. 14 Mia Farrow. 15 1960s. 16 Frank Junior. 17 Chicago. 18 New York. 19 Al Martino. 20 *It Might As Well Be Swing*.

QUIZ 263. AT THE MOVIES
1 Harrelson. 2 Pierce Brosnan. 3 Clarice. 4 Belgium. 5 Irene Cara. 6 Tarzan. 7 Diane Keaton. 8 John Travolta. 9 Christie. 10 1990s. 11 Ryan O'Neal. 12 *The Third Man*. 13 Australia. 14 Matthau. 15 John Wayne. 16 1960s. 17 Raiders. 18 Gwyneth Paltrow. 19 Basinger. 20 Glenn Close.

QUIZ 264. BANDS
1 Coldplay. 2 Radiohead. 3 The Monkees. 4 Police. 5 Illinois. 6 Usher. 7 Pink Floyd. 8 Dire Straits. 9 Creedence Clearwater Revival. 10 5th Dimension. 11 Time. 12 The Beach Boys. 13 Blondie. 14 Van Halen. 15 Foreigner. 16 Tommy James. 17 Five. 18 Bob Dylan. 19 Fleetwood Mac. 20 Tom Petty.

QUIZ 265. HISTORY
1 Kennedy 2 France. 3 UK and Ireland. 4 Romanovs. 5 Eton. 6 Crimean War. 7 Edmund Hillary 8 Hitler. 9 17. 10 Ronald Reagan 11 Mary Robinson. 12 Alabama. 13 Helmut Kohl. 14 Kofi Annan. 15 Flora's maid. 16 Donald Maclean. 17 Argentina. 18 Lord Mountbatten. 19 Axis. 20 Whitechapel.

QUIZ 266. SCIENCE
1 IBM. 2 Star sailor. 3 40 million. 4 Mars. 5 Genetic engineering. 6 Kodak. 7 Orion. 8 Calcium hydroxide. 9 Czechoslovakia. 10 Tibia. 11 Vomiting. 12 Titan. 13 Dialysis machine. 14 Five. 15 Kinetic energy. 16 Neptune. 17 Lungs. 18 Therapeutics plc. 19 Jupiter. 20 1880s.

QUIZ 267. PICTURE QUIZ
B) Elton John. (The others are: A) *Bette Davis Eyes*. C) *Ra-Ra-Rasputin*. D) *Robert de Niro's Waiting*.)

QUIZ 268. DOUBLE TAKE
1 Pupil. 2 Top. 3 Nag. 4 Oasis. 5 Stud. 6 Duck. 7 Truffle. 8 Novel. 9 Kid. 10 Satsuma.

QUIZ 269. CLOCKS AND TIME
1 Switzerland. 2 March (after Mars). 3 Winter. 4 July. 5 12 noon. 6 Orange. 7 Roman Emperor. 8 Daylight. 9 3.10. 10 16thC. 11 Julian. 12 Pendulum. 13 1,440. 14 Boxing Day. 15 Muslim.

QUIZ 270. RECORD BREAKERS
1 Swimming. 2 Brazil. 3 Sixth. 4 Long jump. 5 Australia. 6 Gunnell. 7 Glenn Hoddle. 8 Oxford. 9 15. 10 Torvill & Dean. 11 Mansell. 12 Coe. 13 Africa. 14 Ben Johnson. 15 Davis. 16 East Germany. 17 France. 18 Alan Shearer. 19 Sampras. 20 Edwards.

QUIZ 271. LUCKY DIP
1 Germany. 2 Taurus. 3 3. 4 Abba. 5 Stan Laurel. 6 Lawyer. 7 Jack and Jill. 8 Cycling. 9 Noel Coward. 10 Rule the world. 11 British Telecom. 12 Caffeine. 13 The country mouse. 14 Rugby Union. 15 Water. 16 Eight. 17 Nazareth. 18 Swastika. 19 Dog. 20 Blue and white.

QUIZ 272. AROUND AFRICA
1 Zambia and Zimbabwe. 2 The Sahara Desert. 3 Ethiopia. 4 Organisation of African Unity. 5 Burkina Faso. 6 Wind. 7 Uganda. 8 Namibia. 9 Cocoa. 10 Victoria. 11 Kilimanjaro. 12 Portuguese. 13 Libya. 14 Nigeria. 15 Rwanda. 16 Dutch. 17 Victoria Falls. 18 Sahel. 19 Gold. 20 Botswana.

QUIZ 273. THE ARTS
1 *The Crucible*. 2 Monet. 3 Charlie Parker. 4 Bob Dylan. 5 Blue. 6 Mae West. 7 *The Rainmaker*. 8 Britain. 9 French Revolution (*A Tale of Two Cities*). 10 Margaret Mitchell (*Gone With the Wind*). 11 New York. 12 *Without Remorse*. 13 Michael Ondaatje. 14 *Dr No*. 15 Curtain. 16 Great Ormond Street Hospital. 17 Barbara Taylor Bradford. 18 *Women in Love*. 19 Rodin. 20 Glastonbury Festival.

QUIZ 274. GENERAL KNOWLEDGE
1 Mary. 2 Hannibal. 3 Wilbur Smith. 4 Hyde Park. 5 Canada. 6 William Golding. 7 Cowboy. 8 Retract them. 9 Edgar Rice Burroughs. 10 Suffolk. 11 Caretaker. 12 A wig. 13 Spinning. 14 Chalk. 15 Tights. 16 One. 17 Farming, agriculture. 18 Ice. 19 Democrat, Republican. 20 Louis XVI.

QUIZ 275. WINE
1 Bordeaux. 2 Brut. 3 Australia. 4 Chardonnay. 5 New Zealand. 6 Greece. 7 Madeira. 8 75 centilitres. 9 Spain. 10 Loire. 11 White. 12 Secco. 13 Case. 14 Bulgaria. 15 California. 16 Jancis. 17 South Africa. 18 Eight. 19 Sparkling. 20 Tuscany.

QUIZ 276. PHOBIAS
1 Women. 2 Pain. 3 Dogs. 4 Touch. 5 Darkness. 6 Glass. 7 Snow. 8 Stars. 9 Horses. 10 Gravity.

QUIZ 277. GUESS WHO . . . ?
1 George Bush Snr. 2 David Coulthard. 3 Whitney Houston. 4 Harrison Ford. 5 Roger Bannister. 6 Ben Affleck. 7 Billy Joel. 8 Sir Arthur Conan Doyle. 9 Robert Redford. 10 Sir Steve Redgrave.

QUIZ 278. COMPUTERS
1 1980s. 2 Three. 3 Magenta. 4 Injury. 5 Points. 6 Virus. 7 Cell. 8 Musical. 9 Static. 10 I Love You. 11 V. 12 Justified. 13 Logic. 14 Morphing. 15 Right.

QUIZ 279. PEOPLE
1 Photography. 2 Five. 3 PR man. 4 Kathryn Dawn. 5 Luciano Pavarotti. 6 Jackie. 7 Hands. 8 Branagh. 9 Why not? 10 Victoria. 11 Chelsea. 12 Gymnastics. 13 Film star.14 Cleo Laine. 15 Austria, 16 Pears. 17 Rowing. 18 Gordonstoun school. 19 Arthur Travers. 20 Michael Caine.

QUIZ 280. THE HEADLINES
1 55 hours. 2 London. 3 Bugs Bunny. 4 Chamberlain. 5 First. 6 Gestapo. 7 Cost lives. 8 1916. 9 Morris. 10 Birth control. 11 Lenin. 12 1920s. 13 Munich. 14 Queen Mary. 15 Windsor. 16 Malta. 17 Dresden. 18 Edinburgh. 19 Halls Creek. 20 Richard Harris.

QUIZ 281. MUSICALS
1 Dolls. 2 *Sweet Charity*. 3 *Gypsy*. 4 World War II. 5 *Annie Get Your Gun*. 6 *Hair*. 7 Siam. 8 *Carousel*. 9 Superstar. 10 Horrors. 11 England. 12 *A Chorus Line*. 13 On The Roof. 14 1970s. 15 *Barnum*. 16 Texas. 17 Fosco. 18 *Chicago*. 19 *Annie*. 20 Gershwin.

QUIZ 282. HALF CHANCE
1 *Million Dollar Baby*. 2 Egypt. 3 1950s. 4 Below. 5 *Bergerac*. 6 1930s. 7 Egypt. 8 Nose. 9 Fleet Street. 10 Play it. 11 PLO. 12 Fish. 13 K2. 14 March. 15 Oil pollution. 16 Arab. 17 An insect. 18 Aeronautics. 19 *Mastermind*. 20 Travolta.

QUIZ 283. MANCHESTER UTD
1 Alex Ferguson. 2 17. 3 George Best. 4 Keith Gillespie. 5 Scotland. 6 West Ham. 7 Barcelona and Chelsea. 8 Crystal Palace. 9 Wolves. 10 Gary. 11 10. 12 First sending off in an FA Cup Final. 13 Greenhoff. 14 Ron Atkinson. 15 Eric Cantona. 16 Denmark. 17 PSV Eindhoven. 18 David. 19 Bobby Charlton and Nobby Stiles. 20 Andy Cole.

QUIZ 284. LUCKY DIP
1 Russia. 2 Mark (Deutschmark). 3 Altimeter. 4 George Michael. 5 Burt Reynolds. 6 Edward VIII. 7 Talk. 8 *Porridge*. 9 Thompson Twins. 10 *Genesis*. 11 Housemaid's Knee. 12 Italy. 13 Captain. 14 Black. 15 Cricket. 16 Seven. 17 Fish. 18 On the face. It's a nose. 19 Mersey. 20 Radiohead.

QUIZ 285. PICTURE QUIZ
Titles of musicals. A) *Carousel*. B) *Cats*. C) *Chess*. D) *Hair*.

QUIZ 286. THE 2004 OLYMPICS
1 False. 2 False. 3 True. 4 False. 5 True. 6 False. 7 True. 8 False. 9 True. 10 True.

QUIZ 287. RIVERS
1 Nile. 2 Severn. 3 Danube. 4 Portugal. 5 Clyde. 6 Niagara. 7 Nantes. 8 Mother. 9 Arno. 10 Nile. 11 South. 12 15,000. 13 Victoria. 14 Seine. 15 Murray.

QUIZ 288. GENERAL KNOWLEDGE
1 Druids. 2 Angles. 3 Carbon monoxide. 4 Islands. 5 Study of birds. 6 Australia. 7 Zloty. 8 Yellow. 9 Therefore. 10 Barrels. 11 M62. 12 Bees. 13 Spencer. 14 25th January. 15 Lodge. 16 Four. 17 Dan Dare. 18 The Sphinx. 19 Braille. 20 Guitar.

QUIZ 289. FOOD AND DRINK
1 Orange. 2 Mothering Sunday. 3 Clay ovens. 4 Edible mushroom. 5 Evaporated. 6 Balsamic vinegar. 7 Spinach. 8 Port. 9 Pressure cooker. 10 Roughage. 11 Soup. 12 Japan. 13 Gherkins (pickled cucumbers). 14 Rum. 15 Red. 16 Suet pastry. 17 Sherry. 18 Apple. 19 Scampi. 20 Soya.

QUIZ 290. OPERA
1 New Zealand. 2 Placido (Domingo), José (Carreras), Luciano (Pavarotti).3 Beethoven. 4 *The Yeomen of the Guard*. 5 Benjamin Britten. 6 American. 7 *Faust*. 8 Merry. 9 Puccini. 10 *Tourandot*. 11 *Tommy*. 12 Seville. 13 *The Threepenny Opera*. 14 Spoken dialogue. 15 Stravinsky. 16 Yorkshire. 17 Strauss. 18 Guiseppe Verdi. 19 1990 World Cup. 20 Oratorio.

QUIZ 291. TRAVEL
1 Boliviano. 2 Hudson & East. 3 Maine. 4 Brazil. 5 Bandar Seri Begawan. 6 Angola. 7 Macao. 8 Uruguay. 9 Khartoum. 10 Dzongkha. 11 Australia. 12 Brazil. 13 Algeria and Mauritania. 14 Namib desert. 15 Bogota. 16 Pennsylvania Station. 17 New Providence Island. 18 Wyoming. 19 Mount McKinley. 20 Eilat.

QUIZ 292. THE 1970s
1 Sri Lanka. 2 Graceland. 3 Cambodia. 4 Iran. 5 Princess Anne. 6 Sony. 7 Hot pants. 8 Concorde. 9 Cannes. 10 Lebanon. 11 Louis Armstrong. 12 Spain. 13 Giant Panda. 14 Killing. 15 Egypt. 16 Liza Minnelli. 17 Iran. 18 Nixon. 19 South Africa. 20 Navratilova.

QUIZ 293. TELEVISION
1 Trey MacDougal. 2 Debra Messing. 3 Clampett. 4 Gabrielle Solis. 5 Mrs (Edna) Krabappel. 6 Holby City. 7 Butcher. 8 A scarecrow. 9 Australia. 10 Alan Davies. 11 *Upstairs Downstairs*. 12 Rowan Atkinson. 13 The Addams Family. 14 *2 Point 4 Children*. 15 Run over (by a tram). 16 *Murder She Wrote*. 17 PR executive. 18 A cat. 19 *Minder*. 20 Dudley Moore.

QUIZ 294. NAME GAME
1 Christian Slater. 2 Ben Kingsley. 3 Elaine Paige. 4 Stan Laurel. 5 Eric Clapton. 6 Yves Montand. 7 Axl Rose. 8 Jane Seymour. 9 Doris Day. 10 Nicolas Cage

QUIZ 295. WHO SAID . . . ?
1 Muhammad Ali. 2 Oliver Reed. 3 Picasso. 4 Rose Fitzgerald Kennedy. 5 L.S.Lowry. 6 Sylvester Stallone. 7 Maria Callas. 8 First woman astronaut Valentina Tereshkova.

QUIZ 296. THE BLUES
1 Slowhand. 2 Yardbirds. 3 Bessie Smith. 4 Chicago. 5 Bluesbreakers. 6 Billie Holliday. 7 Hooker. 8 Harmonica. 9 Muddy Waters. 10 France. 11 Baldry. 12 Gary Moore. 13 Baker. 14 Elton John. 15 Blind.

QUIZ 297. LUCKY DIP
1 Kurt Weill. 2 Leonhard Fuchs. 3 Russian. 4 Billy Connolly. 5 Rome and Carthage. 6 Jane Austen. 7 Z. 8 Little Blake. 9 The Valkyries. 10 KGB. 11 Dustin Hoffman. 12 Everything I do. 13 Foo Fighters. 14 Mae West. 15 The 86th Precinct. 16 Plums. 17 Darby and Joan. 18 Bath. 19 Rugby Union. 20 Chukka.

QUIZ 298. INVENTIONS
1 Shorthand. 2 Sony and Philips. 3 Frisbee. 4 Italy. 5 Pullman. 6 Nestlé. 7 Chewing Gum. 8 Homes didn't have electricity. 9 Carpet sweeper. 10 Gillette. 11 Monk. 12 Felt tips. 13 Lego. 14 It doesn't bounce. 15 Paper handkerchiefs. 16 Vaccination. 17 Belgian. 18 Tram. 19 Tomato ketchup. 20 Apple.

QUIZ 299. POP MUSIC
1 Daniel Bedingfield. 2 Stipe. 3 Dire Straits. 4 Kylie Minogue. 5 *It's Raining Men*. 6 *Crocodile Rock*. 7 Mad. 8 *Bohemian Rhapsody*. 9 Frank Sinatra. 10 Four. 11 *Because We Want To*. 12 *Rotterdam*. 13 *Waterloo*. 14 Red. 15 Spice Girls. 16 *Marie* by Blondie. Deborah Harry was on vocals. 17 Bon Jovi. 18 Kate Bush. 19 UB40. 20 Duran Duran.

QUIZ 300. NATURE
1 Stem. 2 Evergreen. 3 Fungi. 4 Linen. 5 Cocaine. 6 Grass. 7 Tequila. 8 True. 9 Leaf stalk. 10 White. 11 Gin. 12 Yellow. 13 Sea. 14 Tapioca. 15 Bulbs. 16 Several. 17 Quinine. 18 Vines. 19 Blue. 20 Turpentine.

QUIZ 301. ARTISTS
1 Gainsborough. 2 Renoir. 3 Mona Lisa. 4 19th century (1853–90). 5 *The Rake's Progress*. 6 *The Laughing Cavalier*. 7 Sphinx. 8 Op Art. 9 Wet plaster. 10 Statue of Liberty. 11 Nude. 12 Engravings. 13 Impressionist. 14 Sculpture. 15 Millais. 16 Henry Moore. 17 Salvador Dali. 18 Glue. 19 Andy Warhol. 20 Portraits.

QUIZ 302. GENERAL KNOWLEDGE
1 Baloo. 2 Valetta. 3 In the neck. 4 A hawk. 5 Aurora Borealis. 6 Spanish. 7 John Milton. 8 Rabbit. 9 Pontius Pilate. 10 Bootlegger. 11 Skye. 12 Benjamin Disraeli. 13 Golf. 14 Mullion. 15 A flower

grows. 16 Ball. 17 Black. 18 Sheep. 19 Nepotism. 20 Neville Chamberlain.

QUIZ 303. PICTURE QUIZ
A The car.

QUIZ 304. NAME THE YEAR
1 1988. 2 1936. 3 1992. 4 1962. 5 1986. 6 1902.

QUIZ 305. SPORT
1 Chicago. 2 Arsene Wenger. 3 Mark O'Meara. 4 Brian Close. 5 Basketball. 6 Republic of Ireland. 7 1970s. 8 America's Cup. 9 Ernie Els. 10 Petit. 11 Hurdles. 12 14 years. 13 Georgia. 14 Skates. 15 Baseball. 16 Tiger Woods. 17 Badminton. 18 Arrows. 19 Fiji. 20 Tennis.

QUIZ 306. SUMMER QUIZ
1 June. 2 15th July. 3 40. 4 Winchester. 5 Cancer, Leo and Virgo. 6 Dog Days. 7 *Grease*. 8 *A Midsummer Night's Dream*. 9 Fruit & bread. 10 Carp. 11 June. 12 Turkey. 13 The fast. 14 Wales. 15 Sydney, Australia. 16 World Environment Day. 17 Barcelona. 18 Elton John. 19 Kansas. 20 Neil Simon. 21 Indian Summer. 22 Dominion Day. 23 London, 1908. 24 Louis XIV. 25 Cricket. 26 Lovin' Spoonful. 27 France. 28 93. 29 Prince William. 30 *Summer Holiday*. 31 France. 32 Bejing 2008. 33 Nelson Mandela. 34 June. 35 Cancer. 36 Helios. 37 9th. 38 Quarantine laws in Australia. 39 1st July. 40 Maple Leaf. 41 John The Baptist. 42 George Gershwin. 43 Buddhism. 44 Ramadan. 45 Elephant. 46 Trees. 47 Stonehenge. 48 1940s. 49 Brothers & sisters. 50 Florida.

QUIZ 307. AMERICAN LITERATURE
1 Spanish Civil War. 2 Henry James. 3 Edward Albee. 4 *Death of a Salesman*. 5 *Billy Budd*. 6 China. 7 Isaac Asimov. 8 F Scott Fitzgerald. 9 James Fenimore Cooper. 10 Ambulance driver. 11 England. 12 Philip Marlowe. 13 Dashiel Hammett. 14 March sisters. 15 *The Armies of the Night*. 16 John Steinbeck. 17 Eugene O'Neill. 18 Cuba. 19 *The Wonderful Wizard Of Oz*. 20 Sylvia Plath.

QUIZ 308. HALF CHANCE
1 Iraq. 2 Baby buggy. 3 French. 4 Beavis. 5 Henry. 6 Ghost. 7 White. 8 29th February. 9 Play. 10 Bolivia. 11 Walkman. 12 Switzerland. 13 *Top Hat*. 14 A barrel. 15 Red. 16 USA. 17 Count. 18 Wear it on the head. 19 Ash Wednesday. 20 White.

QUIZ 309. RICH AND FAMOUS
1 President George W Bush. 2 John D Rockefeller. 3 Madonna. 4 Barbara. 5 Egypt. 6 Chaplin. 7 Lourdes Maria. 8 Douglas Fairbanks. 9 Fred Astaire. 10 Baltimore. 11 Margaret Thatcher. 12 Lanfranco. 13 Explorer. 14 Andrew Lloyd Webber. 15 Grandson. 16 Maurice. 17 South Africa. 18 Her mother Linda. 19 Algeria. 20 Bourret.

QUIZ 310. ANIMALS
1 (African) elephant. 2 Wolf. 3 Warm-blooded. 4 Tooth. 5 Voice box. 6 Alone. 7 Primate. 8 Duck. 9 Dog. 10 Sheep. 11 Sight. 12 Offensive smell. 13 Brown. 14 (South) America. 15 Eye. 16 Hare. 17 Its ears. 18 Alaska. 19 Warm. 20 Carnivorous.

QUIZ 311. AT THE MOVIES
1 Austin Powers. 2 Robert Zemeckis. 3 *Moon River*. 4 Hanks. 5 Fonda. 6 *Chariots of Fire*. 7 Scar. 8 Thompson. 9 Muhammad Ali. 10 Elvis Presley. 11 Arnold Schwarzenegger. 12 *The Thirty Nine Steps*. 13 Barbra Streisand. 14 Gorillas. 15 1980s. 16 *Gone With The Wind*. 17 1950s. 18 Emma Thompson. 19 James Bond. 20 Rowan Atkinson.

QUIZ 312. BEER
1 Hops. 2 Campaign for Real Ale. 3 Dutch. 4 Trouble shooter, John Harvey-Jones. 5 Tetley's. 6 Guinness. 7 Manchester. 8 Adnams. 9 Bitter. 10 Stella Artois. 11 Cider is non alcoholic, hard cider is. 12 Carlsberg. 13 Fuller's. 14 Brown/black. 15 Heineken. 16 Belgium. 17 Yeast. 18 Greene King. 19 Cider. 20 Horse-drawn drays.

QUIZ 313. PICTURE QUIZ
Books of the Bible. A) *Judges*. B) *Kings*. C) *Numbers*. D) *Romans*.

QUIZ 314. DOUBLE TAKE
1 Bishop. 2 Step. 3 Crook. 4 Rap. 5 Address. 6 Organ. 7 Star. 8 Pitch. 9 Scuttle. 10 Bugs.

QUIZ 315. FAST FOOD
1 Onions. 2 Potatoes. 3 1905. 4 Sesame. 5 Fungus. 6 Tube. 7 Toaster. 8 Cheeses. 9 Rice. 10 Toasted sandwich. 11 Eggs. 12 Ice lolly. 13 Buffalo. 14 Mars. 15 Ketchup.

QUIZ 316. LUCKY DIP
1 Christie. 2 Power boat racing. 3 Denmark. 4 House of Hanover. 5 Blur. 6 One. 7 Oxygen. 8 Forget-me-not. 9 Cancer. 10 Highness. 11 Nell Gwyn. 12 Metro. 13 Pack. 14 Orienteering. 15 Wainwright. 16 Bull. 17 Stave. 18 Harold Macmillan. 19 The Comets. 20 General Custer.

QUIZ 317. GEOGRAPHY
1 French. 2 Peter the Great. 3 Italy. 4 Europe. 5 Africa. 6 Ireland. 7 Motorway. 8 Persian Gulf. 9 Canada. 10 Luxembourg. 11 Yugoslavia. 12 Nepal. 13 Wellington. 14 Rhine. 15 Japan. 16 Europe. 17 Italy. 18 Island. 19 London. 20 Sicily.

QUIZ 318. AMERICAN SPORT
1 National Football League. 2 Ice hockey. 3 Pittsburgh Steelers. 4 Baseball. 5 No-one. It was cancelled because of a players' strike 6 Ice hockey. 7 Houston. 8 Washington. 9 George Herman Ruth. 10 Alicia Keys. 11 Boston Celtics. 12 Los Angeles Lakers. 13 American football. 14 Los Angeles. 15 1970. 16 Six. 17 Basketball. 18 Yogi. 19 New York. 20 Basketball.

QUIZ 319. GENERAL KNOWLEDGE
1 W.C. Fields. 2 Mercury. 3 The Strand. 4 Fingal's. 5 Sir Walter Scott. 6 Bottle. 7 Earthquake. 8 Animal. 9 Georgia. 10 Hungary. 11 Internet cafe. 12 Pears. 13 Brooklyn. 14 Violins. 15 Stevie Wonder. 16 Snowdon. 17 North. 18 The Rank Organization. 19 Oedipus. 20 Gemini.

QUIZ 320. HISTORY
1 Bill Clinton. 2 Salvation Army. 3 Louis Pasteur. 4 Nobel. 5 Henry VIII. 6 Guy Fawkes. 7 Henry Ford. 8 Second World War. 9 India. 10 Oil. 11 Glenys Kinnock. 12 Charles. 13 Che Guevara. 14 Queen Victoria. 15 Pankhurst. 16 Saddam Hussein. 17 One. 18 American. 19 W.G.Grace. 20 56.

QUIZ 321. QUEEN
1 Five. 2 John Deacon. 3 Freddie Mercury. 4 Montserrat Caballé. 5 *Killer Queen*. 6 *News Of The World*. 7 *Under Pressure*. 8 *Innuendo*. 9 *Sheer Heart Attack*. 10 *Living On My Own*. 11 Brian May. 12 *Made In Heaven*. 13 Hyde Park. 14 Knebworth. 15 Freddie Mercury. 16 *Bohemian Rhapsody*. 17 1970s. 18 Bicycle. 19 *A Day At The Races*. 20 Ben Elton.

QUIZ 322. WORLD SOCCER
1 Argentina. 2 Iceland. 3 Mexico. 4 Wales. 5 Croatia. 6 Japan. 7 Italy. 8 Sweden. 9 USA. 10 Peru.

QUIZ 323. GUESS WHO . . . ?
1 Michael Hutchence. 2 Elton John. 3 Peggy Lee. 4 Alexandre Dumas. 5 Jodie Foster. 6 Dick Fosbury. 7 Sonny Bono. 8 Madonna. 9 Jack Dempsey. 10 Michael J Fox.

QUIZ 324. PARIS
1 Hunchback. 2 Fortress. 3 Obelisk. 4 July 14th. 5 Tennis. 6 Eiffel Tower. 7 Napoleon. 8 1875. 9 St Denis. 10 Roosevelt. 11 Arc de Triomphe. 12 Léna. 13 1900. 14 Trocadero. 15 Montmartre.

QUIZ 325. HALF CHANCE
1 Mississippi. 2 Smith. 3 Crossbow. 4 Mexico. 5 April. 6 B. 7 Eight. 8 White. 9 Baker. 10 Finland. 11 Moon. 12 The Bangles. 13 1930s. 14 John. 15 *Jerusalem*. 16 Angola. 17 King Duncan. 18 Southampton. 19 Farces. 20 Guitar.

QUIZ 326. SCIENCE
1 Ball point pen. 2 Jeans. 3 German. 4 Tyres. 5 Fountain pen. 6 Hovercraft. 7 Jet. 8 Television. 9 Telephone. 10 Morse. 11 Blind. 12 Deep freezing. 13 Safety lamp. 14 Gramophone. 15 Cornflakes. 16 Wireless. 17 Sony. 18 Dynamite. 19 Pasteurised. 20 Electricity.

QUIZ 327. MURDER MOST FOUL
1 Ronald Goldman. 2 Peter Kurten. 3 A6. 4 John F Kennedy.5 Memphis. 6 Robert LeRoy Parker. 7 Peace Yes Violence No. 8 Joe Orton. 9 Robinson. 10 Wast Water. 11 Tottenham. 12 Model agency. 13 15 victims. 14 10 Rillington Place. 15 King Umberto I of Italy. 16 Salvatore. 17 David Blakely. 18 "The Monster of the Andes". 19 34 years old. 20 Acid bath.

QUIZ 328. LUCKY DIP
1 Sonic. 2 Cancer. 3 Flat. 4 North. 5 Double bogey. 6 Top Cat. 7 Photographic. 8 Libya. 9 Staind. 10 New tricks. 11 Diabetes. 12 David Copperfield. 13 Aberdeen. 14 June. 15 Open spaces. 16 Random Access Memory. 17 Potter. 18 One thousand. 19 Jack. 20 Herb.

QUIZ 329. THE ARTS
1 Sean Connery. 2 Sarah Brightman. 3 RD Wingfield. 4 *Sunset Boulevard*. 5 *La Cage Aux Folles*. 6 *The Sound Of Music*. 7 Tony. 8 Nigel Hawthorne. 9 *Kiss Me Kate*. 10 Theatre Royal. 11 Michael Ball. 12 Don Black. 13 Tim Rice. 14 *Show Boat*. 15 *Happy Talk*. 16 Siam (now Thailand). 17 *West Side Story*. 18 Stripper. 19 Stephen Sondheim. 20 *Carousel*.

QUIZ 330.SPORTING LEGENDS
1 French. 2 Willie Carson. 3 Ravel's *Bolero*. 4 Baseball. 5 Military service. 6 Ballesteros. 7 Manchester Utd. 8 1970s. 9 Michael Johnson. 10 Chess. 11 Bjorn Borg. 12 Squash. 13 20. 14 Chelsea. 15 1970s. 16 400m Hurdles. 17 Tony Jacklin. 18 Barry John. 19 Aberdeen. 20 O. J. Simpson.

QUIZ 331. PICTURE QUIZ
They can all go before the word FISH. A) Angel. B) Monk. C) Jelly. D) Sword.

QUIZ 332. BIRDS
1 True. 2 False. 3 True. 4 True. 5 False. 6 True. 7 True. 8 True. 9 False. 10 True.

QUIZ 333. GARDENING
1 Yellow. 2 Rose. 3 Artichokes. 4 Snapdragons. 5 Bulbs. 6 Cut. 7 Cooking. 8 Hollyhock. 9 Shrub. 10 Lavender. 11 Small. 12 Apple. 13 William. 14 Spit. 15 Elderberries.

QUIZ 334. PEOPLE
1 Ray Charles. 2 *Safety Last*. 3 Conran. 4 Grocer. 5 Diana. 6 Murdoch. 7 74. 8 Bjorn Borg. 9 Paul McCartney. 10 Robbie Williams. 11 Chuck Jones. 12 Queen Mother. 13 Andre Agassi. 14 Louis B Mayer. 15 Geri. 16 Martin Scorsese. 17 Paula Yates. 18 Parker Bowles. 19 Scotland. 20 Twiggy.

QUIZ 335. GENERAL KNOWLEDGE
1 Offenbach. 2 They were Morocco Bound. 3 Architecture. 4 Sir Walter Scott. 5 Prison reform. 6 Noah's Ark. 7 Ben Gunn. 8 (Large) estate/farmhouse. 9 England. 10 Rumpelstiltskin. 11 *The Water Babies* (by Charles Kingsley). 12 May. 13 A dance. 14 Marquetry. 15 Acting. 16 £1. 17 Wagner. 18 Colin Dexter. 19 Cod. 20 Mars.

QUIZ 336. CELEBRITIES
1 Ronald Reagan. 2 Texas. 3 Debbie Reynolds. 4 Elizabeth Hurley. 5 John F Kennedy. 6 Donna Rice. 7 1960s. 8 Ronald Reagan. 9 Burton. 10 Sophia Loren. 11 Farrow. 12 Japan. 13 Jay. 14 Mel B. 15 1958. 16 19. 17 Campbell. 18 Geldof. 19 Fashion design. 20 Versace.

QUIZ 337. FOOD AND DRINK
1 Type of grape. 2 Buck's Club in London. 3 Doner kebab. 4 Belgium. 5 The Dorchester. 6 Caraway seeds. 7 Australia. 8 Salt cod. 9 John Tovey. 10 Chocolate. 11 Top (garnish). 12 Chile. 13 Ullage. 14 Camembert cheese. 15 Chocolate. 16 Greece. 17 Bucket. 18 VDQS. 19 Mixed green salad. 20 Butter made from coconut.

QUIZ 338. THE HEADLINES
1 Harrison Ford. 2 Janet Jackson's. 3 1950s. 4 Russia. 5 Sir Mark Thatcher. 6 Margaret. 7 Robert. 8 Mad Cow Disease. 9 South Africa. 10 Film. 11 Women. 12 Explorer. 13 BBC. 14 Omagh. 15 Angel. 16 Beef. 17 1950s. 18 Book. 19 Northern Ireland. 20 Georgia.

QUIZ 339. HEALTH
1 CJD. 2 Cancer. 3 Womb. 4 Bones. 5 1960s. 6 Swiss. 7 Antibiotic. 8 Legionnaire's. 9 Syndrome. 10 Abdomen. 11 Fleas. 12 Chicken pox. 13 France. 14 Eyes. 15 Soil. 16 T. 17 Tsetse flies. 18 Feet. 19 Japan. 20 Alleviate pain.

QUIZ 340. RIVER CITY
1 Danube. 2 Dnieper. 3 Sumida. 4 Molonglo. 5 Danube. 6 Manzanares. 7 Vilnya. 8 Daugava. 9 Vitava. 10 Han.

QUIZ 341. DOUBLE TAKE
1 Eye. 2 Stop. 3 Coach. 4 Comic. 5 Drill. 6 Tees. 7 Saw. 8 Sap. 9 Globe. 10 Navy.

QUIZ 342. AROUND IRELAND
1 Liffey. 2 Lake. 3 Dublin. 4 Derry. 5 Emerald Isle. 6 County Down. 7 Kells. 8 Lee. 9 Limerick. 10 Neagh. 11 Atlantic. 12 Belfast. 13 Crystal. 14 Two. 15 Blarney Stone.

QUIZ 343. LUCKY DIP
1 Germany. 2 High. 3 Mother of Pearl. 4 Simply Red. 5 Olympus. 6 Sturgeon. 7 Florence. 8 Judy Garland. 9 Winnie The Pooh. 10 Blue. 11 Music. 12 Tank. 13 Blue Whale. 14 Red. 15 Morris. 16 Ten. 17 Numbers. 18 Spike Milligan. 19 Clyde. 20 Swan.

QUIZ 344. TRAVEL
1 Paris. 2 Alaska. 3 South Kensington. 4 Earthquakes. 5 District of Columbia. 6 Zurich. 7 Arizona. 8 Brighton. 9 Corfu. 10 Delaware. 11 Cape Canaveral. 12 Bulgaria. 13 Vatican City. 14 New Orleans. 15 Tagus. 16 Suffolk. 17 Wall Street. 18 California. 19 Venice. 20 Bronx, Brooklyn.

QUIZ 345. JAMES BOND
1 Ian Fleming. 2 *Goldfinger*. 3 *Casino Royale*. 4 Two. 5 Hamburg. 6 *Goldeneye*. 7 *Licence To Kill*. 8 *Dr No*. 9 *Never Say Never Again*. 10 Barbara Bach. 11 George Lazenby. 12 *Live And Let Die*. 13 117 minutes. 14 Stoke Poges. 15 *Thunderball*. 16 *You Only Live Twice*. 17 *A View To A Kill*. 18 Spectre. 19 Auric. 20 *You Only Live Twice*.

QUIZ 346. GENERAL KNOWLEDGE
1 Isle of Wight. 2 Beethoven. 3 Testator. 4 Black.5 Chlorophyll. 6 No 11 Downing Street. 7 Quicksilver. 8 The base of the neck. 9 Sahara. 10 To recognize smells. 11 Otters. 12 Hippocratic Oath. 13 Judaism. 14 Australia and New Zealand. 15 Four. 16 The eye. 17 Mae West. 18 Salisbury. 19 Sulphuric acid. 20 Maeve Binchy.

QUIZ 347. MOTOR SPORTS
1 Canadian. 2 Second decade. 3 Great Britain. 4 Twice. 5 1970s. 6 Italian. 7 24-hour le Mans. 8 Bernie Ecclestone. 9 Motorcycling. 10 Japan. 11 May. 12 Williams. 13 Monte Carlo. 14 Belgium. 15 Brazil. 16 Benetton. 17 Hockenheim. 18 Florida. 19 1920s. 20 Riccardo Patrese.

QUIZ 348. HALF CHANCE
1 Moses. 2 Mozart. 3 52. 4 Circular. 5 USA. 6 Greyish white. 7 Itself. 8 Thigh. 9 Unit. 10 Hour. 11 Painting. 12 Brush. 13 Abbey. 14 Right. 15 Cabbage. 16 China. 17 Mackintosh. 18 Gibson. 19 A bird. 20 Parents.

QUIZ 349. PICTURE QUIZ
C) Telephone 1876. A) Light bulb 1879. B) Paper clip 1900. D) Lawnmower 1902.

QUIZ 350. GUESS WHO . . . ?
1 Ian Fleming. 2 Kelly Holmes. 3 Kylie Minogue. 4 Paul McCartney. 5 Tim Henman. 6 Michael Douglas. 7 Pol Pot. 8 Ellen MacArthur. 9 Brian May. 10 Colin Jackson.

QUIZ 351. SAILORS
1 Erasmus. 2 Chichester. 3 Italy. 4 Pirates. 5 Heath. 6 Nelson. 7 16th. 8 A schooner. 9 William IV. 10 Drake. 11 Three. 12 Derbyshire. 13 America. 14 Trafalgar. 15 Da Gama.

QUIZ 352. WEDDING DAY
1 Platinum. 2 Repent at leisure. 3 30. 4 Mendelssohn. 5 Ireland. 6 Something blue. 7 Choux pastry. 8 Booth. 9 Drew Barrymore. 10 Warren Beatty. 11 Red. 12 Frankie Dettori. 13 Steve McQueen. 14 Greek. 15 Five. 16 Lenny Henry. 17 Arquette. 18 Ronald Reagan. 19 Maria Shriver. 20 Heather Mills. 21 Imran Khan. 22 Melanie Griffith. 23 Adams. 24 Catherine Zeta Jones. 25 Andre Agassi & Steffi Graf. 26 Kate Winslet. 27 Paul McCartney. 28 Richard Burton. 29 Nicolas Cage. 30 Sarah Brightman. 31 Nicole Kidman. 32 40. 33 Frank Sinatra. 34 John McEnroe. 35 Christopher Guest. 36 Clint Eastwood. 37 Three. 38 You've dreamt of a funeral. 39 Sylvester Stallone. 40 Brad Pitt. 41 Jay Leno. 42 Guy Ritchie. 43 60th. 44 Roddam. 45 Gwyneth Paltrow. 46 25. 47 Pledge. 48 19. 49 Marilyn Monroe. 50 Sean Penn.

QUIZ 353. TELEVISION
1 *The Fast Show*. 2 Manhattan. 3 Postman Pat. 4 Bob Mortimer. 5 Mary Alice Youngs. 6 Spain. 7 Nicole. 8 Vulcan. 9 ITV. 10 *Hill Street Blues*. 11 A friend. 12 Mary Tyler Moore. 13 Alexis. 14 Lisa. 15 Anita Dobson. 16 Sabrina. 17 The Meldrews (*One Foot In The Grave)*. 18 Hollyoaks. 19 Adler. 20 Taxi driver.

QUIZ 354. STATESMEN
1 Mikhail Gorbachev. 2 Nelson Mandela. 3 Ehud Barak. 4 Nnamdi Azikiwe. 5 Willy Brandt. 6 Idi Amin. 7 Castro. 8 Reconstruction. 9 Louis Botha. 10 *Red Star*. 11 1952. 12 Papa Doc. 13 Charles de Gaulle. 14 Egon Krenz. 15 Alain Juppé. 16 Showa. 17 Brain. 18 Anthony Eden. 19 1960. 20 Joshua Nkomo

QUIZ 355. w.w.w.
1 Andorra. 2 Peru. 3 Tunisia. 4 Portugal. 5 Spain. 6 Botswana. 7 China. 8 Austria. 9 Togo. 10 Uruguay.

QUIZ 356. CAKES
1 False. 2 False. 3 True. 4 True. 5 False. 6 False. 7 True. 8 False. 9 True. 10 True.

QUIZ 357. WEAPONS
1 Enola Gay. 2 Russians. 3 Assault rifle. 4 Sword. 5 Nitro glycerine. 6 Molotov. 7 1960s. 8 Hand grenade. 9 Rapier. 10 Vengeance. 11 Gunpowder. 12 Colt. 13 Flak. 14 August. 15 Little Boy.

QUIZ 358. LUCKY DIP
1 40. 2 Bunk. 3 Cleese. 4 Mozart. 5 Trug. 6 50. 7 Heap. 8 Egypt. 9 1,000. 10 A bird. 11 November. 12 Grace. 13 Francis. 14 D.H. 15 A farrow. 16 Ballet. 17 Cribbage. 18 1. 19 M8. 20 Stock Exchange.

QUIZ 359. POP MUSIC
1 Dido. 2 Adams. 3 *Changes*. 4 Collins. 5 Canada. 6 Bill Clinton. 7 American. 8 Olympics. 9. Freddie Mercury. 10 Texas. 11 Mariah Carey. 12 Beast. 13 TLC. 14 *I Want To Hold Your Hand*. 15 Westlife. 16 *Blood on the Dance Floor*. 17 *Grease*. 18 Pointer Sisters. 19 Leo Sayer. 20 Never.

QUIZ 360. 1990s SPORT
1 Three. 2 New Zealand. 3 Winter Olympics. 4 Bayern Munich. 5 Buffalo. 6 Williams. 7 (Freshwater) Angling. 8 Blackburn Rovers. 9 Rugby World Cup. 10 Australia. 11 Andre Agassi. 12 Tour de France. 13 Ford. 14 Triple Jump. 15 Green Bay. 16 Turnip. 17 Kieren Fallon. 18 Martina Navratilova. 19 Ipswich Town. 20 Jacques Villeneuve.

QUIZ 361. GENERAL KNOWLEDGE
1 Mars. 2 Cinque Ports (the original five). 3 Left handed. 4 Its stomach. 5 Abraham Lincoln. 6 Jerusalem (Christian, Jewish, Muslim). 7 Tartan. 8 Asia. 9 Denmark. 10 Music Hall. 11 John Lowe. 12 Shooting. 13 A bevy.

14 Dr Kildare. 15 Bankrupt. 16 Euston. 17 *Othello*. 18 1961. 19 Purgatory. 20 *Dead Cert*.

QUIZ 362. SEA LIFE
1 Fish. 2 Skate. 3 Blue whale. 4 Shell. 5 Calf. 6 Sharks. 7 Scorpion. 8 Portuguese. 9 Gold. 10 In the sea. 11 None. 12 Gills. 13 Herring. 14 10. 15 Shark. 16 Whale. 17 Milk. 18 Blubber. 19 Poor. 20 Cartilage (Not bone).

QUIZ 363. AT THE MOVIES
1 *Eyes Wide Shut*. 2 Hawke. 3 Private. 4 Pierce Brosnan. 5 80 minutes. 6 Ireland. 7 Attenborough. 8 1950s. 9 Popeye. 10 Uma Thurman. 11 Vietnam. 12 Willis. 13 Kramer. 14 *Love Story*. 15 Dog. 16 Guinness. 17 Jerry Lewis. 18 Faye Dunaway. 19 John Wayne. 20 *Alien*.

QUIZ 364. PICTURE QUIZ
C Nicolas Cage. B Kevin Spacey. A Russell Crowe. D Denzel Washington.

QUIZ 365. DOUBLE TAKE
1 Court. 2 Grate. 3 Bar. 4 Ball. 5 Beat. 6 Bore. 7 Bow. 8 Bowl. 9 Might. 10 Current.

QUIZ 366. WEDDINGS
1 Breakfast. 2 Third. 3 Silk. 4 Wales. 5 Sugar. 6 Wales. 7 70. 8 Ruby. 9 22. 10 Grey. 11 Sapphire. 12 Shotgun. 13 Crystal. 14 Germany. 15 Lace.

QUIZ 367. HALF CHANCE
1 Australia. 2 Harrison. 3 24 letters. 4 Ship. 5 Go. 6 Hallmark. 7 Jordan. 8 Songs. 9 Provider. 10 Cosmonauts. 11 *Jam*. 12 Square (Trafalgar Square). 13 Two. 14 Ear. 15 Queen Elizabeth I. 16 *Toy Story*. 17 Water. 18 13 letters. 19 Telescope. 20 Globe.

QUIZ 368.CLASSICAL MUSIC
1 Handel. 2 *Enigma Variations*. 3 Beethoven. 4 *Finlandia*. 5 "The Pearl Fishers". 6 *Iolanthe*. 7 *Washington Post*. 8 *Air on a G String*. 9 Johann. 10 "From the New World". 11 *The Four Seasons*. 12 Frederick Delius. 13 Guitar. 14 Elijah. 15 *Eine Kleine Nachtmusik (A Little Night Music)*. 16 Ravel. 17 Animals. 18 Purcell. 19 *The Thieving Magpie*. 20 *The Planets*.

QUIZ 369. LUCKY DIP
1 Scapegoat. 2 300. 3 Italy. 4 Queen Anne. 5 Windscale. 6 Eight. 7 Lead. 8 Slade. 9 Intestate. 10 Spain. 11 *Treasure Island*. 12 Meatloaf. 13 Swarm. 14 Clarinet. 15 Coyote. 16 7. 17 Natural. 18 Nottingham. 19 72. 20 Grape.

QUIZ 370. SPORT
1 Andre Agassi. 2 Throw it. 3 Every four years. 4 Liverpool. 5 Johnny Herbert. 6 New York. 7 Lester Piggott. 8 Washington Wizards. 9 Dawn Fraser. 10 Tony Jacklin. 11 Shergar. 12 Argentina. 13 Gilbert. 14 Kenny Dalglish. 15 Long jump. 16 Geoff Hurst. 17 Czechoslovakia. 18 Brian Lara. 19 Gordon Richards. 20 Four.

QUIZ 371. RAP
1 Eminem. 2 Turbo B. 3 Stevie Wonder. 4 Motocross. 5 Eternal. 6 Will Smith. 7 *Doggystyle* by Snoop Dogg. 8 Faith Evans. 9 Los Angeles. 10 Eminem. 11 Boo-Yaa T.R.I.B.E. 12 Notorious B.I.G.. 13 R Kelly – *Home Alone*. 14 *Fear Of A Black Planet*. 15 P Diddy (was known as Puff Daddy). 16 2Pac – Tupac Shakur. 17 Snoop Dogg. 18 Master P. 19 Gangsta's Paradise. 20 Coolio.

QUIZ 372. GENERAL KNOWLEDGE
1 Fish/eggs/rice. 2 Plucking the strings. 3 Abbey. 4 Gin. 5 Perjury. 6 Sarajevo. 7 Aeroplane. 8 St James's Park. 9 Goldsmith. 10 Sibelius. 11 Martini. 12 A fingerprint. 13 Inner Hebrides. 14 Treason. 15 Bangladesh. 16 Flax. 17 A photograph or illustration. 18 William I. 19 Harmonica. 20 Two.

QUIZ 373. NAME GAME
1 Robbie Coltrane. 2 Billy Idol. 3 Michael Crawford. 4 Demi Moore. 5 Judy Garland. 6 Grandmaster Flash. 7 Rita Hayworth. 8 Elle Macpherson. 9 Richard E. Grant. 10 Tom Jones.

QUIZ 374. GUESS WHO . . . ?
1 Richard Gere. 2 Michael Johnson. 3 Richard Nixon. 4 Melanie Griffith. 5 Freddie Mercury. 6 Marion Jones. 7 Patricia Highsmith. 8 Liza Minnelli. 9 Paul Simon. 10 Jesse Owens.

QUIZ 375. CLASSICAL LINKS
1 Italy. 2 Elton John. 3 Mozart. 4 Electric. 5 Piano. 6 Beethoven. 7 *West Side Story*. 8 Tenor. 9 *Annie's Song*. 10 Manilow. 11 Spain. 12 Morse. 13 Beethoven. 14 Benedictine. 15 Rugby Union.

QUIZ 376. PLANTS
1 Alaska. 2 Parsley. 3 Dead matter. 4 New Zealand. 5 South Africa. 6 Barley. 7 Lamina. 8 Gymnosperm. 9 Hollies. 10 Epiphyte. 11 Cork. 12 Forget Me Not. 13 Small stalk.14. Bamboo. 15 Honesty. 16 Azalea. 17 Pink. 18 Autumn crocus. 19 *Rosa gallica*. 20 Carnations.

QUIZ 377. GEOGRAPHY
1 Rio de Janeiro. 2 Australia & Tasmania. 3 Cairo. 4 Camp David. 5 Martha's Vineyard. 6 Colorado. 7 Florida. 8 Israel & Jordan. 9 Iraq. 10 Nile. 11 Europe. 12 North Sea. 13 Mount Fujiyama. 14 Ecuador. 15 Andes. 16 Death Valley. 17 Grosvenor. 18 New York. 19 Cape Town. 20 Mediterranean.

QUIZ 378. LUCKY DIP
1 Earth. 2 Gemini. 3 Knee. 4 Eric Clapton. 5 Beta. 6 Magenta. 7 Java. 8 June. 9 Gascoigne.10 Nine. 11 Time. 12 Cluedo. 13 Wednesday 14 Diamonds. 15 Animals. 16 Kennedy. 17 Lou Costello. 18 Piaf. 19 Red. 20 Jack Straw.

QUIZ 379. BOOKS
1 Bridget Jones'. 2 4.8 million. 3 Diana Rigg. 4 Martin Amis. 5 Dan Brown. 6 Ronnie Spector. 7 Six. 8 Pat Conroy. 9 Clare Francis. 10 Madonna. 11 Isaac Asimov. 12 *The Ordeal of Gilbert Pinfold*. 13 Pig (created by PG Wodehouse). 14 Noah Webster. 15 John Cleese. 16 Torvill & Dean. 17 South Africa. 18 Her Majesty's Stationery Office. 19 Stephen Hawking. 20 Jilly Cooper.

QUIZ 380. HISTORY
1 Catherine Howard. 2 Spain. 3 President Eisenhower. 4 De Gaulle. 5 Nehru. 6 Al Gore. 7 Fuhrer. 8 Alexandra. 9 Andrei Gromyko. 10 Sir Geoffrey Howe. 11 Beeching. 12 Protestant. 13 Baldwin. 14 One day. 15 Billy Graham. 16 Sebastian Coe. 17 Nelson Mandela. 18 St Augustine. 19 Gerald Ford. 20 Physics.

QUIZ 381. SCIENCE
1 Glass. 2 Computer firms. 3 Moh. 4 1960s. 5 Hovercraft. 6 Inert gases. 7 405. 8 Atomic bomb. 9 Asbestos. 10 0. 11 Mercury. 12 Plant. 13 Carbon dioxide. 14 Bell Telephone Laboratories. 15 Cars. 16 Helium. 17 Human genome. 18 Car (Personal transport vehicle). 19 Q. 20 London and New York.

QUIZ 382. PICTURE QUIZ
C Hilary Swank.

QUIZ 383. CHEERS
1 False. 2 False. 3 True. 4 False. 5 True. 6 False. 7 True. 8 True. 9 False. 10 False.

QUIZ 384. FISH
1 Gills. 2 Red/orange. 3 Tuna. 4 Trout. 5 Roe. 6 Tench. 7 Salmon. 8 Tail. 9 Sardine. 10 Blue/black. 11 Liver. 12 Carp. 13 Around its mouth. 14 Dover sole. 15 Whelk.

QUIZ 385. LEISURE
1 0 to 36. 2 Hang gliding. 3 Chess. 4 Scarlet. 5 Basketball. 6 Stamp collecting. 7 Steel links. 8 Carry it. 9 Alton Towers. 10 Giverny. 11 Clarice Cliff. 12 Military combat. 13 10. 14 Baker Street. 15 Caman. 16 Bungee jumping. 17 Curling. 18 Tramp. 19 Aikido. 20 Four (11 outer 7 inner.)

QUIZ 386. GENERAL KNOWLEDGE
1 Dean Martin. 2 Bell. 3 Two. 4 Norman Tebbit. 5 A mass murderer. 6 Piano. 7 Ass. 8 Julie Andrews. 9 Hydrogen bomb. 10 Mortlake. 11 Dog (King Charles Spaniel). 12 Boris Karloff. 13 George Formby. 14 Lord Nelson. 15 Teddy bear. 16 Shakin' Stevens. 17 Abraham Lincoln. 18 Haemoglobin. 19 Cable News Network. 20 Saint Bernard.

QUIZ 387. FOOD AND DRINK
1 Yorkshire pudding. 2 Beans. 3 Red. 4 Green. 5 Orange-red. 6 Eat. 7 Scotch egg. 8 Cider. 9 Potato. 10 Spaghetti (junction). 11 Round. 12 Strawberries. 13 Tequila. 14 Savoury. 15 Biscuit. 16 Asparagus. 17 Tarragon, chervil. 18 Plums. 19 Geese or ducks. 20 Lime juice.

QUIZ 388. BOXING
1 Five fights. 2 Muhammad Ali. 3 Canada. 4 Chris Eubank. 5 Ken Norton. 6 Muhammad Ali. 7 Ukraine. 8 Jack Dempsey. 9 Sheffield. 10 Evander Holyfield. 11 Las Vegas. 12 Frank Bruno. 13 Bruce Sheldon. 14 Seamus McDonagh. 15 Nevada. 16 33. 17 George Foreman. 18 The cannon. 19 Hungary. 20 Plane crash (August, 1969).

QUIZ 389. NATURE
1 Barley. 2 Lavender. 3 White. 4 Shamrock. 5 Water. 6 Five. 7 Topiary. 8 Monkshood. 9 Yellow. 10 Sweet potato. 11 Bell shaped. 12 Leaf. 13 Ivy. 14 Crops and soils. 15 Apple. 16 Strawberry. 17 Deadly nightshade. 18 It is paralysed. 19 Female. 20 Tea.

QUIZ 390. LUCKY DIP
1 Japan. 2 Rupee. 3 David Gray. 4 64. 5 *Jerry Maguire*. 6 Richard I. 7 Feet. 8 Sting. 9 Harris. 10 Solomon. 11 Gestapo. 12 Netherlands. 13 Kuwait. 14 Mauve. 15 Acer. 16 12. 17 Ostrich. 18 Lodge. 19 Jack Russell. 20 Apron.

QUIZ 391. AIRPORTS
1 Austria. 2 Japan. 3 USA (Florida). 4 Turkey. 5 France. 6 Colombia. 7 Nigeria. 8 USA (Seattle). 9 Sweden. 10 Italy.

QUIZ 392. DOUBLE TAKE
1 Fare. 2 Angle. 3 Back. 4 Dressing. 5 Box. 6 Fan. 7 Figure. 8 Book. 9 Flat. 10 Block.

QUIZ 393. HUMAN BODY
1 Bone. 2 Orbit. 3 Ulna.
4 Backbone. 5 Foot. 6 Arm. 7 650.
8 Abdomen. 9 Skull. 10 Inner ear.
11 Cerebellum. 12 Genome.
13 206. 14 Sartorius. 15 Hyoid.

QUIZ 394. SOLOISTS
1 *Supposed Former Infatuation Junkie*. 2 The Smiths. 3 Dido.
4 Buddy Holly. 5 Smokey Robinson.
6 Engelbert Humperdinck. 7 Robert.
8 Garth Brooks. 9 Madonna.
10 Stevie Wonder. 11 Oliver's.
12 Michael Bolton. 13 Sheryl Crow.
14 Chris de Burgh. 15 Georgie Fame. 16 Australia. 17 Frank Ifield.
18 Jimmy Nail. 19 Enya. 20 Billy Preston on *Get Back*.

QUIZ 395. THE ARTS
1 Utah. 2 David Copperfield.
3 Poems. 4 Tom. 5 *Room At The Top*. 6 Dictionary. 7 Man. 8 Crime fiction. 9 Sherlock Holmes.
10 Koran. 11 *Choral Symphony*.
12 Violin. 13 *Peter And The Wolf*.
14 Ballet. 15 The Ring Cycle.
16 Computer. 17 *Land of Hope and Glory*. 18 Danube. 19 "Britannia rule the waves". 30 France.

QUIZ 396. GENERAL KNOWLEDGE
1 The Union Gap. 2 Parallel. 3 Scott Fitzgerald. 4 Soccer. 5 The Black Death. 6 Somnambulist. 7 Warrant officer. 8 Venice. 9 Elgar. 10 Three.
11 *The Mikado*. 12 Crimean.
13 And. 14 Senorita.
15 Mediterranean. 16 America.
17 Valhalla. 18 International Monetary Fund. 19 Gilbert O'Sullivan. 20 Leonard Bernstein.

QUIZ 397. KINGS AND QUEENS
1 17 Bruton St, London. 2 The Delhi Durbar. 3 Edward VII. 4 Adelaide.
5 George I. 6 Hit with a cricket ball.
7 George V. 8 Henry II's wife, Eleanor of Aquitaine. 9 Edward I (19). 10 It was his second (first when he was a baby). 11 The Pope.
12 Dunfermline. 13 Square, she was so obese. 14 Richard II. 15 River Soar. 16 They were tax collectors.
17 Charles II. 18 St Stephen's Abbey, Caen. 19 Henry I. 20 Edward VIII.

QUIZ 398. INDEPENDENCE DAY
1 Britain. 2 1776. 3 Liberty Bell.
4 Richard Ford. 5 Pam Shriver.
6 Washington. 7 13. 8 Dr Barnardo.
9 Andrew Jackson. 10 Peace of Paris. 11 18th. 12 Harrison.
13 Calvin Coolidge. 14 Panama Canal. 15 Adams. 16 Irish.
17 Spain. 18 Southern. 19 Monroe.
20 1492. 21 Maryland. 22 24 dollars. 23 New Amsterdam.
24 France. 25 New York. 26 Book (of laws) 27 Cape Cod.
28 Delaware. 29 Abraham Lincoln.
30 The (then) Duke of York. 31 It cracked. 32 Buffalo Bill. 33 Neil Simon. 34 19th. 35 Annie Oakley.
36 Gold. 37 They would not renounce polygamy. 38 Arizona.
39 Louis B Mayer. 40 Northern.
41 Hawaii. 42 Lincoln. 43 Three.
44 Louis Armstrong. 45 Jefferson.
46 Wimbledon. 47 Rhode Island.
48 The Alamo. 49 Bailey. 50 20th.

QUIZ 399. PEOPLE
1 Cher. 2 Alexandra. 3 Madonna.
4 Hilary Swank. 5 Egypt. 6 Bath.
7 Lourdes Maria. 8 Elzie Sagar.
9 Don Everly. 10 Motor racing.
11 Margaret Thatcher.
12 Lanfranco. 13 Explorer.
14 Andrew Lloyd Webber.
15 Scrabble. 16 Maurice. 17 South Africa. 18 Her mother Linda.
19 Algeria. 20 Pete Sampras.

QUIZ 400. BLOCKBUSTER MOVIES
1 *Dr No*. 2 Leonardo DiCaprio.
3 Fiennes. 4 Batman. 5 Pryce.
6 Pierce Brosnan. 7 Tornado.
8 1970s. 9 Kidman. 10 *Braveheart*.
11 Jamie Lee Curtis. 12 *The Fugitive*. 13 Seymour. 14 D Day landings. 15 1990s. 16 James Bond.
17 Ursula Andress. 18 Izzard.
19 A POW camp. 20 Burton.

QUIZ 401. GUESS WHO . . . ?
1 Hans Christian Andersen.
2 Christian Dior. 3 Placido Domingo.
4 Neil Armstrong. 5 Margot Fonteyn. 6 Richard Attenborough.
7 Anne Frank. 8 Yuri Gagarin.
9 Indira Gandhi. 10 Yasser Arafat.

QUIZ 402. WHO SAID . . . ?
1 Nelson Mandela. 2 Christopher Lee. 3 Diana, Princess of Wales.
4 Mae West. 5 Clint Eastwood.
6 Tony Curtis. 7 Mark Twain.
8 Michael Caine.

QUIZ 403. TV TRIVIA
1 Revisited. 2 Lake District.
3 *Friends*. 4 Audrey. 5 Robin Hood.
6 West. 7 Thaw. 8 *Coupling*.
9 *Coronation Street*. 10 Two.
11 Antiques. 12 E20. 13 *Dr Who*.
14 Skelthwaite. 15 *The Two Ronnies*.

QUIZ 404. ANIMALS
1 Starfish. 2 Adult. 3 Tadpole.
4 Colour. 5 Skin. 6 Venom. 7 Africa.
8 Bat. 9 Grizzly. 10 Caribou.
11 Seven. 12 Insects. 13 Grey, Red.
14 Cheetah. 15 Scottish. 16 Blue.
17 Man. 18 Trees. 19 Chihuahua.
20 Yes.

QUIZ 405. THE HEADLINES
1 John Kerry. 2 Clothes. 3 Germany.
4 Edward VIII. 5 Three. 6 Russian.
7 Scotland. 8 France. 9 WWII.
10 Women. 11 China. 12 1990s.
13 Glenn. 14 Wales. 15 Italy.
16 East Germany. 17 Mineworkers.
18 Three. 19 Foot and Mouth disease. 20 Brighton.

QUIZ 406. FRENCH CUISINE
1 Very lightly done. 2 Burnt.
3 Pancake. 4 Chocolate. 5 Melted.
6 Nice. 7 South. 8 Raw. 9 Stick.
10 Potatoes. 11 Cauliflower.
12 Garlic. 13 Oysters. 14 Fish.
15 Onions. 16 Pork, pàtés, sausages, etc. 17 Parsley, thyme, bay leaf. 18 Ewe's milk. 19 Stock or broth. 20 White sauce.

QUIZ 407. HALF CHANCE
1 Feb/Mar. 2 Liverpool. 3 North.
4 Bikini. 5 DNA. 6 Hindu. 7 Knife.
8 *Beautiful Day*. 9 None. 10 Crab.
11 France. 12 Victoria. 13 New.
14 Freefall. 15 Longitude. 16 His manager. 17 Two. 18 Latin.
19 Scandinavia. 20 Two.

QUIZ 408. LUCKY DIP
1 Kylie Minogue. 2 Racing on Le Mans track. 3 Henry VIII.
4 Liverpool. 5 Rum. 6 25. 7 Cruelty.
8 Douglas. 9 One. 10 Selleck.
11 Epistle. 12 Harold Pinter.
13 Litmus. 14 J.B. 15 War. 16 900.
17 Ash Wednesday. 18 Washington.
19 The Supremes. 20 Hips and upper leg.

QUIZ 409. 20th CENTURY
1 Hawaii. 2 David Koresh. 3 Ford Bronco. 4 Taiwan. 5 Syphilis.
6 Gallup. 7 Goering. 8 Attlee.
9 Churchill. 10 Washington.
11 Yugoslavia. 12 Philadelphia.
13 Gatwick. 14 *Amoco Cadiz*.
15 1988. 16 Yellow. 17 New Zealand. 18 Reykjavik. 19 House of Lords. 20 Midge Ure.

QUIZ 410. PICTURE QUIZ
A) Bob Geldof/Paula Yates – Peaches. B) Gwyneth Paltrow – Apple. C) Woody Allen/Mia Farrow – Satchel. D) Keith Richard – Dandelion.

QUIZ 411. GUESS WHO . . . ?
1 Nelson Mandela. 2 Bruce Springsteen. 3 George Foreman.
4 Eminem. 5 Victor Hugo. 6 Geri Halliwell. 7 Catherine Cookson.
8 George Best. 9 Mike Tyson.
10 Steve Cauthen.

QUIZ 412. MOTOR SPORTS
1 Ferrari. 2 Automobile. 3 Great Britain. 4 Twice. 5 Luxembourg.
6 29 years old. 7 San Marino.
8 June. 9 Williams. 10 Belgium.
11 Japan. 12 May. 13 San Marino.
14 Twice. 15 Second (1911).

QUIZ 413. AT THE MOVIES
1 Dogs. 2 Gwyneth Paltrow.
3 Wings. 4 Again. 5 Kirk. 6 Tom Hanks. 7 Celine Dion. 8 Scoundrels.
9 *Born On The Fourth Of July*.
10 Streisand. 11 The Beatles.
12 Lombard. 13 Nanny. 14 Griffith.
15 Six. 16 Gould. 17 Woody Allen.
18 *Star Wars*. 19 Sheen. 20 Julia Roberts.

QUIZ 414. TRAVEL
1 Denmark. 2 Mont Blanc.
3 Bulgaria. 4 Finnish and Swedish.
5 Africa. 6 Malta. 7 Rotterdam.
8 Glasgow. 9 Left. 10 Liverpool.
11 Africa. 12 The Algarve.
13 Ukraine. 14 Green. 15 Between East and West Berlin. 16 Chile.
17 Cumbria. 18 Europe & Asia.
19 Gauge. 20 Paris.

QUIZ 415. DUOS
1 Phil Spector. 2 *Wake Up Little Suzie*. 3 Husband. 4 Wham! 5 Dave Stewart. 6 Donkey. 7 Simon and Garfunkel. 8 Lionel Richie.
9 *Homeward Bound*. 10 Kiki Dee.
11 Esther and Abi. 12 L.S. Lowry.
13 Olivia Newton-John. 14 Love you. 15 Marvin Gaye. 16 Pet Shop Boys. 17 Mel and Kim. 18 One.
19 Charles and Eddie. 20 Soft Cell.

QUIZ 416. GENERAL KNOWLEDGE
1 12. 2 Boxing Day. 3 The Troggs.
4 1984. 5 Crescendo. 6 First watch.
7 Mars. 8 Chesterfield.
9 *Clementine*. 10 Diamond.
11 Genealogy. 12 Bears. 13 Cricket.
14 Esperanto. 15 Mount Everest.
16 Lloyds. 17 *Chariots of Fire*.
18 Digitalis. 19 Kent. 20 Quincey Jones.

QUIZ 417. TELEVISION
1 Scully. 2 Woman. 3 Julie.
4 Jebediah Springfield. 5 *The New York Star*. 6 McBeal. 7 Doughnuts.
8 Garden. 9 Rolf Harris. 10 East Anglia. 11 Muppets. 12 QC.
13 Female. 14 Fern Britton. 15 Zoe Ball. 16 Whitehouse. 17 The Spice Girls. 18 Kim Cattrall. 19 Springer.
20 Telephone exchange.

QUIZ 418. BATTLES
1 Spanish Civil War. 2 Panmunjom.
3 Vichy France. 4 Mohne & Eder.
5 Vidkun Quisling. 6 Right arm.
7 MacArthur. 8 Reims.
9 Richthofen's Flying Circus.
10 Gavrilo Princip. 11 Treaty of Sévres. 12 Switzerland & Luxembourg. 13 Anzio. 14 Second Battle of the Somme. 15 Major Johnny Paul Koroma. 16 29.
17 Contras. 18 Japanese.
19 American. 20 Ardennes.

QUIZ 419. ART GALLERY
1 Toulouse Lautrec. 2 Michelangelo.
3 Turner. 4 Monet. 5 Munch.
6 Rembrandt. 7 Leonardo da Vinci.
8 Constable. 9 Dali. 10 van Gogh.

QUIZ 420. TROPHIES
1 False. 2 True. 3 True. 4 False.
5 True. 6 True. 7 False. 8 True.
9 True. 10 False.

QUIZ 421. GUITAR STARS
1 Newcastle University. 2 Old.
3 Astronomy. 4 *From The Cradle*.
5 Hank Marvin. 6 *Neck and Neck*.
7 The Rogues. 8 Roy Harper.

9 London. 10 *Beck-ola*. 11 Sky. 12 R.E.M. 13 Stratocaster. 14 *The Deer Hunter*. 15 Lucille.

QUIZ 422. HALF CHANCE
1 Destiny's Child. 2 1950s. 3 Springboard. 4 Two. 5 Mount Everest. 6 New Orleans. 7 Wall. 8 Rome. 9 Desire. 10 Japan. 11 Little John. 12 Twelve. 13 Carbon dioxide. 14 Musical instrument. 15 Lifeguards. 16 16 letters. 17 Jaune. 18 Ayers Rock. 19 Gomez. 20 Brown.

QUIZ 423. BIRDS
1 Ornithologist. 2 Red. 3 Oology. 4 Larks. 5 A thrush. 6 Green. 7 Feather. 8 The dodo. 9 Condor. 10 Golden crested. 11 Flightless. 12 Pheasant. 13 Murder. 14 They are hollow. 15 Thrush. 16 The pheasant. 17 Smell. 18 It has webbed feet. 19 Ostrich. 20 Archaeopteryx.

QUIZ 424. PICTURE QUIZ
C Clark Gable was the youngest. A Chaplin. B Bogart. D Cagney.

QUIZ 425. NAME THE YEAR
1 1903. 2 1929. 3 1912. 4 1963. 5 1982. 6 1994.

QUIZ 426. POP MUSIC
1 Ignition. 2 Westlife. 3 Angel. 4 Albatross. 5 Madonna. 6 Lonnie Donegan. 7 Blur. 8 Tyrannnosaurus. 9 Five. 10 The Ants. 11 Queen. 12 Love. 13 Enya. 14 "My, my, my Delilah". 15 Dusty Springfield. 16 *Without You*. 17 The Who.18 Iceland.19 Michael Jackson. 20 Stock.

QUIZ 427. LUCKY DIP
1 Mexico and USA. 2 England and France. 3 Sharp. 4 White and yellow. 5 24. 6 Bishop. 7 Animal. 8 Cricket. 9 Van Gogh. 10 Berkshire. 11 Radius. 12 Mont Blanc. 13 H. G. Wells. 14 Everton. 15 Raymond Chandler. 16 90 degrees. 17 Bakewell. 18 Yellow. 19 Bad breath. 20 Enid Blyton.

QUIZ 428. PERFORMING ARTS
1 Simon. 2 Maria. 3 Russian. 4 Shake it. 5 *Cats*. 6 Violin. 7 *The Taming Of The Shrew*. 8 Saturday. 9 Bass. 10 Gertrude Lawrence. 11 *The Crucible*. 12 *The Misfits*. 13 Lillian Hellman. 14 Ezra Pound. 15 Mark Twain. 16 *A Moveable Feast*. 17 *Cat on a Hot Tin Roof*. 18 Washington Irving. 19 Travel. 20 *Blood Brothers*.

QUIZ 429. WHAT COLOUR IS . . .?
1 White. 2 Blue & white. 3 Pink. 4 Yellow. 5 Red. 6 Red. 7 Green. 8 Blue. 9 Light blue. 10 White.

QUIZ 430. DOUBLE TAKE
1 Buck. 2 Hip. 3 Ground. 4 Capital. 5 Cat. 6 Nerve. 7 Catch. 8 Pack. 9 Pine. 10 Chicken.

QUIZ 431. GOSSIP AND SCANDAL
1 Chicago. 2 Whiplash. 3 Forsyth. 4 Eight. 5 Natasha. 6 Mary. 7 Williams. 8 Heather. 9 Jodie. 10 Tiggy. 11 Shamrock. 12 Norway. 13 Barbara. 14 Zeta Jones. 15 Bristol.

QUIZ 432. SPORT
1 Green Bay Packers. 2 Nine. 3 1970s. 4 Ice hockey. 5 Tennis. 6 Rio Ferdinand. 7 Japan. 8 Dominic Cork. 9 Georgia. 10 Bernhard Langer. 11 Pete Sampras. 12 Chris Eubank. 13 Charlton Athletic. 14 Swimming. 15 Marathon. 16 Derby County. 17 Bowls. 18 Arnold Palmer. 19 Four. 20 Yearly.

QUIZ 433. LYRICS
1 She was a showgirl. 2 New York. 3 In the wind. 4 Matchstalk cats and dogs. 5 I feel it in my fingers. 6 Ten. 7 Jolene. 8 All right. 9 Thought control. 10 Midnight. 11 Your lips. 12 This feeling inside. 13 Rosemary and thyme. 14 Guitar George. 15 Tell me more. 16 Good as you (from *Pretty Woman*). 17 River deep mountain high. 18 Eleanor Rigby. 19 Make me cry. 20 A whiter shade of pale.

QUIZ 434. GEOGRAPHY
1 Israel & Syria. 2 Brazil. 3 France. 4 Germany. 5 London. 6 Bass. 7 Switzerland. 8 Netherlands. 9 Czech Republic. 10 Airport. 11 Belgium. 12 Germany. 13 Switzerland. 14 Spain. 15 Indonesia. 16 USSR. 17 Venice. 18 Kingdom. 19 Danube. 20 Balearics.

QUIZ 435. HISTORY
1 Second. 2 Italy. 3 Florence Nightingale. 4 Capone. 5 Nelson Mandela. 6 Jackie. 7 Penn. 8 Peron. 9 Hadrian's Wall. 10 Elephants. 11 Japan. 12 Tsar. 13 Arabia. 14 Lenin. 15 USSR. 16 Macbeth. 17 Scotland. 18 Nelson. 19 Russian. 20 USSR.

QUIZ 436. ACTION MOVIES
1 *Apocalypse Now*. 2 Judi Dench. 3 Tina Turner 4 *Die Hard With A Vengeance*. 5 Marseilles. 6 Sir August De Wynter. 7 Brad Pitt. 8 Channel Tunnel. 9 Frank. 10 *Goldeneye*. 11 Bruce Willis. 12 Pierce Brosnan. 13 *Platoon*. 14 *The China Syndrome*. 15 Charles de Gaulle. 16 Reggie Hammond. 17 Gulf War. 18 Arnold Schwarzenegger. 19 Sheena Easton 20 *The Man In The Iron Mask*.

QUIZ 437. GENERAL KNOWLEDGE
1 Edinburgh. 2 Enid Blyton. 3 The Dandie Dinmont. 4 The Moskva. 5 Mount Olympus. 6 Greece. 7 Michael and John. 8 *The Woman in White*. 9 Roses. 10 The Lord Chancellor. 11 The planet Uranus. 12 Mercury. 13 The Crimean War. 14 Catherine Parr. 15 William Brown (in Richmal Crompton books). 16 Officer of the Order of the British Empire. 17 Jason. 18 Peter Phillips. 19 German. 20 Adam Faith.

QUIZ 438. PICTURE QUIZ
D) Fred Astaire was born in the 19th century. A) John Wayne. B) Gregory Peck. C) Katharine Hepburn.

QUIZ 439. GUESS WHO . . . ?
1 Igor Stravinsky. 2 Daphne Du Maurier. 3 Bjorn Borg. 4 James Joyce. 5 Al Pacino. 6 DH Lawrence. 7 Kiri Te Kanawa. 8 Graham Hill. 9 Andrew Lloyd Webber. 10 Steven Spielberg.

QUIZ 440. CARTOONS
1 Rex. 2 Perdita. 3 Elephant. 4 Jane. 5 Cat. 6 *Antz*. 7 *Aladdin*. 8 *101 Dalmatians*. 9 Blue & white. 10 1930s. 11 Gromit. 12 Thumper. 13 *Jungle Book*. 14 Gibson. 15 *Toy Story*.

QUIZ 441. HALF CHANCE
1 Harvard. 2 Third day. 3 Four. 4 Marathon. 5 Atlantic. 6 Three. 7 Diameter. 8 Caxton. 9 Pottery. 10 Wide. 11 11. 12 The Black Lady. 13 Meringue. 14 Otis Redding. 15 Susan Hampshire. 16 John Le Carré. 17 Nine. 18 January. 19 Ealing Comedies. 20 Desert Storm.

QUIZ 442. LATE GREATS
1 Marc Bolan. 2 Brain. 3 Grace. 4 Never. 5 Grace. 6 Maria Callas. 7 Israel. 8 Gagarin. 9 Oil. 10 Che Guevara. 11 France. 12 Kennedy. 13 Arabia. 14 Violin. 15 World War II. 16 Marilyn Monroe. 17 Elvis Presley. 18 India. 19 Victoria. 20 *Buddy*.

QUIZ 443. LUCKY DIP
1 Chris de Burgh. 2 Leo. 3 Santana. 4 Big Ben. 5 Head. 6 Harry Enfield. 7 Pyrenees. 8 Diving. 9 Baldrick. 10 Deep. 11 Lord Mayor of London. 12 Flamingo. 13 Richard Donner. 14 Ian McShane. 15 Horses. 16 Ravioli. 17 Dane. 18 Alice. 19 Bell. 20 Robert Palmer.

QUIZ 444. FOOD AND DRINK
1 India. 2 Apple. 3 Brother. 4 Bolognaise. 5 Sausage. 6 Fried. 7 Cheese. 8 Rice. 9 Salad. 10 Fish. 11 Red. 12 Italy. 13 Eggs. 14 Crisp. 15 Chicken. 16 Bread. 17 Rectangular. 18 Cheese. 19 Light brown. 20 Lancashire.

QUIZ 445. SHAKESPEARE
1 1564. 2 Capulet. 3 *Macbeth*. 4 Forest of Arden. 5 Two. 6 *Kiss Me Kate*. 7 Ophelia. 8 Anne Hathaway. 9 Iago. 10 37. 11 *Hamlet*. 12 Banquo. 13 King of Naples. 14 Touchstone. 15 *Troilus And Cressida*. 16 King Lear. 17 Friar Lawrence. 18 *Henry VIII*. 19 King of Britain. 20 1616.

QUIZ 446. GENERAL KNOWLEDGE
1 Hara-kiri. 2 Stephen. 3 Rhodes. 4 Guitars. 5 The Avon Gorge. 6 Femur. 7 Atlantic. 8 Comet. 9 Kookaburra. 10 Cyprus. 11 The Brothers Grimm. 12 Danish. 13 Robert Baden-Powell. 14 Chuck Berry. 15 Alchemy. 16 William Bragg. 17 Helicopter. 18 India. 19 Shelley. 20 A biscuit.

QUIZ 447. NAME GAME
1 Jennifer Jason Lee. 2 Michael Caine. 3 David Bowie. 4 Charles Bronson. 5 Billy Ocean. 6 Chris de Burgh. 7 Donna Summer. 8 Charles Aznavour. 9 Carole Lombard. 10 Sting.

QUIZ 448. SAUCES
1 True. 2 True. 3 False. 4 False. 5 False. 6 True. 7 False. 8 True. 9 False. 10 True.

QUIZ 449. CAR CODES
1 Austria. 2 BG. 3 Three (SYR). 4 Jordan. 5 Panama. 6 Tanzania. 7 Azerbaijan. 8 Poland. 9 O. 10 The Gambia. 11 Thailand. 12 Two. 13 Croatia. 14 YV. 15 Egypt.

QUIZ 450. HALLOWEEN QUIZ
1 Samhain. 2 Pomona's Day. 3 Charles Gounod. 4 Bobbing for apples. 5 Pope Boniface IV. 6 *The Castle Of Ontranto*. 7 Pumpkins. 8 The Eve of All Saints, All Saints and All Souls. 9 Fruits (The pumpkin is a type of squash and is a member of the gourd family). 10 Jack O'Lantern. 11 Guy Fawkes Night (Commemorating the execution of the man who attempted to blow up the Houses of Parliament). 12 A fruitloaf. 13 Transylvania (Romania). 14 All Hallow's Eve. 15 *Northanger Abbey*. 16 The druids. 17 Jamie Lee Curtis. 18 Edgar Allen Poe. 19 A pagan religion. 20 Fear of spiders. 21 Paul Dukas. 22 Anne Boleyn. 23 Sarah Michelle Gellar. 24 *Macbeth* (Act IV, Scene I). 25 Voldemort. 26 Bram Stoker. 27 By sprinkling rice by doors and windows. 28 *El Dia De Los Muertos*/ The Day Of The Dead. 29 All Souls' Day. 30 Donald Pleasance. 31 The flying broomstick. 32 The White Witch (of *The Lion, The Witch And The Wardrobe* by C.S. Lewis). 33 Hogwarts. 34 Zombies. 35 Central and South America. 36 Hershey's (Chocolate Company).

37 Strawberry Hill. 38 Dr (Victor) Frankenstein. 39 The Wicked Witch of the West. 40 Osiris. 41 Abraham Lincoln. 42 Dr Johannes Faustus. 43 Cher, Susan Sarandon and Michelle Pfeiffer. 44 *Poltergeist*. 45 The only "normal looking-one" in the Munster Family. 46 Hansel & Gretel (Grimms' Fairy Tales). 47 Trick or treat. 48 Black cats. 49 Pecan nuts. 50 *The Rime Of The Ancient Mariner* (Samuel Taylor Coleridge).

QUIZ 451. SCIENCE
1 Get. 2 1970s. 3 Telecommunications. 4 Steam. 5 USSR. 6 Bar codes. 7 Business. 8 United States. 9 Gates. 10 Birdseye. 11 Modem. 12 Microwave. 13 Long playing records. 14 1990s. 15 Hormone. 16 Japan. 17 Mini. 18 France. 19 Nothing. 20 Frequency.

QUIZ 452. WORLD HISTORY
1 Manchu or Qing. 2 Yugoslavia. 3 China. 4 Shot with her husband Tsar Nicholas II. 5 Kurt Waldheim. 6 Chaim Weizmann. 7 Four. 8 Thomas Stanford Raffles. 9 Cairo. 10 Dissolute. 11 Rheims. 12 Romania. 13 Theodore. 14 The *Anschluss*. 15 The Lion of Judah. 16 Alfred Rosenberg. 17 Dean Rusk. 18 Samora Machel. 19 Egypt. 20 Sandanista.

QUIZ 453. THE ARTS
1 French & English. 2 Michael Crawford. 3 English National Ballet. 4 A cappella. 5 *Cell Mates*. 6 Vanessa Mae. 7 Louis B Mayer. 8 John Ogdon. 9 The Cairo Film Festival. 10 Quintet du Hot Club de France. 11 Dash. 12 Mississippi. 13 Placido Domingo. 14 Phil Collins. 15 *Popcorn*. 16 Maureen Lipman. 17 Laurence Olivier & Ralph Richardson. 18 Double bass. 19 Florence. 20 Jerome Robbins.

QUIZ 454. LUCKY DIP
1 Mecca. 2 Gluttony. 3 Gold Coast. 4 Orange. 5 Bird. 6 Herbivore. 7 Antarctic. 8 *Exxon Valdez*. 9 Asteroids. 10 Cartilage. 11 Blue, white. 12 Sistine Chapel. 13 Netherlands. 14 Venezuela. 15 Julie Andrews. 16 London and New York. 17 Mali. 18 Billy Connolly. 19 William Pitt the Elder. 20 Galileo.

QUIZ 455. FURNITURE
1 Papier mâché. 2 It has legs. 3 A display stand. 4 Pew. 5 Grandfather clock. 6 Form of wood mosaic. 7 Lancaster, Lancashire. 8 Long chair. 9 Music. 10 Small desk. 11 Burr walnut. 12 Marquetry. 13 Wales. 14 18th. 15 Shelf unit. 16 Gilt. 17 A mirror on a four-legged stand. 18 A mirror attached to a cupboard. 19 Rococo. 20 Writing table.

QUIZ 456. HALF CHANCE
1 None. 2 Tsarina. 3 Sydney. 4 The Black Death. 5 Medicine. 6 Gagarin. 7 Stone. 8 Mallet. 9 India. 10 Temple. 11 Red. 12 Ear. 13 Kent. 14 Court. 15 Tyres. 16 Windy. 17 White Coast. 18 Ballet dancer. 19 Baseball. 20 University.

QUIZ 457. PICTURE QUIZ
All names of bands – A) Bread. B) Doors. C) Eagles. D) Queen.

QUIZ 458. DOUBLE TAKE
1 Shop. 2 Slide. 3 Smart. 4 Spirit. 5 Spring. 6 Badger. 7 Table. 8 Stocking. 9 Tank. 10 Strip.

QUIZ 459. PHOTOGRAPHERS
1 French. 2 Scene painter. 3 Arnold. 4 Mountains. 5 Snowdon. 6 Fox Talbot. 7 *Vanity Fair*. 8 David Bailey. 9 Telephoto lens. 10 Man Ray. 11 Patrick. 12 "We do the rest". 13 Women. 14 Lee Miller. 15 Theatrical.

QUIZ 460. GENERAL KNOWLEDGE
1 Ways of ringing church bells. 2 Goat. 3 Nigeria. 4 Eye. 5 Norwegian. 6 Carlisle. 7 Ginger Rogers. 8 Forehead. 9 Palm Sunday. 10 *Take My Breath Away*. 11 Ivor Novello. 12 A watch. 13 Jerusalem. 14 Lemmings. 15 Tax collector. 16 Edinburgh. 17 Dr. Samuel Johnson. 18 Hamlet. 19 Evening. 20 Sheep.

QUIZ 461. LADY WRITERS
1 Rector. 2 *Pride and Prejudice*. 3 Harriet Smith. 4 *Sense and Sensibility*. 5 Jennifer Ehle. 6 Elizabeth, Anne, Mary. 7 Fanny. 8 *Northanger Abbey*. 9 Emma Thompson. 10 Charlotte. 11 Currer, Ellis and Acton Bell. 12 *The Tenant of Wildfell Hall, Agnes Grey*. 13 Brussels. 14 Their brother Patrick Branwell. 15 Nicholls. 16 St John Rivers. 17 Lowood. 18 *Villette*. 19 Emily Brontë. 20 Mrs Gaskell.

QUIZ 462. PEOPLE
1 Stella McCartney. 2 Australia. 3 1920s. 4 The Duchess of York. 5 18. 6 Raymond Blanc. 7 Boys Don't Cry. 8 Gucci. 9 Eurovision Song Contest. 10 Yardley. 11 Tennis. 12 Camilla Parker Bowles. 13 David Bowie. 14 Nicky Clarke. 15 Blythe Danner. 16 David Bailey. 17 Arthur Miller & Marilyn Monroe. 18 Barbara Daly. 19 Czechoslovakia. 20 John Stockton.

QUIZ 463. THE HEADLINES
1 25. 2 Flooding. 3 Westminster Abbey. 4 November. 5 Sound barrier. 6 Monkeys. 7 Oldham General, England. 8 Christopher Reeve. 9 British. 10 Ronald Reagan. 11 Robin Cook. 12 Woodward. 13 Monica. 14 Martina Hingis. 15 Sweden. 16 Space. 17 Revolver. 18 Winnie. 19 Margaret Thatcher. 20 Eric Cantona.

QUIZ 464. SCREEN PARTNERS
1 Woody Allen. 2 Julie Andrews. 3 Joanne Woodward. 4 Richard Burton & Elizabeth Taylor. 5 Robert Carlyle. 6 Colin Firth. 7 Joan Plowright. 8 Sean Connery. 9 Anthony Hopkins. 10 Susan Sarandon. 11 Warren Beatty. 12 Natasha Richardson. 13 Antonio Banderas. 14 Kilmer. 15 Jennifer Aniston. 16 Geena. 17 Sondra Locke. 18 *Enigma*. 19 Diane Keaton. 20 Minnie Driver.

QUIZ 465. NATURE
1 Snapdragon. 2 Geranium. 3 Kidney. 4 Herring. 5 Canterbury Bell. 6 Peace. 7 Cornflower. 8 The smallest mammal. 9 Pollen. 10 Busy Lizzie. 11 Lungs. 12 Acne. 13 The kiss of life. 14 Tuberculosis. 15 Base of the brain. 16 Achilles tendon. 17 Liver. 18 Green. 19 Tulip (tuliban). 20 Honesty.

QUIZ 466. WHAT COLOUR IS . . .?
1 Grey. 2 Yellow. 3 White. 4 Black. 5 Green. 6 Yellow. 7 Pink. 8 Red. 9 Pinkish red. 10 Blue.

QUIZ 467. GUESS WHO . . . ?
1 John Glenn. 2 Helen Mirren. 3 Tessa Sanderson. 4 PD James. 5 Justine Henin-Hardenne. 6 Jennifer Aniston. 7 Halle Berry. 8 Matthew Pinsent. 9 Dustin Hoffman. 10 Geena Davis.

QUIZ 468. THE USA
1 San Francisco. 2 Sacramento 3 Grapes/Wine. 4 Skiing. 5 Columbus. 6 Georgia. 7 Michigan. 8 Five. 9 Pennsylvania Avenue. 10 New York (The Bronx). 11 Black. 12 Lyndon B Johnson. 13 Mississippi. 14 Memphis. 15 Lloyd Wright.

QUIZ 469. LUCKY DIP
1 Tuesday. 2 *Only Fools And Horses*. 3 Paddington. 4 Golf club. 5 Alaska. 6 30. 7 Endive. 8 Tank. 9 Five. 10 Ronnie Barker, Ronnie Corbett. 11 December. *12 Moonlight Serenade*. 13 Trivial Pursuit. 14 Rudolf Hess. 15 Wizzard. 16 Patio. 17 Lenin. 18 Hugh Laurie. 19 T. Rex. 20 Foot.

QUIZ 470. BOB DYLAN
1 *Blowin' in the Wind*. 2 *Times They Are A-Changin'*. 3 *Hey Mr Tambourine Man*. 4 *Blonde on Blonde*. 5 Playing electric guitar. 6 *Mighty Quinn*. 7 *Nashville Skyline*. 8 £35,000. 9 *Tarantula*. 10 *Blood on the Tracks*. 11 *Lay Lady Lay*. 12 *Pat Garrett and Billy the Kid*. 13 The Bible. 14 Accomplice Records. 15 Mark Knopfler. 16 Christianity. 17 *All Along the Watchtower*. 18 *Midnight Cowboy*. 19 Traveling Wilburys. 20 Bob Willis.

QUIZ 471. HALF CHANCE
1 Monica Lewinsky. 2 Horse. 3 Thumb. 4 Austria. 5 Bowl. 6 Thomas Turner. 7 Westmacott. 8 Paris. 9 Rio de Janeiro. 10 Jude (*Hey Jude & Jude The Obscure*). 11 John Barnes. 12 Goldblum. 13 Budgie. 14 13 states. 15 People. 16 Fossils. 17 After death. 18 Jude Law. 19 Joseph Jr. 20 None.

QUIZ 472. ANIMALS
1 Vampire bat. 2 Blue whale. 3 One. 4 Capybara. 5 Algae which grow on it. 6 Mount Everest pika. 7 Exmoor ponies. 8 Bat. 9 Intestine. 10 Behind its eyes. 11 Bootlace worm. 12 On its skin. 13 Teeth. 14 Anywhere above ground. 15 Hummingbird. 16 Flemish horse. 17 Yellow. 18 Europe (bison). 19 Madagascar. 20 Maine coon.

QUIZ 473. IRISH HISTORY
1 Potato. 2 Home Rule. 3 Charles. 4 USA. 5 Daniel. 6 Dublin. 7 Gladstone. 8 Emigrants. 9 USA. 10 Younger. 11 Former. 12 Census. 13 English. 14 Dublin. 15 17th. 16 Scots. 17 Patrick. 18 Cromwell. 19 Vikings. 20 Henry.

QUIZ 474. GENERAL KNOWLEDGE
1 Yew. 2 Greece. 3 February. 4 Portugal. 5 Wore them. They are very wide trousers. 6 It had no toes. 7 Computer languages. 8 Five and a half. 9 Unexploded bomb. 10 A motor car (Model T Ford). 11 Max Wall. 12 Watt. 13 Straws. 14 A spy, informer. 15 Order or command. 16 Stitches. 17 *The Merchant Of Venice* 18 Bob Dylan. 19 Solomon. 20 By rubbing it legs against its wings or together.

QUIZ 475. PICTURE QUIZ
They all have the name Spencer as part of their name.
A) Charles Spencer Chaplin.
B) Lady Diana Spencer.
C) Spencer Tracy.
D) Winston Spencer Churchill.

QUIZ 476. CARTOONS
1 True. 2 True. 3 False. 4 True. 5 False. 6 True. 7 False. 8 True. 9 False. 10 True.

QUIZ 477. DANCE
1 Two. 2 Lopez. 3 Astaire. 4 Red. 5 Diana. 6 *Swan Lake*. 7 Tap. 8 Tchaikovsky. 9 Russia. 10 Royal. 11 On a train. 12 Diaghilev. 13 *Cabaret*. 14 *The King and I*. 15 Yellow.

QUIZ 478. TRAVEL
1 Dublin. 2 Danish. 3 Pacific Ocean. 4 Greece. 5 Mediterranean.

6 Winter sports. 7 Rome (Vatican City). 8 New England. 9 Atlantic. 10 Gibraltar. 11 Europe, 12 Portugal, 13 Paris. 14 West. 15 Divorce. 16 Spain. 17 France. 18 Ireland. 19 Spanish. 20 North.

QUIZ 479. US POLITICS
1 Jefferson. 2 Henry Kissinger. 3 Carl Bernstein, Bob Woodward. 4 John F Kennedy. 5 Gerald Ford. 6 Ronald Reagan. 7 Richard Nixon. 8 Rosalyn Carter. 9 Lyndon Johnson. 10 Bobby Kennedy. 11 Pamela Harriman. 12 William McKinley. 13 Alexander Haig. 14 Tipper. 15 Harry S Truman. 16 Theodore Roosevelt. 17 Dwight Eisenhower. 18 George Bush Snr. 19 Jesse Jackson. 20 Strategic Defence Initiative.

QUIZ 480. TELEVISION
1 Four. 2 *The Rockford Files*. 3 French & Saunders. 4 Clancy. 5 The Dead Donkey. 6 *Sesame Street*. 7 New York. 8 Hutch. 9 Anna Friel. 10 Thomas the Tank Engine. 11 India. 12 Yorkshire. 13 Dickinson. 14 Gervais. 15 *'Allo 'Allo*. 16 Charlotte York. 17 Tom. 18 Robin Hood. 19 Blue. 20 Pascoe.

QUIZ 481. POP MUSIC
1 Busted. 2 R Kelly. 3 Kate Bush. 4 Prodigy. 5 *Unchained Melody*. 6 Shaggy. 7 Phil Collins. 8 Swedish. 9 Stock. 10 Status Quo. 11 Alice Cooper. 12 Australia. 13 The Drugs, 14 Enya. 15 Eric Clapton. 16 Elton John. 17 Two. 18 Orchestra. 19 *My Way*. 20 Ashanti.

QUIZ 482. ANCIENT EGYPT
1 Pharaohs. 2 Embalming. 3 Anubis. 4 1920s. 5 Scarab beetle. 6 Memphis. 7 Papyrus. 8 Rock. 9 Hieroglyphics. 10 Osiris. 11 Lion. 12 Cheops. 13 Falcon. 14 10 years old. 15 Very little. 16 Kohl. 17 Gold. 18 Thebes. 19 Sudan. 20 Ushabtis.

QUIZ 483. LUCKY DIP
1 Fleet. 2 Wrapping. 3 France. 4 Gladstone. 5 Naturalist. 6 Three. 7 Sulphur. 8 Mariah Carey. 9 France. 10 March. 11 Moses. 12 Lady's. 13 Athens. 14 Robin. 15 Denmark. 16 Rhubarb. 17 Earth. 18 A year. 19 Prayer meeting. 20 Knowledge.

QUIZ 484. PICTURE QUIZ
C) Electric cooker 1889. D) Pressure cooker 1905. A) Dishwasher 1932. B) 1945 Tupperware. Specific models will have more recent dates. Well done, gentlemen, if you recognized the items!

QUIZ 485. NAME THE YEAR
1 1815. 2 1930. 3 1984. 4 1978. 5 1964. 6 1979.

QUIZ 486. HALF CHANCE
1 Adams. 2 Bay. 3 Chicago. 4 144. 5 *Transformer*. 6 Alexander. 7 Swimming. 8 20 minutes. 9 Silk screen. 10 Godzilla. 11 Lord Lucan. 12 Gloria Estefan. 13 Carter. 14 Monopoly. 15 Falklands War. 16 George Burns. 17 Diana Ross. 18 Baines. 19 Law. 20 Sally Field.

QUIZ 487. DISNEY
1 Alfred Hitchcock. 2 Flowers and Trees. 3 Kansas City. 4 *Saludos Amigos, The Three Caballeros*. 5 The Skeleton Dance. 6 Alfred & Elma Milotte. 7 Made training films. 8 Laugh O Grams. 9 Julie Andrews (*Mary Poppins*). 10 Sagittarius. 11 One large Oscar and seven small ones. 12 *The Jungle Book*. 13 Leopold Stokowski. 14 *Treasure Island*. 15 Plane Crazy, Gallopin' Gaucho. 16 Dippy Dawg. 17 Victory Through Air Power. 18 *Alice In Cartoonland*. 19 Jungle Cat. 20 29.

QUIZ 488. GENERAL KNOWLEDGE
1 Carbon. 2 Bramwell. 3 Zeus. 4 The Volga. 5 Sir Issac Newton. 6 John Dillinger. 7 The Bilberry. 8 Carmen. 9 Sir Anthony Eden. 10 Surbiton. 11 Fred Astaire. 12 Nagasaki. 13 William of Normandy. 14 Orchestra. 15 Brown. 16 Twentieth. 17 Light. 18 Black Sea. 19 Mandy Rice-Davis. 20 Simba.

QUIZ 489. FOOD AND DRINK
1 Nouvelle cuisine. 2 Aluminium. 3 Spinach. 4 Fish. 5 Black. 6 Soup. 7 Poisonous when raw. 8 Mushroom. 9 Bacon. 10 Basil. 11 Bread. 12 Smoked haddock. 13 Tube shaped. 14 Semolina. 15 Salsify. 16 Escoffier. 17 Mirin. 18 Yellow. 19 Béchamel. 20 Bitter herbs.

QUIZ 490. SAINTS
1 Nicholas. 2 Matthew. 3 Simon Templar. 4 St Lawrence. 5 Catherine. 6 Patrick. 7 Around the head. 8 Stephen. 9 St Trinian's. 10 Andrew. 11 St Pancras. 12 St Bernard. 13 Valentine. 14 St Paul's. 15 St Louis. 16 Astronauts. 17 Mormon. 18 St Peter's. 19 1st November. 20 Luke.

QUIZ 491. SPORT
1 Juventus. 2 Tony McCoy. 3 Gymnastics. 4 Wide receiver. 5 Yvon Petra. 6 Canoeing. 7 147 snooker break. 8 Buffalo Bills. 9 Peter Schmeichel. 10 1940s. 11 The Stilt. 12 Pele. 13 Alain Prost. 14 Martina Hingis. 15 Joe Frazier. 16 Terry Venables. 17 Johnson. 18 Fittipaldi. 19 Steffi Graf. 20 Colombia.

QUIZ 492. GEOGRAPHY
1 Albania. 2 Oberammergau. 3 Yugoslavia. 4 Chechnya. 5 Austria's. 6 Barbados. 7 The Hague. 8 Strait, Turkey. 9 Munich. 10 Greece. 11 Italy. 12 Liechstenstein. 13 Baltic. 14 Italy. 15 Russia. 16 Cologne. 17 Iceland. 18 Denmark and Norway. 19 Moldova. 20 Costa Rica.

QUIZ 493. GUESS WHO . . . ?
1 JM Barrie. 2 Francis Ford Coppola. 3 Leonard Bernstein. 4 Stephane Grappelli. 5 Che Guevara. 6 Al Capone. 7 Alfred Hitchcock. 8 José Carreras. 9 Roald Dahl. 10 Gustav Holst.

QUIZ 494. DOUBLE TAKE
1 Calves. 2 Sound. 3 Mouse. 4 Career. 5 Fine. 6 Cricket. 7 Flag. 8 Cornet. 9 Flannel. 10 Bloomers.

QUIZ 495. FOOD FOR THOUGHT
1 Stewed. 2 Lobster. 3 Chicken. 4 India. 5 Pasta. 6 Lamb. 7 Britain. 8 Rotating. 9 Red wine. 10 Vegetables. 11 Breadcrumbs. 12 Spinach. 13 Chasseur. 14 Melted. 15 Quickly.

QUIZ 496. NUMBERS
1 Million. 2 Hundreds and thousands. 3 Bashful. 4 Thousand. 5 *Twelfth Night*. 6 Three. 7 Roger Bannister. 8 George Clooney. 9 Five thousand. 10 *A Chorus Line*. 11 Seven. 12 Cat. 13 Timmy. 14 Horse riding. 15 Sheila Hancock. 16 Forty niners. 17 Sixth. 18 Dorothy L Sayers. 19 Lady Jane Grey. 20 Forty.

QUIZ 497. LUCKY DIP
1 Two. 2 Virgo. 3 Badminton. 4 Belgium. 5 Microsoft. 6 Kent. 7 Quotient. 8 Vera Lynn. 9 Rick. 10 Look. 11 General practitioner. 12 North Sea. 13 1990s. 14 His heart. 15 Vodka and tomato juice. 16 Sparrow. 17 Squash. 18 Celine Dion. 19 Frisbee. 20 Wimbledon Common.

QUIZ 498. HISTORY
1 December. 2 London. 3 Chicago. 4 Johnson. 5 North Sea. 6 Taj Mahal. 7 China. 8 Reagan. 9 Captain Oates. 10 Philippines. 11 South Africa. 12 Prince Andrew. 13 The Final Solution. 14 Wembley. 15 Mother Theresa. 16 Bonnie Prince Charlie. 17 Falklands. 18 Spain. 19 In space. 20 Kindergarten.

QUIZ 499. SCIENCE
1 Eye. 2 Darwin. 3 Copper. 4 Edwin Hubble. 5 Aluminium. 6 Beaufort. 7 Gold. 8 Sand. 9 James Chadwick. 10 Carbon. 11 Benthos. 12 Lakes. 13 France. 14 Runway. 15 Mir. 16 Observatory. 17 Leonardo Da Vinci. 18 Ernest Rutherford. 19 Thomas Edison. 20 Tokyo, Japan.

QUIZ 500. THANKSGIVING DAY
1 *Mayflower*. 2 Cornucopia. 3 President Roosevelt. 4 Sugar cane. 5 Moses. 6 Turkey. 7 February/March. 8 New England. 9 Shavuot. 10 Autumn. 11 Citron, palm, myrtle and willow. 12 Cattle. 13 Zoroastrianism. 14 Plymouth Rock. 15 *Merci*. 16 Apple. 17 Perennial. 18 Thailand. 19 America. 20 Holi. 21 2nd Monday in October. 22 Vietnam. 23 Zambia. 24 Scotch bonnet. 25 Brazil. 26 Bamboo. 27 Polenta. 28 Rye. 29 Apple. 30 Cotton. 31 Bread. 32 Oats. 33 Honey mushroom. 34 Oats. 35 America. 36 Italy. 37 Gluten. 38 Orange. 39 Rye. 40 Peach. 41 Legume. 42 China. 43 Barley. 44 Biennial. 45 Danke. 46 Festival of Colour. 47 Pumpkin. 48 Rice. 49 Hinduism. 50 Maize.

QUIZ 501. FASHION
1 Shoes. 2 Armani. 3 Vivienne Westwood. 4 Zandra Rhodes. 5 Yves Saint Laurent. 6 Stella McCartney. 7 John Galliano. 8 Jasper. 9 Laura Ashley. 10 Chanel. 11 Pringle. 12 Donatella. 13 Burberry. 14 Mary Quant. 15 Oldfield. 16 Jasper Conran. 17 Christian Dior. 18 Lauren. 19 Alexander McQueen. 20 Calvin Klein.

QUIZ 502. GENERAL KNOWLEDGE
1 James (Jim). 2 Zimbabwe. 3 Titania. 4 Princess Anne. 5 Dorothy. 6 John Paul II. 7 The Wonderbra. 8 What a pity. 9 Bering Strait. 10 Glasgow. 11 Margaret Thatcher. 12 Andorra. 13 Cartoonist. 14 24. 15 African. 16 *Fiddler On The Roof*. 17 Back. 18 Bob Geldof. 19 Parker. 20 Doctor.

QUIZ 503. PICTURE QUIZ
They all link to American Football team nicknames. A) Cowboys (Dallas), B) Dolphins (Miami), C) Giants (New York), D) Vikings (Minnesota).

QUIZ 504. GUESS WHO . . . ?
1 Martin Amis. 2 Kenneth Branagh. 3 Pierce Brosnan. 4 Rowan Atkinson. 5 Phil Collins. 6 Ralph Fiennes. 7 Shirley Bassey. 8 Richard Branson. 9 Frederick Forsyth. 10 Alan Ayckbourn.

QUIZ 505. DIRECTORS
1 *Unforgiven*. 2 Federico. 3 Anthony. 4 *Dirty Dozen*. 5 McEdwards. 6 Stone. 7 Czechoslovakia. 8 Mel Gibson. 9 Vadim. 10 Capra. 11 Huston. 12 Charlie Chaplin. 13 Cubby. 14 Altman. 15 Rosemary's.

QUIZ 506. HALF CHANCE
1 Tuesday. 2 Jewels. 3 F. 4 The White House. 5 A number. 6 Tennis.

7 Baby. 8 The Rockies. 9 Scarlet. 10 Austria. 11 Jason. 12 Boxing. 13 Switzerland. 14 Thursday. 15 Barton. 16 Japan. 17 Monday. 18 60 hurdles. 19 India. 20 18 days.

QUIZ 507. SIMPSONS
1 Bouvier. 2 Sector 7G. 3 Itchy. 4 DMV. 5 Green. 6 Otto Mann. 7 Apu Nahasapeematilon. 8 Martin Prince. 9 Blue. 10 Abraham. 11 His mother. 12 Waylon Smithers. 13 Lisa. 14 Ned Flanders. 15 Fourth. 16 Barney Gumble. 17 Duff. 18 Krusty the Clown. 19 Mr. Burns. 20 Nelson Muntz.

QUIZ 508. THE ARTS
1 Berlin Film Destival. 2 Salzburg. 3 Jim Steinman. 4 Soprano. 5 John Le Carré. 6 *Hello Dolly*. 7 Arpeggio. 8 Leslie Bricusse. 9 *Misery*. 10 Sir Peter Hall. 11 Five. 12 Jeffrey Archer. 13 Rumpole. 14 Barbara Taylor Bradford. 15 Barbara Cartland. 16 Charles de Gaulle. 17 *The Satanic Verses*. 18 Oxford. 19 70. 20 Nigeria.

QUIZ 509. LUCKY DIP
1 Australia. 2 Rouble. 3 Annual. 4 Space. 5 Thesaurus. 6 George VI. 7 Hair. 8 Elvis Costello. 9 A red deer stag. 10 Lion's. 11 Elton John. 12 Scrabble. 13 Roman. 14 Yellow. 15 The Great Fire of London. 16 Four. 17 Corgi. 18 Brass. 19 Robert Zemeckis. 20 An apple.

QUIZ 510. HORSE RACING
1 Best Mate. 2 Frankie Dettori. 3 Lester Piggott. 4 Red Rum. 5 Doncaster. 6 Ireland. 7 November. 8 The Dip. 9 St Leger. 10 1977. 11 National. 12 Chantilly. 13 Corbiere. 14 Richards. 15 United States. 16 Kildare. 17 Goodwood. 18 Derby. 19 Desert Orchid. 20 Kieren Fallon.

QUIZ 511. PEOPLE
1 Martin Luther King. 2 President Kennedy. 3 Walt Disney. 4 McCarthy. 5 Hale and Bopp. 6 Tsar Nicholas II. 7 Burma. 8 Lake Tanganyika. 9 Jacques Santer. 10 "Where's the Bourbon?". 11 Salvador Dali. 12 Brazil. 13 Francois Mitterand. 14 Nelson Mandela. 15 Horatio Nelson. 16 Ronnie Barker. 17 Queen Victoria. 18 Palace. 19 Puccini. 20 Eleanor Roosevelt.

QUIZ 512. w.w.w.
1 Albania. 2 Ukraine. 3 South Africa. 4 Sweden. 5 Mali. 6 Algeria. 7 Bolivia. 8 Greenland. 9 Monaco. 10 Estonia.

QUIZ 513. WHO SAID . . .?
1 Oscar Wilde. 2 Shirley MacLaine. 3 Dolly Parton. 4 Arnold Palmer. 5 Groucho Marx. 6 Duchess of Windsor (formerly Mrs Wallis Simpson). 7 Mick Jagger. 8 Marilyn Monroe.

QUIZ 514. GEMS AND JEWELS
1 Pear shaped. 2 Emerald. 3 Pearl. 4 Victoria. 5 Mountain of light. 6 Cullinan. 7 Ruby. 8 Louis XV. 9 Mars. 10 Blue. 11 Jade. 12 Amethyst. 13 Diamonds. 14 Amsterdam. 15 Koh i Noor.

QUIZ 515. GENERAL KNOWLEDGE
1 Krypton. 2 The longest-serving member. 3 Manhattan. 4 Harry Belafonte. 5 Hydraulics. 6 Ecologist. 7 Martha. 8 Lancaster. 9 221B. 10 Big. 11 Saturn. 12 Greenwich. 13 Campanology. 14 Patrick. 15 Two. 16 William Wordsworth. 17 Baron von Richthofen. 18 China. 19 Clarence Birdseye. 20 Therms.

QUIZ 516. LEISURE
1 Angling. 2 River Cafe. 3 Small cart in harness racing. 4 Plastic shuttlecocks. 5 Abraham Saperstein. 6 144. 7 Gothenburg, Sweden. 8 Art Nouveau. 9 Hunting with dogs. 10 20 minutes. 11 Silk screen printing. 12 Monoboarding. 13 Son et lumiere. 14 Macramé. 15 Uruguay. 16 7 & 11. 17 Kung fu. 18 Swimming. 19 28. 20 Bowling green.

QUIZ 517. AT THE MOVIES
1 Shandling. 2 China. 3 Reynolds. 4 Myers. 5 Piano. 6 Diaz. 7 Samuel L Jackson. 8 Dress in drag. 9 Kate Winslet. 10 Kline. 11 *Raging Bull*. 12 Accept it. 13 *Aladdin*. 14 Eye patch. 15 Costner. 16 West. 17 Never. 18 Park. 19 10. 20 Indiana Jones.

QUIZ 518. THE HEADLINES
1 Fire fighter. 2 Magennis's. 3 Pope John Paul II. 4 Her children. 5 Saddam Hussein. 6 Great Britain. 7 Head teacher. 8 Luciano Pavarotti. 9 Brighton Bomber. 10 Concorde. 11 Oklahoma. 12 Hillary Clinton. 13 Union Carbide. 14 Martin Luther King. 15 Helen Sharman. 16 Belgium. 17 Bolivia. 18 Margaret Thatcher. 19 Light bulb. 20 Virginia Wade.

QUIZ 519. COMPUTERS
1 World. 2 Millennium bug. 3 First. 4 Phone. 5 Question. 6 Service. 7 USA. 8 At. 9 Browser. 10 Navigator. 11 Anna Kournikova. 12 Uploading. 13 Free software. 14 Disconnect. 15 Good behaviour on the net. 16 Two. 17 E. 18 Virus. 19 Sender. 20 *Toy Story*.

QUIZ 520. LUCKY DIP
1 Vanessa Mae. 2 1995. 3 Nudist. 4 Niven. 5 Weathering. 6 Geri Halliwell. 7 Wolves. 8 Mexico. 9 500. 10 Simmer. 11 March. 12 The end of its tail. 13 Exit. 14 CS. 15 Manuel.16 Trifle. 17 Calcium. 18 George II. 19 Sleeve. 20 South Africa.

QUIZ 521. PICTURE QUIZ
They have all had airports named after them. A) Charles de Gaulle. B) Jan Smuts. C) John F Kennedy. D) Leonardo Da Vinci.

QUIZ 522. DRINKS
1 True. 2 False. 3 False. 4 False. 5 False. 6 True. 7 True. 8 False. 9 True. 10 True.

QUIZ 523. ELEMENTS
1 Cyprus. 2 Bluish white. 3 Fe. 4 Silver. 5 Moon. 6 Scottish village. 7 Carbon. 8 1898.9 Yellow. 10 Or. 11 Curie. 12 Calcium. 13 Graphite. 14 Mercury. 15 Tin.

QUIZ 524. HALF CHANCE
1 Howard Carter. 2 Zimbabwe. 3 Nine. 4 Roxette. 5 Archipelago. 6 China. 7 Nixon. 8 Simon. 9 Mine owner. 10 Paris. 11 18th. 12 None. 13 Widow sacrifice. 14 Popes. 15 *Dancing Queen*. 16 I. 17 George Harrison. 18 Peter. 19 Italy. 20 Diana.

QUIZ 525. THEATRES
1 Theatre Royal Drury Lane. 2 New York. 3 The Palace. 4 Puccini. 5 Six hours. 6 UK. 7 Paris. 8 The Old Vic. 9 Tchaikovsky. 10 The Strand. 11 Tom Stoppard. 12 The Savoy. 13 Cameron Mackintosh. 14 Olivier. 15 Blackpool. 16 *Le Nozze di Figaro*. 17 *Hamlet*. 18 Norma (Major). 19 The National. 20 Sam Wanamaker.

QUIZ 526. GENERAL KNOWLEDGE
1 Caves. 2 Vita Sackville-West. 3 The Marx Brothers. 4 Arthur. 5 Chicken Marengo. 6 Joan Collins. 7 The Boer War. 8 Agatha Christie. 9 John Kay. 10 Oxford. 11 The prong of a fork. 12 *Sweeney Todd*. 13 Chesapeake Bay Retriever. 14 Radioactivity. 15 Scientology. 16 Hong Kong. 17 Henry VII. 18 Joan Crawford. 19 Castle. 20 Kali.

QUIZ 527. IRISH LITERATURE
1 Angela's. 2 Wilde. 3 W.B. 4 Samuel. 5 Dracula. 6 Heaney. 7 Day Lewis. 8 Ha Ha Ha. 9 Dubliners. 10 Shaw. 11 Godot. 12 Maeve. 13 Paycock. 14 Reading. 15 Doors. 16 Paris. 17 Film director. 18 O'Brien. 19 Joan. 20 Gulliver's.

QUIZ 528. TRAVEL
1 Greenland. 2 Indonesia. 3 Argentina. 4 California. 5 Casablanca. 6 Two. 7 Azerbaijan. 8 Madrid. 9 North Africa. 10 Cairo. 11 Manhattan. 12 Saigon. 13 Hawaii. 14 Tigris. 15 Brooklyn. 16 Prime Minister, The Earl of Liverpool. 17 Cape Horn. 18 Jodhpur. 19 Johannesburg. 20 Atlantic.

QUIZ 529. TELEVISION
1 Dipsy. 2 *Seinfeld*. 3 Miranda Hobbes. 4 Rolf Harris. 5 Wisteria Lane. 6 Bernard Cribbins. 7 Robson & Jerome 8 Live Aid. 9 Norden. 10 Hughie Green. 11 Clayton Farlow. 12 California. 13 Blue. 14 Televangelism. 15 Sam Malone. 16 Matthew. 17 Ruby Wax. 18 Four. 19 *Father Ted*. 20 Patrick Moore.

QUIZ 530. AIRPORTS
1 Greece. 2 USA (Ohio). 3 Italy. 4 Norway. 5 Cyprus. 6 Canada. 7 Spain. 8 Finland. 9 Italy. 10 Sweden.

QUIZ 531. DOUBLE TAKE
1 Flaw. 2 Hull. 3 Jam. 4 Fling. 5 Ladder. 6 Lake. 7 Fleece. 8 Husky. 9 Galley. 10 Fool.

QUIZ 532. WEIRD WEATHER
1 Red dust. 2 Japanese. 3 Drought. 4 Huang He. 5 Frogs. 6 26th. 7 Death Valley. 8 Siberia. 9 Lightning. 10 Kalahari. 11 Morocco. 12 Flood. 13 Ben Nevis. 14 Coins. 15 Smog.

QUIZ 533. DAVID BECKHAM
1 Leytonstone. 2 Joseph. 3 Preston North End. 4 New York. 5 Ireland. 6 Colombia. 7 £25m. 8 Wimbledon. 9 My Side. 10 OBE. 11 Moldova. 12 Cruz. 13 Argentina. 14 White. 15 Sweden (2002). 16 1996. 17 Real Madrid. 18 Twice. 19 Commonwealth Games. 20 Blackburn Rovers.

QUIZ 534. POP MUSIC
1.Christina Aguilera. 2 Ravi Shankar. 3 "Is this just fantasy?". 4 Clannad. 5 George Harrison. 6 Shakespear's Sister. 7 Four. 8 Philadelphia. 9 Snake. 10 42. 11 *It's In His Kiss*. 12 German. 13 U2. 14 Boyzone. 15 David Bowie. 16 Abba. 17 Rod Stewart. 18 Bruce Springsteen. 19 Slade. 20 *What Makes A Man*.

QUIZ 535. LUCKY DIP
1 The Great. 2 Stripes. 3 Hungary. 4 The House of Tudor. 5 Books. 6 One. 7 Zinc. 8 West. 9 Poison. 10 Blue. 11 Pear. 12 Annie Lennox. 13 Cats. 14 Kabul. 15 Merlin. 16 Romeo. 17 Aintree. 18 South Fork. 19 1,760. 20 Verne.

QUIZ 536. KNIGHTS
1 Four. 2 Order of the Garter. 3 Servant. 4 Knocking an opponent off his horse. 5 Look after the sick. 6 Horsemanship. 7 Page. 8 Knight's esquire. 9 Dubbing. 10 Chainmail. 11 Gauntlet. 12 Lady. 13 White armour. 14 Thigh. 15 Heraldry. 16 Joust. 17 Shin. 18 Herald. 19 Foot. 20 Protect pilgrims to the Holy Land.

QUIZ 537. SPORT
1 Portugal. 2 15 points. 3 1900. 4 Canada. 5 Mile. 6 Geoff Hurst. 7 John McEnroe. 8 Porto. 9 Chris Evert. 10 The visiting team. 11 Jim Clark. 12 Dream Team. 13 Bobby Jones. 14 Peter Fleming. 15 US boycott of the Olympics. 16 US Open. 17 Atlanta. 18 Shoemaker. 19 Six. 20 Shorts.

QUIZ 538. GEOGRAPHY
1 Atlantic. 2 Las Vegas. 3 Canada. 4 Pakistan and Afghanistan. 5 Cape of Good Hope. 6 Wind. 7 Honshu. 8 Australia. 9 Kilimanjaro. 10 K2. 11 Okovango. 12 Indian. 13 Hawaii (a flower garland). 14 China. 15 Namibia. 16 Gobi. 17 Las Vegas. 18 Southern. 19 Michigan. 20 Zambia and Zimbabwe.

QUIZ 539. PICTURE QUIZ
They all had Mary as part of their real name. A) Dusty Springfield. B) Lauren Hutton. C) Kathleen Turner. D) George Eliot.

QUIZ 540. GUESS WHO . . . ?
1 Dawn French. 2 Jerry Hall. 3 Damien Hirst. 4 David Frost. 5 Jeremy Irons. 6 Hugh Grant. 7 Prince Harry. 8 John Galliano. 9 David Hockney. 10 Andrew Lloyd Webber.

QUIZ 541. FICTIONAL DETECTIVES
1 Violin. 2 Poirot. 3 Oxford. 4 Miss Marple. 5 *Charlie's Angels*. 6 David Renwick. 7 *The Rockford Files*. 8 *Crime Traveller*. 9 Cadfael. 10 Imogen Stubbs. 11 *Taggart*. 12 Piet. 13 Sexton Blake. 14 *Gideon's Way*. 15 Cordelia Gray.

QUIZ 542. TV SOAPS
1 Richard. 2 Martin. 3 Richie. 4 Angel. 5 Yorkshire. 6 *Brookside*. 7 Cadbury's. 8 *Eldorado*. 9 *Dynasty*. 10 *Emmerdale Farm*. 11 *Dallas*. 12 Wine. 13 Barlow. 14 *Emergency Ward 10*. 15 Lockerbie. 16 *Coronation Street*. 17 *Neighbours*. 18 *Dallas*. 19 *Home & Away*. 20 Underwear.

QUIZ 543. GENERAL KNOWLEDGE
1 Dancing. 2 360 degrees. 3 Battle of the Boyne 4 Magyar. 5 Alva. 6 Oxygen. 7 Salome. 8 Dunnet Head. 9 Garfield. 10 Photosynthesis. 11 Myology. 12 Rex Harrison. 13 Queen Anne. 14 He was a priest (Father Brown). 15 Pewter. 16 Eurydice. 17 The Eagles. 18 English National Opera. 19 A hybrid. 20 Popeye.

QUIZ 544. GILBERT AND SULLIVAN
1 *The Pirates of Penzance*. 2 *The Yeomen Of The Guard*. 3 Nanki-Poo. 4 Magic and spells. 5 *The Gondoliers*. 6 *Princess Ida*. 7 Tailor. 8 Fairy. 9 Major-General Stanley. 10 Jack Point. 11 *Patience*. 12 *H.M.S Pinafore*. 13 Roses. 14 Josephine. 15 *Iolanthe*. 16 Peep-Bo. 17 Lord Chancellor (*Iolanthe*). 18 Rederring. 19 *Utopia Limited*. 20 Dance.

QUIZ 545. HALF CHANCE
1 Canada. 2 *Daily Planet*. 3 David. 4 1914. 5 Dolly Parton. 6 YMCA. 7 Blondin. 8 *South Pacific*. 9 Painting. 10 Richard Harris. 11 Norwegian. 12 Finland. 13 Doctor. 14 Power. 15 Hoagland. 16 Roller skate. 17 Brazil. 18 New York. 19 Iceland. 20 Jimmy Destri.

QUIZ 546. LUCKY DIP
1 Ronaldo. 2 Libra. 3 Hare. 4 Marmara. 5 Flat. 6 *Dr Zhivago*. 7 Spring. 8 Carburettor. 9 Tongue. 10 A rest. 11 Greenwich mean time. 12 Crystal Palace. 13 E. 14 May. 15 Badminton. 16 An ear. 17 Richard Harris. 18 Music. 19 Lincoln. 20 17th Century.

QUIZ 547. SPEED STARS
1 Lance Armstrong. 2 Gay Lord. 3 Jesse Owens. 4 1920s. 5 100 metre sprint. 6 Bruce McLaren. 7 Joyce Smith. 8 Leroy Burrell. 9 Canada. 10 Lammtarra. 11 Roller skating. 12 Marion Jones. 13 Drum Taps. 14 Stephen Roche. 15 Lotus. 16 Scobie Breasley. 17 Speed skating.18 Nelson Piquet. 19 Cecil Sandford. 20 Rallying.

QUIZ 548. PICTURE QUIZ
B) Nancy Reagan. A) Barbara Bush. D) Hillary Clinton. C) Laura Bush.

QUIZ 549. FABRICS
1 True. 2 False. 3 True. 4 True. 5 False. 6 False. 7 False. 8 True. 9 True. 10 False.

QUIZ 550. FOLK MUSIC
1 Drowned. 2 Drum. 3 Wilson. 4 Ralph McTell. 5 Judy Dyble. 6 Bagpipes. 7 Tom Paxton. 8 Pentangle. 9 Strawbs. 10 Johnny Cash. 11 Clancy. 12 Moore. 13 Humblebums. 14 Strings. 15 Thyme.

QUIZ 551. CHRISTMAS QUIZ
1 The birth of Christ. 2 Boxing Day. 3 Mistletoe. 4 Italy. 5 I'm. 6 Christmas Tree. 7 Mexico. 8 St Wenceslas. 9 Advent. 10 6th January. 11 Bethlehem. 12 Russia. 13 Billy Bob Thornton. 14 *Holiday Inn*. 15 Holly. 16 Clog or stocking. 17 A raw potato and a piece of coal. 18 Scrooge. 19 Natal. 20 Manger. 21 Noel. 22 Marzipan. 23 Elvis Presley. 24 Charlie Chaplin. 25 The Muppets. 26 Ava Gardner. 27 Drink it. 28 Joseph. 29 Decorated orange. 30 Five gold rings. 31 Pierre & Marie Curie. 32 Chocolate log. 33 Pantomime. 34 The Wise Men. 35 Reindeer. 36 *Mary's Boy Child*. 37 Advent calendars. 38 *The Snowman*. 39 Cracker. 40 Carol. 41 26th December. 42 Howard Hughes. 43 Germany. 44 *Hellebores*. 45 Ivy. 46 Nicholas. 47 6th December. 48 Mexico. 49 Humphrey Bogart. 50 Three balls.

QUIZ 552. NATURE
1 Goliath. 2 Mouse. 3 Head. 4 Alpines. 5 Turban. 6 Lime free. 7 Yellow. 8 Yellow. 9 Hooved 10 Insects. 11 Passion Flower. 12 Gypsophila. 13 Buttercups. 14 Nasturtium. 15 Cats (Catmint). 16 Grape Hyacinth. 17 Campion. 18 Viola, Bugle. 19 Salamander. 20 Butterfly

QUIZ 553. HISTORY
1 South Africa. 2 Nixon. 3 Henry Kissinger. 4 John Paul II. 5 Elm. 6 Sweden. 7 Space Shuttle. 8 Bible. 9 Australia. 10 Cambodia. 11 Baader-Meinhof Gang. 12 James Callaghan. 13 Tiger. 14 Afghanistan. 15 Lucan. 16 Margaret Thatcher. 17 Vietnam War. 18 Israel. 19 Switzerland. 20 Andropov.

QUIZ 554. PICTURE QUIZ
They are all left-handed. A) Paul McCartney. B) Prince William. C) Martina Navratilova. D) John McEnroe.

QUIZ 555. DOUBLE TAKE
1 Gilt. 2 Hind. 3 Hives. 4 Grouse. 5 Lash. 6 Habit. 7 Lighter. 8 Guy. 9 Hold. 10 Limbo.

QUIZ 556. ANIMAL GROUPS
1 Peacocks. 2 A watch. 3 Paddling. 4 Troop. 5 Sparrows. 6 Labour. 7 Geese. 8 A barren. 9 Apes. 10 Bears. 11 Cats. 12 Ravens. 13 Skulk. 14 Lions. 15 Larks.

QUIZ 557. IRISH AMERICANS
1 Kelly. 2 John. 3 McEnroe. 4 Westerns. 5 TV. 6 Ed Murrow. 7 Buster. 8 Bing. 9 Novels. 10 Gregory. 11 Cars. 12 Chaplin. 13 Joseph. 14 Newspapers. 15 20th. 16 Reagan. 17 Plane. 18 Monaco. 19 Keystone. 20 Kelly.

QUIZ 558. GENERAL KNOWLEDGE
1 None. 2 Andrew Lloyd Webber. 3 Michael Foot. 4 They were half sisters. 5 Glasgow. 6 The Arctic Ocean. 7 Scandinavian. 8 Nothing at all. 9 *Othello*. 10 Pampas grass. 11 *Swan Lake*. 12 Ewart. 13 Robert Baden-Powell. 14 Colleen McCullough. 15 The 1920s. 16 Finland. 17 Lancelot. 18 Pythagoras. 19 Alsace. 20 212 degrees.

QUIZ 559. FRENCH WORDS
1 Obsession. 2 The woman. 3 Climax. 4 Responsibility. 5 *Enfant terrible*. 6 By the way. 7 *Le mot juste*. 8 Dislike. 9 On a boat (seasickness). 10 Love letter. 11 *Entente cordiale*. 12 Cheese. 13 *Double entendre*. 14 Dover. 15 Eat it – it's a grapefruit. 16 No it's a brawl. 17 Keep to the right. 18 *Nom de plume*. 19 Londres. 20 Park.

QUIZ 560. SCIENCE
1 Adrenalin. 2 Personal. 3 Heating. 4 Earthquakes, 5 Pollution. 6 Wet. 7 Oxygen. 8 Birth. 9 Two. 10 Vitro. 11 Hertz. 12 Becquerel. 13 Copernicus. 14 Stephen Hawking. 15 Nuclear fission. 16 Trigonometry. 17 Kelvin. 18 Atomic particles. 19 A tea-making alarm clock. 20 Radar.

QUIZ 561. LUCKY DIP
1 Linkin Park. 2 Rand. 3 Once. 4 Yul. 5 Guy. 6 Charles I. 7 Phone. 8 Tuna fishing. 9 The Universe. 10 Mark. 11 During the day. 12 Switzerland. 13 Cheshire. 14 Blue. 15 Chalk. 16 Atlas Mountains. 17 Paul Newman. 18 Della Street. 19 Severn. 20 Yellow.

QUIZ 562. WIMBLEDON
1 Boris Becker. 2 Venus Williams in 2000. 3 Nine. 4 Evonne Cawley. 5 Nasty. 6 Arthur Ashe. 7 First female umpire. 8 He never won it. 9 Jo Durie. 10 Jana Novotna. 11 Fell asleep. 12 Betty Stove. 13 Michael Stich. 14 John Newcombe. 15 Roger Taylor. 16 Pete Sampras. 17 Christine Truman & Angela Mortimer. 18 Fred Perry. 19 Green and Purple. 20 Five.

QUIZ 563. NAME GAME
1 Ann Bancroft. 2 Alice Cooper. 3 Bo Derek. 4 Catherine Deneuve. 5 Snoop Doggy Dog. 6 Kiki Dee. 7 Hammer. 8 Edward G. Robinson. 9 Don Johnson. 10 Michael Keaton.

QUIZ 564. GUESS WHO . . . ?
1 Sam Mendes. 2 Harold Pinter. 3 Roger Moore. 4 Simon Rattle. 5 Anita Roddick. 6 Kate Moss. 7 Kristin Scott Thomas. 8 Vanessa Mae. 9 Delia Smith. 10 Emma Thomson.

QUIZ 565. GREAT LAKES
1 Superior. 2 Baikal. 3 Tanganyika. 4 Australia. 5 Lough Neagh. 6 Wordsworth. 7 Baikal. 8 Superior. 9 Canada. 10 9%. 11 Oregon. 12 Four (Illinois, Indiana, Michigan, Wisconsin). 13 Bolivia. 14 Indonesia. 15 Canada.

QUIZ 566. THE ARTS
1 Michael Crawford. 2 Joyce Grenfell. 3 *Wuthering Heights*. 4 Mary Magdalen. 5 *Chess*. 6 Roger Moore. 7 Petula Clark. 8 Jeffrey Archer. 9 *Hair*. 10 *A Chorus Line*. 11 Ruth Rendell as Barbara Vine. 12 Raymond Chandler. 13 *Oliver Twist*. 14 William Blatty. 15 Ellery Queen. 16 Jehovah's Witnesses. 17 Conan Doyle. 18 Cats. 19 Jilly Cooper. 20 Mary Wesley.

QUIZ 567. PEOPLE
1 Cate Blanchett. 2 Stanford. 3 13 years. 4 331. 5 Alexander Graham Bell. 6 Alan Shepard. 7 Hotel de la Reine. 8 Martha Washington. 9 Alfred Hitchcock. 10 John Reed. 11 Reagan. 12 Eric Idle. 13 Dashiel Hammet. 14 John Paul II. 15 Somalia. 16 Bernard Herrmann. 17 Medicine. 18 19th May. 19 London Eye. 20 Elizabeth Arden.

QUIZ 568. SPIELBERG
1 Universal. 2 The bicycle from *E.T.* 3 Sidney Sheinberg. 4 David Geffen & Jeffrey Katzenberg. 5 Kate Capshaw. 6 Martin Brody. 7 Kate Capshaw. 8 Sagittarius. 9 The audience. 10 *The Blues Brothers*. 11 Einstein. 12 Thomas Keneally. 13 *Close Encounters of the Third Kind*. 14 *Indiana Jones & The Temple of Doom*. 15 *Escape To Nowhere*.16 J.G.Ballard – *Empire Of The Sun*. 17 1941. 18 Amblin. 19 *The Sugarland Express*. 20 *An American Tail* and *The Land Before Time*.

QUIZ 569. FOOD AND DRINK
1 Parsley. 2 1905. 3 C. 4 Orange. 5 Buffalo's. 6 Purple. 7 Chickpeas. 8 Aubergine. 9 Australia. 10 Almond. 11 Salmanazar. 12 Mexico. 13 Pine nuts. 14 Kofta. 15 Mulligatawny. 16 Benedictine. 17 Sushi. 18 Earl Grey. 19 Squid. 20 Carignan.

QUIZ 570. GENERAL KNOWLEDGE
1 Yellowstone. 2 Tea. 3 Pole or North Star. 4 Two. 5 Anton Chekhov. 6 Black Prince. 7 Bee. 8 Myxomatosis. 9 The inner ear. 10 Nuts. 11 Crete. 12 Bell Tower. 13 Napoleon Bonaparte. 14 Anaemia. 15 *1984*. 16 Saudi Arabia. 17 Korea. 18 Aneurin Bevan. 19 Golden Gate. 20 Capability Brown.

QUIZ 571. FAMOUS BELGIANS
1 Justine Henin-Hardenne. 2 Saxophone. 3 Hercule Poirot. 4 Eddie Merckx. 5 Jean Claude Van Damme. 6 Jan Ceulemans. 7 The Singing Nun. 8 The Smurfs. 9 King Albert II. 10 Artois. 11 Pieter Brueghel. 12 Joseph Plateau. 13 Audrey Hepburn. 14 Kim Klijsters. 15 Eurovision Song Contest. 16 Jean-Marc Bosman. 17 Django. 18 Electric railway. 19 Leopold I. 20 Hergé.

QUIZ 572. PICTURE QUIZ
C) Petronas Towers 1,482 ft.
B) Empire State Building 1,250 ft.
D) Eiffel Tower 1,050 ft.
A) St Paul's Cathedral, London 364 ft.

QUIZ 573. NAME THE YEAR
1 2001. 2 1983. 3 1926. 4 1956. 5 1960. 6 1951.

QUIZ 574. LUCKY DIP
1 Keystone. 2 *Are You Being Served?* 3 American Civil War. 4 The Dail. 5 Chess. 6 Kuwait City. 7 Covington. 8 Periodic Table. 9 11. 10 Parcel. 11 Status Quo. 12 Osiris. 13 Matinee. 14 W.B. 15 Heather. 16 Pancreas. 17 Liverpool. 18 Paris. 19 Shadows. 20 Head.

QUIZ 575. HALF CHANCE
1 Henry VI. 2 Miss Otis. 3 Kerry blue. 4 Second smallest. 5 Barbed wire. 6 Table. 7 Edinburgh. 8 Seagull. 9 Orlando. 10 Sweden. 11 Sicily. 12 New Jersey. 13 M6. 14 Seven. 15 1789. 16 Portugal. 17 Pennsylvania. 18 Powell. 19 Hungary. 20 Clarinet.

QUIZ 576. FAMOUS FIRSTS
1 Hovercraft. 2 Zip fastener. 3 Neil Armstrong. 4 Chelsea. 5 Israel. 6 United States. 7 Space. 8 *Psycho*. 9 Heart transplant. 10 Severiano Ballesteros. 11 1980s. 12 Lindbergh. 13 Climbing Everest. 14 Ashe. 15 Al Jolson. 16 Sheep. 17 FIFA Soccer World Cup. 18 Fleming. 19 Roald Amundsen. 20 Edward VIII.

QUIZ 577. GENERAL KNOWLEDGE
1 Piano. 2 Lauren Bacall. 3 Ukraine. 4 1990. 5 Rome. 6 New Zealand. 7 Le Mans. 8 Brazil and Colombia. 9 Quito. 10 Inert Gases. 11 Nucleus. 12 Peter Wright. 13 Coco Chanel. 14 Adelaide. 15 *Rainbow Warrior*. 16 24. 17 The Nag's Head. 18 Laurence Olivier. 19 Margot Fonteyn. 20 Rembrandt.

QUIZ 578. MUSICALS
1 Wilkie Collins. 2 Alan Jay Lerner. 3 Paris. 4 Sweden. 5 Florist's. 6 *Jesus Christ Superstar*. 7 Elton John. 8 Los Angeles. 9 *Cats*. 10 Damon Runyan. 11 *How to Succeed In Business Without Really Trying*. 12 Nightclub. 13 Mack Sennett & Mabel Normand. 14 *South Pacific*. 15 *Miss Saigon*. 16 Austria. 17 *Gigi*. 18 *Man of La Mancha*. 19 *The Music Man*. 20 *Oklahoma*.

QUIZ 579. TRAVEL
1 Mansion House. 2 Cork. 3 Porcelain. 4 Paris. 5 Chamonix. 6 Bob Hope. 7 Queen Nefertiti. 8 Finland. 9 Chicago. 10 New York. 11 Leningrad. 12 Barcelona. 13 Virginia. 14 Paris. 15 Basutoland. 16 Madrid. 17 Estonia. 18 New York. 19 Scone Palace. 20 1990.

QUIZ 580. TELEVISION
1 John Rowland. 2 Australia. 3 Beavis. 4 Kristin Davis. 5 Zenith. 6 Selma Bouvier. 7 Rita. 8 Money. 9 Police surgeon. 10 Michelle Pfeiffer. 11 Lindsay. 12 Rebecca Howe. 13 Maigret. 14 Dickinson. 15 *Bergerac*. 16 *Coronation Street*. 17 Pam. 18 *Baywatch Nights*. 19 Music. 20 French & Saunders.

QUIZ 581. WORLD SOCCER
1 Brazil. 2 Republic of Ireland. 3 South Africa. 4 USA. 5 France. 6 Argentina. 7 Germany. 8 Australia. 9 Denmark. 10 Nigeria.

QUIZ 582. CARS
1 True. 2 True. 3 False. 4 True. 5 False. 6 True. 7 False. 8 False. 9 True. 10 True.

QUIZ 583. BEST ACTRESS OSCARS
1 Gwyneth Paltrow. 2 *Boys Don't Cry*. 3 *The Piano*. 4 Julia Roberts. 5 Halle Berry. 6 *Moonstruck*. 7 Shirley MacLaine. 8 Jane Fonda. 9 Hayley Mills. 10 Gwyneth Paltrow. 11 Sally Field. 12 First. 13 Pauline Collins. 14 *The Hours*. 15 Chicago.

QUIZ 584. OSCAR TRIVIA
1 *Saving Private Ryan*. 2 Sammy Cahn. 3 Florence. 4 Michael Douglas (*One Flew Over The Cuckoo's Nest*). 5 Steve Martin. 6 *The Turning Point*. 7 Julie Andrews. 8 Holly Hunter. 9 Best Special Effects. 10 *The Shawshank Redemption*. 11 Ratso Rizzo. 12 Tom Courtenay. 13 Katharine Hepburn. 14 *The Last Emperor*. 15 Three. 16 George Arliss. 17 University Of Hull. 18 Douglas Fairbanks. 19 Carmine. 20 Thomas Newman.

QUIZ 585. LUCKY DIP
1 XY. 2 Disraeli. 3 Atmospheric Pressure. 4 Japan. 5 Gamma. 6 Orange. 7 Indonesia. 8 Thirty. 9 *Literature And Science*. 10 Miles Davis. 11 18. 12 Germany. 13 Opera. 14 Steppes. 15 Oscar Wilde. 16 Solomon Grundy. 17 *Dr No*. 18 Pink Floyd. 19 The Binary system. 20 Stoat.

QUIZ 586. PICTURE QUIZ
A) Sandals 1,560 BC.
C) Wellington boots 1817.
D) Plimsolls 1907.
B) Nylons 1940.

QUIZ 587. DOUBLE TAKE
1 Hamper. 2 Lime. 3 Lock. 4 Hand. 5 Line. 6 Main. 7 Hawk. 8 Madder. 9 Loaf. 10 Hedge.

QUIZ 588. PORTS
1 NW. 2 Le Havre. 3 Vancouver. 4 Mersey. 5 Rio de Janeiro. 6 Hamburg. 7 Yangtze. 8 Hawaii. 9 Ajaccio. 10 Casablanca. 11 Kobe. 12 Pacific. 13 Charleston. 14 Istanbul. 15 Sydney.

The publishers would like to thanks the following sources for their kind permission to reproduce the pictures in this book. The page numbers for each of the photographs are listed below, giving the page on which they appear in the book. Any location indicator (c-centre, t-top, b-bottom, r-right, l-left).

Getty Images: 9tm, 11ml, 35tl, 59tl, 75tl, 75ml, 75m, 79tl, 79tm, 79ml, 83ml, 83m, 93tl, 93ml, 93m, 97tl, 97ml, 105tl, 105tm, 105ml, 105m, 125tl, 125tm, 125ml, 125m, 133tl, 133tm, 133ml, 155tl, 155tm, 179tl, 179tm, 179ml, 179m, 187tl, 187ml, 187m, 207tl, 207tm, 207ml, 207m, 213tl, 213tm, 213ml, 213m, 231tl, 231tm, 231ml, 231m, 253ml, 253m, 261tl, 261tm, 265m, 269tl, 269tm, 269ml, 269m; /AFP: 79m, 83tm, 97tm, 97m, 187tm, 265ml; /America 24/7: 111ml; /Brand X Pictures: 31ml, 59tm, 59m, 67tm, 67m, 141tm, 149tl, 149tl, 163m, 171tm, 201tm; /Comstock Images: 17tl, 23tm, 141ml, 23tm, 141ml, 223tl, 235tl; /Digital Vision: 9ml, 9m, 51m, 111m, 149m, 155ml, 245tm, 283ml; /Foodpix: 23ml, 119tm, 163ml, /Image 100: 171ml; /Image Source: 171tl, 235ml; /Imagebank: 11tl, 11tm, 11m, 35tm, 51tm, 51tm, 67ml, 111tm, 119m, 141tl, 149tm, 149ml, 223ml, 235tm; /National Geographic: 17tm; /Photodisc: 17ml, 35ml, 45tm, 45m, 51tl, 59ml, 67tl, 119ml, 163tl, 163tm, 223m, 283tm, 283m; /Photographers Choice: 23m, 32tm, 111tl, 277tm; /Robert Harding: 277ml, /Stockbyte: 51ml, 171m, 277m, /Stone: 9tl; /Taxi: 31m, 45tl, 141m, 201ml, 223tm, 277tl; /Time Life Pictures: 133m, 253tl, 253tm, 261ml, 261m, 265tl, 265tm; Visual Unlimited: 201tl

Rex Features: 245m; /Stewart Cook: 17m; /Patrick Frilet: 245tl; /Phanie: 201m; /Reso 119tl; /Sunset: 235m

Topham: /Feltz: 31tl; /Fortean: 245ml

Stock.xchng: /http://www.pixelpusher.co.za: 23tl

Every effort has been made to acknowledge correctly and contact the source and/or copyright holder of each picture and Carlton Books Limited apologises for any unintentional errors or omissions that will be corrected in future editions of this book.